PHARMACEUTICAL CHEMISTRY - II

SECOND YEAR DIPLOMA IN PHARMACY

As per E. R. 1991

Dr. A. V. KASTURE
Ex. Prof. in Pharmaceutical Chemistry,
Deptt. of Pharmaceutical Sciences,
Nagpur University,
NAGPUR – 440 010

Dr. S. G. WADODKAR
Ex. Reader in Pharmaceutical Chemistry,
Deptt. of Pharmaceutical Sciences,
Nagpur University,
NAGPUR – 440 010

PHARMACEUTICAL CHEMISTRY – II   ISBN 978-81-85790-20-6

Eighteenth Edition : July 2015

© : Authors

The text of this publication, or any part thereof, should not be reproduced or transmitted in any form or stored in any computer storage system or device for distribution including photocopy, recording, taping or information retrieval system or reproduced on any disc, tape, perforated media or other information storage device etc., without the written permission of Authors with whom the rights are reserved. Breach of this condition is liable for legal action.

Every effort has been made to avoid errors or omissions in this publication. In spite of this, errors may have crept in. Any mistake, error or discrepancy so noted and shall be brought to our notice shall be taken care of in the next edition: It is notified that neither the publisher nor the authors or seller shall be responsible for any damage or loss of action to any one, of any kind, in any manner, therefrom.

Published by :
NIRALI PRAKASHAN
Abhyudaya Pragati, 1312 Shivaji Nagar,
Off J.M. Road, Pune – 411005,
Phone : 25512336/37/39   Fax : (020) 25511379
Email : niralipune@pragationline.com

Printed By :
Repro Knowledgecast Limited
Thane

DISTRIBUTION CENTERS

PUNE
Nirali Prakashan
119, Budhwar Peth, Jogeshwari Mandir Lane,
Pune – 411002, Maharashtra.
Tel : (020) 24452044, 66022708;
Fax : (020) 2445 1538
Email : niralilocal@pragationline.com

Nirali Prakashan
S. No. 28/27, Dhayari,
Near Pari Company, Pune - 411 041
Tel - (020) 24690204
Email : dhayari@pragationline.com
bookorder@pragationline.com

MUMBAI
Nirali Prakashan
385, S.V.P. Road, Rasdhara Co-op. Hsg. Society, Girgaum, **Mumbai** – 400004, Maharashtra
Tel : (022) 2385 6339 / 2386 9976, Fax : (022) 2386 9976
Email : niralimumbai@pragationline.com

RETAIL SHOPS

PUNE
Pragati Book Centre
157, Budhwar Peth, Opp. Ratan Talkies,
Pune – 411002, Maharashtra
Tel : 2445 8887 / 6602 2707

Pragati Book Centre
676/B, Budhwar Peth,
Opp. Jogeshwari Mandir,
Pune – 411002, Maharashtra
Tel. : (020) 6601 7784, 2445 2254

PUNE
Pragati Book Centre
Amber Chamber, 28/A, Budhwar Peth,
Appa Balwant Chowk
Pune : 411002, Maharashtra
Tel : (020) 20240335 / 66281669
Email : pbcpune@pragationline.com

Pragati Book Centre
152, Budhwar Peth,
Near Jogeshwari Mandir,
Pune – 411002, Maharashtra
Tel : (020) 6609 2463 / 2445 2254

MUMBAI
Pragati Book Corner
Indira Niwas, 111-A Bhavani Shankar Road,
Dadar (W), **Mumbai** – 400028
Tel : (022) 2422 3525 / 6662 5254
Email : pbcmumbai@pragationline.com

DISTRIBUTION BRANCHES

NAGPUR
Pratibha Book Distributors
Above Maratha Mandir, Shop No. 3, First Floor, Rani Zanshi Square, Sitabuldi,
Nagpur 440012, Maharashtra, Tel : (0712) 254 7129

JALGAON
34, V. V. Golani Market, Navi Peth, Jalgaon 425001, Maharashtra,
Tel : (0257) 222 0395, Mob : 94234 91860

KOLHAPUR
New Mahadvar Road, Kedar Plaza, 1st Floor Opp. IDBI Bank
Kolhapur 416 012, Maharashtra. Mob : 9855046155

www.pragationline.com   info@pragationline.com

PREFACE

It gives us a great pleasure in presenting this book to the students and teachers of Diploma course in Pharmacy.

This book has been written as per the syllabus under the New Education Regulation 1991 (E. R. 1991) prescribed by Pharmacy Council of India, New Delhi.

As compared to the old syllabus in Pharmaceutical Chemistry for Second Year Diploma Course, the new Syllabus shows no major changes. While all the drugs included in the Syllabus have been adequately dealt with and specifically marked, other related and equally important and clinically useful drugs have also been included to give a more comprehensive outlook. A special Appendix has been included in the book to cover the trade names, name of the manufacturers, dose regeme and the uses. It is hoped that this will make the book more informative.

We hope that the students and the teachers will find this edition useful.

While we are grateful to our colleagues and friends for their valuable comments in the preparation of this book, we look forward to receive creative suggestions in future.

Dr. A. V. Kasture
Dr. S. G. Wadodkar

SYLLABUS

1. Introduction to the nomenclature of organic chemical systems with particular reference to hetero-cyclic system containing upto 3 rings.

2. The Chemistry of following Pharmaceutical organic compounds, covering their nomenclature, chemical structure, uses and the important Physical and Chemical properties (Chemical structure of only those compounds marked with asterisk (*).

The stability and storage conditions and the different type of Pharmaceutical formulations of these drugs and their popular brand names.

Antiseptics and Disinfectants - Proflavine*, Benzalkonium chloride, Cetrimide, Chloro cresol*, Chloroxylene, Formaldehyde solution, Hexachlorophene, Liquified phenol, Nitro furantion.

Sulfonamides - Sulfadizine*, Sulfaguanidine*, Phthalyl sulfathiazole, Succinyl sulfathiazole, Sulfadimenthoxine, Sulfamethoxy pyridazine, Sulfa methoxazole, co-trimoxazole, Sulfacetamide*.

Antileprotic Drugs - Clofazimine, Thiambutosine, Dapsone*, Solapsone.

Anti-tuberculra Drugs - Isoniazid*, PAS*, Streptomycin, Rifampicin Ethambutol*, Thiacetazone, Ethionamide, Cycloserine, Pyrazinamide*.

Antiamoebic and Anthelmintic Drugs - Emetine, Metronidazole*, Halogenated hydroxyquinolines, Diloxanide furoate, Paromomycin Piperazine*, Mebendazole, D.E.C.*.

Antibiotics - Benzyl Penicillin*, Phenoxy methyl Penicillin*, Benzathine Penicillin, Ampicillin*, Cloxacillin, Carbenicillin, Gentamycin, Neomycin, Erythromycin, Tetracycline, Cephalexin, Cephaloridine, Cephalothin Griseofulvin, Chloramphenicol.

Antifungal agents - Undecylenic acid, Tolnaftate, Nystatin, Amphoterecin, Hamycin.

Antimalarial Drugs - Chloroquine*, Amodiaquine, Primaquine, Proguanil, Pyrimethamine*, Quinine, Trimethoprim.

Tranquillizers - Chlorpromazine*, Prochlor Perazine, Trifulo, Perazine, Thiothixene, Haloperidol*, Triperodol Oxypertine. Chlordiazepoxide, Diazepam*, Lorazepam, Meprobamate.

Hypnotics - Phenobarbitone*, Butobarbitone, Cyclobarbitone, Nitrazepam Glutethimide*, Methyprylon, paraldehyde, Triclofos-sodium.

General Anaesthtics - Halothane*, Cyclopropane*, Diethylether*, Metho-hexital sodium, Thiopental sodium. Trichloro ethylene.

Antidepressant Drugs - Amitriptyline, Nortryptyline, Imipramine*, Phenelzine, Tranyl cyromine.

Analeptics - Theophylline, Caffeine*, Coramine*, Dextroamphetamine.

Adrenergic Drugs - Andrenaline*, Noradrenaline Isoprenaline*, Phenylephrine, Salbutamol, Terbutaline, Ephedrine*. Pseudo ephedrine.

Adrenergic Antagonist - Tolazoline, Propranolol*, Practalol, Cholinergic Drugs - Neostigmine*. Pyridostigmine, Pralidoxime, Pilocarpine, Physostigmine*.

Cholinergic Antagonists -Atropine*, Hyoscine, Homatropine, Propantheline*, Benztropine, Tropicamide, Biperiden*.

Diuretic Drugs - Furosemide*, Chlorothiazide, Hydrochlorothiazide*, Benzthiazide, Urea*, Mannitol*, Ethacrynic Acid.

Caardiovascular Drugs - Ethyl nitrite*, Glyceryl trinitrate, Alpha methyldopa, Guanethidine, Clofibrate ,Quinidine.

Hypoglycemic Agents - Insulin, Chlorpropamide*, Tolbutamide Glibenclamide, Phenformin*, Metformin.

Coagulants and Anti-Coagulats - Heparin, Thrombin, Menadione*, Bishydroxycoumarin, Warfarin Sodium.

Local Anaesthetics - Lignocaine*, Procaine*, Benzocaine.

Histmine and Anti histaminic Agents - Histamine Diphenhydramine*, Promethazine, Cyproheptadine, Mepyramine, Rheniramine, Chlorphenitramine*.

Analgesics and Anti-pyretics- Morphine, Pethidine*, codeine, Methadone, Aspirin*, Paracetamol*, Analgin Dextropropoxyphene, Pentazocine.

Non-steroidal anti-inflammatory Agents - Indomethacin*, Phenylbutazone*, Oxyphen butazone, Ibuprofen.

Thyroxine and Antithyroids- Thyroxine*, Methimazole, Methylthiouracil, Propylthiouracil.

Diagnostic Agents - Iopanoic Acid Propyliodone, Sulfobromophthalein, Sodium, Indigotindisulfonate Sodium (Indigo Carmine), Evans blue, Congo Red, Fluoresein Sodium.

Anticonvulsants, cardiac glycosides, Antiarrhythmic antihypertensives and vitamins.

Steroidal Drugs - Betamethazone, Cortisone, Hydrocortisone, Prednisolone, Progesterone Testosterone, Oestradiol Nandrolone.

Anti-Neoplastic Drugs - Actinomycins, Azathioprine Busulphan, Chlorambusil Cisplatin cyclophosphamide, Daunorubicin, Hydrochloride, Fluorouracil Mercaptopurine, Methotrexate Mytomycin.

CONTENTS

1.	Introduction	1	- 1
2.	Central Nervous System Stimulants	2	- 6
3.	Antidepressants and Antiauxiety Agents (Anxiolytic)	7	- 16
4.	Antipsychotic Agents and Hallucinogens	17	- 24
5.	General Anesthetics	25	- 31
6.	Hypnotics and Sedatives	32	- 43
7.	Skeletal Muscle Relaxants	44	- 46
8.	Tranquilizing Agents	47	- 48
9.	Anticonvulsant Drugs	49	- 54
10.	Analgesics (Narcotics)	55	- 65
11.	Antipyretic Analgesics	66	- 69
12.	Nonsteroidal Anti-inflammatory Agents	70	- 76
13.	Adrenergic Agents	77	- 88
14.	Adrenergic Blocking Agents	89	- 95
15.	Cholinergic Agents	96	- 101
16.	Anticholinergic Agents	102	- 116
17.	Cardiovascular Agents	117	- 132
18.	Histaminics & Antihistaminic Agents	133	- 143
19.	Antitussives & Expectorants	144	- 147
20.	Coagulants and Anticoagulants	148	- 151
21.	Diagnostic Agents	152	- 160
22.	Diuretics	161	- 170
23.	Drugs affecting Sugar Metabolism	171	- 178
24.	Local Anesthetics	179	- 186
25.	Steroidal Drugs & Steroidal Hormones	187	- 209
26.	Thyroid and Antithyroid Drugs	210	- 213

27.	Vitamins	214	229
28.	Topical Anti-infective Agents	230	240
29.	Anti-fungal Agents	241	245
30.	Antitubercular and Antileprotic Agents	246	252
31.	Antiprotozoal Drugs	253	259
32.	Antiviral Agents	260	261
33.	Antineoplastic Agents	262	270
34.	Antihelmintics	271	277
35.	Drugs For Urinary Tract Infections	278	279
36.	Sulphonamides, Sulhones as Antibacterial Agents	280	291
37.	Antimalarials	292	301
38.	Antibiotics	302	319
39.	Miscellaneous Pharmaceutical Agents	320	343
40.	Introduction to Heterocyclic Compounds	344	355
	Appendix	356	373

Chapter 1

INTRODUCTION

Pharmaceutical Chemistry is the chemistry of substances used in medicine. In other words, it is the chemistry of drugs. Drugs are used in a medicine to treat illness, protect against disease or improve the health. Pharmaceutical chemistry includes the main branches of chemistry, viz., physical, inorganic, organic and radiochemistry.

Medicinal chemistry is concerned with the determination of structures and the synthesis and isolation of compounds, which may be used in medicine. It involves the study of the metabolism and mechanism of action of drugs. It also involves the relationship between the structures of medicinal compounds and their biological activity.

In this book, drugs of an organic nature are only discussed. Now-a-days, the term, organic chemistry, is defined as the chemistry of carbon compounds. Carbon has the ability to bond successively to other carbon atoms, to form chains of varying lengths and shapes. This property of carbon is called *catenation* and is responsible for the large number and variety of organic compounds. Although organic compounds obey the same fundamental laws of chemistry that are applicable to inorganic compounds, there are marked differences between the composition, structure and behaviour of organic and inorganic compounds. Over two million organic compounds are known today, and about 30,000 new compounds are reported every year.

The great majority of today's new basic drugs consist of organic chemical compounds. The organic drugs may be of natural or synthetic origin. Some vitamins, glycosides, hormones and alkaloids are used as drugs. These drugs are generally obtained from natural sources. In the modern times, more and more of synthetic and organic chemicals are used as drugs.

This book mainly deals with organic substances used as a drugs. The **nomenclature of the drugs, their general properties, storage conditions, dose regions and uses are discussed in this book.**

The study of organic substances that are official mainly in the Indian pharmacopoeia are discussed in this text. The word ' Official ' normally denotes that which is official in the Indian Pharmacopoeia (I.P.), British Pharmacopoeia (B.P.), United State Pharmacopoeia (U.S.P.) and in any other authoritative book of any country. All the important organic compounds, which are commonly used in pharmacy are dealt here with.

Chapter 2

CENTRAL NERVOUS SYSTEM STIMULANTS

The central nervous system (CNS) is highly complex in nature and consists of a number of sub-units and centres, which control the vital functions of the body. There are number of hormones, which are synthesised and act through the transmitters of nerve endings. These hormones are called bioamines and through these the normal functions of the body are maintained.

There are many drugs which act selectively or in general, on the centres of the central nervous system to varying extents in their intensity and duration of action. Thus, they alter the normal activity of the central nervous system. Some drugs stimulate the functions of the central nervous system, while others depress it.

The stimulants of the central nervous system are called the analeptic drugs, which restore the depressed functions of the CNS. Such drugs are useful in a variety of clinical conditions. Another category of drugs are the antidepressants. These drugs reverse profound mental depressions and bring about the feeling of well bein and restore confidence in the patients. Psychoactive drugs are a category of agents which alter the behaviour of patients who are mentally ill. The antipsychotic drugs and their related compounds belong to this category.

In the depressant category, the most potent drugs are the general anaesthetics, which bring about a profound depression of CNS function and bring about unconsciousness in patients, when administered in the required dose. Hypnotic-sedatives is another category of CNS depressants, which calm the nerves and produce sleep or a sleepy condition. These agents produce their action by depressing many centres of the CNS and thus act in a general way. The skeletal muscle relaxants and tranquilizing agents are that category of CNS depressants which act as neuro-sedatives, produce skeletal muscle relaxation acting through the central mechanism and bring about a tranquilizing effect in patients. Anticonvulsants are drugs that prevent or diminish the severity of epilepsy or convulsive seizures. This action is brought through a mechanism involving the CNS. The analgesics which relieve pain by increasing the pain threshold, act through the mechanism at the subcortical and midbrain region of the CNS. The antipyretic–analgesics, which reduce fever and bring elevated body temperatures to normal also act through the midbrain subcortical region.

Besides the major category of the drugs mentioned above some drugs produce different pharmacologal responses partly acting through the CNS mechanism. A detailed discussion of such drugs is beyond the scope of this book. The major category of the drugs, as listed above, are treated separately in the various chapters.

CENTRAL NERVOUS SYSTEM STIMULANTS

Drugs which increase the activities of various functions of the central nervous system are called central nervous system stimulants. These are also called as analeptics as they lessen narcosis and bring about respiratory stimulation. These drugs restore the depressed functions of CNS. Another category of agents called as psychomotor stimulants are used in mental depression.

The central nervous system stimulants have a number of therapeutic applications such as :

(i) They are useful in treatment of narcosis to overcome the depressive effect of depressant drugs.

(ii) They are useful as respiratory stimulants. This action is brought about through chemo-receptors and the vasomotor centre.

(iii) These drugs also act on sensory areas of the brain and increase mental alertness and produce a condition of wakefulness.

(iv) The drugs called " anorexigenic " are useful as appetite controllers.

There are many drugs, belonging to various pharmacological classes, which exhibit pronounced stimulatory effects on the central nervous system e.g. cocaine (local anaesthetics), atropine (parasympatholytic), ephedrine and amphetamine (sympathomimetic), corticoids etc. However, selective central nervous system stimulants can mainly be divided into two major classes : (i) Naturally occurring drugs and xanthine derivatives and (ii) Synthetic agents.

NATURALLY OCCURRING DRUGS

1. Caffeine (I.P. , B.P.) : Caffeine is present in tea and coffee.

1, 3, 7 - trimethyl xanthine

Properties : It occurs as a white, odourless powder and has a bitter taste. It is sparingly soluble in water, and is more soluble in boiling water, alcohol and chloroform. It is a very weak base and readily forms a salt.

The salt, with citric acid (caffeine citrate), is mainly used in formulations with other drugs. It forms a water-soluble complex with sodium benzoate.

Actions and uses : The principal therapeutic actions of caffeine are :

(i) it produces wakefulness.

(ii) enhances mental activity, and

(iii) stimulates respiratory centres.

It is employed in headaches of certain types, e.g. neuralgia, rheumatism, migraine, etc. usually in 200 mg dose, either singly or in combination with other analgesics. In large doses it produces insomnia, restlessness, delirium etc.

Preparations : Caffeine citrate, citrated caffeine tablets (NF), caffeine and sodium benzoate and its injections are some commonly used preparations.

Theophylline and Theobromine are xanthine derivatives. Theophylline is present in tea while theobromine in cocoa. Both these drugs have similar physiological actions like caffeine. Theophylline is mainly used as xanthine bronchodilator. Its salt with ethylenediamine is known as aminophylline. It is widely used in asthamatic conditions.

1, 3 Dimethylxanthine (Theophylline)

3, 7-dimethyl xanthine (Theobromine)

The crude drug lobelia and the alkaloid lobeline show mild CNS stimulant activity. The lobeline hydrochloride was mainly used for its respiratory stimulant activity. This drug is no longer official and not in use.

Picrotoxin and strychine hydrochloride also have powerful CNS stimulant and convulsant activity. These drugs have been replaced by more active and potent synthetic drugs.

SYNTHETIC AGENTS

Compounds from various chemical classes show central nervous stimulant activity of varying degree. The useful drugs in this category are :

1. **Leptazol :** (Pentetrazol) (I.P. B.P.)

Properties : It occurs as a crystalline solid, with a bitter taste. It is soluble in water. The aqueous solutions are stable and can be sterilised by autoclaving.

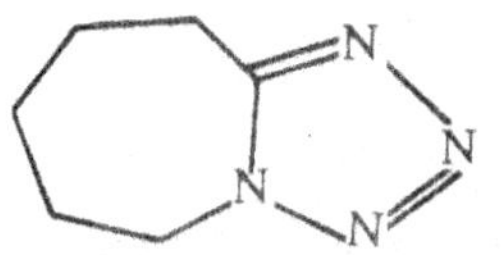

6, 7, 8, 9-tetrahydro, 5-H tetrazoloazepine or
1, 5-pentamethylene tetrazole

Actions and uses : It is used in the form of an injection in 200-500 mg (50 to 100 mg as per I.P.) in the treatment of respiratory depression and also in case of schizophrenia, in small doses.

Preparation : Leptazol injection is official in the I.P.

2. Nikethamide (I.P., B.P.) :

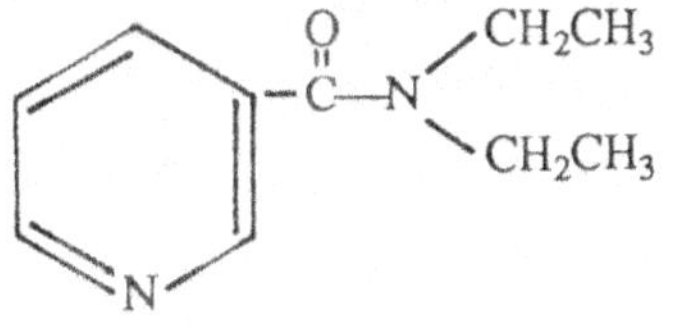

N,N-diethylnicontinamide

Properties : It is a pale yellow liquid with a characteristic odour and bitter taste. It is soluble in water and alcohol. the aqueous solutions are sterilized by filtration or by the autoclaving method. It is given either by intramuscular, subcutaneous or intravenous injection in 25% w/v solution, in 1 to 4 ml doses (0.25 to 1 g according to I.P.) as a respiratory stimulant in respiratory depression produced by morphine or volatile anaesthetics.

3. Bemegride :

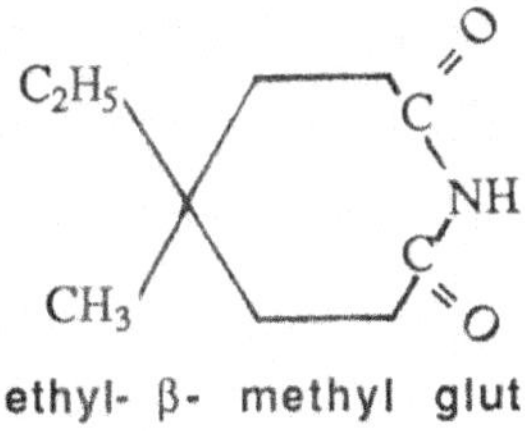

β- ethyl- β- methyl glutarimide

Properties : It is a white crystalline solid, with a bitter taste and is sparingly soluble in water. The solutions are stable and are sterilised by autoclaving.

It is a respiratory stimulant and is employed in barbiturate poisoning in 50 mg doses, at intervals of 10 minutes, upto a total dose not exceeding 1 g.

4. Amphetamine Sulphate (B.P.) :

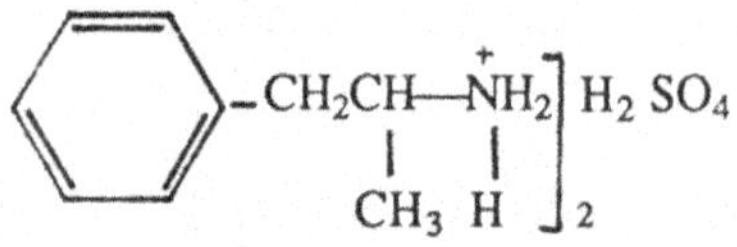

$$\left[C_6H_5\text{-}CH_2CH(CH_3)\text{-}\overset{+}{N}H_2(H) \right]_2 H_2SO_4$$

α-methylphenethylamine sulphate

Properties : Amphetamine sulphate is a salt of an amphetamine base. It occurs as a white powder with a slightly bitter taste. It is soluble in water.

Actions and uses : It is given in 5 to 10 mg doses, either orally or by the patenteral route in the treatment of mental depression in narcolepsy and as an adjunct in the treatment of alcoholism.

5. Methamphetamine hydrochloride (I. P.) :

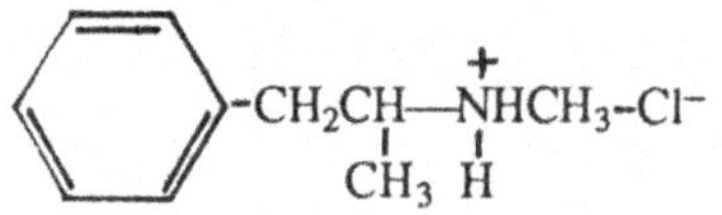

$$C_6H_5\text{-}CH_2CH(CH_3)\text{-}\overset{+}{N}HCH_3(H)\text{-}Cl^-$$

(s)   1-methyl-2-phenylethyl methyl ammonium chloride

Properties : It is a hydrochloride salt of a methamphetamine base. It is white crystalline solid, with a slightly bitter taste. The drug is soluble in water, alcohol and chloroform.

Actions and uses : It is administered orally, in the form of tablets for its euphoretic and antidepressant activity in 5 mg dose. The drug has the tendency to produce habituation and tolerance. It's appetite depressant property is used in the treatment of obesity.

A number of drugs, related to amphetamine and called as sympathomimetics, also possess anorexic, nasal decongescent and a feeble central nervous system stimulant activity. Since, these drugs possess more pressor and adrenergic activity, they are discussed in the chapter on adrenergic drugs.

❑ ❑ ❑

Chapter 3

ANTIDEPRESSANTS AND ANTIANXIETY AGENTS (ANXIOLYTIC)

Antidepressants are drugs which countract or overcome mental depression. These drugs are therapeutically useful in a variety of cases pertaining to mentally ill patients. Mental depression is a phenomenon which may arise in normal individuals or in mentally ill persons. There are various factors which may cause mental disturbances, leading to depression. In mentally ill patients, the mental depression may arise after a schizophrenic of psychotic attack. Patients may also have suicidal tendencies.

It is believed that mental depression arises due to disturbances in the levels of biogenic amines. A certain level of these amines is considered responsible for mental awakening or mental activity. Antidepressant drugs counteract this mental depression by balancing these amines in the brain, through various mechanisms. These drugs appear to be analeptic in their activity but they differ from the latter in their ability in counteracting depression rather than stimulation, as shown by the analeptics.

The desirable properties of antidepressant drugs are : (i) they should have quick action, (ii) they should have a sufficient duration of action and (iii) they should be able to tackle the various phases and degree of severity of mental depression.

Antidepressant drugs may be classified, into two categories, viz., (i) Betaphenylethylamine analogue, which act as monoamino oxidase inhibitors and (ii) Tricyclic compounds.

I. BETAPHENYLETHYLAMINE ANALOGUES

The phenylethylamine derivatives are generally potent adrenergic drugs and due to their structural features exhibit significant analeptic property. These agents exert their action either by (i) inhibition of reuptake of various biogenic anuines or by (ii) increase of neuronal release of bioamines or (iii) by inhibition of monoamine oxidase in higher concentration.

This category of agents show a weak antidepressant activity with considerable side effects. Amphetamine sulphate, methamphetamine sulphate (both discussed under central nervous system stimulants) were the drugs used in mental depression in the early days. Molecular modifications have been attempted in this class, but no useful, potent antidepressant has been evolved.

Monoamine Oxidase Inhibitors :

Monoamine oxidase is one of the enzyme responsible for the metabolism of biogenic amines like norepinephrine. The drugs which inhibit the action of monoamine oxidase thus increase the concentration of bioamine in the brain. The drugs from this category do not elicit an effect in normal individuals and at low doses. They are, however, sufficiently active and potent when used in mentally, depressed patients.

1. Phenelizine Sulphate (B.P.) :

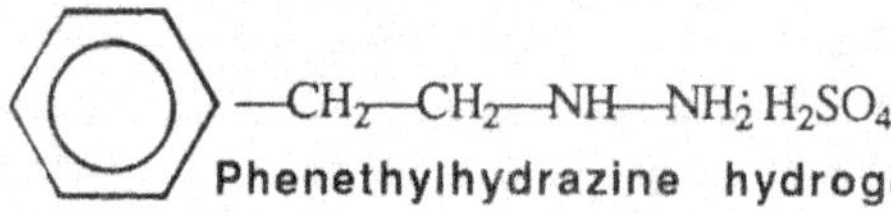

$$C_6H_5-CH_2-CH_2-NH-NH_2 \cdot H_2SO_4$$

Phenethylhydrazine hydrogen sulphate

Properties and uses : It consists of white or pearly platelets with a pungent odour. It is freely soluble in water, but insoluble in alcohol and chloroform. It is administered orally in the form of tablets in 15–45 mg dose in depressed persons.

2. Isocarboxazid (I.P.) :

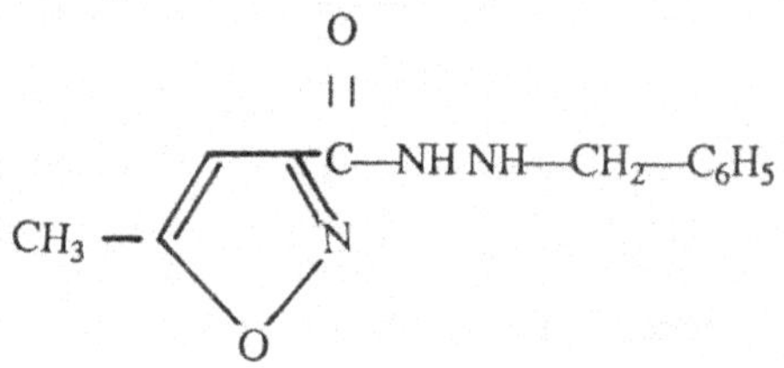

$$\text{(3-methyl-5-isoxazolyl)}-C(=O)-NH-NH-CH_2-C_6H_5$$

**3-N-Benzylhydrazinocarbonyl-5-methylisoxazole or
N-benzyl −N−1(5−methylisooxazole−3−yl−carbonyl)-hydrazine**

Properties and uses : It is a white or creamy white powder, with a faint odour. It is slightly soluble in water, but more soluble in alcohol, ether and chloroform. It is active orally, and is employed in the tablet form in 10-30 mg doses, in treatment of severe mental depression.

3. Pargyline hydrochloride (U.S.P.) :

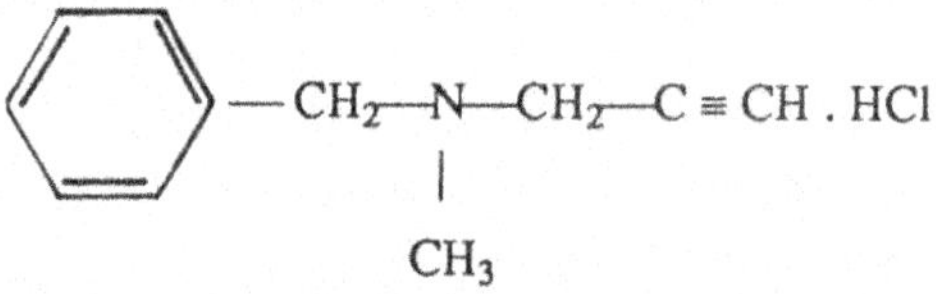

$$C_6H_5-CH_2-N(CH_3)-CH_2-C\equiv CH \cdot HCl$$

N-methyl-N-N-(2−propynyl)−benzylamine hydrochloride

Properties : It is whitish crystalline powder, with a faint odour. It siowly sublimes at elevated temperatures. The salt is very soluble in water and is freely soluble in alcohol and chloroform.

Actions and uses : It is a antidepressant with hypotensive properties. Its hypotensive action is useful in the treatment of patients suffering from mental depression associated with hypertension. Pargyline tablets are available in 10, 25 and 50 mg doses.

4. Tranylcypromine Sulphate (B.P.) :

$$\text{Ph-CH-CH-NH}_2 \cdot \tfrac{1}{2} H_2SO_4$$
$$\quad\ \ \diagdown\text{CH}_2\diagup$$

trans-2-phenylcyclopropiyamine sulphate

Properties : It is a white power, with cinnamaldehyde like odour. It is more soluble in water than in alcohol and solvent ether.

Actions and uses : It is orally active and has a rapid onset of action. The drug is used in severe types of mental depression. Tranylcypromine in a sugar-coated tablet form in 10–20 mg doses are employed.

II. TRICYCLIC COMPOUNDS

The tricyclic antidepressants have been developed by molecular modification of phenothiazines. These compounds belong to the dibenzazepine, dibenzocycloheptene and related three ring class and hence are called as tricyclic compounds. Some compounds, besides possessing antidepressant activity also show sedative and tranquilizing properties. Most of the compounds from this class do not reveal any significant activity in normal individuals at low dose levels. In general the compounds show a slow onset of action. The exact mechanism of action is not known. However, they are believed to inhibit reuptake of norepinephrine into adrenergic neurons.

1. Amitriptyline hydrochloride (I.P., B.P., U.S.P.) :

[Structure: dibenzocycloheptene ring system with numbering 1–11, positions a and d, with side chain HC—CH$_2$—CH$_2$—N—(CH$_3$)$_2$ at position 5] · HCl

3-[10,11-dihydro-5H-dibenzo (a,d) cyclohept-5-ylidene] propyl dimethylamine hydrochloride

Properties : It is a whitish powder with a bitter, burning taste. It is soluble in water and alcohol but is insoluble in solvent ether.

Actions and uses : It has a tranquilizing type, anti-depressant action. It is active orally and is given in the form of tablets. Amitriptyline embonate is official in B.P. The usual dose is 75–150 mg (in divided doses). Amitriptyline injection is official in B.P.

2. **Nortriptyline hydrochloride (B.P.) :**

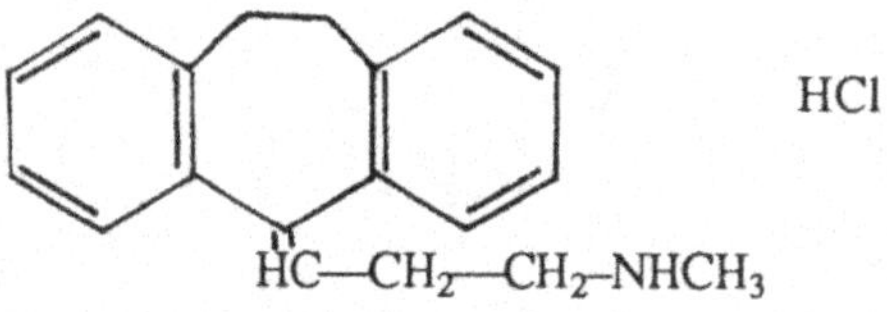

$$3-(10,10-\text{dihydro}-5H-\text{dibenzo [a,d] cyclohept}-5-\text{ylidene})$$
-propyl (methyl) amine hydrochlorde

Properties and uses : It is a whitish powder, with characteristic odour and bitter numbing taste. It is soluble in water and alcohol.

It has similar actions as that of amitriptyline but with fewer side effects. It is administered orally in capsules, tablets or in the liquid form, for treatment of mental depression. The usual dose is in 20–100 mg.

3. **Protryptyline hydrochloride (B.P.)**

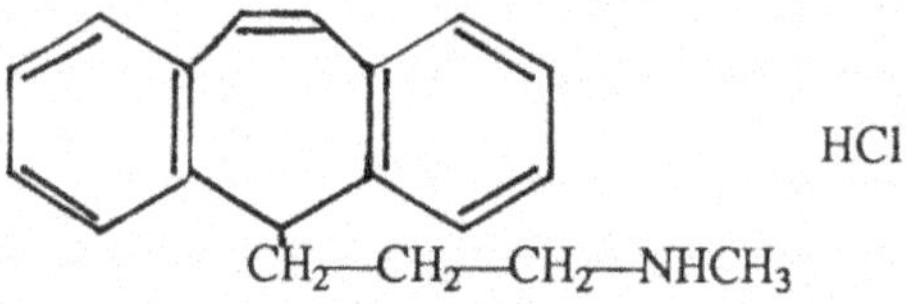

3-(5H-dibenzo-[a, d] cyclohept-5 yl)-propyl (methyl)amine hydrochloride

Properties and uses : It is a yellowish, white powder with a bitter taste and is soluble in water and alcohol. The drug shows a comparatively rapid onset of action. The sedative effect is less. However, it produces drug interactions, and hence should be used with caution. It is active orally, and given in the form of tablets in 15 to 60 mg, in divided doses.

4. **Dothiepin hydrochloride (B.P.) :**

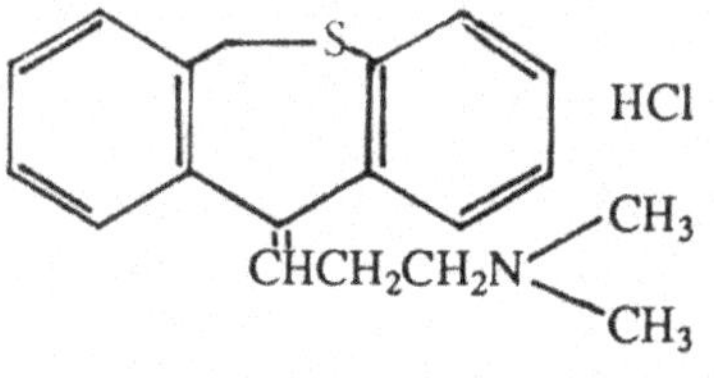

3-(6H-dibenzo (b, e)-thiepin-11- ylidene) propyldimethylammonium chloride

Properties and uses : A white to faintly yellow powder, soluble in water, alcohol and chloroform. The drug is administered orally, as capsules in 75–150 mg dose regime.

5. Doxepin hydrochloride (B.P.)

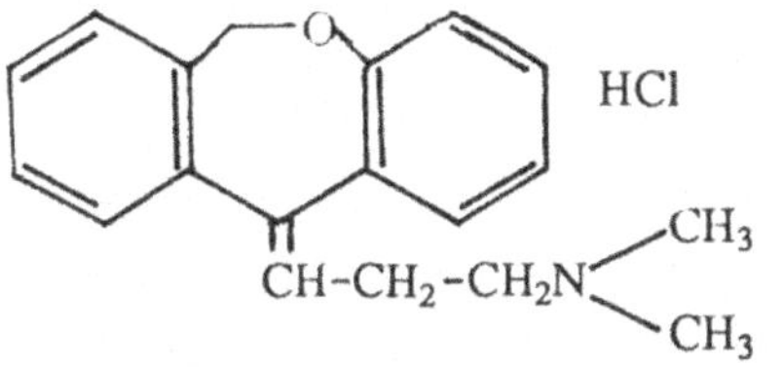

3-(6H-dibenz [b, e]-oxepin-11-ylidene propylimethylamine hydrochloride

Properties and uses : It is a white crystalline powder with an amine like odour and is soluble in water, ethanol and chloroform. The drug shows fewer side effects. It is given as capsules orally, in a 75–150 mg dose.

6. Imipramine hydrochloride (I.P., B.P., U.S.P.) :

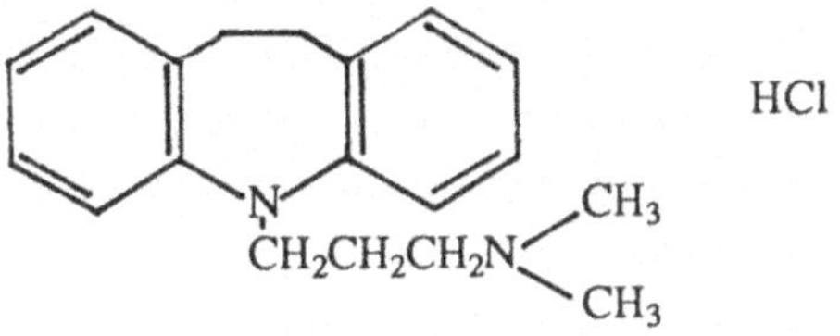

3-(10, 11-dihydro 5H-dibenz [b, f] azepin-5yl) propyldmethylamine hydrochloride

Properties : It occurs as yellowish white crystalline powder and is odourless. It is soluble in water and alcohol.

Actions and uses : It is effective orally. However, there is erratic absorption through the G.I. tract. It is administered as tablets in 10–50 mg for treatment of endogenous depression. Imipramine pamoate is another salt of impramine that is orally active ; and the usual dose is 50 to 150 mg, daily. Ampoules of 25 mg, for intramuscular injection are also available.

7. Desipramine hydrochloride (B.P.) :

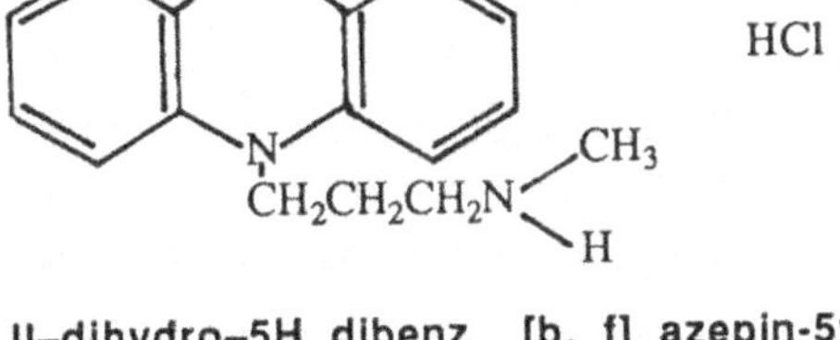

3-(10, II-dihydro-5H dibenz [b, f] azepin-5yl) propyl (methyl) amine hydrochlorde

Properties and uses : It is a white powder with a bitter taste. It is water soluble and has a shorter onset of action than imipramine. Its actions and uses are similar to imipramine hydrochloride. It is effective orally and is available in the form of tablets in 25 mg dose. The usful dose is 25 to 75 mg, daily.

8. Trimipramine maleate (B.P.) :

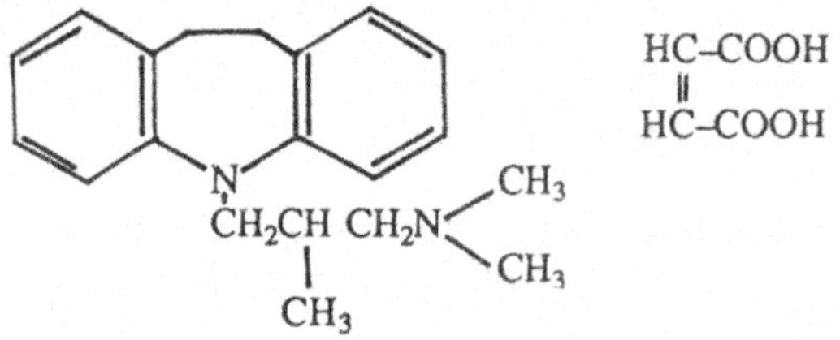

3- (10,11-dihydro-5H dibenz- [b, f] azepin-5 yl)-2-methylpropyl dimethylamine hydrogen maleate.

Properties and uses : It occurs as a white crystalline powder, slightly soluble in water, and more soluble in alcohol. It is active orally and administered as tablets. The usual dose is 50 – 150 mg of base, daily.

9. Clomipramine hydrochloride (B.P.) :

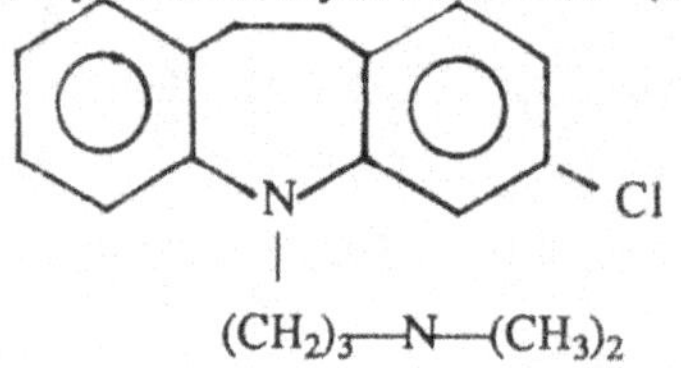

3-(3-chloro-10,11-dihydro 5H dibenz [b, f] azepin-5 yl)
- propyldimethylamine hydrochloride

Properties and uses : It is a yellow crystalline powder, odourless and freely soluble in water, ethanol and in chloroform. It is given in the form of capsule.

10. Mianserin hydrochloride (B.P.) :

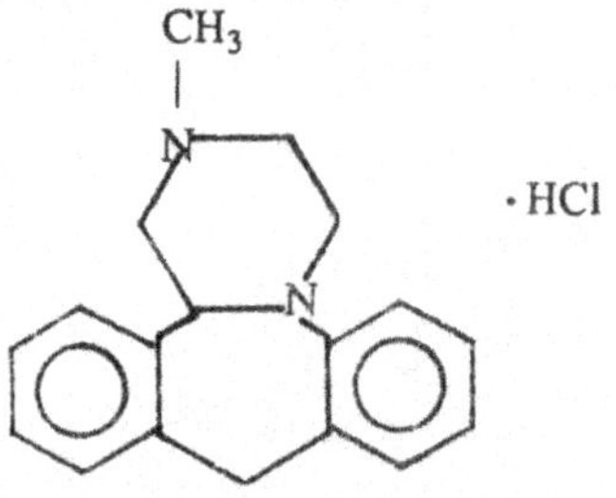

1, 2, 3, 4, 14, b-hexahydro-2-methyldibenzo [c, f] pyrazino [1, 2-a]-azepine hydrochloride

Properties and uses : The drug occurs as almost white crystalline powder, odourless. It is soluble in water and alcohol. It is given in the form of tablets for antidepressant action.

ANTIANXIETY AGENTS (ANXIOLYTIC AGENTS)

Emotional disturbances due to anxiety, worry apprehension, etc. are now-a-days treated with a special class of drugs, called as antianxiety agents. This category is also called as anxyolytic agents. These drugs counteract or reverse anxiety or emotional disturbances in patients. They are believed to act at the cortex and hypothalamus regions of the brain. The exact site and mode of action is not known.

The antianxiety drugs are also used in normal individuals during environmental and emotional stress. The sedative-antianxiety drugs are preferred.

Two major classes of drugs of the sedative hypnotic type have been found useful as antianxiety agents. These are (i) Meprobamate and analogue (ii) Benzodiazepines.

1. Meprobamate (I.P., B.P., U.S.P.) :

$$\begin{array}{c} \text{CH}_3 \quad \text{CH}_2-\text{O}-\overset{\overset{\displaystyle O}{\|}}{\text{C}}-\text{NH}_2 \\ \diagdown \diagup \\ \text{C} \\ \diagup \diagdown \\ \text{CH}_3\text{CH}_2\text{CH}_2 \quad \text{CH}_2-\text{O}-\underset{\underset{\displaystyle O}{\|}}{\text{C}}-\text{NH}_2 \end{array}$$

2-methyl-2-propyltrimethylene dicarbamate

Properties : The drug occurs as a white, crystalline powder with bitter taste. It is sparingly water-soluble but freely soluble in alcohol and organic solvents.

Actions and uses : Meprobamate is active orally. It is used in the form of tablets and capsules. The major therapeutic application is in simple insomnia, anxiety and tension states of psychoneurosis. It is also effective as an anticonvulsant in petitmal form of epilepsy and in muscular spasms. Dose is 0.4 to 1.2 g daily, in divided doses.

BENZODIAZEPINE DERIVATIVES

The development of 1 : 4-benzodiazepines is an accidental one, wherein an unexpected ring enlargement resulted.

The benzodiazepine class for drugs are especially superior because they overcome psychomotor hyperexcitability and also become useful in the treatment of alcohol withdrawal cases. Antianxiety agents being skeletal muscle relaxants also are useful in treating neurologic and musculo-skeletal disorders in patients.

Mechanism of action of benzodiazepines:

Though the importance of role and control of bioamine in brain is accepted, the exact mechanism of action of benzodiazepines in controlling the synthesis, release, storage and metabolism of single neurotransmitter is not known. However, the involvement of γ - aminobutyric acid (GABA) in transmission of neural signals is accepted. Thus the benzodiazepine congeners acting on GABA-containing neurons, which in turn regulates monamines and cholinergic transmission is well known. Presence of benzodiazepine receptor in the brain is also demonstrated.

Clinical use of benzodiazepines :

In general, benzodiazepine drugs exhibit a wide spectrum of activity

1. As a antidepressant they are used in general type of depression, anxiety, tension, worry, apprehension etc.
2. The drugs are also used in treatment of mental depression arising out of psychological disorders as well neurological ones.
3. The sedative-hypnotic action also make then useful in treatment of wide variety of anxiety-tension cases including psychoneurosis.
4. The drugs are also useful as skeletal muscle relaxation in muscular spasm.
5. Some compounds also have strong anticonvulsant activity. Some important drugs used in clinical practice practice are given below :

1. Chlordiazapoxide (B.P., U.S.P.,) :

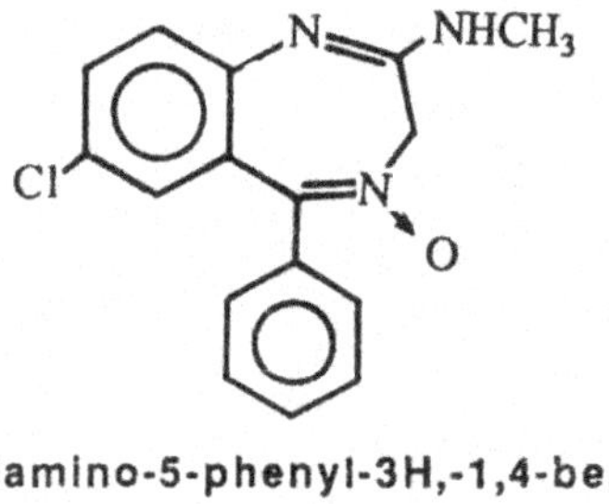

7-chloro-2-methylamino-5-phenyl-3H,-1,4-benzodiazepine-4-oxide

This is a drug developed from 1,4-benzodiazepine. It is used in the form of tablets and capsules (both official) to relieve anxiety and tension states. The usual dose is 10-60 mg daily, in divided doses.

It's hydrochloride is also official in B.P.

2. Diazepam (I.P., B.P., U.S.P.) :

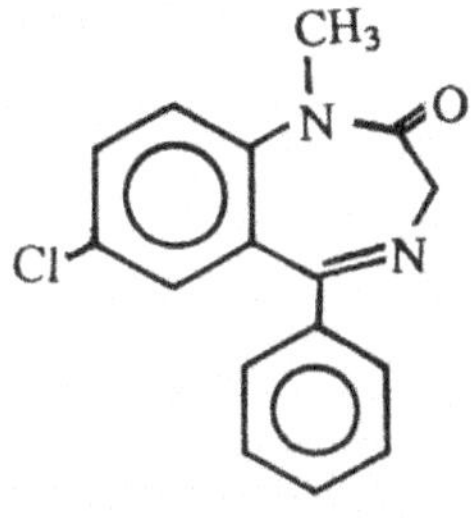

7-chloro-1,3-dihydro-1-methyl-5-phenyl-1,4-benzodiazepine-2-one

The drug has a sedative tranquilizing activity. It is given orally as tablets or capsules in 5 to 30 mg daily in divided doses. The injection, in propylene glycol, is given intramuscularly or intravenously in a 2 to 10 mg dose, in the treatment of anxiety and tension states.

3. Flurazepam monohydrochloride (B.P.) :

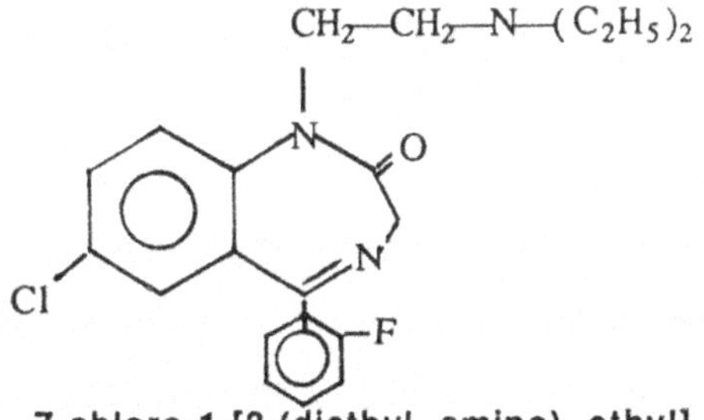

7-chloro-1-[2-(diethyl amino) ethyl] –5-(2-flurophenyl)-1,3 dihydro 2-H-1,4 benzodiazepine-2-one.

Properties and uses : It is white crystalline odourless compound, given in capsules as a hypnotic-antianxiety agent. It is especially useful in insomnia Usual dose is 15-30 mg.

4. Lorazepam (B.P.) :

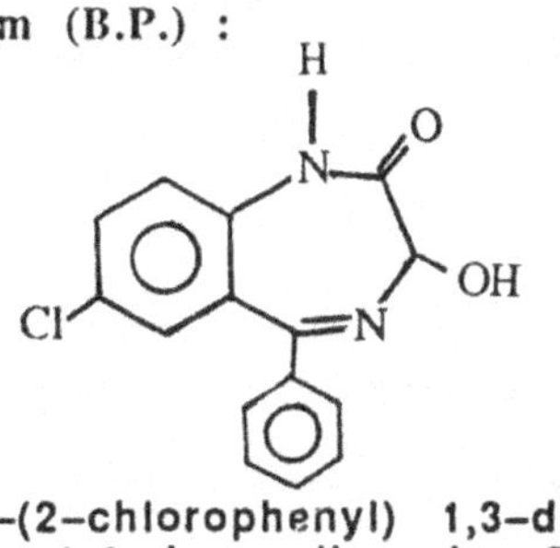

7-chloro-5-(2-chlorophenyl) 1,3–dihydro–3-hydroxy –1,4 benzodiazepine–2-one.

This is related to oxazepam and have higher lipophylicity. Thus lower doses are required to produce anxiolytic effect. It is administered in the form of tablets in 1 to 10 mg dose.

5. Medazepam (B.P.) :

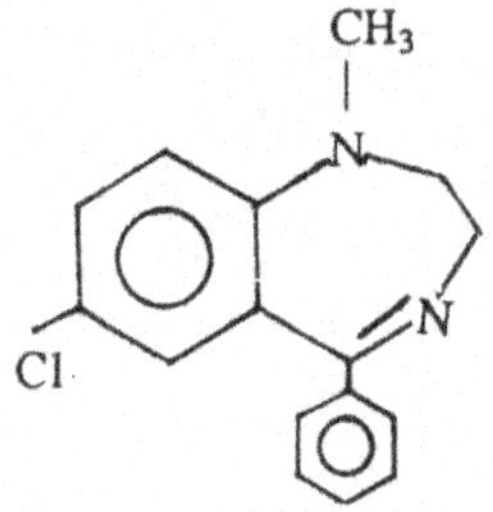

7-chloro-2,3 dihydro-1-methyl-5-Phenyl [1-H] -1,4-benzodiazepine.

Properties and uses : It is a yellowish crystalline powder, insoluble in water, soluble in alcohol. It is a potent anxiolytic agent given in capsules.

6. Oxazepam (B.P., U.S.P.) :

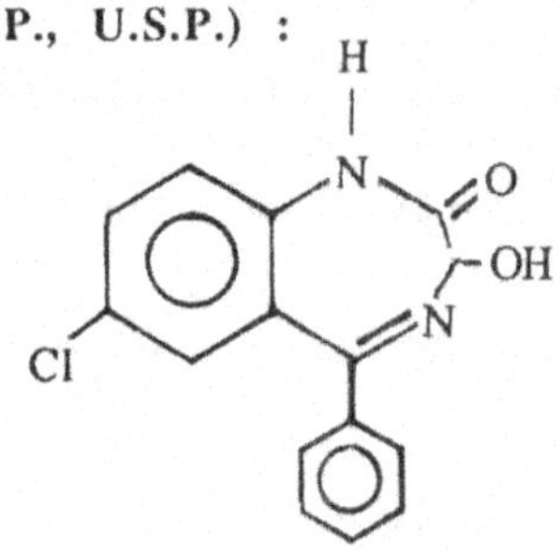

7-chloro-1,3-dihydro-3-hydroxy-5-phenyl-1,4- benzediazepine -2-one

Properties and Uses : It is a white crystalline powder, insoluble in water, slightly soluble in alcohol and chloroform. It is given in capsules and tablet forms for anxiolytic activity. Usual dose is 10–30 mg.

7. Prazepam (U.S.P.) :

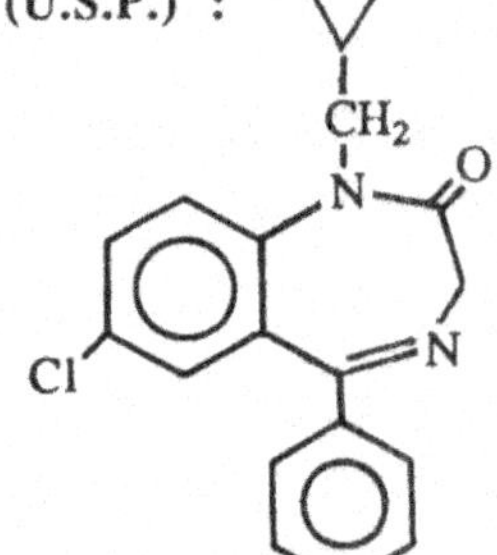

7-Chloro-1-(cyclopropylemethyl)-1,3,-dihydro-5-phenyl-2H- 1,4 benzodazopne-2-one

Properties and uses : It is sedative and antianxiety agent. It is given in tablets in 20–60 mg daily divided doses.

Chapter 4

ANTIPSYCHOTIC AGENTS AND HALLUCINOGENS

Antipsychotics also called as ' ataractics, neuroleptics are the drugs which calm psychotic patients, reduce psychotic manifestations or illness by acting on the central nervous system by a depressant action. Clinically these agents counteract hallucinations or delusion and alleviate psychomotor excitement. Psychosis is a mental disturbance or mental illness, with a varying degree of severity. In milder mental and emotional conditions, anxiety and tension is aggrivated, while in severe types, schizophrenic reactions occur. These reactions are further categorised, depending upon the symptoms and reactions exhibited by the patient.

No biochemical or physiological basis for the psychoses have been known and hence, the exact mechanism by which antipsychotics act is obscure. However, studies indicate that these drugs act at the hypothalamus, brain stem and perhaps at the subcortical parts of the brain by reducing dopaminergic activity in the central Nervous System (CNS). Furthermore, the drugs do not cure the disease, but give relief to the patient.

The antipsychotic drugs act as a calming sedative, neurosedative and psychosedative depending upon the chemical nature of the drug, dose employed and the severity of the mental illness. Some drugs also possess antihistaminic and antiemetic activities, besides weak anticholinergic, local anesthetic, stimulation of gastric secretion actions. etc.

Antipsychotic agents can be broadly classified into the following categories.

(A) Tricyclic compounds (B) Butyrophenones
(C) Reserpine and related compounds (D) Miscellaneous

[A] TRICYCLIC COMPOUNDS

Potent and useful drugs have been developed from the basic three ring nucleus viz., phenothiazine, and ring analog of phenothiazine. The important drugs exhibiting antipsychotic activity are given below.

I. PHENOTHIAZINE CLASS

1. Chlorpromazine hydrochloride (I. P., B.P., U.S.P.) :

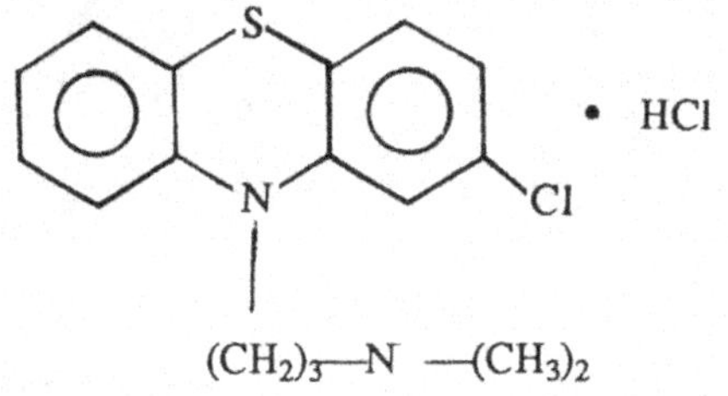

[Structure: phenothiazine ring with S at top, N at bottom bearing $(CH_2)_3-N-(CH_3)_2$ substituent, and Cl on aromatic ring] · HCl

[3-(2-chloro phenothiazine-10-yl) propyl]dimethylamine hydrochloride

Properties : It is a white crystalline powder and is soluble in water and alcohol. Aqueous solutions are stable to heat. Injections are sterilised by autoclaving or by filtration method.

Actions and uses : It is administered orally as tablets, syrups, elixirs or parentally in the treatment of anxiety, tension, agitation, emotional disturbances and in lessening motor activity both in psychoneurotic and psychotic. It also finds use in treatment of nausea and vomiting and also in treatment of acute alcoholism. It potentiates the effects of analgesics, hypnotic and sedatives. Usual dose is 25 – 100 mg daily and in psychiatric states the dose varies from 25 mg to 1 g in divided doses depending on route of administration and purpose.

2. Fluphenazine hydrochloride (B.P., U.S.P.) :

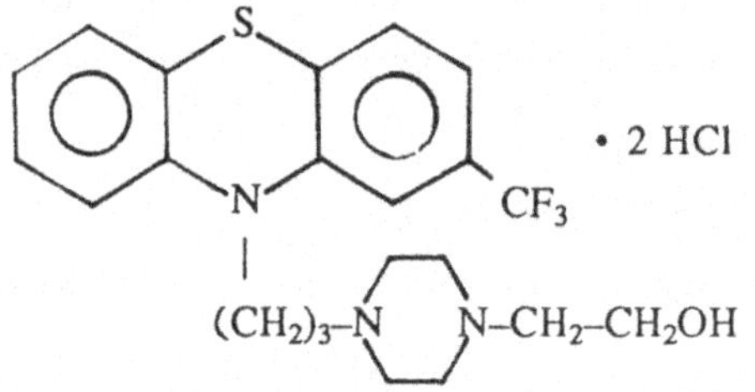

[Structure: phenothiazine ring with S at top, N substituted with $(CH_2)_3-N$ piperazine $N-CH_2-CH_2OH$, and CF_3 on aromatic ring] · 2 HCl

2-{4-[3-(2-trifuromethylphenothiazin-1-yl) propyl] -piperazin-1-yl} ethanol dihydrochloride

Properties and uses : It is a white crystalline odourless powder, soluble in water, less soluble in alcohol and ether. It is most potent tranquiliser used in major psychotic state. The drug is used as tablets in 1.25 mg to 10 mg and as injection 2.5 mg/ml dose. The Fluphenazine decanoate and enanthate are official in B.P. and U.S.P. and are used in the form of injection (in schizophrenia).

3. Prochlorperazine maleate (B.P.) :

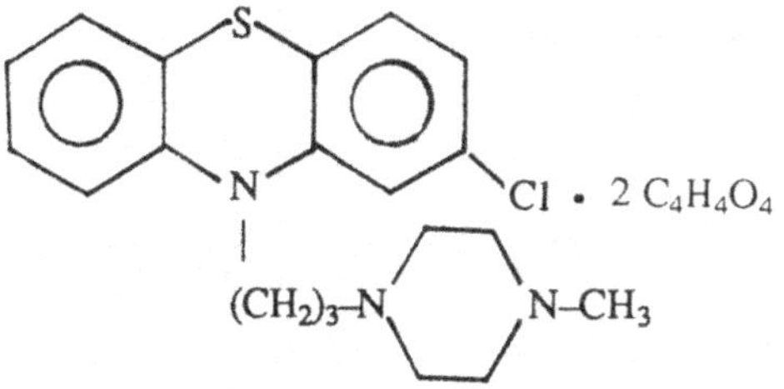

[Structure: 2-chloro phenothiazine with N-(CH$_2$)$_3$-N(piperazine)-N-CH$_3$ substituent; Cl · 2 C$_4$H$_4$O$_4$]

2-chloro-10-[3-(4-methylpiperazine-lyl)-propyl]
phenothiazine maleate

Properties : It occurs as white powder and is slightly soluble in water and alcohol. It is given orally and intramuscularly. It is given as tablets in 10 mg 3, 4 times a day. The drug shows same effect as chlorpromazine but in smaller dose. The mesylate (B.P.) and edisylate (U.S.P.) are water soluble salts and are used for oral and by intramuscular route.

4. Promazine hydrochloride (B.P.) :

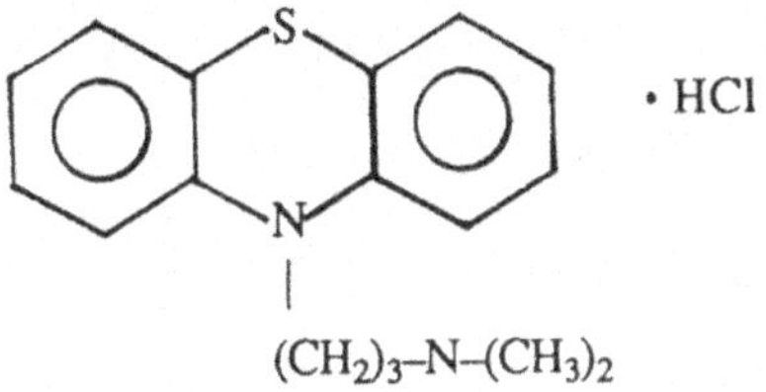

[Structure: phenothiazine with N-(CH$_2$)$_3$-N-(CH$_3$)$_2$ substituent; · HCl]

Dimethyl-(3-phenothiazine-10-yl-propyl)-amine hydrochloride

Properties and uses : It is white to yellowish crystalline solid, soluble in water and alcohol. It gets oxidised on exposure to air and hence should be stored in well closed containers. It is used as antipsychotic agent but is less potent than chlorpromazine. Tablets and injection formulations are commercially available. Oral administration is preferred.

5. Perphenazine (B.P., U.S.P.) :

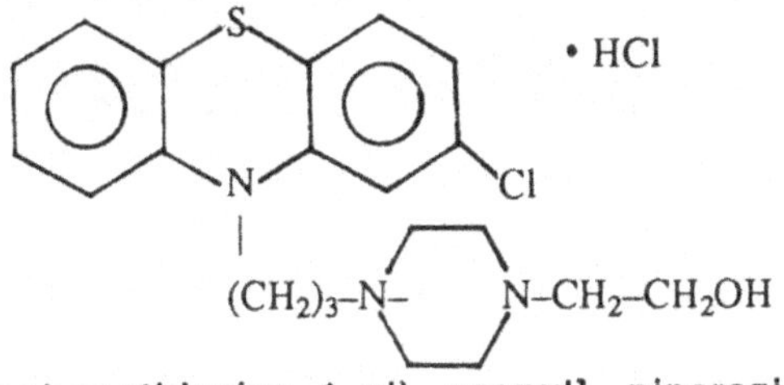

[Structure: 2-chloro phenothiazine with N-(CH$_2$)$_3$-N(piperazine)-N-CH$_2$-CH$_2$OH substituent; · HCl]

2-{4-[3-(2-chlorophenothiazine-1-yl) propyl] piperazine-lyl}
ethanol hydrochloride

Properties and uses : It is a white creamy powder odourless and is practically insoluble in water, soluble in alcohol. It is used in chronic schizophrenia and also as antiemetic.

6. Methotrimeprazine hydrochloride (B.P.) :

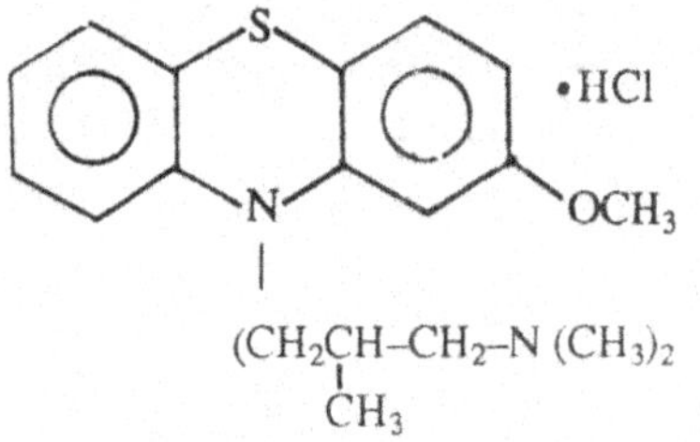

(R)-3-(2-methoxylphenothiazine-10-yl)-2 methylpropyl dimethylamine hydrochloride

Properties and uses : It is a white and slightly yellow crystalline powder and is hygroscopic. It deteriorates on exposure to light and air and should be kept in air tight container and protected from light. It is a potent antipsychotic agent.

7. Thioridazine hydrochloride (B.P., U.S.P.) :

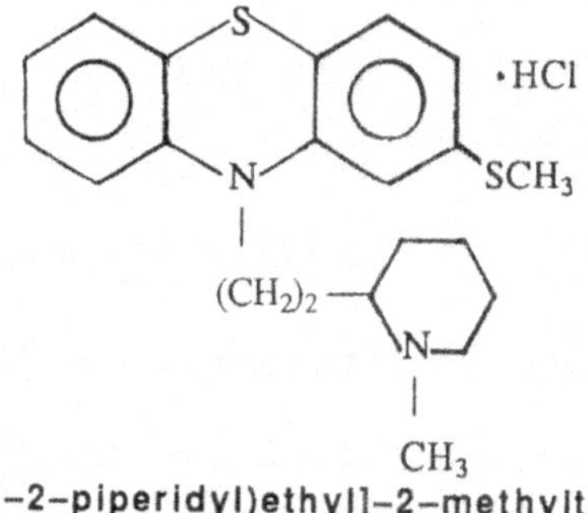

10-[2-(1-methyl-2-piperidyl)ethyl]-2-methylthiophenothiazine hydrochloride

Properties and uses : It occurs as a creamy powder with slight odour, soluble in water and alcohol. It is a potent drug used in the treatment of psychoneurosis and psychosis. It is used orally as tablets in 10 to 100 mg dose.

8. Trifluroperazine hydrochloride (I.P., B.P., U.S.P.) :

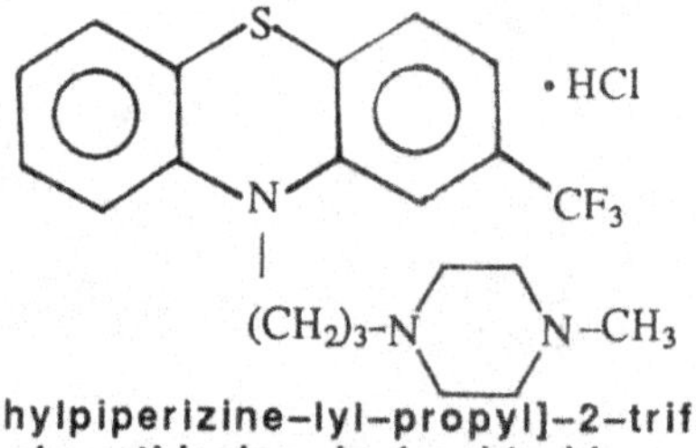

10-[3-(4-methylpiperizine-1yl-propyl]-2-trifluromethyl-phenothiazine hydrochloride

Properties and uses : It occurs as pale yellow crystalline powder, slightly hygroscopic. It is freely soluble in water and alcohol. It is given as tablets in 2 to 5 mg dose daily in psychotic cases.

9. Triflupromazine hydrochloride (I.P., U.S.P.) :

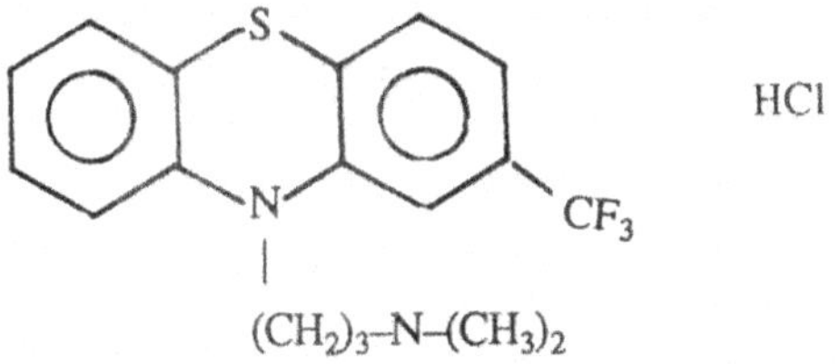

[3-(2-trifluromethyl phenothiazine-10-yl) propyl-dimethylamine hydrochloride

Properties and uses : It is a pale-yellowish brown powder, slight odour, soluble in water, alcohol and acetone. It is used in management of psychotic disorders and also for controlling nausea and vomiting. It is given as tablets, usual dose is 30–150 mg of triflupromazine daily. It is stored in well-closed light resistant containers.

II. RING ANALOG OF PHENOTHIAZINE

(i) **Thiothixene hydrochloride (U.S.P.) :**

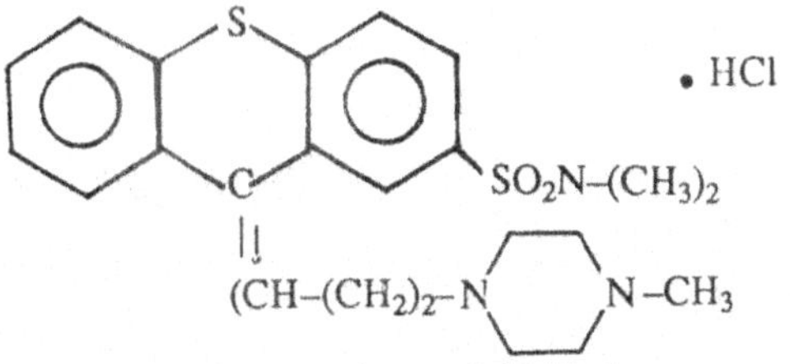

Actions and uses : It potentiates actions of CNS depressants including anaesthetics, hypnotics and alcohol. It is given orally in 3 to 60 mg dose in capsules or by injection. Chloroprothixene is another compound from this class as a potent antipsychlotic agent.

2. Loxapine succinate :

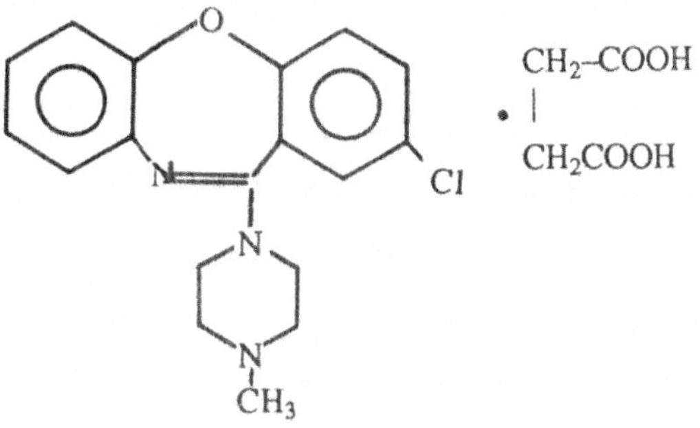

Properties and uses : It is a potent drug used in the treatment of acute and chronic schizophrenia. Side effects are Parkinson like symptoms.

[B] BUTYROPHENONE CLASS

From butyrophenones very potent neuroleptic drugs have been developed. Their mechanism is similar to phenothiazine class by blocking bioamine (dopamine) receptors. The compounds from this class have more potent (20-50 times) antipsychotic activity and are less toxic than phenothiazines. Haloperidol and Droperidal are the two potent dugs used in treatment of manic phase of drpressive illness and in schizophrenia.

Haloperiodol, a prototype related to butyrophenone is a very potent and specific antipsychotic drug.

Haloperidol   (B.P., U.S.P.) :

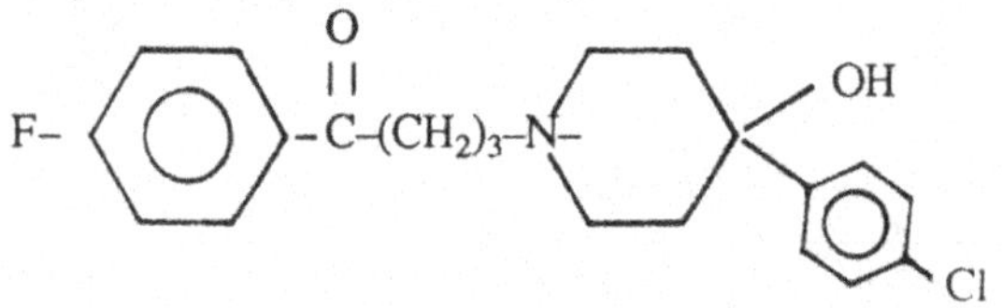

4-[4-(4-chlorophenyl)-4-hydroxypiperiodino)-4-flurobutyro-phenone

Properties, actions and uses : It occurs as a white to yellowish-microcrystalline powder, insoluble in water but soluble in chloroform. It is an effective tranquilliser and is used in the control of agitated states mania and schizophrenia patients. It also potentiates the CNS depressant actions of other drugs. It is given orally as tablets and parantarally by intramuscular injections. Usual dose 1 to 10 mg daily.

Droperiodol (U.S.P.) :

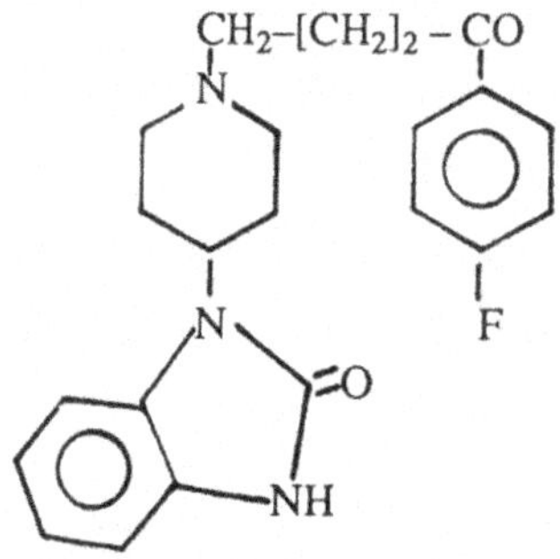

Properties : It is a tan coloured powder, insoluble in water. It darkens on exposure to air. It is used as antipsychotic and is given in combination with

potent narcotic analgesic fentanyl for preanaesthetic sedation and in analgesia.

Some compounds with a central seven membered ring, with or without oxygen in the ring have been under clinical trails. However, they are not as yet official in pharmacopoeias.

[C] RESERPINE AND RELATED COMPOUNDS

Rauwolfia serpentina and its isolated alkaloid, reserpine, is extensively used in treatment of neuroleptic and hypertensive patients. A large number of preparations (both official and non-official) like extracts, isolated alkaloid mixtures; pure reserpine and its tablets and injections are used as antipsychotics, either orally or by parenteral route. For antipsychotic activity, a 3 to 10 mg dose is employed.

[D] MISCELLANEOUS

Miscellaneous compounds with a neuroleptic activity have been found in different chemical classes. However, drugs like Metoclopramide hydrochloride have a more useful antiemetic and accelerator of gastric emptying activity, than neuroleptics.

Metoclopramide hydrochloride :

[Structure: benzene ring with Cl, $CONHCH_2CH_2N(C_2H_5)_2$ · HCl, H_2N, and OCH_3 substituents]

Some benzodioxan derivatives have been attempted for use for neuroleptic activity. However, they have not resulted into therapeutically useful drugs.

HALLUCINOGENS

Hallucination is a peculiar state of mind resulting in alteration of mood and perception. It often shows illusion coupled with feeling of euphoria and a state of exhilliration. This peculiar state is brought about by drugs by altering the levels of biogenic amines and produces stimulating effects on CNS.

The hallucinagens are generally classified into :
(i) True psychotomimetics which exhibit the full range of psychic characters like psychic state and affecting autonomic and somatomotor activities. The drugs from phenylethylamine, indole ethylamine belong to this class.
(ii) **Psychodelics :** Those are agents which bring change in alteration of mood, perceptions and feeling of exhiliration e.g. the LSD, mescaline etc.

The hallucinogenic effects are primarily produced as a toxic side effects of different drugs. Some potent CNS stimulants when used in high doses or when not metabolised produces toxic manifestation in the form of hallucination. such drugs are abuse drugs. No hallucinogenic compound is official for the above reason. However, few compounds find use in experimental animals to act as test models. The following halllucinogens are of recognisable importance.

1. **Dimethyl tryptamine :**

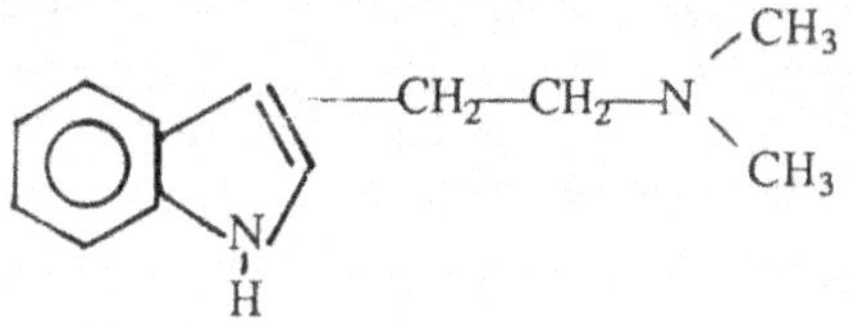

This compound when inhaled produces hallucinogenic condition.

2. **Lysergic acid diethylamide (LSD) :**

This is a very potent agent and produces effect in 100–200 µg when taken orally.

3. **Mescaline :**

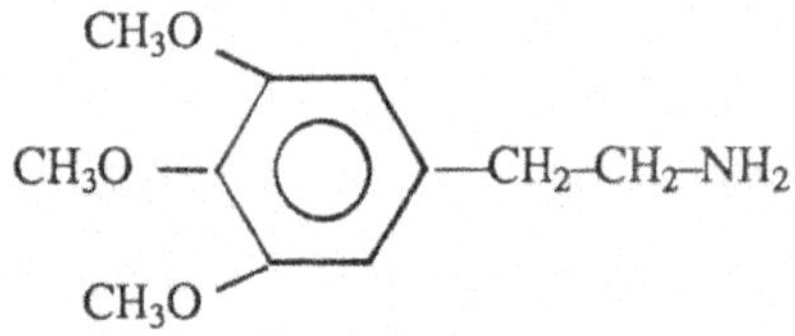

3, 4, 5 trimethoxy phenylethylamine

The drug is orally active in 250–500 mg but is rapidy metabolised.

4. **Phencyclidine hydrochloride :**

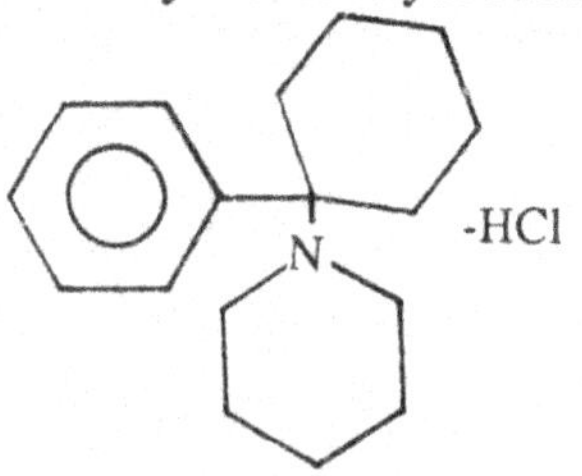

1 (1-phenylcyclohexyl) Piperidine hydrochloride

Properties : The drug has marked analgesic–anaesthetic activity. However, the hallucinogenic effect is predominant when the drug is administered parenterily or inhaled as smoke.

5. **Cannabis (Hashish) :** It is a product derived from *cannabis sativa*. It has marked analgesic, anticonvulsant activity. This a potent hallucinogenie agent and is known for abuse.

None of the above mentioned drugs are used in clinical practice.

Chapter 5

GENERAL ANAESTHETICS

The drugs and chemicals which produce anaesthesia, a condition in which there is a loss of sensation of pain and loss of consciousness, are called general anaesthetics. The general anaesthetics bring anaesthesia to the entire body and patient is made unconscious, with muscular relaxation and insensation to pain. These agents are thus useful to prepare patient for a surgical operation.

Adjuncts to General anesthesia

Some drugs from different pharmacological class like narcotic analgesics, sedatives, anticholinergics, skeletal muscle relaxants, tranquilizers are used before the administration of general anesthetics. These drugs are called as pre-anesthetics medications or as adjuncts to anesthetics. These drugs decrease anxiety, reduce the dose and amount of anesthetic drug. They reduce or minimise some undesirable side effects of anesthetic drug, such as salivation or secretion, bradycardia, postanesthetic vomiting.

Thus narcotic analgesics like morphine or pethedine are used to reduce pain, pentobarb or secobarb to provide sedation and remove anxiety, promazine, or promethazine to induce sedation and antiemetic properties, atropine or scopolamine to inhibit excessive respiratory secretions.

General anaesthetics may be divided into two broad categories:

1. Volatile and gaseous anaesthetics which are administered by inhalation by the open method or the closed method system, and

2. intravenous anaesthetics which are given via the intravenous route. In both categories, the features of safety, effectiveness, general usefulness, freedom from toxicity and after effects, are taken into consideration.

Volatile and gaseous Anaesthetics :

This category of anaesthetics includes liquids which are volatile in nature and belongs to the chemical class of halogenated hydrocarbons (chloroform, ethylchloride, trichloroethylene, etc) and others (diethyl-ether, vinyl ether, methoxyflurane, etc.) while the gaseous substances in this category are nitrous oxide.

1. **Anaesthetics Ether : (I. P., B. P.) :**

$$CH_3\ CH_2\ OCH_2\ CH_3$$

(diethylether) or athody ethane)

Properties : It is a colourless volatile liquid with a burning, sweetish taste and characteristic odour. It is inflammable and when mixed with air and ignited, it exploes violently. It gets slowly oxidised in air with the formation of peroxides. Hence, it is stabilised by the addition of 0.02 % w/v hydroquinone or propyl gallate as preservatives.

Actions and uses : Ether is used as an anaesthetic by inhalation either by itself or with other gaseous anaesthetics. It is administered by the drip method or by a gas machine.

2. **Chloroform (I. P., B. P.) :**

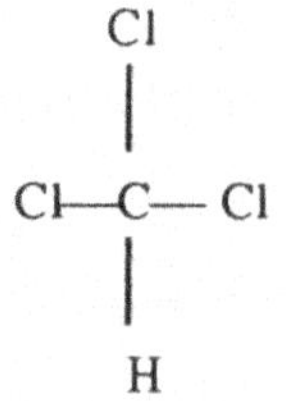

$$\begin{array}{c} Cl \\ | \\ Cl-C-Cl \\ | \\ H \end{array}$$

Trichloromethane

Properties : It is a colourless liquid, with a characteristic sweetish burning taste. It is not inflammable and is mixcible with ether, alcohol and fixed volatile oils. 1 to 2% v/v ethyl alcohol is added to prevent the formation of poisonous phosgene gas.

Actions and Uses : It is a potent anaesthetic and is administered by the open or closed mouth inhalation method. In small doses (0.3 to 1 ml), it act as a carminative. Externally, it is used as a rubefacient. It is used as a preservative and flavouring agent in pharmaceutical preparations.

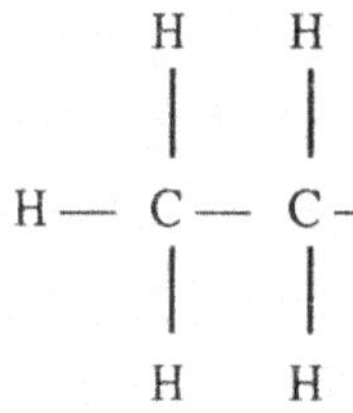

$$\begin{array}{c} H\ \ \ \ H \\ |\ \ \ \ | \\ H-C-C-Cl \\ |\ \ \ \ | \\ H\ \ \ \ H \end{array}$$

1 - chloroethane

Properties : It is a very volatile liquid, with an ethereal odour and a burning taste. It is supplied and stored in compressed cylinders.

Actions and Uses : It is administered by the inhalation method for minor operations. When sprayed, it produces a cool, numbing effect and acts as a local anaesthetic.

4. Halothane (B.P.) :

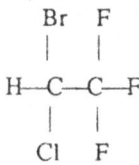

2-bromo-2-chloro, 1,1,1-trifluroethane

Properties : It occurs as a colourless liquid, with an odour like that of chloroform. It is non-inflammable and is miscible with chloroform, ether and other organic solvents. It is protected from light and kept in closed containers. It is light sensitive and is stored in brown bottles and stabilised by addition of 0.01 % thymol.

Actions and uses : It is the most potent anaesthetic and is administered by inhalation. Induction of anaesthesia by halothane is smooth and rapid, and does not cause irritation to the membrane.

5. Methoxyflurane (U.S.P.) :

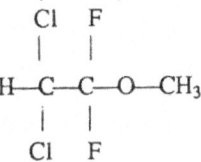

2, 2-dichloro-1,1-difluoroethyl methylether

Properties : It is a clear-colourless, non-inflammable liquid with a sweet fruity odour. 0.01 % w/w butylated hydroxytoluene is used as a stabiliser.

Actions and uses : It is used as an anaesthetic and is administered by the inhalation method. Its irritant action on the mucous membrane is less than that of ether.

6. Trichloroethylene (I.P., B.P.) :

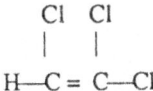

1-chloro 2-2-dichloroethene

Properties : It is a colourless liquid with a chloroform like odour and taste. It is non-inflammable, but decomposed by moisture and light 0.01 % w/w thymol is used as a preservative. It is miscible with chloroform, ether and alcohol.

Actions and uses : It is employed in short surgical operations or in obsterics, and administered by inhalation. It also has a potent analgesic action.

7. Vinyl ether (B.P.) :

$$H-\underset{\underset{H}{|}}{C}=\underset{\underset{H}{|}}{C}-O-\underset{\underset{H}{|}}{C}=\underset{\underset{H}{|}}{C}-H$$

Properties : It occurs as a colourless liquid with a characteristic odour. It is miscible with alcohol, acetone, chloroform and ether. It gets decomposed by oxidation and hence is stabilised by the addition of a suitable antioxidant or by absolute alcohol (4 % v/v).

Actions and uses : It is a more potent anaesthetic than ether and has a more rapid onset of action. It is administered by the open drip method or by the closed method with oxygen.

8. Cyclopropane (I.P., B.P.) :

$$\underset{H_2C - CH_2}{\overset{CH_2}{\diagup\diagdown}}$$

Properties : It is an odourless gas, with pungent taste and an odour like hexane. The gas is soluble in water and alcohol. It is supplied in metal cylinders labled ' inflammable.' The cylinders are painted orange on the neck and its name is engraved on it.

Actions and uses : It is a potent gaseous, non-irritant anaesthetic with rapid induction.

9. Nitrous oxide (I.P., B.P.) : N_2O

Properties : It is a colourless gas, with a slightly sweet taste. It is soluble in water and alcohol. It is supplied in metal cylinders which are painted blue on the collars with the name engraved on the cylinder.

Action and uses : It is a comparatively weak anaesthetic, but has an analgesic action also. It is used, along with oxygen, by the inhalation method.

Intravenous Anaesthetic :

Some drugs are given intravenously as anaesthetics, which produce unconsciousness similar to that produced by volatile or gaseous anaesthetics. This method of administration of drugs, offers many advantages over other methods. The advantages are :

(i) They produce rapid induction of anaesthesia, without the excitment stage.

(ii) They offer freedom from explosion hazards.

(iii) Freedom from pulmonary or mucous membrane irritation and secretion, and ;

(iv) Recovery is without nausea or vomitting.

Important drugs belong to ultrashort acting barbiturates are :

1. Methohexitone Sodium : (B.P.)

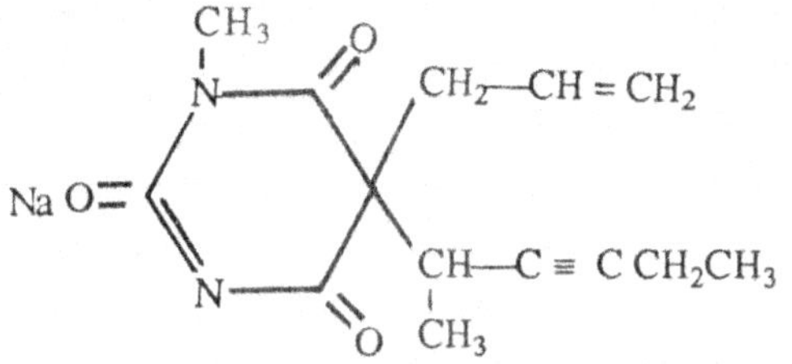

5-allyl-1-methyl 5-(1-methyl-pent-2-ynyl) barbituric acid sodium

Properties : It is a white crystalline powder with a faint odour and soluble in water. The sodium salt is water soluble, and the solution is sterilised by the filtration method.

Actions and uses : It is employed for the induction of anaesthesia intravenously.

2. Thiamylal sodium injection (U.S.P.) :

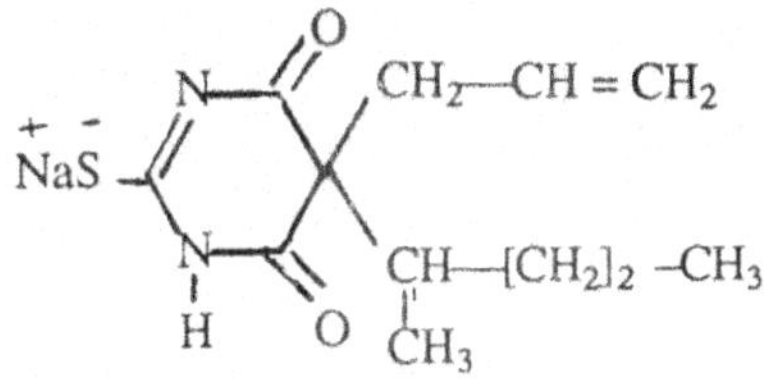

Sodium salt of 5-allyl 5 (1 methyl butyl) 2 - thio barbiturate

Properties : It is a white solid with a faint odour and is water–soluble. The preparation of thiamylal sodium for injection contains about 7 % anhydrous sodium carbonate as a buffer and it is alkaline to litmus.

Actions and uses : It is used to produce anaesthesia of a short duration, in a 3 to 6 ml (2.5 %) dose.

3. Thiopentone sodium (I.P., B.P., U.S.P.) :

It is a mixture of thiopentone sodium with anhydrous sodium carbonate.

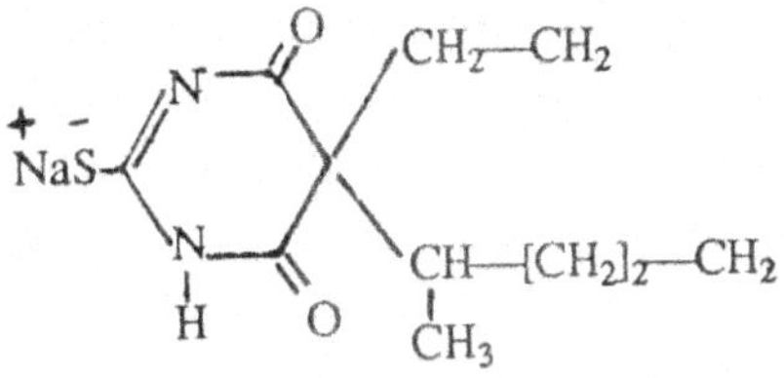

Sodium salt of 5-allyl 5 (1 methyl butyl) 2 - thio barbiturate

Properties : It occurs as a white, crystalline hygroscopic powder, with a disagreeable odour. It is freely soluble in water and its aqueous solution is unstable. Exposure to carbon dioxide results in precipitation.

Actions and uses : It is most widely used as an intravenous, general purpose anaesthetic for short operative procedures in a 100 – 500 mg, dose. For induction of anaesthesia, 2–3 ml of 2.5 to 5 % w/v solution is employed. The maximum dose is of 2g.

4. Propanidid

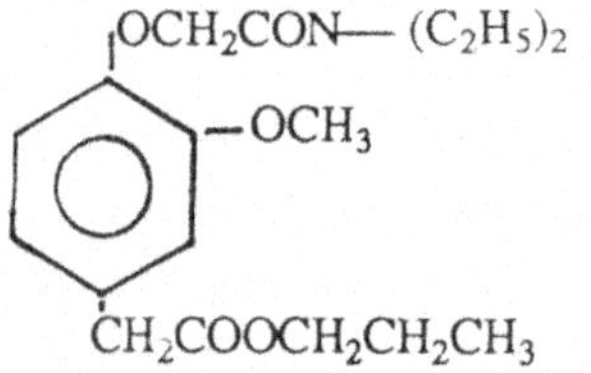

$$\text{OCH}_2\text{CON}-(\text{C}_2\text{H}_5)_2$$
$$-\text{OCH}_3$$
$$\text{CH}_2\text{COOCH}_2\text{CH}_2\text{CH}_3$$

Propyl-4-diethyl-carbamoyl-methoxy-3-methoxyphenylacetate

Properties : It occurs as a pale greenish yellowish hygroscopic liquid. It is less soluble in water, but is miscible with alcohol and ether.

Actions and uses : It is used as an anaesthetic in a usual dose of 5 to 10 mg/kg body weight and is administered via the intravenous route. It gives a short duration of action.

BASAL ANAESTHETICS :

Certain drugs bring about the depression of the central nervous system and produce a state of unconsciousness. Such drugs are called basal anaesthetics. The unconsciousness produced is not of a sufficient depth, and hence, surgical procedures are not possible. However, these drugs are useful in bringing about smooth conduction of anaesthesia, without mental strain or respiratory irritation. The useful drugs from this category are :

1. Hexobarbitone sodium :

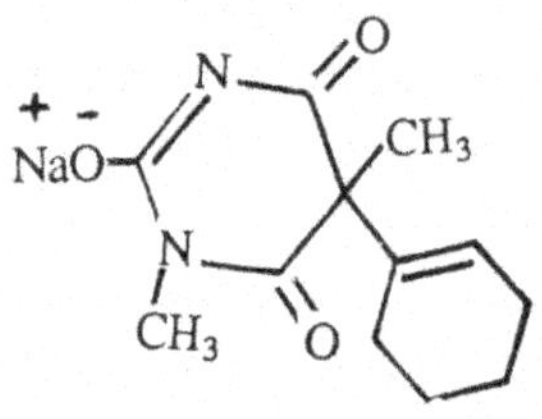

Properties and uses : It is a white, crystalline powder, hygroscopic in nature and very soluble in water and alcohol, but insoluble in ether. The powder gets discoloured on exposure to air. The aqueous solution decomposes on standing. It is an ultra short acting drug. The dose is determined by the physician.

2. Tribromoethanol :

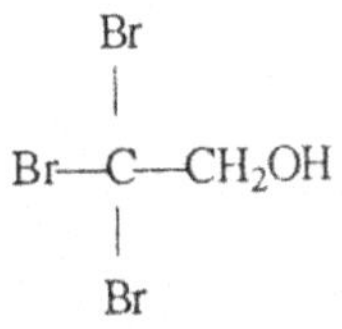

$$\begin{array}{c} Br \\ | \\ Br-C-CH_2OH \\ | \\ Br \end{array}$$

2, 2, 2 Tribromoethanol

Properties and uses : It is a white crystalline powder with a faint aromatic odour. It is soluble in water, alcohol, ether and bezene. It is affected by light and air, and gets discoloured. The aqueous solution also decomposses rapidly. It is employed as a basal anaesthetic in an average dose of 60 mg/kg body weight. The tribromoethanol solution in amylenehydrate(1 %) is employed by the rectal route in 0.06 to 0.08 ml/kg with a maximum upto 8 ml for women and 10 ml for men.

Chapter 6

HYPNOTICS AND SEDATIVES

Hypnotics and sedatives are a category of agents which depress the centra nervous system. Hypnotics are drugs which induce sleep by depression of the central nervous system function, while sedatives are the agents which reduce excitement and motor activity, and produce a calming effect without inducing sleep. Thus, small doses of hypnotics may act as a sedative, while large doses of a sedative may produce a hypnotic effect.

The general characteristics of these agents is the depressant action they produce on the carebrospinal axis. They differ in the time required for onset of depression and duration of the effect. Furthermore, the degree of depression which they produce depends upon the potency of drug, dose and the route of administration. These agents are useful for (i) Insomnia (sleeplessness) (ii) Hypertension (iii) Control of convulsions (iv) Stress and emotional strain, and (v) In potentiation of analgesic effect and as adjuvent to anaesthesia.

The hypnotics and sedatives are classified as follows :

(i) Barbiturates and their derivatives (ii) Non-barbiturates (iii) Alcohols (iv) Aldehydes (v) Ureides (vi) Miscellaneous.

I. BARBITURATES

Brabiturates, in general, are derivatives of barbituric acid which is cyclic ureide formed by the condensation of urea, substituted urea or thiourea with malonic acid ester or substituted malonic acid ester. The skeleton structure for barbituric acid is given below. Due to Keto-Enol tautomerism it forms water-soluble sodium salt. Various barbiturates are prepared by substitution of groups at the 1, 3 and 5 positions of barbituric acid. Substitution of oxygen by sulphur, at position 2, gives thiobarbiturates.

Barbiturates are usually white, crystalline solids and have poor water solubility. Their sodium salts are water soluble and their solutions are alkaline in nature. The solutions are incompatible with acids, acidic substances and ammonium salts.

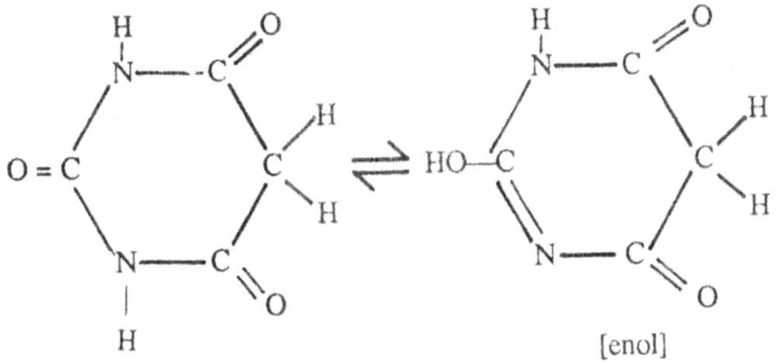

Barbituric acid [keto] ⇌ [enol]

Barbiturates

The barbiturates exert a depressant effect on the cerebrospinal axis. These drugs reduce neuronal activity by modifying the synaptic transmission. They also reduce excitability of the postsynaptic cells by altering permiability of cell membrane. Depending upon the chemical nature of compound, its dose and route of administration, barbiturates produce different degree of depression from slight sedation to deep anesthesia.

Barbiturates are classified according to their biological action (hypnotic action) into long acting, intermediate acting, and short acting categories.

[A] Long Acting Barbiturates

Barbiturates of this class produce the onset of action within 30 minutes to 1 hour, and have a long duration (6 – 12 hours) of action. Some examples are given below.

1. **Barbituric acid –(Barbital) (B.P.) :**

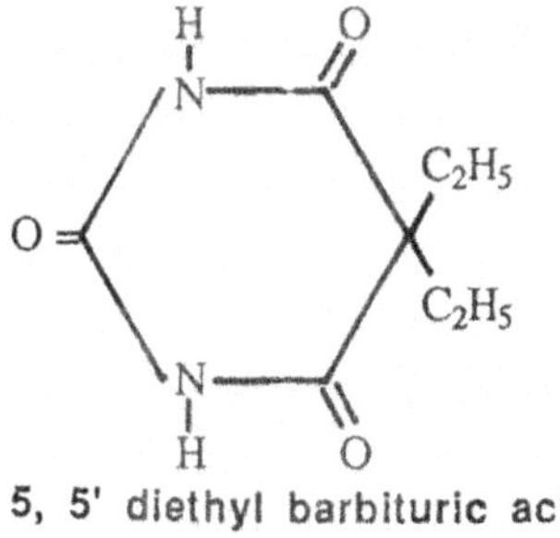

5, 5' diethyl barbituric acid

Properties and Uses : It occurs as colourless crystalline powder odourless, slightly soluble in water but more soluble in alcohol and ether. It is also more soluble in boiling water (1 in 15). The aqueous solution is acidic in nature. The powder is stable in air. It is decomposed by alkalies like NaOH and KOH. It is used in the form of tablets, and the usual dose is 300 mg. It is also available as sodium salt which is more water-soluble.

2. **Phenobarbitone (phenobarbital) (I. P., B. P., U. S. P.) :**

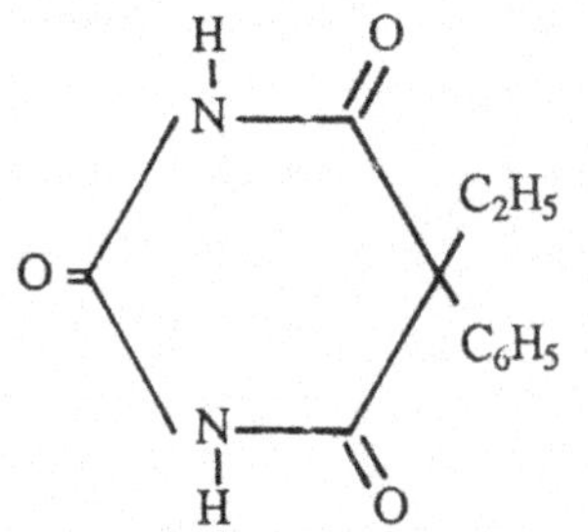

$$\text{5, ethyl - 5 - diethylbarbituric acid}$$

Properties and Uses : It occurs as white crystals, or white crystalline powder, odourless, slightly soluble in water (1 to 100), very soluble in chloroform. It is soluble in aqueous solutions of alkalies. Its saturaed aqueous solution is acidic to litmus. It is stable in air. It acts as a log acting hypnotic and sedative. It is specifically used in the symptomatic therapy of cpilepsy. It is more useful in grandmal and less in petitmal. The usual dose is 15 to 100 mg. for a hyptonic and sedative purpose, and in epilepsy it is 100 mg, two to three times a day.

Phenobarbitone sodium : Phenobarbital sodium (I. P., B. P., U. S. P.) : It is a sodium salt of phenobarbitone.

Properties and Uses : It occurs as white granules or powder, odourless and hygroscopic in nature.It is very soluble in water, soluble in alcohol but practically insoluble in chloroform and ether. Its aqueous solution is alkaline to litmus. It usually decomposes on exposure to air and moisture.

It is used in the form of tablets or as an injection. It can be given intravenously, for the control of actue convulsive syndromes. Its usual dose is 30 to 120 mg orally or 60 to 200 mg as a single dose by intravenous or intramuscular injection.

3. **Methylphenobarbitone, (Mephobarbital) (U. S. P.) :**

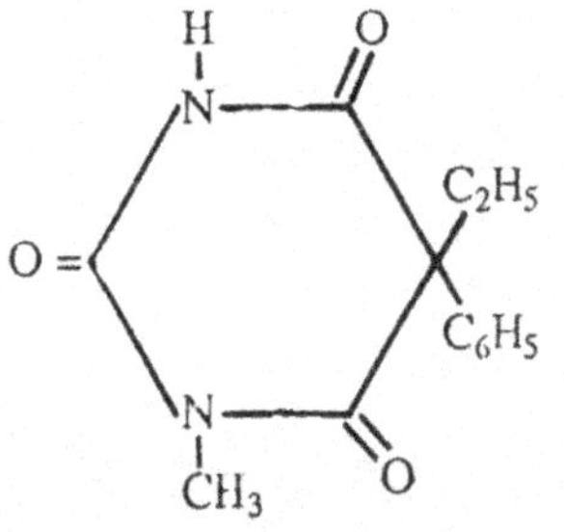

5 - ethyl, 1 - methyl - 5 - phenyl barbituric acid

Properties and Uses : A white crystalline powder, stable in air. It is soluble in chloroform, slightly soluble in ether, water and alcohol. Its aqueous solution is neutral to litmus. It is mainly used in the treatment of grandmal epilepsy. For use as an anticonvulsant, the dose is 30 to 250 mg daily and as a hypnotic and sedative, it is 100 to 300 mg daily.

[B] INTERMEDIATE ACTING BARBITURATES

This category of agents produce onset of action within 20 - 40 minutes, and the duration of hypnotic effect lasts for 2 to 8 hours. Useful drugs in this category are :

4. **Amylobarbitone (I. P., B. P., U. S. P.) :**

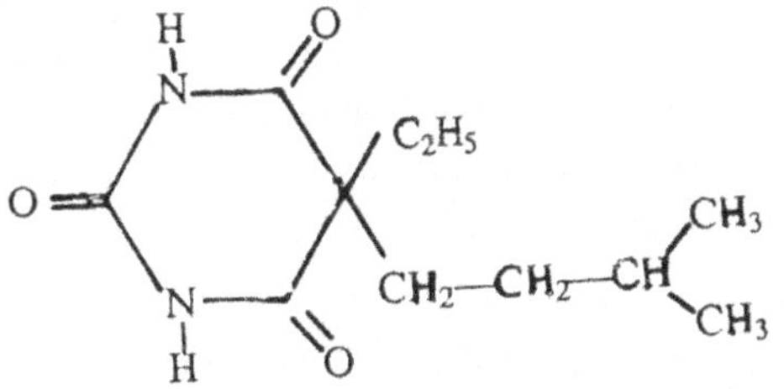

5 - ethyl - 5 - isopentylbarbituric acid

Properties and Uses : A white crystalline powder, highly soluble in alcohol and ether, soluble in chloroform, sparingly soluble in water. It is used in the form of a tablet or elixir (N.F.) as an intermediate acting barbiturate; and the usual dose is 20 to 300 mg.

Amylobarbitone sodium (B. P., U. S. P.) : It is a white, granular powder, very soluble in water and alcohol, practically insoluble in ether and chloroform. It is used in the form of capsules (U.S.P.) or injections. Injections can be given intramuscularly or subcutaneously, in a dose of 20 to 500 mg, the usual dose being 200 mg, once or twice a day.

5. **Butobarbitone (B. P.) :**

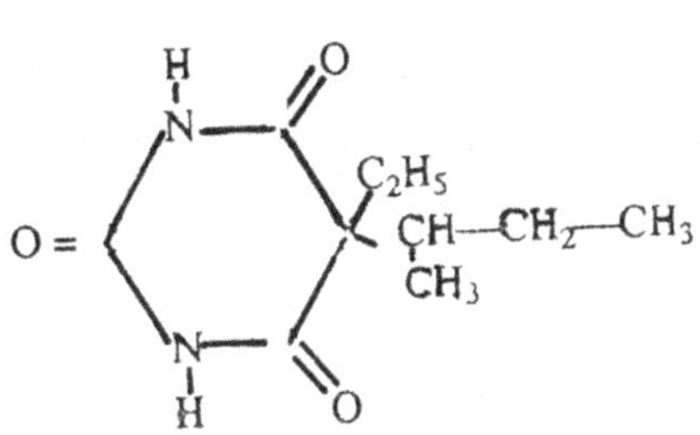

Sodium salt 5 - butyl - 5 - ethylbarbituric acid

Properties and Uses : A white powder, slightly soluble in water and alcohol, it dissolves in solutions of alkali hydroxides, carbonates and ammonia. It is used in the form of tablets, capsules. Usual sedative dose is 30 mg and the hypnotic dose is 100 mg - 200 mg.

6. Cyclobarbitone (I.P., B.P., U.S.P.) :

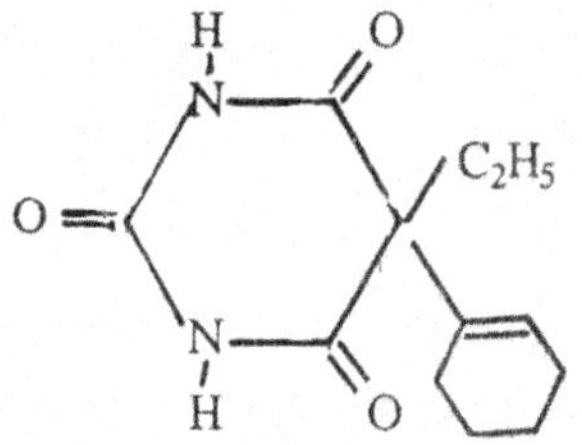

(5-ethyl-5-cyclohex-yl-barbituric acid)

Properties and Uses : A white, crystalline powder, odourless, very slightly soluble in water, soluble in alcohol and ether. Aqueous solutions are acidic to litmus. It is used in the form of tablets. Its calcium salt is official in B.P., and it is also used in the form of tabltes as an anticonvuslant and a hypnotic. Usual dose is 200 to 400 mg.

7. Pentobarbitone Sodium (I.P., B.P., U.S.P.) :

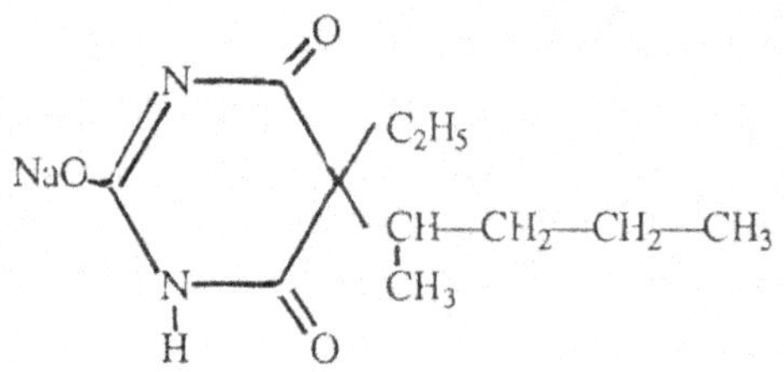

Sodium 5-ethyl-5- (1-methylbutyl) barbiturate

Properties and Uses : It occurs as a white, crystalline powder or granules. It is odourless, very soluble in water and alcohol, and insoluble in ether. Its solutions are alkaline in nature and it decomposes on standing. Its decomposition is accelerated by heating. It is used as a hypnotic and sedative in the form of tablets, capsules, injection and elixir. The last three formulations are official in U.S.P. Its duration of action is shorter than barbiturates. It is given parenterally for the control of convulsive syndormes. Oral dose is 50 to 300 mg, and the intravenous dose is 100 to 200 mg, once or twice a day.

8. Quinal barbitone Sodium (I.P.) :

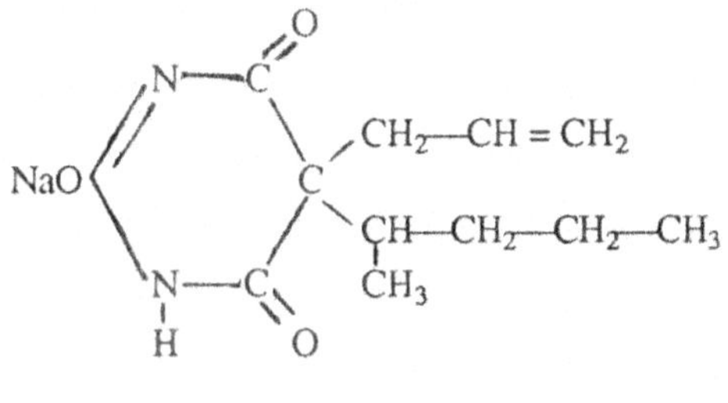

Structure: Sodium salt of 5-allyl-5-(1-methyl-butyl) barbituric acid

Sodium salt of 5-allyl-5-(1-methyl-butyl) barbituric acid

Properties and Uses : It occurs as a white powder hygroscopic in nature, freely soluble in water and alcohol, insoluble in ether. It is used as an anticonvulsant and hypnotic. Its tablets are official in I.P. The usual dose is 100 to 200 mg.

[C] SHORT ACTING BARBITURATES

These barbiturates are given intravenously, and hence produce instant onset of action of a very short duration (1 to 2 hours). These are used in general anaesthesia and to control convulsions. Some of the drugs of this class are as follows :

9. Thiopentone sodium (I.P., B.P., U.S.P.) :

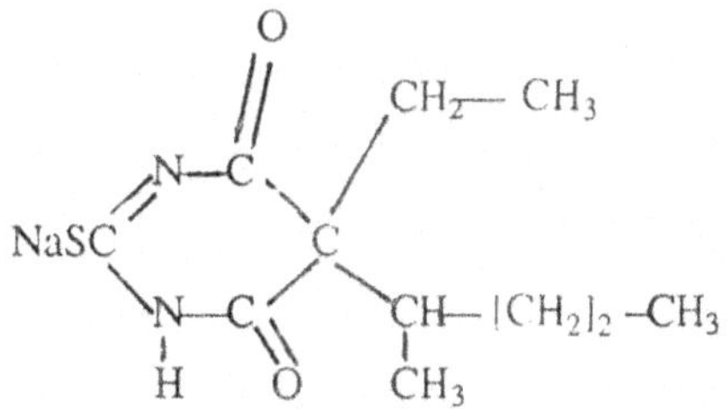

Sodium salt of 5-allyl 5 (1 methyl butyl) 2 - thio barbiturate

Properties and Uses : It occurs as a white to off white, crystalline powder, hygroscopic in nature. It is soluble in water, practically insoluble in ether and benzene. Its solution usually decomposes and precipitates on boilings. Carbon dioxide also causes precipition. It is employed as an intravenous general anaesthetic for minor operations. It should not be used for operations of long duration. As a precaution, facilities for intratracheal oxygen administration should always be ready while using thiopentone sodium. It is used intravenously, 2 to 3 ml of 2.5 % solution, at the rate of 1 ml every 5 seconds.

10. Methohexitone Sodium :

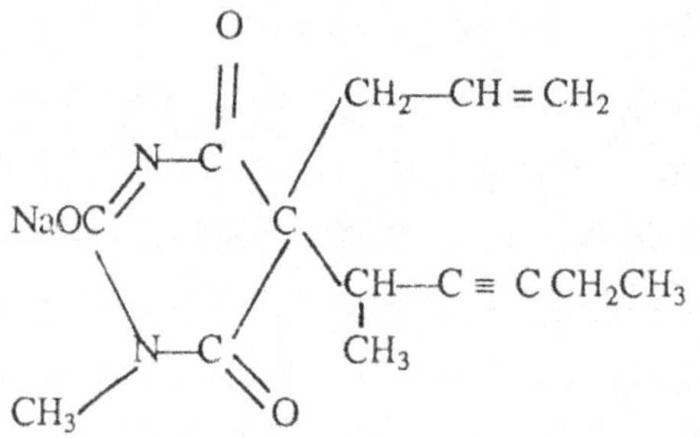

5-allyl-methyl 5-(1-methyl-pent-2-ynyl) barbituric acid

Properties and uses : A white crystalline powder, soluble in water, insoluble in usual organic solvents, it is protected from moisture, CO_2 and light. It is used in the form of an injection. The injection is prepared in CO_2 free water and should be within 24 hours. It is administered via the intravenous route and the usual dose is 30 to 120 mg as a general anaesthetic.

[II] NON - BARBITURATES

It is believed that usually the structure R, R C — CO — NH — appears to be associated with hypnotic sedative agents. However, hypnotic - sedative activity is shown by different groups. Some useful agents are given below :

11. Methylprylon (B.P., U.S.P.) :

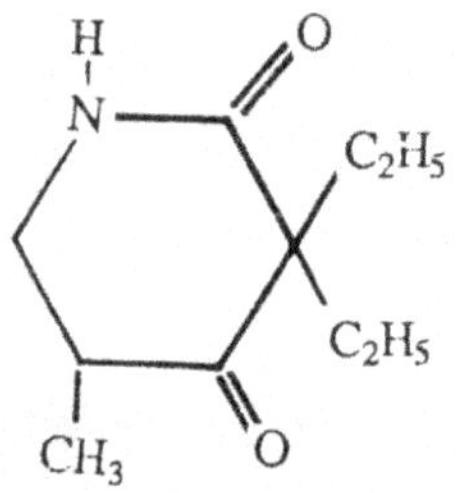

(3,3-diethyl-5-methyl-2,4-piperidinedione)

Porperties and uses : A white, crystalline powder, with slight characteristic odour, soluble in water, very soluble in alcohol, ether, benzene and chloroform. It is affected by light. It is used as a hypnotic and sedative in simple nervous insomnia. Side effects like nausea and vertigo are mild. The hypnotic dose is 200 to 400 mg, and the sedative dose is 50 to 100 mg, 3 to 4 times a day. It is used in the form of tablets and elixir.

12. Methaqualone (B. P. , U. S. P.)

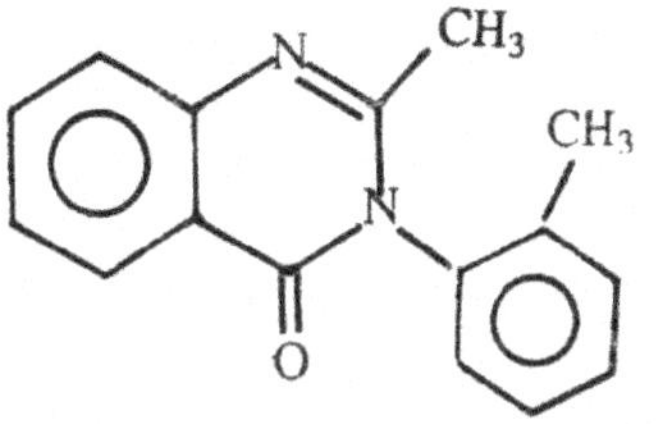

3 4 - dihydro - 2 - methyl - 3-0 tolyquinazolin - 4 - one or
2 - methyl - 3 - O - tolylquinaline - 4 - one

Properties and Uses : It occurs as a white, crystalline powder, insoluble in water, soluble in alcohol and chloroform. It should be protected from moisture and light. It is used as a hypnotic and the usual dose is 150 to 300 mg.

13. Glutethimide (B. P., U. S. P.) :

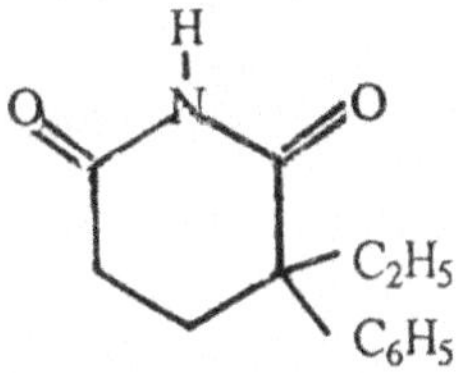

2 - ethyl - 2 - phenyl glutatrimide

Properties and Uses : It occurs as a white crystalline powder, insoluble in water. The saturated solution is slightly acidic in nature. It is soluble in alcohol, acetone and ethyl acetate. It is used in form of tablets. Its onset of action is about one and half hour and hypnosis lasts for about 4 to 8 hours. The usual hypnotic dose is 500 mg and the sedative dose is 125 mg, 3 times a day.

14. Nitrazepam (B. P., U. S. P.)

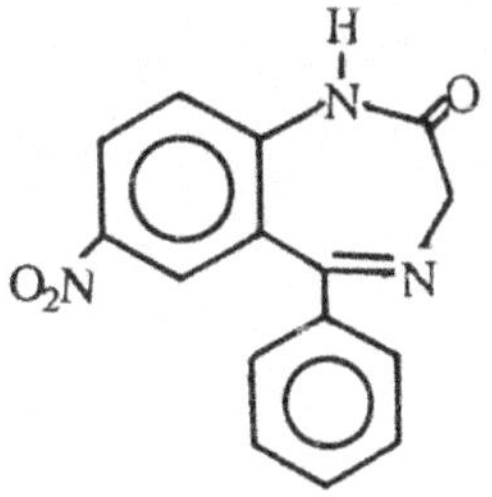

(1, 3 - dihydro - 7 - nitro - 5 - phenyl,
- 2 - H - 1, 4 benzodiazepeine - 2 - one)

Properties and Uses : A yellow, crystalline powder, odourless, insoluble in water, soluble in alcohol, more soluble in chloroform. It is affected by air and light. It is used as a hypnotic and a tranquilizer in the form of tablets. The usual dose is 5 to 10 mg, daily.

15. **Temazepam (B. P.) :**

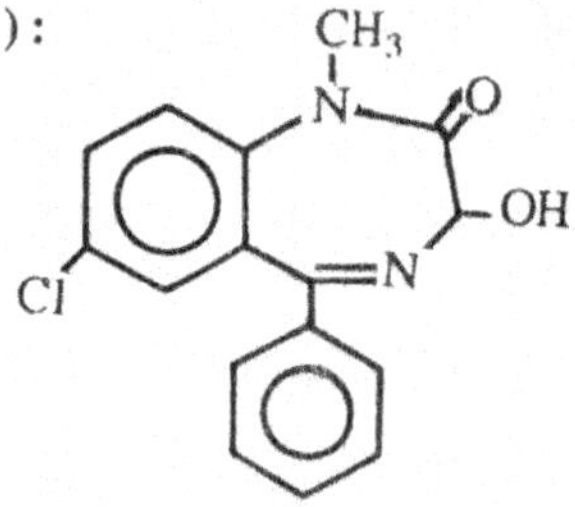

7 - chlor 1,3 dihydro - 3 - hydroxy - 1 - methyl - 5 - phenyl
1, 4 - benzodiazepin - 2 - one

Properties and Uses : It is a white crystalline powder, insoluble in water, slightly soluble in alcohol. The drug is to be protected from light and kept in closed container. This drug is sedative hypnotic with tranquilizing action.

16. **Chlormethiazole (B. P.) :**

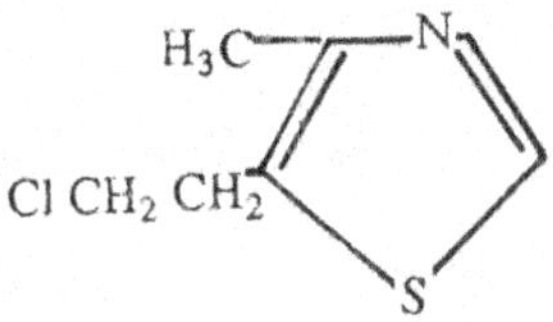

5 (2 - chlorethyl) 4 - methyl thiazole

Properties and Uses : It is a yellowish brown liquid slightly water- soluble, miscible with alcohol. It is administered in capsules for hypnotic and anticonvulsant action. It's edisylate salt is official in B. P.

III. ALCOHOLS

Alcohols have been observed to be hypnotic in nature. Ethyl alcohol depresses the central nervous system and produces a hypnotic effect. However, it is not used clinically. The hypnotic activity of alcohol increases with (i) increase in molecular weight upto 6 carbons, (ii) halogenation, and (iii) unsaturation. Some important compounds in this class are :

17. **Chloral hydrate (I.P., B. P., U. S. P.) :**

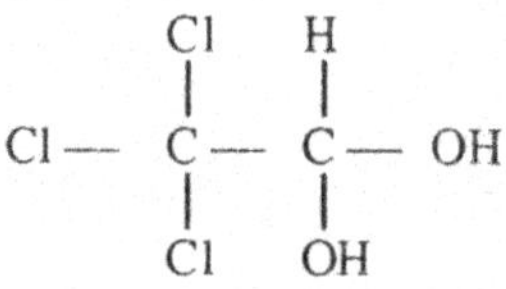

(2, 2, 2 - trichloro ethane, 1 - diol)

Properties and uses : It occurs as colourless, hygroscopic crystals, with a pungent odour, very soluble in water. It is also soluble in alcohol, ether and chloroform. It is stored in a cool place, protected from light. Alkali and alkaline salts cause decomposition. It is used as a sedative and soporific. It is administered as a mixture or elixir in diluted form. Sometimes, it is used for persons undergoing withdrawal therapy from morphine or alcohol addiction. The usual dose is 250 mg to 1.0 g.

18. **Dichloral Phenazone (B. P.) :**

This is complex of chloral hydrate and phenazone. This occurs as microcrystalline white powder with characteristic odour. It is highly soluble in water, alcohol and chloroform. It decomposes in presence of alkali. The drug is given as oral solution or in tablet form for hypnotic action.

19. **Ethchlorvynol (U. S. P.)**

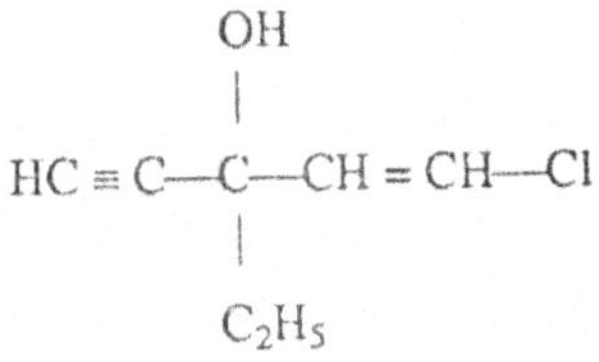

$$HC \equiv C - \underset{\underset{C_2H_5}{|}}{\overset{\overset{OH}{|}}{C}} - CH = CH - Cl$$

(1 - Chloro - 3 - ethyl - 1 - penten - 4 - yn 3 - *ol*)

20. **Triclofos sodium (B. P.)**

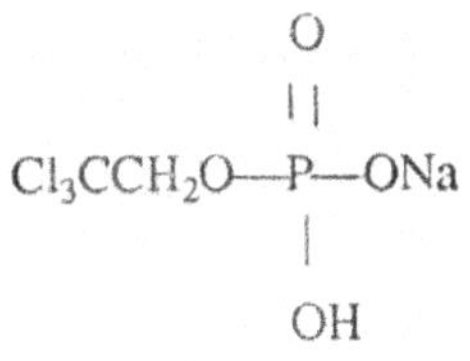

$$Cl_3CCH_2O - \underset{\underset{OH}{|}}{\overset{\overset{O}{\|}}{P}} - ONa$$

(Sodium 2, 2, 2 - trichloral ethanol dihydrogen phosphate)

Properties : It is a white powder, hygroscopic in nature, soluble in water.

[IV] ALDEHYDES

Amongst the aldehyde class, paraldehyde, which is a polymer (trimer) of acetaldehyde, is a powerful, safe and quick acting hypnotic, sedative agent. Furthermore, chlorination of aldehydes increases hypnotic activity.

21. Paraldehyde (I.P., B.P., U.S.P.) :

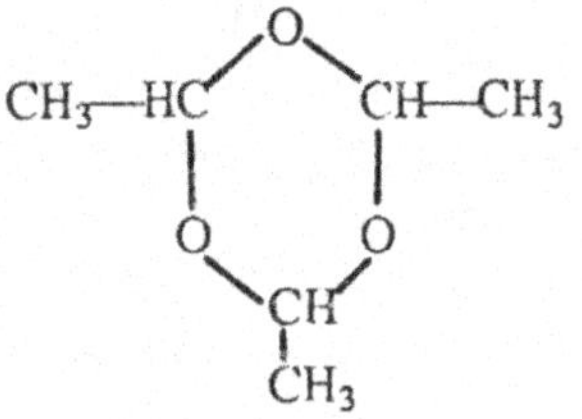

$$\begin{array}{c} \text{CH}_3\text{—HC} \overset{\displaystyle O}{\underset{\displaystyle O}{\diagup\diagdown}} \text{CH—CH}_3 \\ \diagdown \underset{\displaystyle \text{CH}}{\text{O}} \diagup \\ \text{CH}_3 \end{array}$$

Properties and Uses : It is a colourless, transperant, liquid, with a strong odour. It solidifies at low temperature. It is soluble in water and is miscible with chloroform, alcohol and ether. A 0.1 % anti-oxidant is usually added. It is administered as an intramuscular injection for central depression. The usual dose is 2 to 8 ml. By rectal injection as a basal anaesthetic, the usual dose is 15 to 30 ml.

[V] UREIDES

Barbiturates are cyclic ureides. Monoacyl derivatives of ureas, called monoureides, also cause a depression of the central nervous system.

22. Carbromal (I.P., B.P., U.S.P.) :

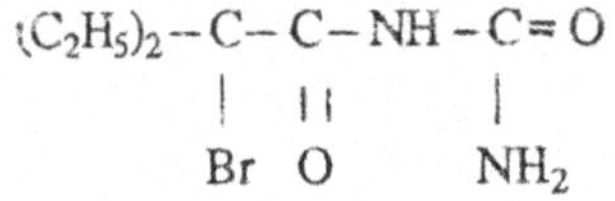

$$(C_2H_5)_2\underset{\underset{\displaystyle Br}{|}}{-}C\underset{\underset{\displaystyle O}{||}}{-}C-NH-\underset{\underset{\displaystyle NH_2}{|}}{C}=O$$

2-Bromo 2 ethyl butyryl urea

Properties and Uses : A white, crystalline powder, sparingly soluble in water, soluble in alcohol and chloroform. It is soluble in alkali-hydroxides.

It is a weak hypnotic and hence now - a - days, it itnot used. Usual dose is 500 mg.

[VI] MISCELLANEOUS

Besides the synthetic agents, some natural drugs also show potent hypnotic-sedative activity. The cannabis extract, opium powder and tincture of opium are important sedative agents. The crude drugs, valerian, has a mild sedative activity.

Other synthetic miscellaneous agents are as follows :

23. Phenacemide :

Properties and Uses : It occurs as a white, crystalline powder, slightly soluble in water and alcohol. The drug is most effective in control of psychomotor seizures as an anticonvulsant agent. The daily dose is 500 mg to 1.0 g.

24. Primidone (I. P., U. S. P.):

Properties and uses : A white, crystalline powder, sparingly soluble in water, more soluble in alcohol. Primidone is useful in grand mal and psychomotor epilepsy. The usual dose in 250 mg, 1 to 3 times daily.

25. Carbamazepine (I. P., B. P., U. S. P.)

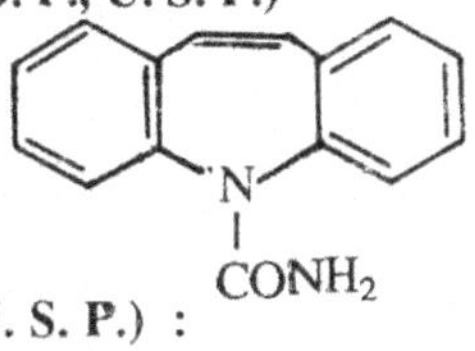

[Structure: dibenzazepine ring system with N-CONH₂ substituent]

26. Diazepam (I.P., B. P., U. S. P.) :

Properties and Uses : An almost white to yellowish white, crystalline powder, sparingly soluble in water, but soluble in alcohol and chloroform. It is affected by light and moisture. It is used in the form of tablets and capsules. It is normally used as a tranquilize. Usual dose is 5 to 30 mg daily, in divided doses. It is also an effective anticonvulsant agent.

27. Promethazone hydrochloride (B. P.):

Properties and Uses : It is white powder, soluble in water. It has H - receptor antagonist action and is also used as antiemetic and sedative.

❏ ❏ ❏

Chapter 7

SKELETAL MUSCLE RELAXANTS

The drugs which produce relaxation of the skeletal muscle and the tone of the muscles are called skeletal muscle relaxants. There are two different categories of agents which bring about skeletal muscle relaxation. One category of agents act by interrupting transmission of the nerve impulses at the neuromuscular junction. They are called as neuromuscular blocking agents. The Curare type of drugs belong to this class. These agents are further divided into sub-classes. viz. (i) depolarising agents and (ii) non-depolarising agents. This category is discussed separately.

The other category of skeletal muscle relaxants is the centrally acting type. They produce muscle relaxation by blockng impulses at the interneurons of the polysynaptic reflex arcs, mainly at the paleocortex and subcortical areas of the brain. This action is brought about by depressing the central nervous system. The skeletal muscle relaxants are used therapeutically in a variety of conditions of muscle spasms like spondylitis, disc syndromes, sprains, backache, etc. Furthermore, because of the depressant effect of this class of compounds, they are useful in simple insomnia and in anxiety, tension and related conditions.

The skeletal muscle relaxants can be classified chemically into two categories viz., (i) glycol and carbamates and (iii) benzodiazepines.

Glycol and the carbamates

Two useful drugs evolved from this class are :

1. Mephenesin (I.P.) :

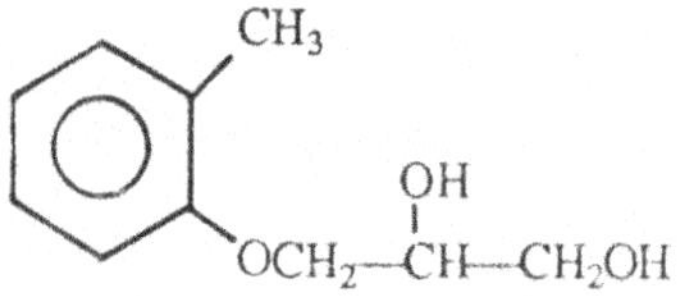

3-O-toloxyl 1,2–propanediol

Properties : It occurs as a white, crystalline powder with a bitter taste. It is sparingly water soluble and is more soluble in alcohol. The solutions are stable to heat and can be sterilised by autoclaving. The drug is metabolised fast, and hence, gives a brief duration of action.

Actions and Uses: It is given orally and/or parenteraly in a 0.1 to 1 mg dose. Mephenesin injection is official (I.P.) and is employed for quick action. The drug is mainly used for symptomatic relief of muscular spasms or cramps.

2. Meprobamate (I.P., B.P., U.S.P.) :

This drug is discussed under anti-anxiety category.

BENZODIAZEPINE DERIVATIVES

The benzodiazepine class of compounds are already discussed under anti-anxiety class. A few important drugs possessing sedative, hypnotic, muscle relaxant and anticonvulsant properties are given below.

1. Chlordiazepoxide hydrochloride (B.P., U.S.P.) :

It is mainly used in the treatment of anxiety and tension. It has moderate anticonvulsant and skeletal muscle relaxant activity. This drug is discussed under antidepressant chapter.

2. Diazepam (I.P., B.P., U.S.P.) :

The drug is used in control of anxiety, tension and muscle spasm. It is also effective in controlling convulsions in epilepsy. This drug is discussed under antidepressant chapter.

3. Oxazepam (B.P. U.S.P.) :

This drug is mainly used as anxiolytic agent and has mild skeletal muscle relaxant action. This drug is also discussed under antidepressant chapter.

NEUROMUSCULAR BLOCKING AGENTS
(Skeletal muscle relaxant)

As stated earlier, there are drugs that act by interrupting transmission of nerve impulses at neuromuscular junction. These are called as neuromuscular blocking agents. Their therapeutic use is as a adjuvant in surgical anaesthesia to produce skeletal muscle relaxation. The skeletal muscle relaxation is brought out similar to that of alkaloid tubocurarine and hence the action is referred as curariform or ' curarimimetic.'

Some important compounds official in pharmacopieia are given below :

1. Tubocurarine chloride (I.P., B.P., U.S.P.) :

The alkaloid is obtained from crude curare and is purified.

Properties and Uses : It occurs as white to yellowish-white powder, odourles and is water soluble. Aqueous solutions are stable. It is used as adjuvant to anaesthesia for skeletal muscle relaxation. It is also employed in diagnosis of myasthenia gravis. The drug is given parentarily by i.m route in 0.1 to 0.3 mg/kg dose (maximum upto 25 mg) usual strength of injection is 10 mg/ml.

2. Succinylcholine chloride (I.P., U.S.P.) :

$$CH_2\text{--}COOCH_2CH_2\text{--}\overset{+}{N}(CH_3)_3 \quad 2\,Cl^-\,.\,H_2O$$
$$|$$
$$CH_2\text{--}COOCH_2CH_2\text{--}\overset{+}{N}(CH_3)_3$$

Properties and Uses : It occurs as a white crystalline powder with salty taste. It is freely soluble in water, slightly in alcohol. The acqeous solutions are unstable in alkaline medium.

It is administered by intravenous injection (20 to 80 mg dose) for skeletal muscle relaxation. It is a depolarising muscle relaxant. It has a short duration of action because of faster hydrolysis.

3. Decamethonium bromide (U.S.P.) :

It is colourless, odourless powder, soluble in water and alcohol. Aqueous solution is comparatively stable. It produces skeletal muscle relaxation especially in combination with barbiturates. It is more potent than tubocurarine and is employed in 500 µg dose.

4. Gallamine Triethiodide (I.P., B.P., U.S.P.) :

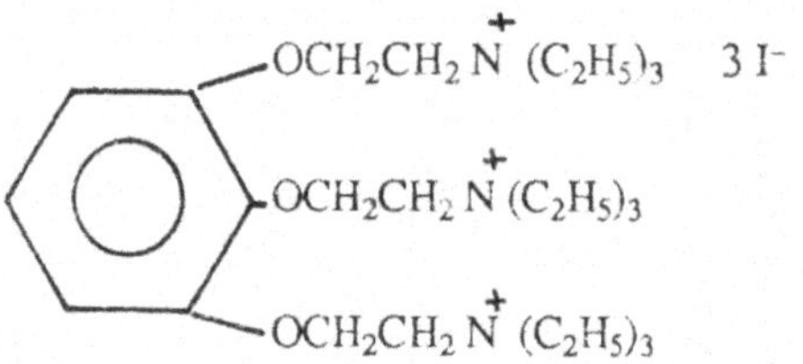

$$\begin{array}{l}\text{--}OCH_2CH_2\overset{+}{N}(C_2H_5)_3 \quad 3\,I^-\\\text{--}OCH_2CH_2\overset{+}{N}(C_2H_5)_3\\\text{--}OCH_2CH_2\overset{+}{N}(C_2H_5)_3\end{array}$$

Properties and Uses : It is a amorphos powder, bitter to taste and very solube in water but sparingly soluble in alcohol. Aqueous solution is acidic in nature. It is employed as muscle relaxant in surgical operations. It is given by i.v. route in 1 mg/kg body weight.

Chapter 8

TRANQUILIZING AGENTS

Tranquilizing agents are drugs which produce selective central nervous system depression. The drugs, in general, reduce excitation, agitation, agressiveness, worry and tension, and calms the patient. These types of agents are also called as neurosedative or calming agents. The tranquilizing action is considered to take place at the subcortical region of the brain. The drugs produce sufficient sedation and bring about a calming and neurosedative action. This action is believed to take place either by interferring in the biosynthesis, uptake, metabolism and site of action of the biogenic amines of the brain. The drugs from this class, thus, have a hypnotic sedative, muscle - relaxant activity.

The tranquilizing agents can be classified into three categories viz.,

(i) Rauwolfia and their alkaloids. (ii) phenothiazine class of compounds, and (iii) miscellaneous compounds.

I. RAUWOLFIA AND ITS ALKALOIDS

The roots of the crude drug, powder of the plant *Rauwolfia serpentina* or related species of rauwolfia, have been used for centuries in various diseases like insanity, hypertention and insomnia. There are number of alkaloids in rauwolfia. The crude drug, its purified alkaloid (reserpine) and related synthetic analogues are now-a-days used in a variety of conditions like agitated states in schizophrenia, psychotic disorders, insomnia and hypertension. Amongst the variety of agents from this category, Reserpine and Rescinnamine are widely used. These drugs acting centrally produce their effect by depleting the levels of brain bioamines.

1. Reserpine (I. P., B. P., U. S. P.) :

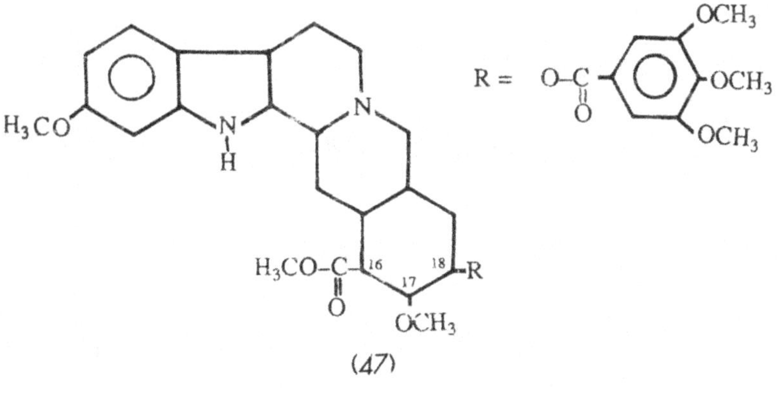

Properties : It is a pale buff-yellowish powder, odourless, and darkens on exposure to light. It is insoluble in water, slightly soluble in alcohol and ether, and more soluble in chloroform and acetic acid. Solutions darken on exposure to light.

Actions and Uses : It is used in 0.5 to 2 mg dose in treatment of anxiety and tension, or 3 to 5 mg orally in disturbed psychotic cases (or 5 to 10 mg by intramuscular injection). The drug is also used in the management of hypertension. Reserpine tablets are official in I.P., B.P., U.S.P. while its injection is official in I.P. and U.S.P.

II. PHENOTHIAZINE DERIVATIVES

A large number of potent drugs have been developed from the phenothiazine class. The drugs, beside bring tranquilizing, potentiates the anaesthetic, analgesic and sedative activities. The drugs are thus useful in quietening psychotic patients and in the treatment of major mental and emotional disordres. A number of drugs also posess antiemetic and antihistaminic activity.

Chlorpromazine hydrochloride, fluphenazine hydrochloride, prochlorperazine maleate and thioridazine hydrochloride are important compounds under this class. These compounds are already discussed under chapter - 4.

III. MISCELLANEOUS COMPOUNDS

1. **Haloperidol (B.P., U.S.P.)**

2. **Droperidol (U. S. P.)**

3. **Thiothixene** are important tranquilisers. These are covered under antipsychotic class.

4. **Hydroxyzine hydrochloride (U. S. P.) :**

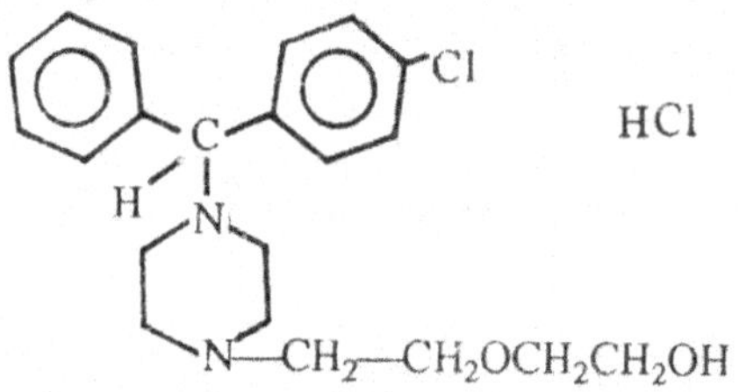

This is an effective tranquilizing agent of the sedative-hypnotic type. It is less potent than the phenothiazine class of drugs and have mild antihistaminic and anticholinergic activity.

5. **Lithium carbonate (B. P., U. S. P.) :** Li_2CO_3

Properties and Uses : It is an inorganic compound. It occurs as a white crystalline powder and is sparingly soluble in water. It is active orally and given in the form of tablets. It is effective in the treatment of mania and related cases of mental and manic depression. It has tranquilizing action also. Dose is up to 1.6 g daily in divided doses.

Chapter 9

ANTICONVULSANT DRUGS

Anticonvulsants are drugs which prevent or control convulsions. These drugs are used in epilepsy. Epilepsy is a disease due to disorder or disturbances in the functions of the central nervous system. This is characterised by fits, frequent occurence of seizures, convulsions, abnormal body movements or a temperorary loss of consciouness. All forms of epilepsy originates in the brain. It results due to abnormal changes in neural activity. These changes may be due to excessive neural discharge, metabolism or disturbance of physicochemical function or eletrical activity of brain. The exact cause of this abnormality is not clearly known. The disease, epilepsy, is categorised into three types, depending upon the types of body reactions produced. They are grandmal, petitmal and psychomotor seizures.

Anticonvulsants belong to different chemical classes and have common structural features as shown below :

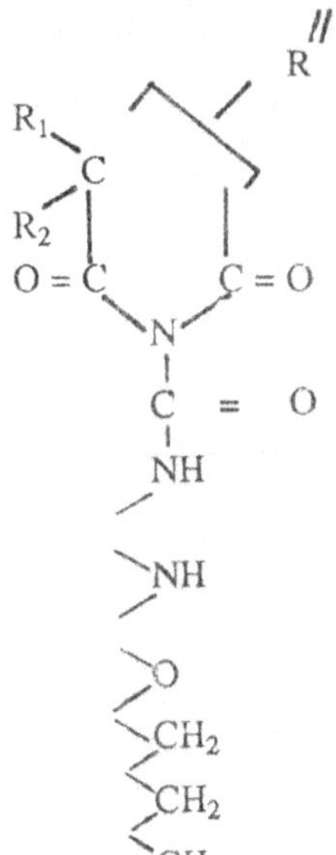

- Barbiturate
- Hydantoin
- Oxazolidinedione
- Succinimide
- Glutarimide

R = Barbiturates, hydantoins, oxazolidinedoines succinimides, phenacemide glutarimides, etc.

I. BARBITURATES

The long acting barbiturates are commonly employed in the grandmal type of epileptic seizures. Barbitone sodium, phenobarbitone and its sodium salt and methylphenobarbitone show selective anticonvulsant activity. These drugs reduce the excitability of the motor cortex.

II. HYDANTOINS

Many hydantoins have been prepared and successfully used in grandmal and psychomotor seizures. They do not have sedative action.

1. Phenytoin (U. S. P.), Phenytoin sodium (B.P., U.S.P.)

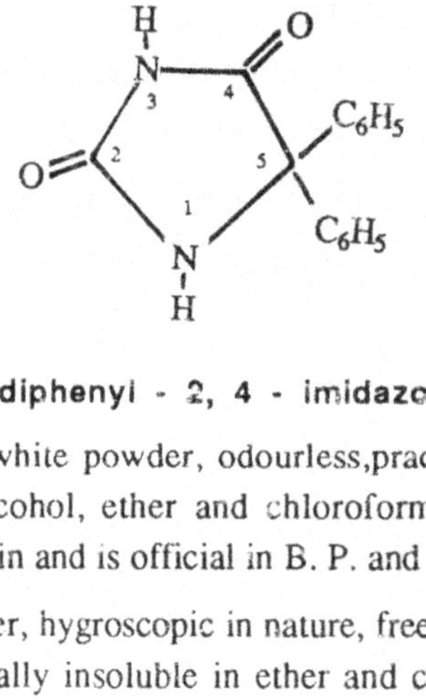

5, 5 - diphenyl - 2, 4 - imidazolidinedione

Properties : A white powder, odourless, practically insoluble in water, slightly soluble in alcohol, ether and chloroform. *Phenytoin sodium* is a sodium salt of phenytoin and is official in B. P. and U. S. P.

It is a white powder, hygroscopic in nature, freely soluble in water, soluble in alcohol and practically insoluble in ether and chloroform. The powder, on exposure to air, gradually absorbs CO_2. It must be stored in airtight containers.

Actions and Uses : It is used in the form of an oral suspension (U. S P.) and its sodium salt is used as such, or as injection (I. P.) in the form of capsules (U. S. P.) It is used in symptomatic therapy of epilepsy. It is the drug of choice in preventing major convulsive seizures. Usual dose 3 to 10 mg/kg or 30 to 200 mg, every 6 to 8 hours. It is also used in cardiac arrhythmias.

2. **Mephenytoin (U. S. P.) :**

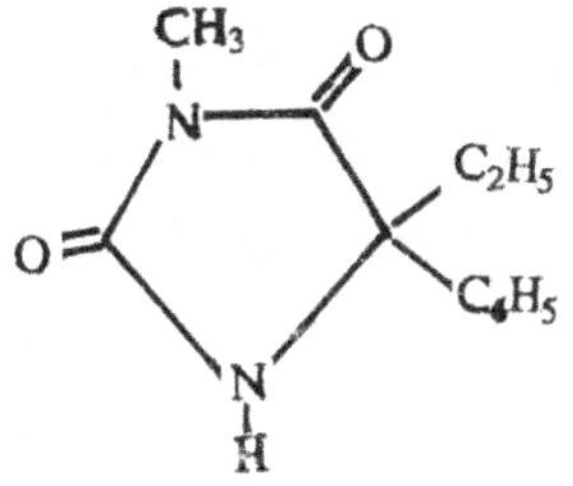

3 - methyl 5 - ethyl 5 - phenylhydantoin

Properties and Uses : It occurs as a colourless, crystalline powder, very slightly soluble in water and soluble in other organic solvents. It is useful in Jacksonian seizures in 200 - 600 mg dose daily in divided doses. The adverse effects are hepatitis, blood dyscarasis and skin rashes.

III. OXAZOLIDINEDIONES

The oxazolidine 2, 4 - dione are compounds which are isosterically similar to hydantoin, wherein oxygen is substituted for the - NH group at position 1. Compounds of this class are useful in petitmal convulsions. They are given below :

1. **Trioxidone, Trimethadione (I. P., B. P. U. S. P.) :**

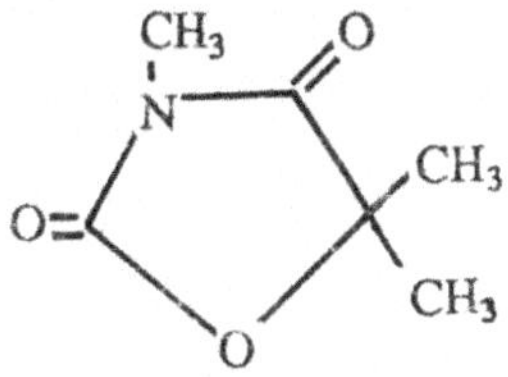

3, 5, 5 - trimethyl - 2, 4 - oxazolidinedione

Properties : A white, crystalline granule with a slight camphoraceous odour, soluble in water, alcohol, ether and chloroform. It is stored in cool place.

Action and Uses : It prevents epileptic seizures and is only useful in petitmal, and not in grandmal epilepsy. Sedation is a common side effect of the drug. It is used in the form of solution (N. F.), capsules (I.P, U.S.P. B.P.) and tablets (N. F.) Usual dose is 300 mg, 3 to 6 times a day. The drug shows toxic effects like gastric irritation, skin rashes, dizziness, etc.

2. Paramethadione (I.P., B.P., U.S.P.) :

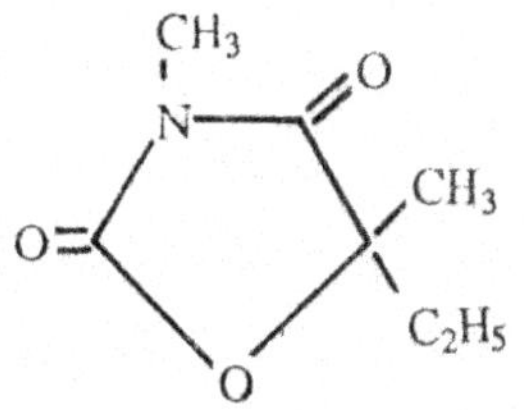

3, 5-dimethyl–5-ethyl-2,4-oxazolidinedione

Properties : A clear, colourless liquid with a characteristic and aromatic, odour sparingly soluble in water, soluble in alcohol, ether and chloroform. It is stored in air tight containers.

Action and uses : Similar to trimethadione the usual dose is 300 mg, three times a day.

IV. SUCCINIMIDES

In the treatment of convulsions, some derivatives of amides, especially of succinimides, proved very useful. The compounds showed usefulness in the petitmal type of epilepsy and also in psychomotor seizures.

1. Ethosuximide (I.P., B.P., U.S.P.) :

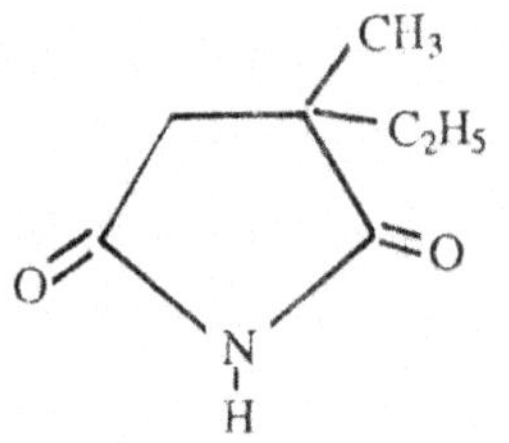

2–ethyl-2-methyl-succinimide

Properties and uses : An almost white powder or waxy solid, practically odourless, soluble in water, alcohol, soluble in water, alcohol, chloroform and ether. It is used in the form of capsules (B.P.) and elixirs. Usual dose is 500 mg, in divided doses up to 2.0 g.

2. Phensuximide (U. S. P.) :

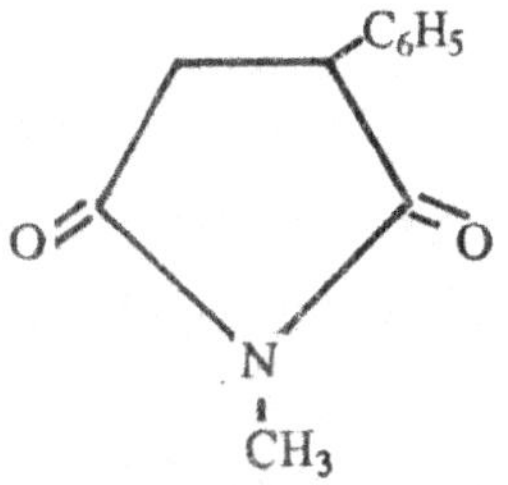

N - methyl - 2 - phenyl - succinimide

Properties and Uses : It is white powder, slightly soluble in water, readily in alcohol. It is given in capsules and suspensions in 500 mg to 1 g dose 2 - 3 times a day.

V. MISCELLANEOUS

A number of compounds with different structural features (some retaining the common features) also show useful anticonvulsant activity. Some therapeutically useful compounds are :

1. Primidone (I. P., B. P., U. S. P.) :

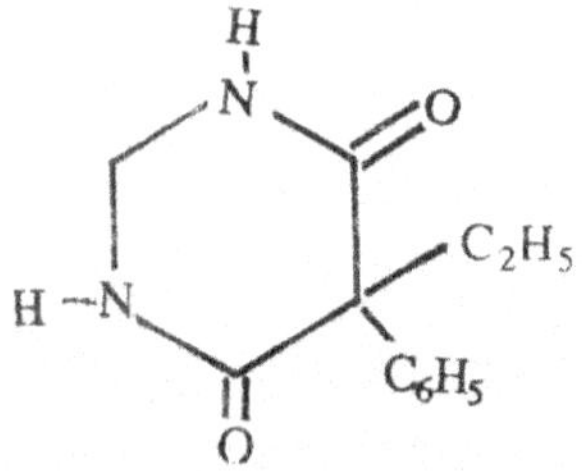

5 - ethylperhydro - 5 - phenyl - pyrimidine - 4, 6 - dione

This compound is similar structurally to Phenobarbitone (2 - deoxy). It displays independent anticonvulsant activity.

Properties and Uses : It is a white powder odourless, sparingly soluble in water and alcohol. It is given as oral suspension or tablets (I. P.) in treatment of grandmal and psychomotor epilepsy.

2. Carbamazepin (I. P., B. P., U. S. P.) :

This drug is convered under hypnotic sedative chapter. The drug is effective in seizure control of epilepsy with few side effects.

3. Clonazepam (U. S. P.) :

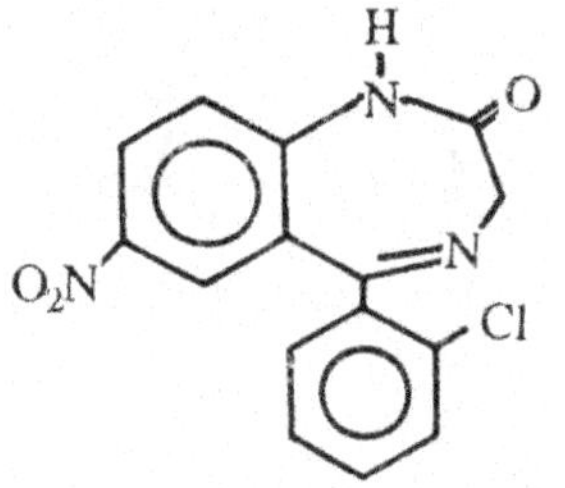

5 - (O - chlorophenol) - 1, 3 - dihydro - 7 - nitro - 2H - 1, 4 - benzodiazepin - 2 - one

Properties and Uses : It is a yellow powder, practically insoluble in water, soluble in alcohol and ether. It is a long acting CNS depressant and especially used as anticonvulsant in treatment of petitmal epilepsy. It is given in tablets to patients where oxazolidinediones or succinimides are not effective. The initial dose is 0.01 to 0.03 mg/kg in divided dose.

4. Sodium valporate (B. P.) :

$$CH_3 — CH_2 — CH_2 — CH — COONa$$
$$|$$
$$CH_3 — CH_2 — CH_2$$

Sodium - 2 - propylpentanoate

The usual dose is 10 - 30 mg/kg. the drug is moderately effective against seizures and exerts anticonvulsant activity, by elevating brain levels through GABA mechanism. The side effects are mild drowsiners, diplopia and gastric irritation.

Properties and Uses : It is white powder odourless, deliquescent in nature, soluble in water and alcohol. It is given in solution and tablet form.

5. Sulthiame (B. P.) :

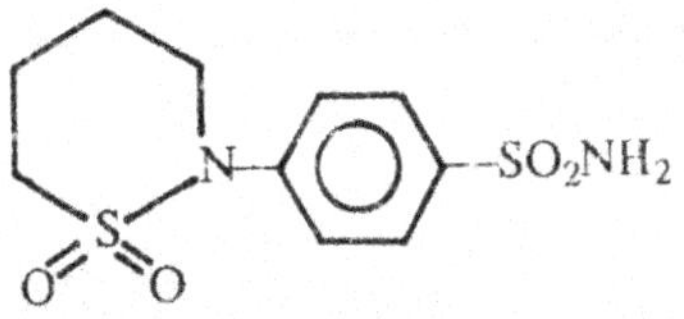

Properties and Uses : This is a white crystalline powder, sparingly soluble in water and alcohol. It is used as anticonvulsant in certain types of epilepsy.

Chapter 10

ANALGESICS (NARCOTICS)

Analgesics are drugs which relieve pain by acting on the central nervous system without loss of consciousness. They increase the pain threshold and give relief from pain. These drugs act by interfering with pain impulses carried by the sensory nerve tracts, at the subcortical region of the brain. Since antipyretics act at the same region, these drugs also act as antipyretics. Analgesics can be

Analgesics (Narcotic)

Analgesics are the drugs which relieve pain by acting on the central nervous system without loss of consciousness. They increase the capcaity to tolerate pain by increasing pain threshold and give relief from pain. The analegesics act by interfering with the pain impulses carried by sensory nerve tracts at the subcortical region of the brain. Since antipyretics act at the same region, these drugs also show antipyretic activity.

Analgesics can be broadly classified into two groups :

(i) Narcotic analgesics (these are called opioid analgesics also), centrally acting.
(ii) Non-narcotic analgesic, acting centrally and peripherally.

The non-narcotic analgesics are discussed separately.

The narcotic analgesics are further classified into (i) Morphine and related compounds and (ii) Synthetic compounds. The morphine and related compounds since are derived from optium they are also called as opioid analgesics. The term opioid is designated to all those drugs (natural or sythetic) which bind specifically to receptors of morphine and evoke morphine like actions. These drugs are called as narcotic analgesics as they have tendencies to produce drug dependence.

Opioid Receptors :

Morphine and related compounds produce selective analgesia by acting on specific receptors (known as opioid receptors) situated in the higher centers and in spinal cord.

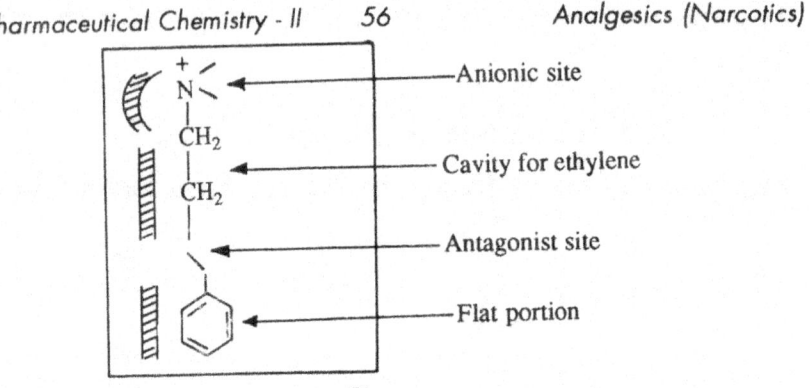

Fig.

The existence of opioid receptors have been established by
(i) Close similarity between opioid agonist and antagonist
(ii) Competitive inhibition of morphine action by narcotic antagonists etc.

The receptor structure comprises of

(i) Anionic site which holds tertiary nitrogen which is assumed to be ionised at physiological pH.

(ii) A cavity for accomodating ethylene (two carbon atom) bridge and

(iii) A flattened part which holds aromatic part of molecular structure by vander walls forces. Further, the receptor holds a natagonist site where narcotic antagonist inhibit access and binding of morphine agonist.

MORPHINE AND RELATED COMPOUNDS

1. Opium (B. P.)

Opium is a dried latex obtained from capsules of *Paver somniferum Linn.*, partly dried by heat of spontaneous evaporation and moulded into masses of uniform shape. It has a strong characteristic odour. It contains about 9.5 % morphine.

Opium powder (I. P.):

Opium is dried at about 65 - 70° and reduced to fine powder, and the morphine content is adjusted to 10 % with a suitable diluent like lactose. It is a light brown powder, with an odour characteristic of opium.

Actions and Uses : Opium and opium powder haven been used over the centuries as powerful analgesic agents. It acts as an antiperistatic and is used for diarrhoeas and dysentries. It further produces sedation and controls cough. It contains about 25 alkaloids, among which morphine codeine and papavarine are important. Since opium is a narcotic, its use is governed by narcotic law. Opium tincture, camphorated opium tincture and opium with chalk are some preparations of opium which were official in I. P., and used clinically.

2. Morphine :

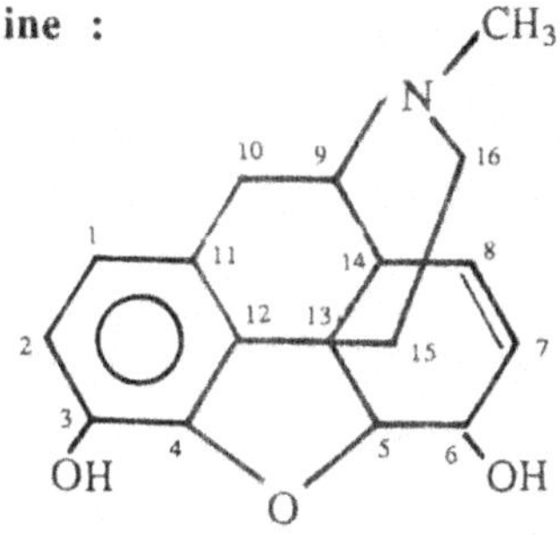

It is the main alkaloid of opium. It has an aromatic ring, with a phenolic OH group (at position 3) hydroxyl group (at position 6), unsaturation (at 7-8), a tertiary nitrogen with methyl group and a etheral linkage (4, 5 position). Its salts, hydrochloride and sulphate, are official in I.P.

Properties and Uses : Both salts occur as white crystalline powder, soluble in water, less soluble in alcohol and practically insoluble in ether and chloroform. Morphine hydrochloride is soluble in glycerine. Aqueous solutions are unstable and decompose at a pH of about 7. The solutions are sterilised by filtration method or by heating with bactericide at 100° for 30 minutes. Morphine and its salts besides being powerful analgesics, suppress cough and relieve anxiety. Morphine hydrochloride solution, injection and morphine sulphate injection are official in I. P. It is given subcutaneously or intramuscularly, the usual dose being 10 to 20 mg Morphine and atropine injection is used as narcotic analgesic and anticholenergic.

3. Codeine (B.P.) :

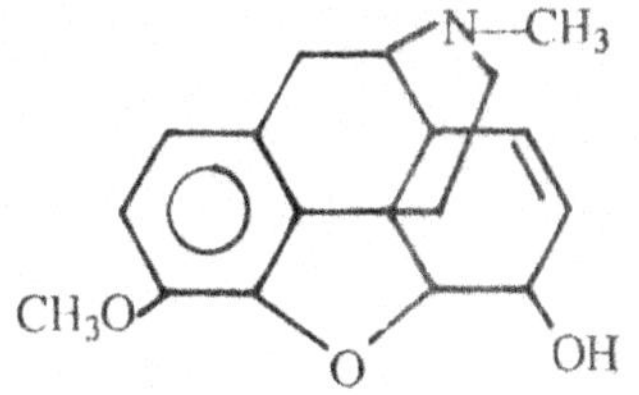

Properties : A white crystalline powder, odourless, less, soluble in water, but more soluble in boiling water, freely soluble in ether, alcohol and chloroform. Aqueous solutions are alkaline in nature. It effloresces in dry air and is affected by light.

Codeine phosphate (I.P., B.P.) :

Properties and Uses : It occurs as colourless crystals or white crystalline powder, highy soluble in water, less in alcohol and practically insoluble in chloroform and ether. The aqueous solutions are sterilised by filtration or by autoclaving. Incompatibilities result with phenobarbitone sodium, alkalies and alkali salts. Codeine and its salts are potent analgesic's similar to morphine. They have an antitussive action, and thus, are used as cough suppresants in cough mixtures. Codeine phosphate syrup, compound codeine tablets are official in I.P. and B.P. The usual dose is 30 mg every 4-6 hours, and as an antitussive, 5 to 10 mg every four hours.

4. Ethylmorphine hydrochloride (I.P.) :

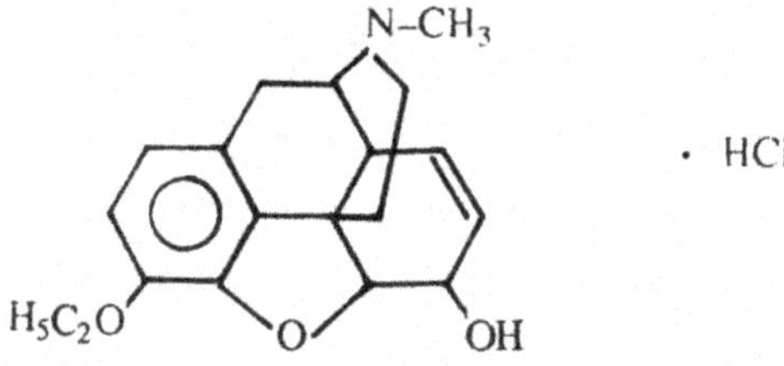

Properties and Uses : A white or faintly yellowish, crystalline powder, soluble in water, but less soluble in alcohol. It is slightly soluble in ether and chloroform. It is preserved in a tight, light resistant container. It is commonly used as a substitute for morphie. When applied locally to the mucous membrane or abraded skin, it causes irritation and hyperemia. So, it is used as a 1 to 5 % solution in chronic inflammatory conditions of the eye.

5. Diamorphine hydrochloride (B.P.) :

It is commonly known as Heroin.

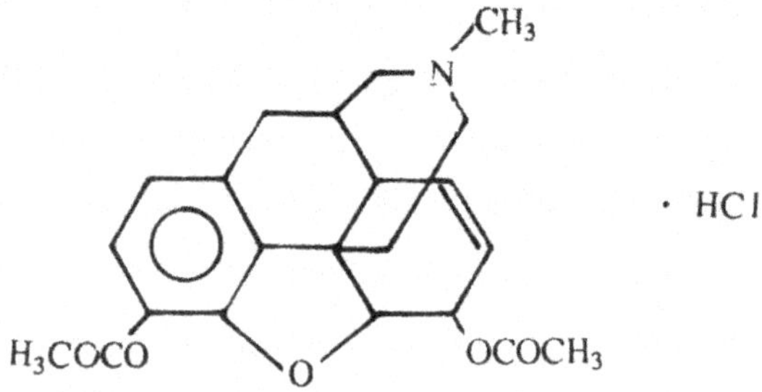

Properties and Uses : It is prepared by acetylation of both, 3 phenolic and 6 hydroxy group of morphine. It occurs as a white, crystalline powder, soluble in water and alcohol. The sterile powder is dissolved in water and a solution for injection is prepared to be used immediately. It is a most potent analgesic, but has a shorter duration of action. It has addiction tendencies.

6. Dihydrocodeinone bitartarate (U.S.P.):

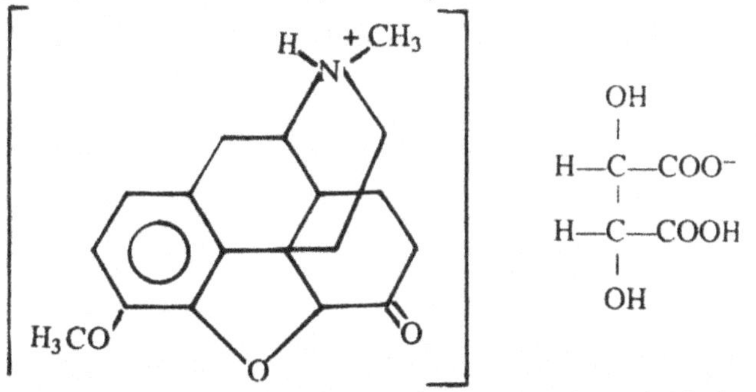

Properties and Uses: A white, fine, crystalline powder, soluble in water, insoluble in ether and chloroform. It is affected by light. It possesses the analgesic and antitussive activity of codeine. Its syrup and tablets are official in N.F. The usual dose is 10 mg. It causes addiction.

7. Dihydrocodeine Tartarate (B.P.):

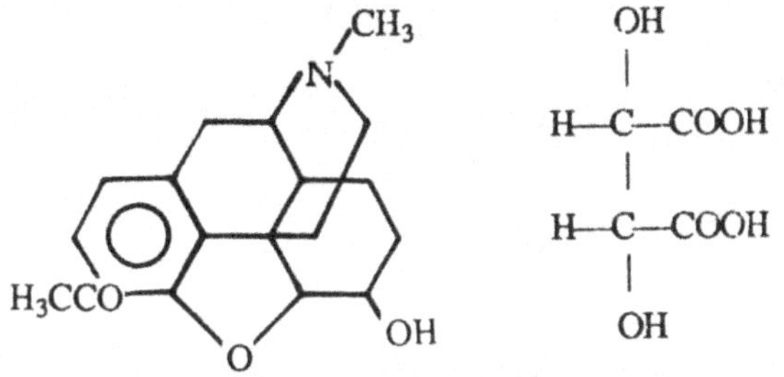

Properties and Uses: It is a white powder, soluble in water but sparingly soluble in alcohol. Solution is acidic in nature. It should be protected from light. It has one third potency of morphine and is used as analgesic and antitussive agent. Usual dose is 10 - 30 mg.

SYNTHETIC ANALGESIC

Considerable work has been carried out on molecular modifications of morphine, to evolve a potent, analgesic without the addiction liabilities and respiratory depressant activity of morphine. This has resulted in the development of new synthetic agents. These agents can be divided into four important categories viz. (i) Pethidine (Meperidine) and (ii) Methadone and analogues (iii) Morphinan and (iv) Benzomorphan analogues.

I. PETHIDINE (Meperidine, analogues)

These compounds, in general, have a strong analgesic activity but are not free from addiction tendencies.

1. Pethidine hydrochloride (I.P., B.P., U.S.P.) :

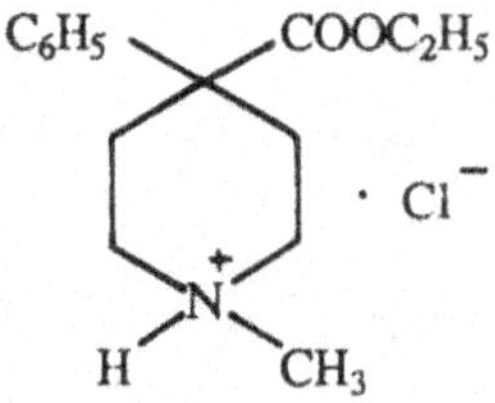

Hydrochloride of ethyl 1 - methyl 4 - phenylpiperidine 4 - carboxylate

Properties and Uses : A white, crystalline powder, odourless, practically insoluble in water, soluble in alcohol and chloroform, sparingly soluble in ether. Aqueous solutions are acidic in nature. The solutions for perenteral use can be sterilised by autoclaving or by the filtration method. It has a pharmacological resemblance with morphine and atropine. It causes sedation and analgesia and also has an antspasmodic action. It has a greater analgesic action than the salicylates. It causes less respiratory depression than morphine. It has an addiction liability. Its tablets and injection are official in I.P. B.P. Usual dose is 25 to 100 mg.

2. Diphenoxylate hydrochloride (B. P., U. S. P.) :

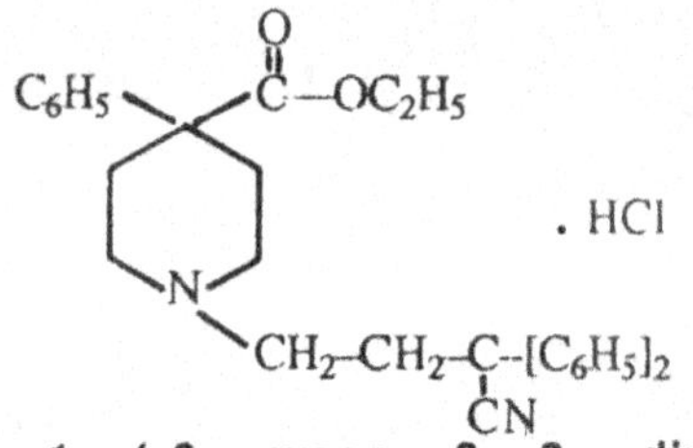

1 - (3 - cyano - 3, 3, - diphenylpropyl) 4 - ethoxycarbonyl - 4 - phenyl piperidine hydrochloride.

Properties and Uses : A white powder, odourless sparingly soluble in water, soluble in acetone and alcohol, insoluble in ether. It is mainly used in diarrhoea usual dose is 5 mg, 4 times a day.

3. Fentanyl citrate (B. P., U. S. P.) :

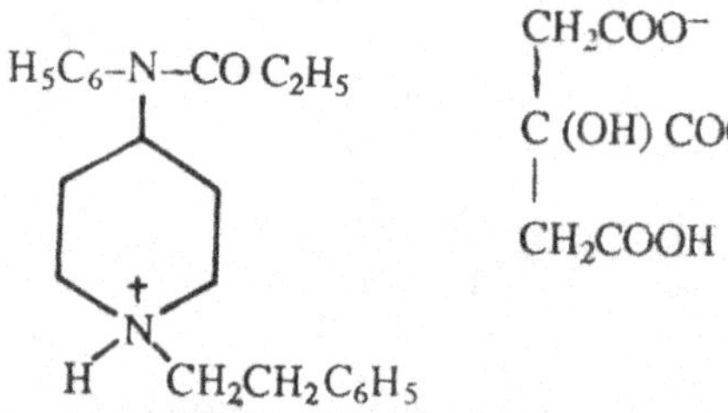

1 - phenethyl - 4 - N - phenyl propinamido piperidium dihydrogen citrate

Properties and uses : A white granule or crystalline powder, soluble in water, less soluble in alcohol and chloroform. It is considered to be 50 times more potent than morphine. It has rapid onset and short duration of action. It is given intravenously, and the usual dose is 50 to 100 micrograms. The dose may be repeated after 2-3 hours.

II. METHADONE ANALOGUES

Using structural fragments, different synthetic compounds have been evolved, one of them being methadone.

4. Methadone hydrochloride (I.P., B.P., U.S.P.) :

$$\text{Structure:}$$

$$\begin{array}{c}
C_6H_5 \\
| \\
C_6H_5-C-C(=O)-CH_2CH_3 \\
| \\
CH_2-CH(CH_3)-N(CH_3)_2
\end{array} \cdot HCl$$

6-dimethylamino, 4, 4-diphenyl 3-heptanone, hydrochloride
dimethyl (1–methyl–4–oxa–3, 3–diphenylhexyl) amine
hydrochloride

Properties : It occurs as a white crystalline powder, almost odourless, soluble in water and freely soluble in alcohol and chloroform. Aqueous solutions are acidic in nature. Incompatability results with alkali and salts of heavy metals.

Actions and uses : Its analgesic action is greater than that of morphine and it produces less sedation and narcosis than morphine. It also controls cough. Its injection and tablets are official in I.P., B.P., U.S.P. Usual dose is 15 to 80 mg, daily. Now-a-days it is mainly used in treatment of drug addiction.

5. Dipipanone hydrochloride (B.P.) :

$$\text{Piperidine}-N-CH(CH_3)-CH_2-C(C_6H_5)(C_6H_5)-C(=O)-CH_2CH_3 \cdot HCl$$

4,4–diphenyl–6–piperidino heptane–3–one hydrochloride

Properties and uses : A white, crystalline powder, almost odourless, soluble in water, more soluble in alcohol and acetone. Its solutions can be sterilised by autoclaving or by the filtration method. It is used as a narcotic analgesic. It is given subcutaneously or intramuscularly, and the usual dose is 25 to 50 mg.

6. **Dextromoramide tartrate (B.P.) :**

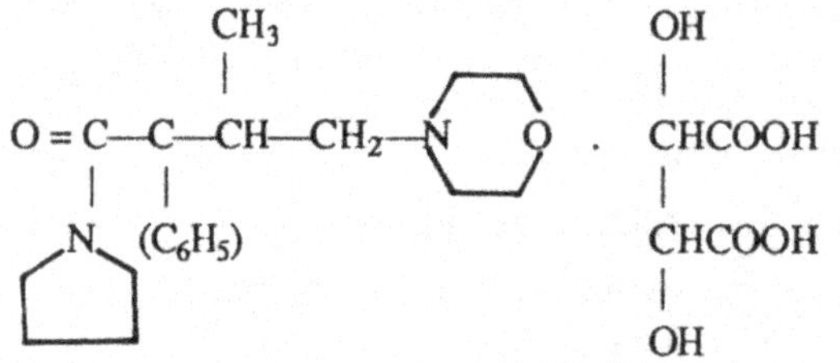

$$O=C-C-CH-CH_2-N\bigcirc O \cdot \begin{array}{c}OH\\|\\CHCOOH\\|\\CHCOOH\\|\\OH\end{array}$$

with substituents: CH_3 on the second C, pyrrolidine-N and C_6H_5 on the first C, and a morpholine ring attached via N.

(+) 1, (3-methyl-4, morpholino ' 2, 2-di,
phenyl-pyrrolidin butane-1–one hydrogentartrate

Properties and Uses : It is occurs as a white, crystalline or amorphous powder. It is soluble in water and less soluble in alcohol. Its aqueous solutions are acidic in nature. It is used as a narcotic analgesic, and the usual dose is 5 mg. of dextromoramide, repeated according ot need. It is used in the form of tablets.

7. **Dextropropoxyphene hydrochloride (I.P., B.P.) :**

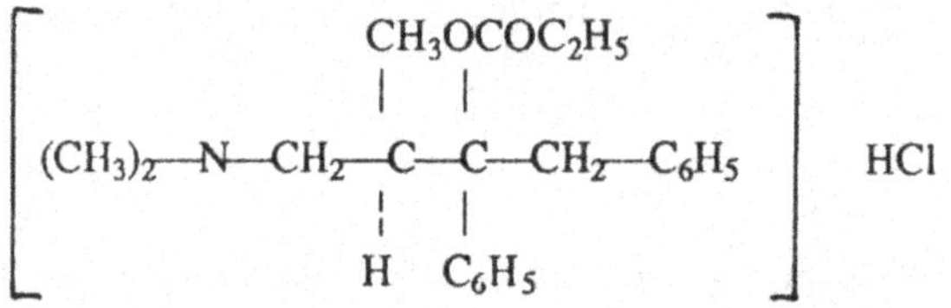

$$\left[(CH_3)_2-N-CH_2-\underset{\underset{H}{|}}{C}-\underset{\underset{C_6H_5}{|}}{\overset{\overset{CH_3OCOC_2H_5}{|}}{C}}-CH_2-C_6H_5\right] HCl$$

1-benzyl-3-dimethylamino-2-methyl-1-phenylpropyl
propionate hydrochloride

Properties and uses : A white or slightly yellowish powder, highly soluble in water, alcohol and chloroform, insoluble in ether. It is used in the form of tablets as an analgesic. The usual dose is 260 mg daily in divided doses.

The other salt which is official in B.P. is Dextropropoxyphene Napsylate, which is insoluble in water. It is used in the form of capsules, and the usual dose is 400 mg daily, in divided doses. The levo form has antitussive action.

III. MORPHINANS

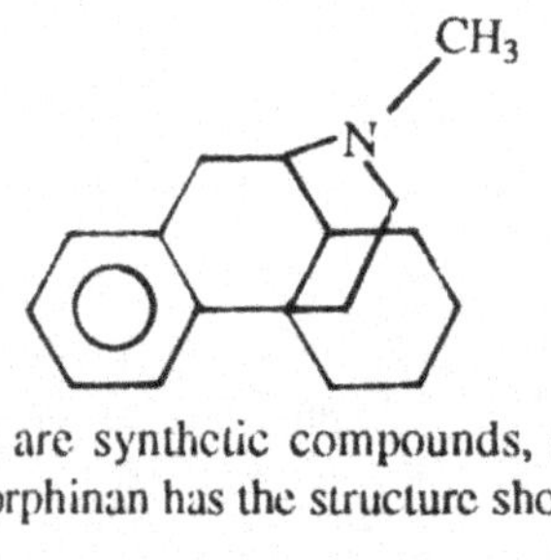

Morphinans are synthetic compounds, structurally similar to morphine. The N–methyl morphinan has the structure shown in the adjacent figure.

8. Levorphanol tartrate (B.P., U.S.P.) :

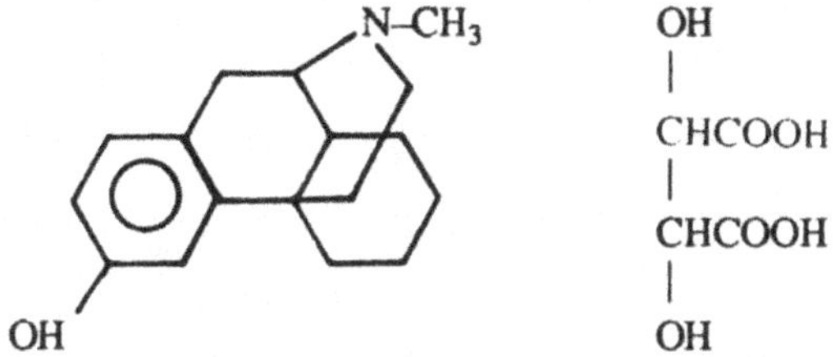

(−)-3 hydroxy-N-methyl morphinan hydrogen tartrate

Properties and uses : A white, crystalline powder, odourless, soluble in water, but less soluble in alcohol. Aqueous solutions are stable and can be sterilised by autoclaving or by the filtration method. It is used in the form of tablets and injections, as a narcotic analgesic ; usual dose being 1.5 to 4.5 mg., intramuscular 2 to 4 mg and intravenous 1 to 1.5 mg. The drug also have addiction liability.

IV. BENZOMORPHAN ANALOGUES

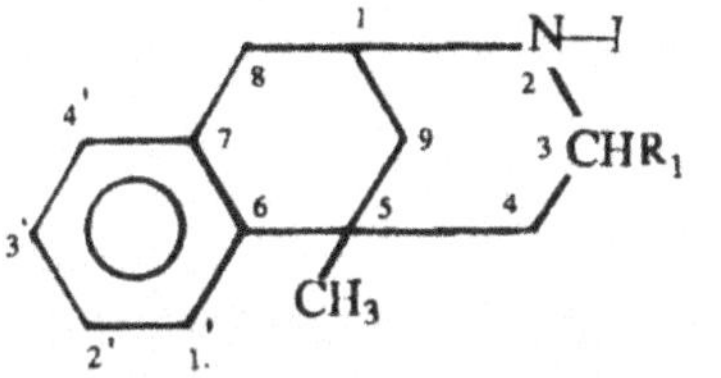

The Benzomorphan nucleus differs from the morphinan due to the absence of alicyclic ring. The structure is R_1, $R_2 =$ H, CH_3 or alkyl.

9. Pentazocine hydrochloride (B.P.)

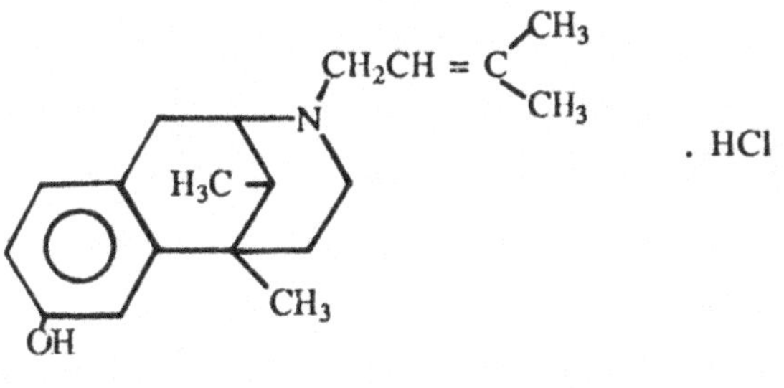

Properties and uses : Pentazocine base is also official in B.P. It occurs as a creamy, white powder odourless, practically insoluble in water, soluble in alcohol. Its hydrochloride is also a creamy white powder, soluble in water, more soluble in alcohol and chloroform. Its aqueous solutions are acidic in nature. It is used in the form of tablets. It is a good substitute for morphine and has a lesser dependence liability.

NARCOTIC ANTAGONIST

There are drugs which counteract or reverse the effect of narcotic drugs. Narcotic drugs like morphine and its related agents produce stupor and have addiction tendencies. Narcotic antagonists are useful in the treatment of over doses of narcotics, and to cure their addiction and habituation tendencies.

1. Nalorphine hydrochloride (I.P., U.S.P.) :

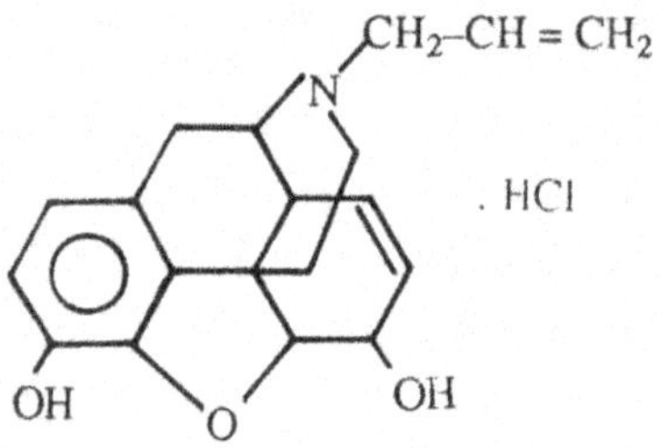

Properties and uses : It is a white, crystalline powder, it is odourless. It darkens slowly on exposure to air and light. It is soluble in water, but is less soluble in alcohol. The aqueous solution is acidic in nature. The aqueous injection is administered by the i.v. or i.m. route, in the dose regime of 2 to 10 mg. Nalorphine produces a direct, antagonistic effect to morphine, pethidine methadone and other related drugs.

2. Levallorphan (U.S.P.) :

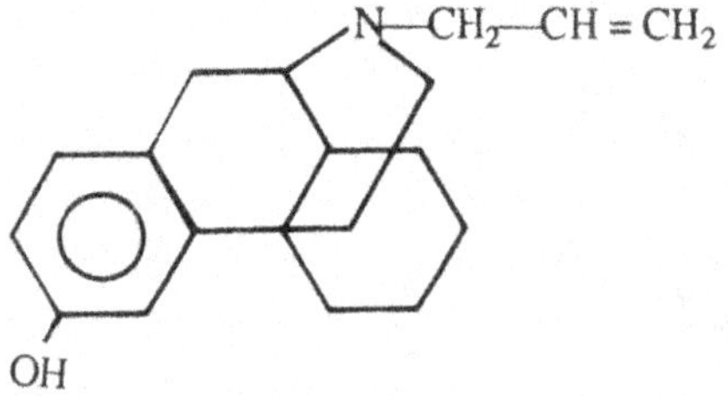

(−) **N-allyl-3-hydroxy morphinan**

Properties and uses : It is used as a tartrate, which is a white powder, soluble in water. It is administered by injection i.v. in 1 mg doses. The drug is about 5 times more potent as a narcotic antagonist than nalorphine.

3. **Naloxone (U.S.P.)** :

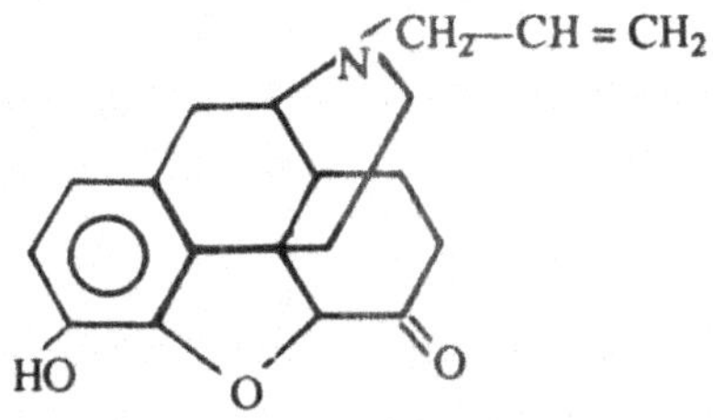

Properties and uses : Its hydrochloride is a white, crystalline powder, soluble in water. It is parenterally administered for treatment of over-doses of narcotics. It is about 7 times more active than nalorphine with a duration of action of about 4 hours. The usual dose is 400 mg.

4. **Apomorphine hydrochloride (B.P., U.S.P.)** :

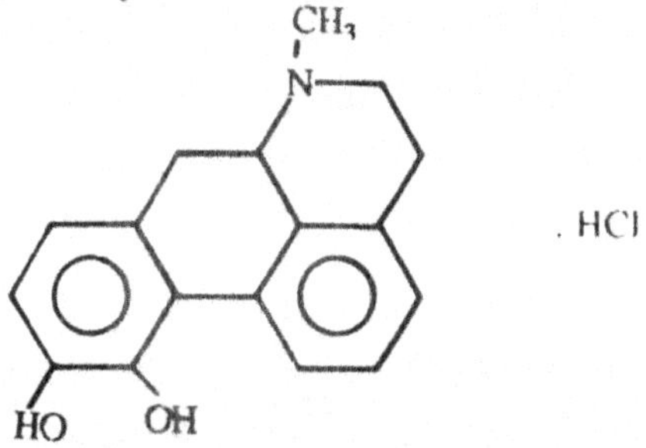

It is obtained by heating morphine with hydrochloric acid in a sealed tube under pressure. This structural change shows different physiological actions. CNS depressant action is reduced and produces stimulation effect. It produces emesis by central mechanism. The drug is sparingly water soluble and is sensitive to light and air. It is mainly used in tablet as well as injection form for emetic action.

Chapter 11

ANTIPYRETIC ANALGESICS

Antipyretics are the drugs which reduces elevated body temperatures while analgesics are the drugs which relieve pain. Many drugs possess both analgesic and antipyretic activities. These are called as non-narcotic anagesics also.

Analgesics - antipyretics as a class include compounds from different chemical categories with no structural resembalance. Most of these compounds are without addiction liabilities and are relatively non-toxic and safe. Since these compounds control both fever and pain they are widely used in pains, aches, bodyaches, febrile conditions and in various musculo-skeletal disturbances.

These drugs are believed to act by blocking biosynthesis of protaglandins and related metabolities and also by central mechanisms. Most of these drugs do not lower normal body temperature. They act at hypothalic temperature control center. Some compounds also show mild anti-inflammatory action.

The important agents in this class are found in (i) aniline (ii) salicylate and (iii) pyrozoline class.

1. Paracetamol (I.P., B.P., U.S.P.) :

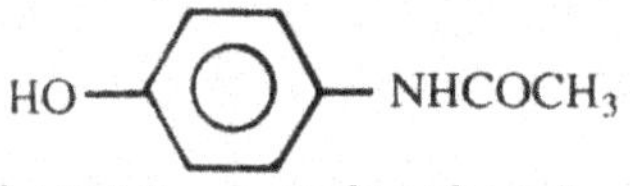

HO—⟨O⟩—$NHCOCH_3$

N-acetyl   p-aminophenol

Properties and uses : It occurs as white crystalline powder, odourless less soluble in water, more in boiling water, soluble in alcohol and alkalies like sodium hydroxide solution. Aqueous solutions are slightly acidic in nature.

Uses : It is used to releive the pain of headaches, myalgias, and other pains arising from muscles and joints. It is used in the form of oral preparations like tablets, suspensions, syrup (pediatric), and the usual dose is 0.5 to 1 g orally, every four hours, maximum upto 4 g in divided doses. It is less toxic than the salicylates.

2. Aspirin (I.P., B.P., U.S.P.) :

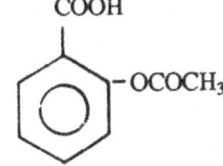

2-acetyl salicylic acid

Properties : It is a white crystals or a crystalline powder, odourless, less soluble in water (1 in 300), soluble in alcohol, ether and chloroform. Aqueous solutions are acidic in nature. It is stable in dry air, but gradually hydrolyses to salicylic acid in moist air. It is incompatible with acetanilide, phenacetin, antipyrine, aminopyrine and phenol, as it forms a damp mass when triturated. Alkali and alkali citrate rapidly hydrolyses it to salicylic acid and acetic acid. It should be stored in a cool and dry place.

Uses : It is employed as an analgesic and antipyretic in a variety of conditions. In gout and rheumatic fever, it has specific action and acts as antiinflammatory drug. It is used in the form of tablets and capsules, and the usual dose is 300 mg to 1 g. Soluble tablet of aspirin is prepared by using citric acid and calcium carbonate which facilitates disolution.

3. Sodium salicylate (I.P., B.P., U.S.P.) :

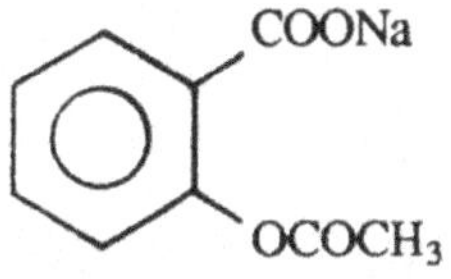

Properties : It is a amorphous or microcrystalline powder, practically odourless or with a slight characteristic odour, very soluble in water, soluble in alcohol and glycerine. Aqueous solution is neutral or acidic to litmus. Its solution darkens on oxidation, which is enhanced due to alkalies or iron. It is precipitated as salicylic acid by mineral acids and with a soluble quinine salt such as quinine salicylate.

Uses : It is widely used for relief of pain and reduction of fever. It is useful in gout and acute rheumatic fever. It causes gastric irritation due to the liberation of salicylic acid and is thus used along with an equivalent amount of sodium bicarbonate. It is normally used in the form of tablets or capsules. The usual dose is 300 mg to 1 g.

4. Aloxiprin (B.P.) :

It is a condensation product of aluminium oxide and acetylsalicylic acid.

Properties and uses : It occurs as a white or off white powder or granules, and has a slight odour. It is insoluble in water and the usual organic solvents. It is used like any other salicylate. Its advantage is that it is free from acetic odour, and its greater stability than aspirin.

5. Analgin (I.P., USSRP) :

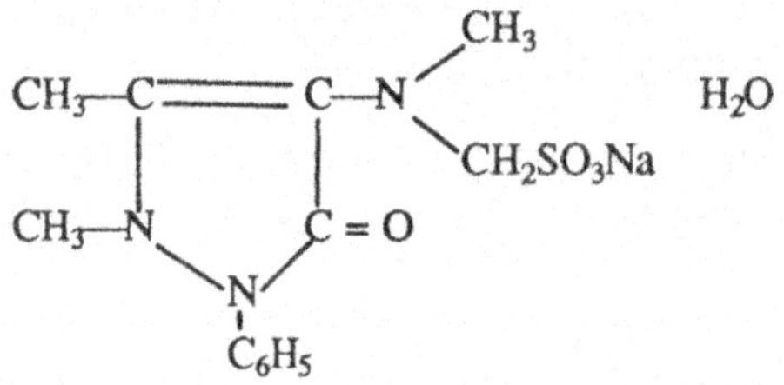

$$CH_3-C=C-N\begin{matrix}CH_3\\CH_2SO_3Na\end{matrix} \quad H_2O$$

2, 3-dimethyl-1-phenyl 5–pyrazolon 4 –yl
N methyl ammonium methane sulphonate

Properties and uses : An almost white, crystalline powder with a yellowish tint, odourless ; very soluble in water and alcohol, practically insoluble in chloroform and ether. As it is affected by air and moisture, it should be kept in tightly closed containers. It is used in the form of tablets as an analgesic and also to relieve muscular pain. Usual dose is 0.5 to 3 g daily, in divided doses.

6. Phenylbutazone (I.P., B.P., U.S.P.) :

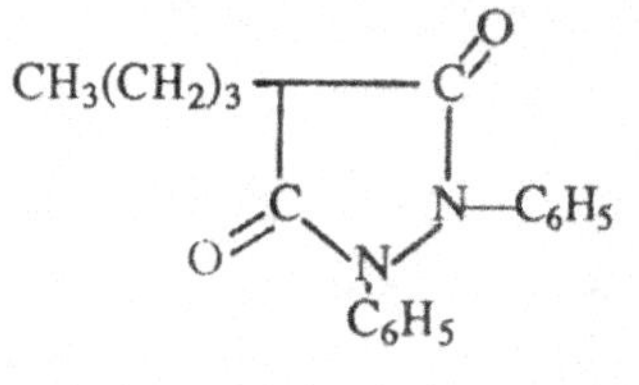

4-butyl-1,2-diphenyl,3,5-pyrazolidine-dione

Properties : It occurs as white, crystalline powder, partially soluble in water. It is affected by moisture and light.

Actions and uses : It is used in the treatment of gout, psoriases, rheumatoid arthritic, etc. It has many toxic effects and it may cause water retension, nausea and vertigo. More serious side effects can be hypertension, hepatitis, leucopenia and agranulocytosis, etc. It is contraindicated in patients with edema, cardiac dysfunction and peptic ulcers. It should be used with due precautions. Usual dose is 300 to 600 mg daily.

7. Sulphinpyrazone (B.P.) :

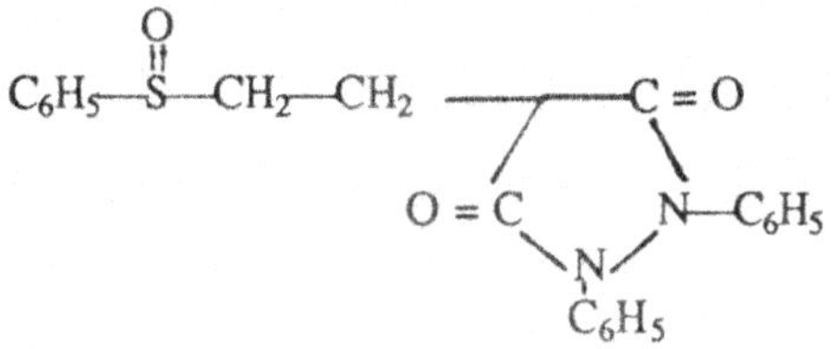

$$C_6H_5-\overset{\overset{O}{\|}}{S}-CH_2-CH_2-\underset{\underset{\underset{C_6H_5}{N}}{O=C}}{\overset{C=O}{\diagup}}\overset{}{\underset{}{N-C_6H_5}}$$

1, 2-diphenyl-4-(2, (Phenyl, sulphinyl) ethyl), 3, 5-pyrazolidinedione

Properties and uses : It is a pyrazolone derivative, related to phenyl butazone. It occurs as a white crystalline powder. It is a potent uricosuric agent, used as a preventive in acute gouty arthritis conditions. It also has several side effects. It is usually taken with milk or food in the dose regime of 50 mg, 4 times a day.

8. Oxyphenbutazone (I.P., B.P., U.S.P.) :

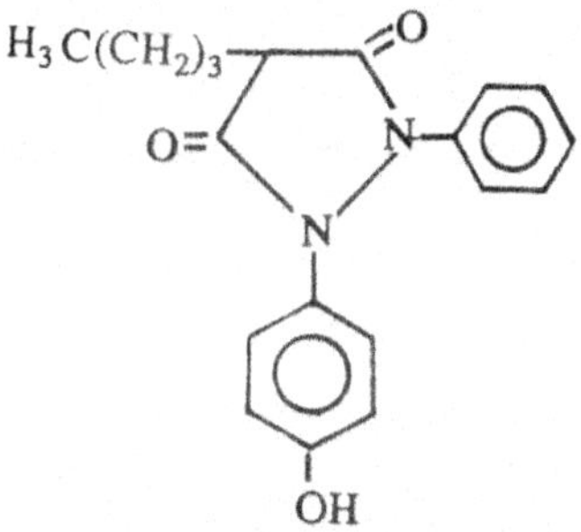

4-butyl-2-(4-hydroxyphenyl) 1 - phenyl pyrazolidine-3, 5 dione

Properties and uses : It is a white, crystalline powder, insoluble in water, soluble in alcohol and dissolves in dilute alkali hydroxides. It is given orally as tablets in combination with other analgesics. It has anti-inflammatory action and hence used in rheumatism, arthritis etc. It's eye ointment is official in B.P.

❏ ❏ ❏

Chapter 12

NONSTEROIDAL ANTI-INFLAMMATORY AGENTS

Nonsterodial Anti-inflammatory Agents

The drugs that inhibit or reduce inflammation and give relief of pain in arthritis and rheumatic diseases are called as anti-inflammaroty agents. Rheumatoid arthritis, rheumatic fever, osteoarturities, anklosing spondylitis etc. are diseases or anilments where the connective tissues are damaged and are affected. The antiinflammatory agents relief in these conditions.

Many mechanisms have been postulated for production and development of inflammation. These are

(i) the tissue damage which initiates in vascular permiability resulting in odema and swelling,

(ii) cellular infiltration of platelets and macrophages from capillaries into the tissue spaces and

(iii) synthesis of extracellular materials like fibroblasts, callogen fibers etc.

Mechanism of Action

The most accepted mechanism is the inhibition of Prostaglandin biosynthesis. Prostaglandins are a group of cyclopetnae derivatives derived from arachiodonic acid. The biosynthesis of prostaglandins is catalysed by microsomal enzymes present in humans and this is inhibited by antiinflammatory drugs.

Classification of Anti-inflammatory agents :

Mainly two different types of drugs are used in inflammatory and related conditions of pain and fever. One category of drus comprise from steroids (particularly glucocorticoids) which provide immense rlief. These steroids are very active and potent. However, these steroids bring undesirable steroidal effects on long and continued use. The second category consists of the nonsteroidal antiinflammatory drugs (NSID) which are equally potent as steroidal drugs and yet are devoid of the undesirable effects of steroidal therapy. These agents have analgesic-antipyretic actions also. They thus become useful in relieving pain and body fever.

The large number of antiinflammatory drugs (non-steroidal) differ considerably in their chemical structure. They can classified into following :

(i) Salicylates e.g. Aspirin, aspirin salts, salicylamide.

(ii) Pyrazolidinediones e.g. phenylbutazone, oxyphenbutazone

(iii) Anthranilic acid derivatives e.g. Mefenamic acid

(iv) Aryl and heteroarylacid derivatives e.g. Ibuprofen, naproxen, indomethacin.

(v) Miscellaneous e.g. Piroxican.

I. SALICYLATES

Compounds belonging to this category are aspirin, sodium salicylate and methyl salicylate. They are discussed under the category of analgesics and antipyretics. Aspirin has uricosuric properties and is used in combination with paracetamol and codeine. It is useful in acute and chronic rheumatic fever and also in gout. Sodium bicarbonate is given along with sodium salicylate as it causes gastric irritation. Methyl salicylate is normally applied in the form of an ointment or liniment, in relieving pain due to lumbago (back ache) and rheumatic conditions.

1. Sal salate (B.P.) :

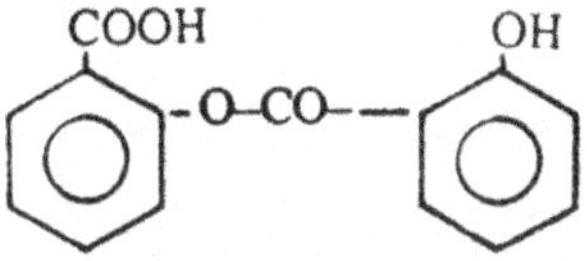

O- (2-hydroxy benzoyl) salicylic acid

Properties and uses : It is a white crystalline powder, very slightly soluble in water, more in alcohol. It is given in capsules in 300 mg - 1 g dose. It has anti–inflammatory-analgesic action.

2. Benorylate (B.P.) :

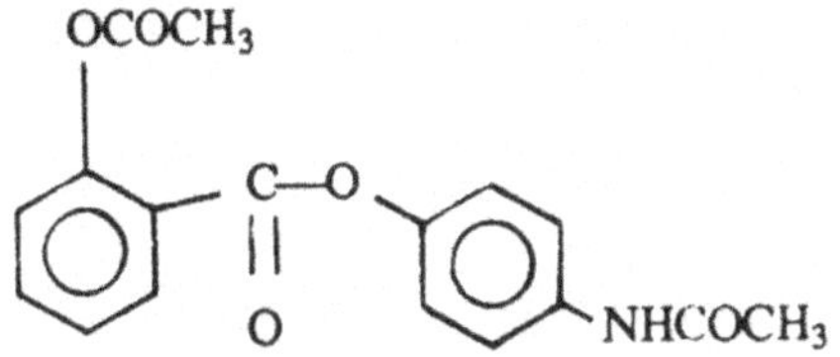

4-acetamidophenyl–O-acetyl-salicylate

Properties and uses : It is white crystalline powder, odourless, insoluble in water sparingly soluble in alcohol. The drug is given in oral suspension or in tablet form for its anti–inflammatory and analgesic action.

3. Diflunisal B.P. :

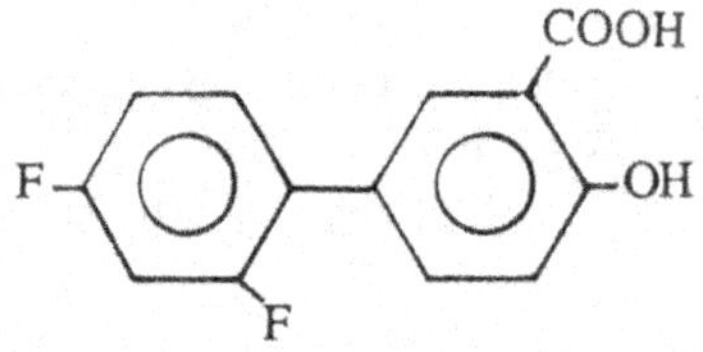

5 (2, 4 diflurophenyl) salicylic acid

Properties and uses : It is white powder insoluble in water, soluble in alcohol. It should be protected from light. It is given orally as tablets for anti–inflammatory-analgesic action.

4. Methyl salicylate (I.P., B.P., U.S.P.) :

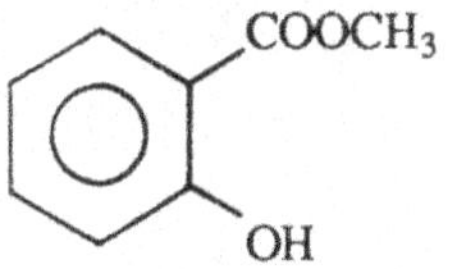

Methyl salicylate is manufactured synthetically or obtained from the leaves of *Gaultheria procumbens* or from the bank of *Betula Centa*.

It is a colourless to yellowish liquid with characteristic odour. It is slightly soluble in water but more soluble in alcohol. It gets hydrolysed by alkali to methanol and salicylic acid. It is commonly used for its rubefacient action in ointments, lotion and creams. It is useful in neuralgia and rheumatism.

II. PYRAZOLIDINE DIONES

This class includes phenylbutazone, oxyphenbutazone, sulphinpyrazone, etc. which have been discussed under analgesic antipyretics. Phenylbutazone is a potent anti-inflammatory agent. It has a marked sodium retention property, and is a mild uricosuric agent. It is more toxic, as compared to other agents. Sulphinepyrazone has enhanced uricosuric activity and is potent against gout.

III. ANTHRANILIC ACID DERIVATIVES

Chemically, anthralinic acid is o-amino benzoic acid. When a substituted phenyl nucleus is attached to the nitrogen of anthralinic acid the compounds exhibit anti-inflammatory activity. The important compounds of this class are given below.

1. Mefanamic acid (B.P.) :

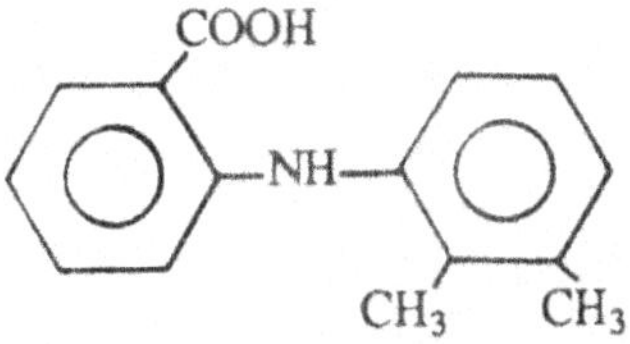

N-2,3-xylylanthranilic acid

Properties and uses : It is a white to greyish white powder, insoluble in water practically soluble in alcohol, ether and chloroform. It should be stored in a well closed container. It is one half times more potent that phenylbutazone. It is used in the form of capsules for minor pains. The usual dose is 1.5 g daily, in divided doses.

2. Flufenamic acid (B.P.) :

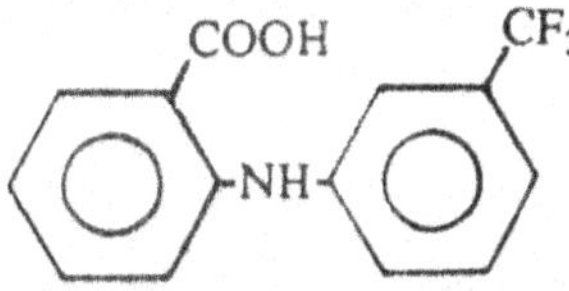

N-(trifluro-m-tolyl) anthranilic acid

Properties and uses : A pale yellowish, crystalline powder, odourless, insoluble in water, but highly soluble in alcohol and chloroform. It is 1.6 times as potent as phenylbutazone. It is used in the form of capsules, and the usual dose is 600 mg daily, in divided doses. It is less effective than prednisone, but is comparable to aspirin in the treatment of rheumatoid arthritis. It is more active than mefenamic acid. It is no longer official in B.P.

Under Antiinflammatory agents

3. Diciofenae and Diciofenacsodium

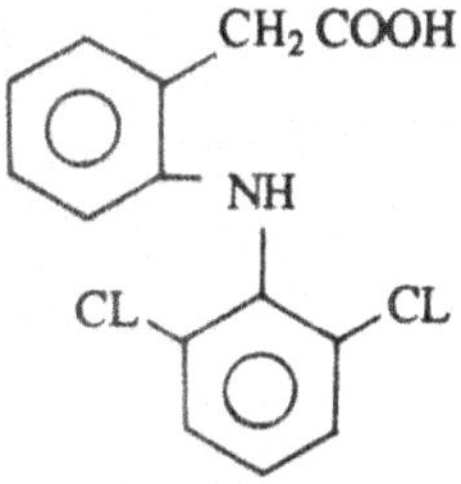

2 - (2, 6 - dichloroantion) Phenylacetic acid.

This is a very potent and popular antiinflammatory drug introduced in market. It is not yet official in I. P. or B. P.

IV. ARYL AND HETEROARYL ACID DERIVATIVES

Various compounds have been developed from aryl acetic acid and aryl propionic acid, naphthyl acetic acid, indole acetic acid etc. These have low prominent antiinflammatory-analgesic action. These compounds are extensively used in variety of rheumatoid and other conditions.

1. Ibuprofen (I.P., B.P., U.S.P.) :

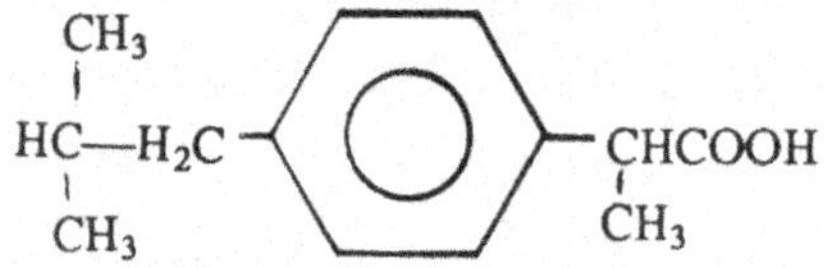

2-(4-Isobutylphenyl), propionic acid

Properties and uses : It occurs as almost white crystalline powder with a characteristic odour, practically insoluble in water, highly soluble in alcohol, ether and chloroform. It is also soluble in solutions of alkali hydroxides and carbonates. It is used as an analgesic anti-inflammatory agent. In the form of tablets, the usual dose is 600 to 1200 mg daily, in divided doses.

2. Flurbiprofen (B.P.) :

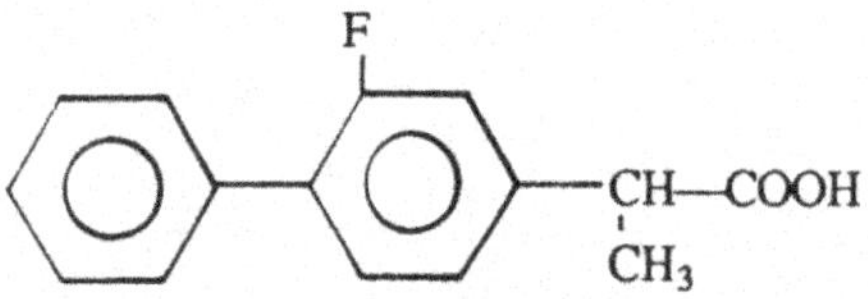

2-(2-flurobiphenyl-4-yl) propionic acid

Properties and uses : It occurs as white crystalline powder, insoluble in water, soluble in alcohol. The drug is administered in the tablet form for antiinflammatory-analgesic action and is more potent than ibuprofen.

3. Fenoprofen calcium (B.P., U.S.P.) :

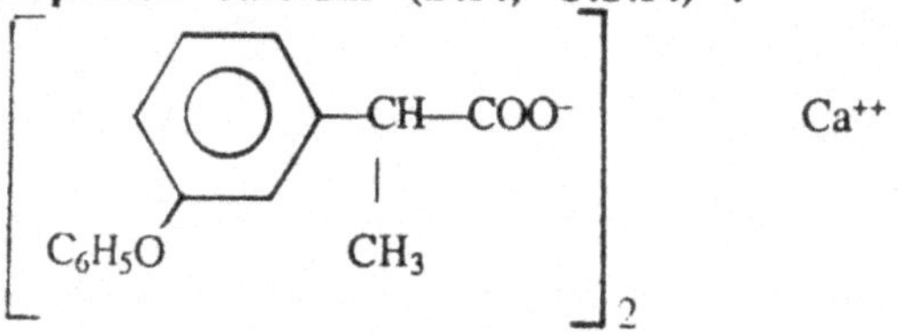

Calcium, 2-(3-phenoxyl-phenyl propionate)

Properties and uses : It is a colourless powder, slightly soluble in water and chloroform soluble in alcohol. It is orally active and given in tablets in 600 mg dose in osteroarthritis and in rheumatoid arthritis.

4. Ketoprofen : (B.P.) :

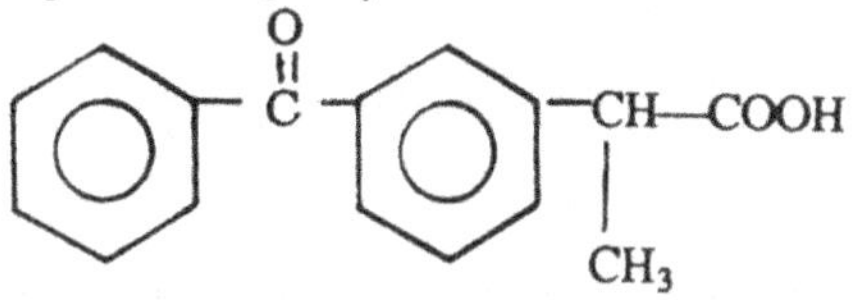

2-(3-benzoyl phenyl) propanoic acid

Properties and uses : It is a almost white powder, insoluble in water but soluble in alcohol. The drug is generally given in capsule form for antiinflammatory-analgesic action.

5. Naproxen (B.P.) :

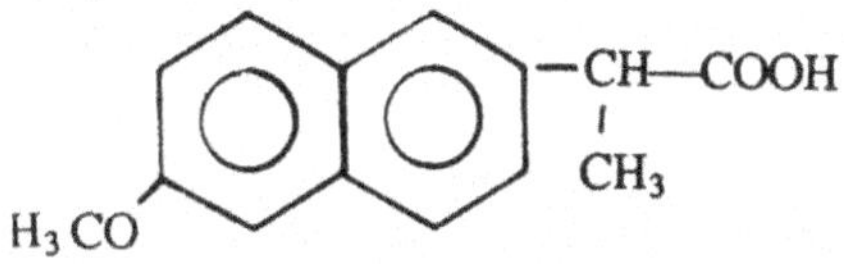

(+)-2-(6-methoxy-2-napthyl) propionic acid

Properties and uses : It is a almost white, crystalline powder, practically insoluble in water, soluble in alcohol, chloroform and ether. It should be stored in a well-closed container protected from light. It is used in the form of tablets and the usual dose is 250 to 1000 mg daily, in divided doses. It is mainly used in rheumatoid and gouty arthritis.

6. Indomethacin (I.P., B.P., U.S.P.) :

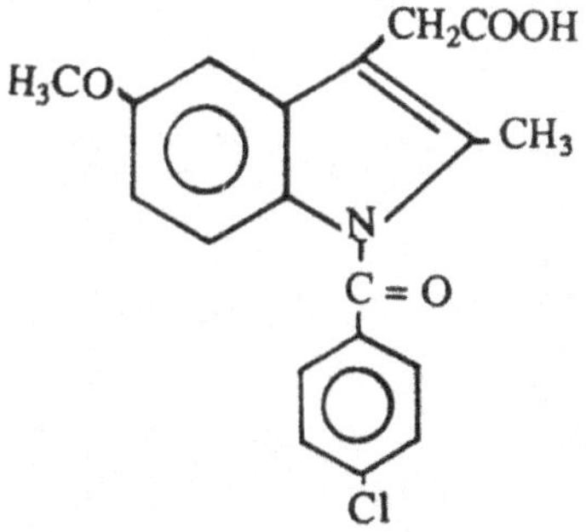

1-(4-chlorobenzoyl)-5-methoxy-2-methylindol-3-yl-acetic acid

Properties : It is a A white to whitish yellowish crystalline powder, practically insoluble in water, soluble in alcohol, chloroform and ether. It shouldbe protected from light.

Actions and uses : It shows excellent effects in gout arthritis and osteoarthritis. It is less effective in rheumatoid arthritis. It is used in the form of capsules, and the usual dose is 75 to 150 mg daily, in divided doses.

7. Sulindac (B.P., U.S.P.) :

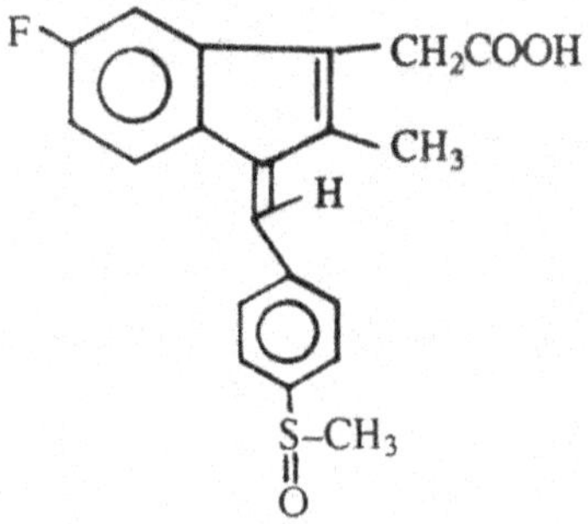

2-(5-fluro 2-methyl-1- (4-,methyl-sulphinyl benzyldien) indene-3-acetic acid.

Properties and uses : The drug is yellow crystalline, odourless powder, sparingly water soluble but soluble in chloroform. It is given in tablets in 150 - 200 mg 2 times a day in rheumatoid arthritis, osteoarthritis and in ankylosing spondglytis.

V. MISCELLANEOUS

Different compounds from varied chemical class possess anti-inflammatory activity of promising order. Some compounds of therapeutical use are.

1. Piroxicam :

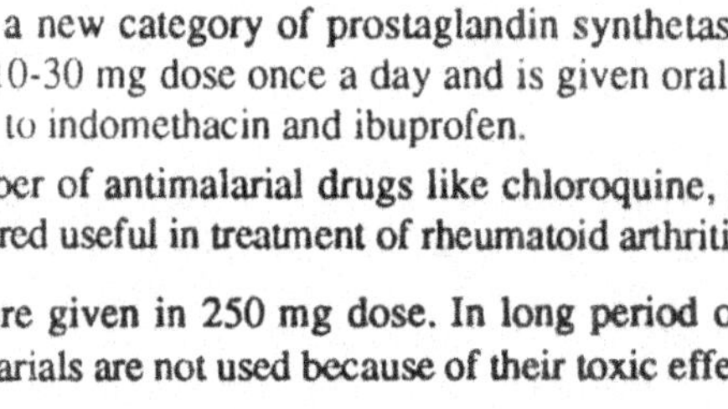

This is a new category of prostaglandin synthetase inhibitor. The drug is effective in 10-30 mg dose once a day and is given orally as tablets or capsules. It is superior to indomethacin and ibuprofen.

A number of antimalarial drugs like chloroquine, hydroxychloroquine etc were considered useful in treatment of rheumatoid arthritis.

They were given in 250 mg dose. In long period of treatment in arthritis, these antimalarials are not used because of their toxic effects.

❏ ❏ ❏

Chapter 13

ADRENERGIC AGENTS

ADRENERGIC AGENTS

These are number of substances which are synthesized and secreted in the body, one such class are the sympathomimetic amines. Adrenaline is a hormone secreted by the adrenal medulla of the adrenal gland. Adrenaline and noradrenaline are the mediators released at the synapse and adrenergic nerve endings. The adrenaline secreted in the body controls a variety of biological activities and functions. Pharmacologically adrenaline evokes a number of actions which include (i) A rise in blood pressure (ii) cardiac stimulation (iii) The constriction of the periferal blood vessels. (iv) relaxation of bronchial muscle and smooth muscle (v) The central nervous system stimulation and (vi) contraction of the ureter and uterus etc. These actions are mediated through α and β adrenergic receptors.

The drugs which exert an action smilar to adrenaline or sympathomimetic agents are called adrenergic agents. Besides pharmacological actions, there are number of therapeutic applications of the agents. They are useful in the treatment of (i) asthma and related conditions of bronchial spasms (ii) cardiac block (iii) hypotension (iv) nasal congestion and (v) stimulation of the central nervous system for mild analeptic effect. They are also useful in obesity for their anorexic action.

A considerable amount of work on the adrenaline and related agents have been carried out by Barger and Dale. There are compounds related to adrenaline that are more or less selective in their action, belonging to a chemical class called β-phenylethylamine. The structure of this is altered in 4 major ways :

$$\underset{1}{\text{Ph}}-\underset{2}{\overset{H}{\underset{|}{\beta C}}}-\underset{3}{\overset{H}{\underset{|}{\alpha C}}}-\underset{4}{\overset{}{\underset{|}{N}}}-H$$

1. The substitution of the hydroxyl group on the aromatic nucleus or replacement of it with other nucleus.

2. Substitution on the beta carbon atom.

3. Substitution on the alpha carbon atom.
4. Substitution on the nitrogen of amino group.

Adrenergic agents can broadly be arranged according to their principle biological actions as given below :

(i) Vasopressor.

(ii) Bronchodilator

(iii) Vasoconstrictor as nasal decongescant

(iv) Miscellaneous.

I. VASOPRESSOR DRUGS

(a) **Adrenaline and other compounds** : The compounds under this category have a catechol(dihydroxy-benzene) nucleus with 2 carbon atom side chain having amine and hydroxy function. These are basic in nature and are unstable. They readily form salts like hydrochloride, sulphate, tartarate etc; which are water-soluble. Aqueous solutions are stabilised by adding 0.1 % sodium metabisulphite as antioxidant. Important compounds of this class are :

1. **Adrenaline [Epinephrine]** : (I.P., B.P., U.S.P.) :

$$HO-C_6H_3(OH)-CH(OH)-CH_2-NH-CH_3$$

(R)-1-(3,4-dihydroxyphenyl-)-2-methyl-aminoethanol

Properties : It consists of white or light buff coloured crystals or powder, sparingly soluble in water and alcohol. It gradually darkens on exposure to light and air and is thus stored in air tight light-resistant containers in cool place. The laevo form is 15 times more active than the racemate. It readily forms salts with acids which are highly soluble in water. It can be precipitated from the solutions by ammonium hydroxide or alkali carbonate solution. The solution of epinephrine is usually prepared by using hydrochloric acid. A slight acidity is necessary for the stability of the solution, otherwise it rapidly oxidises to an inert material. A development of pink or slightly brown colour indicates oxidation. Solutions are usually buffered to pH 4.2 containing 0.1 % sodium metabisulphite as a stabiliser. Metal ions like copper, iron and zinc destroy its activity. The aqueous solutions are sterilised by the filtration method.

Actions and uses : It acts on smooth muscle cells, gland cells and the heart to produce responses similar to those evoked by stimulation of the corresponding sympathetic nerves. Adrenaline stimulates the heart, increases the heart rate, raises blood pressure, relaxes the musculature of intestine and bronchi. It is primarily used to relieve bronchial spasm in asthma. Topically it is applied to control superficial haemorrhages in operative procedures on the nose and throat. It is used in acute coryza as a spray, hay fever and sinusitis. In combination with local anaesthetic, because of its vasoconstriction action, it keeps the local anaesthetic in the desired area and prolongs its action. It is very valuable in complete heart block. It is also useful in a number of allergic disorders and gives relief in cases of serum reaction, serum sickness and giant urticaria.

Epinephrine can be injected subcutaneously or intramuscularly, as 0.01 % solution subcutaneously or 0.05 % solution intravenously, or sprayed as 1 % aqueous solution or applied topically in aqueous solution ; or used in ointment, suppository or jelly. Adrenaline is orally inactive. Official preparations include adrenaline solution, adrenaline maleate injection, adrenaline acid tartrate injection (I.P.). Sterile epinephrine suspension, epinephrine tartrate, opthalmic ointment are official in U.S.P.

2. Nor-adrenaline acid tartrate (nor epinephrine) (I.P., B.P., U.S.P.) :

$$\left[\begin{array}{c} \text{HO-C}_6\text{H}_3(\text{OH})\text{-C(OH)(H)-CH}_2\text{-NH}_3^+ \end{array} \right] \quad \begin{array}{c} \text{OH} \\ | \\ \text{HCCOO}^- \\ | \\ \text{HCCOH} \\ | \\ \text{OH} \end{array}$$

(R)-(2-hydroxy-2,3-hydroxy phenyl)ethyl ammonium hydrogen tartrate)

Properties : It is an almost white crystalline powder, highly soluble in water. Its solubility in alcohol is less and it is insoluble in ether and chloroform. Aqueous solutions are acidic in nature. It slowly darkens on exposure to air and light. It is preserved in tight, light resistant containers.

Actions and uses : Its pharmacological actions are similar to those of adrenaline, but quantitative differences exist between them. When it is given by slow intravenous infusion, or by injection, cardiovascular effects are most prominent. It is used in the treatment of vasomotor collapse, to maintain blood pressure in acute hypotensive states and also in acute cardiac infarction.

3. Isoprenaline sulphate (Isoproterenal sulphate) (I.P., B.P., N.F.) :

$$\text{HO-C}_6\text{H}_3(\text{OH})\text{-CH(OH)-CH}_2\text{-NHCH(CH}_3)_2 \quad . \quad H_2SO_4$$

1-(3,4 dihydroxyphenyl) 2 isopropylamino ethanol sulphate

Properties : It is a white crystalline powder, odourless, freely soluble in water, practically insoluble in alcohol and chloroform. Aqueous solutions are acidic in nature. Its solutions turn pink slowly due to oxidation and immediately in presence of an alkali.

Actions and uses : It causes a decrease in blood pressure and relaxes the smooth muslces of the gastro-intestinal tract. It is a potent cardiac stimulant. It is given sublingually or by inhalation in the treatment of asthma. It is also used in the treatment of bradycardia and as a stimulant in heart attack. It is used in the form of tablets or as an inhalation. The sublingual dose is 10 mg every four hours or as needed, and by inhalation, it is 0.25 mg or as needed. The hydrochloride salt is also official.

4. Phenylephrine hydrochloride (B.P., U.S.P.) :

$$\text{Ar-CH(OH)-CH}_2\text{-NHCH}_3$$
(with 3-OH on phenyl ring)

(S)1-(3-hydroxyphenyl-2-methylamino ethanol hydrochloride

Properties and uses : It is a white crystalline powder, highly soluble in water and alcohol. It is affected adversely by light. Aqueous solutions are acidic in nature. Aqueous solutions are sterilised by the filtration method. Its preparations are incompatible with butacaine. It is active orally, and with oral administration the side effects are less. A 0.25 % solution is used to reduce nasal congestion and hay fever. It is also used as mydriatic agent. Being a vasoconstrictor it prolongs the action of a local anaesthetic. It is systemically used in the treatment of hypotension. As an intramuscular or subcutaneous injection the dose is 5 mg and intravenous dose is 500 micrograms.

5. Mephentermine sulphate (U.S.P.) :

$$\left[\text{Ph-CH}_2\text{-C(CH}_3\text{)(CH}_3\text{)-NHCH}_3 \right]_2 \cdot H_2SO_4$$

N-α, α-trimethyl phenyl ethylammonium sulphate

Properties and uses : It is a white crystalline powder, almost odourless. It is soluble in water. It's solubility in alcohol is less as compared to water. Aqueous solutions are acidic to litmus. The free base is volatile and dispensed as an inhaler or in the form of aqueous solution as a nasal decongestant. In the form of injection, it is given in hypotensive state as it increases the blood pressure immediately for prolonged period. The intravenous dose is 20 to 80 mg and the oral dose is 12.5 to 25 mg, twice a day.

6. Metraminol Tartrate (B.P., U.S.P.) :

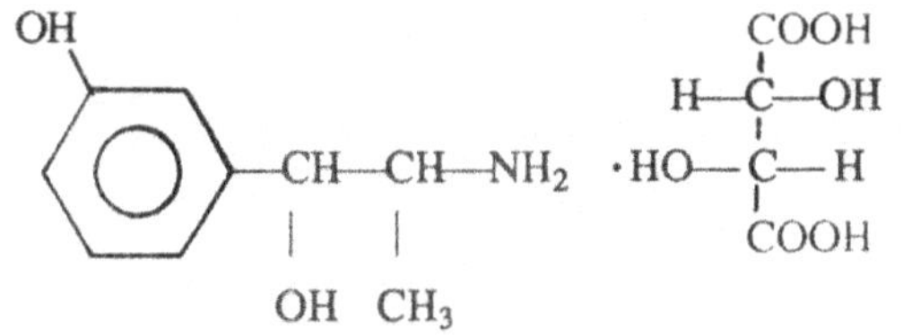

(−)-2-amino-1-(3-hydroxyphenyl propane-1-ol hydrogen tartarate

Properties and uses : It is a white powder, freely soluble in water, less soluble in alcohol, and insoluble in ether and chloroform. The aqueous solutions are acidic in nature. The solutions are sterilised by the filtration method. The drug is used in hypotensive states for sustaining blood pressure under general or spinal anaesthesia and for treatment of shock, for which it is administered by the parenteral route. It is used locally in nasal congestion.

7. Methoxamine hydrochloride (B.P., U.S.P.) :

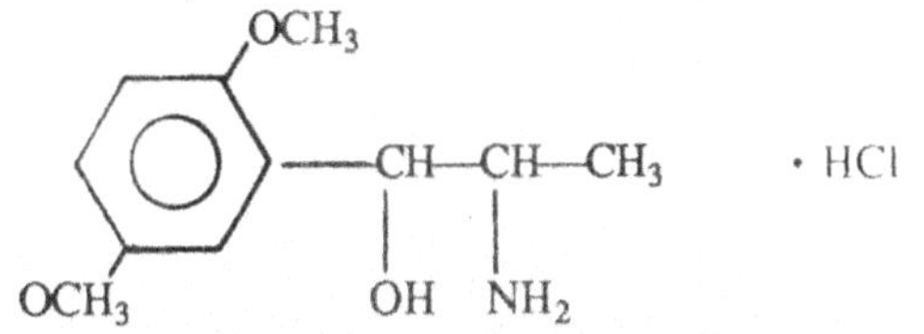

2-amino-1-(2,5-dimethoxy phenyl) propane-1-ol hydrochloride

Properties and uses : The hydrochloride, is a white crystalline powder with a slight odour. It is freely soluble in water and the aqueous solutions have an acid reaction to litmus. It is preserved in light-resistant containers. It is solely used for its pressor action. It is administered intramuscularly in 10 to 15 mg dose or by intravenous route in 3 to 5 mg doses to restore blood pressure during surgical operations and in hypotensive cases.

8. Cyclopentamine hydrochloride (U.S.P.) :

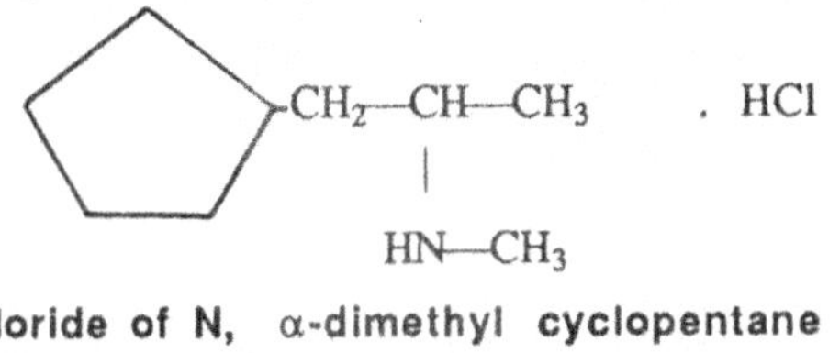

Hydrochloride of N, α-dimethyl cyclopentane ethylamine

Properties and uses : It is a white crystalline powder, with slight and characteristic odour. It is freely soluble in water and alcohol. It is a sympathomimetic and has vasoconstrictor and pressor action. It is used to maintain blood pressure in surgical operations, in spinal anaesthesia and also to relieve nasal decongestion in 0.5 to 1 % solution. Intramuscular dose is 25 mg and intravenous dose is 5 to 10 mg slowly.

9. **Dopamine hydrochloride (B.P.) :**

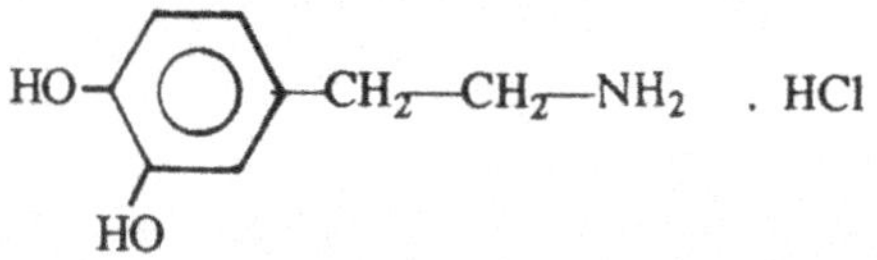

HO—⌬—CH_2—CH_2—NH_2 . HCl
HO

4-(2-aminoethyl) pyrocatechol hydrochloride

Properties and uses : It is a white crystalline powder, freely soluble in water and sparingly soluble in alcohol. It should be protected from light. The drug is given in the treatment of shock. It increases cardiac output and is given by intravenous infusion.

(b) **Ephedrine and other compounds :**

1. **Ephedrine (I.P., B.P., U.S.P.) :**

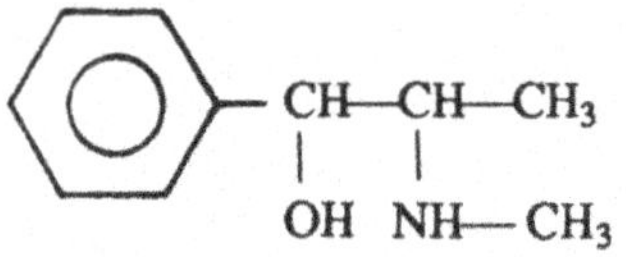

⌬— CH—CH—CH_3
     | |
     OH   NH—CH_3

(1R, 2S)-2-methylamino,-1-phenylpropane-1-ol.

Properties : It is an alkaloid obtained from various species of *Ephedra* or prepared synthetically. It has 2-asymmetric carbon atoms and thus, have 4 stereo isomers. The *erythro* form is called ephedrine, whole the *threo* form is known as pseudoephedrin (φ ephedrin). The biologically active form is D (–).

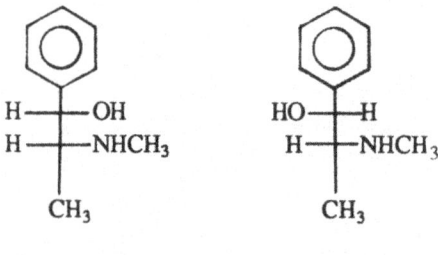

Erythro form   Threo form

It is available as colourless crystals or white crystalline powder and has a slight aromatic odour. It is soluble in water, chloroform, alcohol and ether. It gradually decomposes on exposure to light. It readily combines with acids to form salts. Its aqueous solutions are alkaline to litmus. Ephedrine is soluble in water giving an alkaline solution and incompatibilities may occur due to alkalinity. It forms a compound with iodine which is insoluble in ether, water or oils. Tannic acid precipitates the alkaloid but not its salt. It is incompatible with chlorobutanol.

Actions and uses : It is a sympathomimetic amine and shares some actions of adrenaline but differs in several ways. Because of its stability, it is given orally. It has a longer duration of action than adrenaline. It has a mydriatic action which is valuable in ophthamology. It has a powerful CNS stimulation action which adrenaline does not have. It is used in the treatment of myasthenia gravis. It is employed to bolster the blood pressure in patients undergoing spinal anaesthesia. As it is a vasoconstrictor, it is used in hay fever and acute coryza. Because of its branchodilator action it is used in the treatment of bronchial asthma. Ephedrine is a respiratory stimulant and sometimes useful in treating morphine and barbiturate overdoses.

Ephredric hydrochloride is official in I.P., B.P. and U.S.P. It is soluble in water and insoluble in ether. Aqueous solutions are acidic in nature. Ephedrine salts are insoluble in liquid petrolatum.

Ephedrine sulphate is compatible with silver salts but the hydrochloride gives a precipitate. Ephedrine hydrochloride is used in the form of tablets or capsules. It is a common ingredient of cough mixtures. The usual dose is 25 mg.

2. Pseudophedrine : It is a stereoisomer of ephedrine. It is usually used in the form of a hydrochloride and is useful as an nasal and bronchial decongestant.

3. Phenylpropanolamine hydrochloride (B.P., N.F.) :

$$C_6H_5-CH(OH)-CH(NH_2)-CH_3 \cdot HCl$$

1 Rs, (2SR)-2-amino-2-amino-1-phenyl propane-1-ol hydrochloride

Properties and uses : It is a creamy white crystalline powder, almost odourless. It is soluble in water and alcohol and insoluble in chloroform. The aqueous solutions are acidic in nature. It is active orally and is used in place of ephedrine. It is mainly used as decongestant. The usual dose range is from 25 to 50 mg. It has more of a vasoconstriction and less CNS stimulant action.

II. BRONCHODILATOR DRUGS

Some of the sympathomimetric amines have selective bronchodilatory action and thus find use in asthama and related conditions. The drugs like isoprenaline ephedrine, pseudophedrine are more useful bronchodilator than pressor in their action. The other compounds showing bronchodilator actions are

1. Orciprenaline Sulphate (I.P., B.P.) :

$$\left[\text{(HO)}_2\text{C}_6\text{H}_3-\text{CH(OH)}-\text{CH}_2-\text{NH}-\text{CH(CH}_3)_2 \right]_2 \cdot \text{H}_2\text{SO}_4$$

1-(3,5-dihydroxy phenyl)-2-isopropylaminoethanol sulphate

Properties and uses : It differs in structure from isoprealine in position of hydroxyl group. It is a white crystalline powder, very soluble in water and alcohol. It is affected adversely by light. The aqueous solutions are sterilised by filtration. It is used in the form of tablets and injections in bronchial asthma. The usual dose is 20 to 80 mg, in a single dose or in divided doses. The intramuscular dose is 500 micrograms.

2. Salbutamol (I.P., B.P.) :

$$\text{HO}-\text{C}_6\text{H}_3(\text{CH}_2\text{OH})-\text{CH(OH)}-\text{CH}_2-\text{NH}-\text{C}(\text{CH}_3)_3$$

1-(4-hydroxy-3-hydroxy methylphenyl)
-2-(tert butylamino)-ethanol

Properties and uses : It is an almost white crystalline powder, partially soluble in water, but more soluble in alcohol. It is used in the form of its salt (sulphate) which is freely soluble in water. It must be stored in a well-closed container, and protected from light. It is used in the form of tablets or injection. It is a sympathomimetic drug, used as a bronchodilator and in premature labour. The usual dose is 6 to 16 mg of base daily in divided doses. As a bornchodilator, it is given by intravenous infusion, 3 to 20 micrograms per minute, according to the response of patient.

3. Terbutaline sulphate (B.P., U.S.P.) :

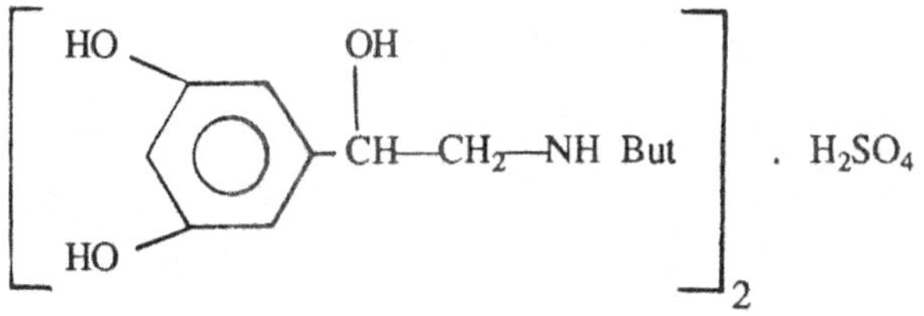

$$\left[\begin{array}{c} HO\text{-}C_6H_3(OH)\text{-}CH(OH)\text{-}CH_2\text{-}NH\text{-}But \end{array} \right]_2 \cdot H_2SO_4$$

2 (tert-butylamino)-1-(3,5-dihydroxyphenyl
-ethanol sulphate

Properties and uses : It is a almost white powder soluble in water, slightly soluble in alcohol. It is employed in tablets in 5 mg dose 3 times a day. The drug acts via beta-receptor and is useful in bronchial asthma and related conditions.

4. Methoxyphenamine hydrochloride (U.S.P.) :

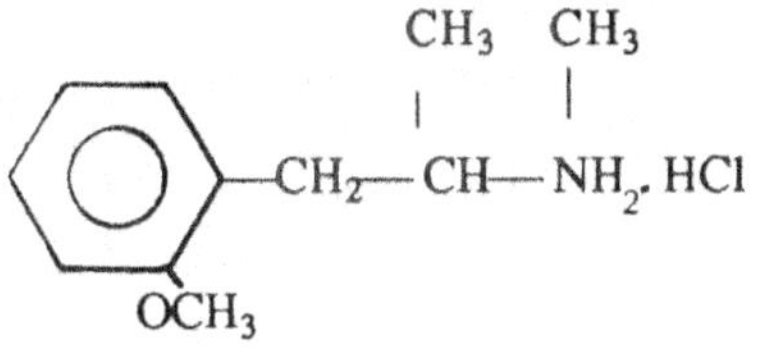

$$C_6H_4(OCH_3)\text{-}CH_2\text{-}CH(CH_3)\text{-}NH(CH_3) \cdot HCl$$

Properties and uses : It is a white bitter powder, odourless, freely soluble in water and alcohol. It has potent action as bronchodilator and has less pressor effect. The drug is used in treatment of asthama and is effective in allergic rhinitis.

5. Aminophylline (I.P., B.P.) :

It is a salt of theophylline and ethylenediamine and is a bronchodilator. This drug do not belong pharmacologically to sympathomimetic class. However, the drug is extremely useful in asthma.

Aminophylline occurs as slightly yellowish granules, with typical odour and has bitter taste It decomposes on exposure to air. It is freely soluble in water, insoluble in alcohol and solvent ether. The aqueous solution becomes turbid (due to decomposition) on keeping. It is administered by slow intravenous injection in 0.2 to 0.5 g dose. Aminophylline tablets are also official in I.P.

III. VASOCONSTRICTOR AS NASAL DECONGESTANT

The drugs like cyclopentamine hydrochloride, phenylpropanolamine, ephedrine hydrochloride, pseudoephedrine phenylephrine discussed earlier have vasoconstrictor action making it useful as nasal discongescant. Besides the above drugs, following are other useful agents.

1. Naphazoline hydrochloride (U.S.P.) (Nitrate B.P.) :

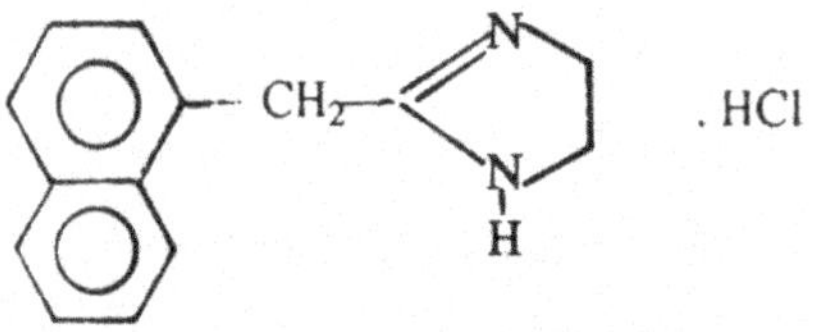

2-(1-naphthyl methyl)-2-imidazoline hydrochloride

Properties and uses : Its nitrate is official in B.P. Both salts are white crystalline powders, soluble in water. Aqueous solutions are acidic to litmus. It is a potent vasoconstricting agent with a prolonged action and is mainly used in nasal congestion. Usual dose is 1 to 2 drops of 0.05 to 0.1 % solution.

2. Tetrahydrozolium hydrochloride (U.S.P.) :

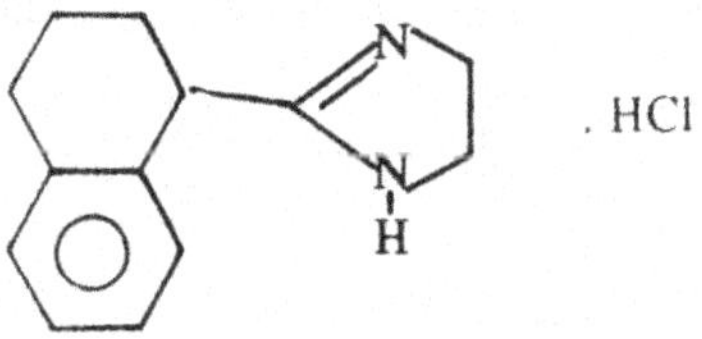

2-(1, 2, 3-4-terarhydro-1-naphthyl)-2-imidazoline

Properties and uses : It is white crystalline powder. It is freely soluble in water and alcohol. It is similar in action to naphazolium hydrochloride. It is used in nasal congestion, but its prolonged use may induce chemical rhinitis. Over-dose may cause drowsiness and sweating. The usual dose is 2-3-drops of 0.1 % solutions, every 3-4 hours. In 0.05 % solution it is useful as occular decongestent.

3. Propylhexedine (U.S.P.) :

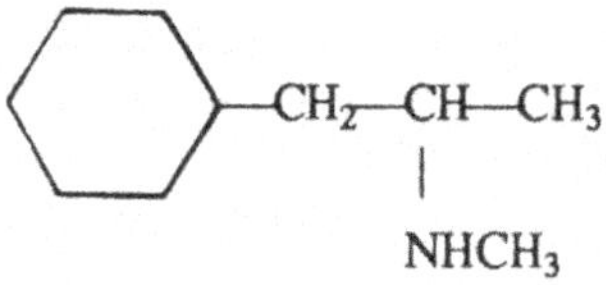

(N α-dimethyl-cyclohexylethylamine)

Properties and uses : It is a clear odourless liquid. It has a characteristic amine like odour, and is very slightly soluble in water, alcohol and chloroform. Its solutions are alkaline to litmus. It absorbs CO_2 from the air and thus it is preserved in tight containers. It slowly volaralises at room temperature. It is used in nasal congestion in the form of inhaler. It has a vasoconstriction effect on the mucous membrane.

4. Xylometazoline hydrochloride (B.P.) :

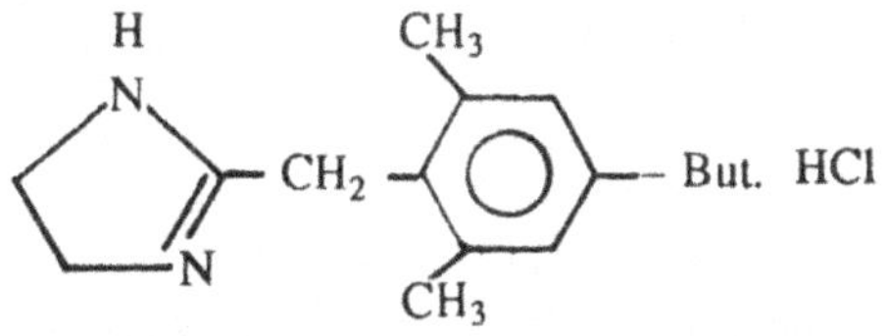

2-(4-tertbutyl-2, 6-dimethyl-benzyl)-2-imidazoline hydrochloride.

Properties and uses : It is white crystalline powder, odourless, soluble in water and alcohol. It is employed in nasal drop in 0.05 to 0.1 % for nasal congestion.

IV. MISCELLANEOUS

Many sympathometric drugs have varying degree of C.N.S. stimulant action. The drugs with more CNS stimulant action becomes useful as analeptic and find use in drowsiness and reversing sedation effect. Other drugs show anorextic action and this makes them useful as anti-obesity drugs. Some useful drugs are given below.

Amphetamine sulphate, methamphetamine hydrochloride are discussed in CNS stimulant chapter.

1. Dexamphetamine sulphate: It is a dextroisomer of amphetamine and is official in B.P. and U.S.P. It is more potent CNS stimulant and is used in the form of tablets (dose 5 to 20 mg) in divided doses.

2. Fenfluramine hydrochloride (B.P.) :

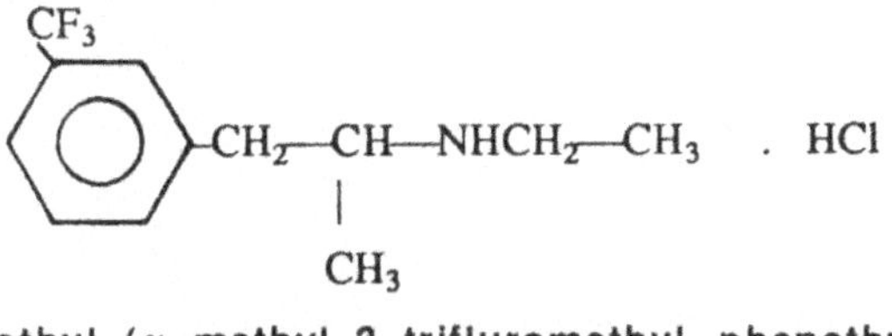

ethyl-(α–methyl–3–trifluromethyl phenethyl)
amine hydrochloride

Properties and uses : It is a white crystalline powder, soluble in water and ethanol. It has no stimulant effect on CNS. It is used as anorexic agent (appetite suppressant) in the form of tablets in the dose 40 to 120 mg daily, in divided doses.

3. Nylidrine hydrochloride (U.S.P.) :

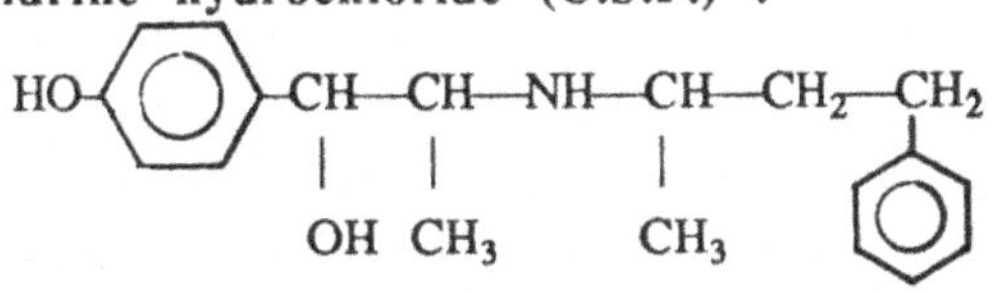

P-hydroxy, (1, methyl 3-phenyl-propyl)
amino) ethyl-benzyl alcohol

Properties and uses : It is a white crystalline powder, soluble in water and alcohol. The drug is periferal vasodilator. It is administered orally or parenterally in various vascular disorders. The side effects are nervousness and palpitation. The usual dose is 6 mg, 3 times a day, orally.

4. **Isoxsuprine hydrochloride (B.P., U.S.P.) :**

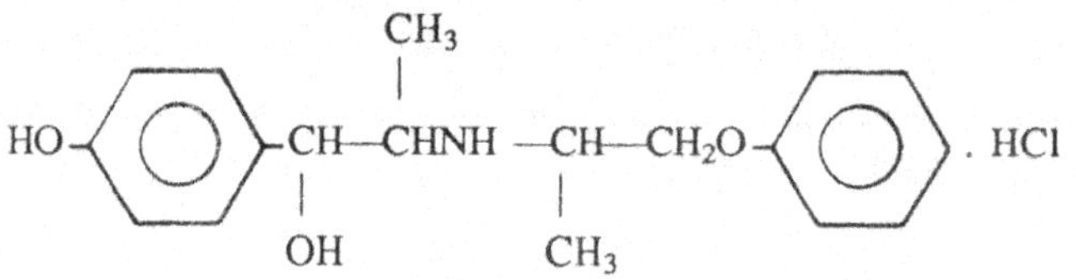

$$HO-\bigcirc-CH-CHNH-CH-CH_2O-\bigcirc \cdot HCl$$
with OH on first CH, CH₃ on CHNH carbon, and CH₃ on the CH before CH₂O

1SR, 2RS)-1-(4-hydroxyphenyl)-2-[2RS)-1-methyl-2-phenoxyethylamino] propane-1-ol hydrochloride

Properties and action : It is a white crystalline powder, odourless, slightly soluble in water and alcohol. The aqueous solution is acidic in nature. This has vasodilator action and is used in peripheral vascular diseases and also as a uterine relaxant. It is administered in the form of tablets and injections in 80 mg in divided doses.

5. **Fenoterol hydrobromide (B.P.) :**

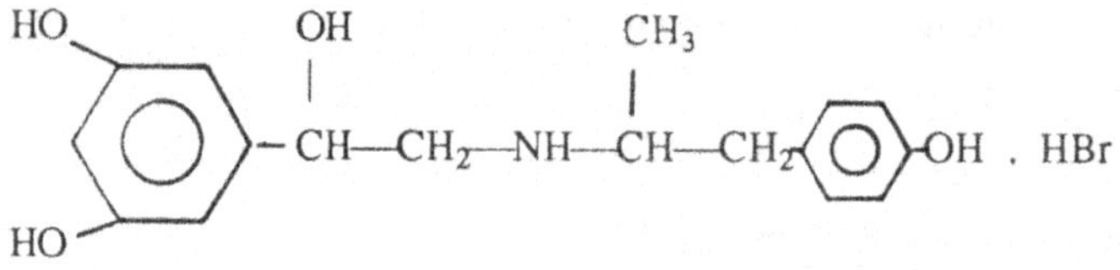

$$(HO)(HO)\text{-}C_6H_3\text{-CH(OH)-CH}_2\text{-NH-CH(CH}_3)\text{-CH}_2\text{-}C_6H_4\text{-OH} \cdot HBr$$

It is mixture of (R)-1-(3,5-dihydroxy phenyl) -2-[(R) 4-hydroxy- α-methyl phenethyl-amino]ethanol hydrobromide and its enantiomer

The drug occurs as a white crystalline powder, soluble in water and alcohol. The drug is beta adrenoceptor agonist.

❑ ❑ ❑

Chapter 14

ADRENERGIC BLOCKING AGENTS

The drugs, which block the response to endogenous or exogenous circulating epinephrine or which block the response to adrenergic nerve stimulation or which prevent the release of the adrenergic transmitter substance at sympathetic nerve ending are the adrenergic blocking agents. Various terms like antisympathetics, adrenolytics etc. were used earlier. However, the adrenergic blocking agent is a much accepted term. Since the postulations of two types of adrenergic receipts (as alpha and beta) the adrenergic blocking agents are classified according to the specific alpha or beta receptors blockers. This classification though useful excludes the category of agents (like xylocholine, bretylium, guanethidine etc.) which prevent the release of adrenergic transmitter substance at the sympathetic nerve endings and produce and adrenergic blocking effect.

ALPHA ADRENERGIC BLOCKING AGENTS

The drugs from this category block the actions of sympathometic agents arising through alpha receptors. Some drugs act by a competitive while others by a non-competitive mechanism. Some therapeutically useful agents under this class are :

1. **Phenoxybenzamine hydrochloride (B.P,.U.S.P.) :**

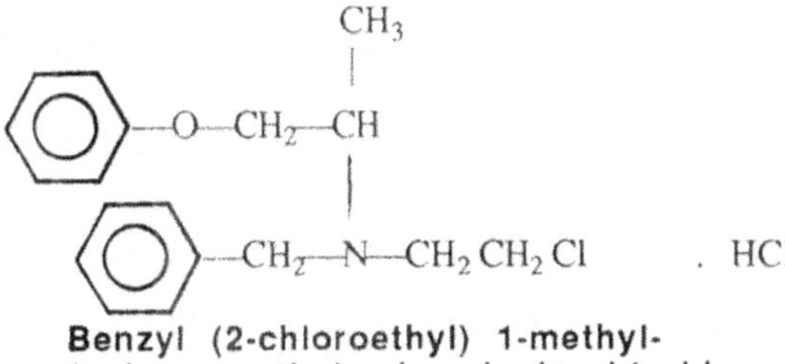

**Benzyl (2-chloroethyl) 1-methyl-
2-phenoxyethylamine hydrochloride**

Properties and Uses : It is a white crystalline powder, odourless, sparingly soluble in water, more soluble in alcohol and chloroform. It slowly hydrolyses in basic and neutral solutions. It acts by it's competitive mechanism. It increases the peripheral blood flow and is useful in peripheral disease like Raynaud's disease, etc. It is used orally in capsules in 10 - 20 mg dose according to the needs of the patient. It is also used to control hypertension caused by Pheuchromocytoma.

2. **Phentolamine hydrochloride (I.P.) :**

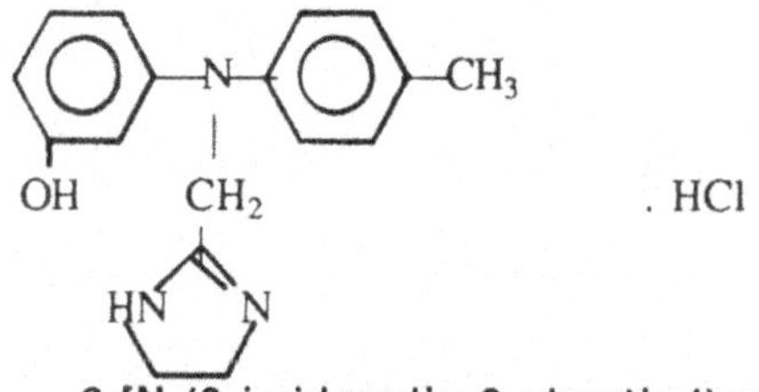

3-[N-(2-imidazolin-2-ylmethyl)-p-toluidino] phenol hydrochloride

Properties : It is found as a white grayish powder, odourless, but bitter to taste. It is sparingly soluble in water and alcohol. The aqueous solution is slightly acidic, and gets adversely affected by light and is unstable.

Actions and uses : This is used orally to control hypertension produced by pheuchromocytoma. A more stable salt of phentolamine with methane sulphonic acid (Mesylate) is used parenterally in the diagnosis and treatment of pheuchromocytoma. The dosage range is 5 to 10 mg.

3. **Tolazoline hydrochloride (U.S.P.) :**

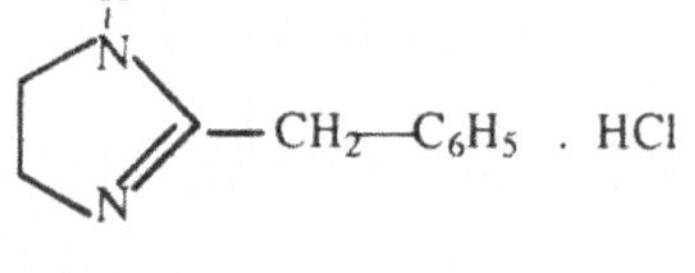

2-benzyl, 2-imidazoline hydrochloride

Properties : It is white-creamy powder slightly odourless. It is freely soluble in water and alcohol. The aqueous solution is acidic in nature. It is stored in tight container protected from light.

Actions and uses : It is used in the treatment of peripheral vascular disorders. It is administered as tablets or injection in (usual dose range of 25 to 75 mg) acrocyanosis, Raynaud's disease etc.

4. Thymoxamine hydrochloride (B.P.) :

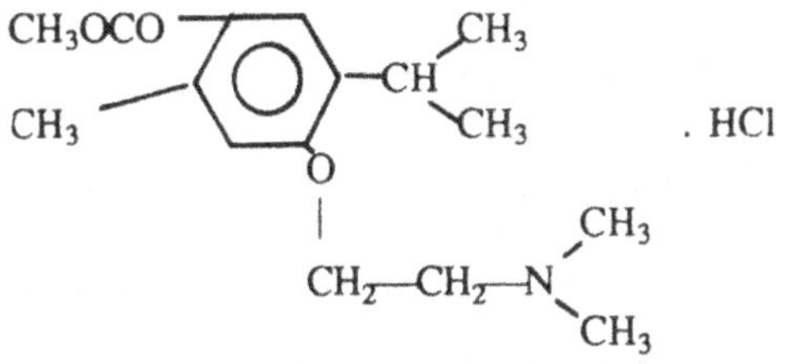

4-(2-dimethylamino ethoxy)-5-isopropyl
2-methyl phenylacetate hydrochloride

Properties and Uses : It is white crystalline powder, odourless. It is soluble in water, alcohol and chloroform. Aqueous solutions are acidic in nature. The drug should be protected from light. The drug is given orally in the form of tablets of 160 to 480 mg. in divided doses to control hypertension. It acts as a peripheral vasodilator through the alpha adrenoeceptor blocking mechanism. It is used in detecting pheuchromochyoma. Thymoxamine tablets are official in B.P.

5. Ergot and Ergot alkaloids : The crude drug Ergot and the alkaloids derived from it are used in variety of conditions. The ergot alkaloids are divided into two classes (i) water-insoluble polypeptide group which exhibits adrenergic blocking activity and (ii) the water soluble group which has a strong stimulating action on the smooth muscle of uterus and hence is used as an oxytosic. The ergotamine and dihydro-ergotamine are useful antiadrenergic agents. They are used as tablets or parenterally.

BETA-ADRENERGIC BLOCKING AGENTS

In recent years new and specific beta-adrenergic receptor blockers are being developed which are considered to be of value in angina pectoris, and cardiac arrhythmias. Drugs useful from a clinical point of view are given below :

1. Propranolol hydrochloride (I.P., B.P., U.S.P.) :

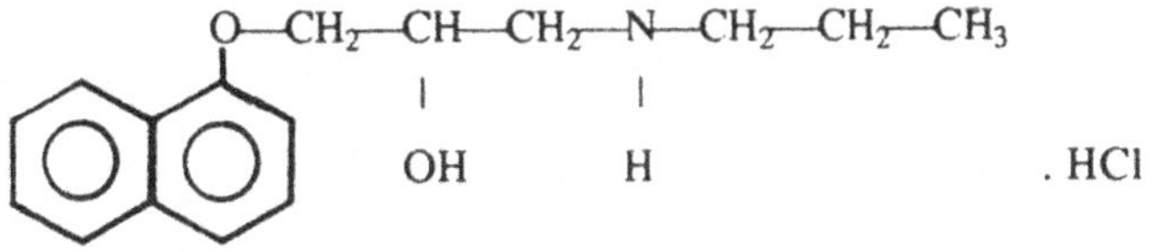

N-[2-hydroxy-3-(1-naphthyloxy) propyl] isopropylammonium
-chloride or 1-(isopropylamino) -3-(1-naphthloxy)-propane–
2–ol hydrochloride

Propeties : It is a white crystalline solid and is odourless. It is soluble in water, alcohol and slightly soluble in chloroform and other non-polar solvents.

Action and uses : It is active orally and parenterally. The tablets or injections are used in 20 to 2000 mg daily, in divided doses as beta adrenoreceptor blocking agent in treatment of angina pectoris, cardiac arrhythmias etc.

2. **Oxprenolol hydrochloride (I.P., B.P.)** :

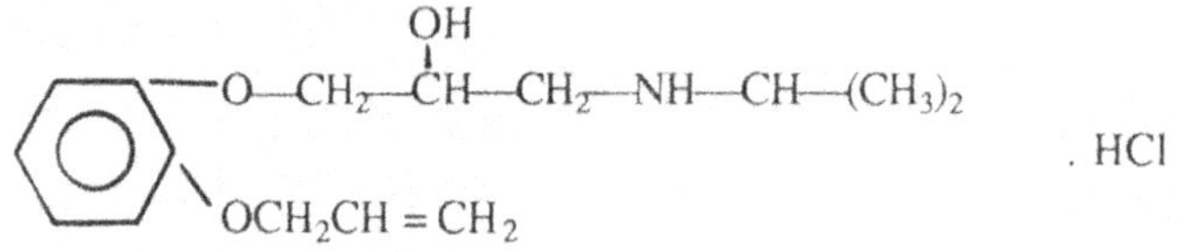

$$\text{Ph}\!\!-\!\!O\!-\!CH_2\!-\!\underset{OH}{CH}\!-\!CH_2\!-\!NH\!-\!CH\!-\!(CH_3)_2 \quad \cdot HCl$$
(with ortho $OCH_2CH=CH_2$ substituent)

1-(2-allyloxy phenoxy)-3-isopropylaminopropane -2-ol hydrochloride

Properties and uses : It occurs as cream coloured crystalline powder, odourless, soluble in water and alcohol. It is used in tablets form of usual strength 40-80 mg.

3. **Prenylamine lactate (B.P.)** :

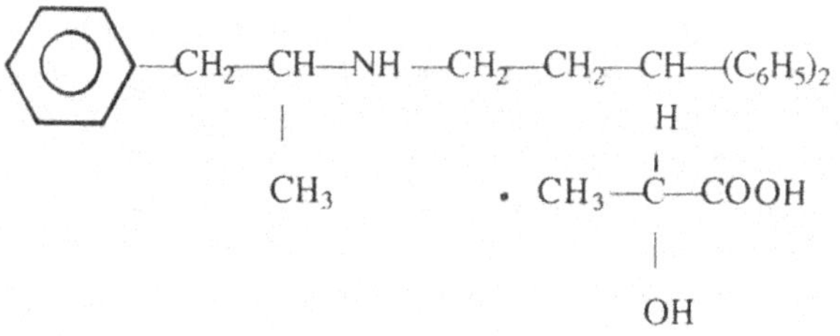

$$\text{Ph}\!-\!CH_2\!-\!\underset{CH_3}{CH}\!-\!NH\!-\!CH_2\!-\!CH_2\!-\!\underset{H}{CH}\!-\!(C_6H_5)_2 \quad \cdot CH_3\!-\!\underset{OH}{\overset{H}{C}}\!-\!COOH$$

2-benzhydrylethyl-(α-methyl phenethyl) amine lactate

Properties and uses : It is a white crystalline powder, odourless and tasteless. It is sparingly soluble in water but easily soluble in alcohol and chloroform. The drug is given in 180-300 mg dose daily (in divided doses) in the treatment of angina pectoris.

4. **Atenolol (B.P.)** :

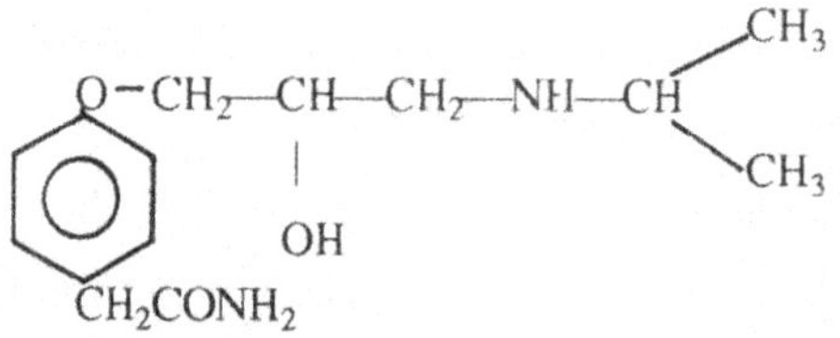

$$\text{Ph}\!-\!O\!-\!CH_2\!-\!\underset{OH}{CH}\!-\!CH_2\!-\!NH\!-\!CH\!\!\begin{array}{c}CH_3\\CH_3\end{array}$$
(with para CH_2CONH_2 substituent)

4-(-2 hydroxy-3-isopropylaminopropoxy) phenylacetamide

Properties and uses : It is a white, odourless powder, sparingly soluble in water, soluble in alcohol. It is given in tablet form as beta adrenoreceptor antagonist in cardiac arrythmias.

5. Debrisoquine sulphate (B.P.) :

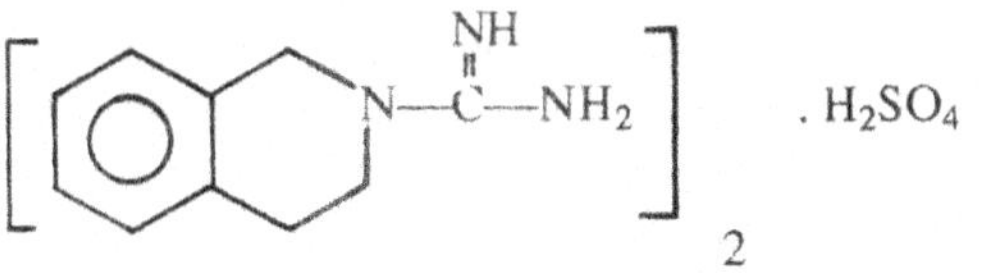

$$\left[\underset{}{\text{isoquinoline}}-N-\overset{NH}{\underset{\parallel}{C}}-NH_2\right]_2 \cdot H_2SO_4$$

1, 2, 3, 4-tetrahydro isoquinoline-2-carboxamidine sulphate

Properties and uses : It is white crystalline, odourless powder, soluble in water. It is employed in tablet form and acts as adrenergic neurone blocking agent.

6. Timolal maleate (B.P.) :

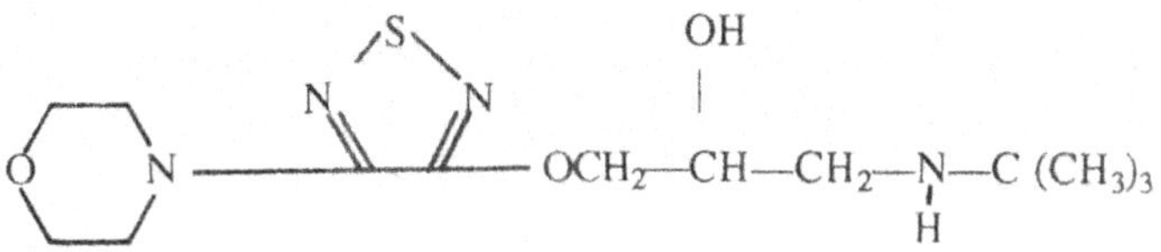

$$\text{morpholine-thiadiazole}-OCH_2-CH(OH)-CH_2-\underset{H}{N}-C(CH_3)_3$$

Properties and actions : It is white powder, soluble in water and alcohol. It is a non-selective beta blocker. It is used as eye-drops in occular hypertension. Timolal tablets are also official.

7. Labetalol hydrochloride (B.P.) :

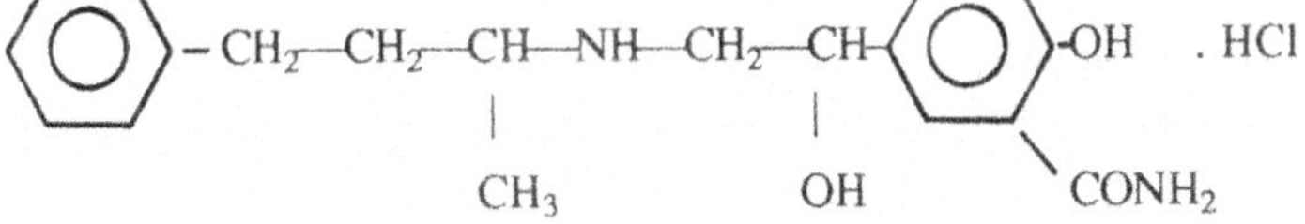

$$\text{Ph}-CH_2-CH_2-\underset{CH_3}{\overset{|}{CH}}-NH-CH_2-\underset{OH}{\overset{|}{CH}}-\underset{CONH_2}{\text{Ph}}-OH \cdot HCl$$

Properties and uses : It is a white granular powder, soluble in water, insoluble in chloroform. It is employed in injection and tablet forms in control of hypertension. It has α and β adrenoceptor blocking action.

Ganglionic Blocking Agents

The autonomic ganglia can be stimulated or depressed (blocked) by various compounds. The drugs or compounds that block or prevent impulses through the autonomic ganglia are called ganglionic blocking agents. The transmission of impulses across the ganglionic synapse is mediated by acetycholine or by related neurotransmitters. The compounds, by blocking the electrical events in the ganglia show both sympathetic and parasympathetic antagonist activity. The nerve impulses are carried through a polarization and depolarisation process. Interference in this process would bring blocking action. The drugs block the impulses either by competitive or non-competitive nondepolarising mechanism.

The drugs of the ganglionic blocking type have been classified into (i) The depolarising type of blocking agent, (ii) non-depolarizing competitive type like tetraethyl ammonium salts, hexamethonium, Mecamylamine etc., and (iii) The non-depolarising non-competitive type like chlorisondamine, trimethiolinium methosulphate etc.

The therapeutic usefulness of ganglionic blocking agents is found in (i) The control of serve hypertension and (ii) In the treatment of peripheral vascular disorders. However, as the parasympathetic ganglia are also blocked the undesirable side effects due to parasympathetic blockade are produced.

The clinically useful drugs and preparations from this class are :

1. Mecamylamine hydrochloride (I.P., U.S.P.) :

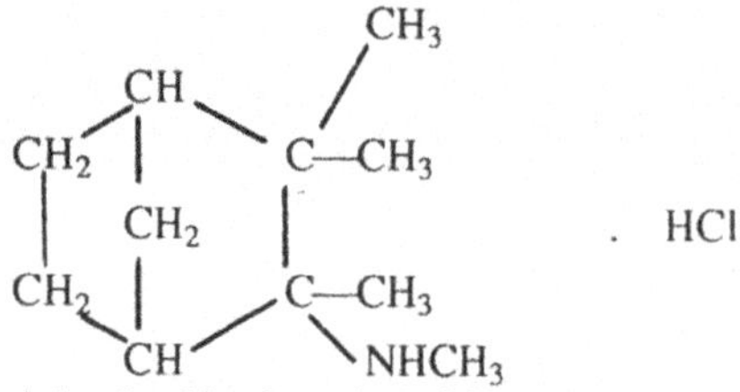

Methyl-2, 3, 3'-trimethyl bicyclo [2-2-1] hept-2-ylamine hydrochloride

Properties : The drug is obtained as white, odouless powder, with bitter-sweet taste. It is freely soluble in water and chloroform. The aqueous solutions are stable and can be autoclaved for sterilization.

Actions and uses : It is given orally in the form of tablets. The drug is absorbed readily and smoothly from gastro-intestinal tract. It has a long duration of action. It is mainly used in the treatment of moderate to severe hypertension with initial 2.5 mg dose which is maintained upto 7.5 mg, 3 times a day, as per the need of patient. The undesirable side effects like dryness of mouth, urinary retension, constipation, visual disturbances etc. associated with parasympathetic blockade are seen.

2. Pentolinium tartrate (U.S.P.) :

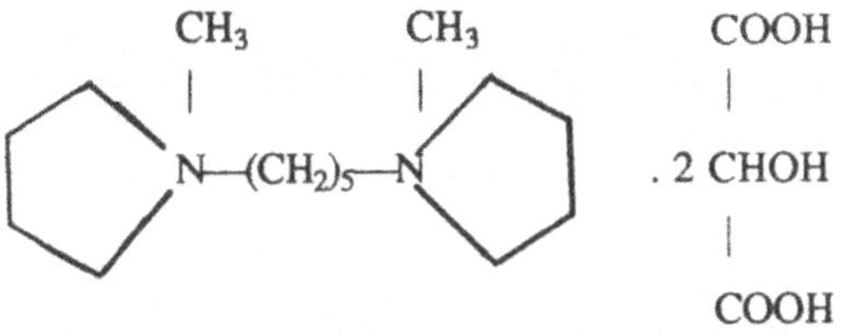

$$\underset{\text{1, 1-pentamethylene-bis-(1-methylpyrrolidinium) tartrate.}}{\text{[CH}_3\text{-N-pyrrolidinium-(CH}_2)_5\text{-N-pyrrolidinium-CH}_3]} \cdot 2 \begin{array}{c}\text{COOH}\\|\\\text{CHOH}\\|\\\text{CHOH}\\|\\\text{COOH}\end{array}$$

1, 1-pentamethylene-bis-(1-methylpyrrolidinium) tartrate.

Properties and Uses : It is a white creamy coloured powder. It is odourless and tasteless. It is freely soluble in water, less soluble in alcohol and insoluble in ether and chloroform. The aqueous solutions are acidic and are stable in the presence of heat. It is active orally as well as parenterally and used in treatment of moderate hypertension and in the diagnosis of peripheral vascular diseases. The standard dose is 20 mg orally.

3. Trimethaphan camsylate (U.S.P.) :

The drug occurs as a white crystalline, odourless and bitter powder that is soluble in water and alcohol but insoluble in ether it is given parentarally by an intravenous infusion, at 200 micrograms to 5 mgs per minute from a mixture of 500 mgs in 500 ml of 5 percent dextrose injection and acts as an antihypertensive agent.

Chapter 15

CHOLINERGIC AGENTS

The autonomic nervous system is divided into the sympathetic and the parasympathetic nervous systems. Acetylcholine is a neuroharmone, which regulates the transmission of nerve impulses in the preganglionic of the sympathetic, the pre and postganglionic of the parasympathetic nerve fibres, and also at the neuromuscular junction in the voluntary system. Acetylcholine is synthesized and stored at the nerve endings from where it is released when needed. Thus, acetylcholine acts as a transmitter of impulses through the para sympathetic system. This is said to be brought about by changing the permeability of K^+ and Na^+ ions, which are the carriers of bioelectric current.

The effects of stimulation on cholenergic system, are divided into two categories : (i) muscarinic and (ii) nicotinic. The effects of acetylcholine include, inhibition of cardiac activity, stimulation of the smooth muscles of the gastrontestinal tract, increased peristalsis, peripheral vasodilation, increased salivation and secretion of secretary glands etc. These effects are similar to those that are produced by the alkaloid muscarine, and hence they are called muscarinic actions. The stimulation of skeletal muscles, blocking of autonomic ganglia and neuromuscular junctions, are the actions of acetylcholine. These are similar to the effect of nicotine and hence are called nicotinic actions. Both these actions are cholinergic. Compounds that have the same effects as acetylcholine, or produce the effects of stimulation of the parasympathetic nerve, are called cholinergic or parasympathomimetic agents.

There is another category of agents known as anticholinesterase that show actions similar to those of acetylcholine. The enzyme cholinesterase, hydrolyses acetylcholine to choline and acetic acid, which are inactive compounds. The drugs which inhibit the enzyme cholinesterase, are called anticholinesterase agents. By inhibiting the enzyme cholinesterase, these drugs cause an accumulation of acetyl choline at the receptor site, and thus produce effects that are similar to the stimulation of the cholinergic system.

The third category of agents exhibits cholinergic action, by acting directly on the cells. Pilocarpin like drugs, act by direct cell stimulation, rather than by a disturbance of the cholinesterase-acetylcholine relationship.

In general, cholinergic agents are employed clinically in certain conditions, and are used to (i) reduce intra-occular pressure in glaucoma, (ii) paralytic ileus and post operative urinary retention (iii) myasthenia gravis, to give relief from muscular weakness.

1. **Acetylcholine chloride :**

$$\left[CH_3-\overset{\underset{|}{CH_3}}{\underset{|}{N^+}}-CH_2-CH_2-O-\overset{O}{\overset{\|}{C}}-CH_3 \right] Cl^-$$

2 acetoxyethyl trimethyl ammonium chloride

Properties and uses : It is a white crystalline solid which is very hygroscopic in nature and freely soluble in water and alcohol. Its aqueous solutions are neutral to litmus. It has to be stored in an air tight container, in a cool and dry place. Since it is rapidly destroyed by cholinesterase in the blood, it has too short a duration of action. It is not used clinically and is not official.

2. **Methacholine chloride (I.P., N.F.) :**

$$\left[CH_3-\overset{\underset{|}{CH_3}}{\underset{|}{N^+}}-CH_2-\overset{\underset{|}{CH_3}}{CH}-O-\overset{O}{\overset{\|}{C}}-CH_3 \right] Cl^-$$

2-acetoxypropyl trimethylammonium chloride

Properties : It is colourless, or white crystalline powder with a slight odour. It is very deliquescent in nature, and very soluble in water, alcohol and chloroform. Its aqueous solutions are acidic to litmus. In an alkaline medium it undergoes hydrolysis. Injections are sterilised by filtration method. It must be stored in an air tight container, in cool and dry place.

Actions and uses : It resembles acetylcholine in its action but it is more stable than acetylcholine. It is used for cardiac disorders like paroxysmal tachycardia, peripheral vascular, diseases like Raynaud's disease, in atonic constipation and in urinary retention. It is also used for the treatment of myasthenia gravis. The usual subcutaneous dose is 10 to 25 mg. It should not be given intravenously.

3. **Carbachol (U.S.P.) :**

$$\left[CH_3-\overset{\underset{|}{CH_3}}{\underset{|}{N^+}}-CH_2-CH_2-O-\overset{O}{\overset{\|}{C}}-NH_2 \right] Cl^-$$

Carbamyl choline chloride

Properties and uses : It is a white or faintly yellowish crystalline powder, with an amine like odour and it is hygroscopic in nature. It is freely soluble in water, less soluble in alcohol and insoluble in ether and chloroform. It is more like acetylcholine and has specific actions. It stimulates the urinary bladder and the intestinal tract, and is used to treat urinary retention and intestinal paresis. It reduces intraoccular tension of glaucoma and is employed in the form of a 0.75 to 1.5 % solution.

ANTICHOLINESTERASE AGENTS

These drugs increase the concentration of acetylcholine at the site of action, by inhibiting the enzyme cholinesterase.

1. Physostigmine salicylate (I.P., B.P., U.S.P.) :

It is a salicylate salt of alkaloid physostigmine which is an alkaloid obtained from the dried ripe seeds of *Physostigma venenosum*.

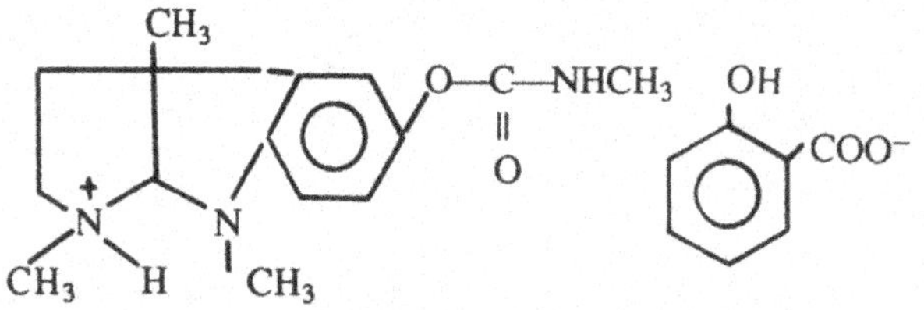

Properties : It is a white or faintly yellowish powder, that is moderately soluble in water, soluble in alcohol and chloroform. A cold saturated solution is neutral to litmus. On exposure to air and light, the powder or its aqueous solution acquires a red tint. It should be stored in an air tight container (glass container free from alkali) which is resistant to light. The solutions are sterilised by the filtration method. It is incompatible with alkaloidal reagents, alkalies and iron salts.

Actions and uses : It has a marked stimulatory action on the bowels, causes more secretion from the glands, and more effect on blood pressure. A 0.1 to 1 % solution is locally applied for glaucoma. Alongwith atropine, it is used to break adhesions between the iris and the lens. Sometimes it is used for conditions of depressed intestinal motality. It is used in the form of solutions or injections.

2. Neostigmine bromide (I.P., B.P., U.S.P.) :

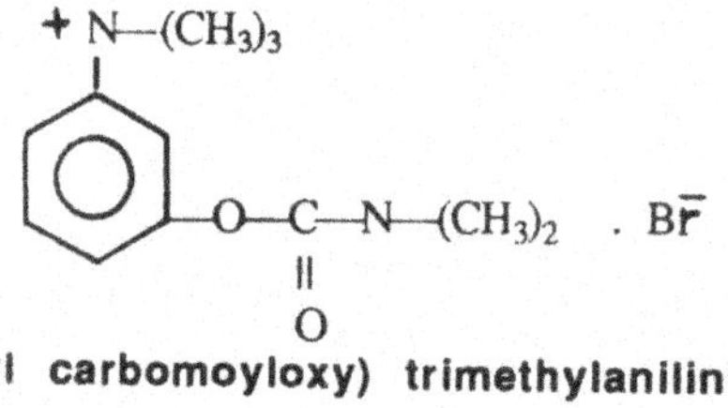

3-(dimethyl carbomoyloxy) trimethylanilinium bromide

Properties and uses : It occurs as a white crystalline powder, it is odourless and has bitter taste and is freely soluble in water and alcohol. Its aqueous solutions are neutral and stable. It is used in the form of tablets and the dosage is 15 to 30 mg daily in myasthenia gravis. It is also used in the treatment of post anaesthetic intestinal paresis, and sometimes as a diagnostic test for early pregnancy.

3. Neostigmine methyl sulpahte (I.P., B.P., U.S.P.) :

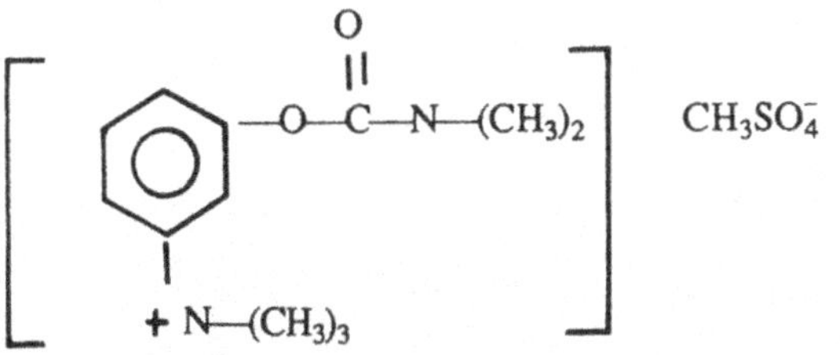

$$\left[\begin{array}{c} \text{Ph-O-C(=O)-N(CH}_3)_2 \\ \text{+N(CH}_3)_3 \end{array} \right] CH_3SO_4^-$$

3-(dimethyl carbomoyloxy
-trimethylanilinium methyl sulphate

Properties and uses : It is a white crystalline powder with bitter taste and soluble in water and less soluble in alcohol. The compound is very hygroscopic and is always used in injection. Its aqueous solutions are neutral to litmus. It is used parenterally for the treatment of paralytic ileus, and post operative urinary retention. It is also used in the diagnosis and treatment of myasthenia gravis. It is given subcutaneously or by intramuscular route in a dose of 0.5 to 2 mg.

4. pyridostigmine bromide (B.P., U.S.P.) :

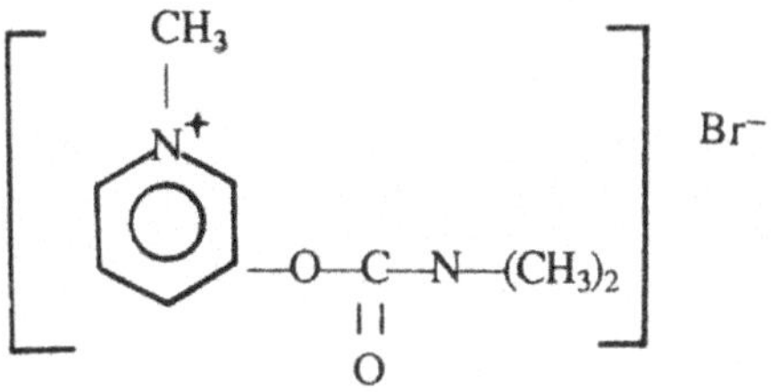

$$\left[\begin{array}{c} CH_3 \\ | \\ N^+ \\ \text{Pyridine-O-C(=O)-N(CH}_3)_2 \end{array} \right] Br^-$$

3-dimethylcarbamoyloxy-1-methyl pyridium, bromide

Properties and uses : It is a white crystalline powder, with a characteristic agreeable odour, and is deliquescent in nature. It is freely soluble be in water, alcohol and chloroform. It should be kept in air-tight containers. Its solutions are sterilized by autoclaving, or by the filtration method. It is less potent and less toxic than neostigmine. Due to its relative affinity for the neuromuscular junctions, it is used in myasthenia gravis. The common formulations are injections and tablets. The usual dose is 60 to 240 mg as per the need of the patient, given orally or by injections of 1 to 5 mg which may be repeated, as per need of the patient.

5. **Ecothiopate iodide (B.P., U.S.P.)** :

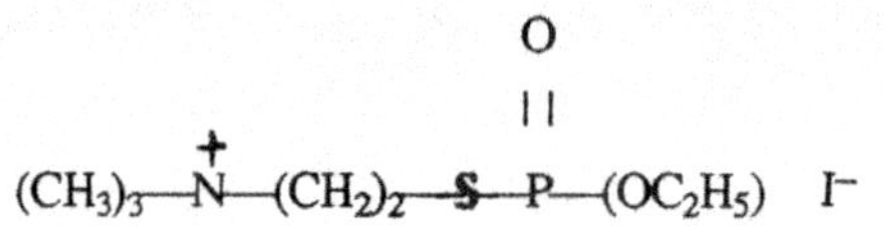

$$(CH_3)_3 \overset{+}{N} - (CH_2)_2 - S - \underset{\underset{O}{\|}}{P} - (OC_2H_5) \quad I^-$$

(2-diethoxyphosphinyl-thioethyl) trimethyl-ammonium iodide

Properties and uses : It is a white crystalline powder. It has an alliaceous, odour, is hygroscopic in nature, freely soluble in water, though less in alcohol. It should be kept in an air-tight container, protected from light, at a temperature between 2° and 8° C. It is an anticholinesterase drug, and is used topically, in the treatment of glaucoma.

6. **Edrophonium chloride (B.P., U.S.P.)** :

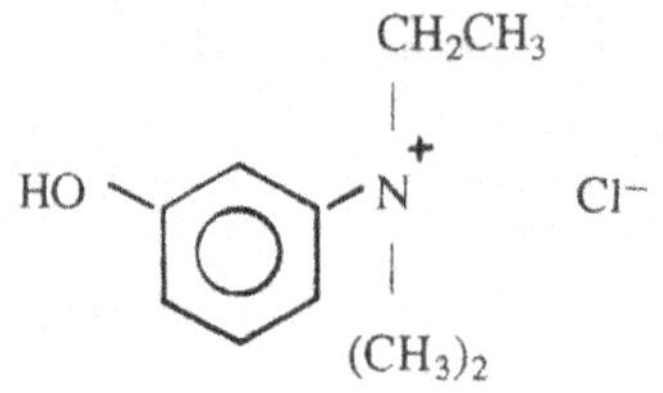

$$HO-C_6H_4-\overset{\overset{CH_2CH_3}{|}}{\underset{\underset{(CH_3)_2}{|}}{N^+}} \quad Cl^-$$

Ethyl (3-hydroxyphenyl) dimethylammonium chloride

Properties and uses : It is a white crystalline powder which is odourless, freely soluble in water soluble in alcohol and practically insoluble in chloroform. It is used as a diagnostic agent for myasthenia gravis, and also to stabilise and abolish neuromuscular paralysis caused by d-tubocurarine or similar drugs. Usually 10 mg are administered, to antagonize the curare overdosage. First 2 mg are given intravenously and if there is no response within 30 seconds the remaining 8 mg are given.

DRUGS ACTING DIRECTLY ON CELLS

1. **Pilocarpine nitrate (I.P., B.P., U.S.P.)** :

Pilocarpine hydrochloride is official in U.S.P. It is a nitrate of alkaloid pilocarpine that is obtained from the leaves of pilocarpus microphyllus. and other species of *Pilocarpus*.

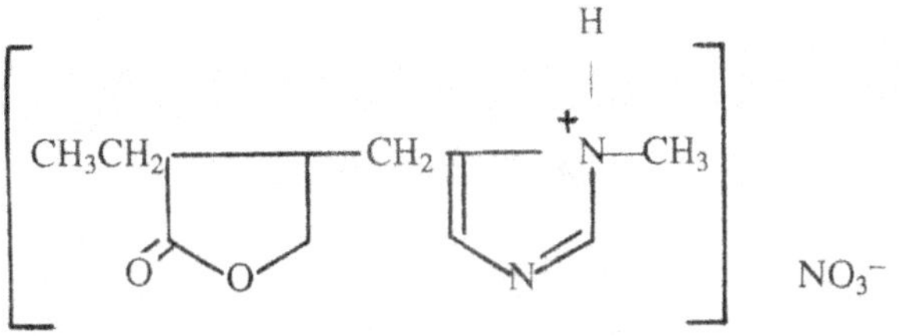

$$\left[CH_3CH_2 \underset{\underset{O}{\overset{\parallel}{C}}-O}{\overline{}} CH_2 \underset{N}{\overline{}} \overset{H}{\underset{}{\overset{|}{\overset{+}{N}}}}-CH_3 \right] NO_3^-$$

Properties : It occurs in the form of colourless crystals, with bitter taste and has a slight odour. It is soluble in water, alcohol, and insoluble in chloroform and ether. Its aqueous solutions are sterilised by filtration, or by autoclaving. It is stored in tight, light-resistant containers.

Actions and uses : It stimulates the smooth muscles and gland cells that are innervated by cholinergic nerves. It is used as 0.5 to 2.0 % solution, topically to the conjunctiva, to act as miotics in glaucoma.

ANTIDOTE FOR CHOLINESTERASE INHIBITORS

Pralidoxime-chloride (I.P., U.S.P.) :

It is commonly known as 2 PAM chloride.

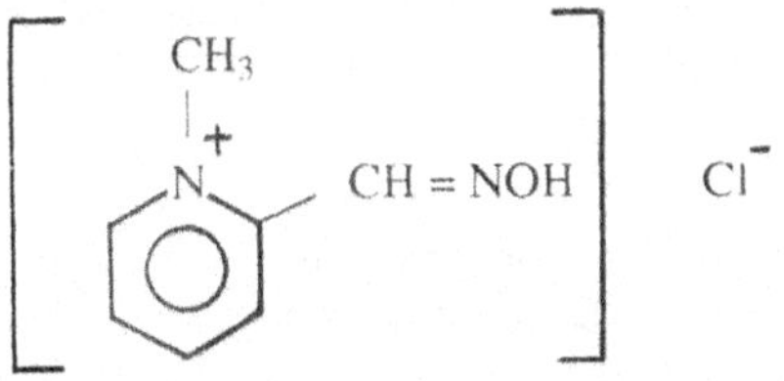

$$\left[\underset{\text{pyridinium with } N^+-CH_3}{} CH=NOH \right] Cl^-$$

2–Hydroxy iminomethyl–1–methyl pyridinium chloride

Properties and uses : It is a pale yellow crystalline powder, odourless and is freely soluble in water. A dose of 1 to 2 g of 5 % solution as injection is given by intravenous route in the treatment of poisoning effects of drugs like neostigmine, pytridostigmine etc.

❑ ❑ ❑

Chapter 16

ANTICHOLINERGIC AGENTS

Antispasmodic, antiulcer, antiparkinsonism, mydriatic and cycloplegic are same of the prominent actions that are exhibited by anticholinergic drugs. Compounds which block the action of acetylcholine, (a neurohormone released in the parasympathetic system), are called as antichlolinergic drugs. Acetylcholine is a chemical mediator, that is released at the post ganglionic parasympathetic nerve endings. This substance is also released at the autonomic ganglia and somatic neuromuscular junction. The anticholinergic activity can thus be shown by drugs that block the action of acetylcholine at the autonomic ganglia, by ganglion blocking agent and at the neuromuscular junction by curare type of drugs.

Anticholinergic drugs interfere with the activities and functions of acetylcholine. These drugs do not prevent the release of acetylcholine at nerve endings, but instead they act by competing with it, for the cholinergic receptor sites. Since these drugs antagonise the actions of the muscarine they are said to be antimuscarinic in nature.

Anticholinergic drugs have the following three major pharmacological actions, for which they are used therapeutically.

(i) **Antispasmodic action** : Motality and tone of gastro-intestinal and genitourinal tract is lowered. The drugs give relief from spasm of colon or bowel.

(ii) **Antisecretory action** : Salivation, perspiration and gastric acid secretion are reduced. The drugs are useful against ulcers.

(iii) **Mydriatic and cycloplegic** : The dilation of pupil and paralysis of the ciliary structure of eye, make these drugs useful in opthalmology.

Anticholinergic drugs, can be broadly classified into the following two classes :

(i) Solanaceous alkaloids and related compounds.

(ii) Synthetic drugs.

SOLANACEOUS DRUGS, ALKALOIDS AND RELATED COMPOUNDS

A number of plants belonging to the family solaneceae like belladonna, hyoscymus, stramonium etc and their preparations, are useful as potent anticholinergic drugs. The crude drugs, the alkaloids and their salts, are also official in various pharmacopoeias. The crude drugs and their preparations are given below.

1. Belladonna herb (I.P., B.P.) : It consists of leaves or leaves and other aerial parts of Atropa belladonna, or Atropa acuminata or a mixture of both species. It consists of not less than 0.3 % alkaloids of bellandonna, calculated as hyoscyamine. It has a slight odour and has a bitter and acrid taste.

2. Belladonna herb powder (B.P.) : It is a coarse powder prepared from the belladonna herb, and it contains not less than 0.3 % alkaloids, calculated as hyoscyamine.

Both the above preparations, should be stored in an air tight container, protected from moisture and light.

3. Prepared Belladonna Herb (B.P.) : It is a finely powdered Belladonna herb, adjusted with a herb powder or exhausted herb powder for its alkaloidal contents which are in the range of 0.28 to 0.32 per cent calculated as hyoscyamine.

4. Belladonna dry extract (I.P.) : The Belladonna herb powder is extracted with 70 % alcohol by percolation, the alcohol is evaporated and the mixture is adjusted to the desired strength, by adding fine Belladonna herb powder, so that it contains 0.25 to 1.05 % total alkaloids, calculated as hyoscyamine.

5. Hyoscyamus leaf (B.P.) : It consists of the dried leaves and flowering tops of *Hyoscyamus niger*. It contains not less than 0.05 % of total alkaloids calculated as hyoscyamine. It has a strong characteristic odour.

6. Hyoscyamus powder (B.P.) and Prepared Hyoscyamus (B.P.) : It is a fine powder that is prepared from leaves and adjusted for strength. It contains 0.05 to 0.07 per cent of alkaloids, calculated as hyoscyamine.

7. Stramonium leaf (I.P., B.P.) : It consists of the dried leaves and flowering tops of *Datura stramonium*. It contains alkaloids which are, calculated as hyoscyamine. It has an unpleasant odour.

8. Stramonium powder (B.P.) and prepared stramonium (B.P.) : It is a moderately fine powder that is prepared from stramonium leaves and it is adjusted to the desired strength with lactose. It contains 0.23 to 0.27 percent of total alkaloids calculated as hyoscyamine.

All the above solanaceous drugs and their preparations, contain atropine, hyoscyamine and hyoscine (Scopolamine) in varying amount. The major biological and pharmacological activities, are due to the above alkaloids and these are discussed under the individual alkaloids.

SOLANACEOUS ALKALOIDS

1. Atropine (U.S.P.) :

It is an alkaloid (±) hyoscyamine, obtained from the various species of Hyoscyamus, or prepared synthetically.

(1R, 3r, 5s)-tropan-3yl (±) tropate sulphate

Properties : It occurs in the form of colourless crystals or white crystalline powder, slightly soluble in water, freely soluble in alcohol and chlorofom and it easily forms salts with acids.

Actions and uses : It has two major actions, (i) on the central nervous system to cause respiratory stimulation and selective sedation, and (ii) depresses the smooth muscles and secretory glands that are innervated by the parasympathetic nerves.

The central action of atropine is to give relief from paralysis, agitants and parkinsonism. It is also used as an antigonist of the central actions of anticholinesterases.

The peripheral actions of atropine are mainly concerned with the secretion of the bronchio-respiratory glands, bronchial muscle, heart, gastro intestinal tract, urinary tract and uterus. In ophthalmology, it is used to dilate the pupil. Its salt solution (aqueous) is usually applied topically. The free alkaloid in the form of an ointment or solution in oil, is also used for the same purpose.

It is useful in bronchial asthama, as it causes relaxation of the bronchial muscles, and dries up the secretions. It is useful in coryza, hay fever and rhinitis. It is widely used along with inhalation anaesthesia, in order to inhibit excessive salivation or secretions. The extract and tincture of belladonna, are mainly use l for their antispasmodic action on the bowels. Atropine is particularly useful for spastic colits and pylorespasm. It is given to children to control frequent urination. It is also used in combination with other drugs, for relief from dysmenorrhea.

2. Atropine sulphate (I.P., B.P., U.S.P.) :

Properties and uses : It occurs in the form of colourless crystals, or a white crystalline powder. It effloresces in dry air, and gets affected by light. It is freely soluble in water and dissolves in alcohol and glycerin. It must be kept in an air-tight container, protected from light. The aqueous solutions are sterilised by the filtration method. It is used in the form of solutions, ointments, injections and tablets. A 0.5 to 1.0 % solution or ointment, is used for mydratic effect. It is administered in small doses as a preanaesthetic medication, to reduce secretions. Atropine and its salts are used in the treatment of gastric ulcers, and to give relief from renal and biliary colic. It is also useful in symptomatic treatment of parkinsonism. The usual dose is 0.25 to 2 mg subcutaneously or intramuscularly.

3. Atropine methobromide (B.P.) : It is a white crystalline powder, which is odourless, and freely soluble in water though sparingly in alcohol. Its aqueous solution is neutral or slightly acidic and the drug is used as parasympatholytic agent.

4. Atropine methonitrate (I.P., B.P.) : It occurs as white crystalline powder, that is freely soluble in water but insoluble in chloroform and ether. It is mainly used in treatment of congenital hypertropic pyloric stenosis of infants.

5. Hyoscyamine (U.S.P.) : Atropine is a racemic modification whereas hyoscyamine is laevo form and is optically active. It is obtained from various species of Hyoscyamus. As a free base it occurs as white needles that are sparingly soluble in water, but soluble in alcohol, chloroform etc. Salts of hyoscyamine are used clinically. They offer an advantage over the base since they are highly soluble in water.

6. Hyoscyamine hydrobromide (U.S.P.) : It occurs as a white crystalline powder, that is freely soluble in water. Its aqueous solutions are unstable when heated. The usual dose is 0.25 to 1.0 mg.

7. Hyoscyamine sulphate (B.P.) : It occurs in the form of colourless crystals or a white crystalline powder, that is highly soluble in water, freely soluble in alcohol but insoluble in chloroform. It is deliquescent in nature. The salts of Hyoscyamine must be protected from light.

Hyoscyamine and its salts are extremely poisonous, and they are used as parasympatholytics.

8. Hyoscine : It is also called Scopolamine. This alkaloid is obtained from mother liquor, after the crystalisation of hyoscyamine. On a large scale, it is obtained from the leaves of Datura metal (Indian) and Datura metelodes. The drug is not official, However, salts are official in I.P., B.P.

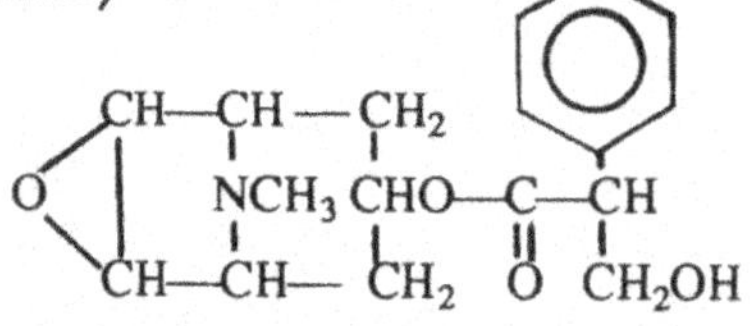

Epoxy hyoscyamine

9. Hyoscine hydrobromide (I.P., B.P., U.S.P.) :
(Scopolamine hydrobromide)

It occurs as colourless crystals, or as a white crystalline or granular powder. It effloresces in dry air. It is freely soluble in water and soluble in alcohol.

Actions and uses : It has a depressant action on the cerebral cortex and is used in treatment of parkinsonism, acute mania, delirium and in calming excited patients. When administered with morphine or pethidine, it produces partial amnesia, a condition known as, 'twilight sleep.' It finds use in obsteries and gynecology. It is used mainly for mydriatic and cycloplegic effects on eyes. This has a rapid onset and a shorter duration of action than atropine. For topical application 0.05 to 0.1 ml of 0.2 to 0.5 per cent solution 2 to 4 times a day, is used. It is also used in the form of eye drops, injections and tablets. The usual dose is 300 to 600 micrograms.

10. Hyoscine butylbromide (B.P.):

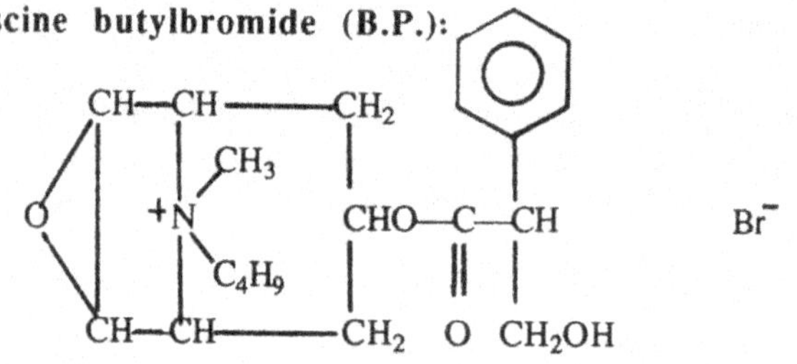

Properties and uses : It is an almost white crystalline powder that is highly soluble in water, soluble in chloroform and alcohol. Its concentrated aqueous solutions are acidic to litmus. It is used in the form of tablets and injections as a spasmolytic. Other uses are similar to hyoscine hydrobromide The usual dose is 30 to 100 mg daily, in divided doses or by an intramuscular or intravenous route in 20 mg dose.

11. Homatropine hydrobromide (I.P., B.P., U.S.P.) :

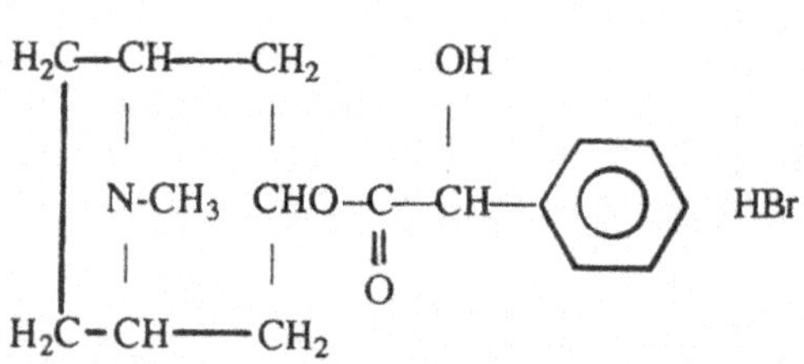

Properties and uses : It is a white crystalline powder, that is soluble in water, though less in alcohol and practically insoluble in chloroform. Its aqueous solutions are neutral to litmus. It is sensitive to light and kept in light-resistant containers. A 1-2 % solution is used for its mydriatic action. It is to be used with extreme care as it is very poisonous.

SYNTHETIC AGENTS

Synthetic agents have been developed from structure action relationship studies of atropine and acetylcholine. These have been carried out with respect of the cationic head, hydroxyl group, ester group, and cyclic substitution in acetylcholine. The following therapeutically useful drugs have been evolved. These are arranged according to their therapeutic usefulness as given below :

I. ANTISECRETARY (ANTIULCER) DRUGS :

1. Clidinium bromide (U.S.P.) :

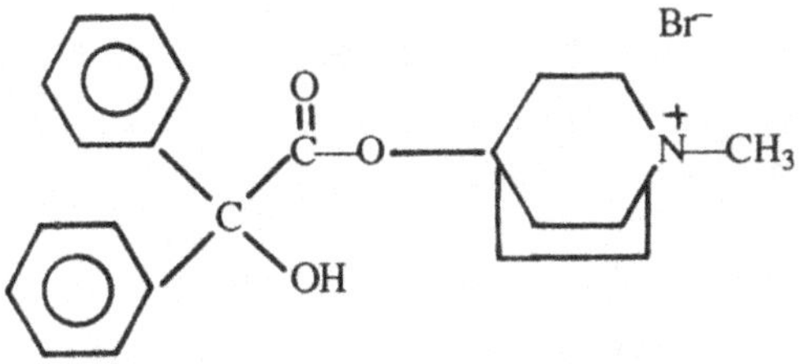

3-hydroxyl-1-methyl quinaclidinium bromide benzilate

Properties and uses : It occurs as white, odourless, crystalline powder, soluble in water and in alcohol. The drug gives relief in peptic ulcer, hyperchlorhydria and in spastic colon. It is given as capsules in 2.5 to 5 mg dose alone or in combination with chlordiazepoxide or other tranquiliser.

2. Diphenanil Methylsulphate (U.S.P.) :

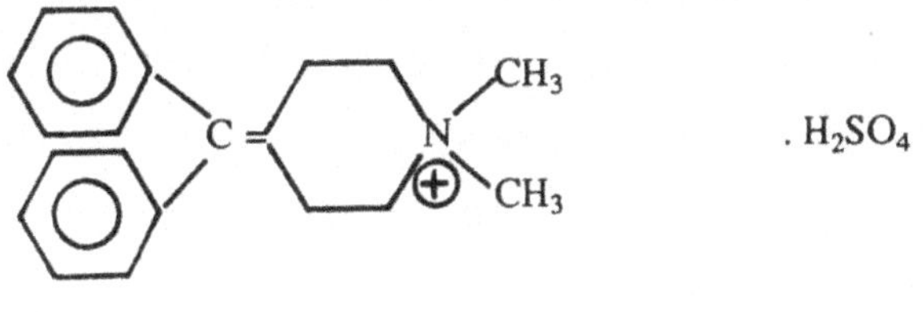

4-(diphenylmethylene)-1,
1-dimethyl piperidium methyl sulphate

Properties and uses : It is a white powder, sparingly soluble in water, alcohol. Aqueous solutions are acidic in nature.

It is highly useful in peptic ulcer and hyperhydrosis. It is used in the form of tablets.

3. Isopropamide iodide (U.S.P.) :

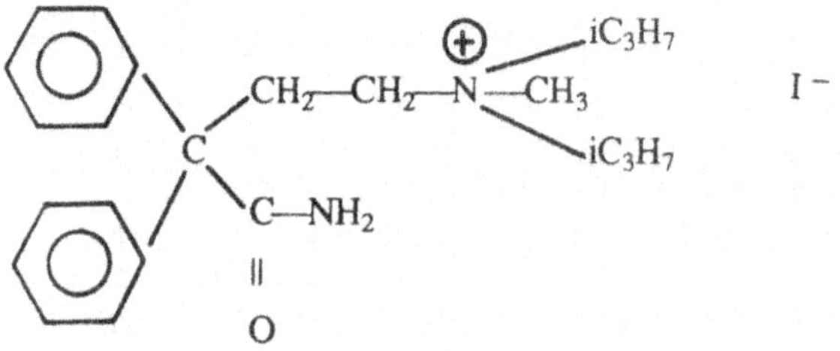

3-(carbamoyl-3, 3-diphenyl propyl) disoproyl methyl ammonium iodide

Properties and uses : It is a white to yellow powder, bitter taste, sparingly soluble in water but freely soluble in alcohol. It is a quaternary ammonium compound and gives antisecretary and antispasmodic action in low doses for long duration of action.

4. Oxyphenonium bromide (I.P.) :

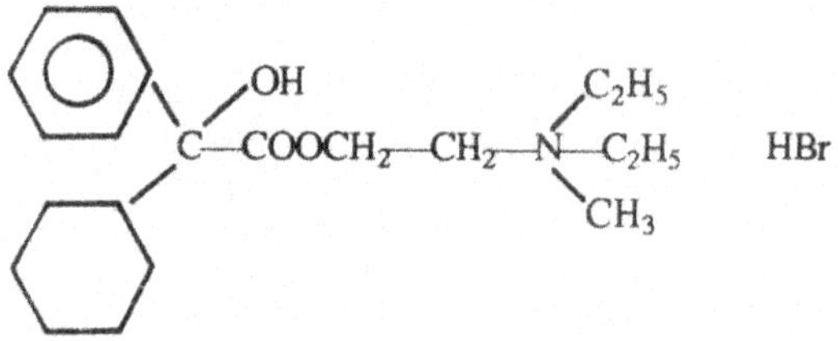

N-[2-(2-cyclohyxyl)-2-hydroxy glycoloxy ethyl]
-N,N'-di-ethyl-methyl ammonium bromide

Properties and uses : It occurs as a white crystalline powder that is freely soluble in water. The drug is active orally. It is used in the form of tablets to control intestinal spasms and in the treatment of peptic ulcers. The usual dose is 10 mg four times a day. It is also given subcutaneously or intramuscularly in 1-2 mgs every 6 hours.

5. Poldinemethyl sulphate (B.P.) :

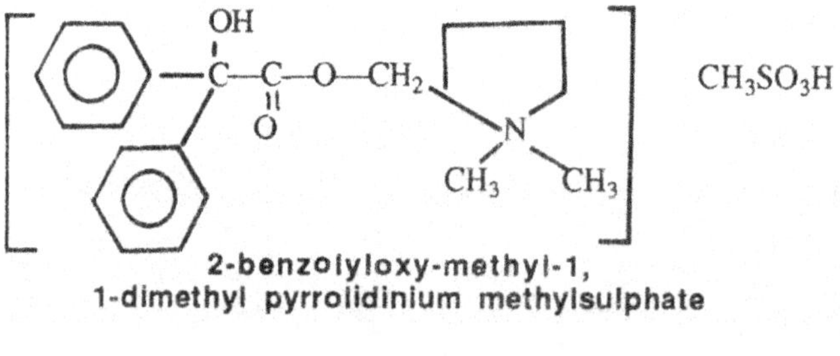

2-benzolyloxy-methyl-1,
1-dimethyl pyrrolidinium methylsulphate

Properties and uses : It is a white crystalline powder, that is odourless highly soluble in water, soluble in alcohol, and sparingly soluble in chloroform. It is used in the form of tablets, as a spasmolytic. The dosage is 10 to 30 mg daily in divided doses and for the treatment of peptic ulcers in 4 mg dose.

II. ANTISPASMODIC DRUGS

1. Dicyclomine hydrochloride (B.P., U.S.P) :

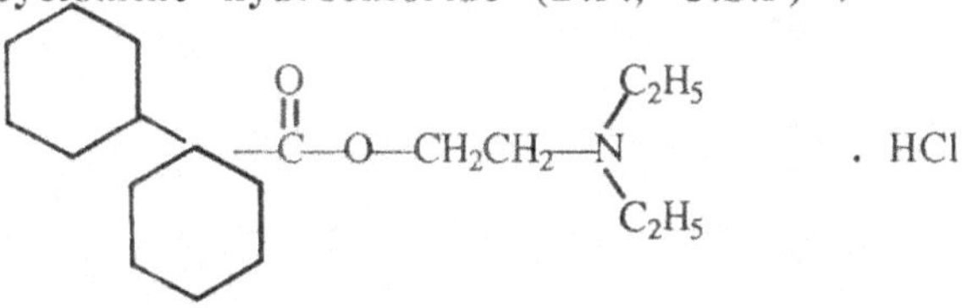

2-(diethylamono)ethyl [bicyclohexyl]-
1-carboxylate hydrochloride

Properties and uses : It is a white crystalline powder, that is soluble in water and freely soluble in alcohol and chloroform. It is used in the form of tablets, elixirs or capsules. It is used in various smooth muscle spasms for its spasmolytic effect. It is useful in dysmenorrhea and biliary dysfunction. The usual dose is 30 - 60 mgs daily, in divided doses.

2. Glycopyrrolate (U.S.P.) :

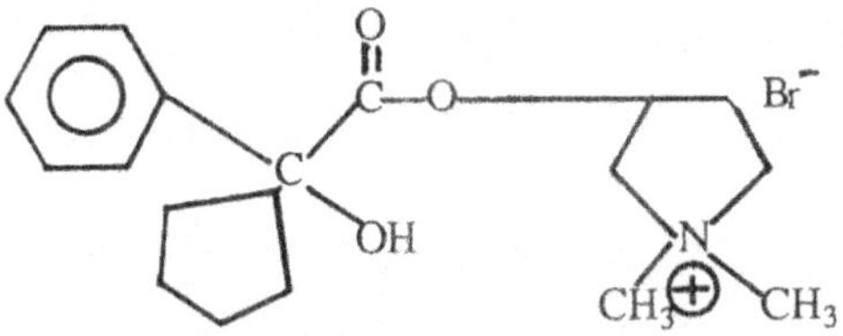

3-hydroxy-1, 1-dimethyl pyrrolidinium bromide
α-cyclopentyl mandelate

Properties and uses : It is white powder, soluble in water and alcohol. The drug is used as adjunct in management of peptic ulcer, hyperactivity, hypermortality of colon etc.

3. Propantheline bromide (I.P. B.P., U.S.P.) :

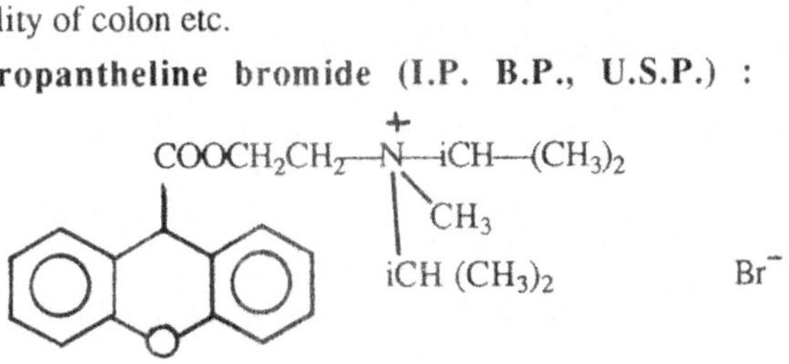

Diisopropylmethyl [2-(xanthen-9-yl
carbonoyloxy) ethyl] ammonium-bromide

Properties and uses : It is a white to off white crystalline powder, that is odourless, and is soluble in water, alcohol and chloroform. It is used in the form of tablets, as an antiulcer and antispasmodic. It has less side effects than other parasympatholytics. The usual dose is 45 mg daily, in divided dose.

4. Piperidolate hydrochloride (U.S.P.) :

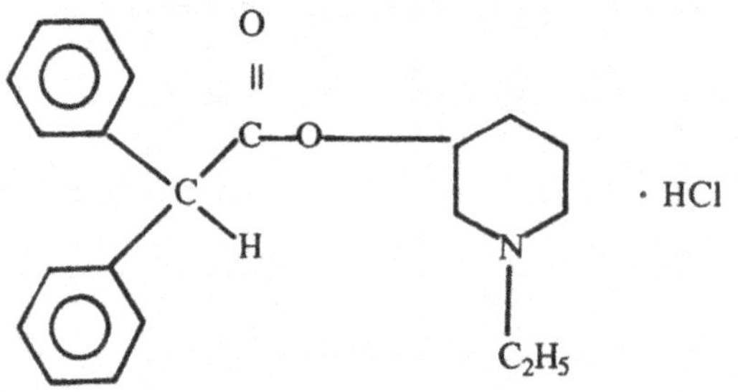

1-ethyl-3-piperidyl diphenylacetate hydrochloride

Properties and uses : It is a white crystalline compound soluble in water. It is given in various gastro-intestinal disorders associated with spasm and hyper motility.

5. Mebeverine hydrochloride (B.P.) :

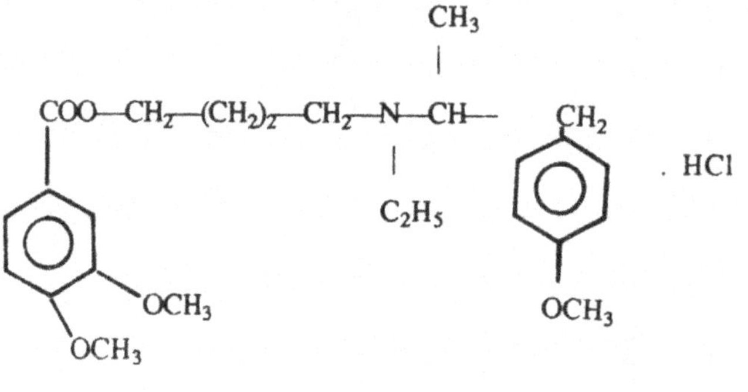

4-[ethyl-(4-methoxy – α-methylphenethyl) amino] butyl veratrate hydrochloride

Properties and uses : It is a white powder soluble in water and alcohol. It is stored in closed container protected from light and at temperature not exceeding 30°. It is given as tablets for antispasmodic action on smooth muscle.

6. Papaverine hydrochloride (B.P., U.S.P.) :

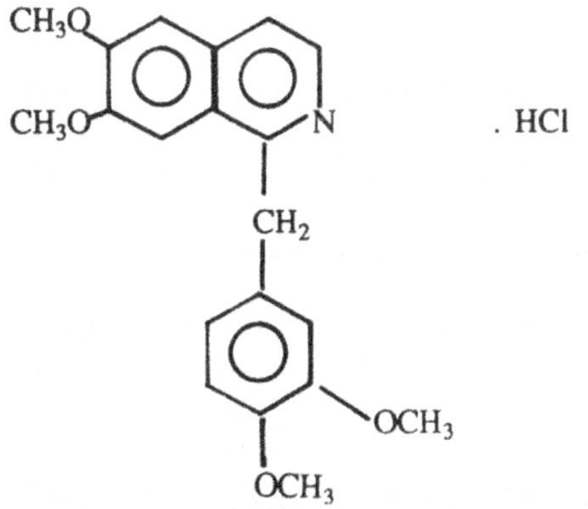

6, 7-dimethoxy-1-(3, 4-dimethoxybenzyl isoquinoline hydrochloride

It is an alkaloid isolated from opium. It's structure and pharmacological actions are different from morphine and other analogous alkaloids.

Properties and uses : It is a white crystalline powder, bitter to taste and is freely soluble in water. Aqueous solutions are acidic in nature and can be sterilized by auticlaving. This is mainly used for its antispasmodic actions on smooth muscle of blood vessels, bronchial tissues. It finds use in relieving spasm. It is given as tablets or in injections by i.m. or i.v. route in 30 to 60 mg dose.

III. MYDRIATIC AND CYCLOPLEGIC DRUGS

1. Cyclopentolate hydrochloride (B.P., U.S.P.) :

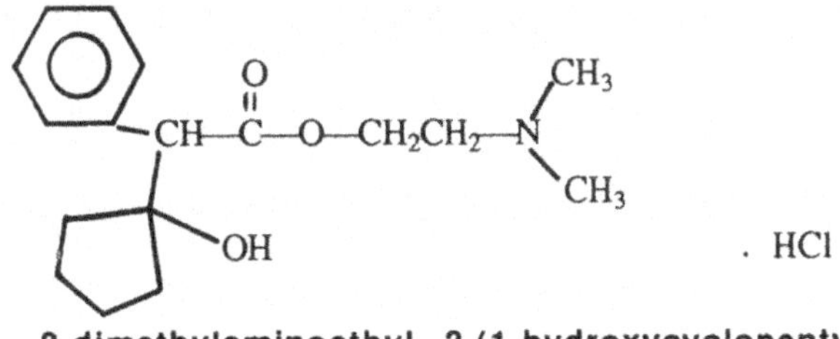

2-dimethylaminoethyl 2-(1-hydroxycyclopentyl) 2-phenylacetate hydrochloride

Properties and uses : It is a white crystalline powder, that is very soluble in water and alcohol. Its aqueous solutions are sterilised by the filtration method. It is used in the form of solution, for its opthalmalogic action. It finds use in the management of iritis, choroiditis, etc. Usually 2 drops of 0.5 to 1 percent solutions are used.

2. Eucatropine hydrochloride (U.S.P.) :

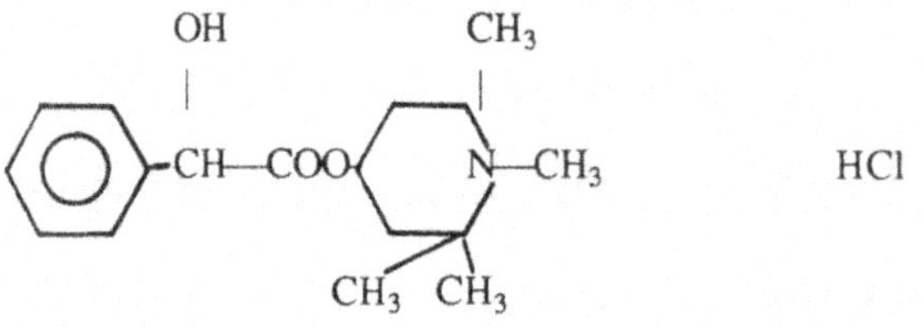

1,2,2,6-tetramethyl-4-piperidylmandelate hydrochloride

Properties and uses : It occurs as a white powder or granules. It is stable in air but is affected by light. It is very soluble in water and alcohol. Its aqueous solutions are neutral to litmus. It is only used as an aid in opthalmoscopic examination as 2.0 % solution using 2 to 3 drops.

3. Tropicamide (B.P., U.S.P.) :

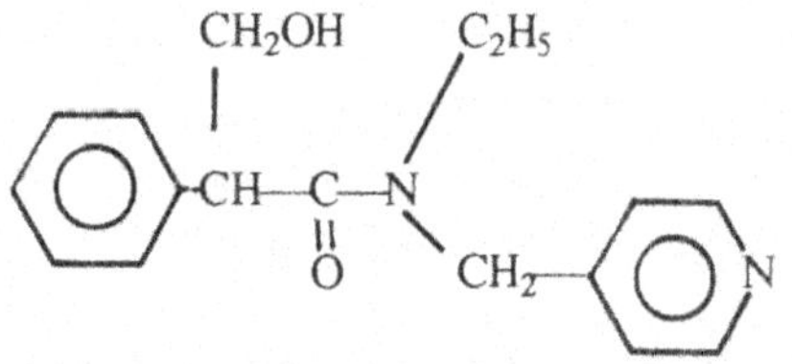

N-ethyl-N-(4-pyridinylmethyl)-tropamide

Properties and uses : It is an almost white crystalline powder that is soluble in alcohol and chloroform, but only slightly soluble in water. It is used for mydriatic and cycloplegic actions. A 0.5 % solution is used for opthalmic purposes.

IV. ANTIPARKINSONISM DRUGS

Drugs that are used for the treatment of the disease parkinsonism (which is characterised by rigidity, tremors, stiffness and disturbed posture etc.), are called as antiparkinsonism drugs. These drugs give relief to the patient, and act by an anticholinergic mechanism. A few clinically useful drugs are given below :

1. Benzotropine mesylate (B.P., U.S.P.) :

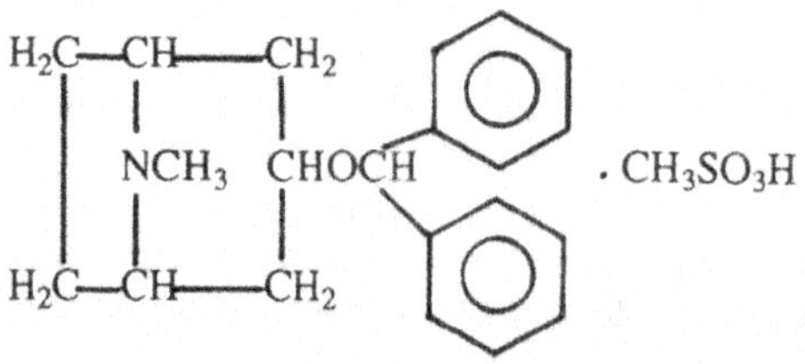

3-benzhydryloxytropane methane sulphonate

Properties and uses : It occurs as white crystalline powder, hygroscopic in nature and very soluble in water and alcohol. Besides being antiparkinsonian it has antihistaminic and local anesthetic action also. It is used in the form of tablets and injections. The usual dose is 1–2 mg once or twice a day.

2. **Benzhexol hydrochloride (B.P.) :**

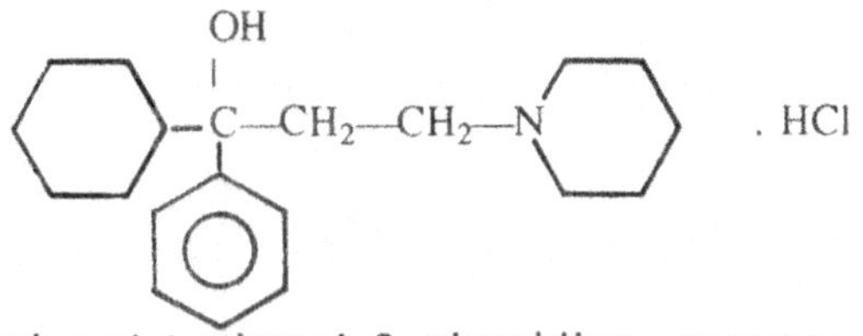

1-(3-cyclohexyl-1-phenyl-3-piperidine propane-1-ol hydrochloride

Properties and uses : It is a creamy, white crystalline powder, that is moderately soluble in water but more in alcohol and chloroform. It is used in the form of tablets. The usual initial dose is 2 mg daily, which is increased gradually up to 20 mg daily, in divided doses as per the need of the patient.

3. **Biperiden (U.S.P.) :**

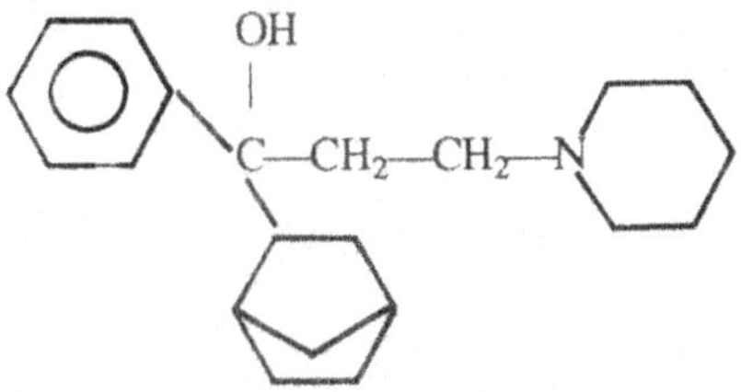

α-5-norborn-2yl α-phenyl-1-piperidiene propanol

Properties and uses : It is white crystalline powder that is freely soluble in chloroform, but almost insoluble in water. A biperiden lactate injection is given intramuscularly or by a slow intravenous route in a 5 mg dose, that is repeated upto 20 mg daily, if necessary. It is employed in all types of parkinsonism diseases.

4. **Chlorphenoxamine hydrochloride (U.S.P.)**

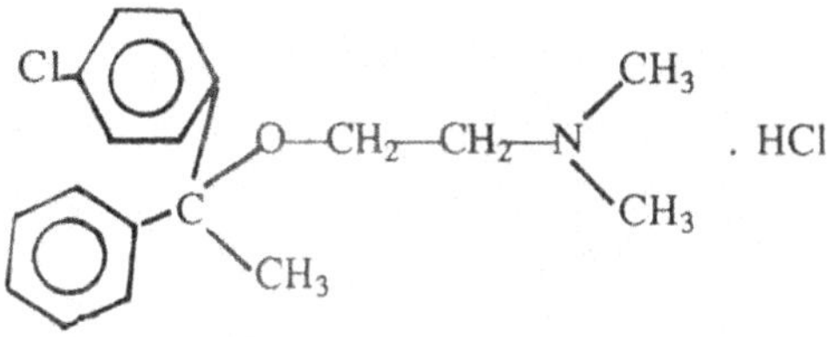

2 [(-p-chloro-α-methyl-phenyl benzyl)-oxy] N,N-dimethyl ethylamine hydrochloride

Properties and uses : It occurs as colourless, needless and is water soluble. It is a antihistaminic drug having anticholinergic activity which is utilized in the treatment of all types of parkinson's disease. It is more useful in relaxation and rigidity of muscle.

5. Ethopropazine hydrochloride (U.S.P.) :

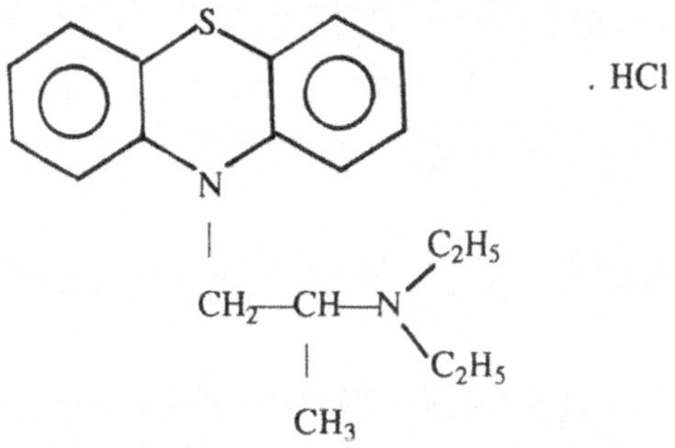

[10 (2-diethylamino) propyl] phenothiazine hydrochloride

Properties and uses : It is a white crystalline powder with no odour. It is soluble in warm water, alcohol and chloroform. It is used in symptomatic treatment of parkinsonism, and in the control of muscular rigidity. The usual dose is 50-600 mg while the initial dose is 50 mg 2-3 times a day.

6. Orphenandrine hydrochloride (B.P., U.S.P.) :

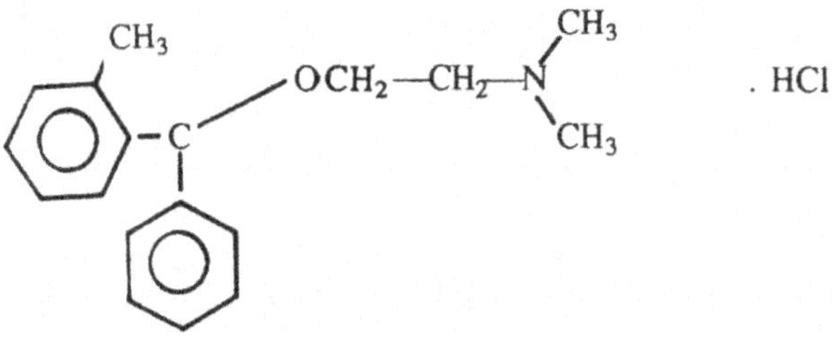

dimethyl [2-(2-o-methyl benzhydryloxy)-ethyl] amine hydrochloride

Properties and uses : It is a white powder, that is soluble in water. Its citrate is also official. It is used in the form of tablets to treat parkinsonism, to relieve the painful spasms of the voluntary muscles. The usual dose is 200 to 400 mg daily, in divided doses.

7. Procyclidine hydrochloride (B.P., U.S.P.) :

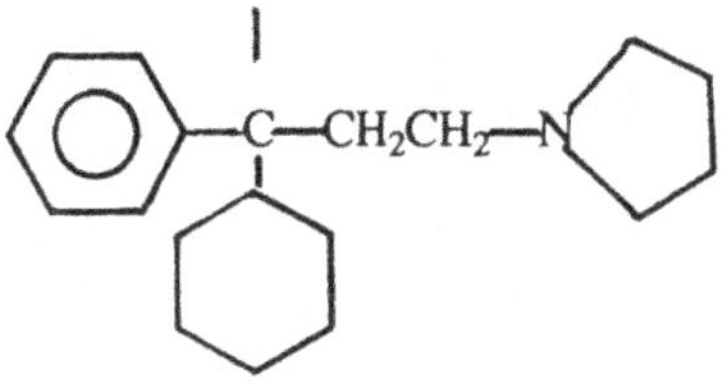

$$\text{Ph-C(OH)(C}_6\text{H}_{11}\text{)-CH}_2\text{CH}_2\text{-N(pyrrolidine)} \cdot \text{HCl}$$

1-cyclohexyl-1-phenyl-3-pyrrolidin-1-ylpropane-1-ol hydrochloride

Properties and uses : It occurs as a white crystalline powder, with a slight odour and it is moderately soluble in water, though more soluble in alcohol. Its tablets are given in an initial dose, of 7.5 mgs daily. The dose is increased to 30 mg daily according to the need of the patient.

8. Levodopa (B.P.) :

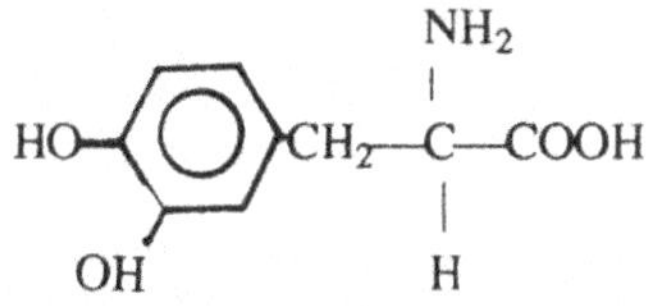

$$\text{HO-C}_6\text{H}_3(\text{OH})\text{-CH}_2\text{-CH(NH}_2\text{)-COOH}$$

3-(3, 4-dihydroxyphenyl)-L-alanine

Properties and uses : A whitish creamy powder, slightly soluble in water, insoluble in alcohol, chloroform. It is used in the form of tablets or capsules in the treatment of parkinson's disease.

9. Carbidopa (B.P.) :

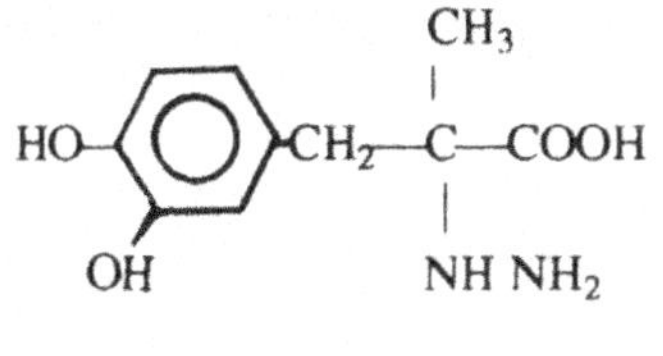

$$\text{HO-C}_6\text{H}_3(\text{OH})\text{-CH}_2\text{-C(CH}_3\text{)(NHNH}_2\text{)-COOH}$$

(s)-2-(3, 4-dihydroxybenzyl)-2-hydrazinopropionic acid

Properties and uses : It's properties and uses are similar to levodopa.

10. **Trihexylphenidyl hydrochloride (U.S.P.) :**

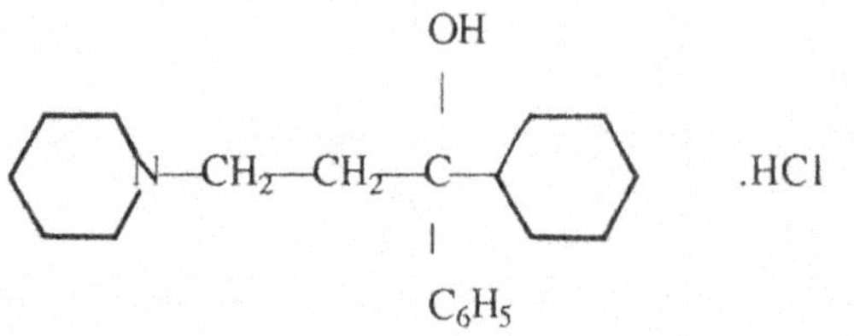

(structure: piperidine-N—CH$_2$—CH$_2$—C(OH)(C$_6$H$_5$)—cyclohexyl · HCl)

α-cyclohexyl- α- phenyl 1-piperidine propanol hydrochloride

Properties and uses : It is a white to off white crystalline powder, with a slight odour. It is sparingly soluble in water but soluble in alcohol and chloroform. It is used in the form of tablets. It has a weak antispasmodic and parasympatholytic action. It is used in the treatment of parkinsonism, and gives relief from mental depression and reduces muscular rigidity.

❑ ❑ ❑

Chapter 17

CARDIOVASCULAR AGENTS

Cardiovascular agents include different types drugs that have an action on the heart or on other parts of the vascular system. They have the ability to alter cardiovascular functions. This category includes cardiotonic drugs like cardiac glycosides ; antiarrhythemic drugs, which regulate the irregular beating of heart ; antihypertensive agents, which regulate blood pressure ; vasodilators which have both coronary and a peripheral vasodilation action and lipid-lowering agents. There are some diuretics and anticoagulants, which are also useful in the treatment of cardiac diseases. The diuretics and anticoagulants are discussed separately, under separate chapters.

CARDIOTONIC AGENTS

Cardiotonic agents have a stimulating action on the cardiac muscles. They increase the force of contraction of the heart, without increasing its oxygen uptake. These drugs are mainly used in the treatment of congestive heart failure. They can cause nausea, vomiting, fatigue and various neuralgic pains.

Digitalis Preparations :

Digitalis (I.P., B.P., U.S.P.) : Digitalis is the leaf of *Digitalis purpurea* Linn., that is dried in the dark below 60'C immediately after collection. It has a slight odour and a bitter taste.

Prepared digitalis (B.P.) : The digitalis leaf is reduced to a moderately coarse powder, and assayed by the biological assay of prepared digitalis. 1 g powder should represent 10 units. The prepared digitalis which contains more than 10 units per gram, is suitably diluted by mixing it with exhausted marc, which is obtained after the preparation of digitalis tincture.

The important constituents of digitalis are the purpurea glycosidee A (Digitoxin, $C_{41}H_{61}O_{13}$), purpurea glycoside B (Gitoxin $C_{41}H_{64}O_{14}$) and digoxin ($C_{41}H_{61}O_{14}$). Digitoxin has digitoxigenin as aglycone and 3 molecules of D-digitoxose. Digoxin and lanatoside C ($C_{49}H_{76}O_{20}$) are important constituents of *Digitalis lanata*. Lanatoside C is made up of digoxigenin as aglycone, with two molecules of Ddigitoxose, one molecule of acetyl digitoxose and one molecule of D-glucose, while Digoxin has digoxgenin as aglycone and 3 molecules of D-digitoxose. The aglycone part of cardiac glycosides namely digitoxigenin, digoxigenin and gitoxigenin, belong to the class called cardenolides. This moiety is responsible for cardiotonic activity. The sugar moiety associated with aglycone, brings solubilty and affinity to the cardiac muscle.

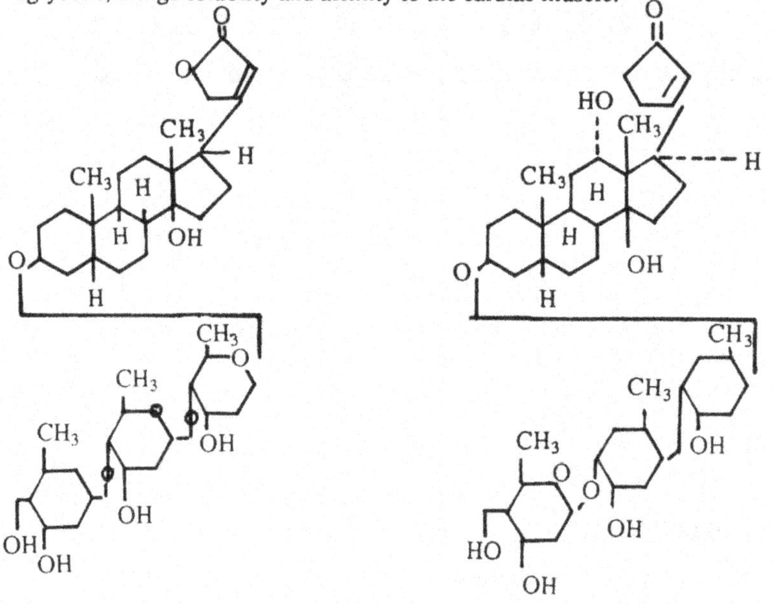

Digitoxin

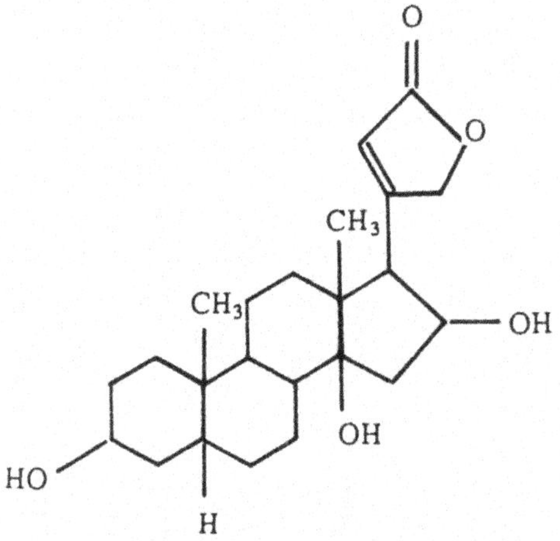

Gitoxigenin

Actions and uses : The important use of digitalis and its preparations, is in the treatment of congestive heart failure. It exerts its salutary effect on a failing heart with a normal sinus rhythm, as well as on the failing heart exhibiting auricular fibrillation. Arrhythmias and valvular defects may modify the action of digitalis. The most outstanding responses are observed in patients with auricular fibrilation and congestive heart failure. It is not indicated for peripheral circulatory collapse or shock. Digitalis has a cardiotonic action on the myocardium and increases the force of contraction, cardiac tone ; and simultaneously the refractory period of the cardiac muscle is prolonged. The heart may slow down by its direct action on the auriculoventricular conduction of sinoauricular node, if digitalis is given in toxic doses. Digitalis to a greater extent abolishes the signs and symptoms of heart failure, but the best results can be seen by bed rest, a sedative and sometimes diuretics along with digitalis. Digitalis is not a true diuretic, even though it increases urine flow, and abolishes oedema. Digitalis can be used as a prophylactic for old people with arteriosclerosis or hypertension, who can develop heart failure. Digitalis glycosides do not cure the arrhythmia, but they improve the condition of the heart. The digital is preparations or the purified digitoxin, are sufficiently absorbed after oral administration.

All digitalis preparations are stored in well closed containers. Two types of digitalis dosages are recognised, the initial dose for digitalization and the second which is a maintenance dose for chronic therapy.

Digitalis Glycosides :

1. Digitoxin (I.P., B.P., U.S.P.) :

Properties and uses : It is a white or buff coloured crystalline powder that is odourless. It is insoluble in water though partially soluble in alcohol and chloroform. Its injection is prepared using 40-50 percent alcohol. It contains glycerine as a solubalising agent and is sterilised by autoclaving. The initial oral dose is 1.5 mg divided over 24-48 hours, and a maintenance dose of 0.1 mg daily. For an intravenous, the initial dose is 0.5 mg and the maintenance dose is 0.1 mg. It is also used in the form of tablets which official in I.P. and B.P.

2. Digoxin (I.P., B.P., U.S.P.) :

Properties and uses : It is white crystalline powder that is practically insoluble in water, chloroform and ether but, freely soluble in dilute alcohol. It is preserved in light-resistant, air-tight containers. It has a cardiotonic activity similar to that of digitalis. As it is purified preparation, it is often used intragvenously, for rapid digitalization. It is also used orally in the form of tablets. The initial dose is 0.5 to 2 mg and the maintenance dose is 0.25 mg.

The initial intravenous dose is 0.5 to 1.5 mg and the maintenance dose is 0.25 to 0.75 mg. It is to be used very carefully, as it is extremely poisonous.

3. Lanatoside C (I.P., B.P.) :

Properties and uses : It is white crystalline powder that is odourless. It is hygroscopic in nature, and absorbs water on exposure to air. It is practically insoluble in water but is soluble in alcohol, pyridine and dioxane. It must be stored in an air-tight container and kept in cool and dry place. It is used in the form of tablets. The initial oral dose is 1 to 1.5 mg and the maintenance dose is 0.25 to 0.75 mg.

4. Oubain (Strophanthin G) (U.S.P.) :

It is a glycoside that is obtained from the seeds of *Strophanthus grantus*, or from the wood of *Acokanthera schimperi*.

Properties and uses : It is a white crystalline powder that is odourless and stable in air but it is affected by light. It is soluble in alcohol. It is not given orally, because of its slow and irregular absorption from the gastrointestinal tract. It is used parenterally, when rapid digital action is desired in extreme congestive heart failure. The usual dose in 0.12 to 0.25 mg intravenously.

5. Deslanoside (B.P., U.S.P.) : It is a digoxigenin glucoside obtained by deacetylation of lanotoside C. It is a white crystalline powder, hygroscopic in nature, insoluble in water and chloroform. It is slightly soluble in alcohol. It is given by injection for rapid digitalization and used in emergency situation.

ANTIARRHYTHMIC DRUGS

Cardiac arrhythima is an irregular beating of a heart. Drugs which correct this defect, are called antiarrhythmic. They bring about a depressant effect on the heart and reduce cardiac activity. They prolong the refractory period of the cardiac muscles and reduce the rate of successive contractions of the heart. The antiarrhythmic drugs exhibit their action by acting through various mechanisms.

A coordination and rhythm is established in the beating of the heart.

Depending upon the condition of arrhythmia, various drugs are used. Some important official compounds in this class are given below :

1. Quinidine sulphate (I.P., B.P., U.S.P.) :

It is an alkaloid obtained from various species of Cinchona or it can be obtained synthetically.

Properties : It occurs in the form of white needle-like crystals. It is slightly soluble in water, freely soluble in alcohol and chloroform. It is to be protected from light, as it darkens on exposure. Its aqueous solutions are sterilised by autoclaving or by filtration. Incompatibilities result with alkalies, iodides, tannic acid etc.

Actions and uses : It depresses myocardial excitability, and prolongs conduction time and refractory period. It finds use in the treatment of atrial tachycardia, flutter and fibrillation. It is used in the form of tablets and the usual dose is 200 to 400 mg repeated as per the need of the patient.

Quinidine bisulphate is offical in B.P. Other salts like gluconate and lactate are employed for intramuscular and intravenous administration.

2. Procainamide hydrochloride (I.P., B.P., U.S.P.) :

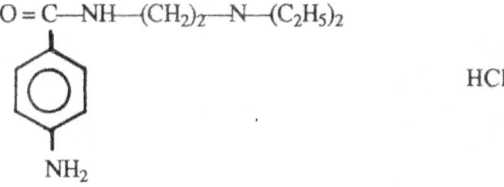

Hydrochloride of 4-amino N-(2-diethylaminoethyl) benzamide

Properties and uses : It is a white to yellowish white crystalline powder that is hygroscopic in nature, very soluble in water, freely soluble in alcohol and slightly in chloroform. Its aqueous solutions are acidic to litmus. It is stable when exposed to air. Its aqueous solutions are sterilized by autoclaving.

It is an antiarryhythmic and antifibrillatory agent. It depresses myocardial excitablity, and prolongs condiction. It is well tolerated by the body. It is used in the form of capsules, tablets and injections. For auricular arrhythmias the initial dose is 1.25 g followed by 500 to 750 mg, 1-2 hourly as necessary. For ventricular arrhythmias, the initial dose is 1 g and then 500 mg 8 times daily.

3. **Disopyramide (B.P.)** :

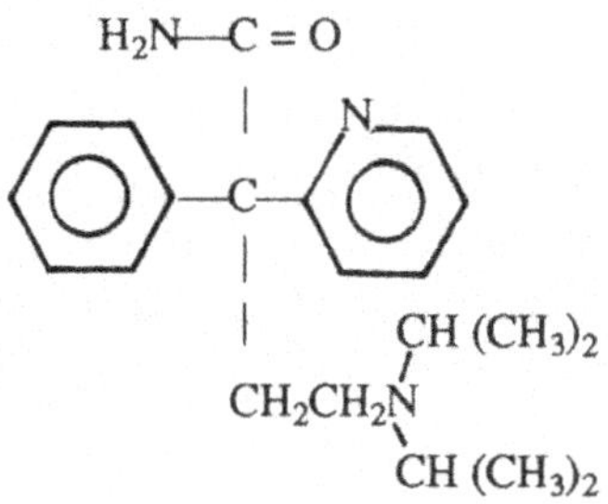

[Structure: H$_2$N—C=O group attached to a central carbon bearing phenyl, 2-pyridyl, and CH$_2$CH$_2$N(CH(CH$_3$)$_2$)$_2$ substituents]

4-di-isopropylamino-2-phenyl-2-(2-pyridyl) butyramide

Properties and uses : It is an odourless powder slightly soluble in water, and freely soluble in alcohol and chloroform. It is used in the form of capsules or intravenous injections. Its phosphate salt is also official in B.P. which is soluble in water, and its aqueous solutions are acidic in nature. Disopyramide and its salt are myocardial depressants and are used in the treatment of arrhythmias. The usual oral dose is 300 to 800 mg in divided dose. Intravenously it is given slowly in 100 to 150 mg of disopyramide, followed by 25 mg hourly upto 500 mg daily.

4. **Lignocaine hydrochloride (Lidocaine) (xylocaine hydrochloride) (I.P., B.P., U.S.P.)** :

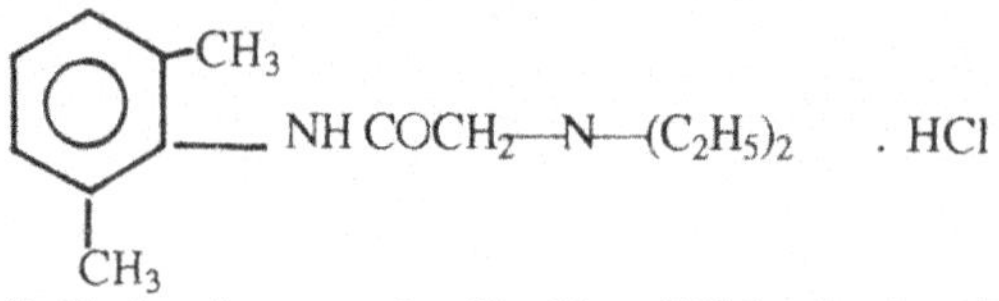

[Structure: 2,6-dimethylphenyl—NHCOCH$_2$—N—(C$_2$H$_5$)$_2$. HCl]

2-diethylamino aceto-2', 6'-xylidide hydrochloride

Properties and uses : It is white crystalline powder, that is freely soluble in water, alcohol and chloroform, but insoluble in ether. It is a local anaesthetic. It is also used in cardiac arrhythmia by an intravenous infusion, of 50 to 100 mg of 1 % solution, and then 1 to 2 mg per minute according to the need of the patient. It increases conduction and decreases the refractory period of heart. It also have membrane depressant property. The lignocaine injections used for this purpose should not contain adrenaline.

5. **Verapamil hydrochloride (B.P.)** :

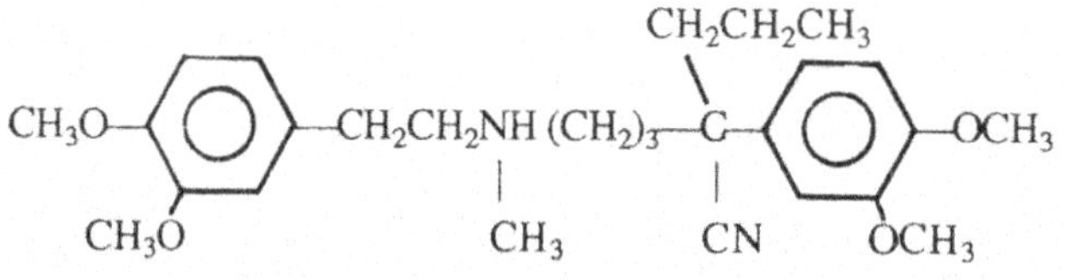

[Structure: CH$_3$O— and CH$_3$O— substituted phenyl —CH$_2$CH$_2$NH(CH$_2$)$_3$—C(CH$_2$CH$_2$CH$_3$)(CN)— phenyl substituted with —OCH$_3$ and OCH$_3$; CH$_3$ on N]

Properties and uses : It is a almost white powder, odourless, soluble in water. Aqueous solutions are acidic. It is used in the form of injections and tablets. It is a selective calcium antagonist and blocks the entry of calcium ions in myocardial cells. It thus acts as antiarrhythmic agent.

6. Mexilentine hydrochloride (B.P.) :

$$\text{2,6-(CH}_3)_2\text{C}_6\text{H}_3\text{—O—CH}_2\text{—CH(CH}_3)\text{—NH}_2 \cdot \text{HCl}$$

1-methyl-2-(2, 6-xyllyloxy) ethylamine hydrochloride

Properties and uses : It is a white powder, freely soluble in water and alcohol. It is given in the form of capsule and injections for antiarrhythmic action. It acts by calcium blockade mechanism.

There are other drugs that belong to the beta-adrenergic blocking agents and anticonvulsant category, which find usefulness in cardiac arrthythmias. From the beta adrenergic blocking class, propranolol hydrochloride in the form of injections and tablets, and practolal in the form of injections acts by blocking catecholamines, which are cardiac stimulants at the beta adrenergic receptor sites. They thus reduce cardiac activity, by inhibiting beta adrenergic stimulation. Pindolol (B.P.) is yet another beta adrenergic blocking agent finds use as antiarrhythmic agent. From the anticonvulsant category, phenytoin sodium is used in the treatment of cardiac arrhythmias. Their exact mechanism of action is still obscure.

ANTIHYPERTENSIVE AGENTS

When the blood pressure is elevated from the normal value of 80-120 mm of mercury, the condition is called hypertension. There are number of factors that are responsible for causing hypertension. When the blood pressure is simply elevated, without any harmful effect on the organs, it is called primary hypertension. When the blood pressure is very high, it causes a delitirous effect other organs, and impairs their functions. This is called secondary or malignant hypertension.

Many drugs are used to lower hypertension, and their actions are varied. The ideal requirement for such drugs is that they should (i) produce slow reduction of blood pressure with a prolonged effect. (ii) with increased doses, it should produce a prolonged effect rather than a pronounced fall of blood pressure. (iii) it should be effective orally (iv) it should act at the small dose level and (v) it should not produce any untoward side effects.

There are many drugs which the lower blood pressure through different mechanisms. They are classified on the basis of their mechanism of action.

Some important mechanisms and the compounds are given below :

I. DRUGS AFFECTING NEURO TRANSMITERS AT NERVE ENDINGS :

The crude drug Rauwolfia which consists of the dried roots and bark of *Rauwolfia serpentina* is known to be antihypertensive. Rauwolfia contains a number of alkaloids of which the significant and important is reserpine. Rauwolfia was offical in number of pharmacopolias. However, only reserpine and methoserpidine are official in (B.P.). These alkaloids exhibit antihypertensive activity by depleting the levels of catecholamine at nerve endings. The antihypertensive effect of reuwolfia alkaloids is mild and have slow onset of action.

1. Reserpine (I.P., B.P., U.S.P.) :

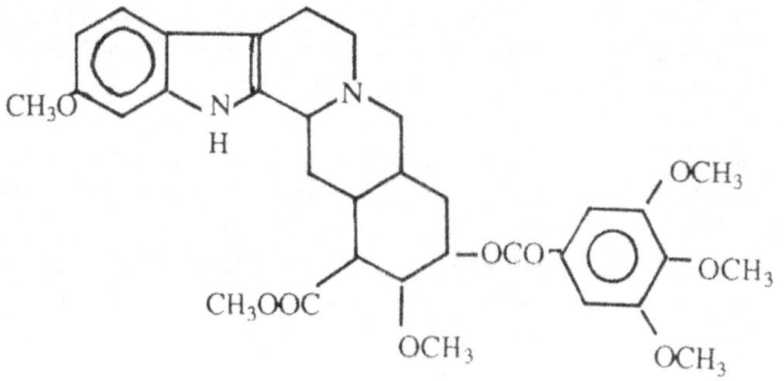

Properties : It is white or pale yellowish white powder that is insoluble in water, very sparingly soluble in alcohol but soluble in chloroform. The powder or solution darkens on exposure to light. It must be stored in air-tight containers in cool and dry places. It aqueous solutions are prepared with the aid of suitable acids and they are sterilized by the filtration method.

Actions and uses : It has central nervous system depressant and sedative action, and hence it is used for mild anxiety and chronic psychosis cases. As an antihypertensive, it acts through a central depression by depleting catecholamines. It is administered in the form of tablets and injections, in doses of 100 to 500 micrograms daily ; in divided doses in mild hypertension.

2. Methoserpidine :

It is similar to reserpine. It is creamy microcrystaline powder, hygroscopic in nature. It is insoluble in water, soluble in alcohol and chloroform. Similar to reserpine, it also undergoes degradation in acidic and alkaline media and is also affected by light. It is given in tablet form for antihypertensive action.

II. ADRENERGIC NEURON BLOCKING AGENTS

Some synthetic compounds selectively block the transmission of neuronal activity at sympathetic nerve ending. They prevent the release of noradrenaline which results due to nerve stimulation. Thus the level and activity of nor-adrenaline is diminished and antihypertensive effect is exhibited. Some clinically useful compounds from this class are :

1. Guanethidine sulphate (I.P., B.P.U.S.P.) :

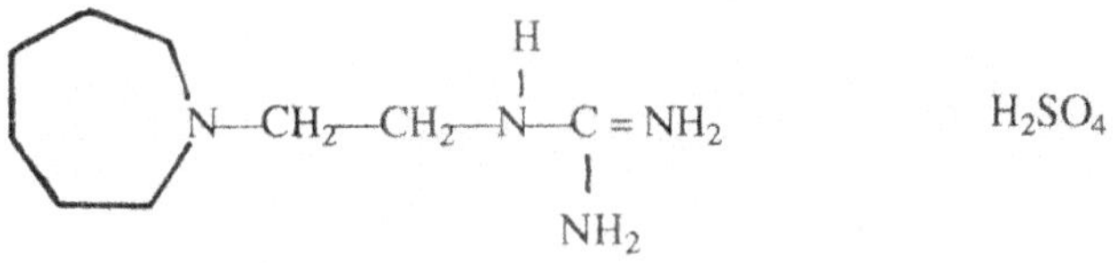

1-[2-(perhydroazocin-1-yl) ethyl] guanidine sulphate

Properties and uses : It occurs as colourless crystals, or a white crystalline powder that is soluble in water. It acts by blocking the release of noradrenaline at the nerve endings thus depleting the noradrenaline stores in peripheral sympathetic nerve terminals. The usual dose is 10-20 mg daily. It is administered orally. It has longer duration of action.

2. Bethandine sulphate (I.P., B.P.) :

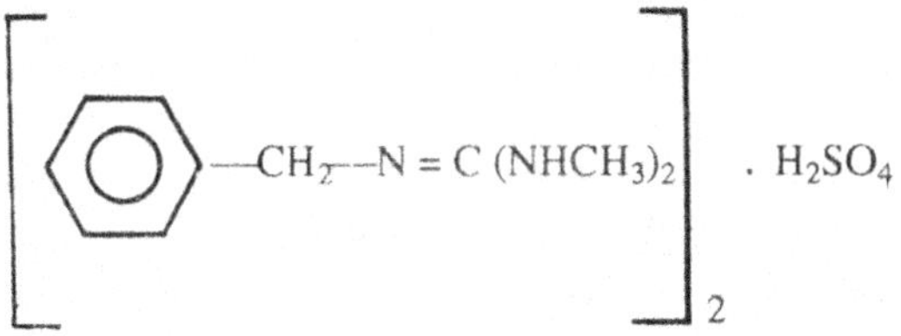

Sulphate of 2-benzyl-1, 3-dimethylguanidine

Properties and uses : It is a white powder, that is freely soluble in water, but less soluble in alcohol and practically insoluble in ether. It is used in the form of tablets. It is an adrenergic blocking agent and its mechanism of action is similar to guanethidine. The usual initial dose is 10 to 20 mg daily in divided doses and a maintenance dose of 200 mg daily in divided doses as per the need of the patient.

III. GANGLION BLOCKING AGENTS

The drugs or compounds that block or prevent the impulses through the autonomic ganglia are called ganglionic blocking agents. The transmission of impulses across the ganglionic synopes is mediated by acetylcholine and by other neurotransmitters. The compounds by blocking the electrical events in ganglia show both sympathetic and parasympathetic antagonist activity. One of the therapeutic usefulness of this category is found in (i) control of servere hypertension and (ii) in the treatment of peripheral vascular disorders. Some useful compounds from this class as antihypertensive drugs are given below :

1. Pentolinium tartrate (U.S.P.) :

1, 1-pentamethylene-bis (1-methylpyrrolidintum) tartrate

Properties and uses : It is an almost white solid that is freely soluble water though sparingly in alcohol and insoluble in chloroform and ether. It is used in the form of injections only, as it shows an erratic absorption when given orally. Its aqueous solutions are acidic in nature, and are sterilized by autoclaving. The drug belongs to the category of ganglion-blocking agents. It therefore interferes wth the nerve transmission of impulses at the ganglions. Since it blocks the sympathetic, it produces peripheral vasodilation and thereby reduces blood pressure. Because of the parasympathetic blockade, it produces side effects, and hence it is not used much now-a-days. The usual dose is 1 mg initially, and then increase as per the need of the patient.

2. Mecamylamine hydrochloride (I.P., U.S.P.) :

Properties and uses : It is a white crystalline powder, that is almost odourless and freely soluble in water and chloroform. It belongs to the category of ganglion blocking agents but differs from other ganglion blocking agents, in the respect that it is not a quarternary ammonium compound. It is well absorbed when administered orally in the form of tablets. It has number of side effects like, nausea vomiting, constipation etc. The usual dose is 2.5 to 60 mg, with the initial dose 2.5 mg twice a day which is then increased by 2.5 mg every alternate day as per the need of the patient.

IV. MISCELLANEOUS CLASS

Different compounds also bring lowering of blood pressure by (i) acting centrally and reducing the tone and stimulation of sympathetic nerve or (ii) by acting peripherally or (iii) by inhibiting the enzyme dopadecarboxylase etc. Clinically useful compounds from this miscellaneous class are :

1. Hydralazine hydrochloride (I.P., U.S.P.) :

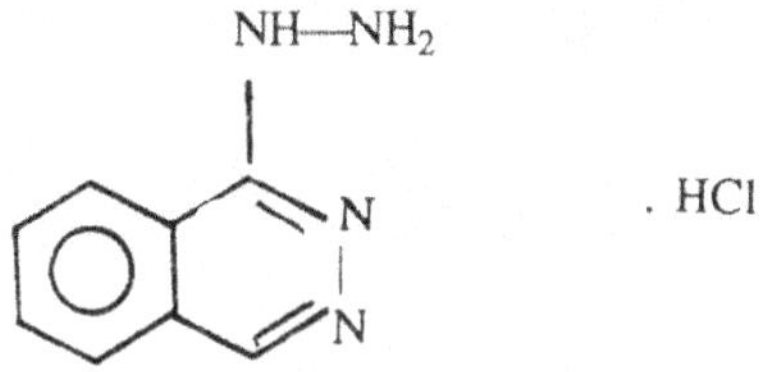

Phthalazin-1-yl hydrazine hydrochloriae

Properties and uses : It is a white crystalline powder, that is soluble in water but sparingly soluble in alcohol and ether. Its aqueous solutions are sterilized by autoclaving or by filtration. It acts as an antihypertensive by the reflux mechanism. It may be used for the treatment of essential and early malignant hypertension. It gives better results when administered alongwith diuretics. Its principal toxic effects are syndromes resembling rheumatoid arthritis and as soon as these are observed the drug must be withdrawn. It is administered in doses of 20 to 40 mg by intramuscular or intravenous routes.

2. Methyldopa (I.P.): (Alpha methyldopa)

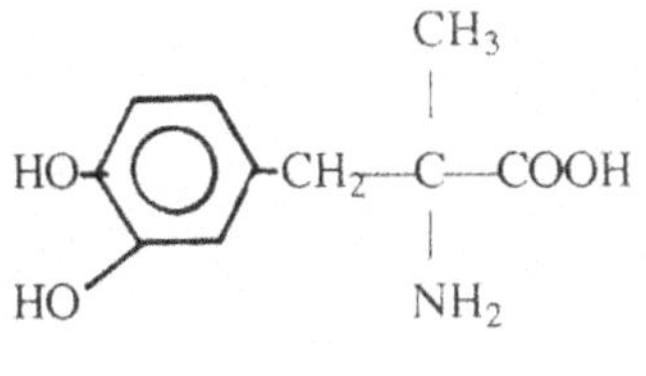

-3-(3,4-dihydroxy-phenyl) 2-methyl-L-alanine

Properties and uses : It is a whitish powder with a yellowish tint and is sparingly soluble in water. It is given orally in the form of tablets. For intravenous administration, Its ethyl ester in the form of a hydrochloride salt is used, which is more water-soluble. It is official in U.S.P. as methyldopate. The solutions are sterilized by the filtration method. Methyldopa acts by inhibiting the enzyme-' dopadecarboxylase.'

Methyldopa : It's hypotensive action is due to its conversion to α-methylnoradrenaline in adrenergic neurons in CNS, where it is stored as a false transmitter. Further, methyldopa supressess release of renin by the kidney, thus action by angiotension mechanism.

The usual dose ranges from 500 mg to 3 g daily, in divided doses.

3. **Clonidine hydrochloride (B.P.)** :

2 [(2, 6-dichlorophenyl) imino] imidozolidine hydrochloride

Properties and uses : It is a white crystalline powder, that is almost odourless and soluble in water and alcohol. Its aqueous solutions are acidic in nature. It is preserved in tight containers. It acts both centrally and peripherally as a antihypertensive. It is also useful in migraine. It is used in the form of tablets and injections. For hypertension the usual intravenous dose is 150 to 1800 micrograms daily, in divided doses, and for migraine it is 50 to 150 mg daily in divided doses.

4. **Diazoxide (B.P.)** :

7-chloro-3-methyl-2H-1-1,2,4-benzothiadiazine-1,1-dioxide

Properties and uses : It is a white crystalline powder, that is insoluble in water, ether and chloroform but very soluble in alkali hydroxide solutions. Its aqueous solutions are sterilized by autoclaving. It is used in the treatment of hypertension and the usual dose is 150 to 1000 mg daily in divided doses but by the intravenous route it is 300 mg daily. It is also used in the treatment of endogenous hyperinsulinism, with the usual dose being 350 to 1000 mg daily in divided doses (hypoglycamic agent). Though it is structurally similar to thiazide diuretic, it does not act as a diuretic.

5. Prazosin hydrochloride (B.P.) :

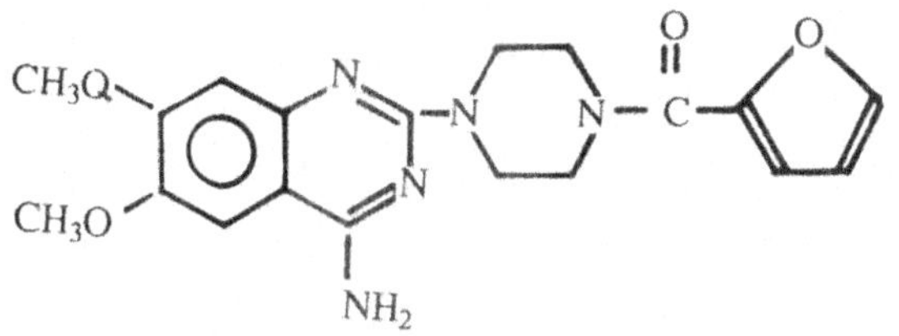

2-[4-(2-furoyl)-pperazine I-yl]
-6, 7-dimethexyqunazoline 4-yl amine hydrochloride

Properties and uses : It is white, odourless solid with negligible solubility in water, alcohol and chloroform. It is given orally as tablets. It is believed to act directly as peripheral vasodilator by direct action on smooth muscle. It also acts by α - adreno receptor blocking mechanism.

6. Pargyline hydrochloride (U.S.P.) :

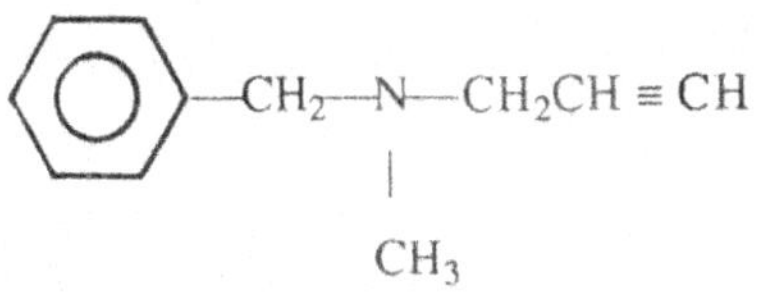

N-methyl-N-2-2propynyl benzylamine hydrochloride

Properties and actions : It occurs as white powder, odourless and is water soluble. It is given orally as tablets. It is a known MAO inhibitor and interestingly acts as a hypotensive agent. It is believed to act by accumulation of false transmitter substance (Octopamine) at the neuron and thus produces hypotension.

LIPID LOWERING AGENTS

Arteriosclerosis is a disease that is caused by the hardening of arteries or blood vessels. High levels of cholesterol, free fatty acids and esters, are considered to be the causative factors for it. In arteriosclerosis, the elasticity of arteries is lost, lumen becomes narrow, and this results in hypertension. It is considered, that substances which reduce the level of lipids in the blood would be useful, and such substances are called lipid-lowering agents. There are various types of hyperliporotenima, some drugs selectively act at particular type.

1. Clofibrate (I.P., B.P.) :

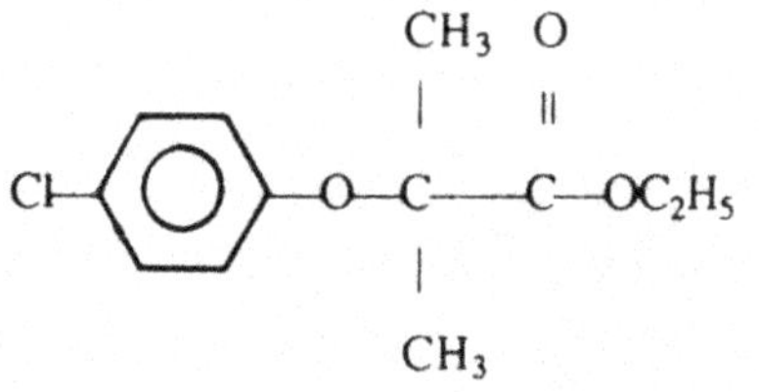

$$Cl-C_6H_4-O-C(CH_3)_2-C(=O)-OC_2H_5$$

Ethyl-2-(4-chlorophenoxy)-2-methylpropionate

Properties and uses : It is a clear colourless liquid, that has characteristic odour practically insoluble in water and is miscible with alcohol, ether and chloroform. It is given in the form of capsules. It is used to reduce the elevated plasma levels of triglycerides and cholesterol, and is thus useful in type III hyperlipoprotenimia as well in coronary heart diseases.

2. Nicotinic acid : (I.P., B.P., U.S.P.) :

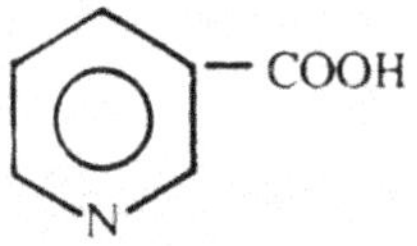

$$\text{Pyridine-3-COOH}$$

Properties and uses : It is a white crystalline powder, almost odourless, partially soluble in water, though more soluble in alcohol and boiling water, and soluble in solutions of alkali hydroxides. It is a component of vitamin B. In large doses it reduces the serum cholesterol levels, and thus helps in reducing hypertension.

VASODILATORS

Drugs that produce dilation of the blood vessels, are called vasodilators. This includes both coronary vasodilators (those that dilate blood vessels of heart) and peripheral vasodilators. Both categories are useful in treating various aliments of the cardiovascular system.

Coronary vasodilators and Anti Anginals :

Coronary vasodilators act directly on the cardiac muscles and produce a relaxation. They also produce a dilation of the coronary vessels and as a result cause an increased supply of blood to the heart muscle. Thus they are useful in angina pectoris. These drugs are useful in anginal attack and are called as antianginal drugs. They are further useful as prophylactices to reduce the severity and frequency of attack.

1. Glyceryltrinitrate :

$$CH_2(ONO_2)$$
$$|$$
$$CH(ONO_2)$$
$$|$$
$$CH_2(ONO_2)$$

Its tablets are offical in I.P. and B.P. while its solution is official in B.P. It is a solid with a characteristic odour and it is highly explosive.

Actions and uses : It is a general relaxant, but it does not paralyse smooth muscle. Its action is not prevented by any agent. It acts as a vasodilator on finer blood vessels, and decreases the blood presure. It is used as prophylaxies and to treat attacks of angina pectories. The effect of the drug appears after about 2-3 minutes and lasts for about 20 minutes. Normally the tablets are allowed to dissolve in the mouth. The usual dose is 0.2 to 0.6 mg which may be repeated if necessary.

2. Amylnitrite (U.S.P.) :

It consists mainly of the nitrite of 3-methylbutane-1-ol [$(CH_3)_2CH$—CH_2—CH_2O NO] and the nitrites of other isomers.

Properties and uses : It is a clear yellowish liquid with etheral and fruit odour. It is practicaly insoluble in water though miscible with alcohol, ether and chloroform. It is volatile even at room temperature. It slowly decomposes on exposure to air and light, and the presence of moisture accelerates its decomposition. It must be preserved in air tight containers and protected from light and heat and kept in a cool place. It is taken by inhaling a few doses of the liquid on a handkerchief, or by crushing a glass ampoule of amyl nitrite to treat attacks of angina pectoris. It is also used for the emergency treatment of cyanide poisoning.

3. Pentaerythitol tetranitrite (U.S.P.) :

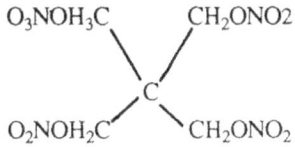

Properties and uses : It occurs as white crystals that are sparingly soluble in water, alcohol and ether but soluble in acetone. It is more sensitive to shock than trinitrotoluene. (i.e. it is more explosive). It is usually diluted with an inert material like lactose, to prevent the danger of explosions. When administered orally, it gets absorbed from the gastrointestinal tract, and it releases the nitrite ion slowly, and shows a prolonged action. The usual dose is 20 mg 3 to 4 times a day.

Peripheral vasodilators :

Peripheral vasodilation is produced by different drugs employing different mechanisms. Adrenaline and catecholamines act through alpha and beta receptors, of which alpha has a vasoconstrictor effect. The drugs of the alpha adrenergic blocking type produce vasodilation by competitive inhibition of alpha adrenergic receptors. Other drugs act directly, by producing a non-specific relaxant effect on the smooth muscles. The clinically useful drugs acting as peripheral vasolilators like (i) phenoxybenzamine hydrochloride, (ii) Tolazoline hydrochloride (iii) Phentolamine (iv) thymoxamine hydrochloride (v) isoxuprine hydrochloride are discussed under adrenergic blocking agents. (vi) Inositol nicotinate and (vii) diluted isosorbide dinitrate are used in the treatment of acute original attack. The dose is 10 mg four times a day. (viii) Methyl nicotinate is employed in various conditions like Raynold's disease, vericose vein as a vasodilator. Usual dose is 50-300 mg per day.

Chapter 18

HISTAMINICS AND ANTIHISTAMINIC AGENTS

Histamine is chemically a β-imidazolethylamine and is widely distributed in nature. It is found in ergot, in plants and is present in the organs and tissues of the human body in small amounts. It is released during allergic and anaphylactic manifestations caused by the action of sensitizing agents (antigen) present in foods, pollen grains or through environmental factors. It is believed that histamine is formed from histidine, which is a naturally occuring amino acid in the body.

Histamine produces a wide variety of physiological actions. These actions are considered to be brought about by two receptors called H_1 and H_2 receptors. Some of the prominent actions of histamine are (i) strong vasodilatation of capillaries and increased permeability, thus resulting in the accumulation of fluid in the body which causes oedema, (ii) on smooth muscle of lungs it produces a bronchiolar constrictor action, (iii) on the uterus, it causes a constrictor action, (iv) through H_2 receptors, it has a stimulating action on secretory and excretory glands. It thus produces secretion of hydrochloric acid in stomach, which in turn produces peptic or duodenal ulcers. Nasal and lacrimal secretions are also stimulated.

The beneficial secretory action of histamine, is utilised clinically to diagnose any impairment of the acid-producing cells of the stomach. It is also used to detect any vascular disease. For test, an intradermal injection of 1 : 1000 histamine solution, produces a wheal or patch on the skin.

Two clinically useful histaminic agents are :

1. **Histamine phosphate (I.P., B.P., U.S.P.)** :

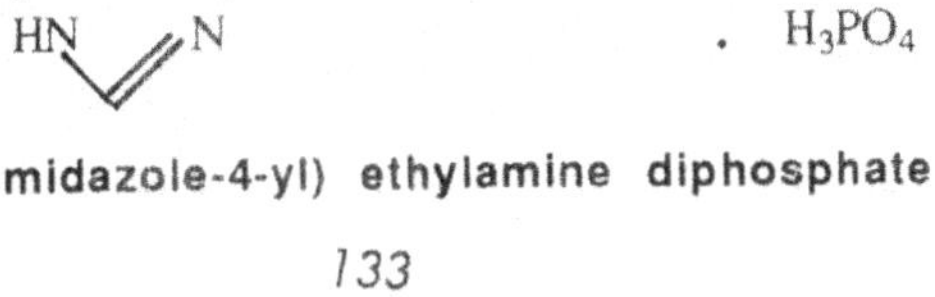

$$\text{imidazole—}CH_2\text{—}CH_2\text{—}NH_2 \cdot H_3PO_4$$

2- (1H-imidazole-4-yl) ethylamine diphosphate

It is phosphate salt of histamine.

Properties and uses : It occurs as long white prismatic crystals. It gets affected by light and so it should be stored in well closed light-resistant containers. It is soluble in water and its aqueous solutions are acidic in nature. Solutions for parenteral use are sterilized by the filtration method. It is also administered by a subcutaneous injection of 10-40 microgram per kg dose, for the diagnosis of the acid secretory capacity of the stomach cells.

2. Betazole hydrochloride (U.S.P.) :

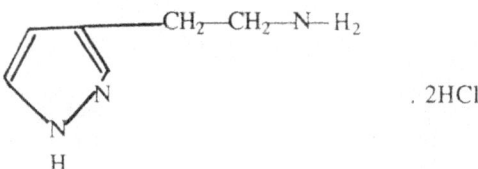

3-(2-amino ethyl) pyrazole dihydrochloride

Properties and uses : It is a white crystalline and odourless powder. It is highly soluble in water. The aqueous solution is acidic. Its solution for injections, are sterilized by the filtration method and are given subcutaneously or intravenously, in 50 mg/ml doses for diagnostic purpose.

ANTIHISTAMINIC AGENTS

Antihistaminic agents are drugs which give relief from histamine reactions in allergic states. These drugs, are also called antiallergic agents.

The release of histamine and histamine-like substances, is considered to be the result of allergic symptoms. Pollen grains, certain foods and a number of unknown antigenic substances, bring about allergic symptoms and anaphylaptic manifestations. The undesirable physiological actions of histamine, bring discomfort and toxic reactions. Antihistaminics become useful in these conditions.

Mechanism of action : Antihistaminics do not combine with histamine and neutralise its action. They do not prevent the liberation of histamine from the cells, nor do they act through enxymes which bring about the destruction of histamine. It is generally believed, that they do not interfere with antigen-antibody reaction. Most of the antihistaminics act by competing at the receptor sites in tissues. The combining of antihistaminics, with the receptive substances present at the receptor sites prevents the action of histamine being exhibited on the tissues and it is thus they act as antihistaminics.

The action of antihistaminic agents is said to be mediated through the H_1 and H_2 receptors. Most of the allergic actions of histamine are evoked through H_1

receptors. The antiallergic type of drugs (antihistaminics) are thus H_1 receptor blocking agents.

Therapeutic uses of antihistaminics :

Antihistaminic agents are used clinically in a number of allergic reactions like hay fever, serum sickness, motion sickness, urticaria, nausea caused by pregnancy etc. Along with analgesics, they are widely used in the treatment of common cold. They are also incorporated in cough, cold and expectorant preparations. A number of antihistaminic agents in varying degrees exhibit local anaesthetic, adrenergic, antispasmodic, analgesic, cholinergic blocking etc. as their overlapping activties. Some common side effects and side reactions of this category of drugs includes sedation, dizziness, muscular weakness diarrhoea, dryness of mouth, nervousness, etc.

A typical feature of the salts of antihistaminics, is the preparation of salts with various dicarboxylic organic aids like succinic, maleic, malic, fumaric, tartaric etc. These salts offer the advantages of increased potency, solubility in water, stability in air and lesser toxicity over the conventional salts like hydrochloride or sulphate.

Pharmaceutical dosage ferms :

Antihistaminics are administered in various dosage forms like capsules, plain and sugar coated tablets, sustained action tablets, elixirs, syrups, nasal drops, ointments and creams. Further, for immediate effect, they are also given parenterally.

Classification of antilistaminics :

The most active antihistaminic (antiallergic) have the following general structural features

$$\begin{array}{c} Ar \\ Ar' \end{array} \!\!\! > \!\! \underset{1}{X} - \underset{2}{C} - \underset{3}{C} - \underset{4}{N}$$

1. Ar = aryl, phenyl or heteroaryl
   Ar' = second aryl or arylmethyl
2. X = N (nitrogen) as ethylenediamine analogs
      O (oxygen) as aminoalkyl other analogs
      C (carbon) as monoaminopropyl analogs.
3. C-C = alkyl chain mostly of two carbon atom i.e. ethylene; branching results in lower activity.
4. N = The terminal nitrogen should be 3° for maximum activity; substituent is lower alkyl i.e. methyl.

I. AMINOALKYL ETHERS

The general chemical-structural feature of this class is

$$R-O-CH_2CH_2-N\begin{matrix}R_1\\R_2\end{matrix}$$

where, R = Benzyl or any other arylalkyl and R_1 and R_2 are methyl groups. Some important compounds from this class are :

1. Diphenhydramine hydrochloride (I.P., B.P., U.S.P.) :

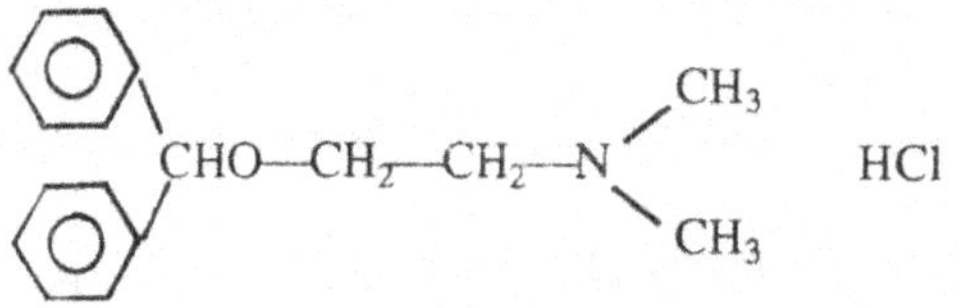

$$(C_6H_5)_2CH-O-CH_2-CH_2-N(CH_3)_2 \cdot HCl$$

2-benzhydryloxy ethyl dimethylamine hydrochloride

Properties and uses : It occurs as a white crystalline powder and has a bitter taste. It is soluble in water, alcohol and chloroform. It darkens on exposure to light and should be stored in well closed container and kept away from light. It is active orally and is given in the form of capsules, elixirs and syrups for antihistaminic and antiemetic effects. The usual dose is 25 to 50 mg 3 or 4 times a day. It is an ingredient of cough mixtures. Intramuscular or intravenous injections in doses of 10-50 mg are given for immediate effects. It is employed in various allergic conditions.

2. Dimenhydrinate (I.P., B.P., U.S.P.) :

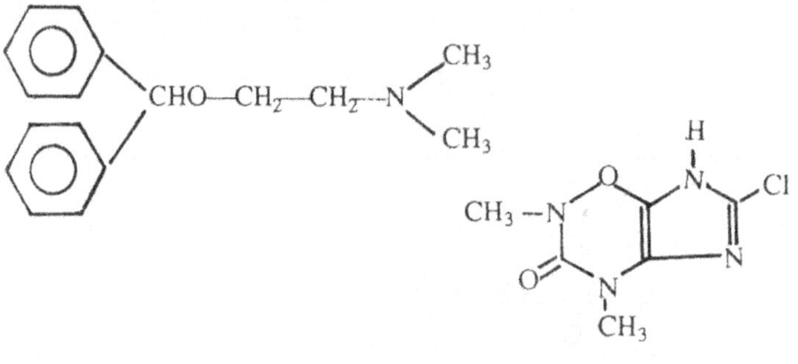

$$(C_6H_5)_2CH-O-CH_2-CH_2-N(CH_3)_2 \quad \cdot \quad \text{8-chlorotheophylline}$$

It is a salt of diphenhydramine with 8-chlorotheophylline.

Properties and uses : It is a white, odourless powder and is slightly soluble in water, though more soluble in alcohol. It is given orally or parenterally. It is mainly used to prevent nausea caused by motion sickness and post-operative vomiting. Solutions are prepared in mixture of propylenegiycol and water. Dimenhydrinate syrup, and tables are official in U.S.P. and are used as antiemetics, in a dose range of 50-100 mg six times a day or as necessary.

II. ETHYLENEDIAMINES

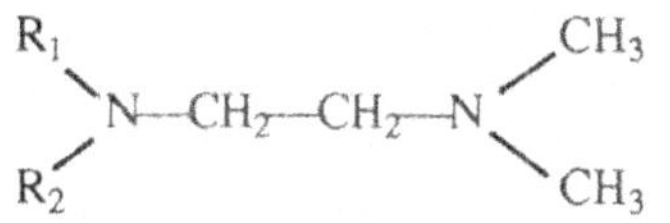

$$R_1\text{-N-CH}_2\text{-CH}_2\text{-N(CH}_3)_2 \text{ (with } R_2 \text{ on first N)}$$

In the ethylenediamine class the structural moiety wherein R_1 and R_2 are various aryl and heterocyclic groups. Some active compounds from this class are :

3. Mepyramine maleate (I.P., B.P.) :

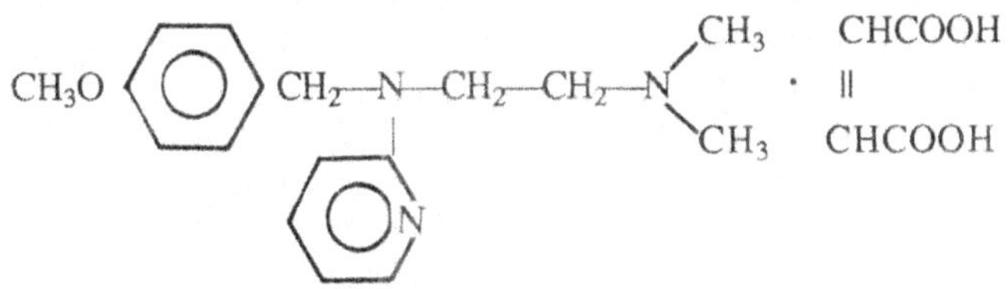

2 (2-p-anisyl-N-2 pyridylamine)-ethyldimethylamine hydrogen maleate
or
2 (2-dimethylamino) ethyl p-methoxy benzyl-amino pyridine bimaleate

Properties and uses : It is a white crystalline powder with bitter taste. It is light-sensitive and is soluble in water, alcohol and chloroform. It is employed to treat hay fever, urticaria and allergic reactions and it also has local anaesthetic effects. Its injection, tablets and elixirs are official in B.P. and the tablets are official in I.P. The usual dose is 0.1 to 0.2 g daily, while the usual range is 300 to 600 mg daily, in divided doses.

4. Tripelennamine hydrochloride (I.P., U.S.P.) :

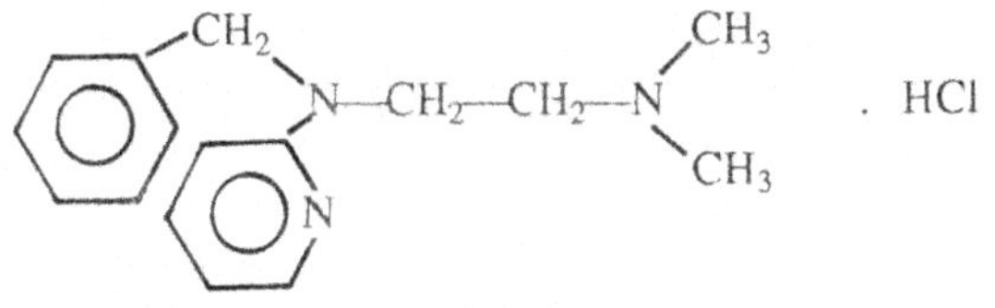

2 {N-benzyl N-2 (dimethylamino) ethyl] -amino} pyridine hydrochloride

Properties and uses : It occurs as a white crystalline powder. It darkens on exposure to light, and should hence be protected. It is freely soluble in water and alcohol. The drug is active orally. Tripelenamine hydrochloride tablets or the tripelennamine citrate in the form of an elixir, are given in doses of 50-100 mg, three to four times a day as antihistaminic of the general type.

III. ALKYLAMINES

In this class there are aryl and heterocyclic groups, on the carbon atom of propylamine.

5. Pheniramine maleate (I.P., B.P.,) :

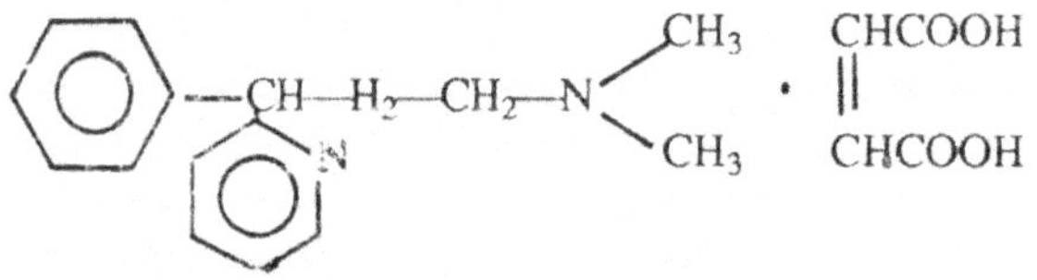

Dimethyl [3-phenyl-3-(2-pyridyl) propyl] amine hydrogen maleate

Properties and uses : It is a white powder with faint odour. It is highly soluble in water and alcohol. It is used orally and given as tablets in various allergic conditions. Usual dose is 25 to 50 mg daily.

6. Chlorpheniramine maleate (I.P., B.P., U.S.P.) :

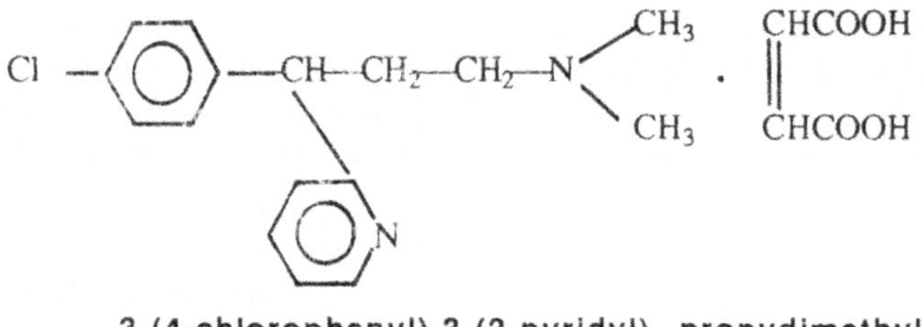

3-(4-chlorophenyl)-3-(2-pyridyl) propydimethyl amine hydrogen maleate

Properties and uses : It is a white crystalline powder. It is soluble in water, alcohol and chloroform. Its aqueous solution is acidic in nature. It is given orally, as tablets or elixirs in dose of 2 to 4 mg, 3 to 4 times a day. The injection is official in B.P. and U.S.P. It is used in 10 to 20 mg doses by intramuscular, or intravenous routes, as a general purpose antihistaminic agent. It shows less side effects. The dextro form known as dexchlorpheniramine inaleate is more active than levo form.

7. Triprolidine hydrochloride (B.P.) :

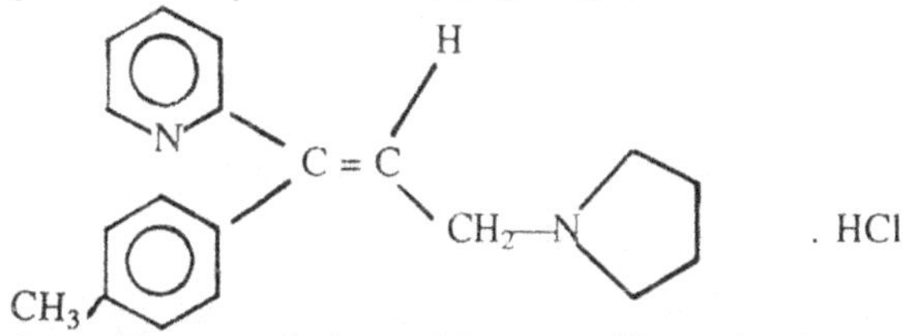

Properties and uses : It is a white crystalline odourless powder. It is soluble in water, alcohol and chloroform and insoluble in ether. The drug is active orally and is given in the form of tablets. The ususal dose is 5 to 7-5 mg daily in divided doses.

IV. PHENOTHIAZINES

Phenothiazine ring compounds exhibit variety of pharmacological actions. The psychotherapeutic agents had shown antihistamic as side reaction which has been utilised in the development of this category of agents. Some important compounds from this class are given below :

8. Promethazine hydrochloride (I.P., B.P., U.S.P.) :

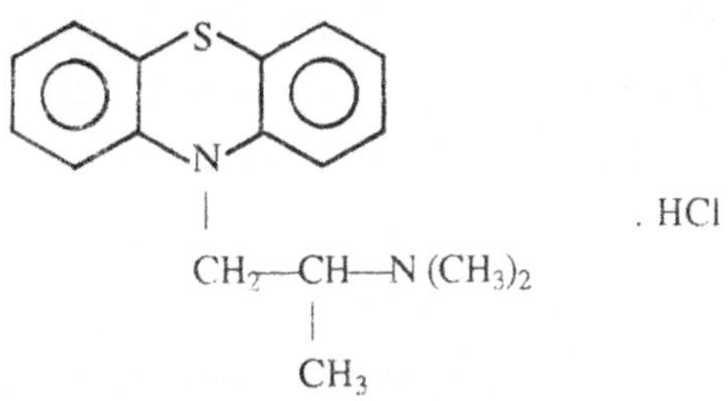

Dimethyl [1-methyl-2-(phenothiazine-10 yl) ethyl] amine hydrochloride

Properties and uses : It is a white to faint yellow crystalline powder, very soluble in water and soluble in alcohol. Aqueous solutions are acidic. It is given orally in the form of tablets and solutions. Besides antihistaminic activity, it has antiemetic and tranquilising action also.

9. Methdilazine hydrochloride (I.P., U.S.P.) :

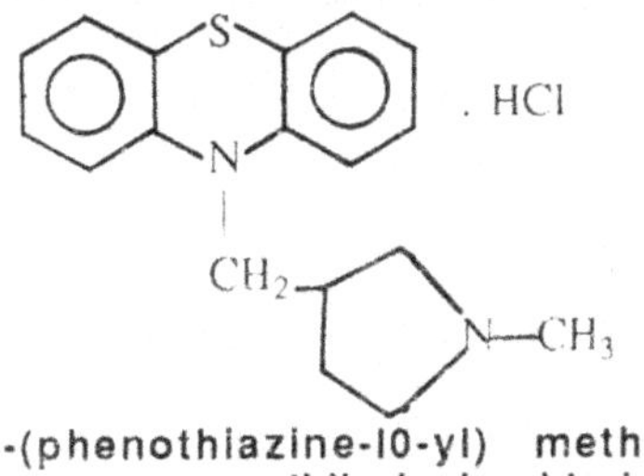

3-(phenothiazine-10-yl) methyl-1-methyl pyrrolidin hydrochloride

Properties and uses : It is a pale-brown powder, slight odour and freely soluble in water. It is stored in light resistant tight container. It is given orally for its antipruritic action.

10. Trimeprazine tartrate (B.P.) :

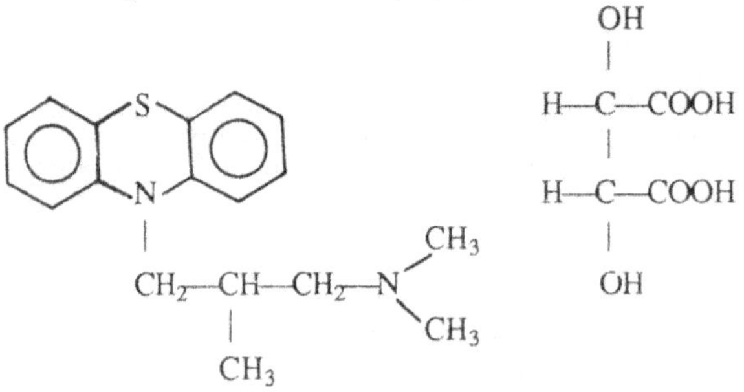

Dimethyl [2-methyl-3-(phenothiazine-10-yl) propyl] amine tartrate

Properties and uses : It is a white-creamcolour powder which darkens on exposure to light. It is soluble in water, alcohol and chloroform. It is given orally in the form of solutions and tablets for its pronounced antipruritic activity.

V. PIPERAZINE DERIVATIVES

This class is also termed as cyclic ethylenediaminium derivatives. Most compounds from this class show slow onset and longer duration of action.

The useful compounds from this class are :

11. Cyclizine hydrochloride (I.P., B.P., U.S.P.) :

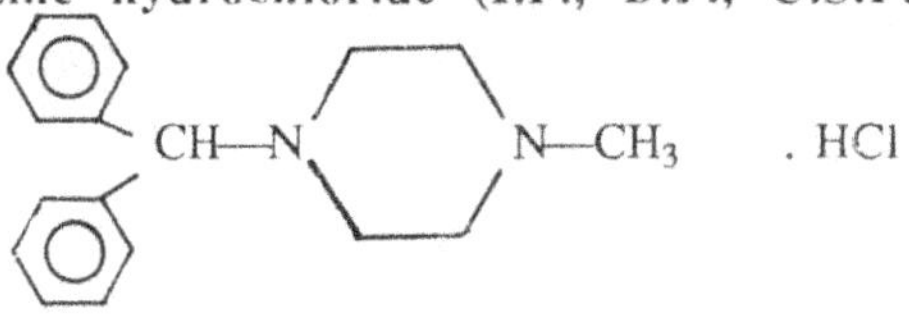

1-benzhydryl-4-methylpiperazine hydrochloride

Properties and uses : It is a white crystalline powder, that is almost odourless and bitter to taste. It is fairly soluble in water and alcohol but almost insoluble in ether. Its aqueous solution is acidic in nature. The drug is used for the treatment of motion-sickness and as an antiemetic. It is active orally, and given in the form of tablets in the dose range of 25 to 50 mg.

12. Chlorcyclizine hydrochloride (I.P., B.P.) :

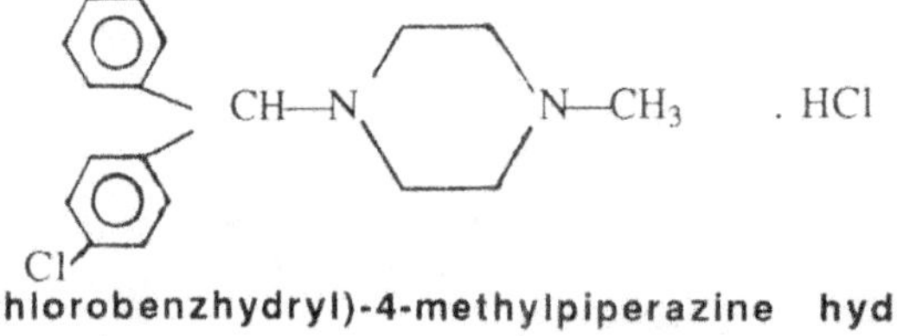

1-(4–chlorobenzhydryl)-4-methylpiperazine hydrochloride

Properties and uses : It occurs as a light sensitive white powder, that is odourless and bitter to taste. It is more soluble in water and alcohol, than cyclizine hydrochloride. Its aqueous solution is acidic. The drug is used for the treatment of allergic conditions as an antihistaminic. It shows a prolonged action and has less side effects. Chlorcylizine tablets are official in I.P. The usual dose is 50 to 100 mg 3-4 times a day.

13. **Meclizine (Meclozine) hydrochloride (I.P., B.P., U.S.P.)**

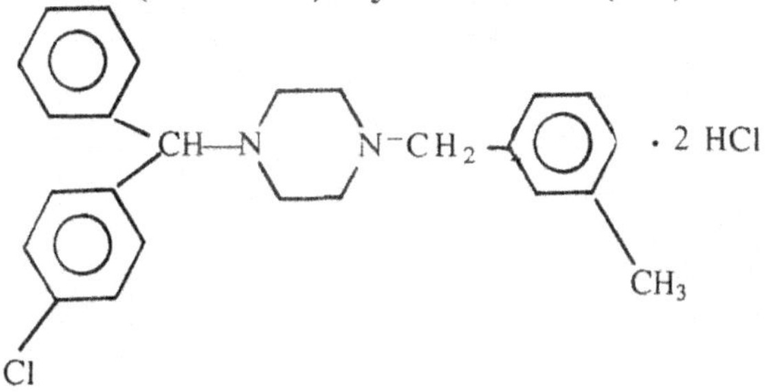

1-(4-chloro benzhydryl)-4-(3m-methylbenzyl)
-piperazine dihydrochloride

Properties and uses : It occurs as a white to creamy white, odourless and tasteless powder. It is slightly soluble in water and alcohol. The drug gives a slow onset but has a longer duration of action. It is used for the prevention or treatment of motion sickness, vertigo, vomiting etc. The drug is active orally and is administered in the form of tablets, in a 25 to 50 mg dose daily.

VI. MISCELLANEOUS AGENTS

14. **Cyproheptadine hydrochloride (I.P., B.P.) :**

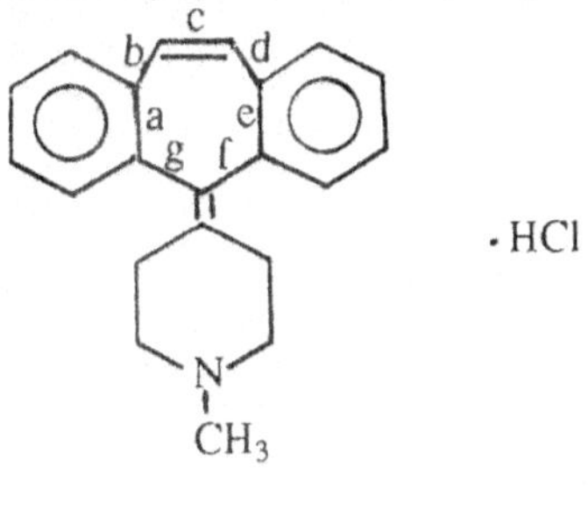

4-(5-H-dibenzo (a-e) cyclohepten-5-ylidene)
1-methyl piperidine hydrochloride

Properties and uses : It occurs as a yellowish white powder that in sparingly soluble in water and alcohol. It has antihistaminic and antiserotonin activity. The principle side effect is sedation and drowsiness. It is given orally in the form of tablets in dose of 4 to 20 mg daily, in divided doses.

15. **Diphenylpyraline hydrochloride (I.P., B.P.) :**

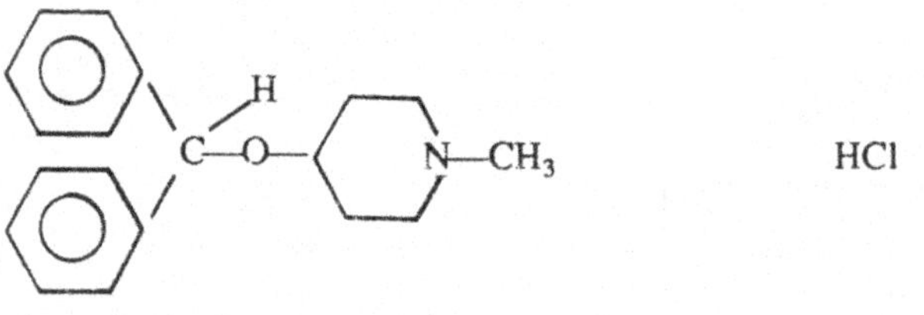

$$(C_6H_5)_2CH-O-\text{[4-piperidinyl]}-N-CH_3 \cdot HCl$$

4-benzhydryloxy 1-methyl-piperidine hydrochloride

Properties and uses : It has a short duration of action, but shows less side effects. The drug is given in 2 mg tablets or in 5 mg, sustained release capsules or tablets.

16. **Phenindamine tartrate (I.P., B.P.) :**

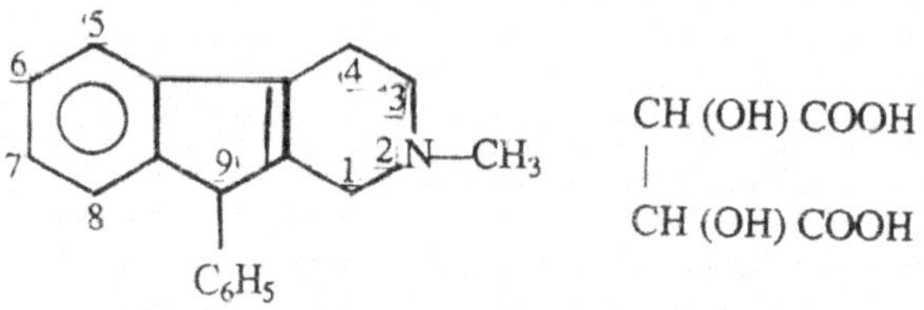

[Structure: 2,3,4,9-tetrahydro-2-methyl-9-phenyl-1H-indeno[2,1-c]pyridine with positions labeled 1-9, with N-CH₃ at position 2 and C₆H₅ at position 9]

$$\begin{array}{c} CH(OH)COOH \\ | \\ CH(OH)COOH \end{array}$$

2, 3, 4, 9-tetrahydro-2-methyl 9-phenyl-
1-H-indeno (2, 1 c) pyridine hydrogen tartarate

Properties and uses : It occurs as a white crystalline powder. It is soluble in water and alcohol, but practically insoluble in ether and chloroform. Its aqueous solution is acidic and its stability is in the pH range of 3.5 to 5.0. Incompatibilities result, with oxidizing agents. It is given orally in the form of tablets, syrups or elixirs, in doses of 75 to 150 mg daily, in divided doses. The drug does not cause drowsiness as a side effect ; on the contrary a mild stimulating effect is exhibited.

H_2 RECEPTOR ANTAGONIST

As stated earlier, prominent action of histamine through H_2 receptor is the stimulating effect on secretary cells and excretory gland. This results in production and secretion of hydrochloric acid in stomach. This excessive secretion of acid in turn results in peptic and duodenal ulcers. H_2 - receptor antagonist inhibit the secretion of acid and thus give relief to the patients suffering from peptic and gastric ulcers. There is no structural resemblance for this category of substances with those of H_1 receptor antagonist. In general, this class has imidazole ring as a part of structural moiety Clinically useful drugs are:

1. **Cimetidine (I.P.) :**

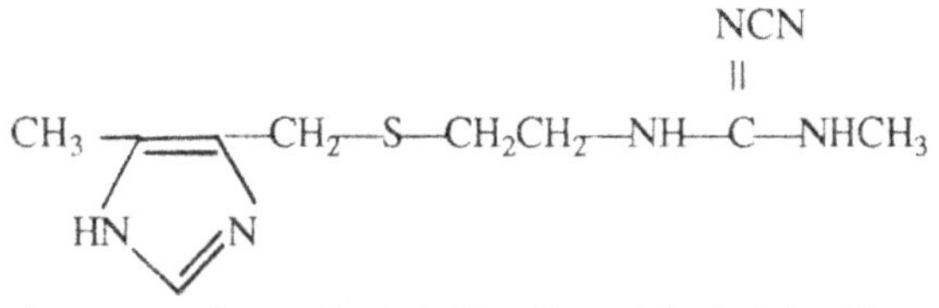

CH₃ — [imidazole ring with HN, N] — CH₂—S—CH₂CH₂—NH—C(=NCN)—NHCH₃

2-cyano-3-methyl-1-[2-(5-methyl-4-imidazoyl methyl thio ethyl] guanidine

Properties and uses : It is white power, odourless, slightly soluble in water, soluble in warm alcohol and in dilute mineral acids. It is administered orally as tablets and in solutions (hydrochloride) for the treatment of ulcers.

2. **Ranetidine**

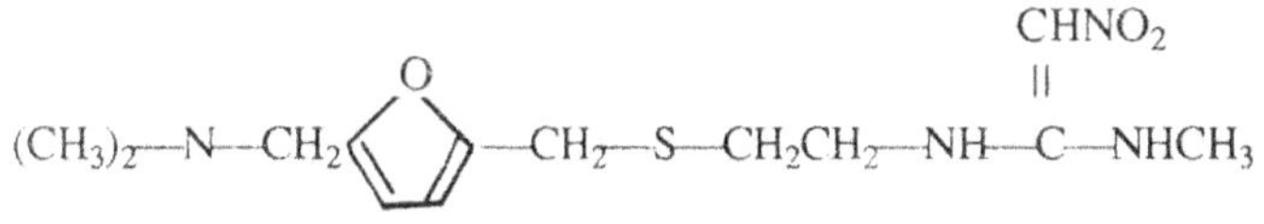

$(CH_3)_2$—N—CH₂—[furan ring]—CH₂—S—CH₂CH₂—NH—C(=CHNO₂)—NHCH₃

N, N-Dimethyl-5-[2-(1-methylamino-2-nitrovinyl amino ethyl thiomethyl] furfurylamine

Properties and uses : It is a yellowish grey powder, freely soluble in water and used in the form of tablets in about 150 - 900 mg dose, daily for treatment of ulcers.

Chapter 19

ANTITUSSIVES AND EXPECTORANTS

An antitussive can be defined as a drug that raises the threshold of the cough centre, and suppresses the irritant non-productive cough. Cough is a phenomenon, wherein irritating substances, mucus and other secretions from the respiratory tract, are expelled out. Under normal conditions cough brings about a clearing of the respiratory tract. However, when it (cough) is excessive, it needs controlling.

It is believed that antitussives act mainly at the cough centre that is situated in the medulla oblongata. A cough is a reflex phenomenon, and potent antitussives act centrally by depressing or suppressing cough by a reflex mechanism.

Compounds that have an antitussive activity can be divided into two categories viz. (i) Narcotic antitussives and (ii) Synthetic non-narcotic antitussives.

NARCOTIC ANTITUSSIVES

Morphine and codeine and are important alkaloids of opium, besides being potent analgesics are also wellknown antitussive agents. These and ethyl morphine, diamorphine, methadone, meperidine (pethidine) are potent antitussive agents. Since all these drugs are narcotic in nature, they are called as narcotic antitussives. These have been covered under the topic on analgesics.

Synthetic Non-narcotic Antitussives :

The clinically useful compounds are discussed below.

1. **Dextromethorphan hydrobromide (B.P.) :**

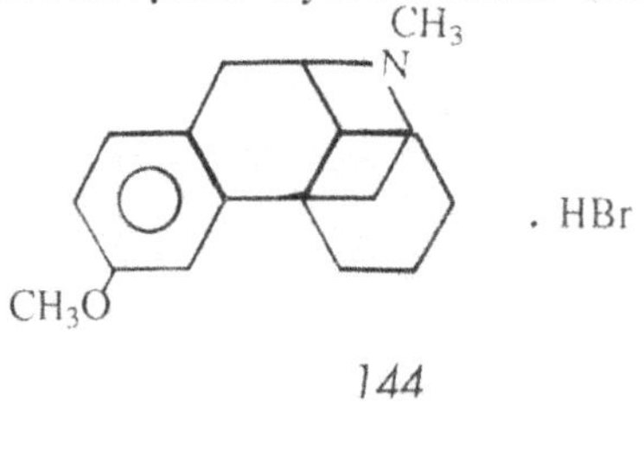

Properties : This salt occurs as a white crystalline powder that is odourless, and has a bitter taste. It is sparingly soluble in water, but is more soluble in alcohol and chloroform. The drug acts as antitussive, without any sedative or analgesic action. The usual dose is 15 to 30 mg, 1 to 4 times a day.

2. **Levopropoxyphene (U.S.P.) :**

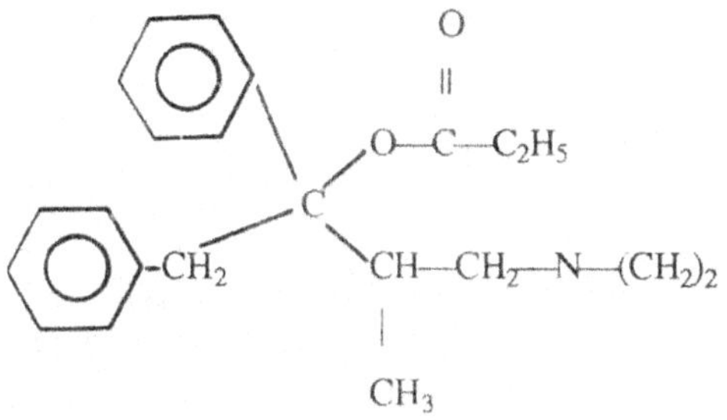

(−)-4-(dimethylamino)-3-methyl-1,
2-diphenyl 2-butanol propionate

Properties and uses : The naphthalene sulphonate salt is called Napsylate. It occurs as a white powder, that is almost tasteless. It is sparingly soluble in water but more soluble in alcohol and chloroform. It can be given in the form of suspension in a 50 mg dose.

3. **Noscapine (B.P., U.S.P.) :**

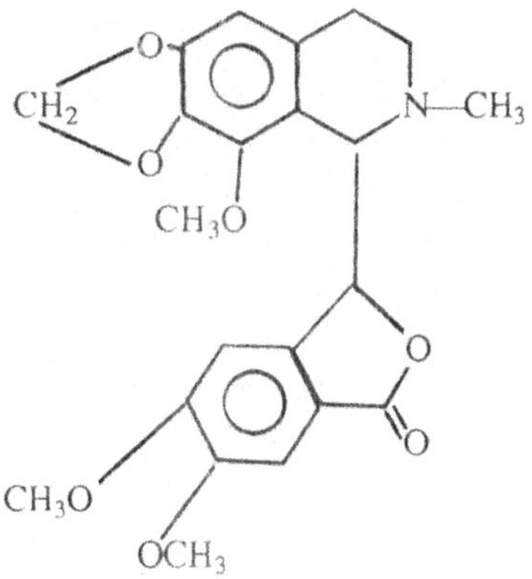

It is an alkaloid of opium.

Properties : It is white powder, odourless, and has intensely bitter taste. It is almost insoluble in water, only slightly soluble in alcohol and more soluble in chloroform. It is orally effective and is antitussive with bronchodilatory action. The drug has no addiction liability, and no analgesic activity. Noscapine Linctus is official in B.P. and noscapine hydrochloride which is its water soluble salt, forms an ingredient of various cough preparations.

4. Pholcodine (B.P.) :

It is a semisynthetic derivative prepared from morphine.

Properties and uses : It is a colourless to white crystalline powder that is odourless and bitter to taste. It is sparingly soluble in water, but more in alcohol and chloroform. It is active orally and is given in the form of linctus upto 60 mg, in divided doses to control unproductive cough. It has a mild sedative action.

EXPECTORANTS

Expectorants are the drugs that remove sputum from the respiratory tract. These drugs either increase the fluidity (or reduce the viscosity) of sputum, or increase the volume of fluids that are to be expelled from the respiratory tract by coughing.

Expectorants can be classified under two categories viz. (i) sedative type and (ii) stimulant type.

The sedative type of expectorants are stomach irritants. They produce their effect through stimulation of gastric reflexes. Drugs that are bitter like ipecac, and compounds like antimony potassium tartrate, ammonium chloride, sodium citrate, and potassium iodide are sedative expectorants. In the stimulant type, the drugs bring about a stimulation of the secretory cells of the respirtory tract directly, or indirectly. Since the drug stimulates secretion, more fluid is produced in respiratory tract, and hence the sputum gets diluted. Turpenoid oils like Eucalyptus, lemon and anise, and active constituents of drugs like terpinehydrate, anethole which are, stimulant expectorants. Amongst phenolic compounds, guaiacol (2-methoxyphenol) and guaiacol carbonate, acetate or glyceryl ethers, are useful expectorants. These compounds are found useful in a number of liquid oral expectorant-cough preparations.

Some crude drugs like cocillana bark, senega root and bark and indian squill are official in B.P. and are used as expectorant.

Two synthetic compounds official in B.P. for their expectorant activity are :

Antitussives & Expectorants

(i) Bromhexine hydrochloride (B.P.) :

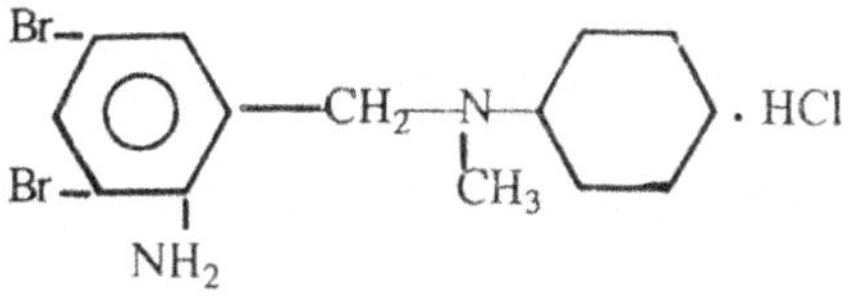

2-amino-3, 5-dibromobenzyl-(cyclohexyl) methylanine hydrochloride

Properties and Uses : It is a white crystalline powder insoluble in water, sparingly soluble in alcohol it is given in tablets form as expectroant.

(ii) Guaiphenesin (B.P.) :

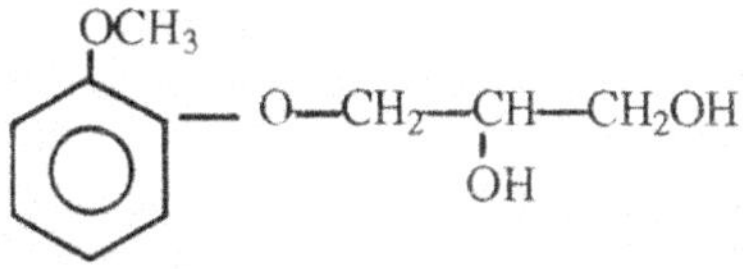

3-(2-methoxyphenoxy)-propane 1,2 diol

In tablet form are clinically used as expectorants.

Properties and Uses : It occurs as crystalline, odourless powder, soluble in water, and alcohol. It is used in tablet form and in cough preparations.

□ □ □

Chapter 20

COAGULANTS AND ANTICOAGULANTS

Drugs which help and bring about the coagulation of blood (called as coagulants) and those which prevent its coagulation and maintain its fluidity (anticoagulants) are clinically used in a variety of conditions. Thus both these categories of agents are useful.

There are number of phases or steps involved in the blood clotting mechanism. Amongst these, the formation of thromboplastin, conversion of prothrombin into thrombin and finally the conversion of fibrinogen into fibrin (the clot) are important. In the blood clotting mechanism, the tissue factors, plasma factors, platelet factors, calcium ions etc. are also involved. In the normal circulating blood, there are factors which prevent the formation of fibrin and the clot. If a blood clot is accidently formed or if one is present in the vascular system then it is broken down by the proteolytic enzyme present in the plasma.

COAGULANTS

The drug which brings about the coagulation of blood are called coagulants. These are employed in the treatment of hamorrhegic or threatened haemorrhagic conditions. Such haemorrhegic conditions are caused by many factors such as platelet defects, plasma coagulation disorder condition, excessive use of anticoagulant therapy etc. The ingestion of vitamine K_1 and other precursers through the diet, usually maintains a normal concentration of prothrombin levels and other clotting factor. However, the following preparations are used for coagulation purposes.

Dried Thrombin (B.P.) Thrombin (U.S.P.)

It is a sterile protein prepared from the prothrombin fraction of bovine origin and it is freeze dried. It appears as a white or greyish, amorphous powder. It can be readily dissolved, and reconstituted in a normal saline solution. It is thermolabile, and sensitive to light. It may contain a suitable antibacterial agent. It is stored in a sealed, sterile container, at a temperature between $2 - 8^oC$. It is supplied in vials in 1000, 5000 and 10,000 units. Solutions of thrombin containing 100 to 2000 N.I.H. units per ml in sodium chloride solution, or in water are applied topically to the wound. The solutions are to be used within a few hours after preparation, and are not injected.

Human fibrinogen (U.S.P.) :

It is a sterile fraction that is derived from normal human plasma and is freeze dried. It appears as a white to greyish amorphous powder. The solution of this gets converted into insoluble fibrin when thrombin is added. It is used by intravenous infusion, in 2 to 6 g as a 2 % solution in water for injection at a rate of 5 to 10 ml per minute, as a coagulant. It is stored in a hermetically sealed container under a vacuum at 2 to 8°C.

Protamine sulphate (U.S.P.) :

Protamine is a protein that is obtained from the sperms of fish and converted into sulphate salt. It occurs as a whitish-grey crystalline powder that is hygroscopic in nature, and is soluble in water. Since it is thermolabile, its solutions are sterilised by the filtration method and are stored in sterile containers between 2 to 8°C. Protamine sulphate powder is stored below 10°C.

Protamine sulphate has an anticoagulant effect. However, in the proper amount, it counteracts the actions of heparin, and thus acts as antidote of heparin. a protamine sulphate injection is given by an intravenous route, in a concentration of 1 mg of Protamine Sulphate for each 80-100 USP units of heparin activity and employed in the treatment of haemorrhegic conditions.

The synthetic compounds menadione and menadiol sodium phosphate have prominent coagulant activity. These help in formation of prothrombin in liver. These compounds are discussed under chapter Vitamin.

ANTICOAGULANTS

Drugs that prolong the coagulation time of blood and prevent coagulation, are called anticoagulants. These drugs find use in a number of clinical conditions such as venous thrombosis, pulmonary embolism, and myocardial infarction. They are employed as prophylactics to prevent thrombosis during and after surgical operations. They are also used in the blood transfusion process and in the preservation and storage of blood, in blood banks.

Anticoagulants are broadly classified into two categories (i) Natural agents and (ii) Synthetic agents. The natural agents like heparin and heparin analogue, are effective only parenterally, and are active both in *vivo* and in *vitro* while the synthetic agents can be given orally, as well as parenterally ; these compounds are inactive in *vitro*.

Natural Agents :

Heparin : Chemically it is mucopolysaccharide that is obtained from the lung or intestinal mucosa of oxen, pigs and sheep. It is a thermolabile material, and is prepared as a calcium or sodium salt (official in B.P.). These salts occur as white, hygroscopic and water soluble powders. The solutions used for injection are prepared in water and strerilized by the filtration method. They are stored in sterile sealed containers and are protected from light.

it is administered by an intramuscular or intravenous route in 5,000 to 15,000 units. It is employed in blood transfusion, and also in arterial or venous thrombolic conditions.

Synthetic Agents :

A number of compounds belonging to the chemical class of coumarins and indanediones, have been developed as orally active anticoagulants. The basic structure of coumarin and indanedione, from which anticoagulants are developed is given below :

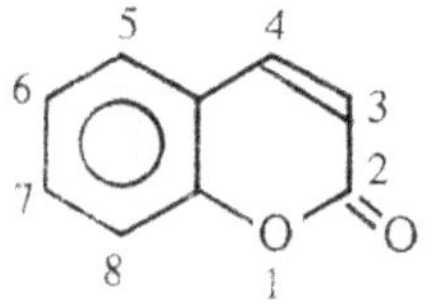

Coumarin 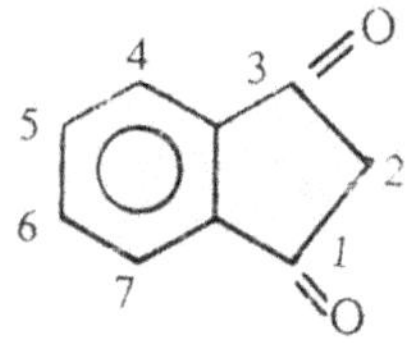   Indandione

Though various compounds were developed from Coumarins and indanediones as potential anticogulants, very few have been accepted after clinical trial. These compounds have poor and irregular absorption from G.I. tract. Further, they differ in their on set and duration of anticogulant activity. These drugs show effect after few days with long tasting effects. Coumarins depress synthesis of clotting factor and hence show slow on set of action. The indane 1,3 diones have slightly greater toxicity and hence are less preferred. The drugs from both the categories are water insoluble.

1. **Dicumarol (U.S.P.) :**

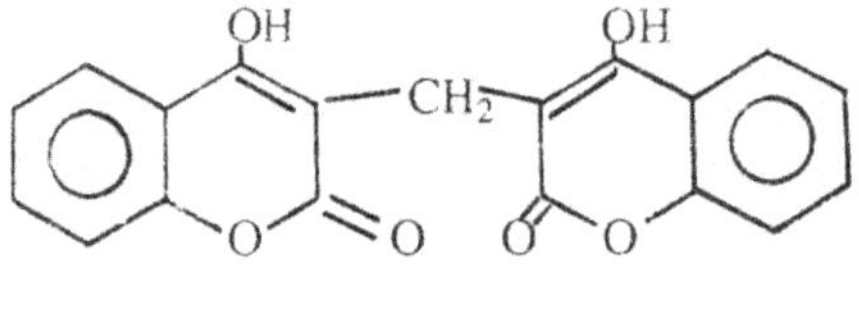

3, 3 methylene bis (4-hydroxy coumarin)

Properties and uses : It occurs as a white-creamy crystalline powder with faint odour. It is insoluble in water and alcohol but soluble in alkali hydroxides. It gives a slow onset of action. The dose after determining the clotting time, is 200 mg. The drug is given orally in the form of tablets or capsules. It is used in the treatment of post-operative thrombophelbitis and pulmonary embolism.

2. Nicoumalone (I.P., B.P.):

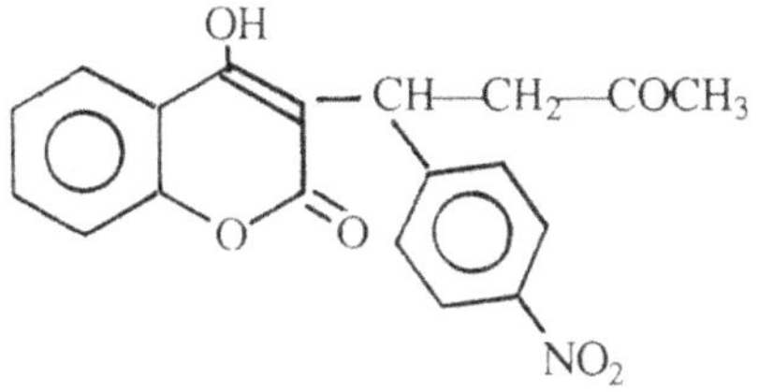

4-hydroxy-3-(1-p-nitrophenyl-3-oxobutyl) coumarin

Properties and uses: It is a white to pale buff coloured powder, that is insoluble in water. It should be protected from light. It is given orally in the form of tablets in 4 to 12 mg dose according to the prothrombin activity of blood.

3. Warfarin Sodium (B.P., U.S.P.):

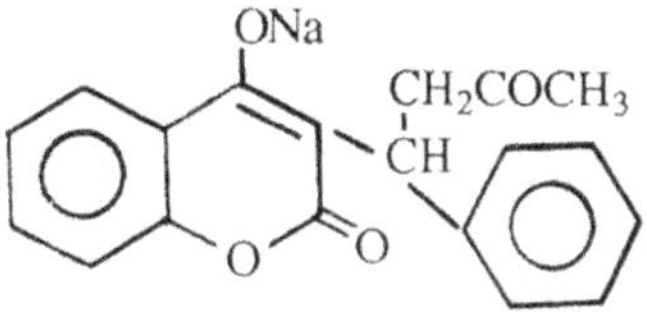

4-hydroxy-3-(3-oxo-1-phenylbutyl) coumarin sodium

Properties and uses: It occurs as a white powder, that is odourless and has a slight bitter taste. It is soluble in water and alcohol. Its aqueous solution is alkaline. It is given orally or intravenously in a 3 to 10 mg dose.

4. Phenindione (I.P., B.P., U.S.P.):

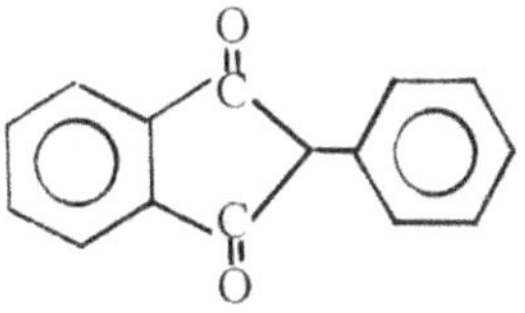

2-phenylindane 1,3 dione

Properties and uses: It occurs as a pale-creamy white, crystalline powder. It is slightly soluble in water, but more soluble in alcohol. It is active orally and is given in the form of tablets in 200 to 300 mg initial doses and subsequently in 50 to 100 mg dose daily.

Chapter 21
DIAGNOSTIC AGENTS

Diagnostic agents are chemicals or substances that are used to detect abnormalities in tissues and organs, or to test an organ function. These are thus useful for the clinical diagnosis of diseases. These agents do not usually have any medicinal values or pharmacological effect. The diagnostic agents are often introduced directly into the body or the specific organ. The chemicals or substances used as diagnostic agents can be divided into two categories :
(i) radiopaque substances, (ii) compounds used to test organ functions.

RADIOPAQUE SUBSTANCES

Radiopaque substances are those compounds (both inorganic and organic) that have the property of casting a shadow on a X-ray film. These substances have the ability to absorb X-rays and hence appear opaque on X-ray examination. **They are also called X - ray contrast media.**

A number of iodinated organic compounds are generaly used as X - ray contred, media. In the iodinated organic compounds iodine is held by a strong covalent liknage and is not released in the ionized form.

Diagnostic agents

The reqirements of satisfactory radiopaque materials are :

(i) For adequate radiopacity, iodine content should be over 50 percent.

(ii) The solutions of material should be selectively concentrated in particular portion to cast shadow.

(iii) The solution should remain in the body till X-ray examination and then should get excreted rapidly.

(iv) The material and its solution should remain stable till use; as well during storage.

(v) The material should have low toxicity as well no pharmacological activity.

Which is toxic. The radiopage iodine compounds are administered by two methods : (i) systemic i.e. orally or intravenously and (ii) retrograde (by mechanical means backwardly). These compounds are useful for the examination of gastrointestinal tract, kidney (urography), liver (cholecystography), gallbladder and bile duct, blood vessels of the heart, uethra, bladder, vagina and fallopian tubes etc.

Radiopaque substances can be divided into two categories : (i) water soluble and (ii) water insoluble contrast media.

Water soluble contrast media :

1. **Diatrizoic acid (U.S.P.)** :

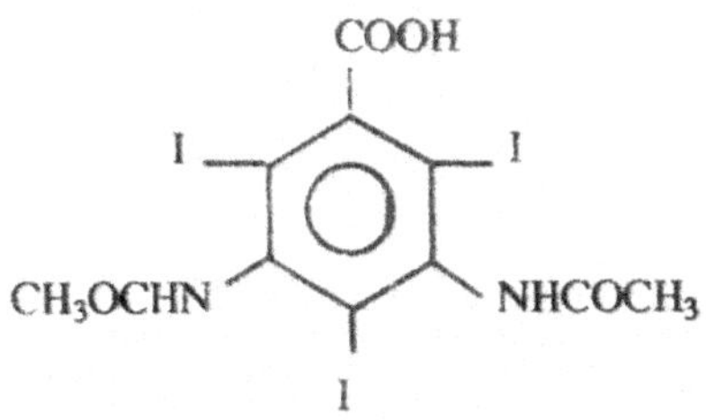

3, 5 bis-(acetylamino) 2,4,6 triiodobenzoic acid

Properties and uses : It is a white odourless powder, that is very slightly soluble in water and alcohol though more soluble in alkali hydroxide solutions. The sodium salt of diatrizoic acid being water soluble is used for radiological examination.

2. **Sodium diatrizoate (B.P., U.S.P.)** :

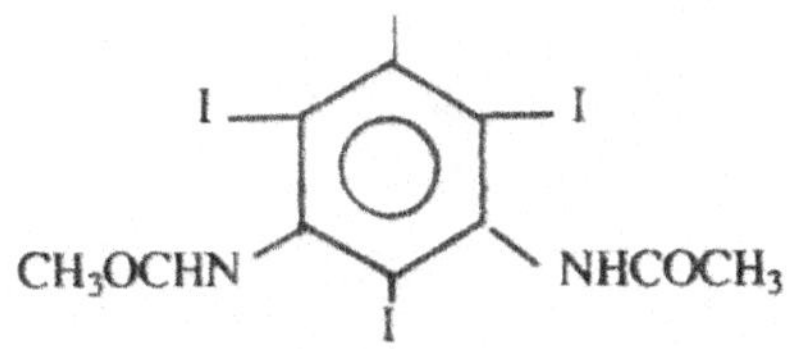

Sodium 3,5-diacetamino-2,4,6-triiodo benzoate

Properties and uses : It is white odourless powder, that is soluble in water and slightly soluble in alcohol, but insoluble in ether. Its aqueous solutions are neutral. The sodium diatrizoate oral solution is official in USP and is used in 30 to 75 ml dose for the examination of the gastrointestinal tract. The sodium diatrizoate injection, which is a sterile preparation containing 20, 25 or 50 % sodium diatrizoate with suitable buffers and calcium or disodium edetate as a stabilizer is employed in cholangiography, excretory urography hysterospingography and in pyleography.

Diatrizoate meglumine is a N-methygulcamine salt of diatrizoate and freely soluble in water. The injection of diatrizoate meglumine is 30, 60, 76 and 85 %, with a suitable buffer and stabilizer like calcium or disodium salt of edetate is employed for various diagnostic examinations. A diatrizoate meglumine and diatrizoate sodium injection preparation is also available and is official in USP.

3. Iothalamic acid (B.P., U.S.P.) :

5-(acetamido)-2, 4, 6-triiodo
N-methylisophthalanic acid

Properties and uses : It occurs as white odourless powder that is slightly soluble in water and alcohol but more soluble in solutions of alkali hydroxide. Sodium salt is highly water soluble. An iothalamate sodium injection is a preparation that is official in B.P. and U.S.P. and contains about 66.6 % of iothalamate sodium in water containing a small amount of buffer and disodium edetate as a stabilizer. It is used in angiocardiography in a dose of 40 to 50 ml, aeortography in a dose of 10 to 100 ml and urography in a 25 to 60 ml dose.

Iothalamate meglumine injection is yet another official preparation of Iothalamic acid, with meglumine prepared in water for the injection. The injections are available in 30 to 60 % strength, containing a phosphate buffer, and calcium or sodium edetate as a stabilizer. The injection is employed in cerebral angiography in 6 to 50 ml of a 60 % solution in excretory urography 25 to 60 ml of a 60 % solution and in peripheral pyelography upto 300 ml of 30 % solution. Yet another injection preparation called iothalamate meglumine and Iothalamate solution is official in USP, and is used as a diagnostic aid.

4. Iodipamide (U.S.P.) :

3, 3 (adipoyldiamino) bis (2,4,6 triiodobenzoic acid)

Properties and uses : It occurs as a white, odourless and crystalline powder that is very slightly soluble in water and less soluble in alcohol. The meglumine salt is highly soluble in water and hence is used in the form of an injection. The iodipamide meglumine injection is official in B.P., and U.S.P. The usual strength is 52 %. It is prepared in water with a suitable buffer and disodium edetate as a stabilizer. It is given intravenously in a 20 ml dose slowly to visualise the gall bladder and biliary duct.

5. Ipodate calcium (U.S.P.) :

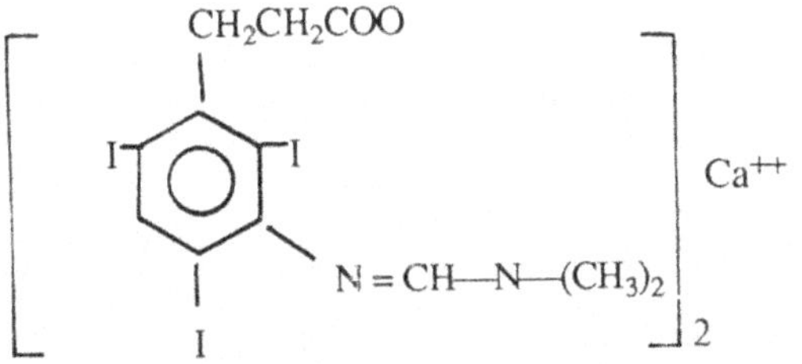

Calcium-3-[(dimethylamino methylene) amino] 2,4,6-triiodo hydrocinnamate

Properties and uses : It occurs as a white, crystalline powder. It is slightly soluble in water, alcohol and in chloroform. It is usually given in the form of an oral suspension, in the dose range of 3 to 6 g in cholecystography.

6. Ipodate sodium (U.S.P.) :

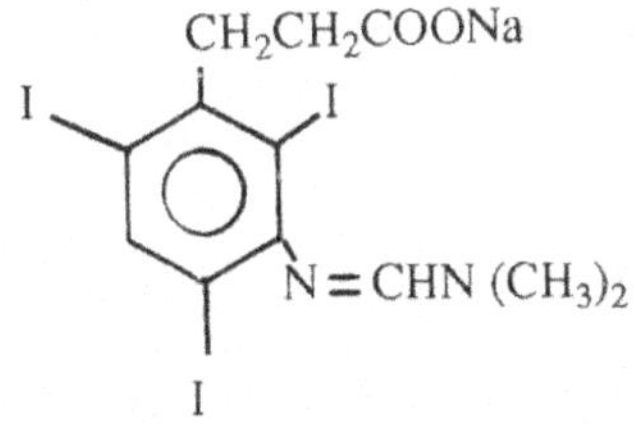

Sodium 3-[(dimethylamino)-methylene] amino]-2,4,6 tri-iodo-hydrocinnamate

Properties and uses : It is a white, odourless fine powder that is freely soluble in water and in alcohol. The compound is stable in the dry state and its aqueous solutions are reasonably stable. This drug should be protected from light. It is given orally as capsules (official in U.S.P.), in 3 to 6 g doses for cholecystography and in cholangrography.

Water Insoluble Contrast Media :

1. Iopanoic acid (B.P., U.S.P.) :

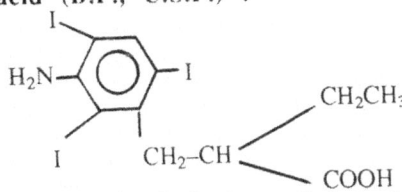

2-(3-amino 2,4,6 triodo benzyl) butyric acid

Properties and uses : It is a cream coloured and almost tasteless powder that gets affected by light, and hence should be protected. It is insoluble in water, but soluble in alcohol and in chloroform. It is also soluble in solutions of alkali hydroxides and carbonates. It is given orally and gets well absorbed through the gastrointestinal tract. It is mainly excreted in the feces. It is given in 3 to 6 g dose, in the form of tablets for cholecystography.

2. Propyliodone (B.P., U.S.P.) :

$$O= \text{[pyridine ring with I at 3,5 positions]} -N-CH_2-COOCH_2-CH_2-CH_3$$

Propyl, 3,5-diiodo-4-oxo-pyridine-1yl acetate

Properties and uses : It is a white, crystalline powder with a faint odour. It is practically insoluble in water but soluble in acetone and alcohol. It is used in a 50 % aqueous suspension (official in B.P.) or a 60 % oily suspension that is prepared aseptically in peanut oil for the examination of the bronchial tract (bronchography) for instillation in the trachea. The usual dose is 0.75 to 1 ml of oily suspension.

Iodised oil fluid injection (B.P.) : It is a sterile iodinated addition product of ethylesters of fatty acids from poppyseed oil. It occurs as a yellowish oily liquid with a characteristic odour. It contains about 37 to 39 % w/w of combine iodine. It is administered by the retrograde technique for the examination of the nasal sinuses and lymphatic system.

3. Iodophthalein (I.P.) :

$$\text{[Structure of disodium tetraiodophenolphthalein]} \cdot 3H_2O$$

Disodium salt of tetraiodophenolphthalein

Properties and uses : It is also called iodophthalein sodium or soluble iodophthalein. It occurs as a blue-violet crystalline powder, that is odourless and absorbs CO_2 an exposure and gradually darkens and decomposes. It is soluble in water, and slightly soluble in alcohol. It is used in cholecystography. The dose is 40 to 60 mg per kg of body weight, upto 5 g.

2. iophendylate (U.S.P.) :

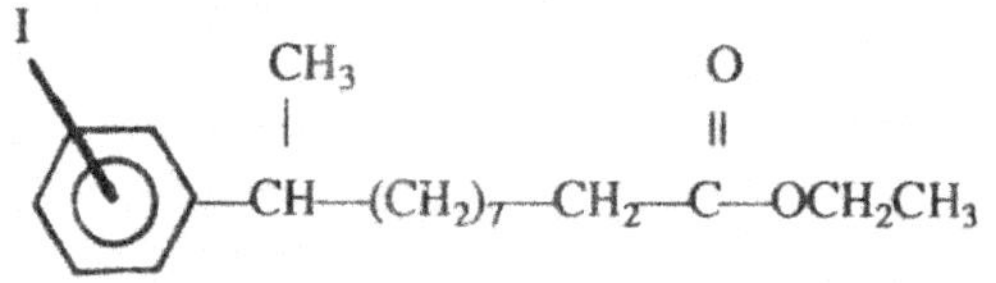

Ethyl 10-(iodophenyl) undecanoate

Properties and uses : It occurs as a pale yellowish odourless and viscous liquid. It is water insoluble, and soluble in most organic solvents and oils. The Iophendylate injection (B.P.) is a preparation containing a mixture of steriosomes of ethyl 10-(4-iodophenyl) undecanoate. It should be protected from light. It is available in 1, 3, 6 and 12 ml volumes, and is employed in doses of 3 to 12 ml, in myelography for the examination of disorders of the spinal cord.

Compounds used to test organ function

There are many compounds which are used selectively, in testing the function of various body organs like the kidney, liver, cardiovascular system and for various diagnostic purposes. The most commonly used agents are :

I. AGENTS FOR KIDNEY FUNCTION TEST

1. Aminohippuric acid (U.S.P.) :

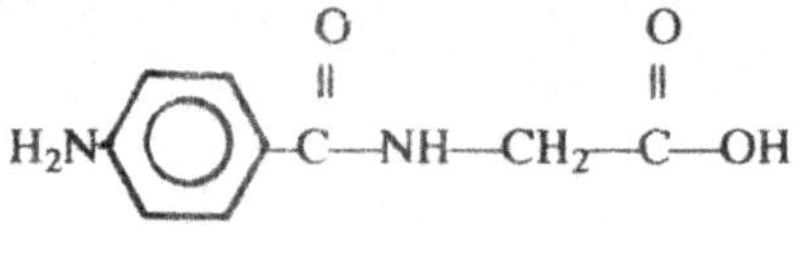

p-aminohippuric acid

Properties and uses : It is a white crystalline solid that darkens o exposure to light. It is soluble in water and alcohol and more soluble in acid and alkalies. The sodium aminohippurate injection is official in U.S.P. Sodium bisulphate is added to prevent the darkening of the solution. It is give intravenously in 2 g dose for renal function determination.
determination.

2. Indigocarmine (I.P.) or Indigotin disulphonate sodiun (U.S.P.) :

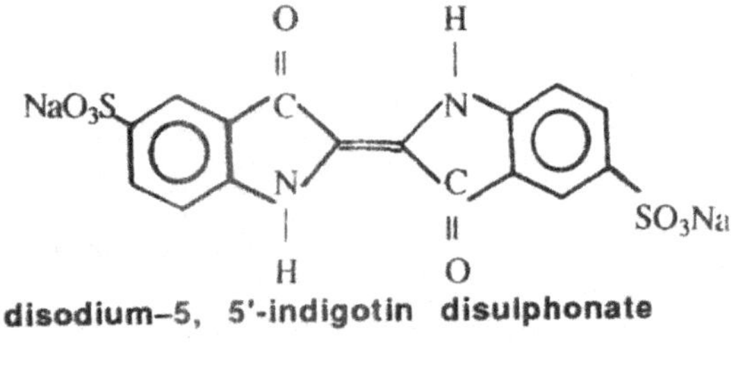

disodium-5, 5'-indigotin disulphonate

Properties and uses : It is a blue coloured powder or crystals, that is sparingly soluble in water and alcohol but almost insoluble in chloroform. It is affected by light. The solutions are sterilized by autoclaving or by the filtration method. It is administered intravenously, in a dose of 40 mg to test renal function (by estimating the rate of excretion in urine) and to locate the ureteral orificies. In the laboratory it is used as colouring agent

3. Phenolsulphophthalein (B.P.) :

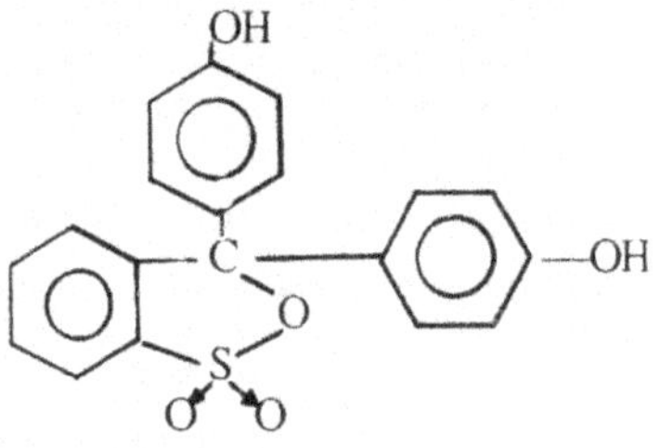

4, 4'- (3H-2, 1-benzoxanthiol-3-ylidene)-di phenol 5 ; 5 dioxi

It is known as phenol red.

Properties and uses : It is a red crystalline powder that is slightly soluble in water and alcohol but more soluble in solutions of alkali hydroxide and carbonates. The solutions for parenteral use are sterilized by autoclaving or by the filtration method. It is used intramuscularly or intravenously, in a 6 mg dose as a diagnostic aid to test renal function. In the laboratory it is also used as an acid-base indicator.

II. AGENTS FOR LIVER FUNCTION TEST

1. Sulphobromophthalein sodium (I.P., B.P., U.S.P.) :

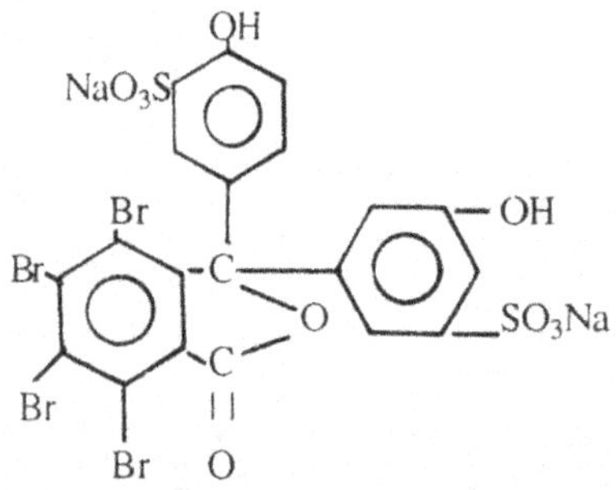

5-5'- (4, 5, 6, 7-tetrabromo-1, 3-dihydro-3-oxo isobenzofuran-
1, 1-diyl) bis (2-hydroxy benzene sulphonate

Properties and uses : It is a white, crystalline powder that is odourless and hygroscopic in nature. It is soluble in water, but insoluble in alcohol and acetone. Sulphobromophthalein sodium injections (official in I.P., U.S.P.) are usually available in a 50 mg per ml concentration. The injection is used in a ratio of 5 mg per kg of body weight given intravenously, as a diagnostic aid to test hepato-biliary function.

III. MISCELLANEOUS DIAGNOSTIC AGENTS

1. **Evans blue (I.P., U.S.P.) :**

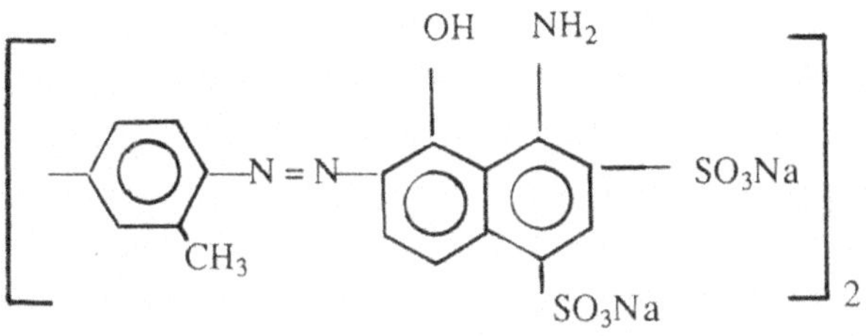

Properties and uses : It is a blue crystalline substance with greenish luster, or a brownish powder. It is very soluble in water but very slightly soluble in alcohol and practically insoluble in organic solvents. Its aqueous solutions are stable and they are sterilized by autoclaving. Evans blue injection (containing 0.45 % of Evans blue), is given intravenously to determine blood volume. The dye combines firmly with the plasma albumin (when injected), and the colour is directly proportional to its concentration.

2. **Fluorescein sodium (I.P., B.P., U.S.P.) :**

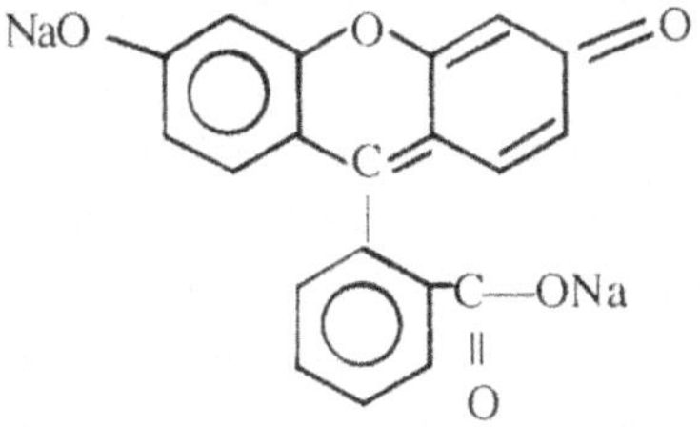

Properties and uses : It is an orange-red hygroscopic, and odourless powder. It is soluble in water but sparingly soluble in alcohol. The fluorescein sodium injection (official in U.S.P.) is available in 50 and 100 mg per ml solutions that are employed in 500 mg doses intravenously for the determination of circulation time. A fluorescein sodium ophthalmic strip is used to detect diseased or damaged areas of the cornea, like corneal ulcers, which get stained green.

3. Indocyanine Green (U.S.P.) :

Properties and uses : It is a dark blue-green or black-powder. Its solutions are deep emerald green in colour and acidic in nature. It is soluble in water and methanol. Its sterile solution, in a concentration of 5 mg in 1 ml, is used to determine cardiac output and in a ratio of 500 microgram per kg of body-weight it is used for the determination of hepato-biliary function.

4. Histamine acid phosphate (I.P.) :

It is histaminic agent that stimulates the secretory cells of the gastric mucosa. This drug (discussed under histaminics) is used to test the secretory function of the stomach.

5. Inulin (B.P.) :

It is a polysaccharide that is obtained from tubers. It occurs as a white, amorphus and hygroscopic powder that is sparingly soluble in water. The aqueous solutions for parentral use are sterilized by filtration. It is given intravenously at a slow rate to measure the glomerular filtration rate of the kidneys.

6. Pentagastrin (B.P.) :

It is a pentapeptide. Its aqueous solutions are sterilized by filtration, and are used to test gastric function. The pentagastrin injection is official in B.P.

7. Xylose (B.P.) :

It is a white powder with a sweetish taste. It is soluble in water. it is given orally for testing the absorbing capacity of the gastro intestinal tract.

8. Congored :

It is brownish red powder, soluble in water and ethanol, insoluble in ether. It is employed as a diagnostic aid in amyloidosis. It is also used as indicator in laboratory.

Chapter 22

DIURETICS

Kidneys are responsible for excretion of water, electrolytes and non-electrolytes from the body. The balance between the normal composition of blood, body fluids and acid-base is maintained by kidneys. Under certain conditions such as hepatic, renal or pulmonary disease or in the case of congestive heart failure salts and water is retained in the body resulting in oedema. Drugs are necessary to promote the excretion of water and electrolytes from body through kidneys. Such drugs are called diuretics.

Clinical uses of Diuretics :

Diuretics are valuable in treatment of edematous conditions associated with various dieseases. They are used in treatment of congestive heart failure, in pulmonary edema, in hypertension. They are also useful in the treatment of drug over dosages or drug poisonig by elimination through kidneys.

Diuretics are classified according to both the mode or mechanism of action and the chemical basis too. There are many useful agents belonging to the different chemical classes, acting by different mechanism. These are administered orally or parenterally.

A chemical Classification is as under :

1. Water and osmotic agents,
2. Acidifying salts,
3. Mercurials,
4. Sulphonamides
5. Thiazides and hydrothiazides
6. Miscellaneous agents.

I. WATER AND OSMOTIC AGENTS

Substances that are poorly reabsorbed by renal tubules and present in a higher concentration than the electrolyte in body fluid brings about elimination of water and electrolytes by osmotic pressure mechanism. Drinking of large quantities of water results in rapid dilution of blood and subsequently its urinary excretion ; but there is no excretion of electrolytes. However, certain non-electrolytes may be used as osmotic diuretics.

1. Urea (I.P., B.P., U.S.P.) :

$$H_2N-\underset{\underset{O}{\|}}{C}-NH_2$$

Properties and uses: It is a white crystalline powder, It is almost odourless It is almost odourless but may develop slight ammonical odour in the presence of moisture. It is freely soluble in water, less in alcohol and insoluble in chloroform. It must be kept in air-tight containers in cool and dry place. It is a excellent diuretic and is not absorbed by renal tubules and is excreted along with the fluid. It is non-toxic and large doses can be given orally. Solutions of 5 to 30 % urea along with 10% inverted sugar are used. Sterile lyophilized urea and inverted sugar solutions should be freshly prepared. It can be administered as an intravenous infusion too in the dose of 1 to 1.5 g per kg of body weight.

It also have keratolytic acton. (B.P.).

2. Mannitol (B.P., U.S.P.) :

$$HO-CH_2-CH-CH-CH-CH-CH-CH_2OH$$
(with OH groups on each CH)

Properties and uses : It is a white crystalline powder, is odourless and freely soluble in water and pyridine, and moderately soluble in alcohol. It is also soluble in alkaline solutions. Mannitol is not metabolised in body. It is filtered by glomerules but is not reasorbed, thus used as a diagnostic agent for kidney function. Mannitol when given intravenously 200 mg per kg body weight, causes cellular dehydration and thus initiates osmotic diuresis. The solutions are sterilized by autoclaving. Usual oral dose is 50 to 100 g given as a 25 % solution. Because of large doses required, osmatic diuretic have been replaced by other potent drugs.

II. ACIDIFYING AGENTS

Compounds like ammonium chloride, potassium nitrate or sodium acid phosphate produces diuretic effect. In the body the ammonium cations are covered into urea whereas the excess of anions (Cl^-, NO_3^-) are excreted. Along with the excess of anions some Na^+ and H^+ ions are eliminated leading to acidosis. The effect of the compounds through this mechanism is very short and weak and hence these compounds are not much in use. The compounds from this class potentiate the action of marcurial diuretics. Ammonium chloride tablets are official in IP, BP, and USP, and the usual dose is 4 g daily. Potassium nitrate can be administered as entertic coated capsules, and the dose is 5 to 10 daily. Sodium acid phosphate is frequently used and the usual dose is 600 mg four times a day.

III. MERCURIALS

In the earlier days inorganic mercurials like mercurous chloride was used as diuretics. Then followed the organic mercurials. The organic mercurials are active orally as well parenterally and give rapid and reliable effect with less side effects. The mechanism of the action of mercurial diuretics consists in the blocking of the action of sulphadryl group on enzymes responsible for tubular reabsorption. When the enzymes is blocked there is marked elimination or excretion of water and sodium chloride. Administration of BAL blocks and reverses this action.

The only therapeutically used agent is :

1. **Mercaptomerin sodium (U.S.P.) :**

$$\text{structure: cyclopentane ring with } H_3C, CH_3, H_3C \text{ substituents and } NaOOC-, \text{ attached to } -C(=O)-NH-CH_2-CH(OCH_3)-CH_2-HgSCH_2-COONa$$

Properties and uses : It is a white powder, or an amorphous solid, hygroscopic in nature, and freely soluble in water and alcohol. It must be stored in tightly-closed containers. It is used parenterally and the usual dose is 130 mg in 1 ml once or twice a week.

The other organomercurials like mercurophyllin and mersalyl were sodium used earlier. They were official also. Because of toxicity and availability of other better drugs, these have been replaced.

IV. SULPHONAMIDES

Sulphonamides, the antibacterial agents were known to produce metabolic acidosis and alkaline urine. This observations led to the conclusion that this results due to the inhibition of an enzyme called carbonic anhydrase. This enzyme is responsible in the conversion of carbon dioxide and water into bicarbonate and hydrogen ions. In the renal tubule there is an exchange of hydrogen ions for sodium ion and thus sodium and bicarbonate ions are excreted in urine. Inhibition of the carbonic anhydranse enzyme supresses the hydrogen-sodium ion exchange and acidosis results. These studies led to the discovery of new diuretic compounds containing sulphamido groups. Thus the natriuretic (excretion of sidium ions) first and then saluretic (excretion of sodium and chloride ions) action compounds were evolved. Amongst the number of compounds studied and tried, some have clinical utility. These are :

1. **Acetazolamide (I.P., B.P., U.S.P.)** :

$$CH_3C(=O)-HN-\underset{S}{\underset{\|}{\overset{N-N}{\diagup\diagdown}}}-SO_2NH_2$$

N-[5-sulphomoyl-1, 3, 4 thiadiazole-2-yl) acetamide

Properties and uses : It occurs as white to yellowish white crystalline powder, slightly soluble in water and alcohol. It is preserved in tight light-resistant containers. It is rapidly absorbed by the stomach, reaches peak level within 2 hours and is eliminated unchanged. It is used in the treatment of moderate congestive heart failure, and in the treatment of petitmal and glaucoma. It is used in the form of tablets, usual dose is 250 mg daily. Its sodium salt is official in U.S.P. and used parenterally. Intravenous or intramuscular dose is 250 mg of acetazolamide base.

2. **Dichlorphenamide (B.P., U.S.P.)** :

[Structure: benzene ring with Cl at positions 4,5; H_2NO_2S and SO_2NH_2 at positions 1,3]

4,5 dichlorobenzene 1, 3-disulphonamide

Properties and uses : It is an almost white crystalline powder with a slight odour. It is insoluble in water and chloroform and moderately soluble in alcohol. However, it is soluble in solutions of alkali hydroxides. It is used in the form of tablets in the treatment of glaucoma and the usual dose is 25 to 50 mg 1 to 3 times a day. It is a carbonic anhydrase inhibitor and causes more excretion of chloride than acetazolamide.

3. **Chlorthalidone (I.P., B.P., U.S.P.)** :

[Structure: isoindolinone ring with OH and NH, attached to benzene ring bearing Cl and SO_2NH_2]

2 chloro–5–(3 hydroxy 1 oxosoindolin–3–yl) benzenesulphonamide

Properties and uses : It is a creamy white crystalline powder, insoluble in water, and sparingly soluble in alcohol. It dissolves in solutions of alkali hydroxides. The drug is similar to benzothiadiazenes. It interferes with renal tubular reabsorption of sodium and chloride. It is used in the form of tablets, usual diuretic dose is 100 to 200 mg daily.

4. **Furosemide (I. P., B. P., U. S. P.) :**

4 chloro-N-furfuryl-5-sulphomyl anthranilic acid

This is a sulphonamide derivative of unthranilic acid. The drug acts by inhibiting reabsorption of Na^+ ions.

Properties and uses : It occurs as an almost white crystalline powder, insoluble in water and chloroform, and soluble in acetone and solutions of alkali hydroxides. It must be preserved in tight containers and protected from light. It is a potent diuretic and has a rapid onset of action. It is used orally in the form of tablets, and the usual dose is 40 to 120 mg daily. Injections are prepared by using its sodium salt and are sterilized by autoclaving or filtration method.

V. THIAZIDES AND HYDROTHIAZIDES

The molecular modification of benzene disulphonamide led to the development of effective saluretics of thiazides and hydrothiazides series. They reduce carbonic anhydrase activity and inhibit the reabsorption of electrolytes. This results in more-excretion of sodium, bicarbonate and chloride ions.

Hydrothiazide differs from thiazide in having 3, 4-bond saturated. This results in a 10-15 times of higher potent diuretic activity. Important structural features in both categories include (i) chloro or trifluro methyl (CF_3) group at postion 6, (ii) free or easily cleavagable sulphomyl group at position 7, (iii) cyclopentylmethyl or dichloromethyl or trifluromethyl,thiomethyl at position 3 and (iv) small alkyl (methyl) group at position 2.

Chlorothazide   Hydrochlorothiazide

1. Chlorothiazide (B.P., U.S.P.) :

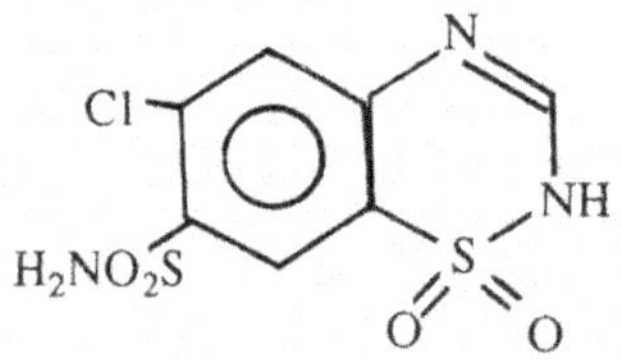

6-chloro-2H-1, 2, 4-benzothiadiazine
7-sulphonamide, 1, 1-dioxide

Properties and uses : It is an almost white crystalline powder, slightly soluble in water, insoluble in ether and chloroform and soluble in solutions of alkali hydroxides and dimethyformamide. It inhibits the renal tubular reabsorption of sodium and is effective orally. It has rapid onset of action and lasts for 6 to 12 hours. It is used singularly or in conjunction with mercurials for management of congestive heart failure. It is also useful in the management of hypertension. It is used in the form of tablets. Usual antihypertensive dose is 250 mg 3 times a day, diuretic dose is 0.5 g to 2.0 g daily as per the response of the patient.

2. Hydrochlorothiazide (I.P., B.P., U.S.P.):

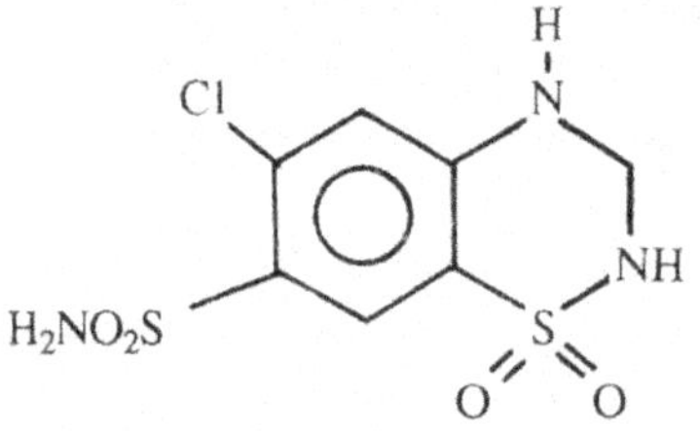

6-chloro 3, 4-dihydro 2H 1, 2, 4 benzothiadiazine
7-sulphonamide 1, 1-dioxide

Properties and uses : It occurs as almost white crystalline powder, practically insoluble in water and chloroform, sparingly soluble in alcohol but soluble in solutions of alkali hydroxides. It is used similar to chlorothiazides but is more potent in action. It is used in the form of tablets, usual diuretic dose is 25 to 100 mg daily.

3. Bendrofluazide (I.P., B.P., U.S.P.) :

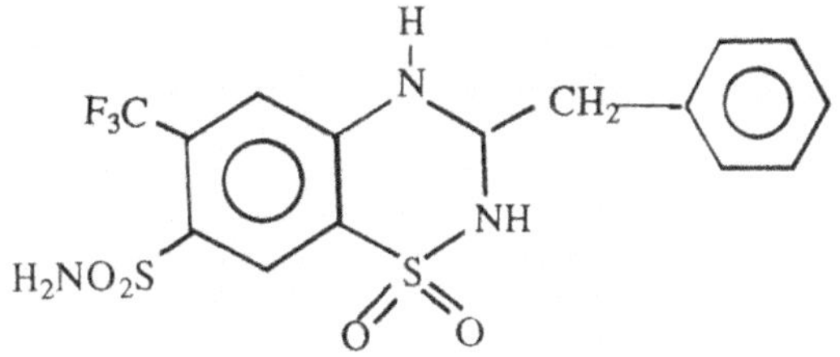

**3-benzyl-3, 4-dihydro-6-trifuromethyl 2-H-1,
2, 4-benzothiadizine-7sulphonamide 1, 1-dioxide**

Properties and uses : It occurs as a white crystalline powder, insoluble in water and chloroform, soluble in alcohol and freely soluble in acetone. It is a more potent diuretic than other thiazides and is used in the form of tablets. The usual dose is 2.5 to 10 mg daily.

4. Cyclopenthiazide (B.P., U.S.P.) :

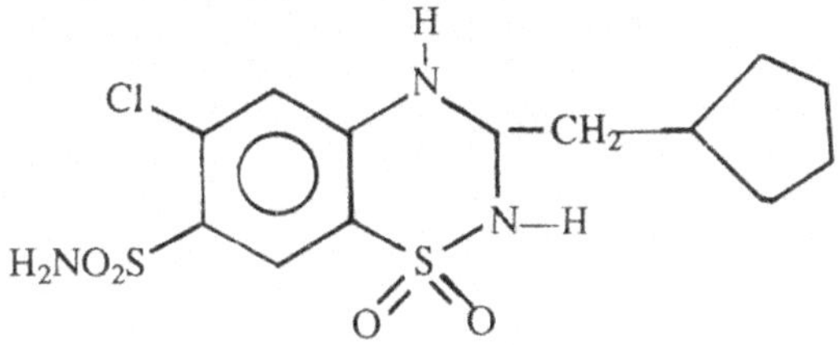

**6-chloro-3-cyclopentylmethyl 3, 4-dihydro
1, 2, 3-benzothiadiazine 7-sulphonamide1, 1 dioxide**

Properties and uses : It occurs as a white powder, insoluble in water, soluble in alcohol and acetone. It is used in the form of tablets, and its usual diuretic dose is 250 to 600 micrograms daily.

5. Polythiazide (B.P., U.S.P.) :

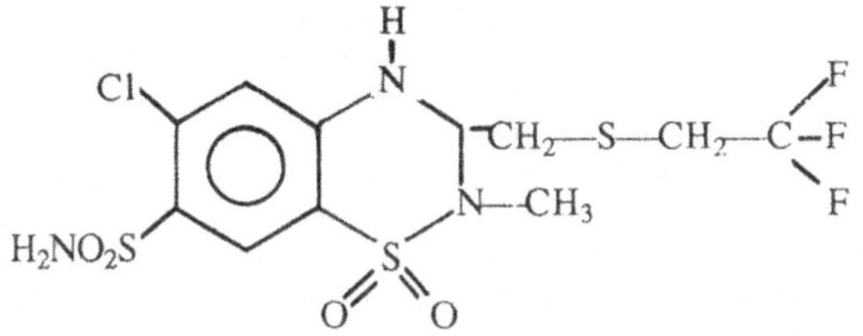

**6-chloro-3-4-dihydro-2-methyl-3-(2,2,2 trifluroethyl   thiomethyl)
1,2,4 benzothiadiazine-7-sulphonamide 1, 1-dioxide**

Properties and uses : It is white crystalline powder, odour alliaceous insoluble in water and chloroform, soluble in alcohol. It is used in the form of tablets and the usual diuretic dose is 1 to 4 mg daily.

6. Hydroflumethazide (B.P., U.S.P.) :

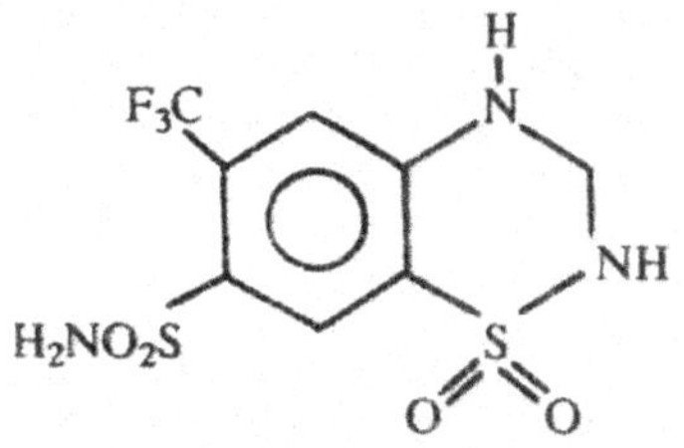

3, 4-dihydro-6-trifluromethyl-2-H 1, 2-benzothiadiazine 7-sulphonamide 1. 1 dioxide

Properties and uses : It occurs as a white shining crystal or crystalline powder. It is very springly soluble in water, but is soluble in alcohol. It is used in the form of tablets and the usual dose is 25 to 100 mg daily.

VI. MISCELLANEOUS AGENTS

Aldosterone is a hormone secreted by the adrenal cortex and is responsible in controlling electrolyte and water excretion through the kidneys. In the absence of this hormone the electrolytes and water is not reabsorbed and this develops into a condition called the diabetic inspidus (watery urine). Attempts have been made to block aldosterone activity or to inhibit biosynthesis which would result in diuresis and such agents are called aldosterone antagonist.

1. Spironolactone (B.P., U.S.P.) :

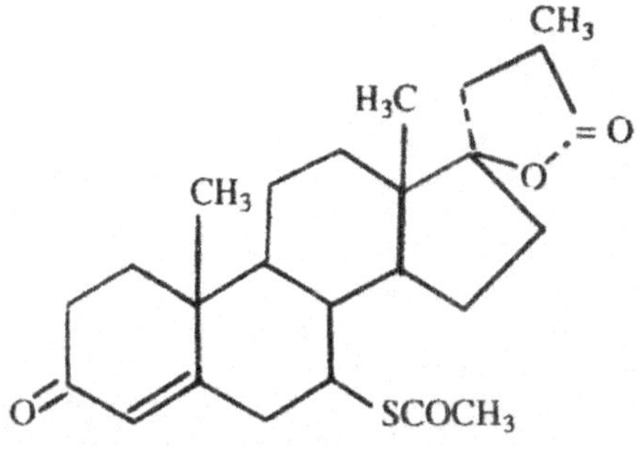

Properties and uses: It is a creamy white powder with characteristic odour, insoluble in water, moderately soluble in alcohol and freely soluble in chloroform. It is protected from light as it is sensitive to it. It is used in the form of tablets as a diuretic. The usual dose is 100 to 400 mg daily. It increases the excretion of sodium ions with less of potassium ions.

2. **Triampeterene (B.P., U.S.P.)** :

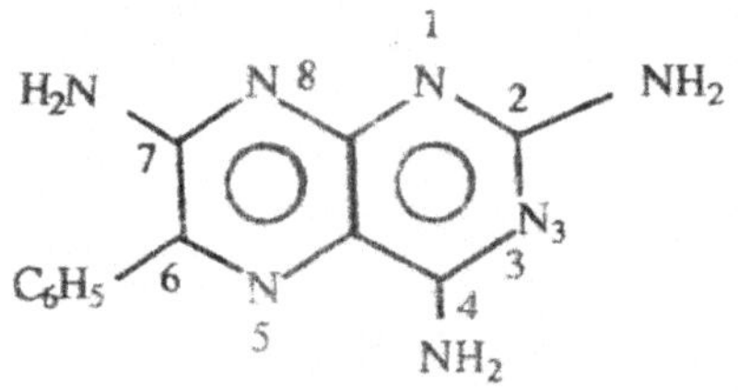

2, 4, 7-triamino-6-phenyl peteridine

Properties and uses: It is a yellow crystalline powder, sparingly soluble in water, less in alcohol and chloroform. It acts by inhibiting aldosterone and brings about the excretion of sodium and chloride in equivalent amount. It is used in the form of capsules and the usual dose is 150 to 250 mg daily in divided doses.

3. **Amiloride hydrochloride (B.P.)** :

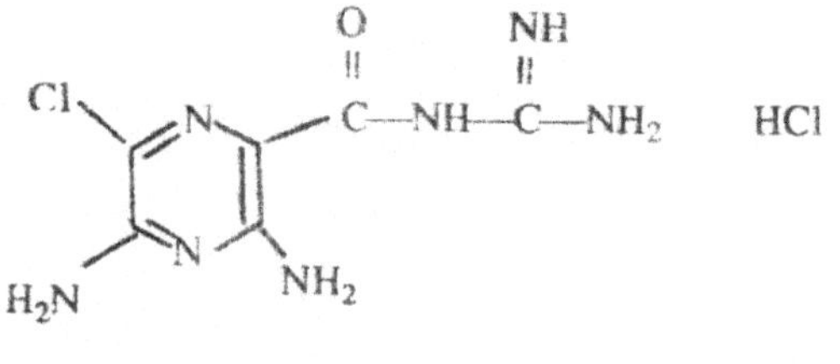

N-amidino-3, 5-diamino-6-chloropyrazine
2-carboxamide hydrochloride

Properties and uses: It is a pale yellowish greenish powder, sparingly soluble in water, less in alcohol and insoluble in chloroform. It should be protected from light. As a diuretic its dose is 5 to 10 mg daily in the form of tablets.

The site of action of triameterine and amiloride is the distal tubule. They block reabsorption of Na^+ and increase excretion of Na^+ and Cl^- in urine.

4. **Ethacrynic acid (I.P., B.P., U.S.P.) :**

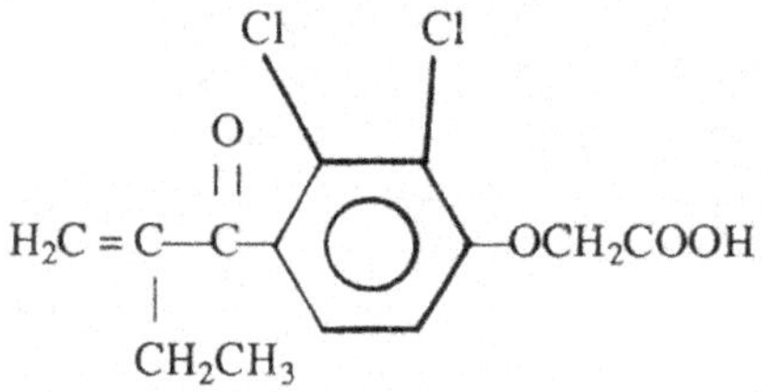

$$H_2C=C(CH_2CH_3)-C(=O)-C_6H_2(Cl)_2-OCH_2COOH$$

[(E-2, 3 dichloro 4 (2-ethylacryloyl) phenoxy] acetic acid

It is a derivative prepared from phenoxyacetic acid. It acts by inhibiting sulphydryl enzyme responsible for tubular reabsorption of Na^+ ions.

Properties and uses : It occurs as white crystalline powder, sparingly soluble in water but freely in alcohol, ether and chloroform. It should be stored in tight containers. The drug is given orally and its usual diuretic dose in 50 to 200 mg daily in the form of tablets.

The extract of tea and coffee were known to exhibit diuretic activity since long. This led to the development of xanthine derivatives as diuretics. Aminophylline, theophylline and theobromine show diuretic activity. These drugs have been replaced clinically by better and more potent drugs.

Chapter 23

DRUGS AFFECTING SUGAR METABOLISM

the condition arising due to abnormal metabolism of carbohydrate, fat and protenies. It is a characterised by hyperglycaemia (excessive sugar in the blood, than the threshold value) and glycosuria (presence of sugar in urine.) There are other symptoms also like polyuria, fatigue, thrist etc. The disease is caused by a deficiency of insulin, a protein hormone secreted by the beta cells of the *slet of langerhas*. This hormone is responsible for proper carbohydrate metabolism. When the blood sugar level is more than the threshold value, it (sugar) gets excreted in the urine and glycosuria results. Besides glucose, ketone bodies are also excreted in urine. In order to control the blood sugar level and to treat the symptoms of the disease, hypoglycaemic agents are used.

The hypoglycaemic agents, which are in use, belong to two main categories : (i) insulin and its preparations (ii) synthetic oral hypoglycaemic agents.

Insulin and its preparations

There are number of insulin preparations. These have been developed to give a desirable onset of action and prolonged duration of action.

Insulin (B.P.) : It is a specific antidiabetic principle, isolated from the pancreas of cattle like ox, pig and purified by precipitation at the isoelectric point.

Chemically, it is a polypeptide containing two chains A and B of 21 and 30 amino acids respectively, which are linked through the disulphide linkage of constituent amino acids. It contains about 0.3 to 0.6 percent zinc.

Properties : It is a white powder, slightly soluble in water, insoluble in alcohol, chloroform and ether. It is an amphoteric protein and dissolves in dilute solutions of mineral acids and bases, but it also undergoes degradation in the above solutions. It gets inactivated by proteolytic enzymes and is sensitive to heat and light. It must be kept in a well closed container and stored at a temperature not exceeding to 20°C.

Functions of Insulin : The important function of insluin are :

(i) It catalyses the synthesis and prevents unwanted breakdown of proteins, glycogen and lipids.

(ii) It regulates red-ox potential of cell surface and facilitates transport of glucose to adipose tissue, cardiac muscle and skeletal muscles.

(iii) It regulates glucose metabolism, stimulates lipogenseis, glycogenesis and controls glycogenolysis (break down of glycogen).

(iv) It lowers plasma amino acid levels and favours synthesis of proteins exhibiting anabolic activity.

Human insulin (B.P.) : It is a protein similar to natural antidiabetic hormone by human pancreas. It is produced from the pancreas of pig by enzymatic modifications or by microbial DNA technique. It contains not less than 26 units per mg calculated with reference to dried material.

Properties : It is a white or almost white powder, insoluble in ether, water, chloroform and alcohol. It dissolves in dilute acids and dissolves in alkaline media with degradation. It is stored in air-tight container and protected from light at a temperature not exceeding 20°.

INSULIN PREPARATIONS

Insulin injection (I.P., B.P., U.S.P.) : It is a sterile, aqueous acidified solution of specific antidiabetic principle of mammalian pancreas. It contains, 20, 40, 80 or more, units per ml. It may be prepared from insulin crystals, using water for injection and the pH is adjusted between 2.5 to 3.5 and contains 1.45 to 1.75 % v/v glycerine and 0.1 to 0.25 % phenol or cresol or a suitable bacteriostatic. It is a clear solution and sterilized by the filtration method and distributed in the final containers, which are sealed aseptically. It is stored below 8°.

Biphasic insulin injection (B.P., U.S.P.) : It is an insulin preparation which gives quick onset and longer duration of action. The preparation is a sterile suspension of crystalline insulin in a solution of porcine insulin. The preparation appears colourless and has the pH adjusted in 6.6 to 7.2 range. It is also standardised to have 40 or 80 units per ml.

Isophane insulin injection (I.P., B.P., U.S.P) : It is a sterile preparation, containing a buffered suspension of insulin, with a small proportion of protamine and zinc. It has a pH range between 6.9 to 7.5. It gives onset of action ranging from 30 to 60 minutes, with a duration of action of about 24 to 30 hours.

Globin zinc insulin injection (I.P.) : It is a sterile aqueous solution of specific antidiabetic principle of mammalian pancreas. It contains 40 or 80 units per ml ; in addition, it has 3.6 to 4.0 mg of globin for each 100 units and a quantity of zinc chloride equivalent to 0.3 mg of zinc per 100 units, 1.6 % v/v glycerine, and a suitable bacteriocide. It is an almost colourless liquid, practically free from turbidity and insoluble matter. pH is between 3.0 to 3.5.

Protamine zinc insulin injection (I.P.) : It is a sterile suspension of specific antidiabetic principle obtained from the mammalian pancreas. It contains 40 or 80 units per ml. It also contains 1.0 to 1.5 mg of protamine sulphate, 0.2 mg zinc, 10 to 11 mg of sodium phosphate per 100 units and 1.6 % w/v glycerine. A suitable bacteriocide is added. It is a colourless turbid liquid.

Insulin zinc suspension (I.P., B.P.) : It is a sterile buffer suspension of the specific antidiabetic principle, obtained from the pancreas of mammals and containing 40 or 80 units per ml. It is prepared by mixing 3 volumes of insulin zinc suspension (amorphous) and seven volumes of insulin Zinc Suspension (crystalline) aseptically. It is an almost colourless, turbid liquid with slightly alkaline reactions (pH 6.9 to 7.5). It is rendered isotonic with blood.

Insulin zinc suspension (amorphous) (B.P.) : It is a sterile, buffered suspension with zinc chloride of the specific antidiabetic principle, obtained from the pancreas of mammals. It contains 40 or 80 units per ml. The preparation is made isotonic with blood.

Insulin zinc suspension (crystalline) (B.P.) : It is sterile, buffered suspension with zinc chloride of specific antidiabetic principle, obtained from the pancreas of mammals. It is isotonic with blood. It contains 40 or 80 units per ml.

Containers for insulin preparations : The containers for insulin preparation are glass vials and are sealed in such way that successive doses on different occasions can be withdrawn.

Labelling of insulin preparations : The label of the insulin container must state the following :

1. Number of units per ml.
2. Date of manufacture and expiry date,(which should not be more than 24 months after the date of manufacture.).
3. The container must be thoroughly shaken before withdrawing the dose
4. The percentage of bacteriocide added and
5. The animal source or other source.

Storage : As insulin is affected by heat and light all insulin preparations must be stored at low temperatures between 2 to 8° in a dark place. It should not be allowed to freeze.

Actions and uses : Insulin is essential for the normal metabolism of carbohydrates. Its specific therapeutic use is in the treatment of diabetic mellitus in controlling the blood glucose levels. As the hormone is destroyed in the gastrointestinal tract, it is given subcutaneously or intramuscularly and not by intravenous route. Insulin injection is rapidly absorbed and exerts its maximum action within three hours. In severe diabetis. It is given as per the need of the patient before meals. *Globin zinc insulin suspension* is intermediate in its action in respect to onset of time and duration. *Protamine zinc insulin suspension* has a slower onset of action and can be given any time once a day as it has a longer duration of action. *Insulin zinc suspension* (amphorous) is short acting and insulin zinc suspension (crystalline) is a long acting insulin preparation. Insulin, in small doses along with other therapeutic agents is used to promote growth by improving appetite in anorexic patients. Insulin is used in psychiatric treatment as hypoglycemic shock therapy. It is also used to test the pituitary function.

Limitations of Insulin Therapy :

In diabetes mellitus it is essential to maintain blood sugar level by administration of insluin and related preparations or by other drugs. Since the treatment involved is of long duration, administration of insulin by parenteral route posses various problems. Some of the problems encountered in insulin therapy are :

(i) In the long term, there is a risk of development of tumours or boils at the site of injection.

(ii) Due to protein nature of insulin, it is likely to maifest allergic reactions in sensitive patients it may even give anaphylactic shock.

(iii) If the dose level is not properly adjusted it may lead to hypoglycaemic shock.

(iv) The antigenic property of insulin slowly leads to the production of insluin antibodies which bind to insulin and decrease its effectiveness.

(v) The long term use often produce visual disturbances, skin rashes and cardiovascular impairments.

Doses : Usual dose cannot be given for insulin preparations. The dose and the frequency of the dose is to be decided by the physician as per the requirements of the patient.

Precautions : An excess of insulin preparation, if taken by a diabetic patient, can cause hypoglycaemia (less sugar), which mainly affects the nervous system. In severe hypoglycemic condition, convulsions may occur. A diabetic patient must keep with him glucose or soluble carbohydrate, and use it immediately when hypoglycemic symptoms occur. Alternatively glycogen (B.P.) which is a polypeptide hormone obtained from beef pancreas is used to increase glucose level.

Synthetic oral hypoglycaemic agents

Though insulin and insulin preparations are very useful in treatment of diabetes mellitus, their limitations and inactivation in GIT encouraged medicinal chemists to develop potent, safe, efficaceous and orally active hypoglycemic agents.

Clinical observations, that certain organic compounds lower the blood sugar level are well recorded. Certain sulphonamides were found to produce hypoglycemia. This stimulated research for more effective, orally acting, synthetic hypoglycemic agents. The effective agents which mainly belong to two groups are : (i) sulphonylureas and (ii) biguanides.

SULPHONYL UREAS

They are derivatives of urea in which the aryl sulphonyl group is attached to one nitrogen while the aliphatic group is attached to another nitrogen atom. The general structure is

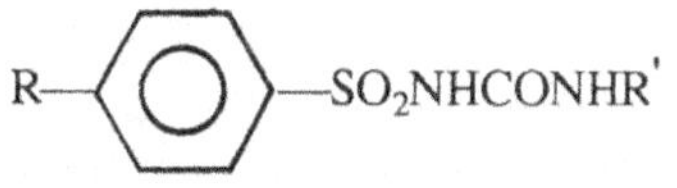

$$R-\text{C}_6\text{H}_4-SO_2NHCONHR'$$

where R may be methyl, carboxyl, chloro, etc., which influences the duration of action and R' aliphatic group of certain size. Maximal activity results when the alkyl group is of 3 to 6 carbon atoms.

Sulphonyl ureas increase the release of insulin from the functioning cells of the pancreas. They are also believed to inhibit glycogenolyses in the liver. However, these are ineffective when the pancreas are not functioning. Some clinically useful agents from this class are :

1. **Acetohexamide (B.P.U.S.P.)** :

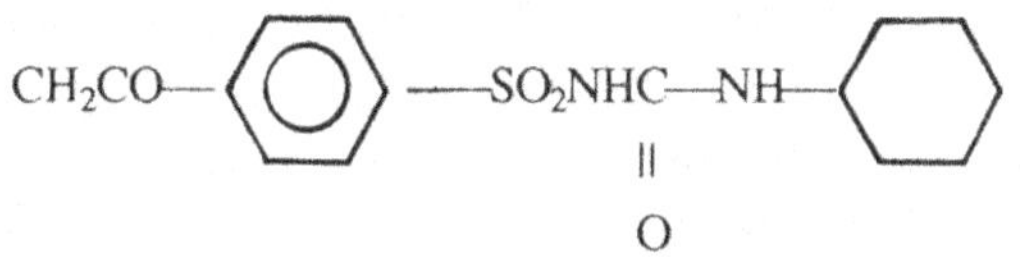

$$CH_3CO-\text{C}_6\text{H}_4-SO_2NHC(=O)NH-\text{C}_6\text{H}_{11}$$

1-(4-acetylbenzenesulphonyl)-3-cyclohexylurea

Properties and uses : It is a white crystalline odourless powder. It is almost insoluble in water, slightly soluble in alcohol and chloroform and more soluble in dilute solutions of alkali hydroxides. Acetohexamide tablets are given in 250 mg to 1 g dose once a day. It acts by stimulating insulin secretion.

2. **Chloropropamide (I.P., B.P., U.S.P.)** :

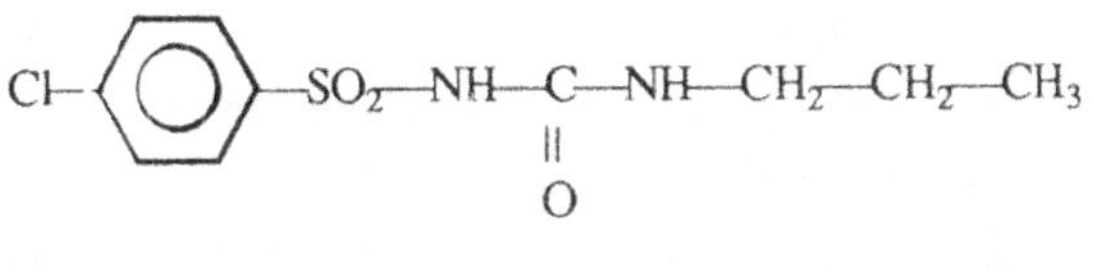

$$Cl-\text{C}_6\text{H}_4-SO_2-NH-C(=O)-NH-CH_2-CH_2-CH_3$$

1-(4-chlorobenzene) sulphonyl-3-propylurea

Properties and uses : It occurs as a white crystalline powder, odourless and tasteless. It is almost insoluble in water, soluble in alcohol and sparingly soluble in chloroform. It becomes soluble in alkali hydroxides. It is given as tablets in 100 to 250 mg dose once or twice a day for reducing blood sugar levels.

The effect of the drug usually lasts for 24 hours. There are fewer side effects with this drug.

3. Glibenclamide (B.P.) :

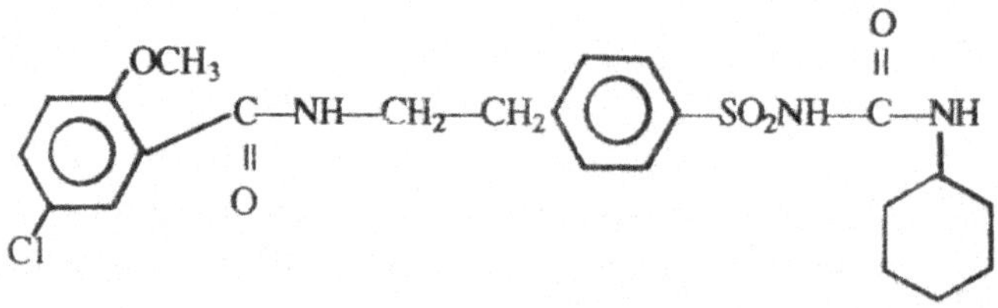

Properties and uses : It is a white odourless powder. It is light-sensitive and hence, should be protected. It is a potent and orally active hypoglycemic-agent and is given in 2.5 to 20 mg once daily, after food, in the form of tablets.

4. Tolazamide (U.S.P.) :

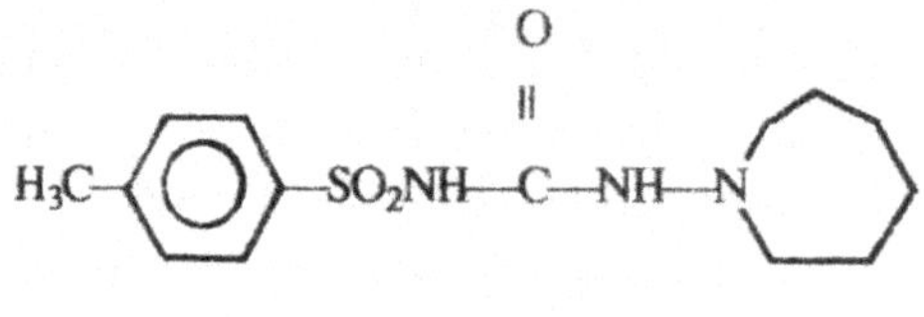

1-perhydroazepin-1-yl-3-p-tolylsulphonylurea

Properties and uses : It is a white to off-white crystalline odourless powder. It is slightly soluble in water and alcohol, but freely soluble in chloroform. Tolazamide tablets are given in a dose of 100 to 250 mg once a day to reduce blood sugar level. The drug is more potent than tolbutamide, with lesser side effects.

5. Tolbutamide (I.P., B.P., U.S.P.) :

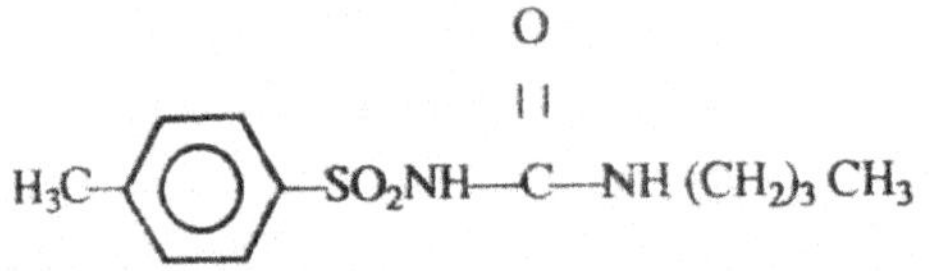

1-butyl-3-tosyl urea

Properties and uses : It is a white crystalline powder, odourless and slightly bitter to taste. It is insoluble in water, but soluble in alcohol, and chloroform. It is soluble in alkali hydroxide solutions and forms sodium or potassium salts which are freely water soluble. Tolbutamide tablets are given in a 500 mg dose twice a day. The sterile tolbutamide sodium (U.S.P.) is a preparation given intravenously in 1 g dose of tolbutamide over a 2 to 3 minutes period as a diagnostic aid in diabetes.

6 . **Glipizide** :

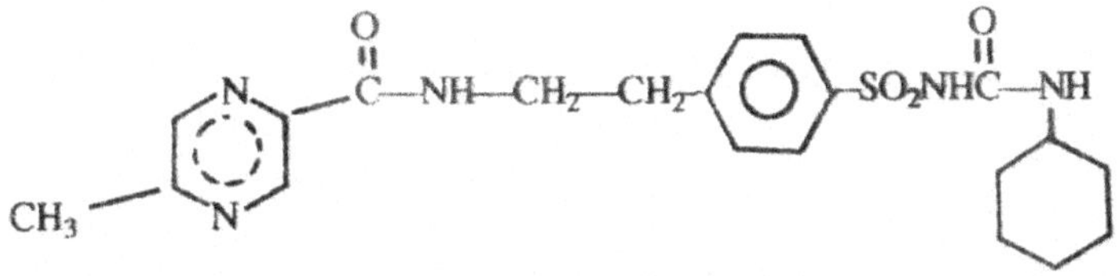

$$CH_3 \text{-pyrazine-} C(=O)\text{-NH-}CH_2\text{-}CH_2\text{-}C_6H_4\text{-}SO_2NHC(=O)\text{-NH-cyclohexyl}$$

Properties and uses : It is a white powder, odourless and is insoluble in water, alcohol, soluble in chloroform. It dissolves in dilute alkali solutions. It is given in tablet form. Usual strength is 5 mg.

BIGUANIDES

Biguanides are the compounds having two guanidino groups attached through –NH bond. For hypoglycemic activity there is arylalkyl group on one of the terminal nitrogen.

in
$$R-N-C=N-C-NH_2$$
$$\quad\;\; |\;\;\; |\;\;\;\; \|$$
$$\quad R'\;\; NH\;\; NH_2$$
moiety

R is alkyl, arylalkyl, pyridyl, thienyl or furanyl white R' is H for maximal activity. The biguanides act as an insulin supporting in their hypoglycemic action. They do not stimulate, insulin release and remain ineffective in absence of insluin. They are believed to act by (i) inhibiting intensinal absorption and transport of sugars. (ii) by potentiating action of insulin on glucose transfer (iii) by inhibiting glyconeogenesis and (iv) by affecting glucose uptake/or oxidative phosphorylation.

1. Phenformin hydrochloride (I.P., B.P.) :

$$\text{C}_6\text{H}_5\text{-CH}_2\text{-CH}_2\text{-NH-C(=NH)-NH-C(=NH)-NH}_2 \cdot \text{HCl}$$

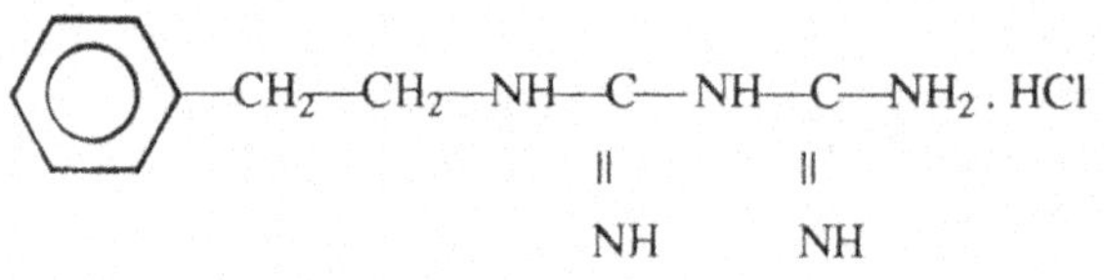

1-phenylethylbiguanide hydrochloride

Properties and uses : It is an almost white crystalline powder, bitter to taste, soluble in water and alcohol, insoluble in chloroform. It is used as an oral hypoglycemic in the form of tablets, the usual dose is 50 to 200 mg daily, in divided doses. It is given alone or with other hypoglycemic agents.

2. Metformin hydrochloride (I.P., B.P.) :

$$(\text{CH}_3)_2\text{N-C(=NH)-NH-C(=NH)-NH}_2 \cdot \text{HCl}$$

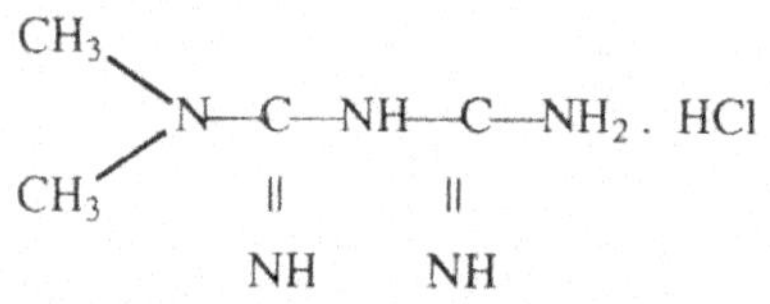

hydrochloride of 1, 1-dimethyl biguanide

Properties and uses : It is a white crystalline powder, almost odourless, freely soluble in water, less in alcohol. It is hygroscopic in nature. It should be stored in a tight container. It is used as an oral hypoglycemic in the form of tablets and the usual dose is 0.5 to 2.0 g daily in divided doses.

Chapter 24

LOCAL ANESTHETICS

Local anaesthetics are the drugs which produce an anaesthetic effect to a limited area of the body when applied externally or injected. They differ from general anaesthetics in the respect that they do not produce depression of the central nervous system which leads to unconsciousness. They act by intercepting the transmission of impulses along the nerve fiber and nerve endings. Thus insensitivity is produced around the area where they are applied or used and the perception of pain is not felt.

Local anaesthetics are of various types. Their differentiation is based upon the route and site of administration employed. They are as follows :

(i) **Surface or topical anaesthetics** : They produce an anaesthetic effect on skin or mucous membrane by blocking the nerve ending around that area.

(ii) **Infiltration anaesthetics** : These drugs are given by injection directly into the area that is subjected to operation.

(iii) **Spinal anaesthetic** : These drugs are injected within the dural membrane surrounding the spinal cord.

Furthermore, certain anaesthetics are used to produce a regional nerve block around the nerve trunk or ganglia, while some are injected into the subarachnoid cavity of the brain. Local anaesthetics are widely used in ophthalmology, dentistry, in minor surgical operations etc. Local anaesthetic agents should have a sufficient duration of action and less toxicity. They should have a good penetrating powder (for topical anaesthetics). A small amount of vasoconstrictor agents like adrenaline is incorporated in some preparations for infiltration anaesthesia.

Local anesthetics :

Mechanism of action : Many hypotheses on mechanism of action have been proposed. The precise mechanism explaining its action at molecular level is not yet known.

However, drugs produce local anesthesia by inhibiting and interfering membrane conductance of sodium ions. This is achieved by inhibiting the release of bond calciumions at the site and thus stabilize membrane to depolarization. Net result is that nerve impulse is not transmitted. It is also suggested that drugs combine with receptors on the inner surface of nerve membrane and inhibit conductance of nerve impulse.

A wide variety of chemical compounds exhibit feeble, moderate to strong local anaesthetic activity. They include hydroxy compounds, esters, amides etc. In general, aromatic pont - intermediate chain - amine part is considered to be anaesthesiophoretic in nature. The nerve impulse blocing properties can be arranged as lipophilic - intermediate - hydrophilic portion. Based on this, many synthetic compounds have been evolved.

Local anaesthetics can be classified into the following classes :

(I) Cocoa, cacaine and related compounds. (II) Esters of benzoic acid (III) Esters of p-amino benzoic acid (IV) Amides (V) Miscellaneous.

1. COCOA, COCAINE AND RELATED COMPOUNDS

Cocoa leaves (Erythroxylon cocoa) and related species of cocoa possess a strong numbening (local anaesthetic) activity. The leaves contains alkaloids like cocaine, cinnamoylcocaine, truxillines ecgonine etc.

1. Cocaine (B.P.) :

It is an alkaloid obtained from the leaves of *Erythroxylon cocoa* and other species, or obtained synthetically from ecogonin.

$$CH_2-CH-CH-C(=O)-OCH_3$$
$$| \quad\quad | \quad\quad |$$
$$NCH_3 \quad CH-O-C-C_6H_5$$
$$| \quad\quad | \quad\quad ||$$
$$CH_2-CH-CH_2 \quad O$$

Properties : It is an alkaloid having a tropane skeleton. It is a benzoic acid ester of (–) Ecogonine methyl ester. It is available as colourless crystals or white powder, odourless and slightly volatile. It is insoluble in water and more soluble in alcohol and the usual organic solvents. It is affected by light and hence should be protected. Saturated aqueous solutions are alkaline in nature.

COCAINE :

Action and Uses: It is the first local anesthetic discovered. The cocaine as base is used in the form of cream, ointment, paste etc;, as a hydrochloride salt it is employed in aqueous solution.

The solutions of cocaine hydrochloride are ordinarily stable but on heating lose it's potency. Solutions are sterilized by filtration method. It is incompatible with alkalis, silver nitrate. mercury salts. It is genrally used in 2 to 5 % strength for opical applications. The drug is not given in the form of injection because it is too toxic. Further, cocaine develops tolerance and is habit forming.

2 Tropacocaine : It is an alkaloid obtained from javanese cocoa or prepared synthetically by esterification of pseudotropine with benzoic acid. The hydrochloride salt has the same anaesthetic activity as that of cocaine.

II. ESTERS OF BENZOIC ACID :

Since cocaine is an ester of benzoic acid a number of benzoic acid esters with aminoalkyl or substituted aminoalkyl groups were prepared. Some of the active compounds from this class are :

3. Hexylcaine hydrochloride (U.S.P.) :

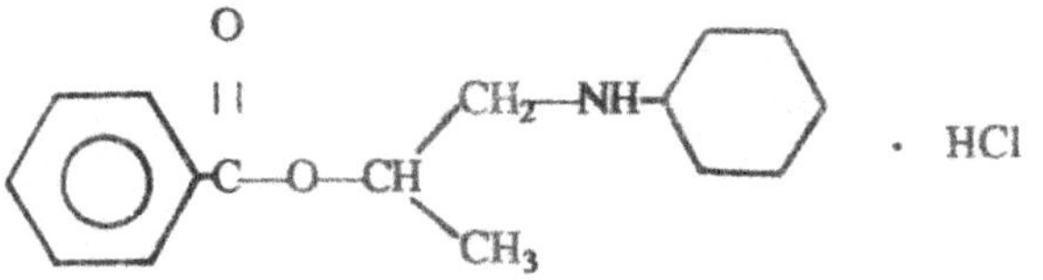

1-(cyclohexylamino) 2-propanol benzoate hydrochloride

Properties and uses : It is a white powder with a slight aromatic odour. It dissolves in water, dissolves freely in alcohol and chloroform. The aqueous solutions are acidic in nature. It is preserved in air-tight containers. It is used in infiltration anaesthesia as 10 % solution and as a nerve block anaesthesia in a 1-2 % solution. Its anaesthetic potency is equal to cocaine and it is used topically.

4. Cyclomethycaine sulphate (B.P.) :

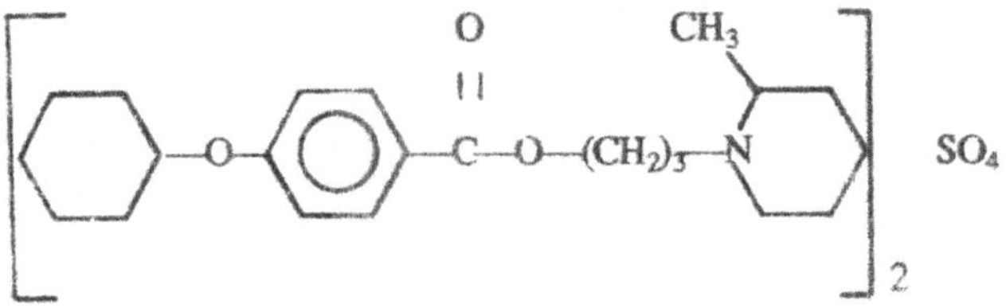

1-{3-4-(cyclohexyloxy) benzoyloxy] propyl }
-2-methyl piperidine hydrogen sulphate

Properties and uses : It is white crystalline powder, moderately soluble in water. The solutions can be sterilized by autoclaving as solutions are stable and retain it's potency. It is used topically in chemical burns, other burns, skin abrassions etc ; usually 0.25 to 1.0 % solutions are used.

5. Proximethacaine hydrochloride (B.P.) :

$$CH_3CH_2CH_2-C_6H_3(NH_2)-COO_2CH_2N-(C_2H_5)_2 \cdot HCl$$

2-diethylaminoethyl-3-amino-4-propoxybenzoate hydrochloride

Properties and uses : It is a white crystalline powder odourless soluble in water and insoluble in chloroform and ether. It dissolves in dilute alkali solutions. It is given in tablets in 5 mg dose. It is kept in closed container, protected from light and used in the form of eye-drops for local anesthetic effect.

III. ESTERS OF PARA-AMINO BENZOIC ACID

6. Benzocaine (I.P., B.P., U.S.P.) :

$$H_2N-C_6H_4-\overset{O}{\underset{\|}{C}}-O-C_2H_5$$

Ethyl 4-amino benzoate

Properties and uses : It can be readily prepared by the esterification of p-amino benzoic acid with absolute alcohol. It is available as a white crystalline powder, soluble in alcohol, chloroform and dilute acids, very slightly soluble in water. It is stable in air but is decomposed by alkali hydroxides. Incompatability occurs with resorcinol, bismuth subnitrate etc. As it is insoluble in water it is not used in the form of injections. It is less active than cocaine but its slower absorption makes it safer than other local anaesthetics. It is used for painful wounds after dental operations and to control or relieve the pain in gastric ulcers.

7. Procaine hydrochloride (I.P., B.P., U.S.P.) :

$$H_2N-C_6H_4-\overset{O}{\underset{\|}{C}}-O-CH_2-CH_2-N(C_2H_5)_2 \cdot HCl$$

2-diethylaminoethyl 4-aminobenzoate hydrochloride

Properties and uses : It is a white crystaline powder, soluble in water but less soluble in alcohol. It is stable in air. Aqueous solutions are acidic in nature. If it is intended for parenteral administration, it should be preserved in such containers so that the sterility of the product is maintained. Aqueous solutions are stable at the pH 3-6. Buffered solutions can be sterilised by autoclaving. It is the most widely used local anaesthetic as infiltration, spinal and nerve block anaesthesia as it has the least toxicity. Its duration of action is prolonged by adding a small amount of adrenaline. Injection of procaine and adrenaline is official and administered subcutaneously as 0.25 to 1.0 % solution and intraspinally upto 150 mg as 1 to 5 % solution.

8. Tetracaine hydrochloride (U.S.P.) :
(Amethocaine hydroxide) (B.P.)

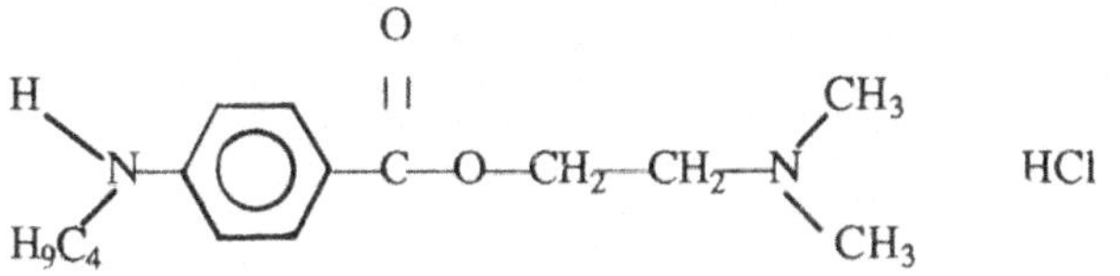

(2-dimethyl amino) ethyl-4-butyl amino) benzoate hydrochloride

Properties and uses : It is a white crystalline powder, very soluble in water, soluble in alcohol and insoluble in ether. Aqueous solutions are neutral to litmus. It is protected from light. It is used as a local anaesthetic in eyes in the form of 0.50 % solution and for nose and throat as 2.0 % solutions. Its injection is offical in U.S.P. Tetracaine base is also official in U.S.P. and used in the form of 0.5 % ointment for the eyes as local anaesthetic.

9. Butacaine sulphate (N.F.P.) :

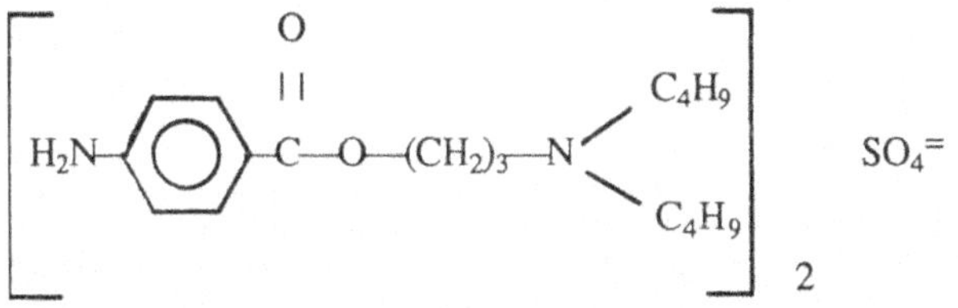

Sulphate of 3-di-n-butylaminopropyl-4-amino benzoate

Properties and uses : It is a white crystalline powder, dissolves in water and is more soluble in warm water. It is soluble in alcohol. The solutions can be sterilized by autoclaving. It finds uses in ophtha.

In the ester class of compounds, the bases are low melting solids. Their solubility is less and are in general less stable. They get affected easily by light. Their salts are soluble in water and solutions are stable at optimum pH. In some cases autoclaving cannot be used for sterilization as it higher temperature decomposition occurs. In such cases the filtration method is used for sterilization. Ester and salts belonging to this class must be protected from light.

IV. AMIDES

This category of compounds possess a potent local anaesthetic activity and are more stable than the ester class of compounds.

10. Lignocaine hydrochloride (lidocaine hydrochloride) (I.P., B.P, U.S.P.) :

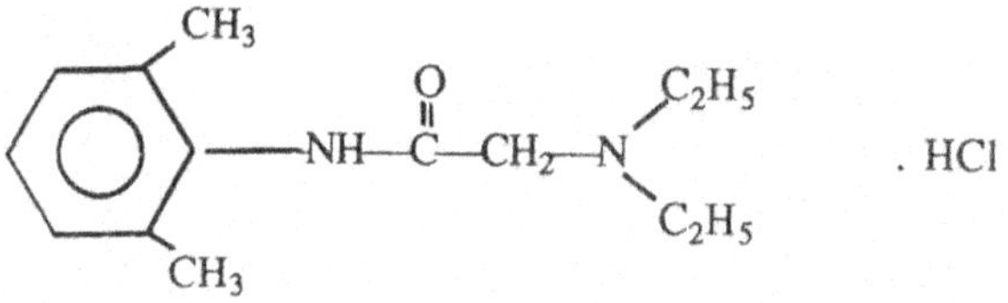

2-diethylaminoaceto-2'-6' xylidide hydrochloride

Properties and uses : It is a white crystalline powder, very soluble in water, freely soluble in alcohol and chloroform. The aqueous solutions are stable and can be sterilized by autoclaving. It has a rapid onset of action and the effects can be prolonged by the incorporation of small amounts of adrenaline.

A 2 % solution is used for application to the muscous membrane. It is also used as infiltration anaesthesia in the concentration of 0.5 %. It is given in the treatment of cardiac arrhythmias where in 5 to 100 mg are administered intravenously in 2 minutes followed by an intravenous infusion at the rate of 1 to 2 mg per minute as per the need of the patient. Lignocaine base is official in U.S.P. and used in the form of ointments and creams as local anaesthetic.

11. Prilocaine hydrochloride (B.P., U.S.P.) :

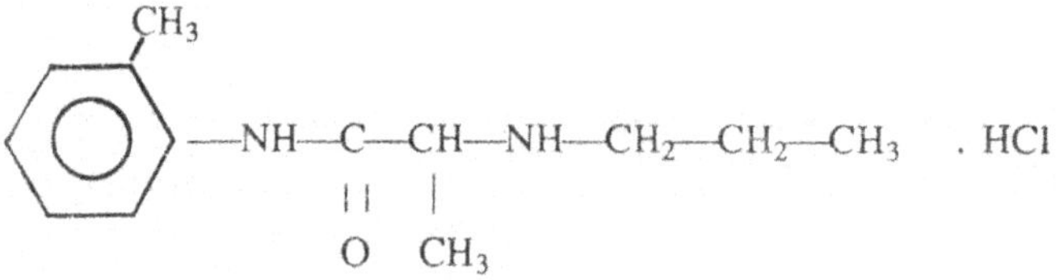

2-propylamino-propiono-o-toluidide hydrochloride

Properties and uses : It is a white crystalline powder, soluble in water and alcohol. The aqueous solutions are sterilized by autoclaving or by the filtration method. It is used in the form of injection in 1 to 2 % strength for nerve block.

12. **Bupivacaine hydrochloride (B.P., U.S.P.) :**

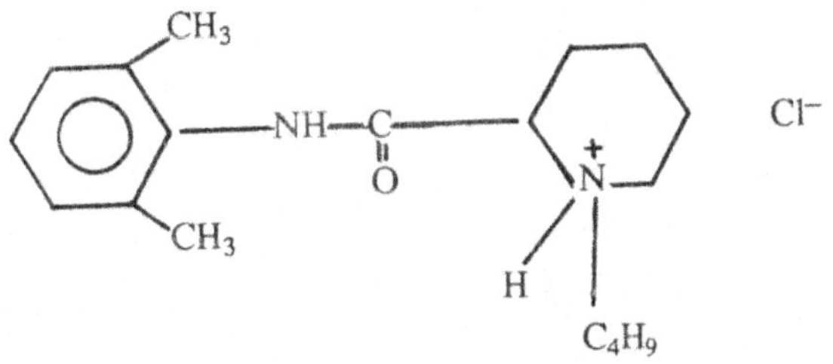

1-butyl-2-piperidyl farmo-2'-6'-xylidine hydrochloride

Properties and uses : It is available as white crystalline powder, soluble in water, but more soluble in alcohol. Aqueous solutions are acidic in nature and are sterilized by autoclaving or by the filtration method. It is used for topical and infiltration anaesthesia. It has a longer duration of action.

13. **Cinchocaine hydrochloride (Dibucaine) (I.P., B.P., U.S.P.) :**

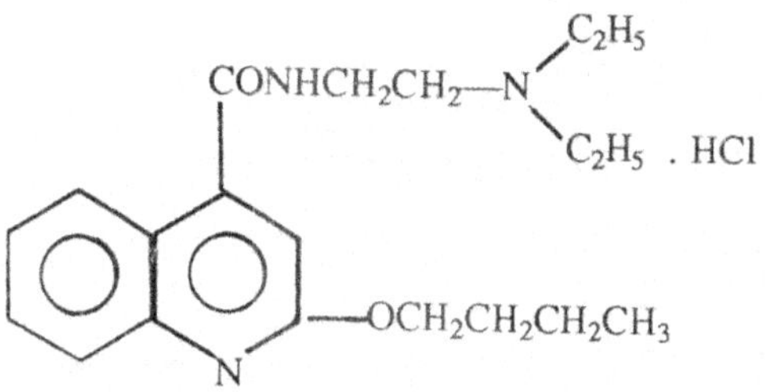

2-butoxy-N-(2-diethylaminoethyl) quinoline-4-carboxamide

Properties and uses :

It is a white crystalline powder, hygroscopic, in nature, very soluble in water, freely soluble in alcohol and chloroform. Aqueous solutions are acidic to litmus. It darkens on exposure to air. It should be preserved in tight, light-resistant containers. It is more active as a local anaesthetic than cocaine when applied to mucous membrane. When used subcutaneously it is more potent than procaine but it is more toxic than procaine and cocaine when administered intravenously. It is used in the form of solutions, aerosols, injections and ointments.

V. MISCELLANEOUS AGENTS

14. **Phenacaine hydrochloride (U.S.P.)** :

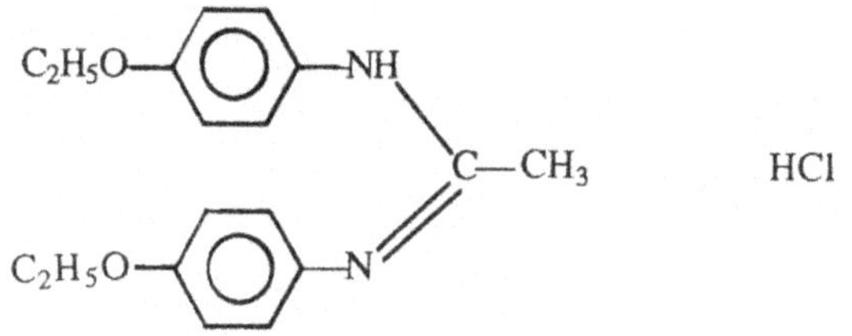

N, N-bis (p-ethoxyphenyl) acetamidine hydrochloride

Properties and uses : It is a white crystalline powder, soluble in water, freely soluble in alcohol, insoluble in chloroform. The solutions are incompatible with alkaloidal precipitating agents and alkalies. Usually a 1.0 % solution is used for producing local anaesthesia for the eye.

15. **Dyclonine hydrochloride (U.S.P.)** :

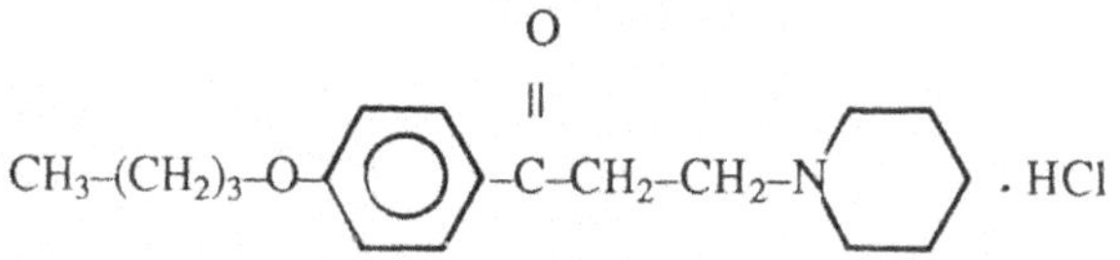

4-butoxy-3-piperidinopropiophenone hydrochloride

Properties and uses : It is a white crystalline powder, soluble in water and alcohol. Aqueous solutions are stable in an acidic media. It is useful for topical applications on skin or mucous membrane. It has a rapid onset of action and has a duration of action between 20 minutes to 1 hour.

16. **Clove oil (I.P., B. P.)** :

Properties and uses : It is a volatile oil obtained from clove and contains 85 to 90 % eugenol. It occurs as colourless or pale yellow liquid. It darkens and becomes thick by ageing and exposure to air. It is soluble in alcohol. Eugenol is official in U.S.P. Clove oil and eugenol are used as anaesthetcs in dentistry.

Chapter 25

STEROIDAL DRUGS AND STEROIDAL HORMONES

Steroids are the complex polynuclear compounds and are widely present both in the plant and animal kingdom. They have in common a tetracyclic nucleus on to which various functional moieties and groups are attached. Because of the rigid chemical structures, steroids have some common physical and chemical properties.

The basic ring structure and the sequence of numbering is shown below :

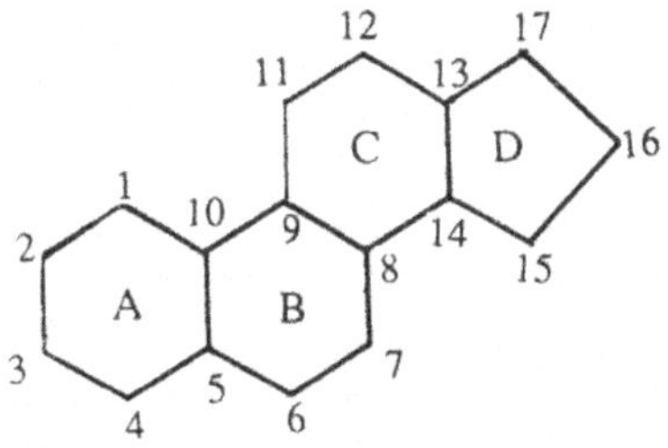

The ring, A, B and C are six numbered and ring D is five membered. In most steroids the ring B and C and D are transfused while ring A and B may be cis or trans. When groups are shown by a thick line as beta (β) and when they are below the plane they are shown by dotted line and termed as alpha (α). Nearly all the steroids are named as the derivatives of cholestane, androstane, *pregnane* and estrane. In cholestane there is 5α (ring A/B trans) with 27 carbon, in androstane the ring A/B is trans (thus 5 α androstane) and contains 19 carbon atoms, in pregnane (5 α pregnane) there are 21 carbon atoms with two carbon side chain attached at position 17. Estrane has 18 carbon and there is no angular methyl group attached to position 10. Some representative examples of steroidal agents of biological importance are covered under the following categories :

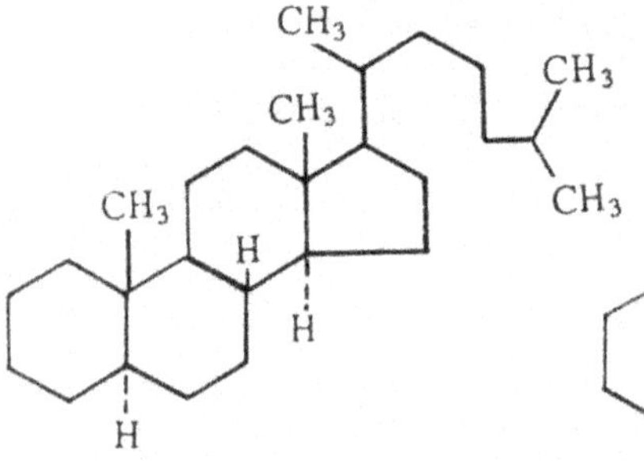

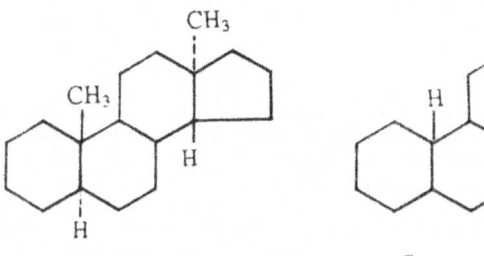

5 α-Cholastane 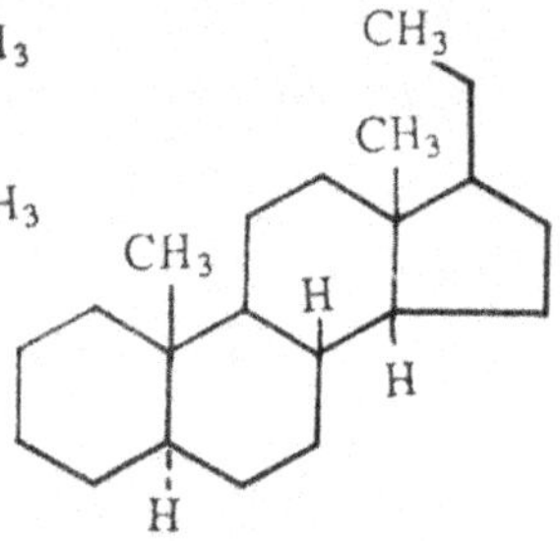   5 α-pregnane

5 α-adrostane 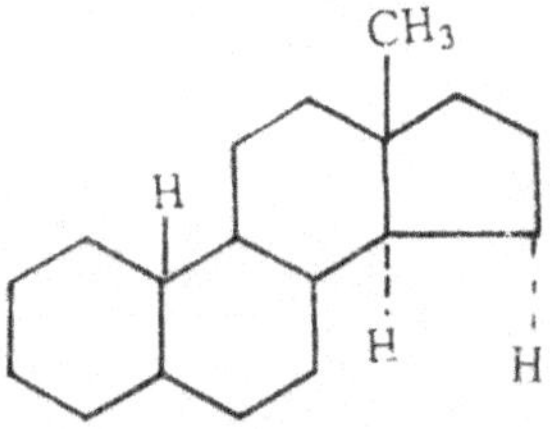   5 α-estane

STEROLS

These are alcohols and they occur in free or in conjugated form in plant and animal kingdom mainly in tissue, oils and fats. They give characteristic colour reactions e.g. Lieberman-Burchard which is used for their identification. They are in general solids insoluble in water but soluble in organic solvents. Some important sterols are :

Cholesterol (U.S.P.) :

It is found in plants and animals. Nerve cells, brain and gall stones contain large amounts of it. It occurs as white-pale yellow odourless, flakes or granules. It is insoluble in water, sparingly soluble in alcohol and more in organic solvents. Biologically it is a precursor of almost all steroidal hormones. A high level of cholesterol in blood is considered harmful as it leads to atheriosclerosis and other cardiovascular diseases. Pharmaceutically cholesterol is used as an emulsifying agent.

Stigmasterol :

It is present in soyabean oil in considerable amount. Its physicochemical properties are similar to cholesterol. It is used as a source for preparation of progesterone and a number of other steroidal drugs.

Ergosterol : It occurs in cryptograms and in small amounts in phanerograms.

It is used as a precursor for synthesizing vitamin D, wherein various sources are used for irradiation.

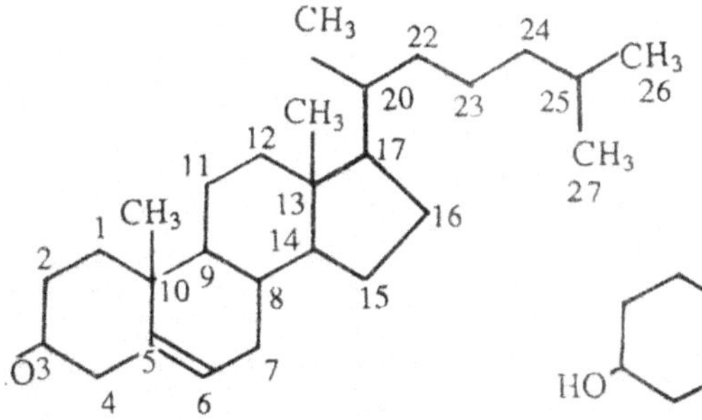

Cholesterol

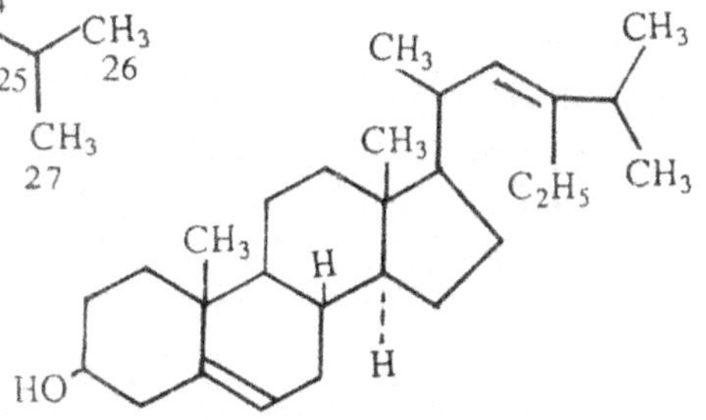

Stigmasterol

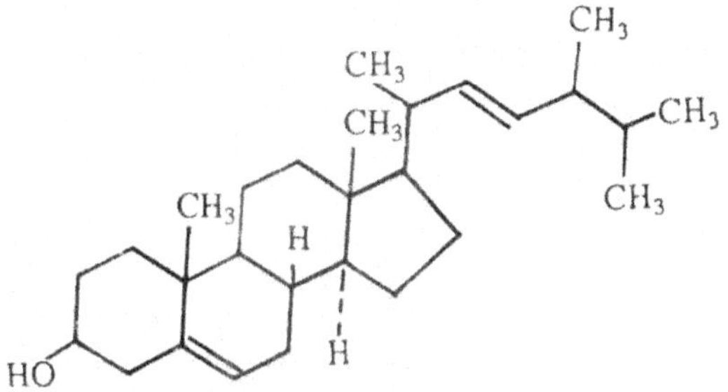

Ergosterol

BILE ACIDS

These are the constituents of bile and are steroidal in nature with carboxylic groups. The cholic acid combines with glycine and taurine and is present as salt in the bile. Bile acids are required in the absorption of fats and fat soluble vitamins. Bile acids and salts are employed in various types of hepatic disorders. They act as choleretics.

The cholic acids are the derivatives of cholanic acids. These are :

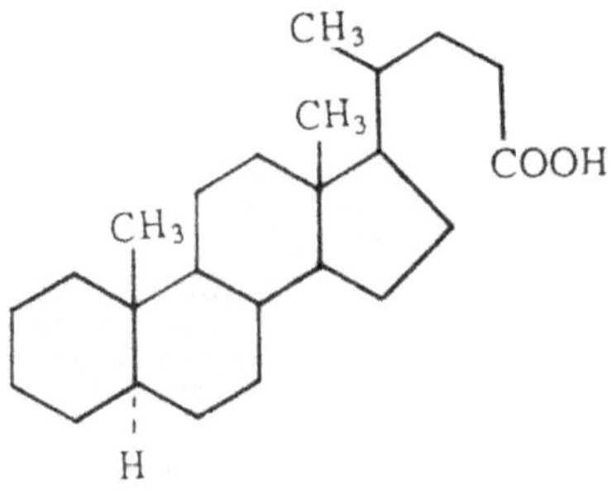

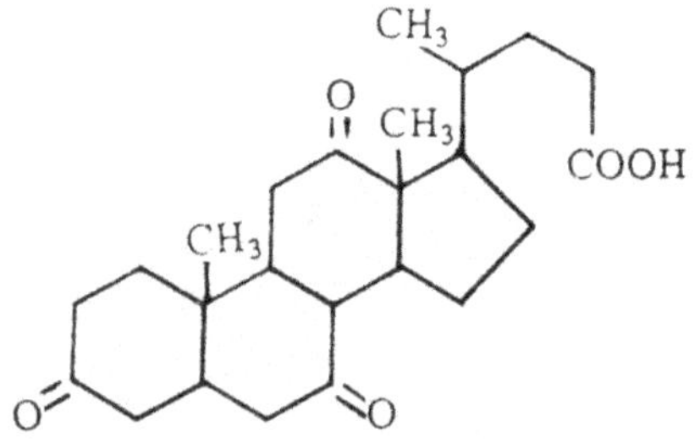

      Cholanic acid   dehydrocholic acid

Cholic acid : It is $3\alpha, 7\alpha, 12\alpha$ Trihydroxy cholanic acid.

Desoxycholic acid : $3\alpha, 12\beta$ dihydroxy cholanic acid.

Lithocholic acid : 3α hydroxy-cholanic acid.

Dehydrocholic acid : 3, 7, 12 Trioxocholanic acid.

SEX HORMONES

Sex hormones are steroidal in nature. Androgens are the main hormones in reproductive physiology of male while oestrogens and progestagens are hormones in female.

MALE SEX HORMONES

Androgens : Androgens are the hormones which are responsible for the secondary sex character in males. These are synthesized in the body, metabolised and excreted. Some analogues are prepared semisynthetically or synthetically for a more potent and longer duration of action. Androgenic agents are used clinically in the treatment of certain types of cancers like mammary cancer in females. A modification in this category have been made to have anabolic activity (retension of nitrogen, water and an increase in the skeletal muscle growth is a anabolic activity). Important androgenic-anabolic compounds are :

Derivatives : Decanoate
Enanthate
Isocaproate
Propionate

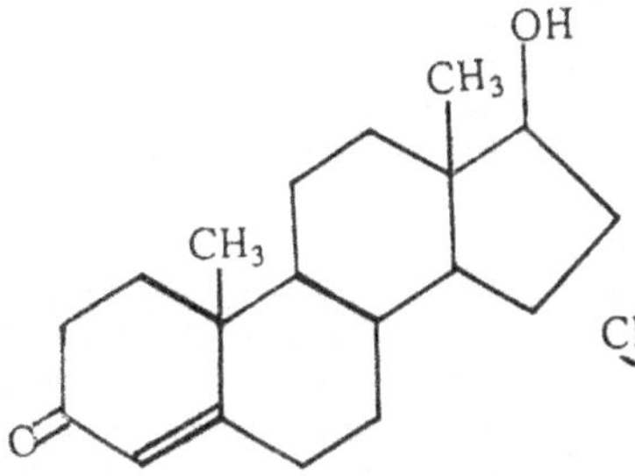

Testosterone
17-β-hydroxy
and rosta-4-en-3-one

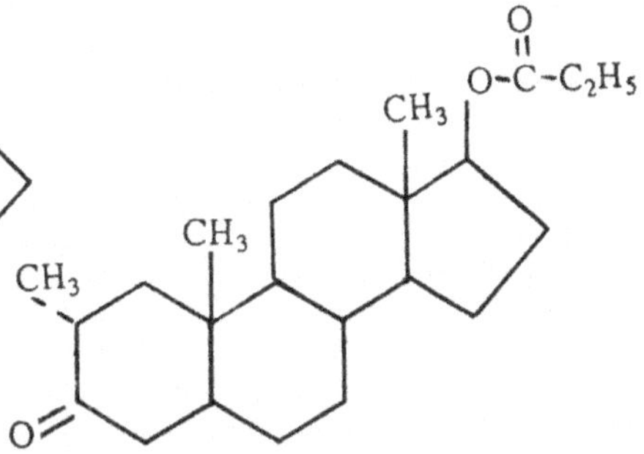

Drostanolone propionate
2 α-methyl-3-oxa-5 α-androstan-
17 β-yl propionate

Testosterone (B.P.) :

Properties and uses : It occurs as white, odourless crystals. It is practically insoluble in water, soluble in chloroform and fixed oils. Incompatabilities result with oxidising agents. It is not orally active hence given either parenterally or as implants in 100 to 600 mg doses (official in B P.) Being an androgen, it is administered in the treatment of hypogonadism. It is also used in the treatment of breast cancer in females. Testosterone in the form of esters like propionate (I.P., B.P., U.S.P.) and phenylpropionate (B.P.) are used in the form of an oily injection and administered intramuscularly and phenylpropionate subcutaneously in a 5 to 25 mg dose once or twice a week.

Testosterone isocaprioate, testosterone enanthanate, testosterone decancate injections are official and are used as androgens.

Methyltestosterone (I.P., B.P., U.S.P.) : It is a semisystemetic analogue of testosterone. It's structure is similar to testosterone having an additional alpha methyl group at 17 position.

Properties and uses : It is a whitish crystalline, odourless powder. It is almost insoluble in water, soluble in alcohol, ether and sparingly soluble in vegetable oils. Because of methyl groups at the 17 position it becomes orally active. It is thus administered in the form of tablets in 25 to 50 mg for men and 5 to 20 mg daily for women.

Drostanolone Proponate (B.P.) : It is white powder insoluble in water. It is protected from light and used in the form of injection for androgenic activity.

ANABOLIC AGENTS

The steroids which bring retention of nitrogen and building up of muscles and help in protein metabolism are called the anabolic agents. The androgenic steroid on suitable molecular modification results in an increased anabolic activity. A favourable anabolic to androgenic ratio is useful in the treatment of underdeveloped, convulsive patients to increase their body weight and to have overall body growth. However, care is to be exercised in administering these drugs to females who may develop masculine characters. A few useful anabolic agents are given below :

Ethyloestrenol (B.P.) :

Properties and uses : It is a white, crystalline powder, practically insoluble in water, soluble in ethanol and chloroform. It should be protected form light and stored at a temperature below 15°C. It is given orally in 2 to 4 mg doses, daily, in the form of tablets as an anabolic agent.

2. Fluoxymesterone (B.P., U.S.P.) :

Properties and uses : It is a white-creamy powder, practically insoluble in water, soluble in alcohol and chloroform. It is effective orally and 5 to 10 times more potent that testosterone. Fluoxymesterone tablets are official. They are administered in 1 to 10 mg dose in case of deficiency of androgenic activity.

3. Methandienone (B.P.) :

Properties and uses : A whitish crystalline powder, odourless, insoluble in water, soluble in ethanol and chloroform. It is active orally. The standard dose is 5 to 10 mg daily, in the form of tablets.

4. Nandrolone decanoate (B.P.) :
It is a decanoate ester of nandrolone.

Properties and uses : It is a creamy white powder with a faint characteristic odour. It is soluble in water, alcohol and fixed oils. The oily injection is given by the intramuscular route in 25 to 50 mg dose.

Nandrolone phenpropionate :

It is a phenylpropinate ester of nandrolone. It is also used as an oily injection administered by the intramuscular route in 25 to 50 mg doses weekly.

5. Oxymetholone (B.P.) :

Properties and uses : It is a creamy white powder and is soluble in 50 parts of alcohol and, chloroform. It is orally active. It should be kept in containers, free from ferrous metals and protected from light. It is given in 5 to 30 mg dose daily, as tablet.

6. Stanozolone (B.P.) :

Properties and uses : It is a white odourless, powder, practically insoluble in water, soluble in alcohol and ether. It should be protected from light. It is given in a 50 to 75 mg daily dose as an anabolic agent.

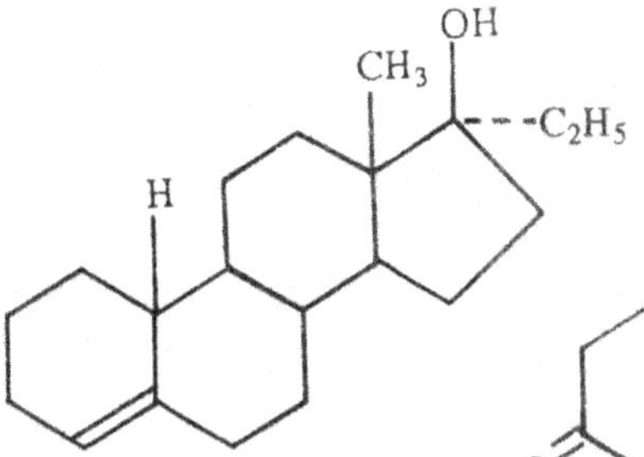

Ethyloestrenol
17-α-ethyl ester-4en-17β ol

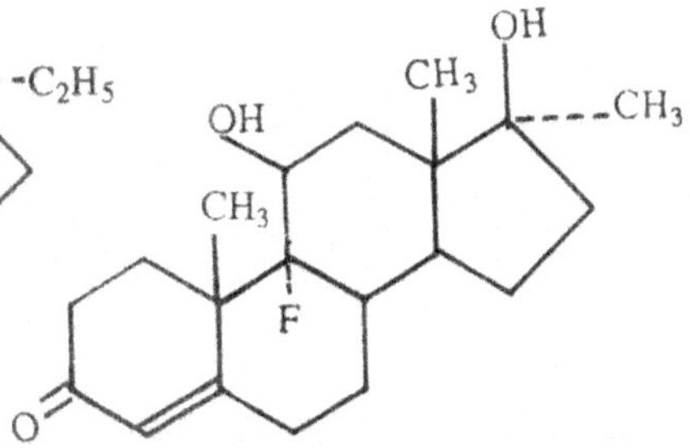

Fluoxymesterone
9 α-fluro-11β, 17β-dihydroxy-
17 α methyl androst-4-en-3-one

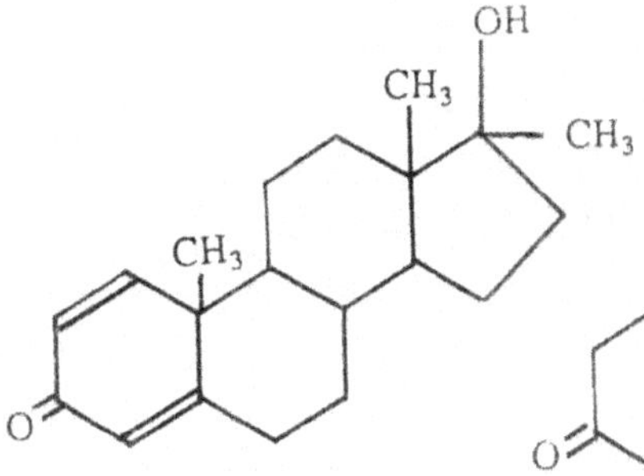

Methandrostenolone
(Methandienone)-α-methyl
17 β-hydroxy-17α emthyl-
1,4-androstadiene-3-one

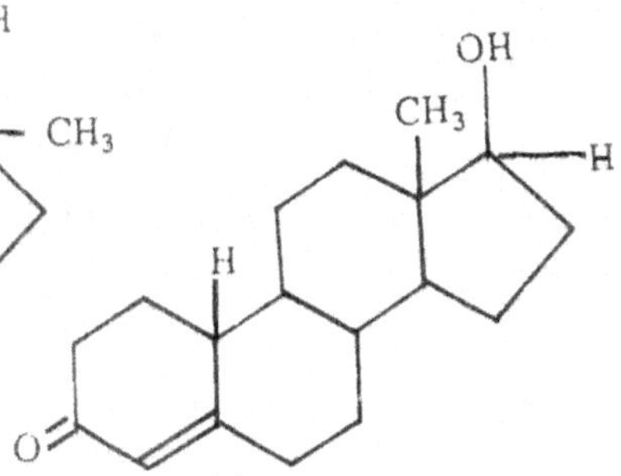

Nandrolone
3-oxa-estra-4-en-17 β-ol
Derivatives : Decanoate
phenpropionate

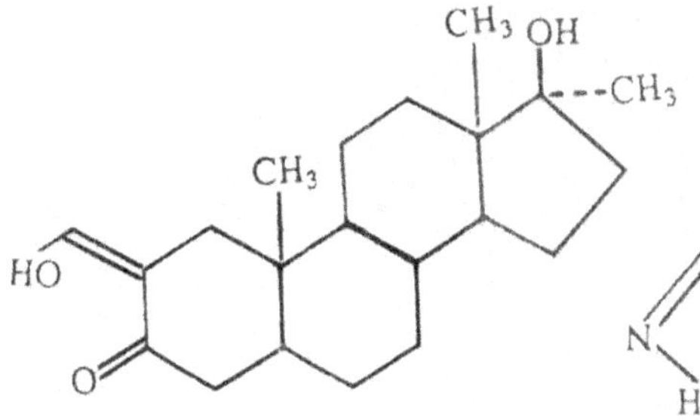

oxymetholone
17-β-hydroxy-2-dydroxymethylene
17α-methyl-5-α-androstan-3-one

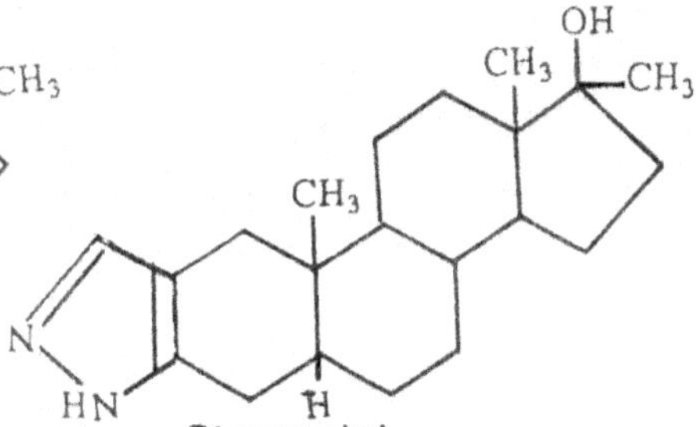

Stanazolol
17-α-methyl-2'H-5α-
androst-2eno [3,2-c]
pyrazole-17β-ol

FEMALE SEX HORMONES
Oesterogens

Oestrogen is a female sex hormone and is concerned with the development of secondary sex characters in female and regulates the menstrual cycle. Estrogens are used in the conditions of estrogen insufficiency in menopause, amenorrhae, ovarian failure, and hypogenitalism. Estrogens in combination with progestins are used to control excessive uterine bleeding, It is also used to stimulate the development of the uterine endometrium and also in appropriate combinations as contraceptives. Oestradiol is the main oestrogenic hormone synthesized in body. It is metabolised and is interconvertible into estrone and estriol.

Some important oestrogenic agents are :

Oestradiol benzoate (I.P., B.P.) :

Properties and uses : It occurs as a white crystalline powder, practically insoluble in water soluble in alcohol and acetone, slightly soluble in oils. It should be protected from light. The solutions in oil for injection are sterilized by heating the oil at 150°C for 1 hour. It is given by intramuscular injection in 1 to 5 mg dose, daily, as an ostrogenic agent.

Oestroadial dipropionate (I.P.) :

It is a preparation similar to estradiol benzoate and is given by intramuscular injection in 1 to 5 mg dose daily. *Estradiol cypionate* is other ester, which is official in U.S.P.

Ethinyloestradiol (I.P., B.P.) :

Properties and uses : It is a white or yellowish white powder and is odourless. Because of the ethynyl groups at the 17-position, it is active orally. Ethinylestradol cyclopentyl ether is official in U.S.P.

Mestranol (B.P., U.S.P.) : It is 3-methylether of ethinyl estradiol.

Properties and uses : It is also a white crystalline powder, almost insoluble in water but soluble in alcohol. It is used in the form of tablets as an oral contraceptive.

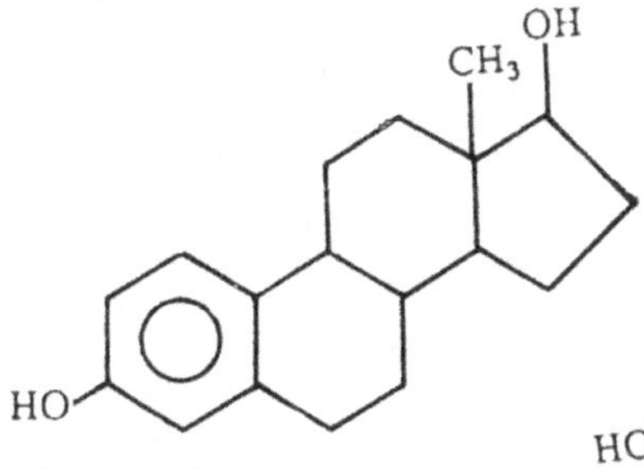

Oestradiol
Esta 1,3,5 9(10) triene-3, 17β-diol

Derivatives : 3,17β dipropionate
17 β-cyclopentyl propionate

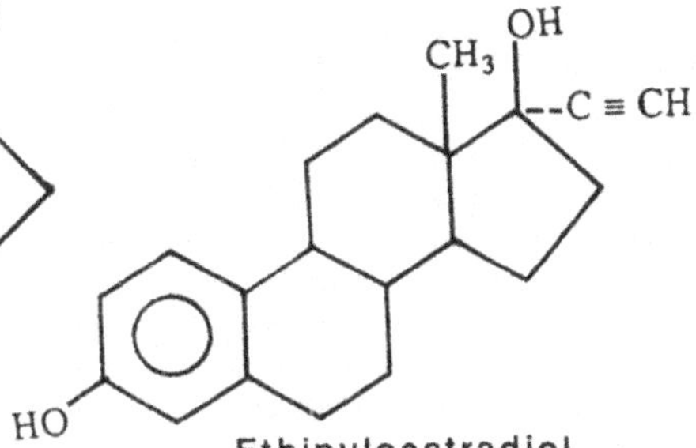

Ethinyloestradiol
19Nor-17α-
3-benzoate
pregnal, 3,5 (10) triene-
20-yne-3, 17 β-diol
Derivatives :
3-methylether
3-cyclopentyl ether

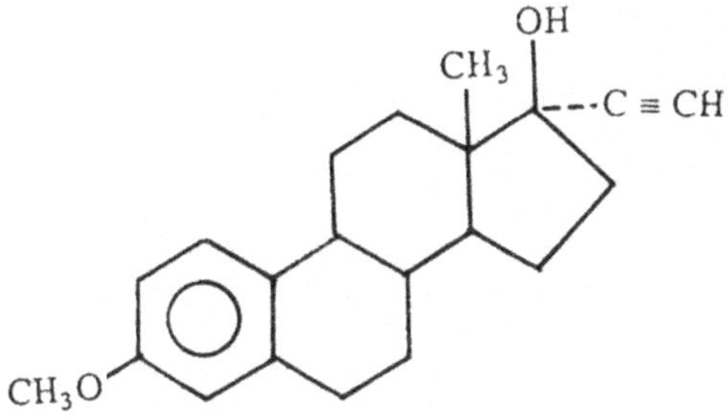

Mestranol
3-methoxy-10-nor-17α-pregna
1,3,5 (10) triene-20 αyl-17β-ol

Estrone
Estra-1, 3, 5 (10) triene
3β-hydroxy 17-one

Estriol
Extra-1, 3, 5 (10) triene
3β, 17β, 17α-triol

Oestrogen
Female sex hormones

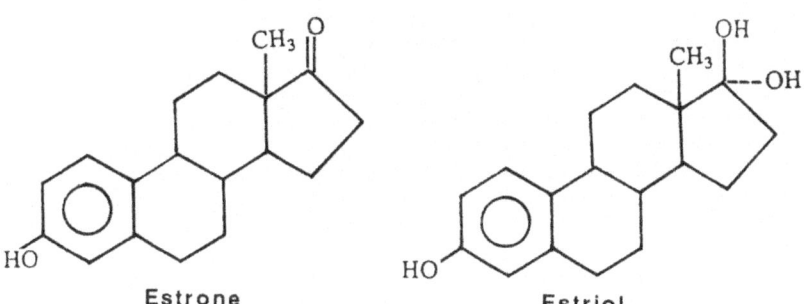

NONSTEROIDAL OESTROGENS

Certain simple compounds exhibit potent oestrogeniic activity. These compounds have the advantage of being orally active and potent. The compounds in trans configuration show a striking resemblance to estradiol. Some useful compounds are .

(i) **Dienoestrol (I.P., B.P.)** :

Properties and uses : It is white powder, practically insoluble in water, soluble in ether, alcohol and also in solutions of alkali hydroxides. It is protected from light. It is given in 500 to 5000 micrograms daily in the treatment of menopause and in 15 to 30 mg daily in treatment of carcinoma of prostate and mammary carcinoma. Dienoestrol tablets are official in I.P., B.P.

(ii) **Hexoestrol**

Properties and uses : It is a colourless crystalline powder. It has no odour, practically insoluble in water, soluble in alcohol and in solution of alkali hydroxide. It is given in 1 to 5 mg dose daily in the treatment of prostrate and mammary carcinoma. It is also used to supress lactation. Hexoestrol tablets are official in I.P.

(iii) **Stilboestrol (I.P., U.S.P.) : (Diethyl stibostrol)** :

Properties and uses : It is a white powder, insoluble in water, soluble in ethanol, ether and aqueous solution of alkali hydroxide and is protected from light and kept in well-closed containers. It is gven in the form of tablets, in 100 to 1000 micrograms. It is used in cases of menopause and in 10 to 20 mg daily in treatment of prostrate cancer and mammary cancer. It is also used to supress lactation in 5 mg doses, three times a day for three days, followed by 5 mg once a day for six days.

(iv) **Chlorotrianisene (B.P.)** :

Properties and uses : It is a white crystalline powder, slightly soluble in water, partially soluble in alcohol, more soluble in fixed oils. It is more active orally than by injection, probably being converted into a more active form in the liver. It has a slow onset but longer duration of action. It is given in 12 to 48 mg dose, daily, for thirty days, in cases of menopause, while in 12 to 24 mg dose, daily in treatment of carcinoma of prostate either in the form of capsules or tablets.

(v) **Benzestrol (U.S.P.)** : Structurally it is similar stilbostrol and is used for oestrogenic activity. It is given in 1 to 2 mg dose daily in the form of tablets.

(vi) **Fosfestrol sodium (B.P.)** : It is tetra sodium salt of phosphoric acid ester of stilbosterol. It is a orally active ostrogenic drug.

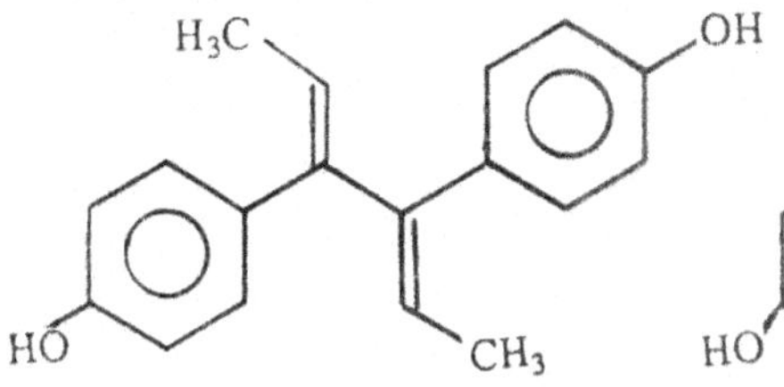

Dienoestrol
(z,z)-4-4'-bis (ethyldiene) ethylene) di phenol

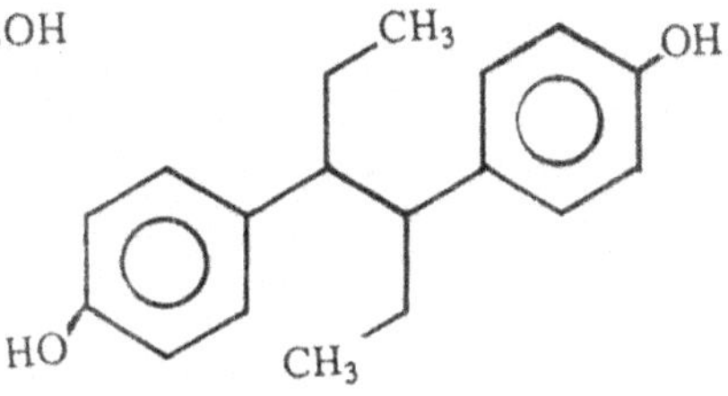

Hexastrol
3,4-dip-hydroxy phenyl) hexane

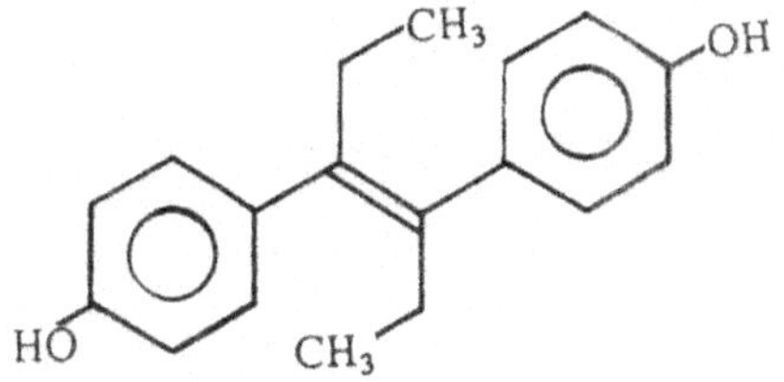

Stilbesterol (diethyl stilbosterol)
(E)-a, b-diethylstilbene-4, 4'-diol

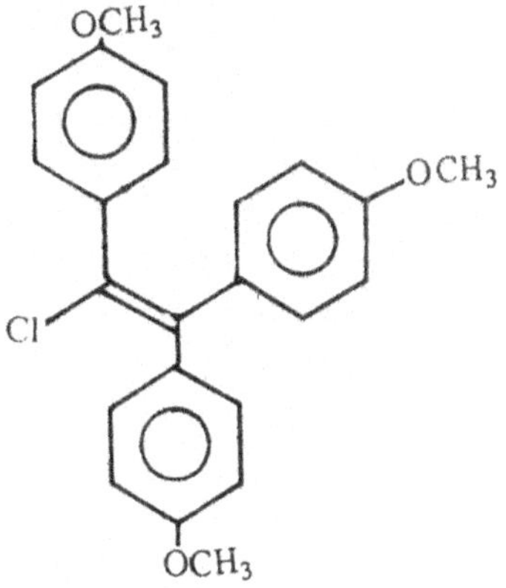

Chlorotrianisene
chlorotris-(4-methoxy phenyl) ethyene

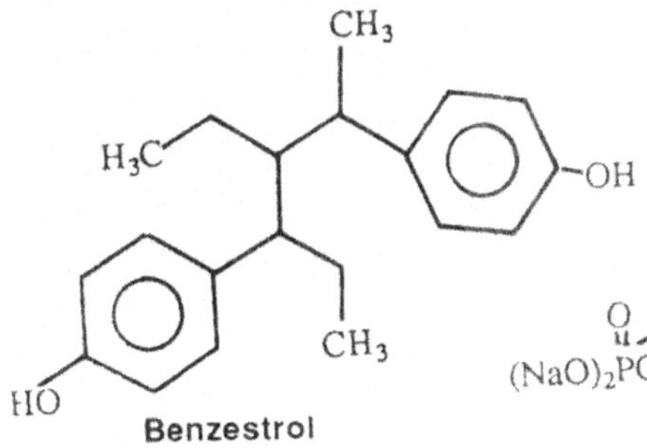

Benzestrol
4-4'-(1,2-diethyl 1-3-methyl 1-3-propanediyl)-bisphenol

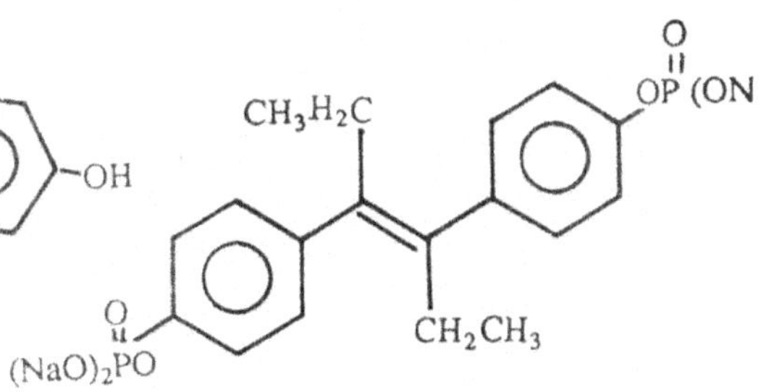

Fostestrol sodium
Tetrasodium (E)-4, 4'-(1, 2-diethyl vinylene) bis (phenylorthophosphate)

Synthetic oestrogenic hormones

PROGESTOGENS

It is a female sex hormone which is responsible for bringing changes in the uterus and vagina during the menstrual cycle. Progestines are used in correcting menstrual disorders in the treatment of uterine bleeding, in the maintenance of pregancy and in the treatment of cancer of breast. These are administered as oily injections by the intramuscular route. The new synthetic agents offer an advantage over the natural agents being orally active and more potent. Furthermore, the combination with oestrogenic agents are widely used as oral contraceptives in female. The clinically useful agents are :

1. Progesterone (I.P., B.P., U.S.P.) :

Properties and uses : It is available as colourless crystals or yellowish white powder. It is practically insoluble in water, soluble in alcohol, chloroform and fatty oils. It is light sensitive and should be kept in well-closed containers protected from light. It is not effective orally as it gets very rapidly metabolised. It is administered as an intramuscular injection. The oily injection is sterilized by heating the oil to 150° for 1 hour and then aspecially dissolving the drug in oil. The standard dose is 20 to 60 mg daily as a progestational agent. Progesterone caproate is an ester of progesterone and is given parenterally.

2. Hydroxyprogesterone hexanoate (B.P.) :

Properties and uses : The drugs is a white powder, almost insoluble in water, but soluble in alcohol, chloroform, fixed oils and esters. It is administered parenterally by intramuscular injection in 250 to 500 mg dose, once or twice weekly.

3. Dydrogesterone (B.P.) :

Properties and uses : It is a white crystalline powder, practically insoluble in water, soluble in alcohol, chloroform and fixed oils. It is active orally and is given as tablets in 5 to 30 mg doses daily, in single or divided doses.

4. Medroxyprogesterone acetate (B.P., U.S.P.) :

Properties and uses : It is a white crystalline powder, odourless, insoluble in alcohol, fixed oils. It is effective orally as well as parenterally. Usual dose is 25 to 40 mg daily, by intramuscular injection. and 50 to 150 mg dose daily in the treatment of neoplasma.

5. Ethisterone (I.P., B.P.)

Properties and uses : It is a white crystalline powder insoluble in water, soluble in alcohol and chloroform. It should be protected from light. It is given as tablets in 25-100 mg dose daily (single or divided doses) as a progestinal steroid.

6. Megestrol (B.P.) :

Properties and uses : It is a white creamy powder and mainly used as an oral contraceptive and progestational agent.

7. Norethynodrel (B.P.) :

Properties and uses : It is white crystalline powder. Soluble in ethanol, ether but insoluble in water. It is active orally and used as oral contraceptive agent.

8. Lynoestrenol (B.P.) :

Properties and uses : It is a white powder, insoluble in water, soluble in alcohol, chloroform etc., and is orally active as a progestational steroid.

9. Norethisterone (I.P., B.P.) Norethindrone (U.S.P.) :

Properties and uses : It is whitish-creamy powder, insoluble in water, soluble in alcohol but insoluble in vegetable oils. It is effective orally, given in the tablet form in 5 to 20 mg dose daily, in single or divide doses.

10. Norethisterone acetate : It is 17β acetate of norethisterone. It is given in a 2.5 to 20 mg dose daily either in single or divided doses in combination with ethinyl estradiol in the form of tablets. It is used as an oral contraceptive in a single day for 20/21 days.

11. Levonorgestrel (B.P.) : It is a white powder. It's solubility is similar to other similar drugs. It is stored at a temperature not exceeding 15°. The drug is employed for similar progestogenic activity.

12. Ethynodiol diacetate (B.P.) :

Properties and uses : It is available as an almost white powder. It is also used as protestinal agent and administered parentarally.

Progestogens (Female sex hormones)

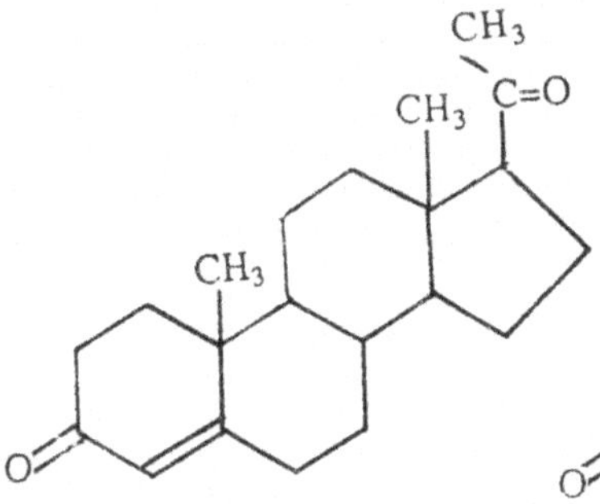

Progesterone
Pregna-4-ene-3, 20-dione

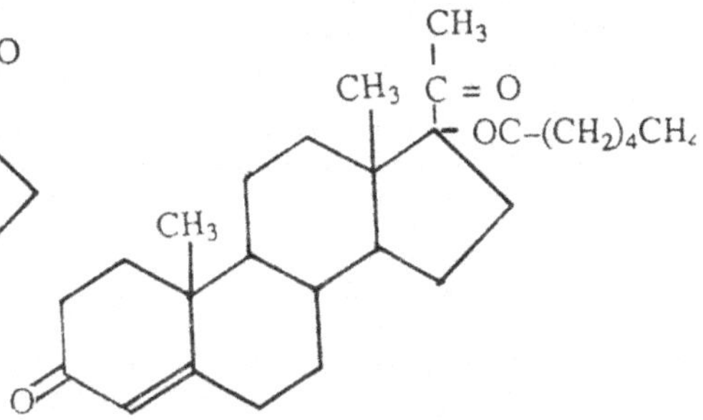

Hydroxyprogesterone hexanoate
3, 20-dioxy pregn-4-en-17α yl hexanoate

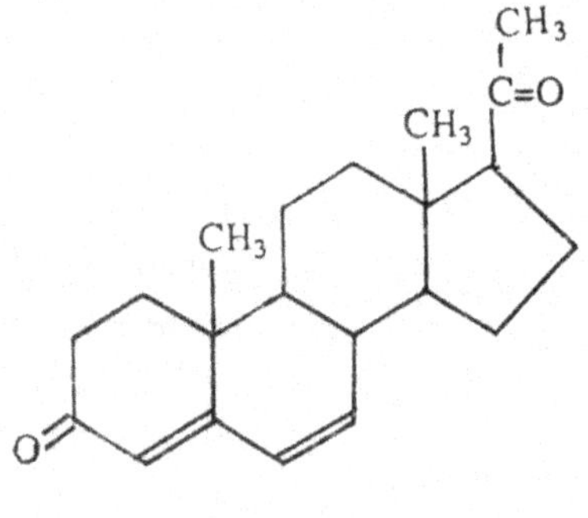

Dydrogesterone
9β, 10α-pregna-4,6-diene
3, 20-dione

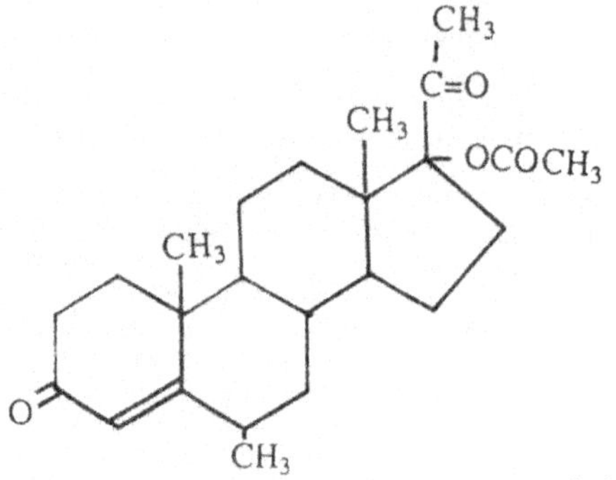

Medroxyprogesterone acetate
6α-methyl-3,20-dioxopregn-
4-en-17α-yl acetate

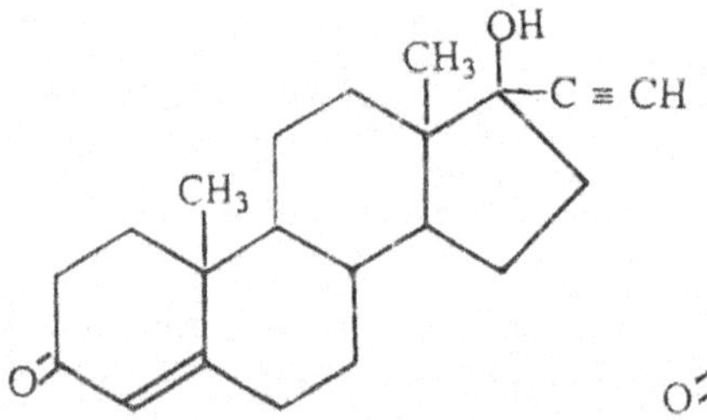

Ethisterone
17β-hydroxy-17α-pregna
4–en–20–yn–3–one

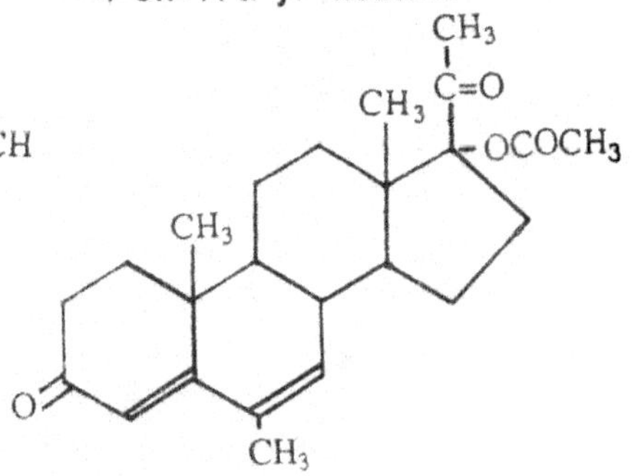

Megestrol acetate
6-methyl-3, 20-dioxopregna-
4,6-diene-17α-yl acetate

Progestogens [Synthetic 19-nor compounds]
Female Sex Hormones

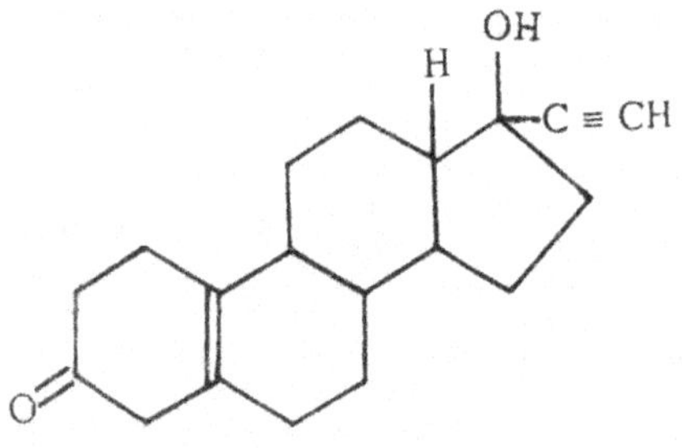

Nor ethy nodrel
17β-hydroxy-19-nor
17α–preg–5 (10) en
–20–yn–3–one

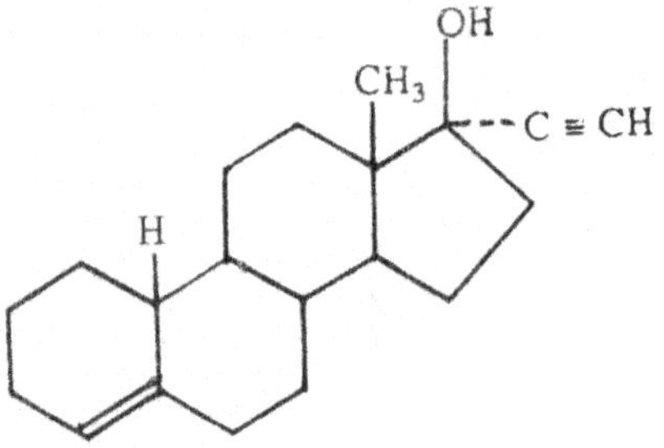

Lynestrenol
19-nor-17α-preg-4en-20-yn
-17β-ol

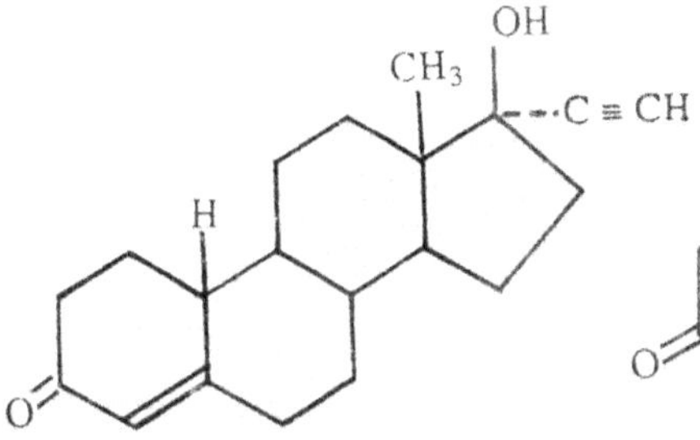

Norethisterone
17β-hydroxy-19-nor-17α-pregn-4-en-20-yn-3-one
Derivatives : 17acetate

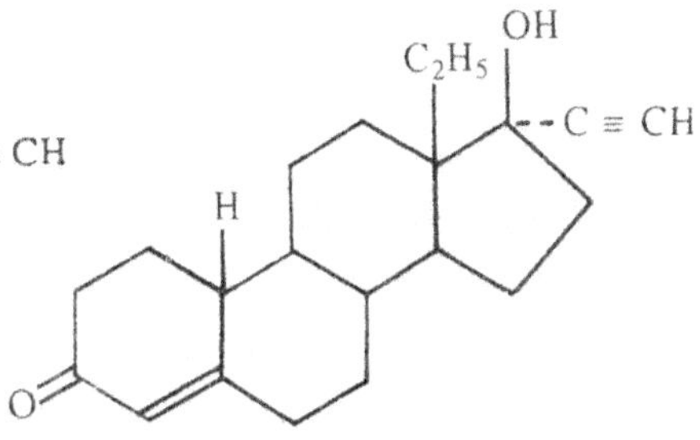

Levonorgestrel
(-) 13 β-ethyl-17β hydroxy-18,19-dinor-17α-pregn-4-en-20 yn-3-one

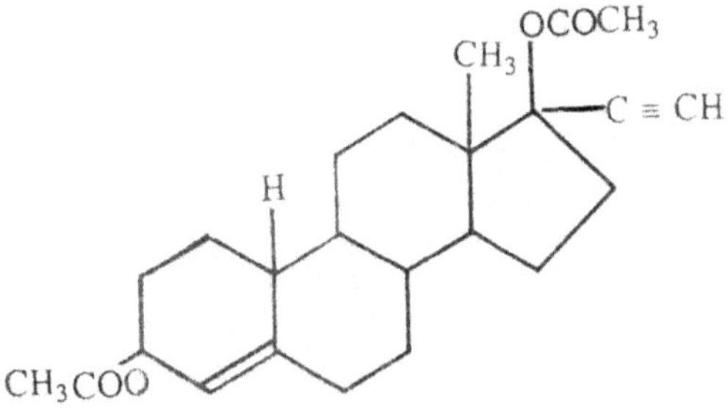

Ethynodiol diacetate
19-nor-17α-pregn-4-en-zoyne-3β, 17β-diol diacetate

ADRENAL CORTEX HORMONES

The adrenal gland consisting of the medulla and cortex secretes two different types of hormones. The medulla secrets adrenaline and the cortex, a group of closely related steroidal hormones. The adrenocorticoid hormones are broadly categorised into two types (i) Glucocorticoids (ii) mineralocorticoids. The glucocorticoids (hydrocortisone and related analogs) are primarily involved in intermediary metabolism and in gluconeogenesis, glycogen deposition etc. This group of compounds have medicinal importance. They are useful as antiflammatory, antiallergic agents. The mineralocorticoids to which deoxycortisone, aldosterone belong, one primarily concerned with electrolyte and water metabolism. The synthetic agents from this class have advantage of being useful in Addison's disease.

Some important therapeutic uses of modified adrenocortical steroids are immunosuppression, antinflammatory, antiallergic, in the treatment of collagen vascular diseases, rheumatoid artheritis and in Addison's disease, cushing's syndrome etc. They are also used topically and also in chronic lymphocyctic leukemia in combination with other antineoplastic agents.

The natural and synthetic glucocorticoids of medicinal interest are :

Hydrocortisone (I.P., B.P., U.S.P.) :

Properties and uses : It is a white crystalline powder insoluble in alcohol and sparingly soluble in chloroform. It is sensitive to light and should be protected from it during storage. There are a number of hydrocortisone derivatives and formulations available like creams, lotions ointments and tablets.

Hydrocortisone Acetate : It is an acetate of 21-hydroxyl group of hydrocortisone which is a white powder, odourless, tasteless and is practically insoluble in water, soluble in alcohol and chloroform.

Hydrocortisone acetate injection : It is a sterile suspension of hydrocortisone acetate in 25 mg/per ml concentration in sodium chloride injection containing a suitable dispersing agent. It is prepared by an aseptic technique. It is administered intravenously in a 5 to 10 mg dose.

Hydrocortisone eye ointment : It contains about 2.5 % w/w of hydrocortisone.

Hydrocortisone acetate ointment : It is a preparation containing 0.5, 1 and 2.5 % hydrocortisone acetate for topical applications.

Hydrocortisone hydrogen succinate : This is an ester prepared from hydrocortisone with succinic acid. It is a white powder and is sparingly soluble in water. It is used in the form of injection.

The hydrocortisone sodium succinate : It is a water-soluble sodium salt of hydrocortisone succinate. When rapid action is required this drug is given by slow intravenous injection in 100 to 500 mg hydrocortisone four to six times a day.

Hydrocortisone sodum phosphate : It is a whitish yellow powder, hygroscopic in nature and is freely soluble in water, and slightly in alcohol, its injection is used in 25 to 50 mg of hydrocortisone four to six times a day.

The hydrocortisone with neomycin is used in eye drops, ear drops and in ointments while with clioquinol it is used for topical applications.

Cortisone acetate (I.P., B.P., U.S.P.) :

Properties and uses : It is a white, odourless crystalline powder. It is stable in air. It is used in the form of tablets in a standard dose range of 50 to 400 mg daily, orally in divided doses or by intramuscular injection in 50 to 300 mg. dose. Sterile cortisone acetate suspension in 25 to 50 mg per ml in a aqueous medium is used as anti inflammatory steroid.

(Glucocorticoil Hormones)

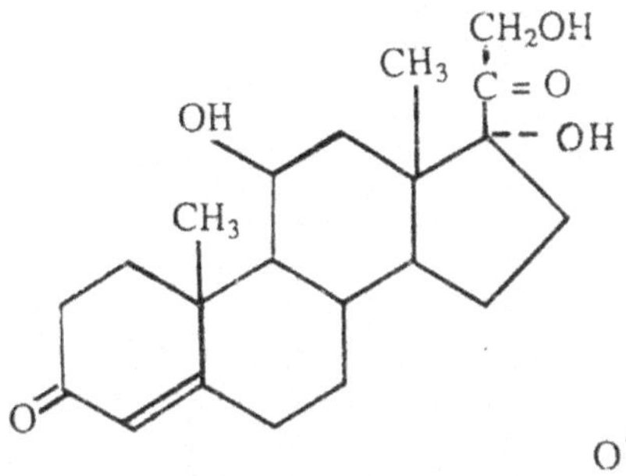

Hydrocortisone
11β, 17α, 21-trihydroxy-pregn-4-ene-3, 20-dione
Derivatives : 21-acetate
21-hydrogen succinate
21-sodium phosphate

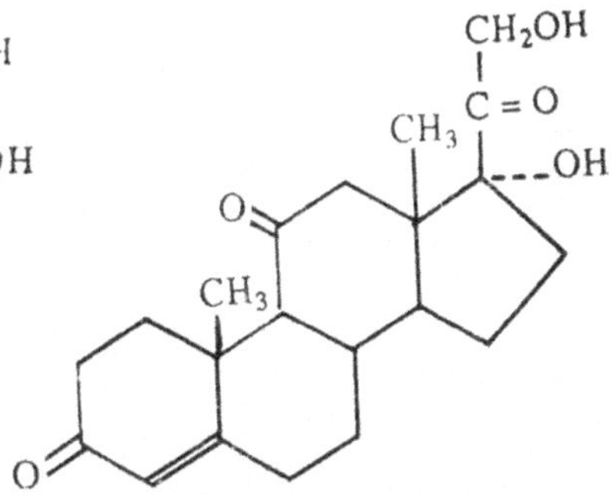

Cortisone
17α, 21-dihydroxy-pregn-4-ene-3, 11, 20-trione
Derivatives : 21-acetate

(Mineralocorticoid hormones)

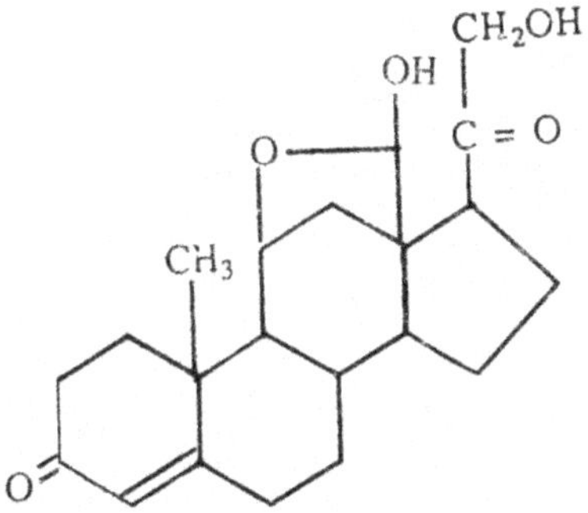

Aldosterone
(Non official non commercial)

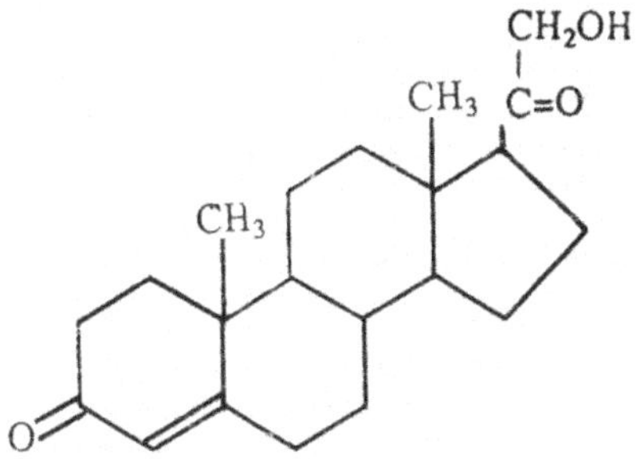

Deoxycortiosone
(Deoxycortisone)
3, 20 dioxo pregn
−4−en−21−yl
Derivatives : 21-acetate

Mineralocorticoids : Aldosterone is a major corticoid secreted by the adrenal cortex and is responsible for salt electrolyte and water balance. Since this hormone is formed biosynthetically and is active parenterally only synthetic analogs have been prepared and used in Addison's disease and in other adrenocortical deficiency states. Useful compounds under this category are :

Deoxycortisone acetate (I.P., B.P.) Desoxycorticostorone acetate (U.S.P.) :

Properties and uses : It is a white creamy powder, and odourless. It is stable in air. It is mainly used in the form of injection. The injection is a sterile solution of deoxycortone acetate in vegetable oil. The oil is sterilized by heating at 150° for 1 hour. The drug is dissolved aseptically into it. The oily injection in (5 mg per ml) is used in 2 to 5 mg daily, by intramuscular injection for it's salt regulating activity. Deoxycortisone acetate implants are official in I.P. Total implantation dose is 100 to 400 mg.

MODIFICATION IN STEROIDS

Attempts have been made on steroidal nucleus to improve its activity, potency and also to alter its pharmacokinetic profile. In these attempts many compounds have been prepared from steroid which would be more lipid-soluble (by introducing alkyl groups, alkyl side chain etc.) or more water soluble (by introducing hydroxyl groups or increasing polarity). Besides, attempts have been made to prevent the susceptible rapid metabolism or inactivation. This is to increase the drug's half-life.

In persuing the modification in corticoid steriods, significantly potent antirvheumatic, antiinflammatory, low salt retaining steroids have been prepared. Some very popular drugs from this category are given below.

1. Prednisone (I.P., B.P. U.S.P.) :

Properties and uses : It is a white, odourless crystalline powder, very slightly soluble in water, sparingly soluble in alcohol. It is active orally and given in the form of tablets in 5 to 15 mg, 1 to 4 times a day.

2. Prednisolone (I.P., B.P., U.S.P.) :

Properties and uses : It is white, odourless powder, very slightly soluble in water, soluble in methanol and alcohol. It is used in the form of tablets in 5 to 15 mg one to four times a day (10 to 100 mg as a corticosteroid.)

Prednisolone acetate is a 21 acetate of prednisolone. It is used in the form of tablets. It's sterile suspension is used as anti inflammatory agent.

The prednisolone sodium phosphate is a sodium salt of phosphoric acid ester of prednisolone. It is slightly hygroscopic and is freely soluble in water and in alcohol. It is employed in the injection form and in the ophthalmic solution, as an anti-inflammatory preparation and for topical treatment of proctocolitis. Prednisolone succinate and prednisolone sodium succinate (U.S.P.) and prednisolone pivolate are the other forms prednisolone and are used clinically for corticoid activity.

3. Methylprednisolone (B.P.):

Properties and uses: It is a white crystalline powder. The drug is administered as tablets in 4 to 48 mg daily, in divided doses, as corticosteroid. Methylprednisolone acetate is used in the form of injection by intramuscular route in 40 to 120 mg dose for local treatment.

4. Triamcinolone acetonide (B.P., U.S.P.):

Properties and uses: It is a cream coloured powder with a slight odour. It is practically insoluble in water, very slightly soluble in alcohol, in chloroform. It has sodium retaining effect. It used in creams, ointment and dental paste (in 0.025 to 0.5 %) for topical applications to skin or mucous membrane as antiinflammatory preparation. The sterile suspension in 10-40 mg per ml is used intradermally intramuscularly as an adrenocortical agent.

Triamcinilone hexacetonide is a sterile suspension (5 to 20 mg ml) is used in affected skin.

5. Fludrocortisone acetate (B.P., U.S.P.):

Properties and uses: It is a pale yellow crystalline powder, hygroscopic in nature; insoluble in water, sparingly soluble in alcohol and chloroform. It is protected from light. The tablets available in 100 microgram are used for salt regulating activity.

6. Fluocinolone acetonide (B.P., U.S.P.):

Properties and uses: It is a white, odourless crystalline powder, practically insoluble in water, soluble in methanol. It is used in creams in 0.01 to 0.2 % concentration to be applied to the skin, 2 to 4 times a day as a potent anti-inflammatory agent. Fluocinolone acetonide ointment and solution are also official in U.S.P. Fluocortolone hexanoate and Divalate are official in B.P. and are used as anti-inflammatory agents.

7. Betamethasone (I.P., B.P., U.S.P.):

Properties and uses: It is a whitish powder, insoluble in water, and soluble in organic solvents. It can be applied topically or taken internally for glucocorticoid activity. Betamethasone tablets are official in I.P. and B.P.

Betamethasone sodium phosphate is a salt prepared from betamethasone. It is water soluble and hence used as an aqueous injection. Its tablets are also official in I.P. and B.P.

Betamethasone valerate: This drug is presented in many dosage forms like aerosol, cream, lotion, ointment etc. in 0.1 to 0.2 % strength to be applied to the affected area 1 to 3 times a day.

8. Fluclorolone acetonide (B.P.):
It is a chloro and fluoro containing corticoid with potent activity. It is mainly used as an eye ointment.

9. Dexamethasone (I.P., B.P., U.S.P.):
It essentially has the same chemical structure as that of betamethasone except the methyl group at

position 16 has α-configuration.

Properties and uses : It occurs as white, odourless, crystalline powder, stable in air. It is insoluble in water, sparingly soluble in alcohol, methanol etc. It is used in the form of tablets in 500 micrograms to 2.5 mg two to four times a day. Dexamethasone elixir is official in U.S.P.

The dexamethasone sodium phosphate is presented in many pharmaceutical formulations. The injection is an official preparation containing dexamethasone sodium phosphate in 4 mg per ml concentration. Besides dexamethasone sodium phosphate cream, opthalmic ointment, ophthalmic solutions are official in pharmacopoeias and are used as an antiinflammatory agent.

10. Beclomethasone dipropionate (B.P.) : It is a creamy powder used in creams and ointments for corticoid activity.

Modified Corticoid Hormones

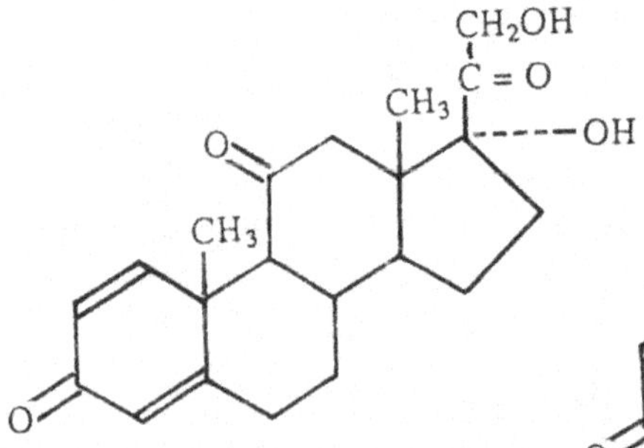

Prednisone
17α, 21-dihydroxy pregna-1, 4-diene-3, 11, 20-trione

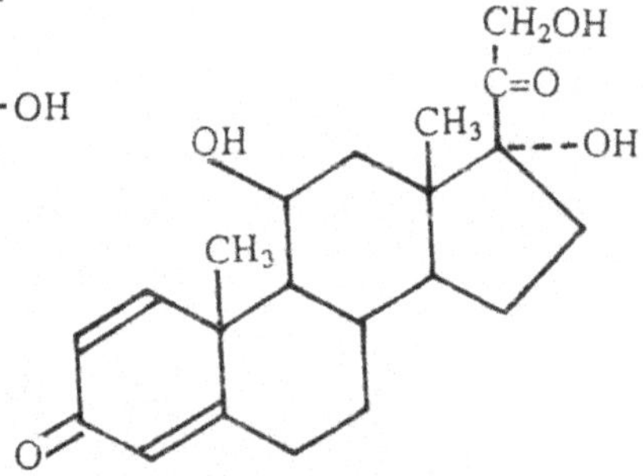

Prednisolone
11 β,17α, 21-trihydroxy pregna-1, 4-diene-3, 20-dione
Derivatives : 21-sodium phosphate
21-sodium acetate

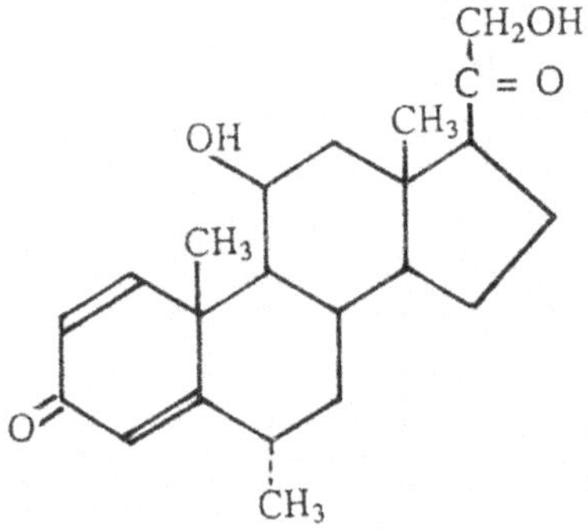

Methylprednisolone
11β, 17α, 21-trihydroxy--6α-methyl pregna.1, 4-diene-3, 20-dione
Derivative : 21-acetate

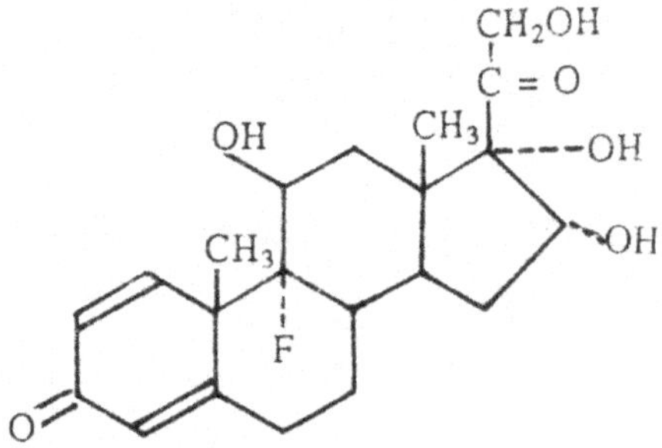

Triamcinolone
9α-fluro-11β,16α, 17α, 21-tetahydroxy pregna--1, 4-diene-3, 20-dione
Derivatives : Acetonide

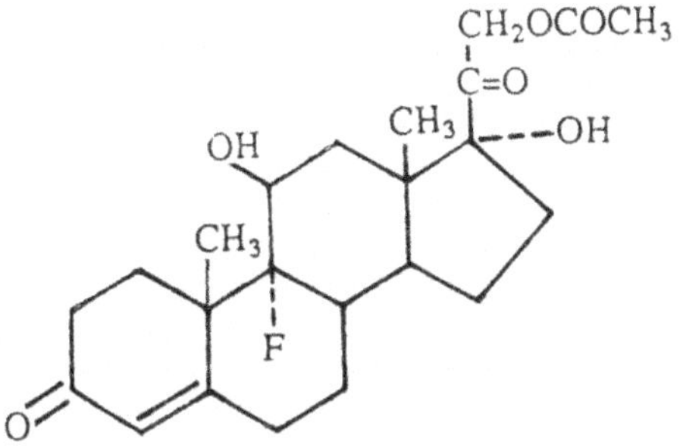

Fludrocortisone acetate
9α-fluro-11β, 17α, 21-trihydroxy
pregna-4-ene-3, 20-dione 21-acetate

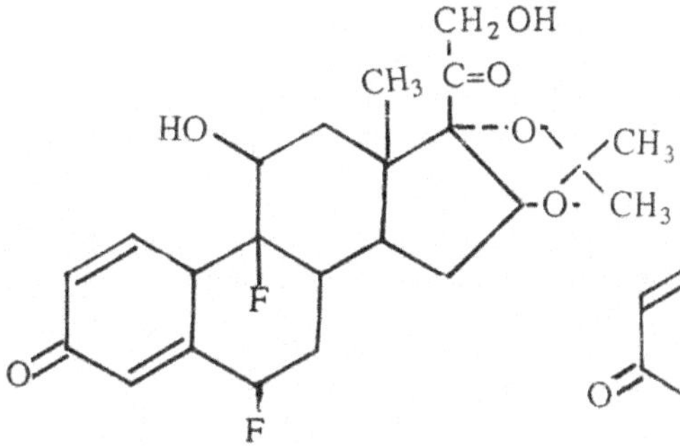

Fluocinolone acetonide
6α, 9α-difluro-11β,
21-dihydroxy
16α, 17α-iso propylidine dioxy
pregna-1,4-diene-3, 20-dione

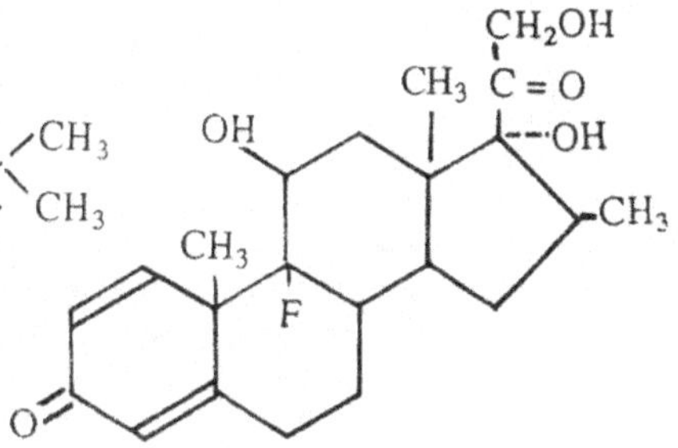

Betamethosone
9α-fluro-11β, 17α,
21-trihydroxy
-16βmethyl pregna-1,4-diene,
-3, 20-dione
Derivatives : 21-acetae
21-sodium phosphate
17-valerate

Fluclorolone acetate
9α, 11β-dichloro-6α-fluro
pregna21—hydroxy dioxy
16α, 17α iso propylidise
-1,4-diene-3, 20-dione

Dexamethadone
9α-fluro-11β, 17α, 21-
trihydroxy-16α-methyl
pregna-1, 4-diene-3, 20-diene
Derivatives : 21-sodium phosphate

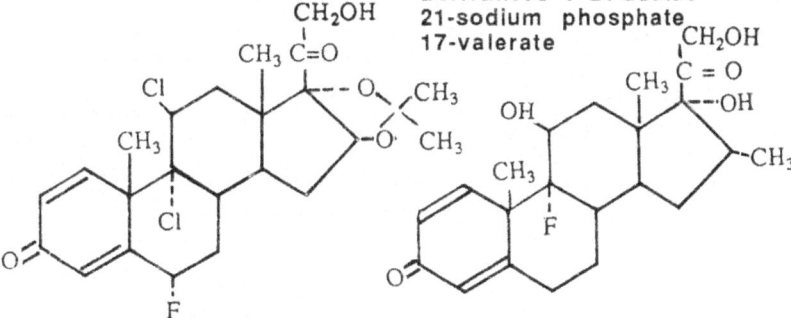

Beclomethasone dipropionate
9α-chloro-11β, 17a, 21-trihydroxy-16b-methyl pregna-
1,4-diene-3, 20-dione 17, 21 dipropionate
Modified Corticoid Hormones

Contraceptives

The problem of population control has been of severe concern. The government, various bodies and societies are trying to counteract the menace of population growth by many methods. The methods adopted are (i) The use of intra vaginal spermicides agents (ii) use of oral contraceptives (iii) Adoption of postcoital contraceptives, abortifacients and hormone-releasing intrauterine devices. (iv) use of condoms diaphragm, cervical caps, loops etc. and (v) The sterilization for both male (vasoctomy) and for female (tubectomy).

The criteria by which contraceptive methods should be judged are effectiveness, acceptability and freedom from toxic effects. Amongst the drugs, materials, articles ease of availability and cost are the other criterias for selection.

Vaginal contraceptives or spermicidal agents : Certain substances act as sperimicidal and are used as contraceptives. These include sulface active agents like monoxinol - 9 octoxinol, bactericides like betadine (Poviodone-iodine) in pessary, or 10 % betadine in varginal gel and acids like acetic acid 1 % boric of tartaric acid etc. These substanes are marked in a form of aerosol, gel, creams or pessaries and introduced deep into vagina before the intercourse.

ORAL CONTRACEPTIVES

The oral contraceptives are the drugs/agents which when taken orally effects contraception. There are many drugs, mostly steroids, which act by following methods.

(a) **Combination preparation** : These are the preparations which contain a balance of estrogen and progestin. The pills generally contain 20 to 50 microgram of ethinyl oestradio or mestranol as oestrogen and varying amounts of progestin such as norethinodrel, norethistrone acetate, norgestrel or lynoestrenol. The combination pills act by inhibiting the ovulation.

The combination preparations (pill) are taken for 21 days, starting with first pill on the 5th day of menstrual cycle. The next course is started 7 days after the last dose or the 5th day after the onset of menstrua cycle. Marketed preparations containing highdose estrogen, medium dose estrogen and low dose estrogen are available.

(b) Sequential Preparations : In this, pills containing only oestrogen ( ) are taken for the first 15 days starting with 5th day of the cycle. Estrogen acts by inhibiting ovulation by blocking FSH release and because of absence of progestin maturation of endometrium do not occur. The sequential preparations are no longer popular being less reliable and less efficacious.

(c) Progestin Pills : These contain small dose of progestin only. The pills are taken daily without break. The pills are used when patient is sensitive to oestrogen. These are more suitated for older patients in whch oestogens cause side effects. Oral preparations are stated on the 1st day of cycle and taken everyday at the same time of a day. The progestins used as ethynodiol diacetate 500 microgram, norethisteral 350 micrograms Levonorgestrel 30 micrograms.

(d) Postcoital Pills : These are used to prevent implantation of ovum. The preparation is given orally as ethynil estradiol 5 mg daily for 5 days or diethyl stibestrol 25 mg. twice a day continuous for five days even if there is nausea and vomiting. The large dose of estrogen produces imbalance of hormone and lutecolytic action. Withdrawal of larges of estrogen induces bleeding. This preparation is used only termergency for e.g. in treating rape victims.

(e) Long action preparations (once-a-month) : These are preparations containing long action estrogen like 3 - cyclopentylether of ethonyl estradinal 2.0 mg with 2.5 mg of quinestanol acetate as progestin. The preparation is taken on 22nd day of menstrual cycle and then every 28 days thereafter. The long term use of this preparation is not advisable for various reasons.

INTRA UTERINE DEVICES (IUD)

These are medicated prearations containing progestin intended to release a small amount into uterus in a sustained manner over prolonged period. The preparations containing 38 mg or 52 mg of progesterone suitably dispersed in a silicone oil within a flexible T shaped polymer. It release about 65 micrograms progesterone per day over about one year. The inserted device remains effective for a long period. It is acive locally in nonsystematic manner and side effects are generally less.

Other devices : These include the condom mode for latex rubber. They are marketed as lubricated or nonlubricated and are used by men as mechanical barrier during coitus. Similar to condom are diaphragm which are inserted into vegina. The copper T is a plastic carrier wound with copper wire is placed in vagina which prevents implantation of fertilised ovum.

Chapter 26

THYROID AND ANTITHYROID DRUGS

The Thyroid gland plays an important role in the body. It regulates the growth and metabolism. It synthesises two hormones namely thyroxine and tri-iodo tyronine. These hormones are secreted by thyroid gland and they are circulated in the blood. For synthesis of these hormones the necessary amino acid (tryonine) and inorganic iodide which are present in the body, are utilised.

The important functions of thyroid hormones are to increase metabolic rate through increasing the oxidation processes in body. It maintains growth of the body. Deficiency of thyroid hormone causes hypothyrodism, a condition wherein all the metabolic processes are slowed down. Cretinism (mental retardation and dwarfism) is a clinical condition where there is deficiency of thyroid hormones since birth. This cannot be cured. Hyperthyrodism results from excessive secretion of thyroid hormones. The severe form of this malady is manifested by exophthalmos (enlarged eye ball). To treat hypothyroidism or hyperthyroidsm drugs of appropriate type are needed. Dried thyroid gland or Thyroid hormones are used in its deficiency (i.e. in hypothyroidism) and antithyroid drugs are used in the treatment of hyperthyroidism.

Thyroid hormones and preparations

Thyroid (I.P., U.S.P.) : It is a dried powder obtained from the defatted thyroid gland of either an ox or pig. It contains 0.09 to 0.11 % of iodine (IP) and 0.097 - 0.23 % of iodine (U.S.P.) in combination as thyroxine and is free from iodine in inorganic or any form of combination other than that peculiar to the thyroid gland. A dried thyroid powder may be brought to a standard by the addition of dried thyroid of a lower iodine content or by mixing with sodium chloride, starch, sucrose etc.

Properties and uses : It is a cream coloured amporphous powder. The odour and taste is faint and meat like. It is preserved in a tight container in a cool place. It is used in the form of tablets. It has a slow onset of action and its effect may continue to a certain extent upto 2 to 3 days, so it should be used cautiously. In the treatment of adult myxedema about 100 mg a day and in cretinism depending upon the age low doses are administered. It is also given to patients with chronic constipation, menstrual disorders, sterilty etc. associated with low metabolic rate.

Thyroxin sodium (I.P., B.P., U.S.P.) :

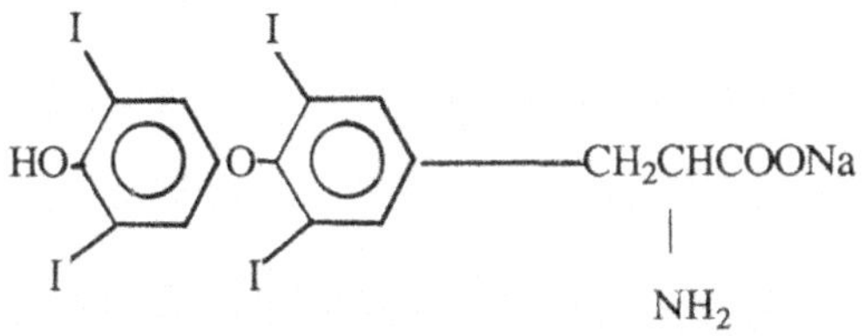

Sodium-O-(4-hydroxy-3, 5-diiolodophenyl)
-3,5-diiodo-L-tyrosinate

Properties and uses : It is a buff coloured or pale yellowish brownish powder. It is hygroscopic in nature and is affected by light and thus should be stored in tight, light resistant containers. It may be isolated from the thyroid gland or prepared synthetically. Its uses are similar to that of thyroid, and it is used in the form of tablets. The standard dose is 50 to 300 microgram daily.

Sodium liothyronine (B.P., U.S.P.) :

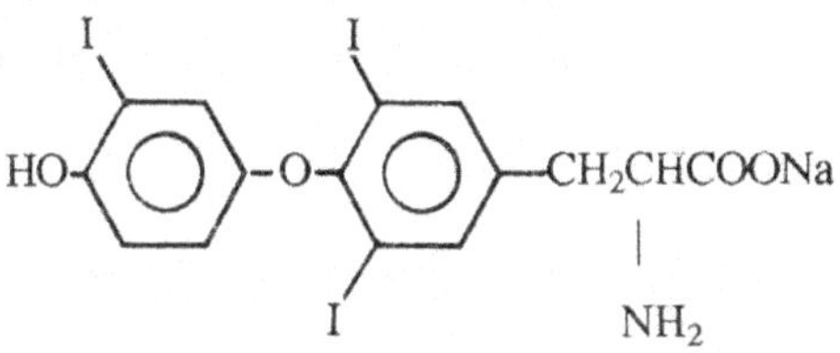

Sodium-O-(4-hydroxy-3-iodo-phenyl)-3,5-diiodo-L-tyrosinate

Properties and uses : It is a white to buff coloured powder. It is odourless, and very slightly soluble in water. It is soluble in alcohol. It is stored in air-tight containers. It is used in the form of tablets. It is said to be more active than sodium thyroxine and its uses are similar. The usual dose is 5 to 200 microgram, as per the need of patient.

ANTITHYROID DRUGS

Antithyroid drugs are used in the treatment of hyperthyroidism and are of value in thyrotoxicosis.

Antithyroid drugs : Antithyroid drugs act by inhibiting the synthesis of thyroid hormone thyroxine. These drugs block the iodination process of the hormone by antagonizing the iodide oxidation by peroxidase. They prevent the formation of iodothyronines. These drugs do not affect the release of thyroid hormones.

Propylthiouracil (B.P., U.S.P.) :

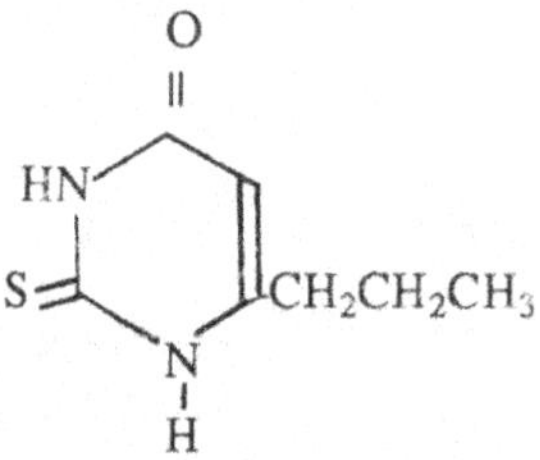

6 propyl 2-thiouracil   OR
2,3- dihydro-6-propyl-2-thioxopyrimidine-4 (1H) -One

Properties and uses : It is a white powder, with starch like appearance, and touch. It is slightly soluble in water, sparingly soluble in alcohol and easily soluble in alkalihydroxides. It is affected by light. It interferes with the synthesis of thyroxine by the thyroid gland and thus it is used in the treatment of hyperthyroidism. It is used in the form tablets. The controlling dose is 0.2 to 0.3 g daily while the maintenance dose is 50 to 300 mg. It exhibits toxic effects in number of patients.

Methylthiomacil

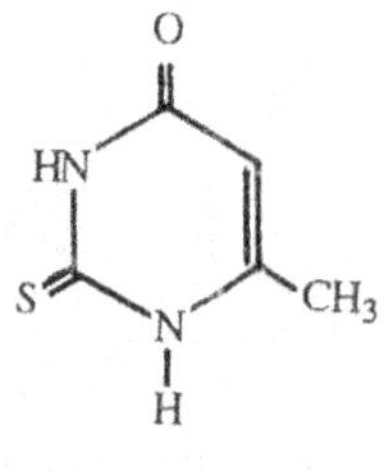

6 - methyl - 2 thiouracil

Properties and Uses : It is a white crystalline Powder, odourless, slightly soluble in water, ether and chloroform but freely soluble in solutions of alkali hydroxides and ammonium hydroxide. It is used in the treatment of hyperthyroidism in the form of tablets. Dose is 150 - 250 mg. Usual dose is 50 mg four times a day.

Carbimazole (I.P., B.P.) :

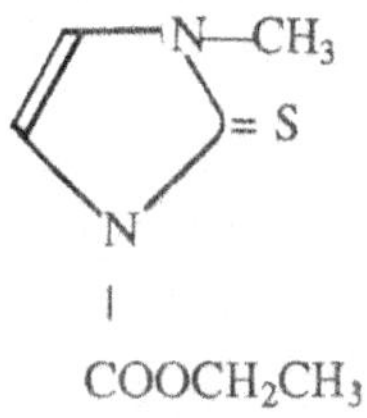

Ethyl-3-methyl-2-thiaoxo-4-imidazoline-1-carboxilate

Properties and uses : It is a white to creamy white crystalline powder. Its odour is characteristic, it is sparingly soluble in water, soluble in alcohol, freely soluble in chloroform. It is used in chloroform. It is used in the form of tablets as an anti-thyroid drug. The standard dose is 0.5 to 4.5 mg, given daily, in divided doses.

Methimazole (U.S.P.) :

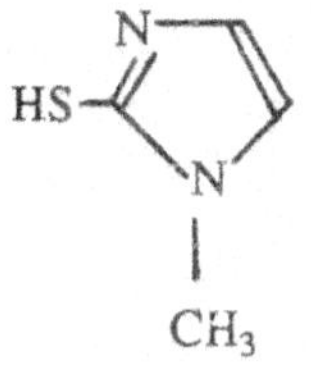

1-methylimidazole-2-thiol

Properties and uses : It is a off-white crystalline powder with characteristic odour. It is freely soluble in water. It is stored in light resistant container. The drug is more potent than propylthiuracil as antithyroid drug. The standard dose range from 5 to 60 mg daily.

Chapter 27

VITAMINS

Human beings consume a lot of food, and the purpose of food is to provide energy for growth and maintenance of the body and its functions. The energy required is provided by carbohydrates, fats and proteins. In addition, body also requires certain other chemicals, which do not provide energy but are required for the normal growth and maintenance of the life viz., vitamins, minerals, amino acids etc.

The term vitamine was first used by Funk in 1913. Later on it was observed that certain other substances which are also required but do not contain nitrogen, and it was thus suggested by Drummond to drop terminal ' e ' and the term vitamin came into use.

A number of diseases and symptoms which are known today are due to dietary deficiencies of vitamins. These were known for a long time, e.g. beriberi, scurvy, rickets, night blindness etc. Man and animal are unable to synthesize the vitamins themselves. All the known vitamins which occur naturally are synthesized by plants with the exception of vitamin A and D. Plants however synthesize precursers of vitamin A and D. Only some birds and animals synthesize vitamin and provitamin such as ascorbic acid and 7 dehydro cholesterol. If the diet is lacking in vitamins, then normally there is a breakdown of the normal metabolic processes which retards growth, particularly in children. The symptoms of malnutrition are called deficiency diseases.

Vitamins can be taken in a dose far exceeding the normal daily requirements, without much side effects. The excess of vitamins are either stored in liver ; (e.g. vitamin A and D) or excreted through urine (the water-soluble vitamins).

Vitamins are divided broadly into two classes :

(i) Fat soluble.

(ii) Water soluble Vitamin.

A summary is given below :

FAT SOLUBLE VITAMINS

Vitamin A : The main source of vitamin A is fish liver oils, like halibut liver oil, shark liver oil, burbot liver oil and cod liver oil. Milk and eggs are also good source of this vitamin. Alpha, beta and gamma carotens are called provitamin A which occur in green parts of plants. Carrots, apricots and peaches are common plant sources for vitamin A.

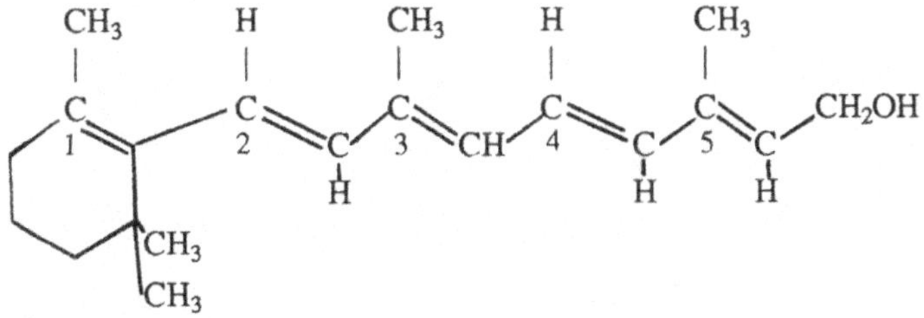

Number indicate the position of double bond.

All trans (Retinol)

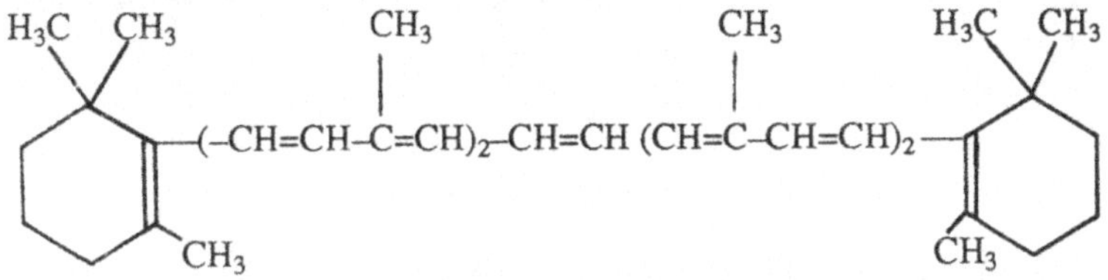

β-Carotene

Vitamin A (I.P., B.P., U.S.P.) :

It consists of an ester, usually acetate or palmitate or mixture of esters of retinol. It may be diluted with edible vegetable oils or it may be incorporated in solid edible carriers or excipients. Esters of natural or synthetic origin or mixtures of such esters can be used. It may contain suitable preservative, diluent and antioxidants. I.P. states that each gram contains not less than 3,00,000 units of vitamin A activity.

Properties : It is a yellow to red oily liquid or a mixture of oil and crystalline material. It has a slight fishy odour (but not rancid). The liquid form is insoluble in water and glycerine, freely soluble in absolute alcohol and vegetable oils, soluble in chloroform, ether and liquid paraffin. The solid form is dispersable. It is stored in containers, in the atmosphere of inert gas and kept in cool place.

Pure vitamin A can be isolated from natural sources or can be prepared synthetically from β-carotene. It is a pale yellow crystalline compound, soluble in fatty solvent. It is not easily destroyed by heat but is easily oxidised and is less stable in acidic than in alkaline media.

Deficiency symptoms, action and uses : It is called the growth vitamin. Its deficiency causes degradation of mucus membranes, affects eye and causes xeropththalmia. Severe deficiency causes dryness and scaliness of skin. It also regulates the activity of osteoblasts and osteoclasts. It is used in correcting night blindness and xerophthalmia and in acne-vulgaris as 0.05 % solution in propylene glycol.

The following are the preparations offical in I.P. (1) Vitamin A and D capsules (2) Concentrated vitamin A solution. (3) Concentrated vitamin A and D solution. (4) Shark liver oil. (5) Dilute shark liver oil. (6) Shark liver oil with vitamin D.

Following vitamin A forms are official in B.P. :

(1) Vitamin A ester concentrate (Natural) (2) Synthetic vitamin A concentrate (oil form) (3) Synthetic vitamin A concentrate water dispersable form.

Vitamin D : The main sources of vitamin D are fish liver oils, obtained from the livers of Bluefin-tuna, Yellowfin-tuna, Halibut, Burbot, Cod and Shark. The provitamins to vitamin D are ergosterol and 7-dehydrocholesterol which in presence of ultraviolet light are converted to vitamin D_2 (ergocalciferal) and vitamin D_3 (chole calciferal) respectively.

These provitamins are found both in plant and animal tissues. Ergosterol is found in large amounts in yeast and 7-dehydrocholesterol is found in animal skin.

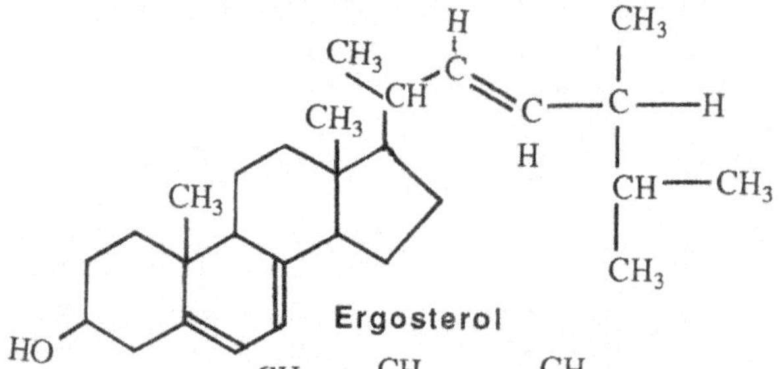

Ergosterol

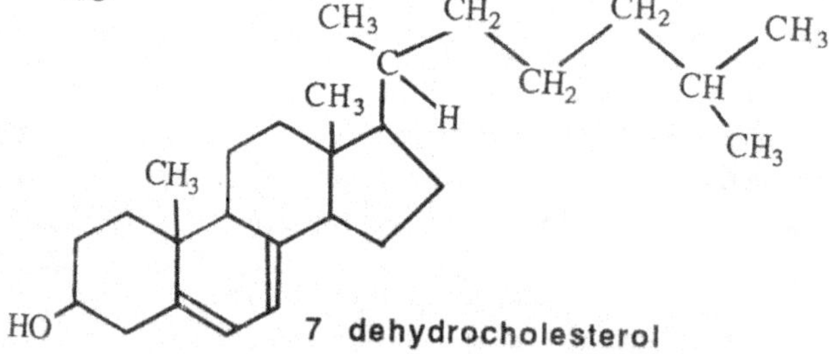

7 dehydrocholesterol

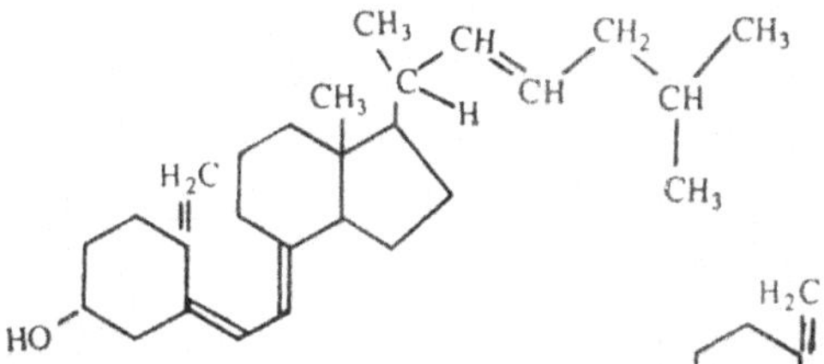

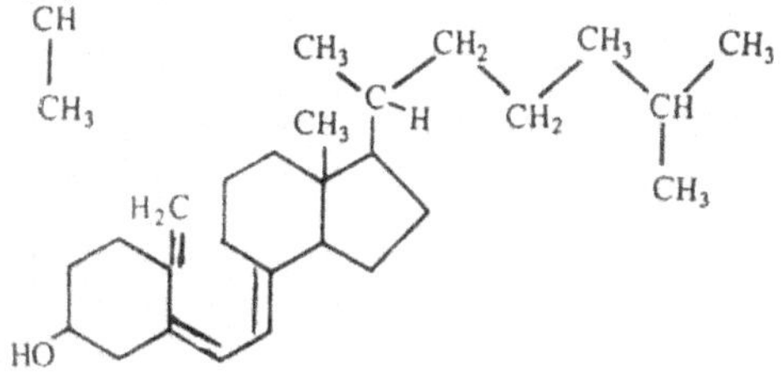

Ergocalciferol (Vitamin D₂)   **Cholecalciferol (vitamin D₃)**

Ergocalciferol (I.P., B.P., U.S.P.) :

It is usually obtained by exposing ergosterol to ultraviolet light for a proper length of time. It occurs as white crystals, insoluble in water but soluble in alcohol, ether, chloroform and fatty oils. It is slowly oxidised in oils by the oxygen in the air. It is preserved in an harmetically sealed container under nitrogen, kept in cool place and protected from light.

Cholecalciferol (B.P., U.S.P.) :

It is obtained by irradiation of 7-dehydrocholesterol. It is made up of white crystals or crystalline powder and it is odourless. It is soluble in usual fatty solvents and vegetable oils but is insoluble in water. It is more stable compared to vitamin D_2. It should be preserved in harmetically sealed containers under nitrogen, in cool place, protected from light.

Both vitamins can withstand the autoclaving temperature of 120° in absence of air but are destroyed completely at 170°.

Other offical forms

Dihydrotachysterol (B.P., U.S.P.) :

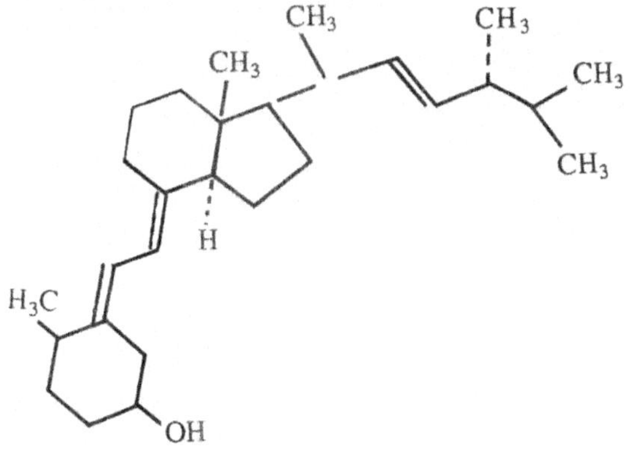

It is a colourless white, crystalline powder, odourless, insoluble in water, soluble in organic solvents. It is stored in well closed container, protected from light at a temperature not exceeding 25°. It is used in treatment of hypocalcaemia as it increases calcium concentration in blood.

Calciferol injection and high strength calciferol tablets are official in B.P.

Codliver oil (B.P., U.S.P.) :

It is obtained from livers of *Gadus morrhua* and other species of Gadidae. Each gram contains not less than 255 micrograms of vitamin A and 2.125 micrograms of vitamin D. It may be flavoured with suitable flavouring agents. It is an oily liquid, with a characteristic slight fishy odour and is soluble in alcohol, ether, chloroform and ethylacetate. It is stored in a vacuum and kept in a cool place, protected from light.

Halibut liver oil (B.P., U.S.P.) :

The oil is obtained from the livers of the halibut species. Each gram of oil contains not less than 18 milligram (60,000 USP units of vitamin A and not less than 15 micrograms (600 USP units) of vitamin D. It may be flavoured suitably. It occurs as yellow to brownish yellow oily liquid with a characteristic fishy odour. Its solubilities and storage conditions are similar to cod liver oil.

Deficiency symptoms action and uses : Deficiency of vitamin D results into " Rickets ", which is characterised by lack of calcificaton of bones. The hypertrophic cartilage zone of the bones are affected. Vitamin D plays an important role in the absorption of calcium and phosphorous from intestinal tract. In ricketic persons the phosphatase blood serum level is high which is brougth down to a normal value by this vitamin. Vitamin D and other preparations are used for the treatment of the rickets and also for management of hypocalcemia. An usual dose is 1200 to 1500 USP units in rickets, and upto 20,000 USP units in hypocalcemic tetany.

Vitamin E : It designates the biological effect of a group of compounds called tocopherols. It includes, α, β and δ tocopherols out of these only α-tocopherol is biologically important. Vitamin E is widely distributed in nature and normally any diet will not be deficient in Vitamin E. Tocopherols are abundant in wheat germ, corn germ and other seed germs. It is present in soya and cotton seed oil and is also found in some green leafy vegetables. Tocophero can be isolated from oils. They can also be prepared synthetically.

α - Tocopherols

Vitamin E (U.S.P.) : It consists of d or dl-α-tocopherol or their acetates of succinates. It may be mixed tocopherols concentrate containing not less than 33 per cent of total tocopherols of which not less than 50 percent is dl or d-tocopherol obtained from edible vegetable oils. It may also be a 25 per cent dl or d - α - tocopheryl acetate concentrate in edible oil as vehicle.

Properties : The tocopherols and their acetates are oily liquids, with light yellowish colour and characteristic taste. They are soluble in alcohol, ether, chloroform and fixed oils but are insoluble in water. They are slowly oxidised in air, but undergo oxidation rapidly in presence of alkali in air or mild oxidising agents and ferric salts. They are affected by ultra violet light and are deactivated, and hence are preserved in tight containers, protected from light.

Actions and uses : The exact role played by vitamin E in the body is still not understood completely. But it is observed that it is essential part in the metabolism of skeletal muscles. Tocopherols are concerned with bogenesis of coenzyme Q which is necessary for α-ketoglucuronidate and succinate oxidation. It is given as a supplement to diet of new borns particularly premature one.

Another important salt is *d-Alpha tocopheryl acid succinate*. Alpha tocophenyl acetate is offical in (I.P., B.P.).

Vitamin K : It refers to a group of chemical substances occurring in nature having similar biological activity to one isolated from alfa alfa and other forms from putterfied fish meal. It is an essential constituent in the clotting of blood. Vitamin K_1 is found in green plants for example alfa alfa and spinach leaves. Vitamin K_2 is found in puterified fish meal. It is also occurs in hog liver fat, tomatoes and soya bean oil. Certain micro-organism like *Bacillus cereus, B. Subtalis, Proteus vulgaris, Sarcina lutea* etc. contain antihaemorrhagic agent.

Chemically vitamin K is naturally occurring derivatives of 2-methyl 1, 4-napthoquinone.

Vitamin K_1 is known as Phytomenadione (B.P.) or hlytonadione (U.S.P.)

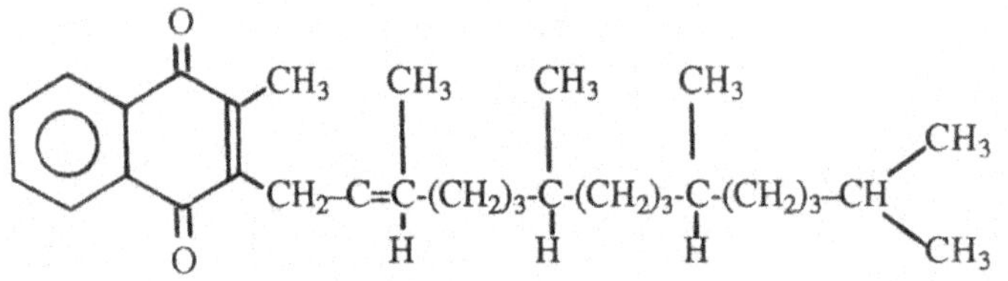

Vitamin K - 1

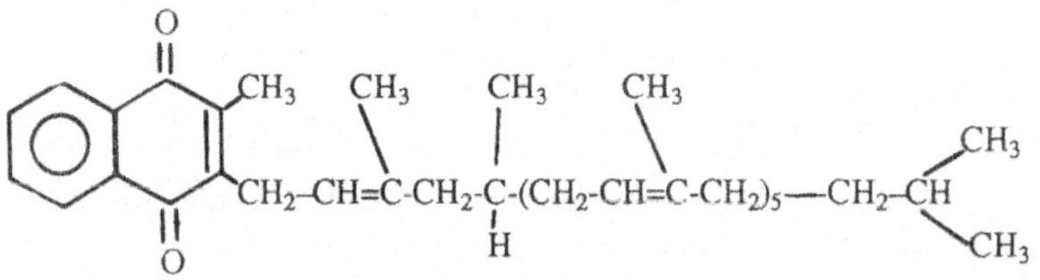

(Structure: 1,4-naphthoquinone with 2-methyl and side chain)
$CH_2-C=C-(CH_2)_3-C-(CH_2)_3-C-(CH_2)_3-CH(CH_3)_2$
with CH_3 groups at indicated positions and H substituents.

Vitamin K - 1

Vitamin K - 2

$CH_2-CH=C-CH_2-C-(CH_2-CH=C-CH_2)_5-CH_2-CH(CH_3)_2$

Vitamin K - 2

Properties : The pure compounds isolated from the natural sources are pale yellowish liquids. They are soluble in fatty solvents and oils but are insoluble in water. They are sensitive to light and are destroyed during saponification.

Actions and uses : Vitamin K is important for the coagulation of blood as it is needed in the formation of prothrombin in liver it helps in clotting of blood Vitamin K is absorbed from intestinal tract but only in presence of bile salts. In certain conditions like jaundice or pyloric or intestinal obstruction there is defective secretion of bile salts which reduces the absorption of vitamin K. It is used to prevent or treat hypoprothrombinemia in infants either by administering to mother shortly before parturition or single dose to newborn in first week of life.

Phytomenadione injection and tablets are official in B.P. and U.S.P.

As vitamin K is insoluble in water, the menadione and its salts are now-a-days used clinically.

These are given below :

Menadione (B.P., I.P.) :

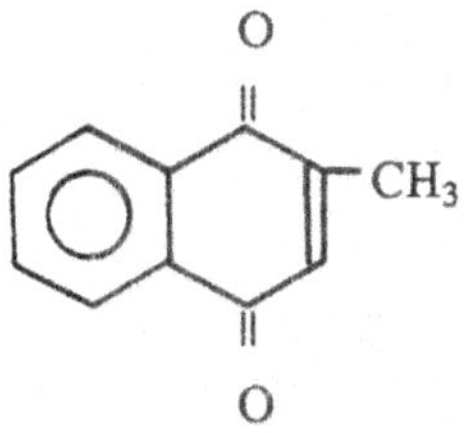

2-methyl-1,4-naphthoquinone

Properties and uses : It occurs as yellow crystalline powder, insoluble in water, sparingly soluble in alcohol, soluble in chloroform. It is protected from light. It is a synthetic Vitamin K analogue.

Menadiol sodium phosphate (I.P.) :

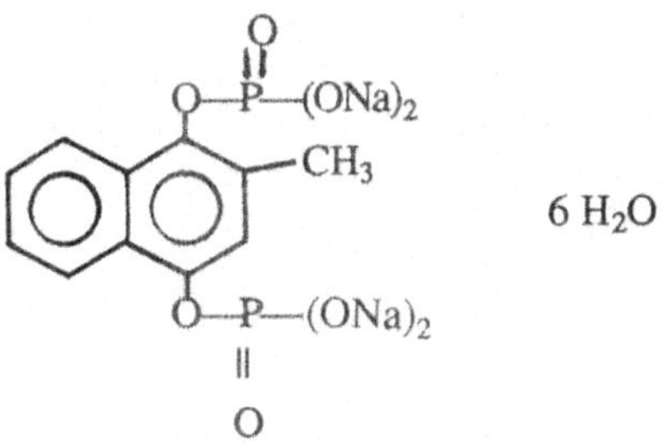

$6 H_2O$

tetrasodium-2-methyl naphthalene–
1, 4-diyl di (orthophosphate) hexahydrate

Properties and uses : It is a white powder, odourless hygroscopic and is soluble in water. It is administered as tablets in Vitamin K deficiency.

Acetomenaphthone (I.P.) :

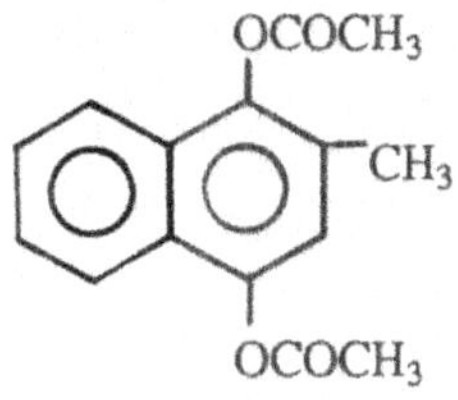

1, 4-diacetoxy-2-methylnaphthalene

Properties and uses : It is a white crystalline powder, odourless with slight bitter taste. It is practically insoluble in water, slightly soluble in alcohol. The drug is stored in well-closed containers. It is given as prophylaxis of neonatal hemorrhage in 5 to 10 mg daily for one week before delivery.

WATER SOLUBLE VITAMINS

Vitamin C (ascorbic acid) and all the vitamins belonging to B group are soluble in water. Some of the vitamins belonging to B group still retain their designation such as B_1, B_6 and B_{12} and other have become obsolete. Because of the multiple nature of vitamins belonging to this class, they were called as vitamin B complex, but this terminology is not much used.

Ascorbic acid [Vitamin C] : It is atiascorbutic vitamin known since very long. It is synthesized during germination of seeds, and more amount is present in growing parts of the plant. Human beings also synthesize it in small amount. The best sources for vitamin C are citrus fruits like lemon, orange, strawberies, lime etc. Green vegetables like cabbages and lettuce are also good sources. Now-a-days it s prepared onlarge scale by fermentation process. In nature it exists in reduced and oxidised form (dehydroascorbic acid). Both forms have the same biological activity.

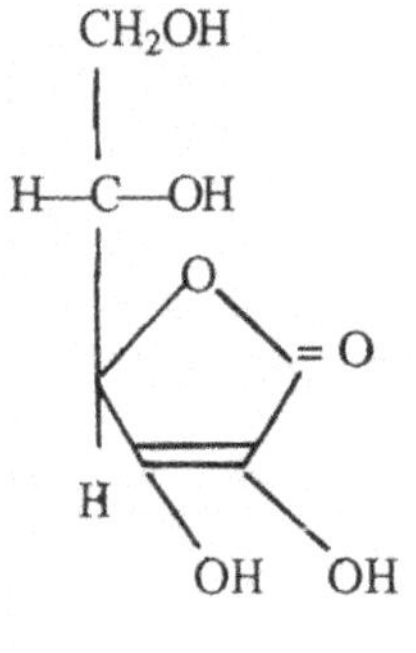

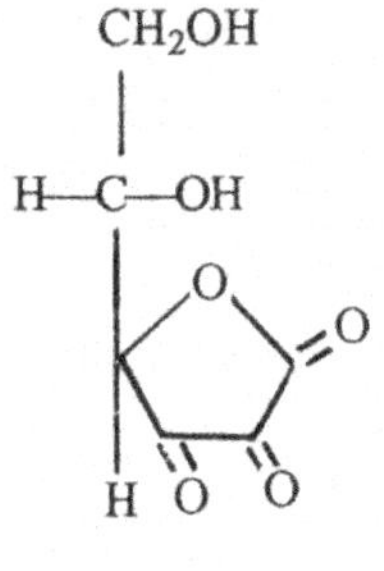

L-ascorbic acid   Dehydroascorbic acid

Vitamin C (I.P., B.P., U.S.P.) :

Properties : It is white crystalline powder, with a faint yellowish tint. It is freely soluble in water, less in alcohol and insoluble in chloroform and ether. On exposure to light, it darkens. It is somewhat stable in dry state but in solutions it rapidly darkens in the presence of air. The oxidation is accelerated by heat, light, alkalies and oxidative enzymes. Aqueous solutions are strongly acidic in nature. It forms salt with metal easily. It must be preserved in tight containers, and protected from light. Aqueous solutions are sterilized by filtration method.

Deficiency symptoms, actions and uses : Deficiency of ascorbic acid results into scurvy which is characterised by general break-down of intracellular collagen, bleeding and pin-point hemorrhages in the skin. Vitamin C is lost during cooking. It is essential for healing of bones, as in deficient patient healing of fractured bone is slow. It also functions in the metabolism of tyrosine. It is one of the factors whch resists infection. It is used in the form of tablets or injection in scurvy, idopathic methemoglobeinemias, and microcytic anaemias. Usual dose for adults in scurvy is 1 g daily in divided doses for 8 days then 500 mg till symptoms disappear. It is used as antioxidant in food products.

VITAMIN "B"

The water soluble B group vitamins have been now dfferentiated into distinct chemical moieties. They are thiamine, riboflavine, niacine, pyridoxine, pantothenic acid, folic acid and cyanocobalamine which are required in human nutrition.

Thiamine, Aneurine (Vitamin B_1) : It is found in cereal grains, milk, nuts, eggs and pork, wheat,rice polishing. Yeast contains larger proportion of thiamine. It is also prepared synthetically.

Thiamine hydrochloride (I.P., B.P., U.S.P.) :

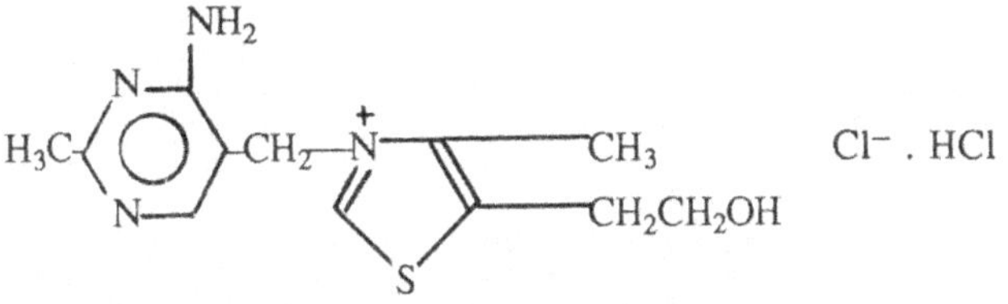

It consists of a substituted pyrimidine ring connected by a methylene bridge to the nitrogen of substituted thiazole ring.

Properties : It occurs as white crystals or white crystalline powder with slight characteristic odour. Anhydrous powder rapidly absorbs water up to 4 per cent when exposed to air. It is freely soluble in water, soluble in glycerine, less soluble in alcohol and insoluble in ether. Dry product is stable in air. Aqueous solutions are acidic in nature and are relatively stable between 3.5 to 5 pH. It is destroyed in alkaline solution. It is precipitated by reagents like mercuric chloride, iodine, picric acid, tannins, Mayer's reagent etc. It is sensitive both to oxidising and reducing agents. In alkaline media it is oxidised to thiochrome a biologically inactive fluroscent substance. It is incompatible with acid neutralising substances. The aqueous solutions are sterilized by filtration method.

Deficiency symptoms, action and uses : Beriberi or polyneuritis (disfunctioning of the nervous system) is associated with deficiency of thiamine. In peripheral neuritis, nerves of extremities are affected. The deficiency symptoms include anorexia, loss of weight-muscle cramps and general muscular weakness. It is readily absorbed from small and large intestine and carried to the liver. In cells and liver, it exists in the form of pyrophosphate of carboxylase. It serves as prosthotic group of enzyme systems which are concerned with decarboxylation of α-ketoacids. Thiamine deficiency is not very common. It plays important role in the metabolism of carbohydrates and possibly fats and amino acids. It is used in the treatment of " Beriberi ", and employed in the form of tablets or injections. Usual dose is 1 to 50 mg. The daily requirement is 1 to 2 mg and therapeutic dose 5 to 50 mg.

Thiamine mononitrate (I.P., U.S.P.) :

Properties and uses : It is a white crystalline powder with slight characterisitc odour. It is soluble in water, less in alcohol and chloroform. Aqueous solutions are slightly acidic or neutral. It is more stable than thiamine hydrochloride. Action and uses are similar to that of thiamine hydrochloride. Prophylactic dose is 2 to 5 mg and therapeutic dose is 25 to 100 mg.

Riboflavine (Vitamin B_2) : It is also known as Lactoflavin. It is widely distributed in nature, in plants and animals. It is an essential constituent of living cells. The best natural sources are rice polishing, wheat germ, milk, spinach, eggs, meat, beef and other food materials. It is also synthesized by number of micro-organism, including some bacterias of human intestinal tract. It is also prepared synthetically.

Riboflavine (I.P., B.P., U.S.P.) :

$$CH_2-CH-OH-CHOH-CHOH-CH_2OH$$

Properties : It is a yellow to orange-yellow crystalline powder with slight characteristic odour. It is slightly soluble in water, more soluble in alkaline solutions, slightly soluble in alcohol, insoluble in chloroform and soluble in solutions of alkali hydroxides. In dry state, it is much affected by light, but in alkaline media it rapidly deteriorates. It is unstable to light and heat (thermolabile) and is converted to lumaflavine which is fluorescent but is devoid of biological activity. It is more stable in acidic medium between pH 1 to 6.5. It is rapidly reduced by hydrosulphite or hydrogen in the presence of zinc in acidic media to lucoriboflavine which is easily oxidsed by the air. Due to this oxidation-reduction property it owes its biological importance.

Riboflavine sodium phosphate : It occurs as yellow to orange yellow crystalline powder, hygroscopic in nature, soluble in water, sparingly soluble in alcohol and insoluble in chloroform and ether. Aqueous solutions are acidic in nature. It must be stored in tight containers, protected from light. It is mainly used in multivitamin formulations, because of its high water solubility. Usual prophylactic dose is 1 to 4 mg and therapeutic dose is 5 to 10 mg.

Deficiency, actions and uses: Deficiency symptoms of riboflavine includes reddening of lips and tissues at the corner of mouth, colour change of mucus membrane. There is sensation of itching, burning of eye lids, lacrimation and photophobia. Riboflavine plays an important role as prosthetic groups of number of enzyme systems, which are involved in the oxidation of carbohydrates and amino acids. It is used in the form of tablets and injection. Prophylactic dose is 1 to 4 mg daily and therapeutic dose is 5 to 10 mg daily. It is used to treat riboflavine deficiency and with other vitamins in the treatment of pelegra and beriberi.

Niacin : This covers both nicotinic acid and Nicotinamide (niacinamide), which have similar properties as vitamins. It is synthesized in growing plants and is present in most of the food articles in small amount. Good sources for niacin are pork, lamb, hog kidney, bakery yeast, wheat germ, green peas etc. It is manufactured synthetically from β-picoline and also from quinoline.

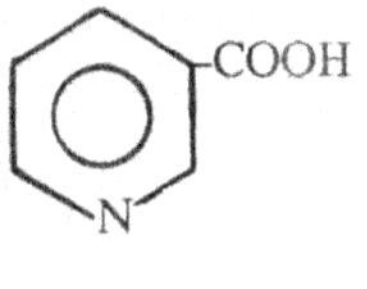

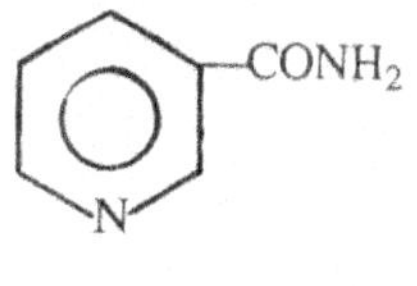

Nicotinic acid   Nicotinamide pyrdine
pyridine 3, carboxylic acid   pyridine 3 - carboxylic acid anide

Nicotinic acid (I.P., B.P., U.S.P.) :

Properties : It occurs as white to creamy white crystalline powder, moderately soluble in water, freely soluble in boiling water, boiling alcohol and solutions of alkali hydroxides and carbonates. It is stable in air but gets affected slowly by light. It is stored in a light resistant container

Niacinamide (I.P., B.P., U.S.P.) :

Properties : It is a white crystalline powder, practically odourless, freely soluble in water and alcohol and dissolves in glycerine. Its aqueous solutions are neutral to litmus.

Deficiency, actions and uses : Deficiency of niacin leads to a disease known as " Pellagra ", which is characterised by development of typical dermatitis with pigmentation, reddening and swollening of tongue, ulceration of mucus membrane of alimentary tract. Vagina is also affected. In the body, niacin is converted to niacinamide which is a constituent of co-enzyme I and II that occurs in enzyme systems involved in oxidation of carbohydrates. Niacin is absorbed readily from the intestinal tract and it can be given in large doses orally or parenterally. It is given in pellagra in the form of tablets, capsules or injections. Uusal prophyactic dose is 15 to 30 mg daily and therapeutic dose is 50 to 250 mg daily.

Pyridoxine (Vitamin B_6) : Pyridoxine is the term used for the group of the naturally occuring pyridines which are related to each other metabolically and functionally, and are interconvertible in vivo in their phosphorylated forms. It is widely distributed in plant and animal kingdoms. Yeast and rice bran are good sources for vitamin B_6 activity. It is also found in cereals, seeds, milk, eggs and green vegetables.

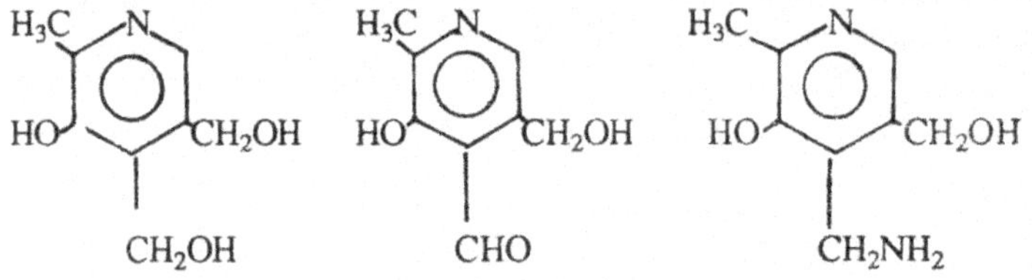

Pyridoxine   Pyridoxal   Pyridoxamine

Pyridoxine hydrochloride (I.P., B.P., U.S.P.) :

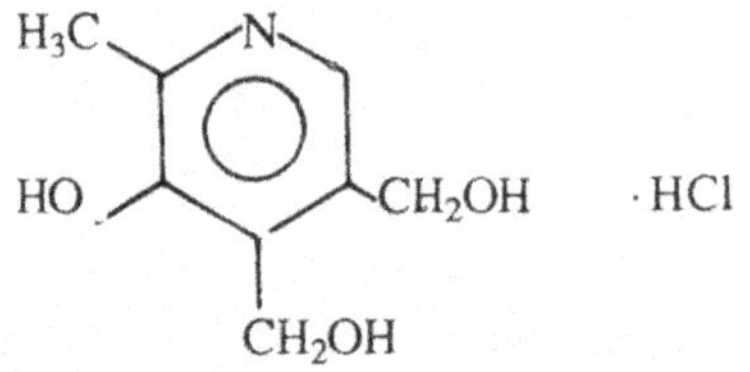

3-hydroxy-4,5 bis- (hydroxymethyl) - 2-methylpyridine hydrochloride

Properties : It occurs as colourless crystalline powder, soluble in water, less in alcohol, and insoluble in chloroform. In dry state, it is stable in light and air. concentrated solutions(10 % w/w) has a pH between 2.6 and 3. Aqueous solutions are sterilized at pH 5 by autoclaving. It is easily oxidised by oxidising agents like H_2O_2. It is stable in multivitamin preparations.

Deficiency, symptoms, actions and uses : Pyridoxine deficiency normally do not exist as it is widely distributed in nature. It is essential for normal growth and functions and is related with protein and amino acid metabolism. It is also related to carbohydrate metabolism. The deficiency symptoms are characterised by edema, loss of hair, and convulsive seizures. It is mainly used for muscular weakness, epilepsy scizures, acne, radiation sickness and nausea and vomitting in pregnancy. It is used in the form of tablets or injections. Usual oral or parenteral dose is 5 mg or as per need of the patient.

Pantothenic acid : It is widely distributed in plant and animal tissues, Good sources for pantothenic acid are yeast, liver, kidney and eggs. Many organisms are capable of synthesizing pantothenic acid. Another commercial liquid preparation available is D-pantothenyl alcohol (panthenol). It is also available in the form of calcium or sodium salt. Panthothenic acid is white crystalline powder, freely soluble in water. In neutral solution it is fairly stable but is sensitive to acid, alkali and heat.

Calcium pentothenate (I.P., U.S.P.) :

Properties : It is a white powder, slightly hygroscopic in nature. It is freely soluble in water, and insoluble in alcohol. Aqueous solutions are neutral or slightly alkaline in nature. In dry state it is stable in air, but unstable to heat. In the form of solutions both in acidic or alkaline media it is unstable to heat. It is most stable at pH 5.5 to 6.5 and the solutions are sterilized at this pH by autoclaving in short time without much loss. It must be preserved in tight and light resistant containers.

As pantothenic acid is widely distributed in plant and animal tissue deficiency is not normally observed. It is a normal constituent of cell and is essential in cellular metabolism. Its biological importance is because of the fact that it is incorporated into coenzyme A (CoA) which is involved in many enzymatic reactions. Calcium pantothenate tablets are official in U.S.P. and usual dose is 10 mg orally.

Folic acid (I.P.B.P.) : The vitamin was first isolated from spinach leaves. It occurs in the form of conjugates as pteroyltriglutamic and pteroyl heptaglutamic acid. Cereals, green vegetables, liver, kidney and muscle are good sources of folic acid. It is manufactured by synthetic methods.

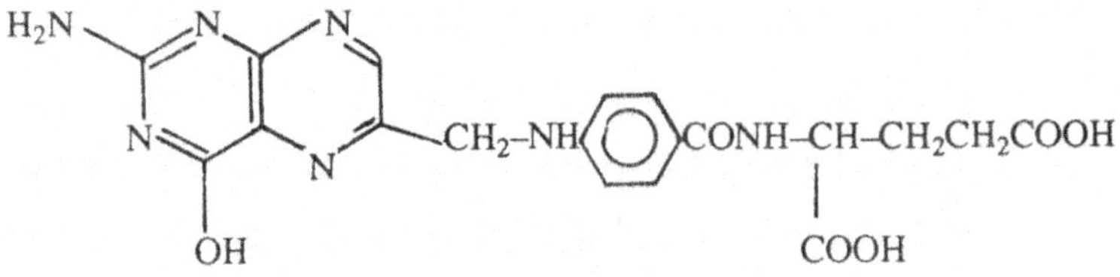

4-(2-amino-4-hydroxy-6-pteridin-6-yl) methyl amino benzoyl-L glutamic acid

Properties : An orange yellowish crystalline powder. On heating it decomposes without melting. It is sparingly soluble in water, insoluble in alcohol, ether but soluble in solutions of alkali hydroxides, carbonates, dilute hydrochloric acid and sulphuric acid. It is easily destroyed by heat in acidic media but is quite stable in pharmaceutical processing and storage. It undergoes oxidation easily. The aqueous solution can be sterilized by autoclaving.

Deficiency symptoms, actions and uses : Deficiency of this vitamin is caused by vitamin deficient diet or by giving sulphonamides which reduces synthesis of this vitamin in intestine by bacterial flora. Its deficiency is characterised by anaemia. It is involved as coenzyme in the metabolic reactions in which one carbon unit is transferred. It seems that folinic acid is the natural factor in liver digest and folic acid arises from it.

Folic acid is used in the form of tablets and injection in the treatment of certain megaloblastic anaemia, pernicious anaemia of pregnancy and macrocytic anaemia. It also finds use with vitamin B_{12} in pernicious anaemia. Usual oral or intramuscular dose is 5 to 20 mg.

Cyanocobalamine (Vitamin B_{12}) :

It is was first isolated from liver. It is also formed during fermentation process of antibiotics from micro organisms such as *Streptomyces griseus, S aureofaciens* etc. Commercially it is obtained from the microbial source.

Cyanocobalamine (I.P., B.P., U.S.P.) :

Structure is very complex. It occurs as red crystals, or crystalline powder, hygroscopic in nature. It is soluble in water and alcohol, and insoluble in acetone, chloroform and ether. When anhydrous form is exposed to air it absorbs about 12 per cent moisture. Vitamin B_{12} and its solutions are affected by light. Folic acid and vitamin B_{12} are stable at pH 6 to 6.5. It is stable in solutions of sorbitol and glycerine. Aqueous solutions can be sterilized by autoclaving for 15 minutes only.

Hydroxycobalamine (U.S.P.) : It is an analogue of cyanocobalamine wherein cyano radical is replaced by hydroxyl radical. It occurs as red crystals or crystalline powder, hygroscopic in nature. It is sparingly soluble in water and alcohol and insoluble in acetone, chloroform etc. Aqueous solutions (2 %) has pH 8 to 10. Its solution is prepared in acetate buffer at pH 3.5 to 4.5.

Following are the radioactive cyanocobalamine official preparations and are used as diagnostics and in pernicious anaemia.

1. Cyanocobalamine Co 57 capsules U.S.P.
2. Cyanocobalamine Co 57 solution U.S.P.
3. Cyanocobalamine Co 60 capsules N.F.
4. Cyanocobalamine Co 60 solution N.F.

Deficiency symptoms action, and uses : A prolong deficiency of this vitamin results in pernicious anaemia. An intrinsic factor which is normally present in gastric secretion is essential for the absorption of cyanocobalamine. In absence of intrinsic factor in permicious anaemia vitamine B_{12} is not satisfactorily absorbed. The vitamin B_{12} preparation with intrinsic factor should be given orally in pernicious anaemias. Vitamin B_{12} is also required for normal blood formation. It is effective in the treatment of macrocytic anaemia. It plays an important part in preventing the neurological changes common in pernicious anaemia. In vitamin deficiency it is administered intramuscularly, in initial dose 1 mg, repeated ten times at the interval of 2-3 days, and maintenance dose is 250 micrograms every month as per the need of the patient.

Besides, the number of individual vitamins in tablets or injection form which are official in pharmacopoeias there are many formulations available in the market in the form of vitamin B complex (which contains mainly the water-soluble group of vitamins in syrup, tablete injections etc.,) and multivitamins. The multivitamin preparations are available in various liquid-oral dosage forms containing all the vitamins of fat-soluble and water soluble group in appropriate dosage as required to cover up the deficiency of the vitamins. Few such preparations like Hexavet, Decevet capsules are official in N.F.

Chapter 28

TOPICAL ANTI-INFECTIVE AGENTS

This broad based terminology includes a wide variety of agents which are toxic to the organism, frees the host from infectious organisms. These drugs do not allow micro-organisms to grow but kill them before they invade the host and thus act as anti-infectives.

The classification of antinfective agents can be done in many ways. For example, they may be classified according to the diseases or infections against which they are used, or they may be classified according to their chemical class or groups of related compounds.

Anti-infective agents comprise antiseptic, disinfectant, germicides, etc. These are found in several chemical classes. Clinically useful offical antiinfective agents can be considered under the following categories :

I. ALCOHOLS AND ALDEHYDES

The simple aliphatic alcohols are known to possess antiseptic activity. The antibacterial activity increases with increase in molecular weight in the straight chain alcohols. Halogenation increases activity. However, with increase in molecular weight, water solubility decreases and so also the antibacterial activity. Some useful agents in this class are :

1. Alcohol (I.P., B.P., U.S.P.) : Ethyl alcohol is a clear colourless, volatile liquid with characteristic odour and burning taste. The dehydrated alcohol (contains not less than 99 % by weight of ethyl alcohol) and specially denatured alcohol (it is the ethyl alcohol containing woodnaphtha, methanol etc. rendered unfit for human consumption) are two forms of ethyl alcohol with antibacterial properties. Ethyl alcohol is extensively used as solvent and pharmaceutically has astringent, rubefacient and slight anaesthetic action.

2. Formaldehyde solution (I.P., B.P., U.S.P.) : It is called as formalin and contains about 37 % of formaldehyde with methanol (as stabalizer) in water. It can be mixed with water and alcohol and has pungent odour. On keeping at low temperature, the solution becomes cloudy. It can get easily oxidised and or polymerised. It should be stored in well closed containers in a moderately warm place. Formaldehyde has powerful effect on all kinds of cells and tissues. It thus inhibits the bacterial growth and kills them. It acts as a germicide. The gas is employed to disinfect various articles. Formaldehyde solution in saline is used as a preservative for pathological specimens.

II. HALOGEN COMPOUNDS

Some halogenated organic compounds are very good antiseptic and disinfectant in nature. These compounds owe their activity due to slow release of halogen atom which acts as antibacterial. The chlorine containing compounds act by oxidation of sulphydryl groups of bacterial enzymes or by deactivating certain bacterial proteins. The iodine compounds act by foreving irresible complxes with protein of backterial enzymes or oxidation of sulphydryl enzyme or by direct iniodination of unsaturation.

3. Chloramine T (B.P.) :

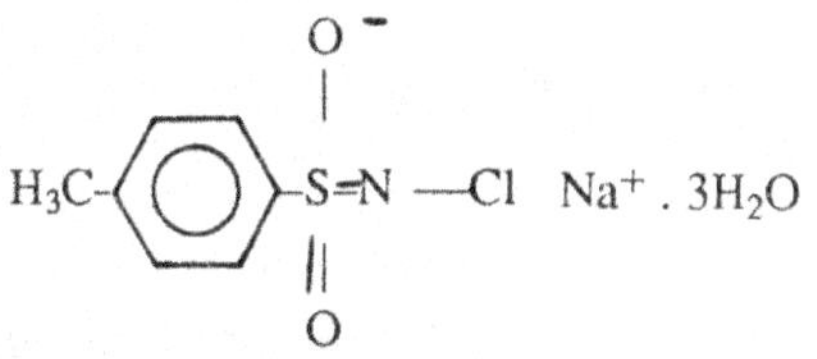

$$H_3C-C_6H_4-S(=O)(=N-Cl)-O^- \ Na^+ \cdot 3H_2O$$

N-chlorotoluene-p-sulphonimidate

It is also called as chloramine or chlorazene. It occurs as white or slightly yellow crystalline powder, with a chlorine like odour. It is soluble in water and alcohol, insoluble in ether and chloroform. It gets affected by light and liberates chlorine. Aqueous solutions slowly decompose to give sodium hypochlorite. A freshly prepared 1 to 2 % solution is used for washing wounds.

4. Chlorhexidine acetate (B.P.) :

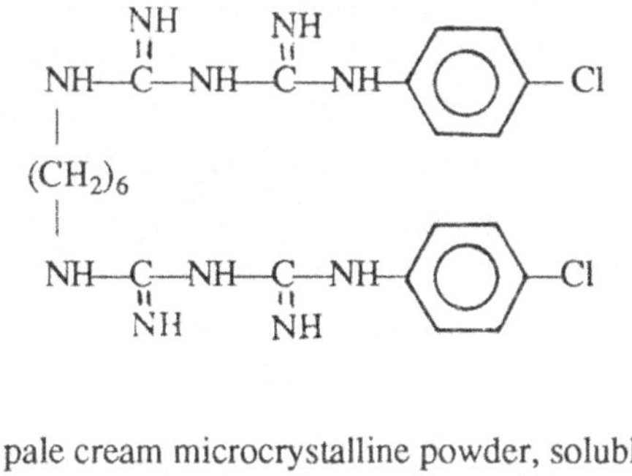

$$NH-C(=NH)-NH-C(=NH)-NH-C_6H_4-Cl$$
$$|$$
$$(CH_2)_6$$
$$|$$
$$NH-C(=NH)-NH-C(=NH)-NH-C_6H_4-Cl$$

It is a pale cream microcrystalline powder, soluble in water and alcohol but slightly soluble in glycerol. *Chlorhexidine hydrochloride* is another salt of chlorhexidine and is very slightly soluble in water. Both the salts are used in creams, dusting powders, lozenges and ointments for antiseptic action.

Chlorhexidine cream and dusting powder are official in B.P. Chlorhexidine gluconate solution is an aqueous solution containing about 20 % w/v of chlorhexidine gluconate. This is official in B.P. and is employed as nontoxic antiseptic in treatment of burns and wounds as a general disinfectant solution.

5. Dibromopropamidine isethionate (B.P.):

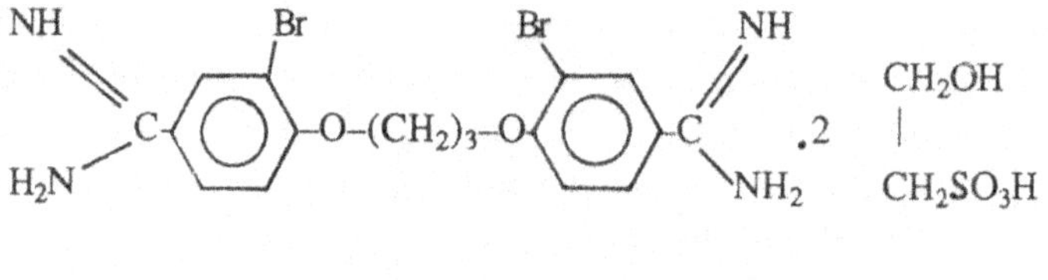

$$\underset{H_2N}{\overset{NH}{\diagdown}}C-\underset{}{\overset{Br}{\diagdown}}-O-(CH_2)_3-O-\underset{}{\overset{Br}{\diagdown}}-C\underset{NH_2}{\overset{NH}{\diagup}} \quad .2 \quad \begin{array}{c} CH_2OH \\ | \\ CH_2SO_3H \end{array}$$

3, 3'-dibromo-4, 4'-trimethylenedioxy-
dibenzimidine bis (2-hydroxy ethane sulphonate)

It is a white powder, odourless and is soluble in water and alcohol. It is used for treatment of eye infections in the form of eye ointment or opthalmic solution. It is employed externally in the form of cream for its antibacterial action.

III. PHENOLS AND RELATED COMPOUNDS

A number of phenols occurring in nature and prepared synthetically are known to possess antiseptic activity. The most widely useful agents are:

6. Phenol (I.P., U.S.P.):

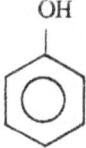

It is known as carbolic acid and is one of the oldest known antiseptic. It occurs as colourless to pink deliquescent crystalline material with characteristic odour. It is less soluble in water, more soluble in alcohol, glycerine fixed and volatile oils. Phenol is susceptible to oxidation. Exposure to air turns it pink. It is stable and solutions can be sterilized by autoclaving. A violet colour is formed with ferric chloride solution.

Aqueous solutions (0.2 to 1 %) act as bacterostatic and are used for dressing minor wounds and as antipruritic in phenolated calmine ointment. A strong solution of phenol is caustic in nature as it precipitates proteins. The caustic property is reduced by dissolving in alcohol, glycerinae or in fixed oils. It is employed in dentistry because of its local anaesthetic effect.

Phenol glycerine is a solution of phenol in glycerine acts as antiseptic and is employed in treatment of ulceration of mouth and tonsilitis.

7. Chlorocresol (I.P.) :

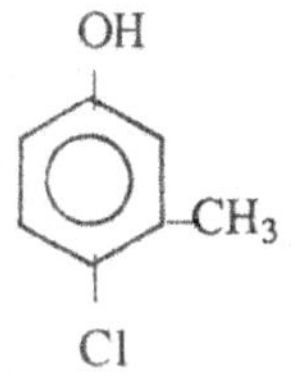

[Structure: phenol with OH on top, CH₃ at position 3, Cl at position 4]

4-chloro-3-methyl phenol

It is a colourless white crystalline solid with phenolic odour. It is sparingly soluble in water but more soluble in alcohol. It is used in 0.2 % as bactericide in sterilization process. It is used as preservative in paste, creams and other preparations meant for external use. It is usually employed in 0.1 to 0.2 % for its antibacterial effect in various formulations and has low toxicity.

8. Chloroxylenol (I.P., B.P.) :

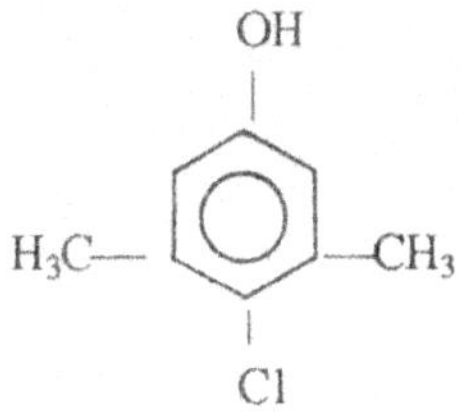

[Structure: phenol with OH on top, two CH₃ groups and Cl]

4 chloro 3, 5 dimethyl phenol

It occurs as a white to cream coloured crystals with characteristic odour. It is volatile in nature and is very sparingly soluble in water but soluble in alcohol. The chloroxylenol solution contains 1 % chloroxylenol and is used as disinfectant for skin and general purpose antiseptic.

9. Cresol (I.P.) :

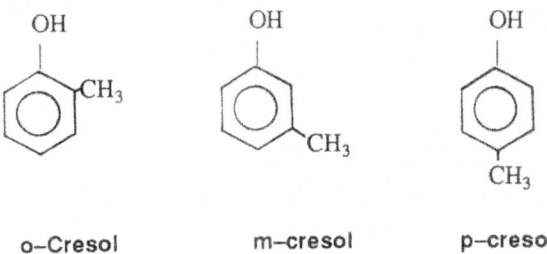

o-Cresol   m-cresol   p-cresol

The official form of cresol is a mixtrue of o, m and p isomers. It occurs as pale yellow or brownish yellow liquid with characteristic smell of phenol. The colour darkens on exposure to light. It is slightly soluble in water and more in alcohol. It is mainly employed as disinfectant of general type in hospitals and in homes in the form of soap solution. Solution of cresol with soap is a very popular preparation.

10. Hexachlorophene (I.P., U.S.P.) Hexachlorophane (B.P.)

It is a white to pale buff powder with characteristic odour. It is insoluble in water, soluble in alcohol, stable in air. It is used in 2 to 3 % concentration in creams, dusting powders, ointments, soaps and in articles and similar preparations for disinfectant effect. It is effective against wide range of Gram-positive and Gram-negative organisms and is less irritating to cells and tissues. However, it is not used in treatment of burns because of its systemic toxicity.

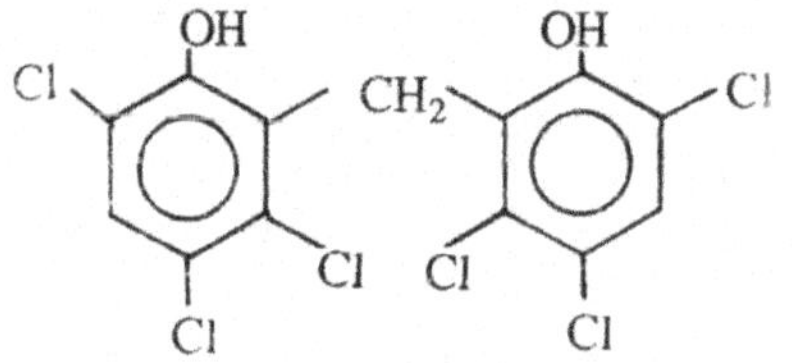

2, 2'-methylene-bis-(3,4,6-trichlorophenol)

11. Thymol (I.P., B.P.) :

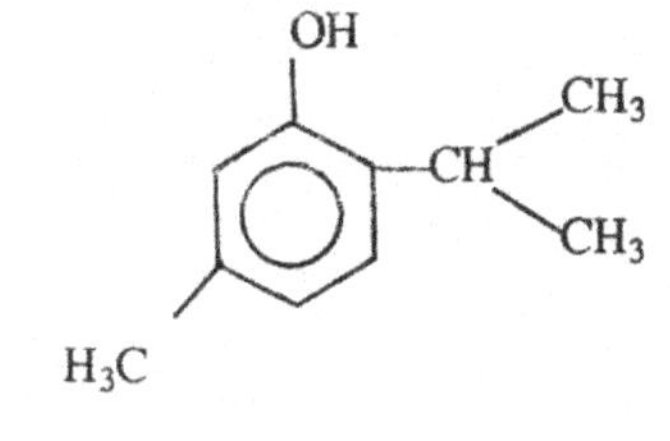

2-isopropyl-5-methyl phenol

It occurs in nature in various volatile oils and can be prepared synthetically. It is a white large crystalline solid or tears with pungent charateristic odour. It is practically insoluble in water, soluble in alcohol and in vegetable, volatile oils. It is stable and forms eutectic mixture with menthol and camphor. It acts as deodorant and antiseptic and hence is employed in mouth washes, gargles etc. It is an ingredient of dusting powder, pain-balm, kaolin poultice, toothache drops and various other similar preparations.

IV. MERCURY COMPOUNDS

Mercury and its salts have been used in early days as anti-infectives. Metallic mercury in the ointment base was used for skin infections. Similarly, inorganic mercury compounds as bacteriostatic through inhibition of sulphydryl enzymes of bacteria. Since inorganic compounds are irritating and toxic in nature, organic mercurial compounds have been developed.

12. Merbromin (Mercurochrome):

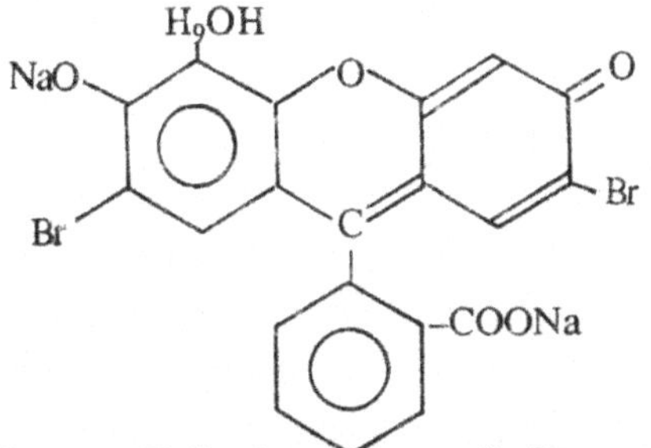

2', 7'-dibromo-8'-(hydroxymercuri) fluorescein)

It is the first organic mercury compound developed as antiseptic.

It is red coloured solid, freely soluble in water, insoluble in alcohol and ether. It is used in 2 % aqueous solution or hydroalcoholic solution for external application on skin, mucous membrane as a general purpose antiseptic. It is nonirritating and less toxic agent.

13. Thiomersal (B.P.):

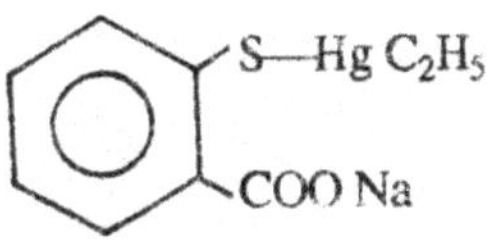

Sodium-(2--carboxyphenyl)thio-ethylmercury

It is a cream coloured powder, soluble in water. It is susceptible to light and hence stored in light resistant containers. It is used in 0.1 % aqueous solution for preoperative treatment to skin and in very dilute solution (0.01 to 0.2 %) as antiseptic for irrigation purpose. It acts as preservative and used in some biological products. It is also non-irritating and doses not stain clothes or tissues.

V. DYES

A large number of organic days have been developed for various purposes. Out of these some are used in pharmaceutical products, cosmetics and foods. The dyes need certification and hence are called as certified colours.

The important dyes which are used for antiseptic, disinfectant and similar medicinal purposes belong to acridine, triphenyl methane and thiazine classes. Some dyes ionise and carry negative charge and these are called acid dyes. Usually they contain sulphonic acid group and the salts of these are water-soluble. The other type of dyes on ionization have positive charge and are called as basic dyes. The medicinally useful dyes are –

14. Aminacrine hydrochloride (I.P.) :

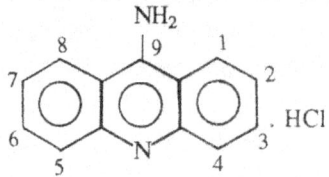

9-aminoacridine hydrochloride

It occurs as a pale yellow crystalline powder odourless, bitter to taste. It is soluble in water, alcohol and glycerine. It is used as general purpose antiseptic for topical applications in creams, ointment etc. or for pressing of wounds in 0.1 to 1 % concentration.

15. Proflavine hemisulphate (I.P.) :

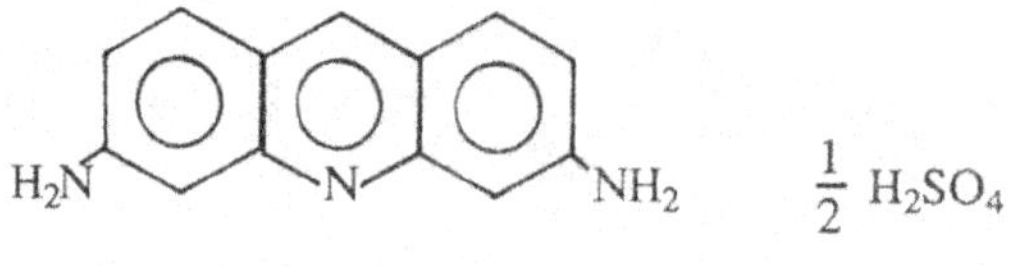

3, 6-diaminoacridine sulphate

It occurs as red coloured hygroscopic powder and is odourless. It is sensitive to light. It is soluble in water and aqueous solution shows green fluorescence. It is employed similarly to aminacrine hydrochloride in 0.1 to 1 % concentration as disinfectant.

16. Acriflavine :

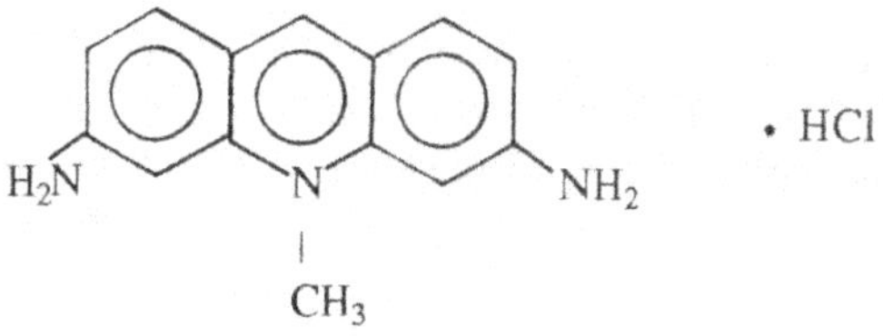

3, 6, diamino 10 methyl acridine hydrochloride

The acriflavine base is neutral and occurs as deep orange coloured granules. It is soluble in water and sparingly soluble in alcohol. It exhibits fluorescene and is sensitive to light. The acriflavine solution is slightly basic and is less irritant to mucous membrane than its hydrochloride. The hydrochloride salt is also water-soluble and acts as antibacterial in 0.01 to 0.1 % solution for local application.

17. **Brilliant green (I.P., B.P.)** :

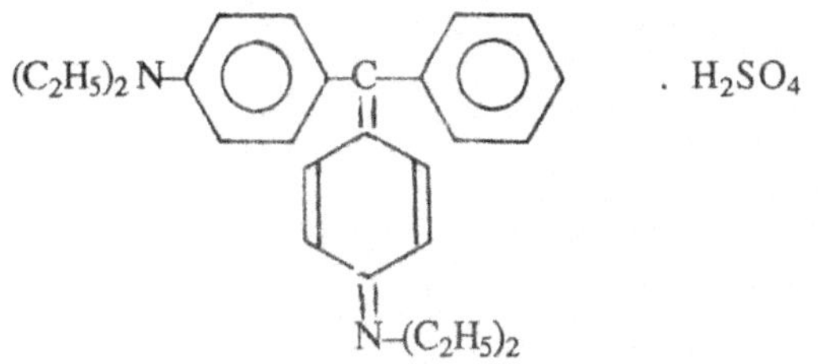

$$(C_2H_5)_2N-\phi-C(-\phi)=\phi=N(C_2H_5)_2 \cdot H_2SO_4$$

It belongs to class triphenyl methane dye and occurs as sulphate as dark shining crystals. It is soluble in water and alcohol. It is used as 0.05 to 0.1 % aqueous solution as antiseptic in treatment to wounds and burns and along with gentian violet (crystals violet) as throat paint.

18. **Crystal violet (I.P., B.P.) Gentian violet (U.S.P.)** :

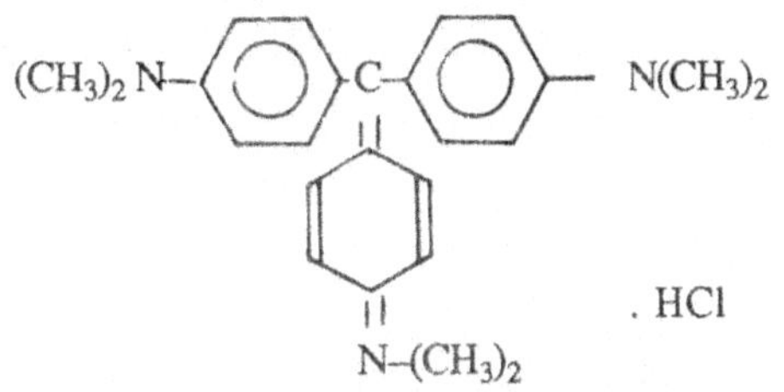

$$(CH_3)_2N-\phi-C(-\phi)=\phi=N(CH_3)_2 \quad N(CH_3)_2 \cdot HCl$$

It occurs as green crystals or granules with metallic luster. It is soluble in water, alcohol and glycerine. The dye is more-effective against Gram-positive organisms than Gram-negative. It is employed externally in 0.5 to 1 % solution in various bacterial and fungul infections of skin and also in applications to burns, boils etc.

19. **Methylene blue (U.S.P.)** :

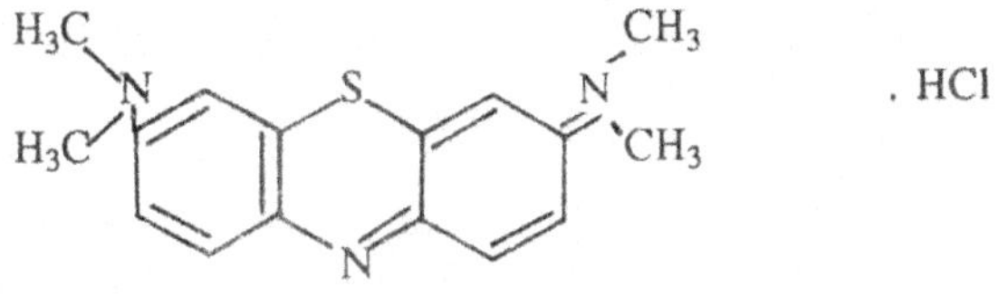

$$\begin{array}{c} H_3C \\ N \end{array} S \begin{array}{c} CH_3 \\ N \end{array} \cdot HCl$$
$$H_3C CH_3$$

3, 7-bis (dimethylamino) phenazathionium chloride

The dye belongs to phenothiazine class. It is a dark green crystal or granules with bronze luster. It is soluble in water, alcohol and also in chloroform. It is thermostable and solutions can be sterilized by autoclaving. It is a weak antiseptic and is used for external application in skin diseases. Because of its low toxicity, it is employed as a dye to test renal function. It is also used in staining of nerve cells. Methylene blue also acts as antimalerial and as antidote in cyanide and nitrate poisoning.

VI. SURFACE ACTIVE AGENTS

The surface active agents are classified into ionic and non-ionic types and the ionic types are further subdivided into cationic and anionic types. These agents, in general, have various pharmaceutical applications. The cationic surface active agents have ability to precipitate proteins (of micro organisms also) and thus become useful as antimicrobial agents.

The quaternary ammonium compounds on ionization become cationic in nature and act as antibacterial against a number of Gram-positive, Gram-negative and many fungi and viruses. Some of the official compounds under this category are :

20. Benzalkonium chloride (B.P., U.S.P.) :

$$\text{C}_6\text{H}_5\text{-CH}_2\text{-}\overset{+}{\underset{\underset{\text{CH}_3}{|}}{\overset{\overset{\text{CH}_3}{|}}{\text{N}}}}\text{-R} \quad \text{Cl}^-$$

$$R = C_8H_{17} \text{ to } C_{18}H_{37}$$

This drugs is a mixture of alkylbenzyldimethyl ammonium chloride. The alkyl groups have eight to eighteen carbon atoms. It is used in the form of solution.

It occurs as a clear colourless or pale yellow thick syrupy liquid with characteristic odour. Aqueous solutions are alkaline to litmus and foam on shaking. The solution possesses wetting detergent and emulsifying properties. It is effective against many pathogenic organisms A 0.05 % solution is used for storage of surgical instruments. It is employed in 0.02 % solution as a detergent antiseptic for skin and mucous.

21. Cetrimide (B.P.) : It occurs as whitish, hygroscopic granular or powder with characteristic odour. It is soluble in water and alcohol. It is a non-toxic agent and is employed in the form of cream for cleansing wounds, burns and as a general purpose antiseptic. A 0.1 % in aqueous solution is employed for disinfecting utensils, apparatus, surgical wares etc.

22. **Cetylpyridinium chloride (B.P., U.S.P.)** :

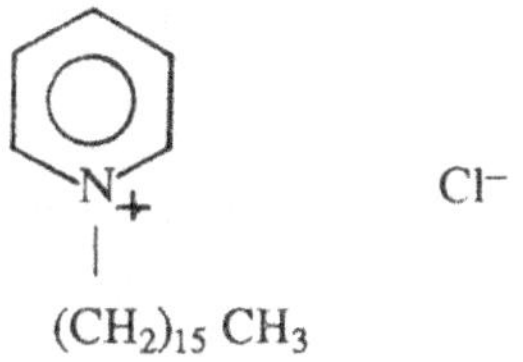

$$\underset{(CH_2)_{15}CH_3}{\underset{|}{C_5H_5N^+}} \quad Cl^-$$

It is white powder with characteristic odour, soluble in water and alcohol. It is employed in 0.1 to 1 % in aqueous solutions for cleaning wounds and skin, in 0.05 to 1 % for disinfectant effect on softer tissues. It is employed in throat lozenges and 0.5 % solution as mouthwash.

23. **Domiphen bromide (B.P.)** :

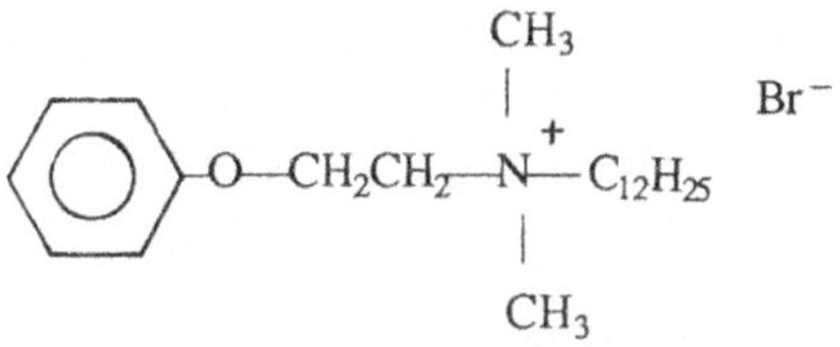

$$C_6H_5-O-CH_2CH_2-\underset{\underset{CH_3}{|}}{\overset{\overset{CH_3}{|}}{N^+}}-C_{12}H_{25} \quad Br^-$$

deodecyldimethyl-2-phenoxy ethyl ammonium bromide

It is a white microcrystalline powder with faint odour. It is soluble in water and alcohol. The drug has low toxicity and good disinfectant as well antifungal activity. It is employed in 0.2 % aqueous solution in mouthwash, cleansing wounds and also in surgical dressings. It is used in throat lozenges also.

24. **Octaphonium chloride (B.P.)** :

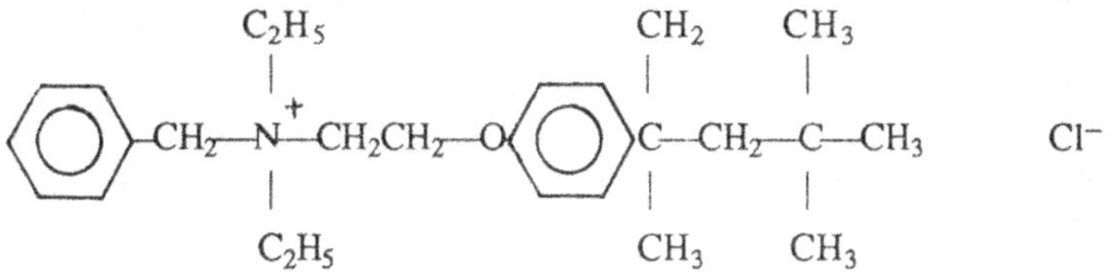

$$C_6H_5-CH_2-\underset{\underset{C_2H_5}{|}}{\overset{\overset{C_2H_5}{|}}{N^+}}-CH_2CH_2-O-C_6H_4-\underset{\underset{CH_3}{|}}{\overset{\overset{CH_2}{|}}{C}}-CH_2-\underset{\underset{CH_3}{|}}{\overset{\overset{CH_3}{|}}{C}}-CH_3 \quad Cl^-$$

It is a white crystalline powder, almost odourless and is soluble in water. It is employed similarly to domiphenbromide as general purpose antiseptic in .05 % aqueous solution. It acts as antiseptic-detergent.

VII. MISCELLANEOUS AGENTS

25. Dequalinum chloride (B.P.) :

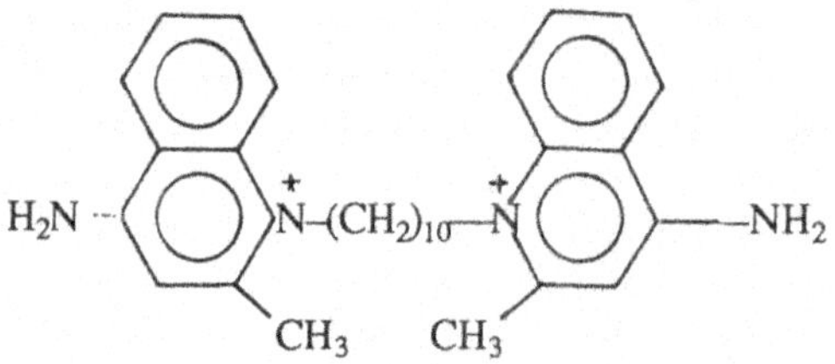

$$H_2N-\text{[quinolinium]}-N^+-(CH_2)_{10}-N^+-\text{[quinolinium]}-NH_2$$
(with CH_3 substituents)

It is a creamy white powder, odourless and slightly soluble in water. It iis used in the treatment of bacterial infections of gums, throat etc. for which it is employed in the form of paint.

26. Nitrofurazone (B.P.) :

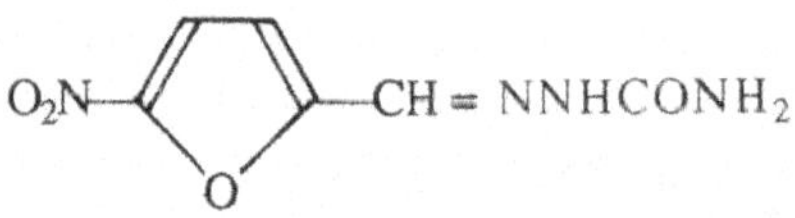

$$O_2N-\text{[furan]}-CH=NNHCONH_2$$

5-nitro-2-furfuraldehydesemicarbazone

It occurs as lemon yellow crystalline powder, odourless, stable to heat but darkens on exposure to light. It is slightly soluble in water propyleneglycol, alcohols and almost insoluble insoluble in ether and chloroform. It is used in ointments, solutions and suppositories usually as 0.2 % strength for topical applications in treatment of injections of skin, burns, cleaning wounds and ulcers.

Chapter 29

ANTI-FUNGAL AGENTS

Similar to bacterial infection, fungus infection is also very common. A large number of chemical agents are used in a variety of fungal infections. Newer synthetic agents are tried as antifungal agents since the ideal antifungal agent has not yet been evolved. Some compounds like fatty acids and their copper and zinc salts act as fungistatic, while other as fungicidal. The antifungal agents are used in variety of fungal infections. Some are active orally while others are mostly applied topically in the form of ointment, creams, liniments, lotions, suspensions etc. The antifungal agents can be broadly classified into two categories : (i) chemical antifungal agents and (ii) antibiotics.

CHEMICAL ANTIFUNGAL AGENTS

A number of chemical agents have antibacterial-antifungal properties. The simplest are the aromatic acids like benzoic ; salicylic acid etc. The antifungal agents in clinical use are :

1. **Benzoic acid (I.P., B.P., U.S.P.) :**

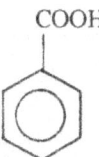

It occurs as a colourless crystals, scales, flakes, odourless and is sparingly soluble in cold water, more soluble in hot water, alcohol, chloroform, ether and alkali hydroxides. It is stable, gives buff coloured precipitate with ferric salt, forms insoluble salt with heavy metals like silver, lead, mercury etc.

Benzoic acid is used externally as antiseptic in lotions, mouth washes etc. Benzoic acid in combination with the salicylic acid acts as antifungal agent. Officially it is known as whitefields ointment. It is an effective food preservation as an acid and as sodium salt.

2. Salicylic acid (I.P., B.P., U.S.P.) :

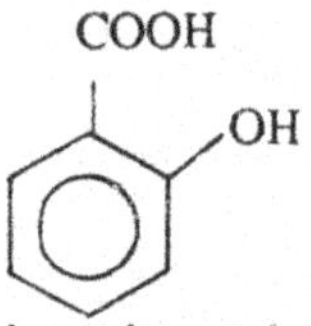

COOH
OH

2-hydroxybenzoic acid

It occurs as white crystals or fluffy powder. It is slightly soluble in water and soluble in usual organic solvents and alkali hydroxides. It produces violet colour with ferric salts. Coloured compounds are produced with oxidising agents. It forms salts with heavy metals. It has strong antiseptic properties and it acts as antifungal in 3 to 5 % in concentration the form of ointment, cream, lotions etc.

3. Clotrimazole (B.P.) :

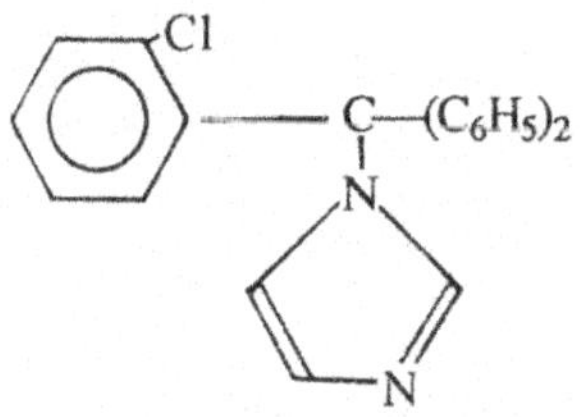

$$\text{Ar-Cl} - C - (C_6H_5)_2$$
with imidazole N

1-(2-chlorotrityl)imidazole

It is a pale yellow odourless powder. It is insoluble in water, soluble in alcohol and chloroform. It is stored in closed container, protected from light. Clotrimazole is mainly used in cream and pessaries in the treatment of Tinea infections and candiasis by *Candida albicans*.

4. Dithranol (I.P., B.P.) :

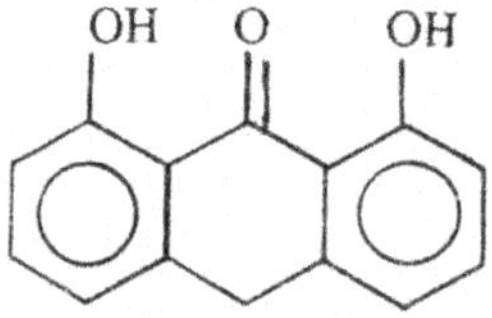

OH O OH

1, 8-dihydroxyanthrone

It is yellow powder, odourless, practically insoluble in water, slightly in alcohol, soluble in chloroform. It acts as fungicide and primarily employed externally on the skin in treatment of ringworm infections. It is also used in the treatment of psoriasis in 1 % strength as ointment or paste.

5. Econazole nitrate (B.P.) :

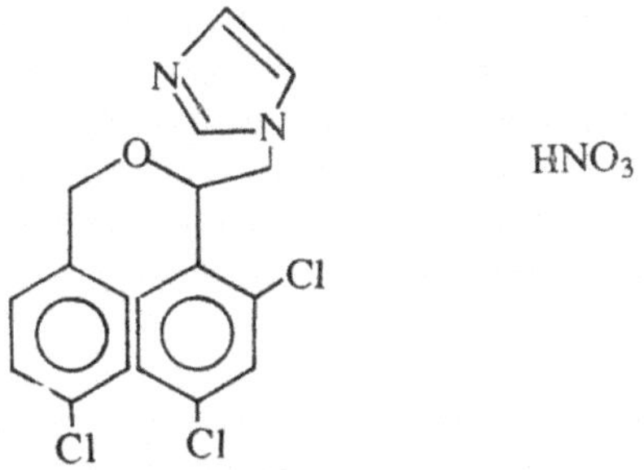

[Chemical structure with HNO₃]

1 [2, 4-dichloro-β-(p-chlorobenzyloxy) phenethyl]immidazole

It occurs as white powder, soluble in water and in ether. The drug is effective antifungal and is used in creams.

6. Flucytosine (B.P., U.S.P.) :

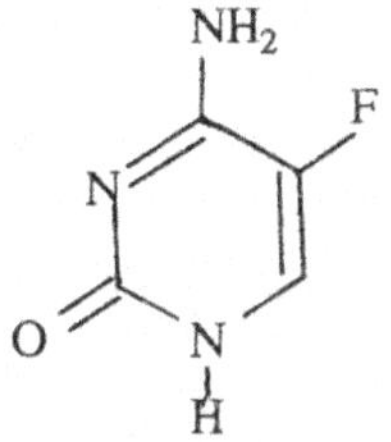

[Chemical structure]

5-flurocytosine

It is a white to offwhite powder, odourless and is sparingly soluble in water and alcohol. It is given orally and is used in 250 to 500 mg dose in capsules as antifungal agent.

7. Miconazole Nitrate (B.P.) :

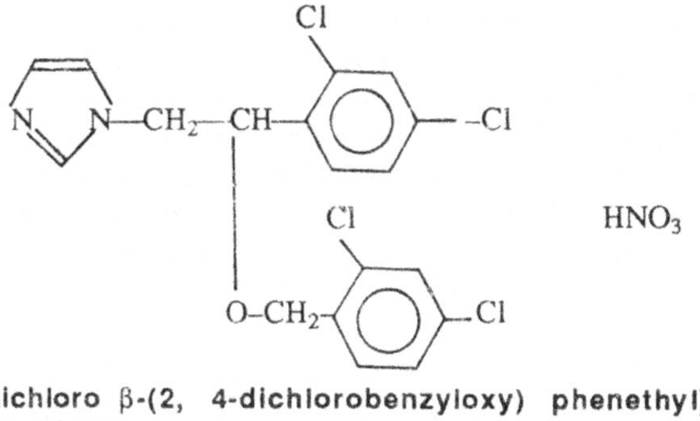

[Chemical structure with HNO₃]

1-[2, 4 dichloro β-(2, 4-dichlorobenzyloxy) phenethyl] imidazole nitrate

It occurs as white crystalline or microcrystalline powder, slightly soluble in water, more soluble in alcohol. It is used in 2.0 % in creams to be applied externally in the treatment of tinea and other fungal infections.

8. Sodium caprylate [$CH_3(CH_2)_5 CH_2 COONa$]

It is a sodium salt of caprylic acid (found in coconut and palm kernel). It is white cream coloured granule or powder, soluble in water and sparingly soluble in alcohol. It is used in solution, powder or ointment as antifungal effective against microsporous and *candida albicans*. No skin reaction occurs even on continued use.

9. Tolnaftate (B.P.) :

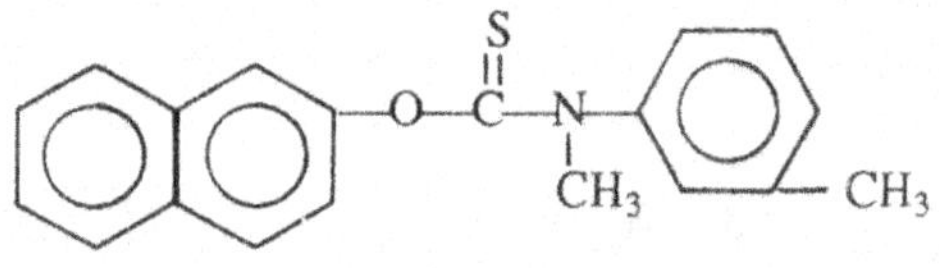

O-2-naphthyl N-methyl-m-tolylthiocarbamate

It occurs as white to creamy-white powder, odourless ; practically insoluble in water, soluble in chloroform and ether. It is a very potent antifungal agent. In 1 to 2 drops of 1 % solution in propylene glycol it is applied externally in the treatment of fungal infections.

10. Undecylenic acid (I.P., U.S.P.), Undecanolic acid (B.P.) :

$$CH_2 = CH-(CH_2)_8-COOH$$

It is obtained by cracking castor oil. It occurs as yellow liquid with characteristic odour. It is practically insoluble in water but can be mixed with organic solvents. It is employed in 10 % strength in emulsions, lotions, ointments or powders as effective fungistatic agent. It is also used in capsules for treatment of psoriasis.

Zinc undecylenate or zinc undecanolate : It is a zinc salt of undecylenic acid. It is used as antifungal agent in combination with free undecanoic acid and applied externally.

11. Furazolidone (B.P.) :

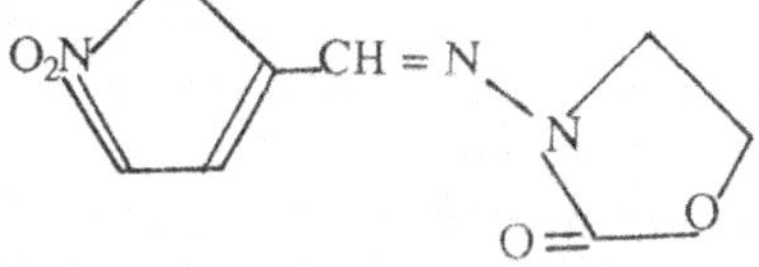

It is a yellow crystalline powder, slightly soluble in water and alcohol. It is given orally in 400 mg daily in divided doses as antibacterial, antifungal and antiprotozoal agent.

ANTIBIOTICS

Certain substances are effective orally as antifungal agents. These include flucytosine and some antifungal antibiotics.

Anti-fungal Agents

1. Amphoterian B (I.P., B.P.) :

It belongs to the polyene macrolide class. It is a mixture of antibiotics produced by *streptomyces nodasus* named as amphotericin A and B. The B component is more active. It occurs as yellow orange coloured powder, odourless and is soluble in water. It is amphoteric in nature. It is unstable in aqueous medium as it deteriorates rapidly. It is given in the form of colloidal suspension along with sodium deoxy-colate for oral administration or by intravenous infusion of fungal infection in 100 to 250 mg per kg dose. It can be applied externally also.

2. Candicidin (B.P., U.S.P.) : The antibiotic is obtained from *streptomyces griseus*. It is yellow powder, practically insoluble in water. It is used for local treatment in the form of ointment and vaginal tablets in vaginal infection.

3. Griseofulvine (B.P., U.S.P.) :

It is a macrolide antibiotic produced by the growth of *penicillium greseofuluum*. It occurs as white pale cream powder, practically insoluble in water. It is effective orally but gets slowly absorbed from gastro-intestinal tract. It is given in 500 mg to 1 g dose in the form of tablets in the treatment of variety of fungal infections. Griseofulvin tablets are official in B.P., U.S.P. while capsules are official in U.S.P. Tablets are usually available containing 125, 250 or 500 mg of microcrystalline grisiofulvin.

4. Nystatin (B.P., U.S.P.) :

The antibiotic belongs to polyene class The antibiotic is produced from *streptomyces noursei*. It is a yellow to light tan powder. It is a slightly soluble in water, sparingly soluble in organic solvents. It is unstable to heat, light, air and moisture. The solutions of nystatin are rapidly inactivated by acids and bases. Nystatin is used orally as tablets (offical in B.P.) and as oral suspension (1 lack units per ml) in 4 to 6 lack units four times a day.

5. Homycin

It is polyne class of antibiotic produced by *streptomyees pimprina*. It has antifungal and trichomonocial activity. It is used topically as well by oral route in fungal infection.

Chapter 30

ANTITUBERCULAR AND ANTILEPROTIC AGENTS

The bacterial species called as *Mycobacterium* is characterised by formation of nodules and is responsible for two diseases namely tuberculosis and leprosy. In tuberculosis, the causative organism is *Mycobacterium tuberculosis*. This organism affects or attacks almost any tissue and lungs being the most common target of this organism. After the preliminary phase, the organism spreads effecting other tissues and organs. Affected person develops anorexia, grows weaker and loses weight.

The disease leprosy is caused by the micro-organism *M. leprae*.

The chemical agents of clinical use as antitubercular and antileprotic are as follows:

ANTITUBERCULAR DRUGS

The usual antibacterial agents are not effective against mycobacterium. Specific chemical agents which act as antitubercular have been developed. These drugs can be categorised into (i) synthetic drugs and (ii) antibiotics.

I. SYNTHETIC DRUGS

The important drugs are:
1. **Paraamino salicylic acid : (PAS)**

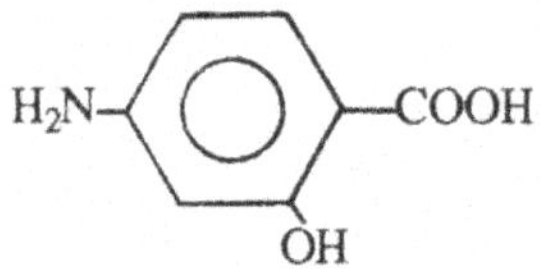

$$H_2N-\underset{OH}{\underset{|}{C_6H_3}}-COOH$$

This is commonly known as PAS and it occurs as white powder which darkens on exposure to light and air and has slight odour. It is sparingly soluble in water (0.1 %) but more soluble in alcohol. PAS is known to possess remarkably selective action against human tubercular bacilli. In combination it is usually employed along with streptomycin or isonazid wherein PAS enhances the clinical response or permits lower doses to be employed as antitubercular. PAS is used alone only when the strain of organism has developed resistance to other agents. PAS was official in various pharmacopoeias, however, it is replaced by its sodium and calcium salt.

Calcium aminosalicylate (I.P.), Calcium PAS :

$$[H_2N-C_6H_3(OH)-COO]_2 Ca \cdot 3H_2O$$

Calcium-4-amino-2-hydroxy-benzoate

It occurs as white-creamy powder or granules with unpleasant odour and saline taste. It is freely soluble in water and alcohol. Aqueous solutions decompose rapidly and rate depends on the pH and the temperature. It is potent tuberculostatic, shows less gastrointestinal irritations, and is employed in the form of tablets in 10 to 20 g daily in divided doses.

Sodium aminosalicylate (I.P., B.P., U.S.P.) : known as **Sodium PAS** : It is a sodium salt of para-aminosalicylic acid dihydrate. It occurs as yellowish-white powder or crystals with slight odour. It is readily soluble in water, sparingly in alcohol, almost insoluble in ether. The aqueous solutions are unstable and darken on exposure to light. Incompatibilities result with acids, ferric salts and oxidising agents. It is used as tablets or granules (both official) in 4 to 5 g three times a day along with streptomycin or isoniazid in reatment of various forms of tuberculosis.

2. **Ethambutol hydrochloride (I.P., B.P.) :**

$$CH_3CH_2-CH(CH_2OH)-NH-(CH_2)_2NH-CH(CH_2OH)-CH_2CH_3 \cdot 2HCl$$

(R,R)-N, N'-ethylenebis-(2-aminobutan-1-ol)dihydro-chloride

Chemically it is an aliphatic diamine. The dextro isomer ismore potent than levoisomer. It is a white crystalline powder, freely soluble in water. It is used in 15 to 25 mg per kg body weight daily in treatment of pulmonary tuberculosis. It is more effective in combination with isoniazid or rifamycin. It is active orally and gets absorbed well from gastrointestinal tract and administered in the form of tablets which are official in I.P. and B.P.

3. Ethionamide (I.P., B.P., U.S.P.) :

[Structure: pyridine ring with N, C₂H₅ substituent at 2-position, and S=C—NH₂ at 4-position]

2-ethylpyridine-4-carbathioamide

It is a bright yellow powder with faint characteristic odour. It is slightly soluble in water and chloroform and more soluble in methanol. It should be protected from light. The drug is active orally and given in the form of tablets in 250 mg, two to four times a day in resistant type of pulmonary tuberculosis.

4. Prothionamide (B.P.) :

[Structure: pyridine ring with C₃H₇ at 2-position and S=C—NH₂ at 4-position]

2-propylpyridine-4-carbothioamide

This drugs is similar to ethionamide but having propyl group. It also occurs as yellow crystalline powder, insoluble in water and used in pulmonary tuberculosis in the form tablets in 0.75 to 1 g daily in divided doses.

5. Isoniazid (I.P., B.P., U.S.P.) :

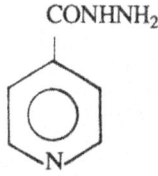

isonicotinhydrazide

This well known drug occurs as colourless or white crystalline powder, odourless, gets affected by exposure to air and light, it is freely soluble in water, sparingly in alcohol. Incompatibilities occur with ferric salts, oxidising agents. Isoniazed is well absorbed after oral administration and gets rapidly excreted. It is active on growing strain of organism and not on resting forms. Isoniazid tablets (official) are usually available in 50,100 and 300 mg and administered in 5 mg per kg of body weight upto 300 mg daily. For prompt action, it is administered by intramuscular injection. The injections are available 100 mg per ml strength. Isoniazid syrup is also official in U.S.P. in 50 mg per 5 ml concentration.

6. Pyrazinamide (B.P., U.S.P.) :

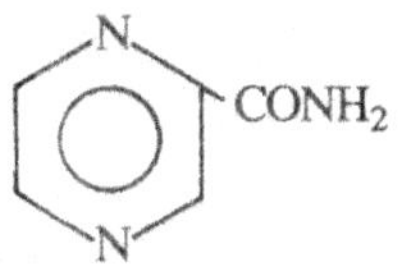

pyrazine-2-carboxamide

The drug is similar to isoniazid. It is a white, odourless, crystalline powder, sparingly soluble in water, soluble in ether and in chloroform. The drug gets absorbed fairly well from gastrointestinal tract. However, it is likely to be hepatotoxic hence it should be used when need arises. It is available in the form of tablets of 500 mg and usually given in 5 mg per kg body weight upto 3 g daily (in divided doses in various types of tuberculosis.

7. Thiacetazone (I.P.) :

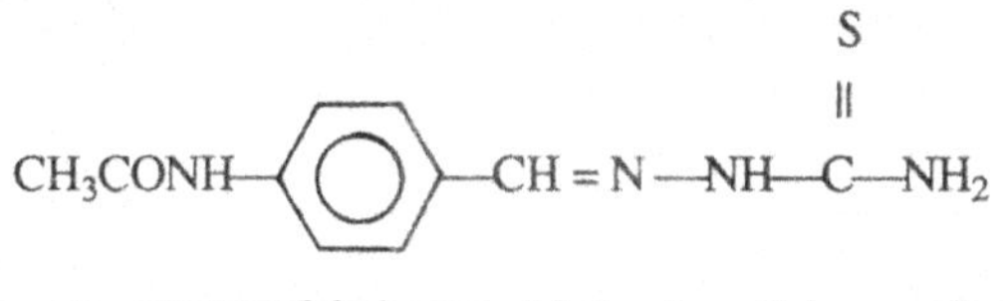

p-acetamidobenzaldehyde thiosemicarbasone

It occurs as pale yellow crystals odourless, slightly soluble in water, soluble in propylene glycol. Thiacetazone is tuberculostatic and antileprotic in its action. It is usually administered in combination with isoniazid in the form of tablets in pulmonary tuberculosis. The combination tablets are official in I.P. and are given in thiacetazone 150 mg and isoniazid 300 mg, daily, in divided doses.

ANTIBIOTICS

From the variety of antibiotics, certain antibiotics are found be of specific use in the treatment of tuberculosis. These antibiotics are :

Capreomycin sulphate (B.P., U.S.P.) :

Capreomycin is a strongly basic cyclic peptide type of antibiotic obtained from *Streptomyces capreolus*. It is analogous to viomycin chemically and is specific tuberculostatic. It is converted into water soluble sulphate salt and given intramuscularly in 1 mega unit daily.

Cycloserine (B.P., U.S.P.) :

$$\begin{array}{c} H_2N-C=O \\ | \quad\quad | \\ H_2C \quad\quad NH \\ \diagdown O \diagup \end{array}$$

It is obtained from *streptomyceus orchidaceus,* and *S. laveudulus.* It is whitish powder and is freely soluble in water. It is unstable in acid medium. Usually it is given orally as tablets or capsules in 250 to 750 mg daily, in divided doses.

Kanamycin sulphate (B.P., U.S.P.) :

It is obtained from *Streptomyces kanamyceticus* which gives three closely related Kanamycins as A, B and C. It is similar to streptomycin chemically and is basic in nature. It readily forms salt with acids through its amine group. It is stable to heat and solutions can be sterilizzed by autoclaving. It is poorly absorbed from intestinal tract (can be used as antiseptic of bowel) and hence given intramscularly or in emergencies intravenously in 0.5 to 1 mega unit of Kanamycin base in divided doses. It is slightly toxic and mycobacterias develop resistance rapidly, hence it is used with caution.

Rifampicin (B.P.), Rifampin (U.S.P.) :

It is a group of cycle polypeptide antibiotic obtained from *Streptomyces mediaterrani*. It occurs as orange, brown-crystalline powder, sparingly soluble in alcohol, and unstable to moisture and heat. It is absorbed well from intestinal tract. Since the mycobacterias develop resistance rather rapidly, it is administered along with isoniazid or other antitubercular agents. It shows hepatotoxicity on continued use. It is usually given in capsules in 450 to 600 mg dose.

Streptomycin sulphate (I.P., B.P., U.S.P.) :

This antibiotic (discussed under antibiotics) is used in the form of tablets (500 mg every 6 to 8 hours) or by intramuscular injection in all types of tuberculosis.

Viomycin sulphate (U.S.P.) :

The antibiotic viomycin is a cyclic peptide isolated from various species of streptomyces. It is basic in nature and its salt sulphate is a white to yellow, odourless powder and is freely soluble in water. It acts as tuberculostatic and administered intramuscularly (usually in 20 mg per kg of body weight or 600 mg of viomycin base).

COMBINATION THERAPY

Treatment of the tuberculosis is a continual and lengthy process, since complete elimination of mycobacteria from the body takes long time. Drugs are given over a long period and hence development of resistance by the mycobacterium develops. The drug becomes useless and new drug has to be tried. It is for this reason certain combination of antitubercular drugs are given as the first choice of drugs. These, include isoniazid, streptomycin, ethambutol, PAS and thiacetazone. When microbial resistance develops or the toxicity with the drugs used becomes more serious the drugs of second choice (like pyrazinamide, ethionamide, prothionamide, kanamycin, cycloserine capreomycin etc.) are used. Thus, toxicity is less, the drug dose regim is also reduced and chances of developing drug resistance are minimised.

ANTILEPROTIC DRUGS

Leprosy takes a long time to be eliminated for its organism from human body. A number of synthetic drugs of antibacterial like (sulfadoxine) antitubercular like (thiacetazone, ethionamide) and antibiotics like (Kanamycin, rifamycin) and some special other drugs are used. The clinically used drugs and remedies are :

Chaulmoogra oil (I.P.) :

It is a fixed oil obtained from seeds of *Hydnocarpus kurzii* and from other species of Hydnocarpus. It is a yellowish brown liquid (above 25°C) with characteristic odour and is insoluble in water but soluble in organic solvents. It is used externally.

1. Clofazimine (I.P., B.P.) :

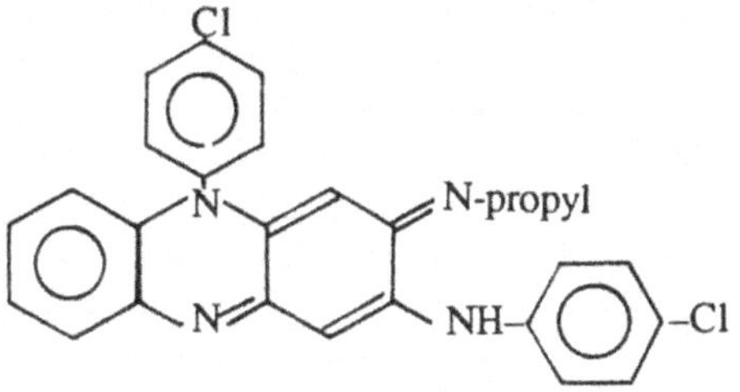

3-(4-chloroanilino)-10-(4-chlorophenyl)-2,
10 dihydrophenazin -2-ylidine isopropylamine

It is red- brown powder , practically insoluble in water but soluble in chloroform. It is given in capsules in 100 mg three times in fresh patients and in dapsone resistant patients in 100 mg six times weekly.

2. Dapsone (I.P., B.P., U.S.P.) :

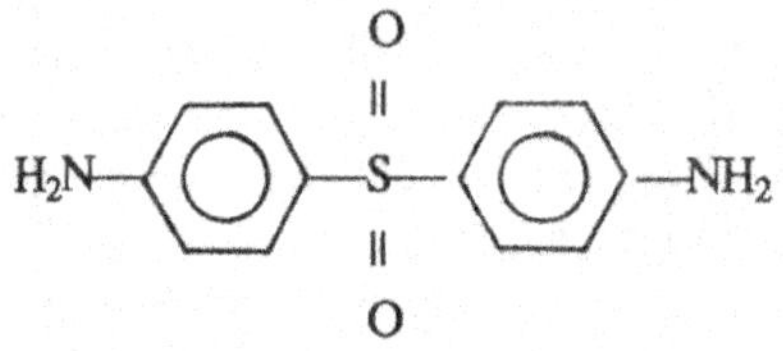

$$H_2N-\underset{}{\underset{}{\bigcirc}}-\underset{\underset{O}{\|}}{\overset{\overset{O}{\|}}{S}}-\underset{}{\underset{}{\bigcirc}}-NH_2$$

bis-(4-aminophenyl) sulphone

It is white, yellowish-white powder, odourless, slightly soluble in water. It gets discoloured on exposure to light. It is given orally as tablets in 25 to 50 mg twice weekly as initial dose increasing by 50 to 100 mg every month and maximum of 200 to 400 mg twice weekly. It is found effective in all types of leprosy, especially in dermatitis herpetiformis.

3. Thiambutosine (U.S.P.) :

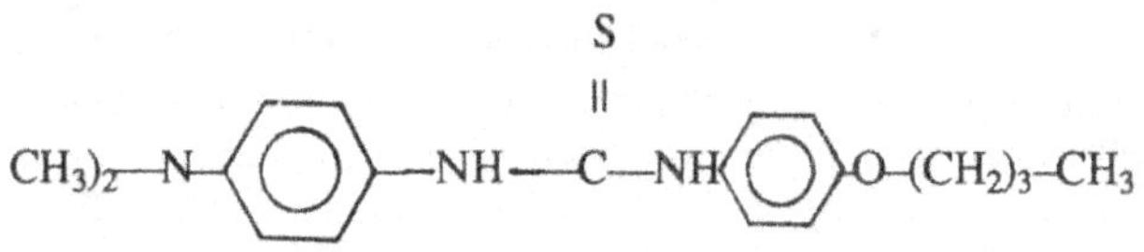

$$(CH_3)_2-N-\underset{}{\underset{}{\bigcirc}}-NH-\overset{\overset{S}{\|}}{C}-NH-\underset{}{\underset{}{\bigcirc}}-O-(CH_2)_3-CH_3$$

1-(4-butoxyphenyl)-3-(4-dimethyl-amino phenyl) thiourea

It is a white crystalline powder, odourless, bitter to taste. It is practically insoluble in water, soluble in chloroform and solvent ether. It is active orally and given in the form of tablets in 500 mg daily, increasing every fort-night by 500 mg. maximum up to 2 g daily divided doses. It is found useful in the treatment of lepromatous and tuberculoid leprosy. The drug and preparation should be protected from light.

❏ ❏ ❏

Chapter 31

ANTIPROTOZOAL DRUGS

This category includes antiamoebic, trypanocidal, leishmanicidal, trichomonacidal and drugs useful in giardiasis. The clinically useful drugs in various types of the above mentioned protozoal diseases are as follows :

ANTIAMOEBIC DRUGS

Amoebiasis is a protozoal disease. It affects human beings and animals. In man, it is caused by the infection of Entamoeba histolytica. This organism affects intestine and thus cause amoebic dysentery or may invade other organs like liver, lung, kidney etc. Various antiamoebic drugs are used to combat amoebiasis. The clinically useful drugs can broadly be divided into following causes : (i) Arsenicals (ii) Quinolines derivatives (iii) Miscellaneous agents and (iv) Drugs from natural source.

(i) **Arsenicals** : Organo-arsenicals have been known to possesses antiprotozoal action. Some compounds are even now clinically used as antiamoebic. They are :

1. **Acetarsol (B.P.)** :

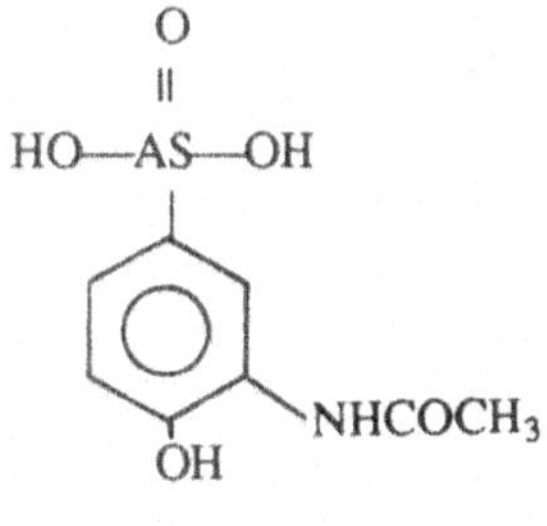

3-acetamido-4-hydroxy
phenyl arsonic acid

Properties and uses : It occurs as white crystalline powder, odourless, practically insoluble in water, soluble in aqueous alkali. It is used orally in treatment of intestinal amoebiasis. It is used locally in the form of pessaries in 500 to 750 mg twice daily in vagina in treatment of trichomonal vaginities.

2. Carbarsone (U.S.P.) :

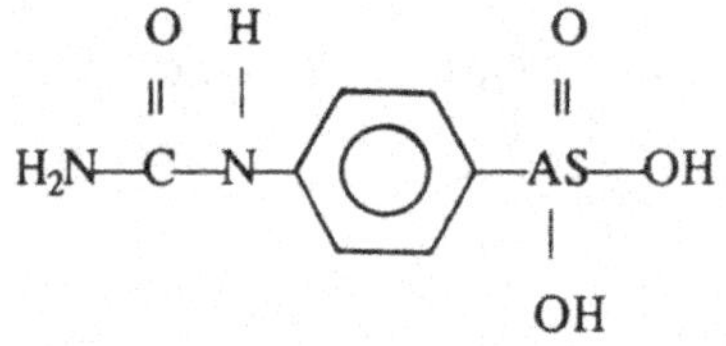

$$H_2N-\underset{\underset{}{\overset{O}{\|}}}{C}-\underset{\underset{}{\overset{H}{|}}}{N}-\underset{}{\bigcirc}-\underset{\underset{OH}{|}}{\overset{\overset{O}{\|}}{As}}-OH$$

N–carbomyl arsanilic acid

Properties and uses : It is a white crystalline powder slightly soluble in water and alcohol, more soluble in aqueous alkali. It is effective orally and employed in the treatment of intestinal amoebiasis and trichomonal vaginalis in the form of pessaries.

3. Glycobiarsol (I.P.) :

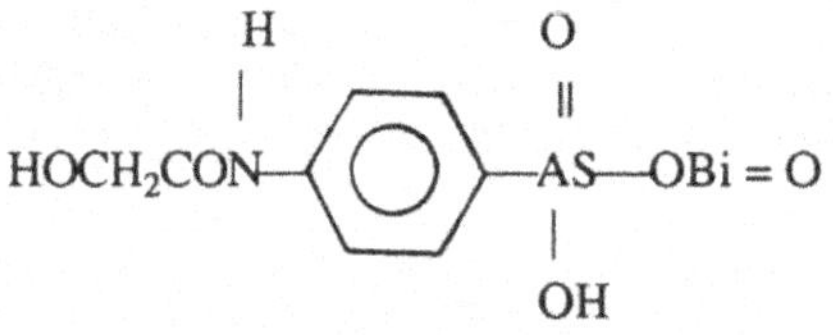

$$HOCH_2CON\underset{\underset{}{\overset{H}{|}}}{}-\bigcirc-\underset{\underset{OH}{|}}{\overset{\overset{O}{\|}}{As}}-OBi=O$$

N-glycoloyl arsenilate

Properties and uses : This is a bismuth glycolyl arsanilate. It occurs as yellowish-white amorphus powder, slightly soluble in water. It is given orally in 0.5 to 1.5 g daily in the treatment of chronic intestinal amoebiasis.

(ii) Quinoline derivatives : Certain quinoline derivatives are used as antimalarial and antiprotozoal agents ; among them the following are official:

4. Clioquinol (B.P.), Quiniodochor (I.P.) :

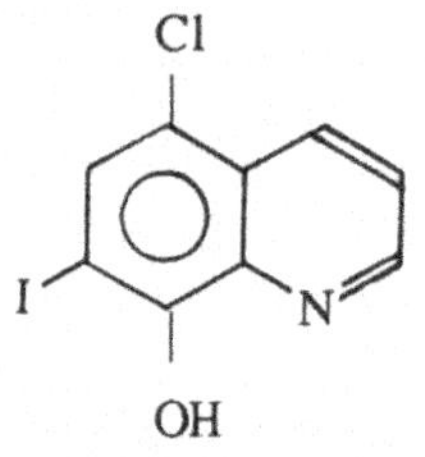

5-chloro-8-hydroxy-7-iodoquinoline

Properties and uses : It occurs as a yellowish-white or brownish amorphus powder with characteristics odour. It darkens on exposure to light. It is almost insoluble in water and also in alcohol. The drug is effective orally and is give as tablets in 0.25 to 0.75 g daily in divided doses mainly for the treatment of intestinal amoebiasis. Quiniodochor tablets are official in I.P.

5. Diiodohydroxyquinoline (I.P.) :

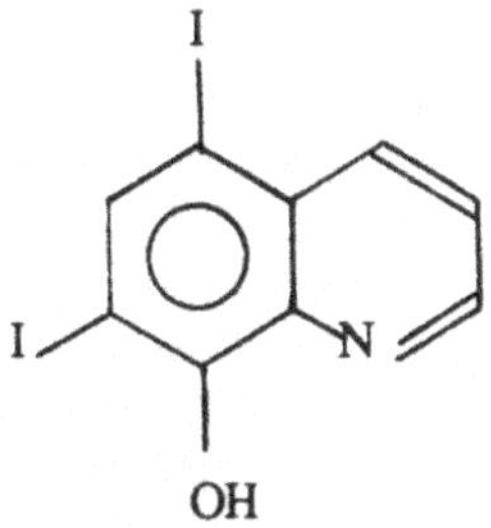

5, 7-diiodo-8-hydroxyquinoline

Properties and uses : It is a yellowish brown microcrystalline powder. It is almost odourless and is insoluble in water. It is a useful drug in the treatment of intestinal amoebiasis and in giardiasis in 1 to 2 g dose in the form of tablets.

6. Chloroquine phosphate and chloroquine sulphate (both official in I.P. and B.P.) are in quinoline derivatives of value in amoebic hepatitis in 0.5 to 1.0 g and 0.4 to 0.8 g dose respectively. These drugs are employed in the form of tablets and injection along with other antiamoebic drugs (Chloroquine is covered under antimalarials).

(iii) MISCELLANEOUS SYNTHETIC AGENTS

7. Bialamicol hydrochloride :

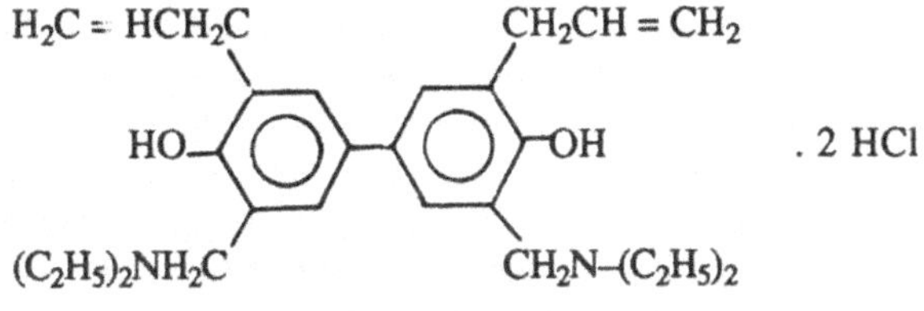

6-6'-diallyl 2-2' - bis (diethylamino) 4,4'-bicresol dihydrochloride

Properties and uses : The drug is a whitish powder soluble in water. It is active orally and usually given in 250 to 500 mg, 3 to 4 times a day, for five days in treatment and control of intestinal amoebiasis. It is usually administered with food to minimise the gastric irritation.

8. Diloxanide furoate (I.P., B.P.) :

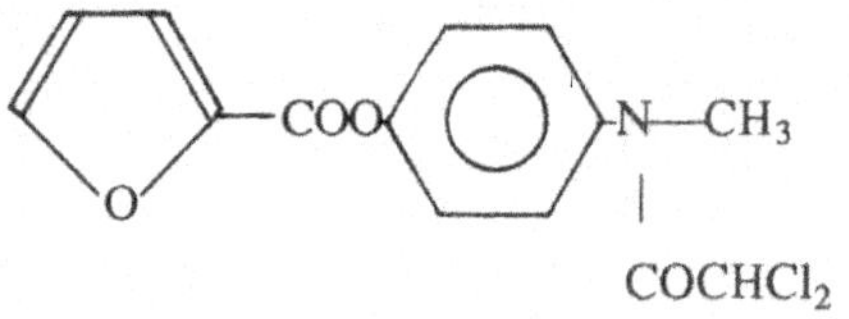

$$\text{Furan-COO-C}_6\text{H}_4\text{-N(CH}_3\text{)-COCHCl}_2$$

4-(N-methyl-2, 2-dichloroacetamido)-phenyl-2-furoate

Properties and uses : It occurs as white crystalline powder, odourless and sparingly soluble in water. It is given orally as tables in 1.5 g daily, divided doses, for ten days in treatment of acute and chronic intestinal amoebias and along with chloroquine in hepatic amoebiasis. Diloxanide furoate tablets are official in I.P. and B.P.

9. Metronidazole (I.P., B.P.) :

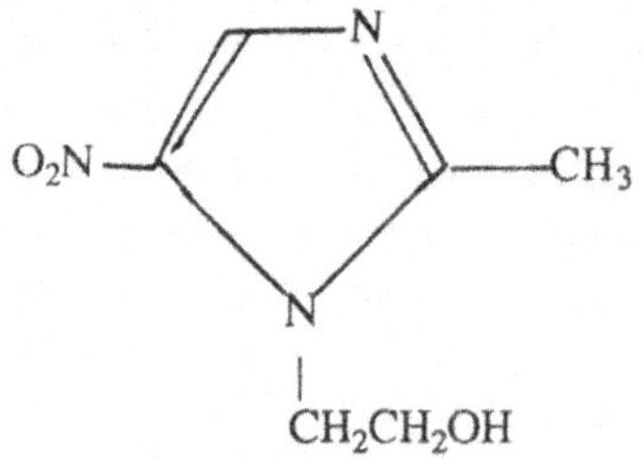

$$O_2N\text{-imidazole-}CH_3,\ N\text{-}CH_2CH_2OH$$

1 (hydroxyethyl)-2-methyl 5-nitroimidazole

Properties and uses : It is a creamy-white powder, odourless, bitter in taste. It is slightly soluble in alcohol. Metronidazole is effective orally and absorbed well from gastrointestinal tract. It is effective in wide variety of protozoal infections like T. vaginalis, E. histolytica and Giardia intestinalis. The drug is used in the treatment of amoebic dysentery, amoebic hepatitis, trichomoniasis of genitourinary tract and in giardiasis. It has wide range of antibacterial action. The drug is given as tablets in 200 mg three times a day for seven days in trichomaniasis and in 400 mg. three times a day for five to ten days in amoebic dysentery. Vaginal pessaries are used in treatment of Trichonaniasis vaginalis.

(iv) DRUGS FROM NATURAL SOURCE

The crude drug, the prepared drug powder and extract of ipecaucanha are used clinically as emetic-expectorant and in treatment of amoebic dysentery.

The alkaloid emetine obtained from ipecaucanha is a potent antiamoebic agent.

10. Emetine hydrochloride (I.P., B.P., U.S.P.) :

Properties and uses : It occurs as white or yellowish white crystalline powder, odourless, with bitter taste. It darkens to yellow colour on exposure to light. It is soluble in water and in alcohol. Aqueous solutions are acidic in nature. It is given parenterally (being bitter and it produces emetic action) in the treatment of amoebic hepatitis and other types of amoebic infections. It is best in symptomatic control of acute amoebic dysentery. The aqueous solutions for parenteral use are sterilized by heating with bactericide method. Usual dose is 30 to 60 mg daily by intramuscular or subcutaneous injection. Dehydroemetine hydrochloride as injection and tablets is also given in amoebiasis and is official in I.P.

The antibiotics like erythromycin, paromomycin are effective antiamoebics. The antibiotics, in general, act by interferring in development of intestinal bacterial flora which is used by the pathogenic protozoas. Thus they act indirectly as antiprotozoal. The paromomycin, however, acts directly as amoebicidal and is given orally in capsules in the treatment of bacillary and amoebic dysentery.

TRYPANOCIDAL DRUGS

The disease trypanosymiasis is known as sleeping sickness. It is caused by parastic infection by various species of genus *Trypanosma*. The clinically used drugs under this category are :

Pentamidien isethionate (I.P., B.P.) :

$$H_2N\diagdown C-\langle O\rangle-O-(CH_2)_5-O-\langle O\rangle-C\diagup^{NH}_{NH_2} \cdot 2 \begin{vmatrix} CH_2OH \\ CH_2SO_3H \end{vmatrix}$$

4-4-(Pentameteylenedioxy) dibenxamidine
bis-(2-hydroxyethanesulphonate)

Properties and uses : It is a white hygroscopic powder with bitter taste. It has butyric odour. It is soluble in water and glycerine, slightly soluble in alcohol, Aqueous solutions are acidic, and they deteriorate on storage The injections are prepared by aseptic technique and administered by intramuscular route in 50 to 250 mg dose. It is effective in African trypanosaniasis and also in leishmaniasis. The side effects re vertigo, nausea, convulsions etc.

Tryparsamide :

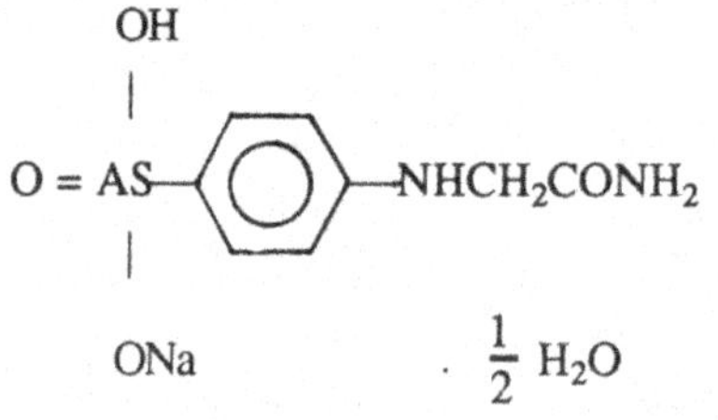

$$O=As\text{-}C_6H_4\text{-}NHCH_2CONH_2 \quad \cdot \frac{1}{2}H_2O$$

with OH and ONa on As

p–carbomylmethylaminophenylarsonate

Properties and uses : It is a colourless crystalline powder. It is freely soluble in water. The solutions for injection are prepared aseptically. Aqueous solutions deteriorate on storage. It is given in 1 to 3 g by intravenous injection. The drug is effective as trypanocidal and also in syphilis. It affects optic nerve and may cause blindness and hence should be used with caution.

LEISHMANICIDAL DRUGS

Leishmanias is another type of protozoal disease caused by Leishmania Organisms : The disease is spread by sandflies. *L. donovani, L. tropica* are the organisms responsible for Kala-azar. The drugs used in the treatment are :

The Pentamidine isothionate : In the form of injection, besides being useful as antitrypanocidal it is also useful in Kala-azar. The other compound of clinical significance is a antimony compound.

Sodium stibogluconate : The aqueous solution of sodium stibogluconate is stable and the injection preparations can be sterilized by autoclaving. It is given by intramuscular injection in 0.6 to 2 g daily for ten to thirty days in the control of Leishmaniasis.

TRICHOMONACIDAL DRUGS

Trichomonias is caused by various species of Trichomonas. The infection due to the organism usually occurs in genito-urinary tract. The effective drugs in the treatment are the Acetarsol, carbarsone, glycobiarsol and arsenic compounds and metronidazole.

DRUGS USED IN GIARDIASIS

Giardiasis is another type of protozoal infection caused by organism *Giardia lamblia*. The infection is characterised by diarrhoea or dysentery. The infection usually occurs in gastrointestinal tract and treated with antimalarial and or antiprotozoal drugs.

Antimalarial drugs *Mepacrine* (quinacrine) is found effective in giardiasis and is used in 300 mg daily in divided doses for five days.

Metronidazole is also useful in treatment of giardiasis where in it kills the protozoa.

Furazolidone : It is a drug with antibacterial, antifungal and antiprotozoal action. It is given in 400 mg daily, in divided doses.

❏ ❏ ❏

Chapter 32

ANTIVIRAL AGENTS

Viral infection and viral diseases are very difficult to treat. Viruses are the submicroscopic organisms which thrive on living host cells. They can be brodly divided into (i) smaller group (rickettsia etc.) and (ii) larger viruses. The main difficulty in finding useful antiviral drugs is because of close relation between virus and the host cell. Thus a compound toxic to virus is found toxic to the host cell. However, now-a-days virus specific enzymes have been identified and specific enzyme inhibitors are developed. The agents which act as antiviral are :

Adamantadine hydrochloride (I.P.) :

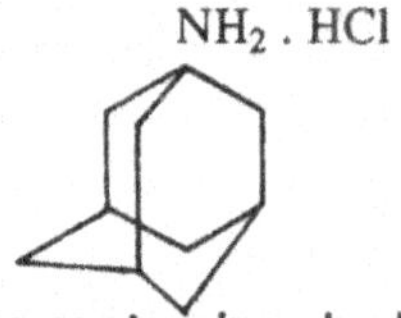

$NH_2 . HCl$

1-adamantamine hydrochloride

Properties and uses : It occurs as white crystalline powder, odourless, easily soluble in water, insoluble in alcohol. It has bitter taste and hence administered orally as syrups or capsules. It is given in 200 mg daily dose in prevention of influenza virus A_2 strain.

Idoxuridine (B.P., U.S.P.) :

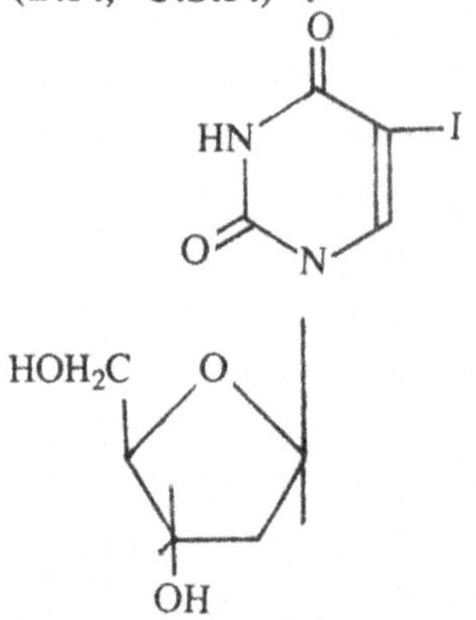

2-deoxy-5-iodouridine

Properties and uses : It is slightly soluble in water and insoluble in ether, chloroform. Aqueous solutions are stable in acidic medium if kept in refrigerator. It is used in treatment of dendritic keratitis caused by Herpex simplex. It is applied externally to the conjunctiva as it is useful in infection of eye in the form of eye drops or eye ointment in 0.1 and a 0.5 % concentration respectively.

Methisazone :

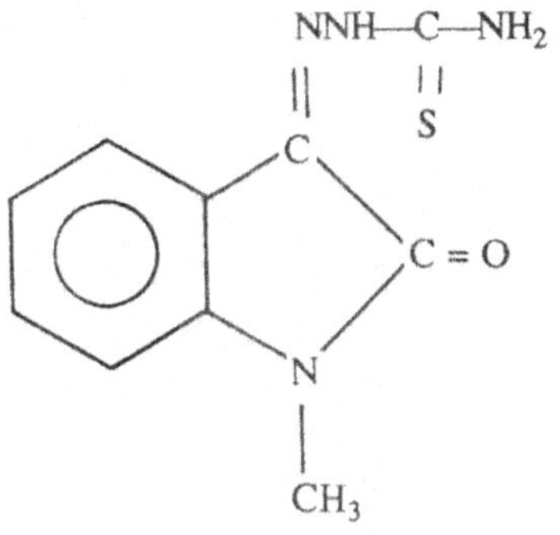

1-methyl-isatin-3-
thiosemicarbazone

Properties and uses : It occurs as orange-yellow powder, odourless, insoluble in water. It is given orally in the form of mixture as a prophylaxis of small pox. It is also employed in the treatment of eczema vaccinatum and vaccinia gangrenosa.

Chapter 33

ANTINEOPLASTIC AGENTS

These are the drugs which are used in the management of malignant disease (i.e. cancer). Cancer is a very difficult disease to treat. This has been because of lack of reliable diagnostic tests for the early detection and not having the compounds which will cure any form of cancer. The therapy which is utilised today is the use of ionizing radiation, surgery and use of chemotherapeutic agents.

Anti cancer agents are now-a-days available which increase survival time, suppress the growth of developing neoplasm and give relief of pain. Immunosuppressive agents are also used to prolong the life of organs and tissue transplants during surgical procedural methods in cancer.

Since cancerous cells grow fast and abnormally from the host cells, attempts in developing anti-cancer drugs have been in the direction of arresting, their growth. The anti-cancer agents thus can be categoriesed into the following types depending upon ther mechanism of action (i) Alkylating agents (ii) Antimetabolities (iii) antibiotics (iv) Hormones (v) Plant products and (vi) Miscellaneous compounds.

I. ALKYLATING AGENTS

Alkylating agents are the drugs belonging to different chemical classes and act by mechanism of alkylation. By the alkylating mechanism, they act upon and fix by cross linking to guanine base of RNA and thereby arrest cell division and multiplication. The important clinically useful agents from this class are :

1. **Busulfan (I.P., B.P., U.S.P.)** :

$$CH_3 . SO_2 . O . (CH_2)_4 . O . SO_2 . CH_3$$

tetramethylene-di (methane sulphonate)

Properties and uses : It occurs as white powder and is practically insoluble in water. It is active orally and is given as tablets in 2 to 4 mg daily in the treatment of myeloid leukemia, Bsulfan tablets are official in pharmacopoias.

2. Chlorambucil (B.P., U.S.P.) :

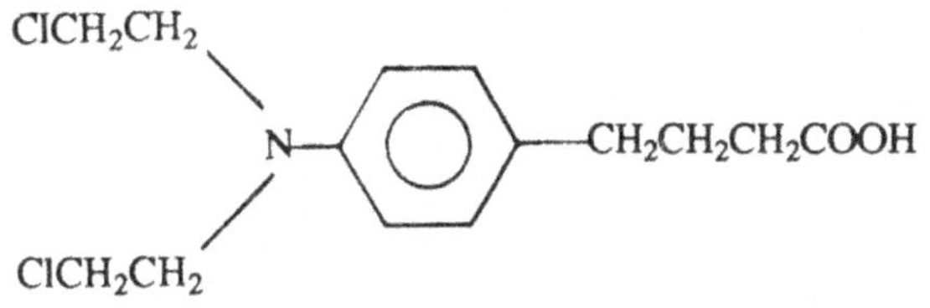

$$\text{ClCH}_2\text{CH}_2\text{-N(CH}_2\text{CH}_2\text{Cl)-C}_6\text{H}_4\text{-CH}_2\text{CH}_2\text{CH}_2\text{COOH}$$

4 {4-[bis-2 (-chloroethyl) amino]-phenyl} butyric acid

Properties and uses : The drug belongs to nitrogen mustard class. It occurs as white, odourless powder and is slightly soluble in water. It is active orally and given in 2 to 4 mg dose in sugar coated tablets. It is useful in chronic leukemia, Hodgkin's disease and in lymphocytic lymphoma.

3. Cyclophosphamide (I.P., B.P., U.S.P.) :

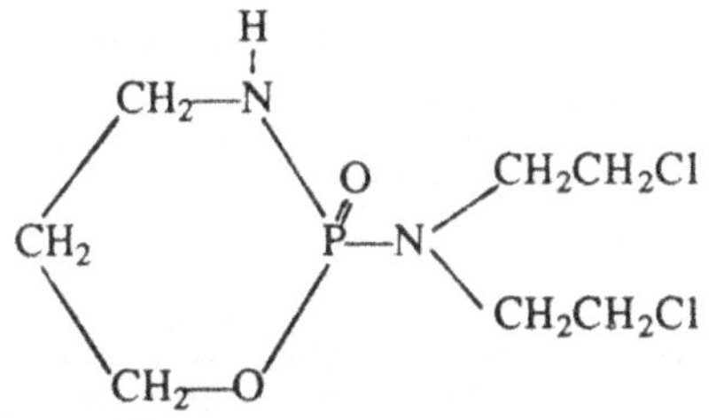

[Structure: perhydro-1,3,2-oxazaphosphorine ring with P=O, P–N(CH$_2$CH$_2$Cl)$_2$, and NH in ring]

2-bis (2-chloroethyl) amino perhydro 1,3
2-oxazaphosphorine, 2-oxide

Properties and uses : It is modified type of nitrogen a mustard. It occurs as monohydrate white crystalline powder, which gets discoloured on exposure to light. It is stable, but at higher temperature it forms anhydrous material and then becomes unstable. It is soluble in water but solutions are to be used immediately after preparation. The drug is employed in the treatment of Hodgkin's disease, reticular sarcoma, in chronic lumphocytic leukemia, tumours of brain, breast and also in carcinoma of bronchorial tract. The usual dose is 100 to 150 mg daily given orally as tablets or by intravenous injection.

4. **Dacarbazine (B.P.) :**

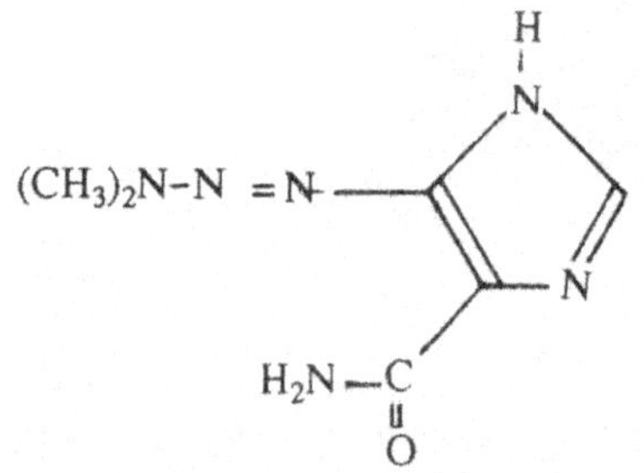

(CH$_3$)$_2$N-N=N- [imidazole ring with H$_2$N-CO- substituent]

5-(3, 3-dimethyltriazeno)
imidazole-4-carboxamide

Properties and uses : It is a pale yellow crystalline powder, slightly soluble in water. The drug is given by injection. It should be stored below 8º.

5. **Lomustine (B.P.) :**

[cyclohexyl]—NHCON(CH$_2$CH$_2$Cl)(NO)

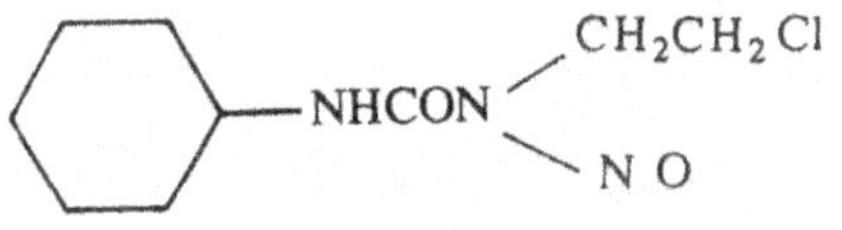

1-(2-chloroethyl)-3-cycloexyl-1-nitrosourea

Properties and uses : It occurs as a yellow powder, insoluble in water, soluble in alcohol. It is employed as cytotoxic agent in capsule form.

6. **Melphalan (B.P., U.S.P.) :**

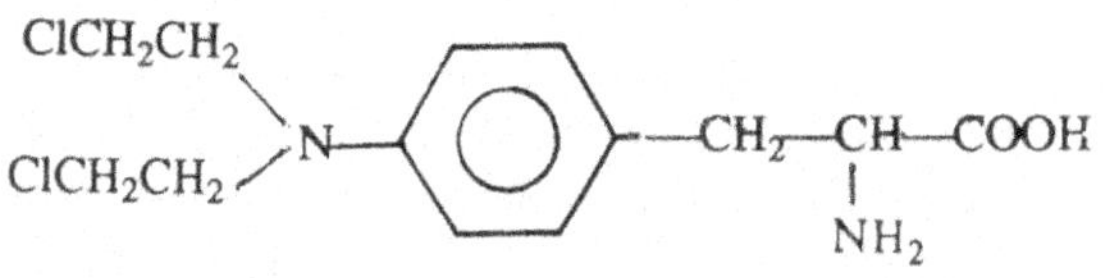

(ClCH$_2$CH$_2$)$_2$N—[phenyl]—CH$_2$—CH(NH$_2$)—COOH

4-bis (2-chloroethyl) amino-L-phenylalanine

Properties and uses : It is a white powder, odourless, stable in air in dry state. It is sparingly soluble in water, more soluble in alcohol and propylene glycol. The drug is active orally and is given as tablets in 6 mg initial and 2 mg maintenance dose once a day in lymphocytic leukemia and myeloma. It is given by intravenous injection in the treatment of malignant neoplasm.

7. **Mustine hydrochloride (B.P.) Mechlorethamine hydrochloride (U.S.P.) :**

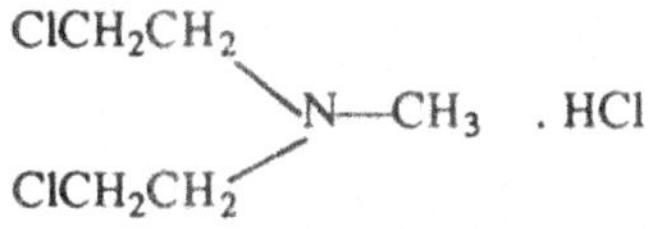

$$ClCH_2CH_2\text{-}N(CH_3)\text{-}CH_2CH_2Cl \cdot HCl$$

N-bis (2-chloroethyl) methylamine hydrochloride

Properties and uses : It occurs as white hygroscopic crystalline powder and is soluble in water. Aqueous solutions are unstable and lose their activity. Solutions for injection purpose are prepared immediately before use, adopting aspectic method. It is given with saline as intravenous infusion in 400 micrograms per kg of body weight in the treatment of Hodgkin's disease and in reticulum cell sarcoma.

8. **Thiotepa (B.P., U.S.P.) :**

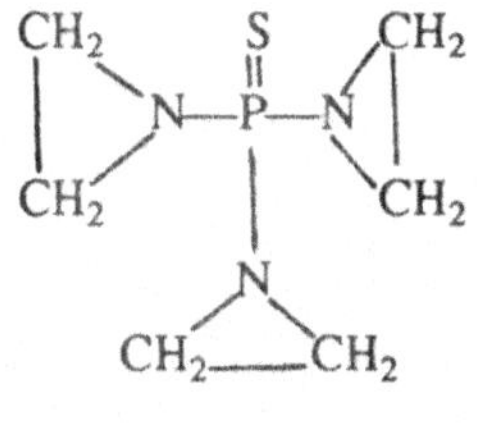

Tris-(1-aziridinyl) phosphine sulfide

Properties and uses : It occurs as white crystalline flakes. It is freely oluble in water, but solutions are to be used immediately. The injections are repared by aseptic method and are employed in 15 to 30 mg dose (repeated if eed arises) by intravenous route in the treatment of cancer of breast, ovaries etc.

I. **ANTIMETABOLITES**

Antineoplastic agents have been developed on the theory of metabolite intagonism. Accordingly, the antineoplastic agents on administration blocks the physiological enzymes which are utilised by normal body metabolite. Thus they prevent normal body metabolite utilization resulting in stoppage of cellular multiplication. The drugs act as antagonist of folic acid, purine and pyrimidine and thus nucleic acid synthesis is arrested. In this category, the effective dose is very often close to the toxic dose. The useful agents from the category are :

9. Azathiopurine (B.P., U.S.P.) :

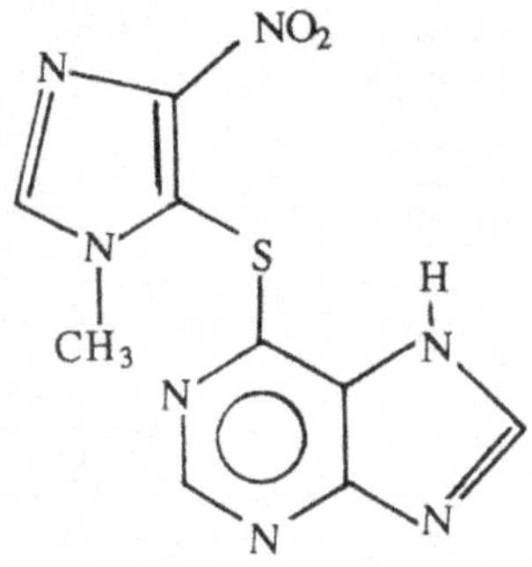

6-(1-methyl-4-nitroimidazol-5-ylthio) purine

Properties and uses : It occurs as pale yellow powder, insoluble in water, soluble in alcohol and dilute alkali solutions. It is stable in neutral or acidic medium but gets rapidly hydrolysed to mercaptopurine in alkaline media. It is active orally (given as tablets) or by intravenous injection in 100 to 150 mg dose. It is mainly used as immunosuppressive agent.

9. Cytarabine (B.P.,U.S.P.) :

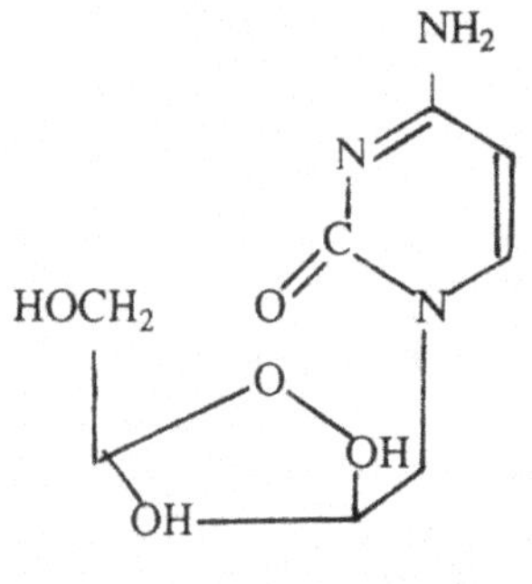

1-β-D-arabinosylcystosine

Properties and uses : It occurs as white to off-white crystalline, odourles powder. It is supplied in vials as freezedried preparation which is prepared in solution with water for injection. The solutions are used within 48 hours and any solution showing turbidity is discarded. It is given by intravenous infusion in 2 mg per kg body weight in treatment of acute leukemia. The toxic effects are bone marrow suppression, leukopenia and anemia.

11. **Flurouracil (I.P., B.P., U.S.P.) :**

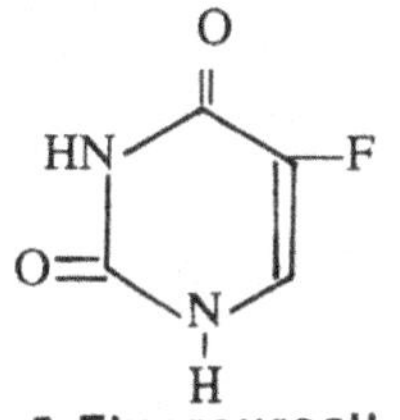

5-Fluorouracil

Properties and uses : It is a white crystalline powder, sparingly soluble in water and alcohol. It is stable to heat. However, solutions should be protected from light. It is given in the form of injection (50 mg per ml) in the dose of 12 mg per kg of body weight once daily for 4 to 5 days for the treatment of certain tumors. It is also employed as solution or cream externally in treatment of aclinic keratoses.

12. **Mercaptopurine (I.P., B.P., U.S.P.) :**

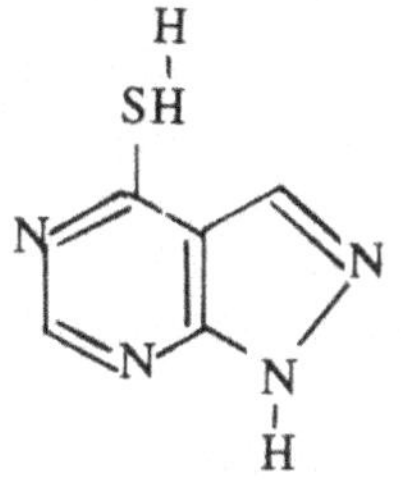

6-mercaptopurine

Properties and uses : It occurs as yellow crystalline powder, odourless and is insoluble in water, soluble in alcohol and dilute alkali solutions. It is given orally in 100 to 200 mg, daily, as tablets. It acts as antimetabolite for adenine and finds use in various types of leukemias.

13. **Methotrexate (I.P., B.P.) :**

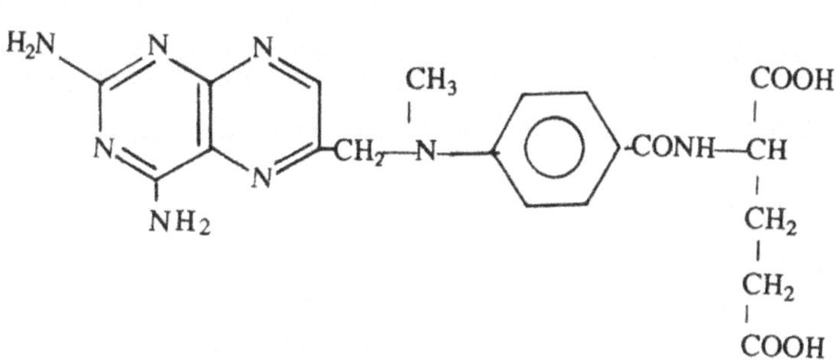

4-amino-4-deoxy-1o-methyl pteroyl-L-glutamic acid

Properties and uses : It occurs as yellow to orange crystalline powder, almost insoluble in water, soluble in dilute solutions of acids and alkalies. It is active orally and given as tablets in 5 to 100 mg at suitable intervals as needed by patient or given parenterally by intramuscular or intravenous injection in the treatment of lymphoblastic leukemia and in carcinoma of tumor or chorionic tissues.

14. **Thioguanine (B.P., U.S.P.) :**

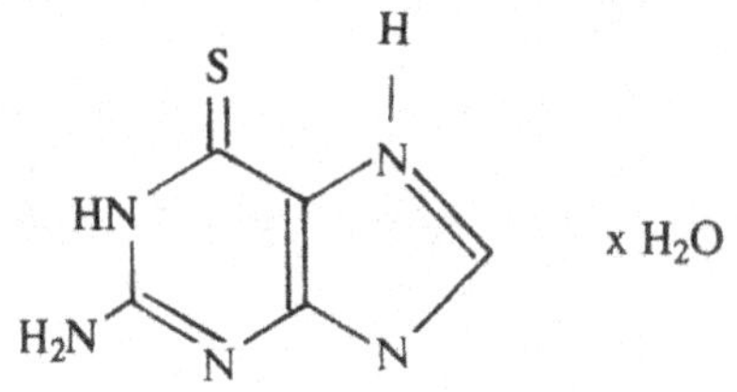

2-aminopurine6-(1-H) thione

Properties and uses : It occurs as pale yellow crystalline powder, odourless. It is insoluble in water and alcohol but soluble in dilute solutions of alkali. It is active orally and is absorbed well. It is given as tablet in the dose of 2 mg per kg of body weight once daily. Dose is increased if toxicity is not encountered. The drug acts like mercapto purine as antimetabolite in purine metabolism. Clinically, it is employed in the treatment of leukemia.

III. ANTIBIOTICS

From the several antibiotics, now available, some antibiotics have been found effective especially in the treatment of malignant tissues. These are believed to act at DNA level by interferring in its synthesis. The antibiotics of Useful nature are given below :

ACTINOMYCIN (DACTINOMYCIN)

This antibiotic though discovered in 1940 its utility as antineoplastic-antitumor was recognised in 1958. It is obtained from *Streptomyceous parvullus*. The actinomycins comprise number of closely related compounds. All of them contain 3 - phenoxazone - 1, 9 - dicarboxylic acid as active group.

It occurs as red powders, soluble in alcohol and alcohol-water mixture. It is sensitive to light. Vials containing 0.5 mg of lyophilized powder are used. The drug is used against sarcoma and wilm's tumor. The mode of action is that it intercalate into double helical DNA. This results in inhibition of DNA and RNA synthesis and the depletion of RNA and proteins leads to cell death.

DAUNORUBICIN HYDROCHLORIDE

It is obtained from the fermentation of *Streptomyces peucetius*. The salt occurs as red coloured crystalline powder. It is soluble in water and alcohol. It is available as lyophillised powder in 20 mg vials.

It is used in the treatment of acute lymphocytic and granulocytic leukemias. Usual dose is 30 to 60 mg per sq/m for three days.

MITOMYCIN - C :

It is obtained from *Streptomyces caespisosus*. It is a blue-violet crystalline powder, soluble in water and polars solvents. The crystalline material is stable at room temperature but is unstable in acids and bases.

It is commonly used in combination with flurouracil in treatment of breast, gastric and pancreatic carcinomas. Dose is 10 - 20 mg per sq/m. in single dose.

Cisplatin : It is a complex obtained by treating potassium chloroplatinate with ammonia.

It is a white solid, soluble in water. It is supplied as 10 g of lyophilised powder. It is employed in combination with bleomycin and vinblastin for treatment of metastatic testicular tumor. It is also used in ovarian tumors. The usual dose is 20 mg per sq/m for five days.

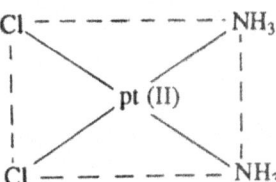

IV. HORMONES

In certain types of cancer like breast cancer, prostate cancer and other tissue cancers, hormone treatment has been reported to be of clinical use. The exact mechanism by which they show effectiveness is unknown. Amongst the hormones, Dromonstanalone propionate (U.S.P.) in metastatic breast carcinoma in post menapansal women and magestrol acetate (B.P.) in treatment of advanced breast cancer is wellknown.

V. PLANT PRODUCTS

Certain plants, their extracts and isolated active principles are found active in various types of tumors and leukemias. Amongst this category, the important drugs -

Vinca alkaloids : The extract from the flowers of Vinca rosea was first found effective in Hodgkin's disease and in certain types of lymphomia and carcinoma. Amongst the various alkaloids present in the plant two alkaloids have been found extremely useful in the treatment of cancer and these are :

15. Vinblastine sulphate (B.P., U.S.P.) :

It is effective in Hodgkin's disease, monocytic leukemia and related conditions. It is given intravenously in 100 micrograms per kg of body weight initially until the maximum dose (500 microgram per kg of body weight) determined by white blood cellcount. The drug is supplied in lyophilized form. It is protected from light *Vincristine sulphate* (B.P., U.S.P.). This is another alkaloid of Vinca rosea relatd to vinblastine. It is water-soluble and is mainly used in the treatment of acute leukemias. The drug is given by the intravenous route in the same dose regime as that of vinblastine sulphate. It is also protected from light.

VI. MISCELLANEOUS COMPOUNDS

Amongst the miscellaneous class certain drugs, given below, are found useful :

17. Hydroxyurea (B.P.) : $HONHCONH_2$

Properties and uses : It is white, crystalline powder, very hygroscopic in nature, and decomposes when in contact with water. It is given in capsules, being active orally in the treatment of chronic mycloid leukemia.

18. Mitobronital (B.P.) :

$$\begin{array}{c} CH_2Br \\ | \\ HO-C-H \\ | \\ HO-C-H \\ | \\ H-C-OH \\ | \\ H-C-OH \\ | \\ CH_2Br \end{array}$$

Properties and uses : It is white crystalline solid and is sparingly water soluble. It should be protected from light. The drug is used as cytotoxic in tablet form.

Chapter 34

ANTIHELMINTICS

Helminthiasis is broadly a class of disease, caused by parasitic worms. Different types of worms affect human beings and animals. Different types of chemical agents and drugs are used to destroy or remove the infecting worms from the host. These are called as anthelmintics. The drugs which are employed against various types of helminthiasis are as follows :

DRUGS USED IN TAPE WORMS

Tape worms belongs to the class cestoda. It affects the gastrointestinal tract and causes dysentery. The infection is carried to the human being though infected meat and related articles. The effective anthelmintics are -

1. **Dichlorophen (B.P.) :**

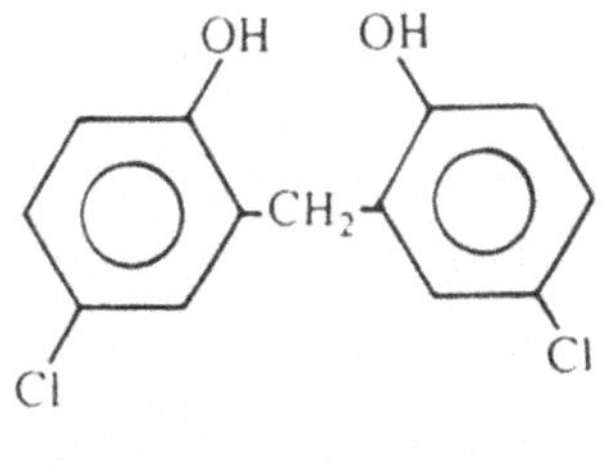

4,4'-dichloro-2,2' methylenediphenol

It is a synthetic, biphenyl compound, specifically active against tape worms.

Properties and uses : It occurs as a white-to cream coloured powder, practically insoluble in water and alcohol. It is given in form of tablets in a dose of 6 g on two successive days, in divided doses for adult, and in 2 to 4 g in divided doses for children.

2. Niclosamide (I.P., B.P.):

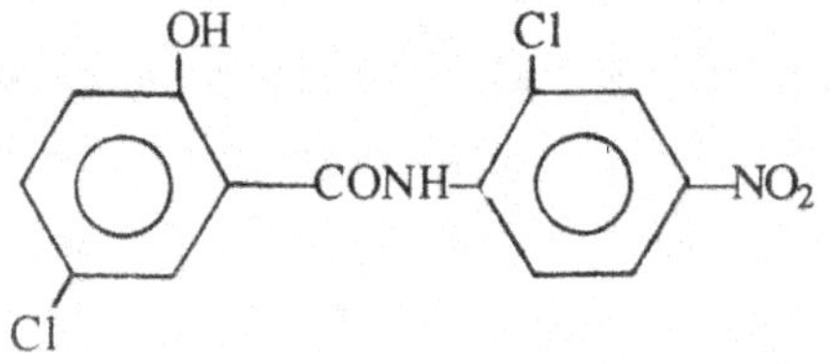

2', 5-dichloro-4'-nitrosalicylanilide

Properties and uses : It is a cream coloured, odourless powder. It is practically insoluble in water. It is active orally and is given in the form of tablets, in 2 g doses daily, in divided doses.

DRUGS USED IN FLUKES

Flukes are parasitic worms which belongs to the class Trematodes and look similar to tape worms. They are also flat in nature and have a leaf like body. They mainly invade and reside in the intestine or may be found in the lumen of veins. The main source of infection is through aquatic animals. The disease caused is called schistosomiasis. The drugs used are :

3. Antimony sodium tartrate (I.P., B.P.):

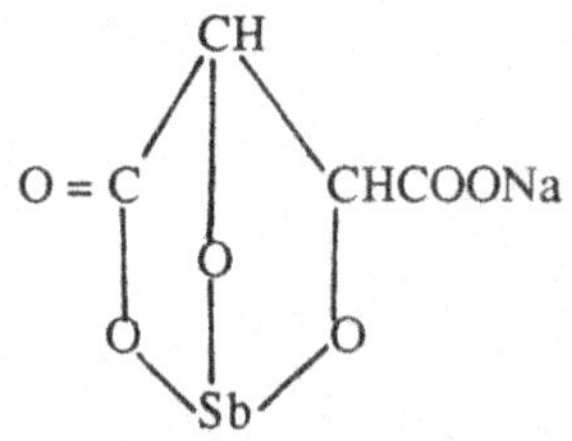

Properties and uses : It is a salt of trivalent metal antimony with sodium tartrate. It occurs as colourless, hygroscopic crystals, soluble in water. Solutions are stable and sterilized by autoclaving for parenteral use. It is given by the intravenous route in a 30 mg initial dose, increased by 30 mg on alternate days, until a total quantity of 1.2 to 1.5 g is administered.

4. Stibophen (I.P.) :

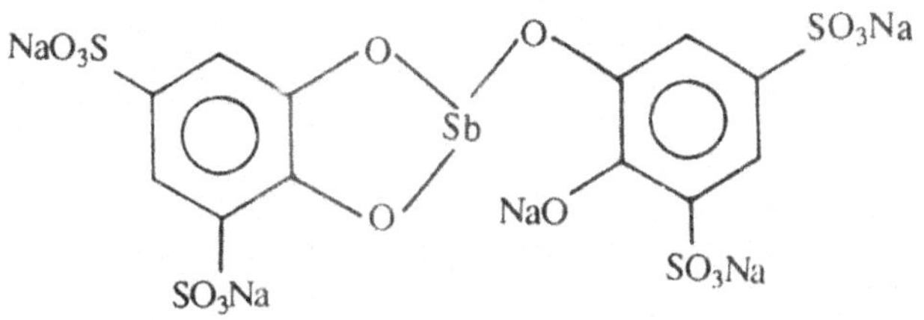

[Structure: Sb complex with two 4,6-disulfonate-catecholate ligands shown, with SO₃Na groups and NaO substituent]

Properties and uses : It is a white powder, odourless and soluble in water. Its solution darkens on exposure to light and air. It can be stabilized by adding acid. Stibophen injections are sterilized by autoclaving and administered intramuscularly in 0.1 to 0.3 g dose.

DRUGS USED IN ROUND WORMS, THREADWORMS AND PINWORMS

The round worms, thread worms and pin worms belong to the class called Nematodes. These are considered as higher organisms and they spread a disease called filariasis. Anti-filarial agents are used in filarasis. Useful drugs in this category are :

5. Bephenium hydroxynaphthoate (I.P., B.P.) :

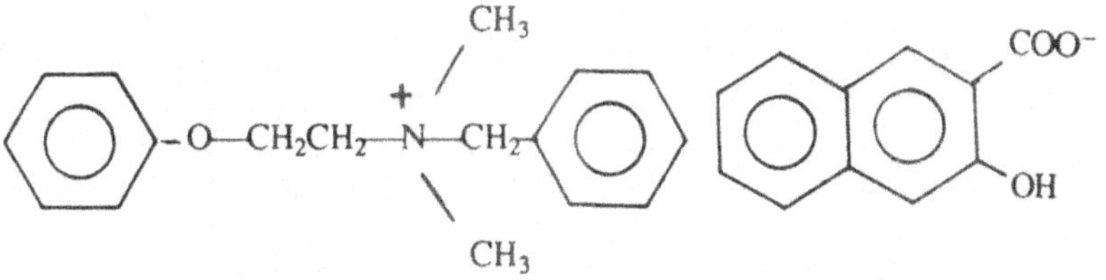

[Structure of benzyldimethyl-(2-phenoxyethyl) ammonium cation with 3-hydroxy-2-naphthoate anion]

Benzyldimethyl-(2-phenoxyethyl) ammonium 3-hydroxy-2-naphthoate

Properties and uses : It is a pale yellow crystalline powder, bitter in taste and is sparingly water soluble. It is effective in hook worm and mixed infestations. Since it has a bitter taste some palatable food is given prior to this drug. The granule form is also official in I.P.

6. **Diethylcarbamazine citrate (I.P., B.P., U.S.P.)** :

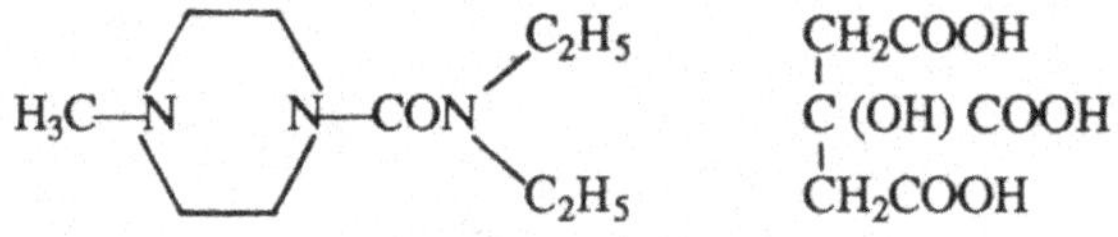

$$H_3C-N\underset{}{\overset{}{\bigcirc}}N-CON\underset{C_2H_5}{\overset{C_2H_5}{<}} \quad \underset{CH_2COOH}{\overset{CH_2COOH}{\overset{|}{C(OH)COOH}}}$$

**N, N'-diethyl-4-methyl-piperazine
-1-carboxamide dihydrogencitrate**

Properties and uses : It occurs as a white, crystalline powder almost odourless and is soluble in water. The base (diethylcarbamazine) is precipitated by an alkali and alkaline substances. It is active orally and is absorbed well from the gastrointestinal tract. It is given in an initial dose of 50 mg followed by increasing doses from 150 to 250 mg, in treatment of eosinophilia and to treat filariasis.

7. **Hexylresorcinol (B.P.)** :

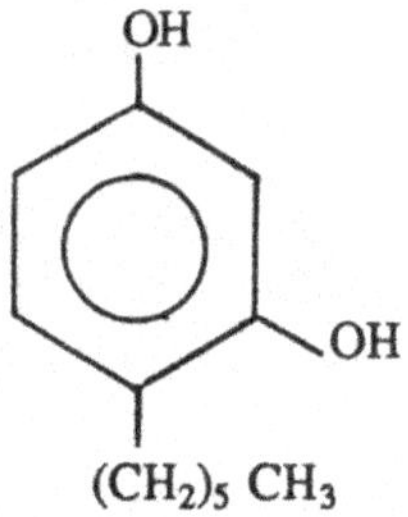

4-n-hexyl resorcinol

Properties and uses : It occurs as a white, odourless crystalline powder. It is sparingly soluble in water, and more soluble in alcohol. It is given as tablets in 1 g single dose for adult or 100 mg for each year of age up to 1 g in children in treatment of round worms (Ascaris) and also against hook worms, treadworms etc.

8. **Levamisole hydrochloride (B.P.)** :

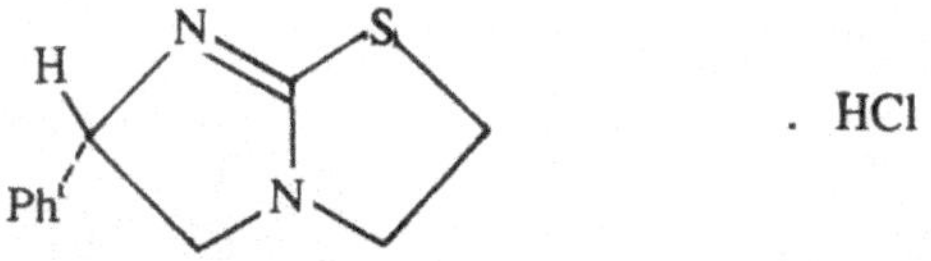

. HCl

Properties and uses : It is a creamy white powder, odourless, soluble in water. It is given the treatment of various nematoda infestations. It is claimed to have immunosuppressant action.

9. **Mebendazole (I.P., U.S.P.) :**

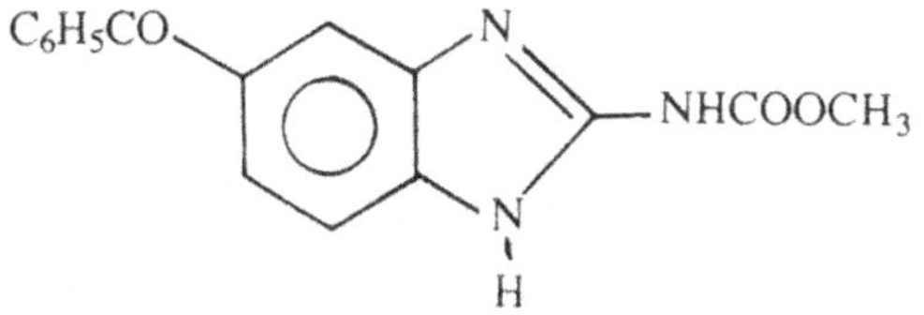

Methyl 5-benzoylbenzimidazole-2yl-carbamate

Properties and uses : It occurs as slight yellow amorphous powder, insoluble in water. The drug is given as tablets in 100 mg single dose for threadworm and 100 mg twice daily for two days for other infestations. It is contraindicated in preganant women.

10. **Pyrantel pamoate (U.S.P.) :**

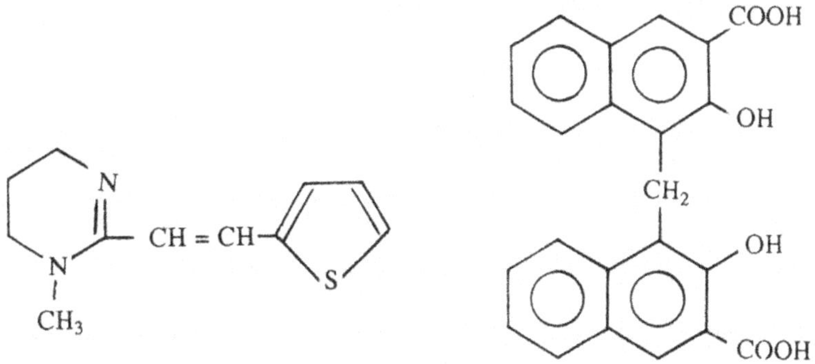

trans-1, 4, 5, 6-tetrahydro-1-methyl 2-[2-(2 thienyl) vinyl] pyrimidine pamoate

Properties and uses : It is a coloured dye and is water soluble. The drug is useful against pin-worms and round-worms.

11. Pyrvinium pamoate (U.S.P.) :

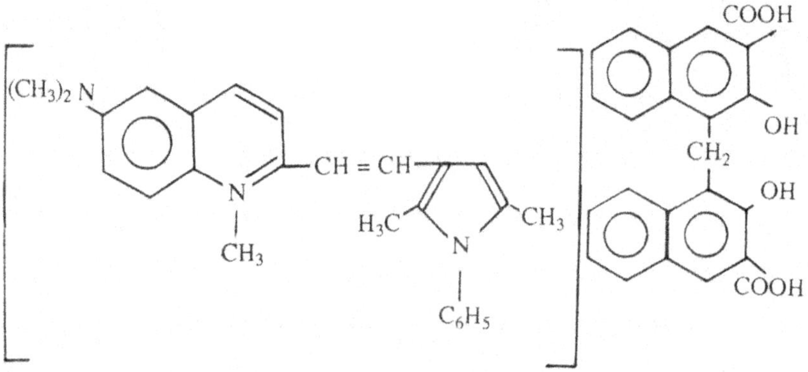

Properties and uses : It occurs as red colour dye and is sparingly soluble in water. It is poorly absorbed through G.I. tract. It has local irritant action and hence causes nausea vomitting. The drug is effective against pin-worms.

12. Piperazine adipate (I.P., B.P.) :

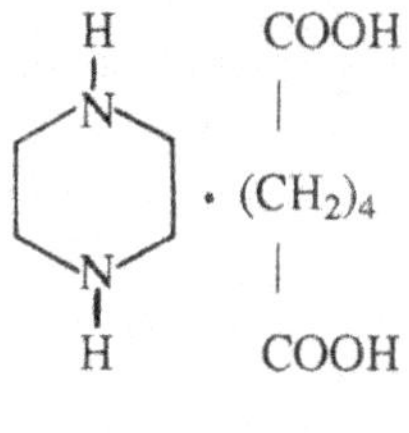

Properties and uses : It is a white crystalline powder, almost odourless, contains water of crystallization and is hygroscopic. It is water soluble and administered as tablets in 1 to 2 g daily, for the treatment of thread a worm, 4 to 5 g single dose in round worm infestations or 40 mg of piperazin hydrate per kg of body weight in divided doses.

Piperazine citrate (I.P., B.P., U.S.P.) :

Properties and uses : It is another salt of piperazine which also occurs as a white, crystalline powder, with water of hydration. It is soluble in water and is administered orally as tablets or elixirs, in 0.6 to 4.5 g in divided doses for treatment of thread worm infectations and upto 5 g in a single dose for round worm infestations.

Piperazine phosphate (I.P.) is given as tablets in thread worm infections. Piperazine hydrate is also official in I.P. and B.P.

13. **Tetrachloroethylene (I.P., B.P., U.S.P.)** :

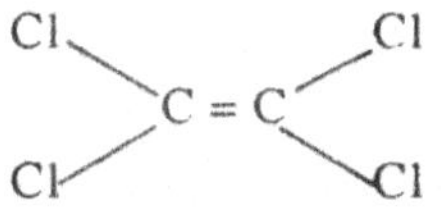

$$Cl_2C=CCl_2$$

Properties and uses : It is a clear, colourless, mobile liquid, with a characteristic odour. It is non-in-flammable. It is insoluble in water, and miscible with alcohol. It is given orally in capsules, as treatment against hook worms and intestinal flukes in a 1 to 3 ml dose maximum upto 5 ml. The capsules usually contain 0.2, 0.5, 1, 2.5 and 5 ml of tetrachloroethylene.

14. **Thiabendazole (B.P., U.S.P.)** :

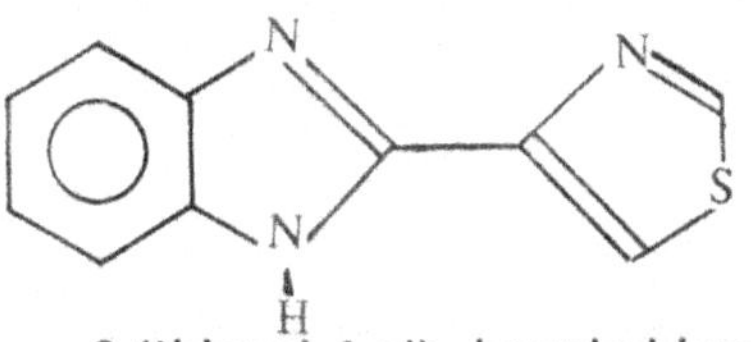

2-(thiazol-4-yl) benzimidazole

Properties and uses : It is a cream-coloured, odourless powder. It is insoluble in water but soluble in alcohol. Thiabendazole is active orally and is administered as tablets in a 1.75 g dose twice daily, in divided doses for two to three days. The drug is a potent anthelmintic against a wide range of worms like pinworm, threadworm, whip worm, round worm, hookworms etc. Thiabendazole oral suspension is official in U.S.P. and is available in 500 mg per 5 ml concentrations.

❑ ❑ ❑

Chapter 35

DRUGS FOR URINARY TRACT INFECTIONS

The substances which act as anti-infectory agents in urinary tract infections are called urinary tract antiseptics or anti-infectives. This class of substances, in general, act as an antiseptic or anti-infective. However, they are selectively more effective in the treatment of urinary tract infections.

Certain antbiotics and sulphonamides are effective in urinary tract infections (discussed eleswhere) and are used alone or in combinations. However, when resistance is developed against antibiotic or when they are contraindicated, different types of drugs are used in the treatment of urinary tract infections. Some clinically useful drugs are :

1. **Mandelic Acid** :

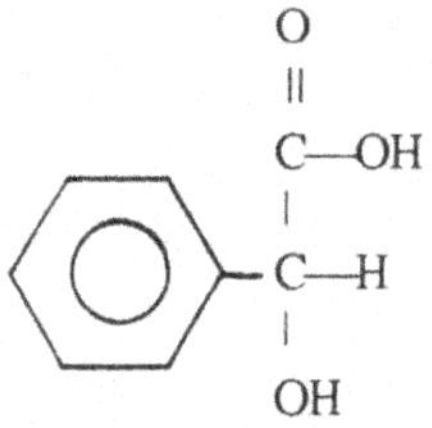

$$\text{C}_6\text{H}_5-\underset{\underset{OH}{|}}{\overset{\overset{O}{\parallel}}{\underset{|}{C}}}\text{H}-\text{C}-\text{OH}$$

Properties and uses : The racemic form is biologically active. It occurs as a white crystalline powder with an aromatic odour and darkens on exposure to light. It is sparingly soluble in water. Its sodium and ammonium salts are more water-soluble. It shows good bacteriostatic activity against a variety of organisms. It is active orally and is exerted in the urine unchanged (as it is not metabolised). The calcium salt is used clinically because gastric irritation is less. The usual dose is 3 g.

2. Nalidixic acid (B.P., U.S.P.) :

$$\text{Structure of Nalidixic acid with CH}_3, \text{N, N-C}_2\text{H}_5, \text{COOH, and 4-oxo groups}$$

**1-ethyl-7- methyl-4-oxo-
1, 8-napthyridine-3-carboxylic acid**

Properties and uses : It occurs as a whitish to pale yellow, crystalline powder, almost odourless and insoluble in water. The drug is administered orally as tablets or in mixtures (both official in B.P.). It is rapidly absorbed and excreted in the urine. It is claimed to be more effective in the treatment of urinary tract injections caused by Gram negative organism than other micro-organisms. The usual dose is 2 to 4 g, four times a day.

3. Nitrofuantoin (B.P., U.S.P.) :

$$O_2N-\text{furan}-CH=N-N\overset{\displaystyle C=O}{\underset{\displaystyle CH_2-C=O}{\diagup\diagdown}}NH$$

1-[(5-nitrofurfurylidine) amino] imidazolidine-2, 4-dione

Properties and uses : It occurs as pale yellow crystals, odourless, sparingly soluble in water, and more soluble in alcohol. It should be kept in a closed container, protected from light. It is readily absorbed from the gastrointestinal tract and is excreted in urine. It is given in the form of tablets or as a mixture, for treatment of various types of microbial infections of the urinary tract. Usual dose is 400 mg, in divided doses daily.

Chapter 36

SULPHONAMIDES, SULPHONES AS ANTIBACTERIAL AGENTS

Sulphanilamide was synthesized in the year 1908 by ' Gelmo'. However it became impotant as a drug only after the synthesis of ' prontosil', which was found to have a stron bateriostatic action. Afterwards, large number of sulphanilamides have been prepared and screened for their antibacterial action. Sulphanilamide derivatives are collectively called ' Sulphonamides ' Sulphanilamide was official in older pharmacopoeias, but it is no longer official as it is replaced by the more effective sulphonamides. Sulphonamides, as a class, are easier to prepare in the laboratory or on an industrial scale.

The nomenclature of sulphanilamide derivatives is based on the following numbering system.

(i) Substituents on the nitrogen of the sulphonamido nitrogen are called as N^1-substituents, and

(ii) Substituents on the amino nitrogen are called as N^4 substituents.

(iii) The nomenclature radical is called the sulphanilamido group.

(iv) In naming a heterocyclic substituted sulphonamido, the point of attachment of the hetero ring is given. For e.g. sulphadimidine.

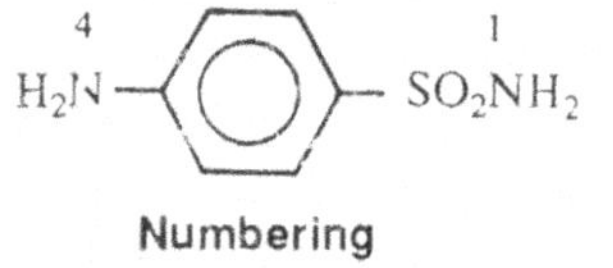

Numbering

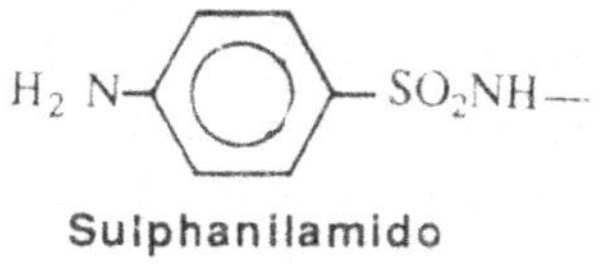

Sulphanilamido

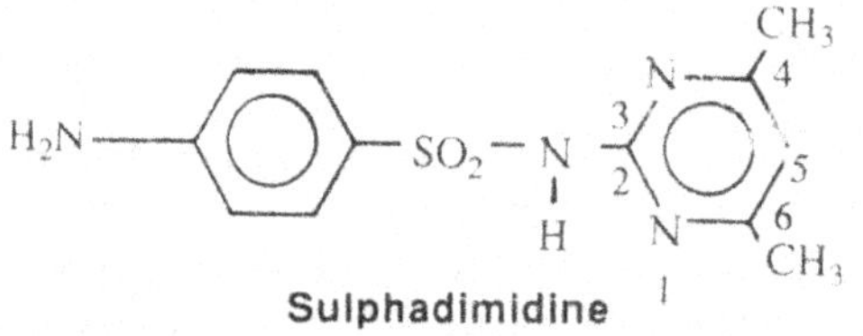

Sulphadimidine
N^1-(4,6-dimethyl-pyrimidine-2-yl) sulphanilamide
or 2-sulphanilamido-4,6-dimethyl pyrimidine

Sulphonamides have very broad anti-microbial spectrum. They were effective against all Gram-positive cocci, except enterococci, all Gram-positive bacilli. Enterobacteriaceae and Gram negative cocci, H *influenzae B. Pertussis*, and some pseudomonas. But as the micro-organisms have developed resistance to sulphonamides, the spectrum is reduced greatly. These are effective against the following micro-organisms : *gonococcus, meningococcus, pneumococcus streptococcus hemolyctus, Stereptococcus viridans, Haemophilus influenzac, Shigella disper, Bacillus coli, Clostridium Septicum. Friedlander's bacillus*, etc. Most of the staphylococci are resistant to sulphonamides. Against viral infection sulphonamides are not effective.

Classification of Sulphonamides : Sulphonamides can be classified by many methods

(A) **The Chemical basis of classification is :**

(i) Substituents on aromatic amino group e.g. Prontosil,

(ii) Substituents on sulphonamido nitrogen e.g. sulphadiazine, sulphamethoxazole.

(iii) Substituents on both amino and sulphonamido group e.g. succinylsulphathiazole, phthalyl sulphathiazole.

(iv) Sulphas without aromatic amino group e.g. Mefenide.

(B) **The pharmacological basis of classification is :**

(i) As antibacterials, e.g. Sulphadimnidine, sulphadiazine etc.

(ii) As oralhypoglycemics i.g. Tolbutamide.

(iii) As diuretics e.g. furosemide, chlorthalidone.

(iv) As antimaterial e.g. sulphadoxine.

(v) As antidiarrheal e.g. phthalylsulphathiazole.

(C) **Another method of classification is based on duration of action (i.e. the half life of drug) :**

Thus, sulphas can be classified as

(i) Long acting : Sulphas having t/2 of about 24 hours. e.g. sulphamethoxy-pyridazine, sulphadiamethoxine.

(ii) Intermediate acting : sulphas having t/2 between 10-24 hours. e.g. Sulphamethoxazole, sulphasomizole

(iii) Short acting : Sulphas having t/2 less than 10 hours e.g. Sulphathiazole, sulfisoxazole.

Sulphomides are dissused as under

I. Sulphonamides used in Eye infections.
II. Sulphonamides which are used for intestinal infection.
III. Sulphonamides which are used for systemic infections.
IV. Sulphonamides useful in burn infections.
V. Sulphonamides used in urinary tract infections.

During sulphonamide therapy, untoward side effects are observed. The most frequent side effects are crystalluria and related renal damage. In a few cases, hematuria is noted, particularly when sulphadiazine of sulphonamides contain pyridine nuclei. The possibility of hematuria can be lessened by using alkali and fluid therapy, or by using a mixture of sulphonamides. In a few patients, hypersensitivity reactions like dermatitis, lupoid syndrome, hepatitis and pulmonary eosinophilia are observed. In patients receiving sulphapyridine, a plastic anaemia, leukopenia and agranulocytosis are observed. Long acting sulphonamides cause a serious side reaction known as the Stevens Johnson syndrome. Sulphonamides should be used only after a proper bacteriological diagnosis.

Mechanism of action : The antibacterial action of sulphonamide have been explained on the basis of competitive antagonism. Sulphonamides act as bacteriostatic and arrests growth and multiplication of infectious organism. The infection is eradicated by hosts cellular and humaral defance mechanism.

According to Woods-Fildes, the para-aminobezoic acid (PABA) is essential in the biosynthesis of various folate enzymes as co-factors. The structural similarity between PABA and sulphonamides act as antimetabolite and prevent formation of pteroylglutamic acid and folinic acid Certain sulpha drugs exhibit synergistic effect when combined with other drugs like trimethoprim/ pyrimethamine, tetracycline etc.

Metabolism : All sulphas get bond to the body plasma proteins and also to the erythrocytes to a varying extent. The free sulphonamide is eliminated from body partly as the unchanged and partly as acetyl derivatives. The acetylated forms are less water soluble than the parent drug and have large quantity of water need to be taken to prevent crystalluria. Long term use of sulphonamide produces metabolic acidosis and hence alkaline salts like potassium citrate or sodium bicarbonate are given along with sulpha drugs to keep the urine alkaline.

I. SULPHONAMIDES USED IN EYE INFECTIONS

Sulphacetamide (I.P.):

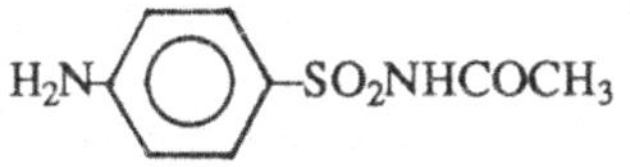

$$H_2N-C_6H_4-SO_2NHCOCH_3$$

N¹-acetylsulphanilamide

Properties and uses : It occurs as a white crystalline powder, soluble in water and alcohol. It is very soluble in hot water and solutions of alkali hydroxides and mineral acids. Its aqueous solutions are acidic to litmus. It is readily absorbed because of its high water solubility and is easily eliminated through urine. Usual dose is 0.5 to 1 g initially, with a maintenance dose 1 g, every four hours. in urinary tract infections.

Sulphacetamide sodium (I.P., B.P., U.S.P.) :

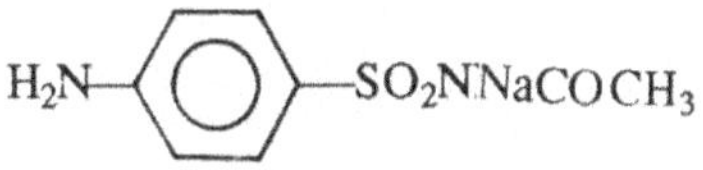

$$H_2N-C_6H_4-SO_2NNaCOCH_3$$

Sodium salt of N¹-acetylsulphanilamide

Properties and uses : It is a white to yellowish white, crystalline powder, highly soluble in water, slightly soluble in alcohol and insoluble in chloroform. Aqueous solutions are alkaline in nature. They are incompatible with all acidic substances. Sulphacetamide eye ointment (ophthalmic ointment) is official in I.P., B.P. and U.S.P. and ophthalmic solution is official in U.S.P. Usual strength is 10 to 30 per cent. The antibacterial spectrum is similar to sulphonamide but it is less potent. In high concentrations it is mainly used for eye infections caused by pyogenic coccgonococcus, E. Coli and Koch Weeks bacilli. As the drug is non-irritating, it is used in high concentrations to achieve penetration of the occular tissue. Usually, the ointment is applied topically, 2 to 8 times a day, and the solution is used in 0.1 ml every 2 to 3 hours.

II. SULPHONAMIDES USED IN INTESTINAL INFECTION

Sulphonamides for the intestinal infections have poor water solubility and are not absorbed through G.I. tract.

Sulphaguanidine :

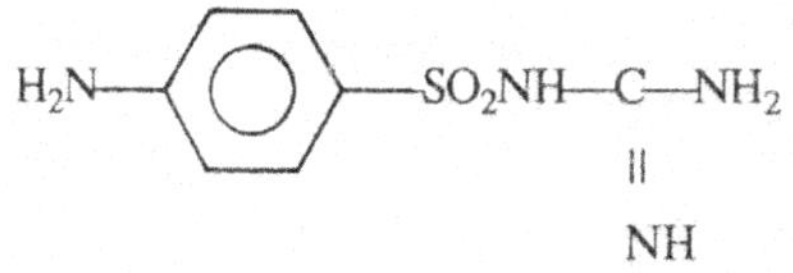

$H_2N-\langle\text{C}_6H_4\rangle-SO_2NH-C(=NH)-NH_2$

N¹-guanidyl sulphanilamide

Properties and uses : It occurs as white, needle shaped crystals or crystalline powder. It is sparingly soluble in water, but dissolves in boiling water. It darken slowly on exposure to light. It is used for intestinal infection as it is poorly absorbed from the intestine. The drug is no longer official.

Phthalyl sulphathiazole (I.P., B.P.) :

[Structure: 2-carboxybenzamide linked via CONH to para-aminobenzenesulfonamide, with SO₂NH attached to thiazol-2-yl]

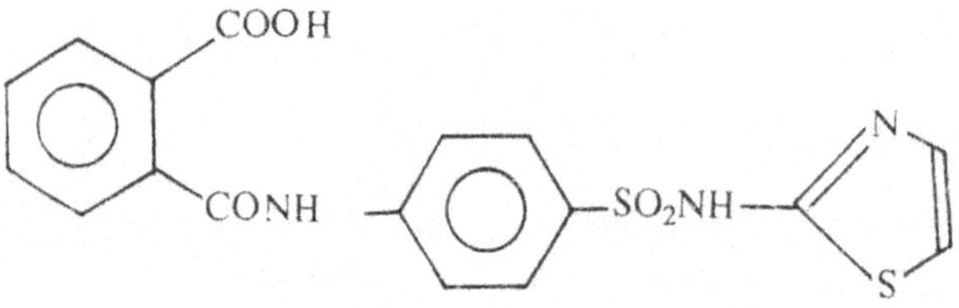

4-(thiazole-2-yl sulphamoyl) phthalanilic acid

Properties and uses : It is a white powder, insoluble in water and chloroform, slightly soluble in alcohol and soluble in aqueous solutions of alkali hydroxides and mineral acids. It darkens slowly on exposure to light. It is used in the form of tablets, occasionaly for intestinal infections and mainly in the preparation of bowel surgery. It also finds use in chronic ulcerative colitis and in intestinal amoebiasis. Usual dose is 4 to 12 g daily, in 6 divided doses.

Succinyl sulphathiazole (I.P., B.P.) :

$HOOC-COCH_2CH_2CONH-\langle\text{C}_6H_4\rangle-SO_2NH-\langle\text{thiazole}\rangle$

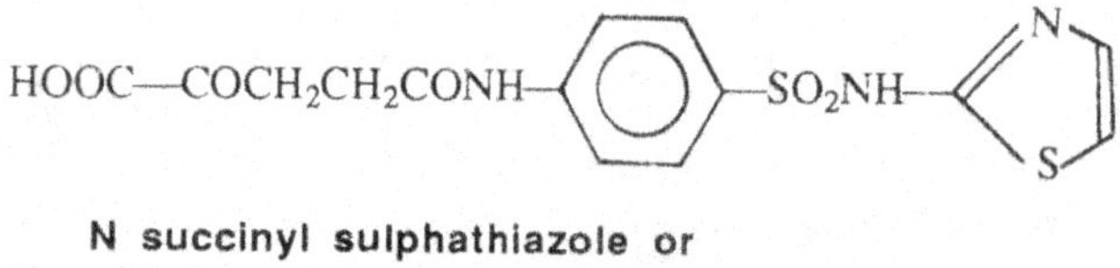

N succinyl sulphathiazole or
4' - (N thiazol-2yl sulphamoyl) succinalic acid

Properties and uses: It is a white to yellowish white, crystalline powder, very slightly soluble in water. It is soluble in aqueous solutions of alkali hydroxides and carbonates. It is stable in air, but slowly darkens on exposure to light. It is used in the form of tablets (I.P.). It is very poorly absorbed from the gastro-intestinal tract, and thus it finds used in infections of large intestine. The usual dose is 10 to 20 g daily, in divided doses.

III. SULPHONAMIDES USED IN SYSTEMIC INFECTIONS

Sulphadiazine (I.P., B.P., U.S.P.) :

$H_2N-\langle\bigcirc\rangle-SO_2NH-\langle pyrimidine \rangle$

N^1- (pyrimidine-2yl) sulphanilamide

Properties and uses : It is a white or whitish-yellowish crystalline powder. It is soluble in solutions of alkali hydroxides and carbonates, and in dilute solutions of mineral acids. It is practically insoluble in water. It is used in the form of tablets. It is one of the most widely used sulphonamide for systemic infections. It is useful in meningococcal infection, as it penetrates the cerebrospinal fluid better than sulphadimidine. Sulphadiazine powder is sterilized by drying at 100°, then, filled in a final container and heated at 150°C for 1 hour. It is also used topically for infection caused by *Hemophlus vaginalis*. Initial dose is 3 g, followed by a 2 to 4 g dose daily, in divided doses. Sulphadiazine is also effective as a antimalarial drug.

Sulphadimidine (I.P., B.P.) Sulphamethazine (U.S.P.) :

$H_2N-\langle\bigcirc\rangle-SO_2NH-\langle 4,6-dimethylpyrimidine \rangle$

N^1-(4,6 dimethyl pyrimidin-2-yl) sulphanilamide

Properties and uses : It is a white or creamy white, crystalline powder, soluble in aqueous solutions of alkali hydroxide, carbonates and dilute mineral acids. Its tablets are official in I.P. and B.P. and is used for treating systemic infections. It is excreted slowly by the kidney as compared to sulphadiazine.

Sulphadimidine sodium (I.P., B.P.) :

It is a sodium salt of sulphadimidine. It occurs as a white to creamy white powder hygroscopic in nature, very soluble in water, but less soluble in alcohol. Aqueous solutions are alkaline in nature. It must be stored in tight containers, protected from light. Its injections are official in I.P. and B.P. It is administered intramuscularly or intravenously when higher blood levels are required, while treating severe systemic infections. The usual dose is 1 - 2 g.

The use of sulphadimidine and its sodium salt is not favoured as chances of kidney damage are greater.

Sulfisoxazol Acetyl (U.S.P.) :

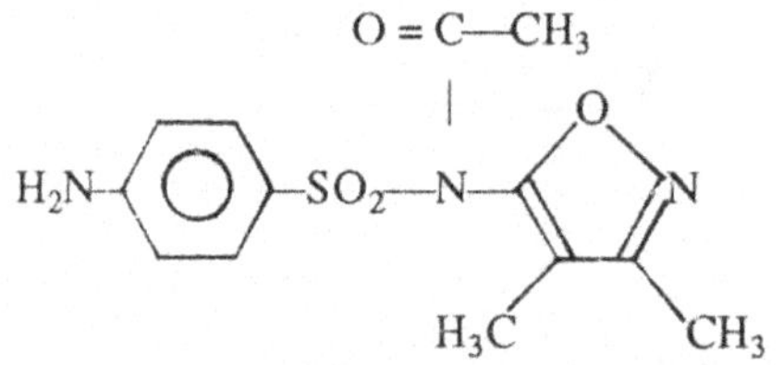

N^1- N^1, (3,4,- dimethylisoxazol-5-yl) sulphanilamide

Properties and uses : It is a white to whitish-yellowish crystalline powder, practically insoluble in water slightly soluble in alcohol. As the powder is tasteless, it is used in the form of an oral suspension. Uses are similar to sulfioxazole. Usual initial dose (adult) is 2 to 4 g, followed by a maintenance dose of 4 to 8 g daily, in 4 to 6 divided doses.

Sulphathiazole (B.P.) :

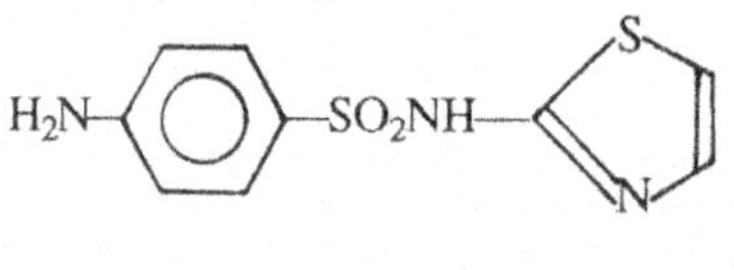

N^1-thiazol-2-yl-sulphanilamide

Properties and uses : It occurs as an almost white, crystalline powder, very slightly soluble in water, soluble in dilute solutions of mineral acids and alkali hydroxides. The crystalline powder, dried at 100º, can be sterilized by heating at 150º for 1 hour. After sterilization, it shows a slight discolouration. It is used in the form of tablets as sulphonamide, in the dose regime of 2 to 6 g daily, in divided doses.

Sulphapyridine (B.P., U.S.P.) :

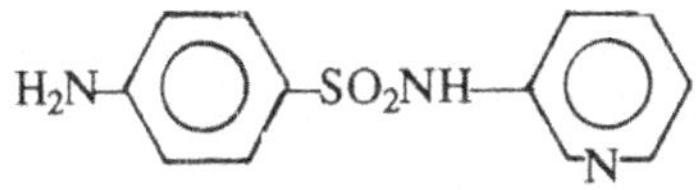

$$H_2N-\phenyl-SO_2NH-\text{(pyridin-2-yl)}$$

N^1-2-pyridylsulphanilamide

Properties and uses : It occurs as a white or faintly yellowish white, crystalline powder, very slightly soluble in water, soluble in dilute solutions of mineral acids and alkali hydroxides. It is stable in air, but darkens on exposure to light. It was the first drug used as a curative for pneumonia. It also finds use in the treatment of dermatitis herpetiformis. Tablets in the dose of 0.5 to 3.0 g daily, in single or divided doses, are employed. Sulphapyridine sodium is very soluble in water and is used as an intravenous injection. When quick action (high blood level) is desired. It should not be given subcutaneously or intramuscularly, as the high alkalinity of the solution causes tissue damage.

LONG ACTING SULPHONAMIDES

Sulphadimethoxine (I.P., B.P.) :

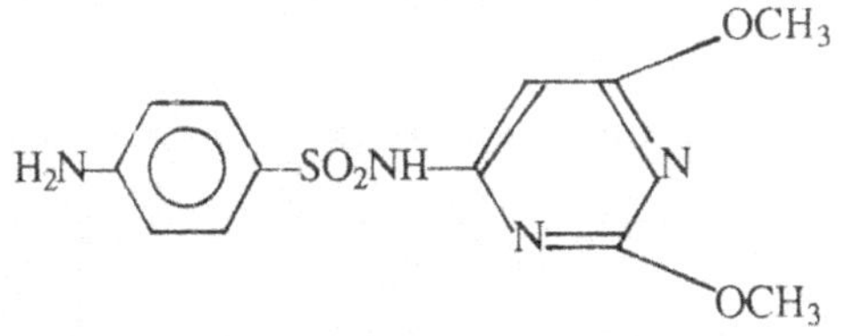

$$H_2N-\phenyl-SO_2NH-\text{(2,6-dimethoxypyrimidin-4-yl)}$$
with OCH_3 groups at 2 and 6 positions

N^1- (-2, 6-di-methoxy-pyrimidin-4-yl) sulphanamide

Properties and uses : A creamy white, crystalline powder, insoluble in water, moderately soluble in alcohol, soluble in aqueous solutions of mineral acids and alkali hydroxides. It is a long acting sulphonamide (has a longer duration of action). Its excretion is slow, so the chances of crystalluria are less. It is used in the form of tablets, for systemic infection treatment. Initial dose is 1 to 2 g and subsequent dose is 500 mg daily.

Sulfadoxine (I.P., B.P.) [Sulphormethoxine] :

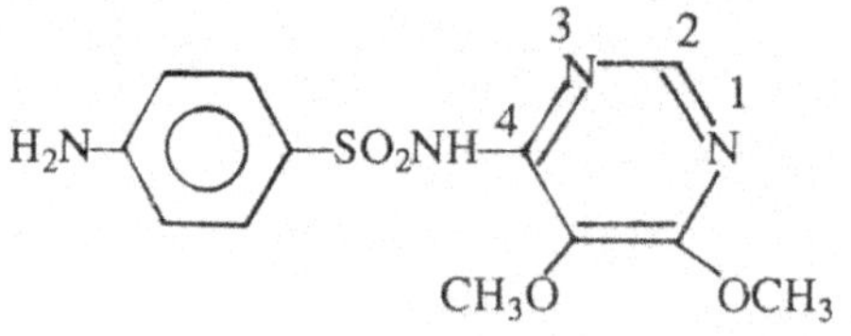

N^1-5, 6-dimethoxypyrimidin-4-yl) sulphanilamide

Properties and uses : It occurs as a creamy white, crystalline powder, very slightly soluble in water, sparingly soluble in alcohol, soluble in aqueous solutions of mineral acids and alkali hydroxides. It is mainly used as an antimalarial against *P. falciparum* infections. The usual dose is 1 g, as a single dose.

Sulphalane (I.P.) : Sulphamethoxypyrazine :

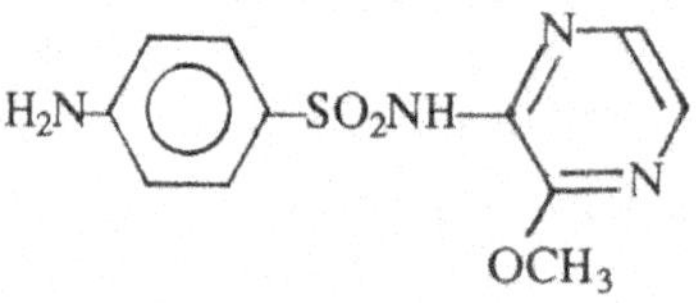

N^1-(2-methoxy-3-pyrazin-3-yl) sulphanilamide

Properties and uses : It is a yellowish white powder, slightly bitter in taste. It is given orally in 800 mg dose followed by 200 mg for systemic infections. It is also used as antimalarial drug.

Sulphamethoxypyrida-z-ine (B.P.) :

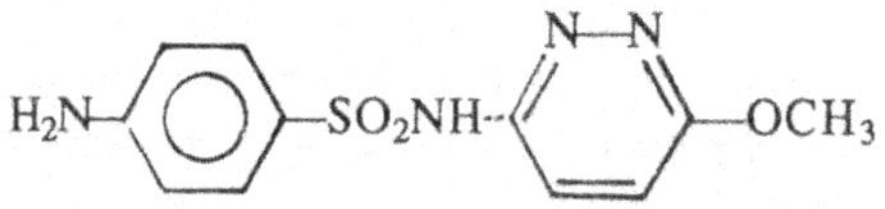

N^1, (6-methoxy-pyridazin 3-yl) sulphanilamide

Properties and uses : It occurs as a white to yellowish white, powder, very slightly soluble in water, sparingly soluble alcohol, soluble in dilute solutions of mineral acids and alkali hydroxides. It is a long acting sulphonamide used in the form tablets for the treatment of systemic infections. The initial dose is 1.0 g, followed by a 500 mg daily.

VI. SULPHONAMIDES FOR BURN THERAPY

Certain sulphamides are specially useful in burns and hence are clinically used.

Silver sulphadiazine : It is a silver salt of sulphadiazine. It is very slightly soluble in water and is very effective against pseudonomal species. The drug is applied externally in cream on the affected part.

V. SULPHONAMIDES USED IN URINARY TRACT INFECTION

Sulphafurazole (I.P., B.P.) : Sulfioxzole (U.S.P.) :

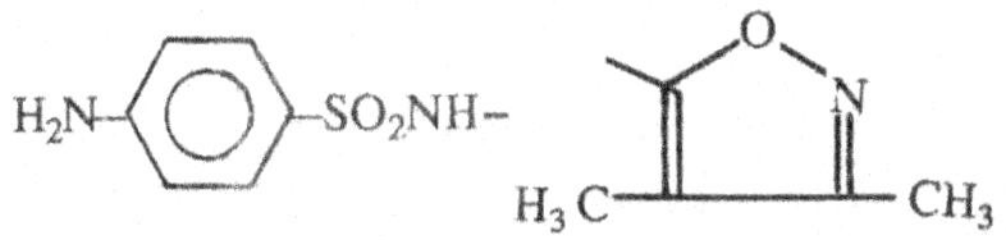

N^1- (3-4 dimethyl isooxazole-5-yl) sulphanilamide

Properties and uses : It is white to yellowish white, powder, practically insoluble in water, soluble in alcohol. It is used in the form of tablets. For treatment of systemic infections. The usual dose is 3 g initially followed by a 6 g dose daily, in divided doses, and in urinary tract infections, the initial dose is 2 g and then a 4 g dose daily, in divided doses.

Sulphaphenazole (I.P.) :

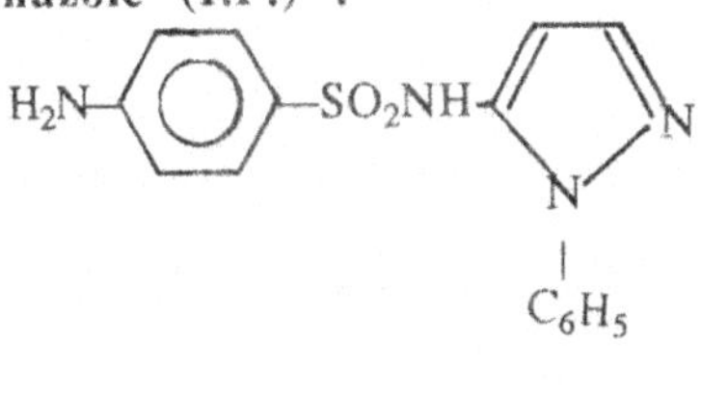

N^1-(1'-phenylpyrazol-5-yl) sulphanilamide

Properties and uses : This is white to creamy white, crystalline powder, very slightly soluble in water, soluble in dilute solutions of mineral acids and alkali hydroxides. It is an intermediate acting sulphonamide, and is readily absorbed from the gastro-intestinal tract. Tablets are used in the treatment of systemic and urinary tract infection caused by susceptible organisms. Usual initial dose is 1 g every 12 hours for 2 days, and subsequently, 500 mg every 12 hours for 2 to 5 days.

Sulphamethizole (B.P.) :

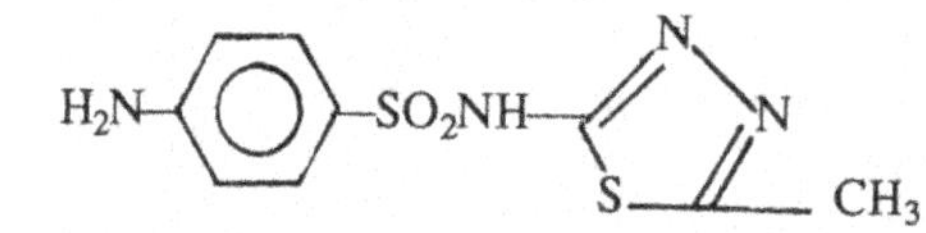

$H_2N-\langle C_6H_4 \rangle-SO_2NH-\text{(5-methyl-1,3,4-thiadiazol-2-yl)}$

N–1(5-methyl-1,3,4-thiadiazole-2-yl) sulphanilamide

Properties and uses : It is a white, crystalline powder sparingly soluble in water, soluble in alcohol, dilute solutions of mineral acid and alkali hydroxides. It is specially useful in the treatment of urinary tract infections, and is usually employed in the form of tablets. The usual dose is 100 to 200 mg, every 4 to 6 hours.

Sulphamethoxazole (I.P., B.P.) :

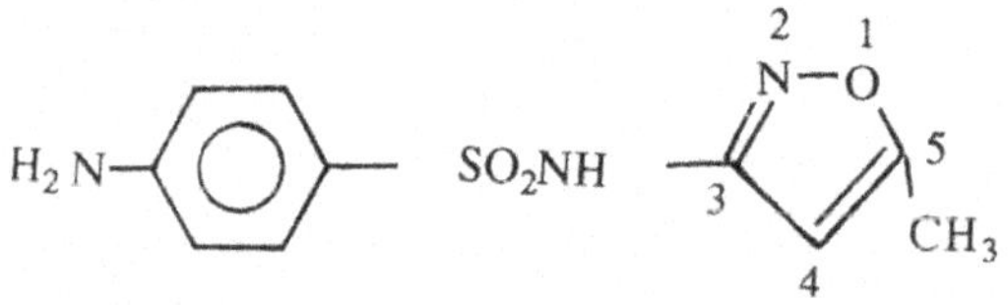

$H_2N-\langle C_6H_4 \rangle-SO_2NH-\text{(5-methylisoxazol-3-yl)}$

N^1-(5-methylisoxazole 3-yl) sulphanilamide

Properties and uses : It occurs as a white crystalline powder, stable in air. It is slightly soluble in water, ether and chloroform, soluble in alcohol, dilute solutions of mineral, acids and alkali hydroxides. It is normally used in combination with 'Trimethoprim for an antibacterial action.

Trimethoprim (I.P., B.P.) :

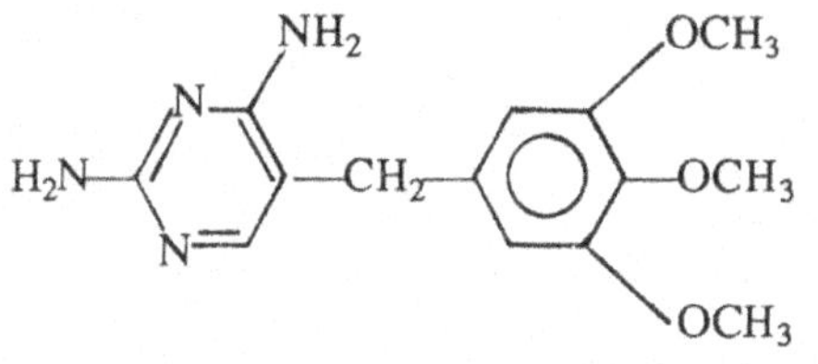

$H_2N-\text{pyrimidine(NH}_2\text{)}-CH_2-\langle C_6H_2 \rangle-(OCH_3)_3$

5 (3, 4, 5 trimethoxybenzyl) pyrimidine 2, 4-diamine

Properties and uses : A white to yellowish white, crystalline powder, very slightly soluble in water, more soluble in alcohol and chloroform. it is used as an antibacterial agent along with sulphamethoxazole.

The following formulations of sulphamethoxazole and trimethoprim are official pharmacopoeias. Sulphamethoxazole and trimethoprim tablets are official in I.P. and Co-trimoxazole injection, Co-trimorazole tablets, Dispersible Co-trimoxazole tablets and Paediatric Co-trimoxazole tablets are official in B.P.

The combination is useful clinically, as both are excreted approximately at the same rate and cause a ' sequential blockade ', in the pathway of the formation of tetrahydrofolic acid. Sulphamethoxazole inhibits the biosynthesis of dihydropteroic acid and trimethoprim inhibits the conversion of dihydrofolic acid to tetrahydrofolic acid. This combination is useful for systemic infection treatment and for urinary tract infections. The usual strength is 400 mg of sulphamethoxazole and 80 mg of trimethoprim and in divided doses. The double strength is 800 mg sulphamethoxazole and 160 mg trimethoprim.

Besides the sulphamethoxazole and trimethoprim combination ; certain mixed sulphonamides are in use and some of these are official in U.S.P. They are as follows :

1. Trisulphapyrimidines oral suspensions (U.S.P.) :

It contains 9.3 to 10.7 % w/v of total sulphapyrimidines. It contains 3 to 3.7 g of sulphadiazine, sulphamerizine and sulphamethazine in each 100 ml.

2. Trisulphapyrimidines tablets (U.S.P.) :

It contains 95 – 105 % w/w of the labelled amount of total sulphapyrimides, consisting of sulphadiazine, sulphameriazine and sulphamethazine. The amount of each sulphapyrimidines is 31.5 to 35 % w/w of the labelled amount of total sulphapyrimidines.

The above combinations have the same usefulness as that of indivdual sulphonamides and the advantage is the lesser incident of crystallurea and renal injury normally associated with their therapeutic use.

Storage of sulphonamides : Practically all sulphonamides are stable in air, but are affected by light. Thus, they should be stored in light resistant containers.

SULPHONES

Dapsone (I.P., B.P., U.S.P.) :

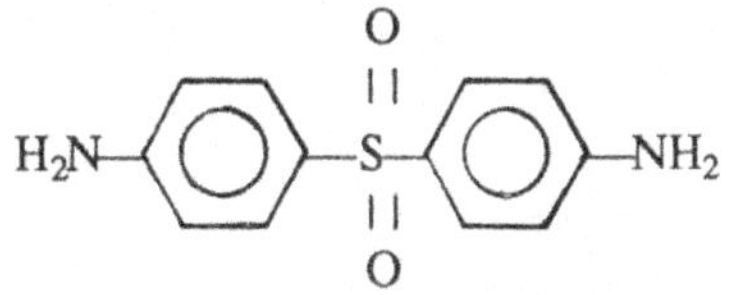

$$H_2N-\bigcirc-\underset{\underset{O}{\|}}{\overset{\overset{O}{\|}}{S}}-\bigcirc-NH_2$$

Properties and uses : It occurs as a white, crystalline powder, very slightly soluble in water and alcohol. In the presence of moisture, it is susceptible to discolouration in light. Thus, it must be protected from light. In the form of tablets it is used in the treatment of leprosy. The usual dose is 25 to 300 mg per week.

Modifications have been attempted with a view to get increasingly active compounds. However, no other useful agent has yet been developed.

Chapter 37

ANTIMALARIALS

Amongst the infectious diseases, malaria is most widely spread disease in tropical and subtropical regions which has disabling and lethal effects. Malaria is caused by protozoan plasmodium, and the four species for which man is the natural host are *P. vivax, P. falciferum, P. malariae* and *P. ovale.* The characteristic symptoms of malaria are successive chills, fever, sweating and body pains. The fever tends to reoccur every third or fourth day and infections are called tertian or quartan. Infection with *P. malariae* is characterised by a quartan type : *P. vivax* is begin tertian, *P. ovale* is tertian and *P. falciferum* is estivo-aututinal and malignant tertian.

All species of plasmodium have two hosts : a vertebrate and mosquito that acts as both vector and host. Mosquitoes which belong to genera Anopheles are the vectors for human malaria. The malaria organism requires human (or avian) and mosquito to complete its life cycle. Since febrile condition (fever) is associated with malaria, antifibrialatory drugs were tried in the olden days. Subsequently, the use of cinchona bark and the isolated active principles from it proved useful. Then followed the use of synthetic agents as antimalarials. The problem of disease malaria is complicated because of development of resistance to the drugs, lack of specific, potent drugs and different stages involved in the life cycle of plasmodium. Furthermore, the complete, irradication of the mosquito, the carrier of plasmodium has not been possible as yet. Hence the search for newer, potent antimalarial drugs is being carried out all-over the world.

Antimalarials are the drugs which prevent or cure malaria. As these drugs act at different stages of the life cycle of organism, they are classified into different classes as follows :

(A) **Sporozoitocides** are the drugs which are capable of killing the sporozoites as soon as they are introduced in the blood by a mosquito bite.

(B) **Exoerythrocytic schizontocides** are the drugs which kill the parasite as it exists in schizont the stage in the exoerythrocytic form. These are also called *tissue schizontacides.* These drugs are curative as they are capable of destroying the organism, before their entry in the red blood cell or dormant are in the host.

(C) **Erythrocytic schizontoicides** are the drugs which are capable of inhibiting the development of schizonts during the erythrocytic stage. They are also called *supperessive* or clinical prophylactics as they keep the number of blood forms of the organism below the level of showing clinical symptoms of malaria.

(D) **Gamatocytocides** are the drugs which are capable of killing parasite in the gametocyte stage ; as a result, these drugs prevent the spreading of the disease.

(E) **Sporontocides** are the drugs which prevent sporogony in the mosquito by their effect on the gametocytes in the blood of the vertebrate bost. These drugs are useful as exoerythrocytes and schizontocides.

The widely used antimalarials are broadly divided into the following chemical classes.

(1) Cinchona alkaloids. (2) 4-aminoquinolines (3) 8-aminoquinolines. (4) 9-aminoacridines (5) Biguanides (6) Pyrimidines (7) Miscellaneous.

1. CINCHONA ALKALOIDS

About twenty-five alkaloids have been obtained from various species of Cinchona. The important alkaloids are quinine, quinidine, cinchonine and cinchonidine. They have diastereomeric relationship with each other.

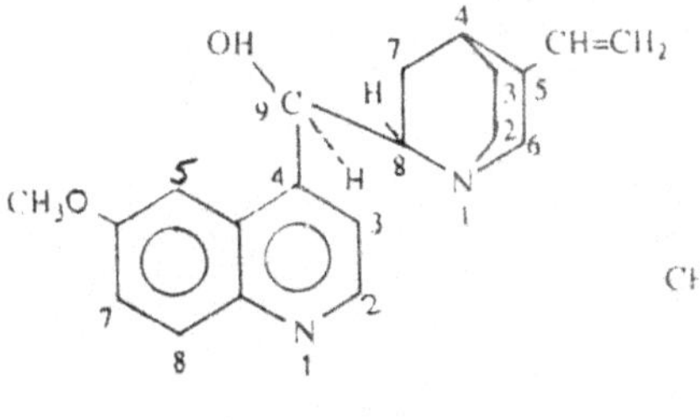

Quinine 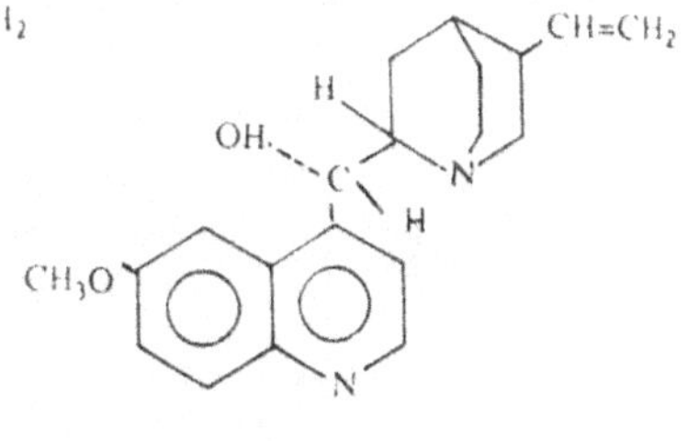   Quinidine

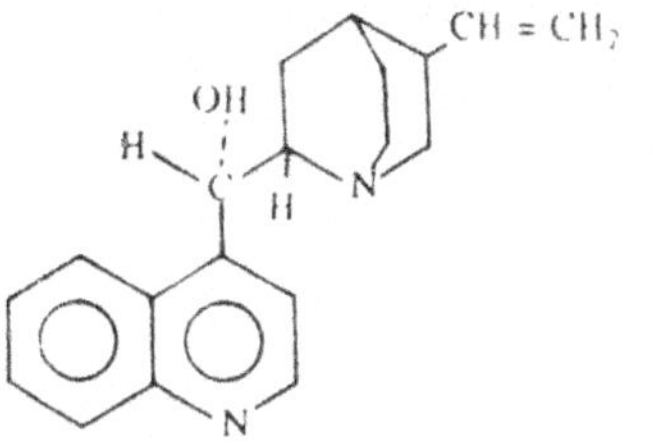

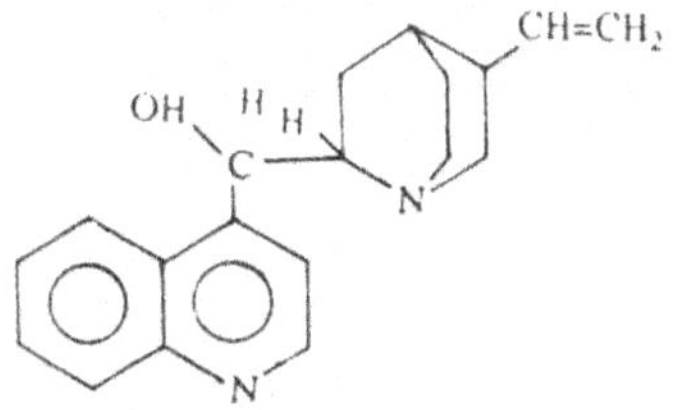

The percentage of the total alkaloids and quinine are highest in bark of cultivated cinchona. Quinine behaves as diacidic base and forms salts easily. These salts are of two types : (i) the acid or bisalts and (ii) the neutral salts. Many salts of quinine are official in pharmacopoeias.

Cinchona bark (B.P.) :

It consists of the dried bark of the *Cinchona succirubra* or its variates and contains not less than 6.5 % of the total alkaloids, of which 32 to 60 per cent are alkaloids of the quinine group. It has a slight characteristic odour.

Powdered Cinchona bark (B.P.) :

It is a powder, prepared from the bark and requirements are same as cinchona bark. Cinchona extract, compound cinchona tincture and cinchona febrifuge were official in I.P.

All cinchona preparations should be stored in tightly sealed containers protected from light.

Actions and uses : Cinchona alkaloids are absorbed rapidly and completely after oral administration, and , the blood level falls quickly after the administration is stopped. Thus repeated doses must be administered. The soluble salts of quinine produces a higher initial blood level than that of a free base. Both the free base and salts are good for maintenance doses. The toxic reactions of the cinchona alkaloids is referred to as cinchonism, which are characterised by allergic skin reactions, slight deafness, vertigo and slight mental depression. In the treatment of faciforum quinine or cinchona alkaloids are given which may cause hemoglobinuria with development of black water fever. If pregnant women are treated with cinchona alkaloids it may lead to foetal blindness or may cause abortion.

The cinchona alkaloids act only as erythrocytic schizontocides of the malarial parasite. They are used in beningn, tertian and quartan malaria as suppressive rather than for curing malaria. The cinchona alkaloids can be administered orally, intramuscularly or intravenously. Quinine dihydrochloride and hydrochloride are used for parenteral administration. An intravenous administration may be hazardous as it may cause cardiovascular depression to a great extent leading to generalised collapse. Therefore parenteral administration should not be done. Besides antimalarial action, cinchona alkaloids have antipyretic, local anaesthetic and antiseptic action ; however, better drugs for these purposes are available.

The salts of cinchona alkaloids which are official are :

Quinine bisulphate (I.P., B.P.) :

It occurs as colourless crystals or white crystalline powder as heptahydrate, efflorescent in dry air. It is soluble in water but less in alcohol. Aqueous solutions are strongly acidic in nature. It is preserved in tight containers, protected from light. It is used in the form of tablets for the supression of malaria, a dose of 300 to 600 mg daily and for the treatment of malaria, a dose of 1.2 to 2.0 g, daily, in divided doses.

Quinine sulphate (I.P., B.P., U.S.P.) :

It is made up of white needlelike crystals as dihydrate. It is sparingly soluble in water, slightly in chloroform and moderately soluble in alcohol. 1.0 per cent aqueous suspension is acidic to litmus. It is used in the form of tablets. Uses and doses are similar to quinine bisulphate.

Quinine dihydrochloride (I.P., B.P.) :

It is an almost white crystaline powder, freely soluble in water and soluble in alcohol. Aqueous solutions are strongly acidic in nature. The aqueous solutions are sterilised by autoclaving or by the filtration method. It is used in the form of tablets and injection ; the intravenous dose is 300 to 600 mg.

Quinine hydrochloride (I.P., B.P.) : It usually occurs, as colourless silky crystals, usually clusters as dihydrate. It is soluble in alcohol and chloroform. Its tablets are offcial in I.P. The uses and doses are similar to quinine dihydrochloride.

2. 4-AMINO QUINOLINES

Amodiaquine hydrochloride (I.P., B.P., U.S.P.) :

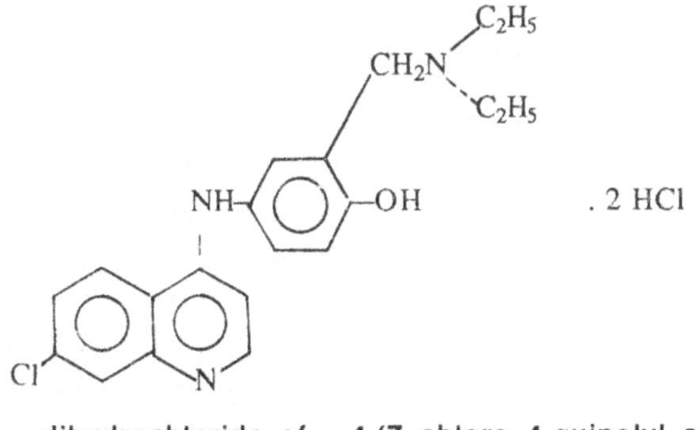

dihydrochloride of -4-(7-chloro-4-quinolyl amino) -2-(ethylaminomethyl) phenol

Properties and uses : It is a yellow crystalline powder. It is odourless. It is soluble in water, less soluble in alcohol and insoluble in chloroform and ether. It is used in the form of tablet. The suppressive dose is 400 mg of amodiaquine base every week and the therapeutic dose is 400 to 600 mg of the base daily for 3 to 4 days.

Chloroquine (U.S.P.) :

$$NH-CH-(CH_2)_3-N(C_2H_5)_2$$

(attached to 7-chloro-4-aminoquinoline with CH$_3$ on the α-carbon)

4-(7 chloro-4-(-4-quinolylamino)-pentyldiethylamine

Properties and uses : It is a white crystalline powder with a yellowish tint. It is very slightly soluble in water but more soluble in chloroform, ether and dilute mineral acids. Chloroquine is normally used in the form of its salts.

Chloroquine phosphate (I.P., B.P., U.S.P.) :

Properties and uses : It is a diorthophosphate of chloroquine base. It is a white-crystalline powder, freely soluble in water, partially soluble in alcohol and not at all soluble in ether and chloroform. Concentrated aqueous solutions are acidic in nature. Aqueous solutions are sterilized by autoclaving or by filtration method. It is used in the form of tablets (I.P., B.P., U.S.P.) and injection (B.P.). It is a suppressive and is useful in acute attacks of vivaxmalaria too. It is also useful in the treatment of amoebic hepatitis and to a certain extent in tape worm infections and rheumatoid arthritis. It is less toxic than quinacrine. In acute attacks of malaria, higher doses are used. It can cause gastric disturbances (nausea, vomiting), mild headache and some visual disturbances. As a prophylactic, and a suppressive in malaria, the standard dose is 500 mg weekly, the therapeutic dose is 1 g initially and then 500 mg in 6 hours and then 500 mg on 2nd and 3rd day. As an antiamoebic 500 mg to 1 g in divided doses for 2 days and then 500 mg daily for 2 to 3 weeks, but the total amount of the drug should not exceed 11.0 g. Chloroquine phosphate injection is official in I.P. and B.P.

Chloroquine sulphate (I.P., B.P.) :

Properties and uses : It is a white crystalline powder, a monohydrate. It is freely soluble in water, sparingly soluble in ether and insoluble in alcohol. Concentrated aqueous solutions are acidic in nature. Aqueous solutions are sterilized by autoclaving or by the filtration method. It is used in the form of tablets and injections. It is used as a suppressive in malaria in a dose of 400 mg, once a week, and in treatment of malaria 400 mg to 1200 mg daily. The intravenous or intramuscular dose is 200 to 300 mg of chloroquine base to treat malaria. It is given in hepatic amoebiasis in a dose of 400 to 800 mg daily, in divided doses.

Hydroxy chloroquine sulphate (B.P., U.S.P.) :

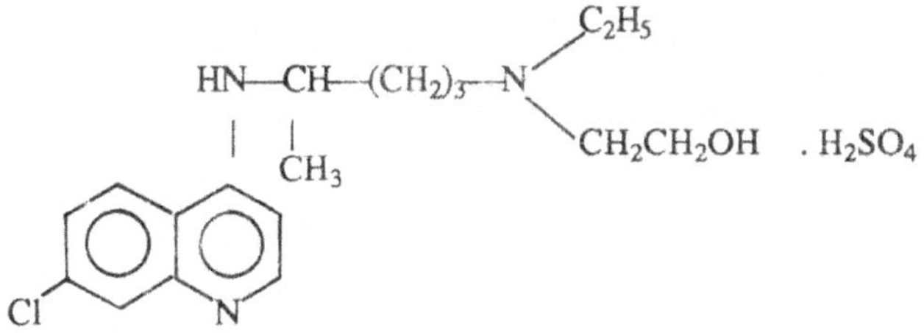

$$\text{7-Cl-quinolin-4-yl-NH-CH(CH}_3\text{)-(CH}_2\text{)}_3\text{-N(C}_2\text{H}_5\text{)(CH}_2\text{CH}_2\text{OH)} \cdot \text{H}_2\text{SO}_4$$

2-{ N-[4-(7-chloro 4-quinolylamino) pentyl] N-ethyl amino} ethanol sulphate

Properties and uses : A white crystaline powder, freely soluble in water, practically insoluble in alcohol and chloroform. Aqueous solutions are acidic in nature. It is preserved in tight containers protected from light. It is used in the form of tablets in lupus erythematosus in a dose of 200 to 400 mg, 1 to 2 times a day, for faciparum malaria 1.25 g in a single, or, in two divided doses. In rheumatoid arthritis, 400 mg is administered daily.

3. 8-AMINO QUINOLINES

A large number of compounds of this series were synthesized and screened as antimalarials. The important ones are pamaquine, primaquine, pentaquine and isopentaquine.

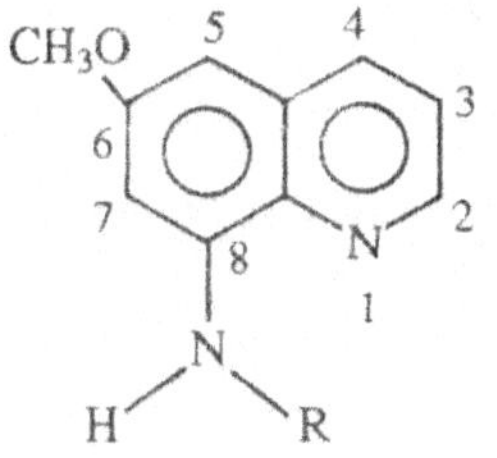

6-methoxy-8-(NHR)-quinoline

Pamaquine $R = -CH(CH_3)-(CH_2)_3-N-(C_2H_5)_2$

Primaquine $R = -CH(CH_3)-(CH_2)_3-NH_2$

Pentaquine   R = —CH$_2$—(CH$_2$)$_4$—N(H)—CH(CH$_3$)$_2$

Isopentaquine R = —CH(CH$_3$)—(CH$_2$)$_3$—N(H)—CH(CH$_3$)$_2$

Amongst these primaquine is official in pharmacopoeas. It is mainly used for their exoerythrocytic schizontocidal activity against P. vivax and P. malariae. Some compounds of this class have good gametocytocidal activity.

Primaquine phosphate (B.P., U.S.P.) :

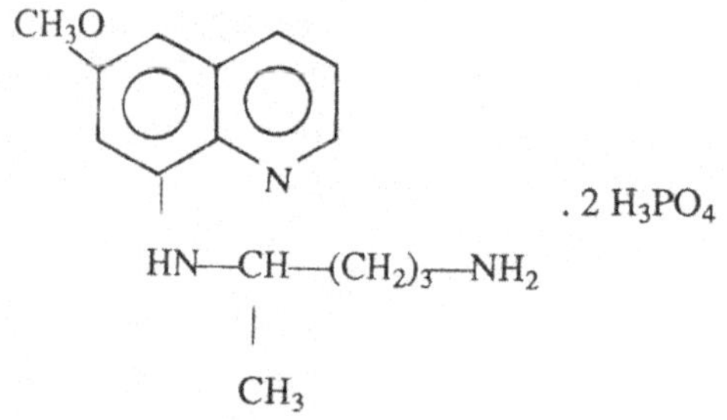

[Structure: 6-methoxy-8-aminoquinoline with HN—CH(CH$_3$)—(CH$_2$)$_3$—NH$_2$ side chain] . 2 H$_3$PO$_4$

4-amino-1-methylbutyl-(6-methoxy-8-quinolyl)-amine diortho—phosphate

Properties and uses : It is an orange red crystalline powder, soluble in water and insoluble in chloroform and ether. Aqueous solutions are strongly acidic in nature. The drug is well tolerated with less toxic effects that includes hemolytic anaemia, leucopenia, abdominal pain and vomitting. It is used for the radical cure of P vivax malaria. Its tablets are official and usual dose is 15 mg of primaquine base for fourteen days.

4 9-AMINO ACRIDINES

The intensive research in synthetic antimalarials in acridine derivatives led to the invention of 9-amino acridine derivative known as quinacrine a widely

Mepacrine hydrochloride : Quinacrine hydro-chloride (U.S.P.) :

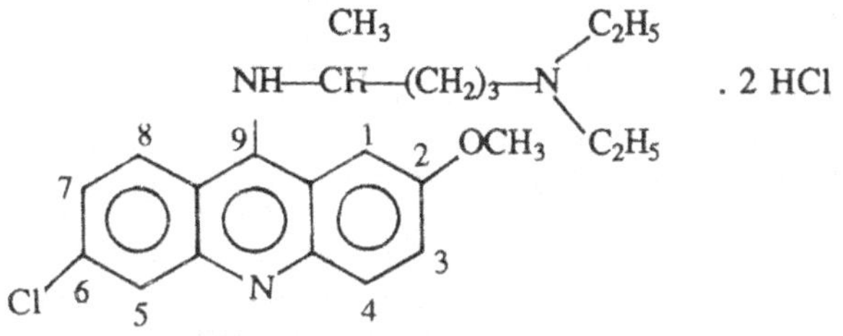

$$NH-CH(CH_3)-(CH_2)_3-N(C_2H_5)_2 \text{ (acridine ring with OCH}_3 \text{ at 2, Cl at 6)} \cdot 2HCl$$

5-chloro 9-(-4-(diethylamino)-1-methyl butyl aminol-2-methoxy acridine-dihydrochloride

Properties and uses : It is a bright yellow coloured crystalline powder, soluble in alcohol and water and insoluble in chloroform. The aqueous solutions are acidic in nature and shows a fluorescence. Solutions of dihydrochlorides are not stable. It acts as an erythrocytic schizontocide in all kinds of human malaria. It is used in the treatment of black water fever where quinine is contraindicated. Sometimes its used in amoebasis, tapeworm and pin-worm infections. The usual anthelmintic dose is 200 mg with 330 mg of sodium bicarbonate for 4 days. Therapeutic dose is 200 mg with sodium bicarbonate every 6 hours for 5 days then 100 mg 3 times for 6 days in malaria and as a suppressive 100 mg daily. It is usually given in the form of tablets. This drug is no longer official in I.P. and B.P.

5. BIGUANIDES

Proguanil hydrochloride (I.P., B.P.) : Chloroguanide hydrochloride (U.S.P.) (Paludrine) :

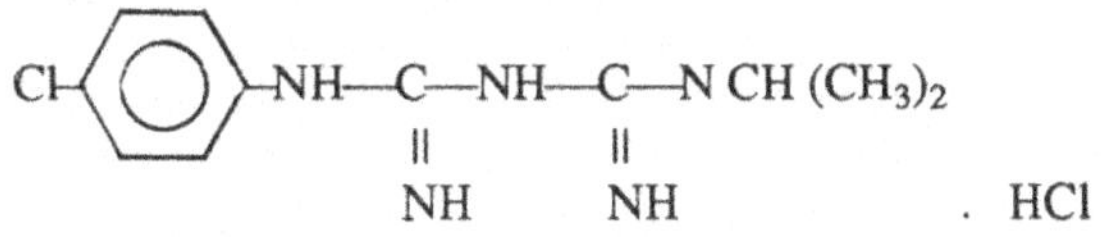

$$Cl-C_6H_4-NH-C(=NH)-NH-C(=NH)-N-CH(CH_3)_2 \cdot HCl$$

1-(4-chlorophenyl)-5-isopropyl biguanide hydrochloride

Properties and uses : It is a white powder moderately soluble in water, more in alcohol and insoluble in chloroform. The saturated aqueous solutions are acidic in nature. In *P. falciparum* the drug destroys the extra erythrocytic form and eradicates the infection. In vivax it only act on the erythrocytic phase. Thus it is used as suppressive drug in acute attacks. The disadvantage is that the resistant to this drug has occurred to a great extent in many parts of the world.

It is used in the form of tablets and the standard dose (as suppressant) is 100 to 300 mg daily.

PYRIMIDINES

A large number of compounds was synthesized in this series known as 2, 4-diamino 5-aryl pyrimidines. The most useful compound from thsi class is pyrimethamine. It is an effective erythrocytic schizontocide against all human malarias. In infection due to p vivax and P. falciparum it acts as exoerythrocytic schizontocide. It also exhibits sprontocidal action which breaks the chain of transmission of malaria.

Pyrimethamine (I.P., B.P., U.S.P.) :

It is also known as " Daraprim."

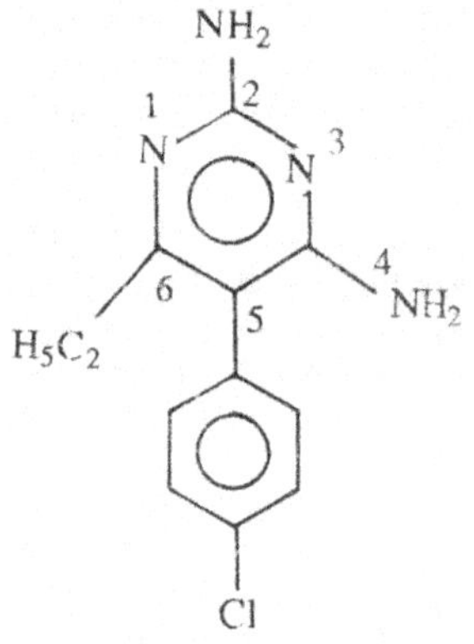

5 (4-chlorophenyl) 6 ethylpyrimidine 2,4 diyldiamine

Properties and uses : It is a white crystalline powder, insoluble in water, moderately soluble in alcohol and chloroform, soluble in warm dilute mineral acids. It is used in the form of tablets in the suppression of malaria in the dose of 25 to 50 mg once weekly.

7. MISCELLANEOUS

Dapsone belongs to the category called sulphone and is official in I.P., B.P. and U.S.P. It has a very limited value as an antimalarial specially in malaria caused by P. falciparum. It has broad antibacterial activity spectrum and hence becomes useful in malaria (It is discussed under antimycobacterial agent).

Sulfadoxine (I.P., B.P.) :

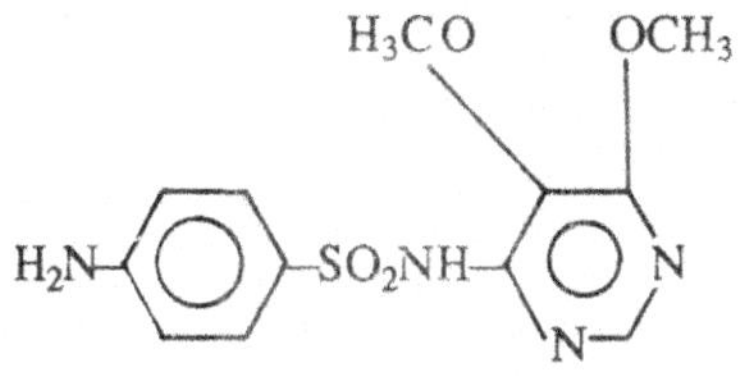

$$H_2N-C_6H_4-SO_2NH-\underset{\underset{H_3COOCH_3}{}}{pyrimidine}$$

N¹ (5, 6 dimethyl pyrimidin 4 yl) sulphanilamide

Properties and uses : It is a creamy white crystalline powder, very slightly soluble in water, and in alcohol and insoluble in ether. It is used in treatment of P, falciparum infection in 1 g single dose.

Mefloquine is a most promising drug currently tried as a antimalarial in some countries. It is said to act at erythrocytic stage and has very less side effects. The drug is said to be especially effective against resistant type of malaria.

Chapter 38

ANTIBIOTICS

Antibiotics are defined as substances produced by microorganisms which have the capacity of inhibiting the growth, or destroying other microorganisms. A broader definition includes chemical compounds derived form, or produced by living organisms and their synthetic analogues which even in small concentrations are capable of inhibiting the life processes of microorganisms.

Since the successful use of penicillin, hundreds of antibiotic substances have been successfully isolated. Of these some are used in medical practice. For antibiotic to be successful in clinical use (i) it should be effective against pathogens without producing toxic effects on the host. (ii) it should be stable during isolation, storage and use (iii) it should have a desirable degree of safety and (iv) It should have a satisfactory rate of absorption and elimination.

Some antibiotics have a high degree of selectivity and specificity against organisms and are called as narrow spectrum antibiotics ; e.g. bacitracin, nystatin while some are effective against a wide variety of pathogenic organisms and are called broad spectrum antibiotics. All antibiotics do not act in the same manner. Though no details of the exact mechanism is known, in many cases, they act at a cell wall by interferring with the mucopeptide synthesis or by interrupting cell-wall crosslinking or by altering membrane function of the cell wall, while others, act by interfering with the protein synthesis or m-RNA synthesis.

Antibiotics belong to different chemical class and hence the chemical classification of antibiotics is very difficult. However, some general structural features are common in them and thus they can be considered under the following categories.

I. Beta lactum antibiotics e.g. : Cephalosporin and Penicillins

II. Polypeptide antibiotics e.g. : Bacitracin, Colistin and Polymyxins

III. Polyenes Antibiotics e.g. : Nystatin, Amphotericin and Candicidin.

IV. Aminoglycoside Antibiotics e.g. : Streptomycin, Kenanycins Neomycin, Gentanycin, Vancomycin, Tobramycin.

V. Microlide and Linomycins Antibiotics e.g. : Erythromycins and Linomycins and clindamycin.

VI. Tetracyclines e.g. : Tetracycline, Chlortetracycilin Oxytetracyclin etc.
VII. Other Miscellaneous Class e.g. : Cycloserine
    Chloramphenical
    Griseofulvin
    Sodium fusidate
    Novobacin, rifamycins.

I. BETA LACTUM ANTIBIOTICS

1. Cephalosporins :

Cephalosporins are similar to penicillins in having β-lactam structural moiety. It contains dihydrothiazine as it's heterocyclic nucleus. Cephalosporins are produced from the growth of strains of fungus cephalosporium and from semisynthetic processes. The general structure is given below.

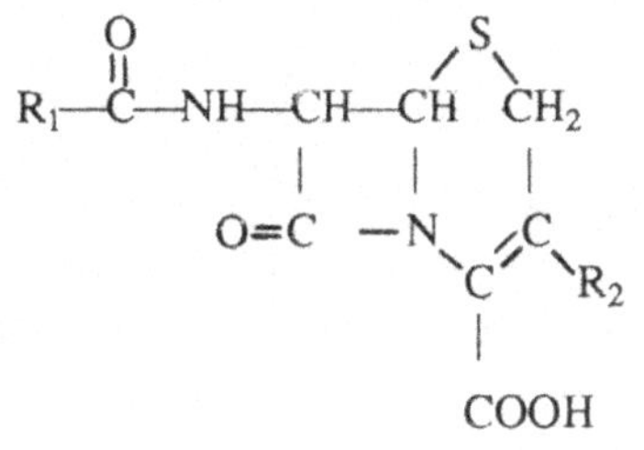

$$R_1-\overset{O}{\underset{\|}{C}}-NH-CH-CH\underset{\underset{C-R_2}{\overset{|}{COOH}}}{\overset{S}{\diagup\diagdown}}CH_2$$

Parental active

Cephalothin $R_1 =$ thiophene–CH_2 and $R_2 = CH_2OCOCH_3$

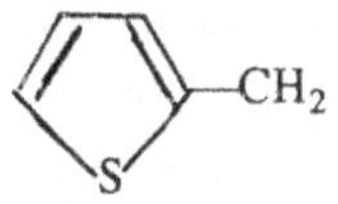

Cephaloridine $R_1 =$ thiophene–CH_2 and $R_2 = -\overset{+}{N}$–pyridinium

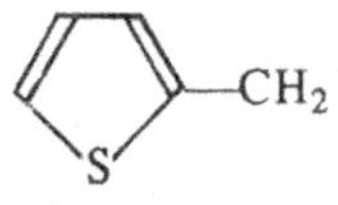

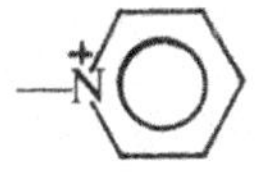

Cephalexin $R_1 =$ phenyl–$\underset{\underset{NH_2}{|}}{CH}$ and $R_2 = CH_3$

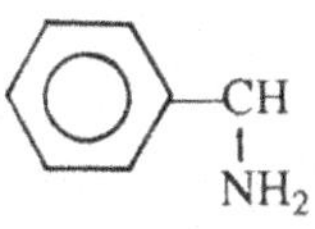

Cephradine $R_1 =$ cyclohexenyl–$\underset{\underset{NH_2}{|}}{CH}$ and $R_2 = CH_3$

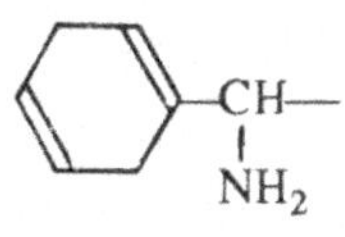

(i) Cephalexin (I.P., B.P., U.S.P.) :

Properties and uses : It is a white crystalline powder. It is odourless and freely soluble in water. It is well absorbed orally. It is stable and is resistant to acid. The antibiotic has low protein binding and is mainly excreted in urine. It is used in the treatment of urinary tract and respiratory tract infections. It is given in the capsules and tablets (official in I.P., B.P.U.S.P.) in 1 to 4 g daily, in divided doses.

(ii) Cephradine (B.P.) :

Properties and uses : It is a white crystalline hydrate and is readily soluble in water. It is absorbed well by oral route and is stable to acid reaction. It is given in the form of capsules in 250 to 500 mg four times a day in urinary tract and respiratory tract infections.

(iii) Cephaloridine (I.P., B.P.) :

Properties and uses : It is a white crystalline powder and darkens on exposure to light. It is very soluble in water ; however, aqueous solutions decompose rapidly and thus are to be used within 24 hours. The drug is stored in a refrigerator. It is poorly absorbed from the gastrointestinal tract and hence administered parenterally. The sterile cephaloridine is administered by intramuscular route in 0.5 to 1 g (I.P.) daily, in divided doses to treat infections of a wide range of Gram positive and Gram-negative organisms. It finds main use in meningitis, respiratory and urinary tract infections. The injection preparations are official in I.P., B.P.

(iv) Cephalothin sodium (B.P., U.S.P.) :

Properties and uses : It is a white to off-white powder, odourless and is freely soluble in water. It is poorly absorbed when administered orally and hence given parenterally. It is usually administered by slow intravenous injection in 2 to 10 g of cephalothin daily, in divided doses. Sensitivity reactions are observed with this drug.

2. PENICILLINS

Penicillin is the first antibiotic discovered. The various penicillins are obtained by fermentation, using various strains of mould *Penicillium*. Some 30 penicillins have been isolated by the fermentation method using mixtures of various strains. The variations have been achieved by adding different side-chain precursers to the fermentation broth of *Penicillium crysogenum* or *P. notatum*.

Different penicillins are derived from 6-amino-penicilanic acid, which is fused thiazolidine ring to β–lactum. The structure of 6-amino pencillanic acid is :

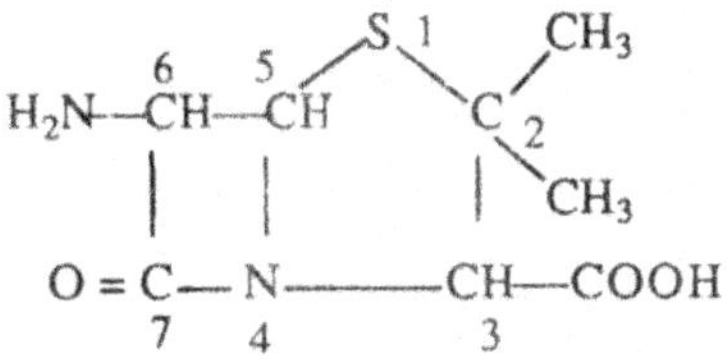

6-aminopenicillanic acid

From this, various salts and esters are prepared. The natural penicillins through biolotically active have of late, been limited applications and semisynthetic and synthetic penicillins are used. The natural penicillins, in general, are parenterally active as they get cleavaged in the gastrointestinal tract and get affected by the enzyme (penicillinase). The synthetic types are either acid resistant or enzyme action resistant.

General Structure of Penicillin :

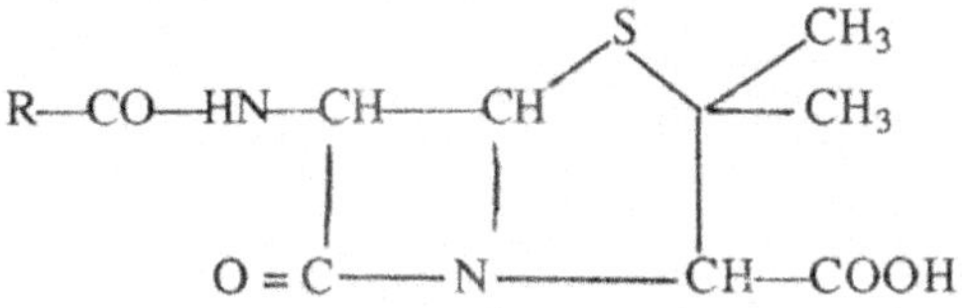

Structures of various penicillins :

R = phenyl-CH_2— penicillin G (Benzylpenicillin)

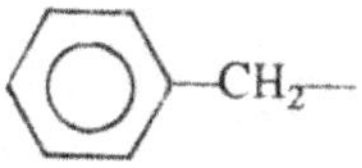

R = phenyl-O-CH_2— Penicillin V (Phenoxymethyl penicillin)

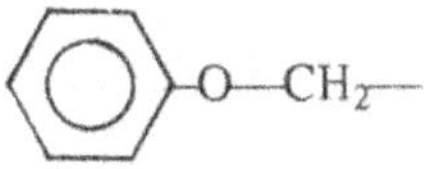

R = phenyl-O-CH(CH_3)— Penethicillin

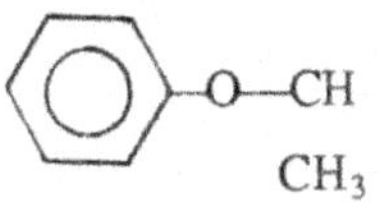

R = (3-chlorophenyl-isoxazolyl-CH_3) Cloxacillin

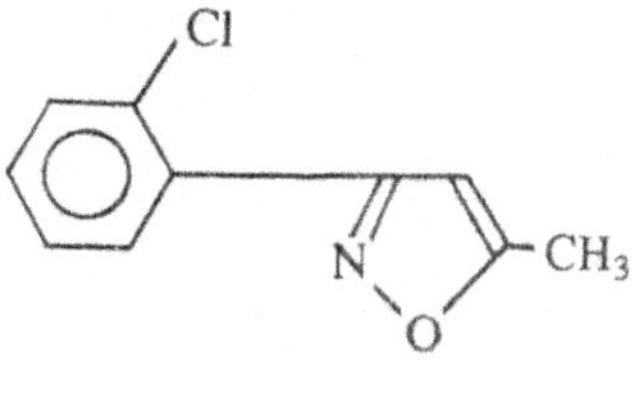

R = [2-chloro-6-fluorophenyl-5-methylisoxazole]   Flucloxacillin

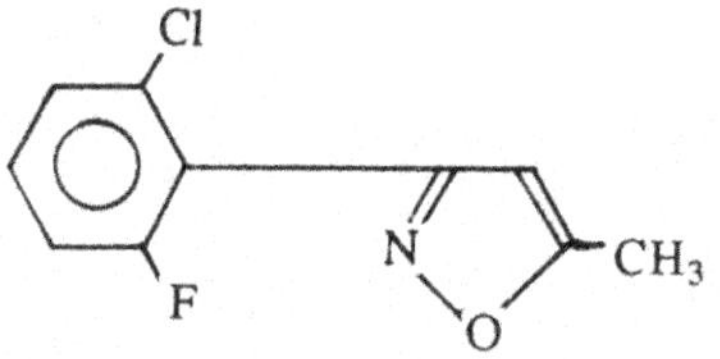

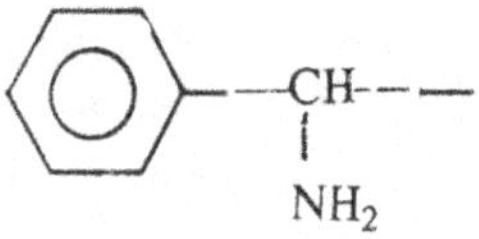

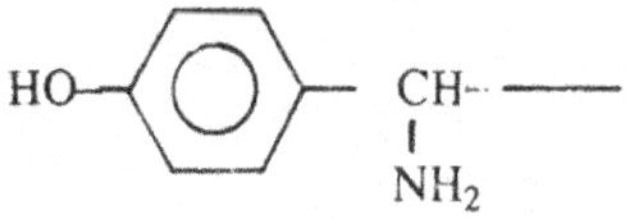

R = [phenyl]—CH(NH₂)—   Ampicillin

R = HO—[phenyl]—CH(NH₂)—   Amoxicillin

R = [phenyl]—CH(COOH)—   Carbenicillin disoda salt

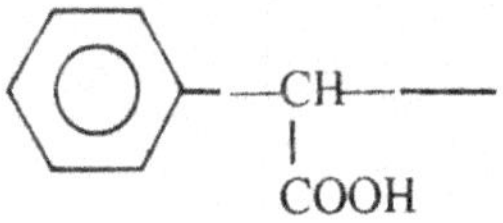

Important penicillins of clinical utility are :
(i) Benzylpencillin (Penicillin G) (I.P.) :
Benzylpenicilline is affected by acid and alkali and gets hydrolysed. At higher temperature it lose it's potency. It is stable in powder form when it contains less than 0.5 % moisture and is stored in airtight containers. The aqueous solutions are unstable and to be used immediately after preparation. The solutions for parenteral use are sterilized by the filtration method, or may be prepared by an aseptic technique. Benzylpenicllin is effective against a wide range of Gram-positive organisms. It is less effective orally and is administered either by the intramuscular or intravenous route in 0.5 to 3 g daily, in divided doses. One unit activity is considered equivalent to 0.6 microgram of penicillin G. Benzyl penicillin injection and Benzylpenicillin eye ointment are official in I.P.

(ii) Benzyl penicillin sodium (B.P.), Benzyl penicillin potassium (B.P.) :

Properties and uses : These two salt form fo penicillin are available as a white crystalline, slightly hygroscopic powder and are water soluble. These salts are given orally or parenterally for rapid high blood level concentrations. The salts get inactivated by gastric juice. To counteract this effect antacids are usually administered alongwith the drug. The aqueous injections of penicillin salts are sterilised by the filtration method. The salts are very water-soluble and are rapidly eliminated by the kidneys. To counteract the rapid elimination from the blood stream, the suspension of penicillin, in vegetable oils or with procaine are used. The salts in the form of tablets, injections and fortified procaine penicillin injection are official in B.P. The oral dose is 0.5 to 3 g of penicillin daily, in divided doses or in 0.3 to 6.0 g by intramuscular or intravenous injection in divided doses.

(iii) Benzathine penicillin (I.P., B.P., U.S.P.) :

Properties and uses : It is a salt of benzyl penicillin with N, N dibenzyl ethylenediamine. It is a white powder and is almost insoluble in water. It is less affected by the hydrochloric acid of the stomach. It gets well absorbed orally when administered in the form of tablets. Because of its poor water solubility it has great stability and has prolonged duration of effect. The activity of this form is equivalent to 1,211 units per mg. Benzathine penicillin tablets are official.

(iv) Phenoxymethyl penicillin (I.P., B.P.) Penicillin V (U.S.P.) :

Properties and uses : It is a white odourless crystalline powder, it is poorly water soluble. Penicillin V gives uniform concentration in the blood and is resistant to acid hydrolysis. It has activity of 1695 units per mg. Because of its acid resistant activity it is given orally in the form of tablets.

(v) Phenoxymethyl penicillin potassium (I.P., B.P.) :

It is potassium salt and is available as white powder. It is very soluble in water. For rapid action injections of potassium salt of phenoxy methyl penicillin are used. However. capsules and tablets are official in B.P., while only tablets are official in I.P., It is given in 0.5 to 1.5 g equivalent to phenoxymethyl penicillin, daily in divided doses.

(vi) Phenethicillin potassium (B.P., N.F.) :

This drug is similar to penicillin V and differs in having methyl group on acyl moiety. This makes that carbon atom asymmetric and optically isomers are produced. However, the racemic mixture is biologically active.

Properties and uses : It is a white crystalline powder and is very soluble in water. The drug has high stability in acidic solutions and gives resistance to degradation by penicillinase. It is usually given in the form of capsules or tablets orally in 0.5 to 1.5 g of phenethicillin daily, in divided doses. The drug gives high blood level concentrations after oral administration as compared to the parenteral route. It is effective against Gram-positive organisms and is used against a number of streptococci.

(vii) **Cloxacillin sodium (I.P., B.P., U.S.P.) :**

Properties and uses : It is a white, odourless crystalline powder that is freely soluble in water. This penicillin is resistant to acid and penicillinase. The drug is effective orally and administered in the form of capsules and parenterally by intramuscular injection in 1.5 to 3 g of cloxacillin daily in divided doses. The capsule and injection forms are official.

Cloxacillin with ampicillin in capsules and suspension is used clinically.

(viii) **Flucloxacillin sodium (B.P.) :**

This contains an additional fluoro atom at *ortho* in the benzyl ring of the cloxacillin. The drug is similar in its activity profile to that of cloxacillin sodium. This is used in treatment of infection due to strepto and staphyllococci which are resistant to natural penicillins. The usual dose is 1 to 2 g daily, in divided doses. The drug is administered either intramuscularly or by the intravenous route. Capsules and injections are official B.P.

(ix) **Ampicillin (I.P., B.P., U.S.P.) :**

Properties and uses : It is a white, crystalline anhydrous powder. It is also available as a slight buff coloured crystalline trihydrate. It is soluble in water and is stable towards acid hydrolysis and alkaline hydrolysis. However, it is not resistant to penicillinase, thus a few allergic reactions appear. The drug is effective orally and usually given either in capsules or as suspensions. Ampicillin has broader antibacterial activity. It is thus effective not only against Gram-positive but Gram-negative bacteria and also against organisms succeptible to other forms of penicillins. *Ampicillin sodium* (I.P., B.P.) is a sodium salt of ampicillin and is very soluble in water. It is used for parenteral administration of the drug. The solutions are not stable and hence are to be used within 1 hour after its preparation. The standard range of the dose is 1 to 6 g daily, in divided doses.

The ampicillin trihydrate is used in pediatric tablet preparations.

(x) **Amoxycillin trihydrate (I.P., B.P.) :**

Properties and uses : It is a white to off white fine crystalline powder. It is sparingly soluble in water. Aqueous solutions are fairly stable. It is stable towards acid hydrolysis. It gives low protein binding. It is effective orally and given in the form of capsules. The drug is absorbed well and gives high blood concentrations. It has greater antibacterial spectrum than natural forms of penicillin. It is mainly used in the treatment of certain systemic and urinary tract infections. The standard dose ranges from 750 mg to 4.0 g daily, in divided doses.

(xi) Carbenicillin sodium (B.P.) :

Properties and uses : It is a whitish powder and is soluble in water. It is comparatively unstable in acid and gets inactivated by penicillinase. However, it penetrates into the cell wall of bacterial and exhibits broad spectrum activity and is effective against pseudomonas and coliform bacteria. The drug is administered by intravenous in 12 to 30 g of Carbenicillin or by intramuscular injection in 4 to 8 g daily, in divided doses.

II. POLYPEPTIDE ANTIBIOTICS

This group of antibiotics are composed of a number of aminoacids joined through as peptide linkage and have a cyclic structure. They contain unnatural, D-configuration aminoacids. Chemically they are of three main types ; acidic, basic and neutral. The cyclic acidic types are a free carboxyl group while basic are of the amino group. In the neutral type, there are no free amino or carboxyl groups.

This group of antibiotics is mainly derived from the genus Bacillus. These are active against Gram-positive, while others are active against Gram-negative organisms. Mostly they are used for topical applications.

(i) Bacitracin (I.P., U.S.P.) :

This is produced by the *Bacillus licheniformis* group of organisms like *B. subtilis*. It is a complex mixture of polypeptides.

Properties and uses : Bacitracin is a white to pale buff, odourless powder and is hygroscopic in nature. It is stable in the dry state. It is soluble in water. However, the aqueous solutions deteriorate rapidly. Comparatively it is stable between the pH 4 to 5 in an aqueous medium. Heavy metals bring precipitation and inactivation. Bacitracin is not absorbed well from the gastrointestinal tract and hence is not much used orally, except for the treatment of amoebic infections. It is used locally in topical preparations. Bacitracin tablets are official. The standard dose by intramuscular injection is 30,000 to 100,000 units.

(ii) Capreomycin sulphate (B.P.) :

It is produced by *Streptomyces capreolus*.

Properties and uses : It is white crystalline odourless powder. It is freely soluble in water. The aqueous solutions are stable, however, incompatibility results with heavy metals. Capreomycin injection is official in B.P. and used to treat tuberculosis. The standard dose is 1 mega units daily.

(iii) Colistin sulphate (B.P., U.S.P.) :

The antibiotic is produced from *Aerobacillus colistinus*. Chemically it is a polypeptide resembling polymyxin B.

Properties and uses : It is a white powder. It is soluble in water. Aqueous solutions are stable in an acidic (pH 2 to 6) medium. Colistin tablets (official in B.P.) are given orally to treat gastroenteritis and also in refractory urinary tract infections caused by Gram -ve strains. It is also given in the form of an oral pediatric suspension. For parenteral use colistin methanesulfonate (colistimethate sodium U.S.P.) is used by intramuscular injection. The dose is 9 to 18 mega units daily, in divided doses.

(iv) Polymyxin B sulphate (B.P., U.S.P.) :

It is produced from *Bacillus polymyxa*. It is found to contain polymyxins A, B_1, B_2, C, D_1, D_2, M etc. wherein polymyxin B predominates. The sulphate salt is official.

Properties and uses: It is a white to buff coloured powder, odourless and soluble in water. Aqueous solutions are stable in an acidic media but decompose in alkaline conditions.

It is used to treat infections caused by Gram-negative organisms. It is commonly used against infections in wounds and burns topically. It is poorly absorbed from the intestinal tract and thus becomes useful in intestinal infections. The dose is 1 to 2 mega units daily, in divided doses. The injection form as sterile polymyxin B sulphate is official in U.S.P.

III. POLYENE ANTIBIOTICS

Some antibiotics contain a conjugated polyene system and are called polyene antibiotics. Furthermore, they contain a large lactone ring in which there is a conjugated polyene system. A sugar moiety in the form of glycosidic linkage is also found in some antibiotics. The macrolide polyene antibiotics principally act as antifungal agents.

(i) Nystatin (B.P.) :

It is obtained from *Streptomyces nourser*. It is discussed under antifungal agents.

(ii) Amphotericin B (B.P., U.S.P.) :

This antibiotic is produced from *Streptomyces nodosus*. It is a mixture containing amphotericin A and B of which the B component is more active.

Properties and uses : It is a yellow orange powder, with a faint odour and is water insoluble. It is amphoteric in nature. It is unstable in an aqueous medium and deteriorates rapidly. The drug is poorly absorbed from gastrointestinal tract hence it is given parenterally, as an infusion in fungal infections in 100 to 250 mg per kg dose. It is applied topically in treatment of fungal infection.

(iii) Candicidin (U.S.P.) :

It is produced from streptomyces - Griseus.

Properties and uses : It is a yellow powder almost odourless and is practically insoluble in water. It is mainly used to treat fungal viginal infections in the form of an ointment or tablets. The candicidin is kept in a well-closed containers, protected from light.

IV. AMINOGLYCOSIDE ANTIBIOTICS

Antibiotics from this class are derived from sugars and contain some sugar or substituted sugar moiety. In general, the antibiotics are basic in nature, and form salts readily which are water-soluble. These are produced from the genera *Streptomyces.* Some important antibiotics from this class are :

(i) **Streptomycin sulphate (I.P., B.P.) :**

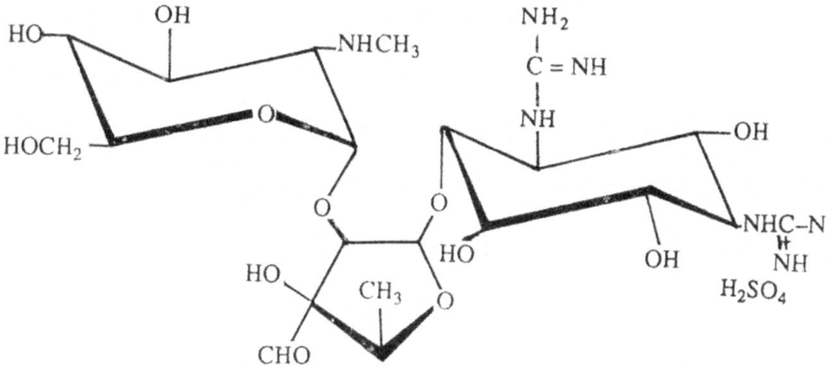

N-methyl-L-Glucosamine   L-streptose   Streptidine

The antibiotic is produced from the strains of *Streptomyces griseus*. Chemically it consists of three units, streptidine, N-methyl-L-glucosamine and streptose jointed through glycosidic linkage. Being basic it forms salts (sulphate is official) and are stable in the dry state. Streptomycin sulphate is water-soluble. Aqueous solutions are comparatively stable in a pH range of 5 to 6.5 when stored at a low temperature. Decomposition results with acids, alkalies, oxidising and reducing agents.

It is not absorbed well from the gastrointestinal tract. However, the streptomycin tablet (official in I.P.) is administered orally to treat infections of the intestinal tract. The injections cannot be sterilized by the heating method. Sterile solutions are prepared by dissolving sterile powder in distilled water. The streptomycin sulphate injecton is used to trat tuberculosis. Streptomycin develops a resistance quickly and on continued use produces achromic toxicity. The intramuscular injection equivalent to 0.5 to 1 g of streptomycin base is given daily in cases of the systemic infection of tuberculosis.

(ii) **Dihydrostreptomycin sulphate :**

Properties and uses : It is prepared synthetically by hydrogenation from streptomycin. The sulphate salt is a white crystalline powder and is soluble in water. This drug has the same activity profile as that of streptomycin. Dihydrostreptomycin sulphate injection is given by the intramuscular route iin 0.5 g dose daily. It is no longer official.

Kanamycins : These are produced from *Streptomyces kanamyeticus*. The mixture of kanamycin contains predominantly kanamycin A.

(iii) **Kanamycin sulphate (B.P., U.S.P.) :**

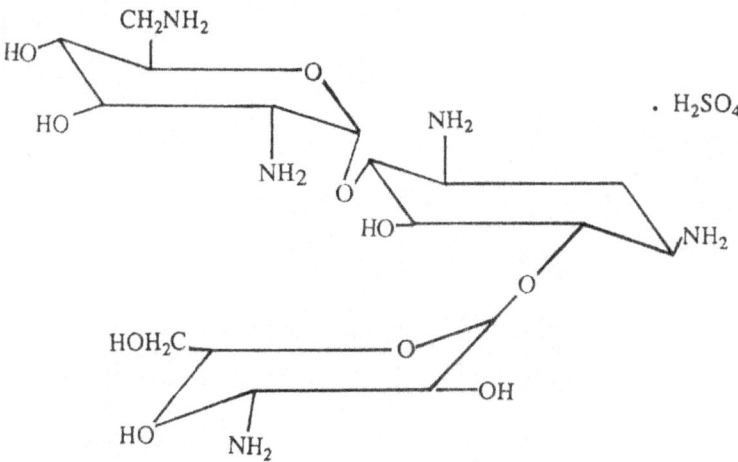

Properties and uses : It is a white powder, soluble in water and is stable in the presence of heat and chemicals. It is poorly absorbed orally and hence used intramuscularly to treat infections caused by Gram negative organisms. It is used orally as an intestinal antiseptic and to treat intestinal infections including bacillary dysentry. Kanamycin sulphate is usually given parenterally by intramuscular injection in 0.5 to 1 mega unit daily, in divided doses to treat systemic infections.

NEOMYCINS

Neomycin is mixture of antibiotics produced by *Streptomyces fradiae* consisting of A, B and C components, Neomycin C is present in a large amount in a mixture consisting a four carbohydrate units and is the active moiety.

(iv) **Neomycin sulphate (I.P., B.P., U.S.P.)** :

Properties and uses : It is a white or slightly yellow crystalline powder and is soluble in water. It is hygroscopic and hence stored in tightly-closed containers. The solutions darken on exposure to light. Solutions for injection are sterilized by filtration and are administered in doses of 0.5 to 2 g, every four hours intramuscularly to treat systemic infections. It has a broad spectrum activity against a large number of organisms. Neomycin sulphate is also used in topical applications against the infections of the skin, eye etc.

GENTAMYCIN

This antibiotic is a mixture consisting of Gentamycin C_1, C_1 A, C_2 etc. and is obtained from *Micromonospora purpurea*.

(v) **Gentamycin sulphate (I.P., B.P., U.S.P.)** :

Properties and uses : It is a white to buff coloured substance, odourless and is soluble in water. The aqueous solutions are stable and can be sterilized by the autoclaving method.

This antibiotic has a broad spectrum activity and is particularly effective against Gram-negative organisms. The Gentamycin injection is official in I.P. B.P. and used to treat septicaemia, urinary tract infections and hospital aquired infections. Gentamycin cream, eyedrop and ointment (official in B.P.) are used to treat a variety of skin infections.

(vi) **Tobramycin (B.P.)** :

The antibiotic is produced from *Streptomyces tenebrarius*. Structurally it is related to kanamycin.

Properties and uses : It is a white powder and is freely soluble in water. The aqueous solutions for injection are sterilized by the filtration method and given by the intramuscular or intravenous route. Tobramycin is particularly effective against *Pseudomonas* and resistant types of Gram negative organisms. Tobramycin injection is official in B.P. Usual dose by intramuscular or intravenous injection is 210 to 350 mg daily in divided doses.

(vii) **Framycetin sulphate (B.P.)** :

This antibiotic is obtained from the strain of *streptomyces fradiac* or *streptomyces decaris*. It occurs as yellowish-white, odourless powder hygroscopic in nature. It is soluble in water. It is stored in closed container protected from light. It is used as general antibacterial antibiotic for external use like in surgical dressing.

(viii) **Vancomycin hydrochloride (B.P., U.S.P.)** :

The antibiotic is produced from *Streptomyces orientalis*

Properties and uses : It is a granular brownish powder, odourless and is very soluble in water and insoluble in organic solvents. It is stable in the dry from and a aqueous acidic medium. This antibiotic is administered by intravenous infusion or by slow injection in treatment of staphylococcal infections. The usual dose is 500 mg of vancomycin base in 100 to 200 ml of 5 % Dextrose injection.

V. THE MACROLIDE AND LINCOMYCIN ANTIBIOTICS

Macrolide antibiotics constitute a group of antibiotics which have three common chemical characteristics : (i) a large lactone ring (ii) a ketone group and (iii) an amino sugar linked glycosidically to the lactone ring. Usually the lactone ring has 12, 14 or 16 atoms containing unsaturated olefinic groups conjugated with ketone functional moiety. Since the structural features contain the dimethylamino group, they form salts readily. The free bases are partially soluble in water. Aqueous solutions, in general, are stable at low temperatures but are deactivated by acids and bases. This group of antibiotics are generally active against Gram positive organisms. Some clinically useful antibiotics from this class are :

(i) **Erythromycin (I.P., B.P., U.S.P.) :**
It is produced form *Streptomyces erythreus*.

Properties and uses : It is a white or yellowish-white crystalline powder with a very bitter taste. It is slightly soluble in water and more soluble in alcohol. It readily forms salts with acids which are soluble in water and also forms ester. Aqueous solutions are alkaline and get inactivated in a pH less than 4. Erythromycin tablets are official in I.P. and B.P. The tablets are usually coated (film or enteric) as the drug is very bitter to taste. Since the drug gets partly destroyed by the gastric acid, the ester forms (Estolte and stearate) are given orally in capsules or tablets. The standard range of dosage is 1 to 2 g daily in divided doses. Erythromycin is active against many Gram positive organisms like cocci and in upper respiratory tract infection. It is found to be useful in the treatment of intestinal amoebiasis. Erythromycin ointment in a strength of 1 % and in ophthalmic ointment in 0.5 % are available for external use.

LINCOMYCINS

(i) **Lincomycin hydrochloride (B.P.) :**
This is antibiotic is produced from *S, lincolinensis*. The hydrochloride salt is official (in B.P.)

Properties and uses : It is a pale creamy powder with a characteristic odour and bitter taste. It is readily soluble in water and alcohol and aqueous solutions are stable. It gets slowly hydrolysed in an acidic medium. Lincomycin is absorbed well when administered orally in the form of capsules or by oral suspension. It is also given parenterally by the intramuscular route in 600 mg doses once or twice a day. This antibiotic is mainly used in the treatment of infections causes by staphylococci, haemolytic streptococci, pneumococci and also against nonspore forming anaerobic bacteria

(ii) Clindamycin hydrochloride (B.P., U.S.P.) :
It is related to lincomycin and is 7-S-deoxy-lincomycin.

Properties and uses : It is a white crystalline powder. It is odourless and is water soluble. It is rapidly absorbed from the gastrointestinal tract and hence administered orally in the form of capsules or oral suspension. The usual dose is 150 to 450 mg 3 to 4 times a day or 8 to 25 mg per kg body weight given in divided doses. Clindamycin phosphate injection is administered either by intramuscular or intravenous route for a rapid effect. Clindamycin is claimed to be more effective in treatment of respiratory tract, skin, tissue, infections caused by staphylococci, streptococci, pneumococci etc. than other antibiotics.

VI. TETRACYCLINS

Tetracycline is a group of broad spectrum antibiotics having octahydronaphthacene (Hydrocarbon made up of 4 fused ring) skeleton structure. Various tetracyclins have been derived from the parent tetracycline. The tetracyclines are amphoteric compounds and form salts with acids and bases. Some salts like sodium, potassium, hydrochloride etc. are water insoluble, while salts with divalent and polyvalent metals are water-soluble and form chelates. Tetracyclins undergo epimerization at a slightly acidic pH and the epimer has less activity than natural isomers. Strong acids and bases bring changes in its structure resulting in decreased activity. Tetracyclins are active orally and are absorbed reasonably well from the gastro intestinal tract. However, soluble alkalinizers decrease its absorption. Tetracyclins are broad spectrum antibiotic and are active against a wide range of Gram positive, Gram negative, Rickettsiae and Viruses. Thus, this group of antibiotic is used in a variety of infectious diseases. Resistance develops but slowly. Various tetracyclins have been developed with the idea of modifying pharmacokinetic properties and increase in clinical utility. The structures of important tetracyclins are given below.

Tetracyclines

		R_1	R_2	R_3	R_4	R_5
1.	Tetracycline	H	CH_3	OH	H	H
2.	Chlorotetracycline	Cl	CH_3	OH	H	H
3.	Oxytetracycline	H	CH_3	OH	OH	H
4.	Democycline (desmethyl chloro tetracycline)	Cl	H	OH	H	H
5.	Doxycycline	H	H	CH_3	OH	H
6.	Minocycline	$N(CH_3)_2$	H	H	H	H
7.	Rolitetracycline	H	CH_3	OH	H	$CH_2-N\langle$ 

Tetracyclines (I.P., B.P., U.S.P.) :

Properties and uses : It is the first antibiotic from this class and it is obtained from *Streptomyces aureofaciens*. It is a bright yellow crystalline powder, stable in air but darkens on exposure. It is sparingly water soluble. It is used in oral suspensions (official in I.P.) in a variety of infectious diseases. The standard dose is 1 to 4 g, in divided doses.

Tetracycline hydrochloride (I.P., B.P.) :

Properties and uses : It is a hydrochloride salt of tetracycline. It is most commonly used in medicine because of its stability and solubility in water. This salt is used in capsules, eye ointment, injections and tablets. The solutions for patenteral purpose are either prepared asceptically or sterilized by the filtration method. The standard dose is 1 to 4 g daily. For external use 0.05 to 0.1 ml of 1 % suspension or 1 % ointment is used.

(ii) **Chlortetracycline hydrochloride (I.P., B.P., U.S.P.) :**

It differs from tetracycline in having an extra chloro group at position 7.

Properties and uses : The compound is of a bright-yellow colour (hence was formerly called aueromycin). It is stable in air. It is water soluble. It is most commonly used orally in the form of capsules (as it is bitter to taste) and for quick blood levels by parenteral route.

(iii) **Oxytetracycline (I.P.) :**

Properties and uses : It is a yellow crystalline, odourless powder. It is slightly soluble in water and sparingly soluble in alcohol. It is odourless and has a bitter taste. The hydrochloride salt (official in B.P. and U.S.P.) is a crystalline powder with a pale-yellow colour and bitter taste. It is stable in air but darkens on exposure to light. It is soluble in water and alcohol. Both the base and its salt gets deactivated by alkali hydroxide. The drug is absorbed well from the gastrointestinal tract and hence administered orally in the form of capsules. The salt being more water-soluble is used intravenously in 0.1 % w/v as infusion in 1 to 2 g dose daily or by intramuscular injection in concentrations not exceeding 5 % w/v for adults in 0.2 to 0.4 g daily and for children 5 mg per kg of body weight daily. It's calcium salt is official in use.

(iv) **Demeclocycline hydrochloride (B.P.) :**

It is modified from chlortetracycline. It is obtained from *S. aureofaciens*. In physico-chemical properties it is similar to tetracycline hydrochloride. It is a yellow, crystalline powder, odourless, and bitter to taste. It is sparingly soluble in water. A 1 % solution is acidic to litmus. It is slightly more active than other form of tetracycline. It shows photosensitivity as a side reaction. It is administered in the form of capsules in a 150 to 900 mg daily dose. This antibiotic is orally active and because of its bitter taste it is administered in the form of capsules.

(v) **Doxycycline hydrochloride (B.P., U.S.P.) :**

Properties and uses : It is a yellow crystalline powder, soluble in water, in methanol and in solutions of alkali hydroxides and carbonates. This antibiotic is very stable in the presence of acids and bases and has a long biological half life. It is absorbed well from the gastrointestinal tract and high tissue levels are obtained. It is given in 100 mg doses in the form of oral suspension or in capsules as a general purpose, broad spectrum antibiotic.

(vi) **Minocycline hydrochloride (B.P., U.S.P.) :**

This tetracycline occurs as yellow, crystalline powder, soluble in water and slightly soluble in ethanol. It is the most potent tetracyclin used clinically. It is stable in acid medium. It is especially active against gram positive organism in chronic bronchitis, upper respiratory tract and urinary tract infections.

(vii) **Rolitetracycline (U.S.P.) :**

Properties and uses : This antibiotic is prepared from tetracycline with pyrrolidine and formaldehyde. It is soluble in water and hence mainly used in the form of injection in 150 to 250 mg every 12 hourly by the intramuscular route or in 350 to 700 mg by intravenous infusion.

VII. OTHER MISCELLANEOUS CLASS

1. Cycloserine (B.P., U.S.P.) :

This antibiotic is obtained from *streptomyces orchidaceus*. Now-a-days it is mainly produced synthetically.

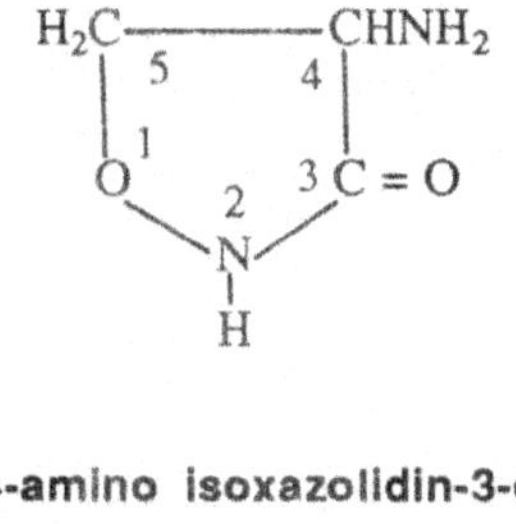

(R) 4-amino isoxazolidin-3-one

Properties and uses : It is a white to pale yellow powder. It is soluble in water. It absorbs water and loses it's activity. It is stable in an alkaline medium but gets inactivated in acid. It is mainly used alongwith other agents in the treatment of tuberculosis. The standard dose is 260 to 750 mg, daily, in divided doses. It is normally used in the form of capsules and tablets.

2. Chloramphenical (I.P., B.P., U.S.P.) :

The antibiotic is produced from the *streptomyces venezuelae* and also synthetically. It has two asymmetric carbon atoms and give D-threo, L-threo, D-erythro and L-erythro isomer of which D-threo is biologically active.

$$O_2N-C_6H_4-\underset{\underset{H}{|}}{\overset{\overset{OH}{|}}{C}}H-\underset{\underset{NHCOCHCl_2}{|}}{\overset{\overset{H}{|}}{C}}-CH_2OH$$

D (−) threo-2-dichloroacetamido
1 p-nitrophenyl propane 1, 3-diol
or
2,2-dichloro-N-[(αR, βR)-β-hydroxy-α- hydroxymethyl-
-4-nitrophenethyl] acetamide

Properties and uses : It is a white powder with a very bitter taste. It is slightly soluble in water but very soluble in alcohol and other polar organic solvents. It is stable. Chloramphenicol is used mainly in typhoid fever. It is a broad spectrum antibiotic. Chloramphenical is mainly used against these gram positive and gram negative organisms that have developed resistance to penicillium G and ampicillin. It acts by strong inhibition of protein systhesis. It is usually given in capsules or oral suspensions in 1.5 to 3 g daily in divided doses for adults and in 25 to 50 mg per kg of body weight for children. The clinically useful preparations for chloramphenicol are capsules, dry syrup and suspension which are used in systemic infections and Ear drops, Eye drops and Eye ointments (official in B.P. and U.S.P.) for topical applications against affecting sensitive organisms.

Chloraphenicol being very bitter, various modifications have been tried to make it palatable. Chloramphenicol palmitate is an ester (3–OH group esterified) with a bland taste. It is insoluble in water and administered in suspension form orally. Chloramphenicol palmitate mixture is official in B.P. while oral suspension is official in I.P. and U.S.P. For parenteral use a very soluble salt of chloramphenicol sodium succinate (official in I.P., B.P. and U.S.P.) is used. The injection of chloramphenicol sodium succinate is administered either subcutaneously, intramuscularly or by intravenous route in equivalent of 3 to 4 g of chloramphenicol daily, in divided doses.

3. Griseofulvin (B.P., U.S.P.) :

It is discussed under as antifungal agents.

4. Sodium fusidate (B.P.) :

Properties and uses : It is a white cyrstalline powder, slightly hygroscopic in nature and is soluble in water, alcohol and partially in acetone. A 1.25 % aqueous solution is alkaline is nature and has pH 7.5 to 9.0. The antibiotic is effective against Gram positive bacterial infections particularly when patients who are penicillin-sensitive. It is used orally in the form of tablets and also locally in ointment. The dose ranges from 1 to 2 g daily, in divided doses.

5. Novobocin sodium (I.P.) :

It is produced from *Streptomyces niveus* and related species.

Properties and uses : It is a pale yellow crystalline photosensitive compound. It is soluble in water and other polar solvents. Aqueous solutions are precipitated by acid and alkaline solutions and deteriorate when it is preserved for a long time.

The antibiotic is markedly effetive against Gram positive organisms particularly against staphylococcal resistance strains of oranisms. The sodium salt is used for parenteral purpose and also administered in oral capsules. The usual dose is 250 to 500 mg every 6 hourly or 500 mg to 1 g every 12 hourly.

6. Rifampicin (B.P.) :

Properties and uses : It is a brick-red coloured crystalline powder, very slightly soluble in water. It is readily absorbed from the gastrointestinal tract when administered orally. It is used in the form of capsules in 600 mg once daily in the treatment of pulmonary tuberculosis and in leprosy. Rifamycin sodium is a brick-red coloured fine granular powder and is soluble in water. It is given parenterally. The intramuscular injections are given to treat infections caused by Gram positive bacterial and also in Tuberculosis.

Chapter 39

MISCELLANEOUS PHARMACEUTICAL AGENTS

'Pharmaceutical aids' or 'Pharmaceutical necessities' is a very broad term normally used to describe substances which have very little or no therapeutic value but are necessary in the manufacture of various dosage forms like tablets, liquid preparations, ointments, injections and also in the manufacture of cosmetics. These include a variety organic, inorganic, chemicals, oils, fats and number of natural products.

The most commonly used pharmaceutical aids are classified into the following categories:

    I. Antioxidants and preservatives,
    II. Colouring, flavouring and sweetening agents,
    III. Emulsifying and suspending agents,
    IV. Ointments and suppository bases.
    V. Diluents, binding agents disintegrating agents and lubricants and
    VI. Surface Active agents.
    VII. Solvents and vehicles.

I   ANTIOXIDANTS AND PRESERVATIVES

Antioxidants are agents which inhibit oxidation and are commonly used to prevent rancidity of oils and fats or deterioration of other meterials through the oxidative processes.

Preservatives are agents which are added to prevent microbial growth and spoilage of preparation. Both categories of agents find wide application in pharmaceutical dosage forms, cosmetics and food.

ANTIOXIDANTS

1. Ascorbyl palmitate (U.S.P.) :

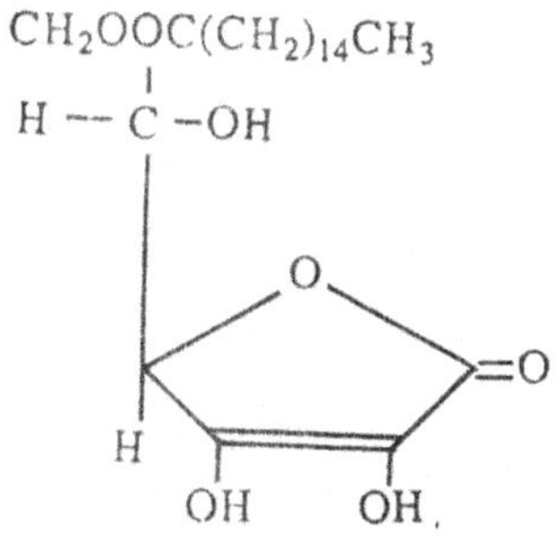

$$CH_2OOC(CH_2)_{14}CH_3$$
$$H-C-OH$$

(ascorbyl palmitate ring structure with OH, OH, =O)

Properties and uses : It is a white to yellowish white powder. It's odour is characteristic. It is slightly soluble in water, soluble in vegetable oils, alcohol. It is a reducing agent and thus used as an antioxidant in the preservation of food and to prevent rancidity in oils and fats.

2. Butylated hydroxyanisol (I.P., B.P.) :

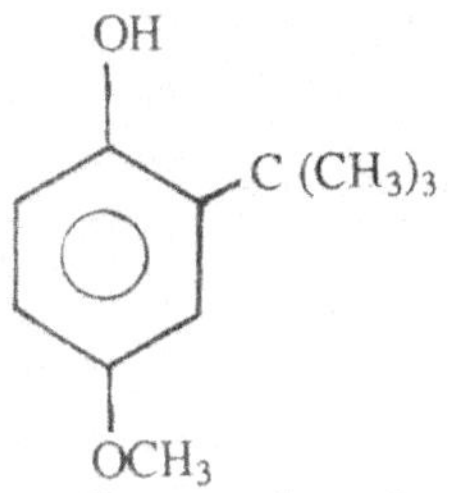

(structure: phenol ring with OH, $C(CH_3)_3$, and OCH_3 substituents)

2-t-butyl-4-methoxy phenol

Properties and uses : It is a white to yellowish white solid with a faint odour. It is waxy in nature. It is insoluble in water, soluble in alcohol, chloroform, ether and propylene glycol. It is used as an antioxidant in pharmaceutical preparations containing oils and fats.

3. Butylated hydroxy toluene (I.P., B.P.) :

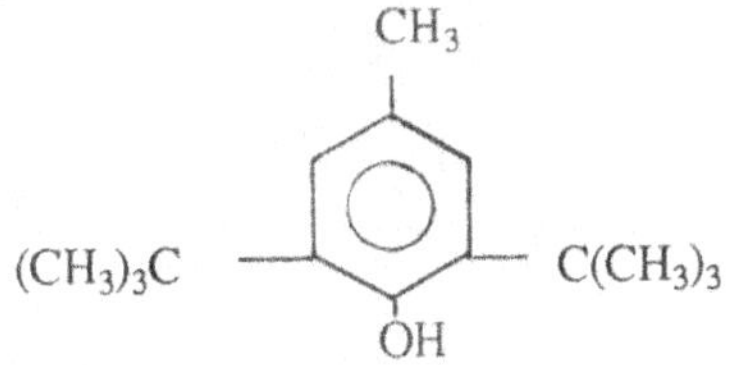

(structure: phenol ring with CH_3, two $C(CH_3)_3$ groups, OH)

2, 6-ditert-butyl-p-cresole

Properties and uses : It is white crystalline solid. It's odour is slight. It is insoluble in water, freely soluble in alcohol, chloroform and ether. It is less effective as an antioxidant as compared to butytated hydroxy anisole.

The above antioxdants are stored in tight containers protected from light.

4. Esters of gallic acid : The following four esters of gallic acid are official in B.P. and are used as antioxidants :

ANTIOXIDANTS

Esters of Gallic acid : These are deodecyl gallate, octyl gallate, propyl gallate and ethyl gallate. These occur as white to creamy white powders which are soluble in alcohol. All the above compounds should be kept in tight containers, protected from light. Their contact with metals should be avoided. These are used in 0.1 - 0.5 % concentration in various pharmaceutical preparations.

Sodium metabisulphite ($Na_2S_2O_5$) and sodium sulphite anhydrous (Na_2SO_3) are two inorganic compounds which extencively are used to retard oxidation of easily oxidisable drugs like ascorbic acid, adrenaline, phenylephrine hydrochloride etc. They are used as food preservatives also.

PRESERVATIVES

Preservatives are the agents which are added to prevent microbial growth, spoilage of preparation and are used in pharmaceutical dosage forms, cosmetics and food. They may be bacteriostatic, bactericidal, antibacterial and antifungal in their action. Sometimes they are referred to as antimicrobial preservatives.

Some agents besides being preservatives have specific actions and uses, and are discussed under suitable chapters. They are given below :

1. Benzoic acid (discussed under antifungal agent)

It is used in 0.1 % concentration as an antibacterial preservative. It is a fairly strong acid and is therefore active only to the extent to which it exists as an undissociated molecule. (which depends on the pH of the solution).

Chlorocresol, Cresol, Phenol and Thiomersal are the other Antiinfective agents.

2. Chlorocresol : It is used in a 0.1 % concentration as an bacteriostatic.

3. Cresol : It is used in a 0.3 % concentration as a disinfectant.

4. Phenol : It is used in 0.5 % concentration as a preservative and has a rather non-selective action on different micro-organisms.

5. Thiomersal : It is a non-toxic antibacterial agent and has weak bacteriostatic and fungistatic activity. It is used as preservative.

6. Benzalkonium chloride (discussed under surface active agent)

The solution is mainly used as antiseptic detergent.

The other compounds which are used as preservatives are discussed below.

7. Cetrimide (I.P., B.P.) :

It consists of mixture of dodecyl, tetradecyl and hexadecyl-trimethyl ammonium bromide and contains 94-102 % w/w of alkyl trimethyl ammonium bromide calculated as $C_{17}H_{28}NBr$. It is a creamy white light powder, with a odour characteristic. It is very soluble in alcohol. Its aqueous solutions are clear or slightly opalescent. It is used in a 0.001 % concentration as a bactericide.

8. Chlorobutanol is a antimicrobial preservative :

Esters of p-hydroxy benzoic acid : They are the most common preservatives.

9. Ethyl paraben (B.P., U.S.P.) : Ethyl hydroxybenzoate :

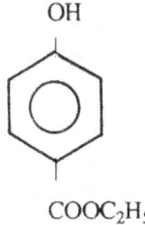

ethyl4-hydroxybenzoate

It is a white crystalline powder, practically odourless, sparingly soluble in water, freely soluble in alcohol, ether and solutions of alkali hydroxides. It is used as antifungal preservative in a 0.5 % concentration in aqueous preparations and 0.15 % concentration in oils and creams.

10. Butyl paraben (B.P., U.S.P.) : Butyl hydroxybenzoate

butyl-4-hydroxy-benzoate

It is a crystalline powder, very sparingly soluble in water, highly soluble in alcohol. It is used as antifungal preservative in an 0.01 % concentration in aqueous preparations and 0.15 % concentration in oils and creams.

11. Methyl paraben (I.P., B.P., U.S.P.) : Methyl hydroxybenzoate :

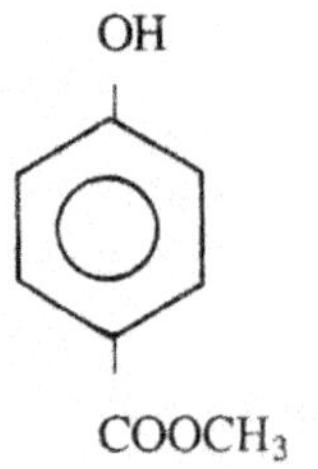

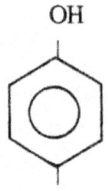

methyl-4-hydroxybenzoate

It is a available as colourless crystals or a white crystalline powder. It is sparingly soluble in water but soluble in alcohol. It is used as an antifungal preservative in a 0.1 % concentration in aqueous preparations and in 0.2 % concentration in oils and creams.

12. Propylparaben (I.P., B.P.) : Propyl hydroxybenzoate :

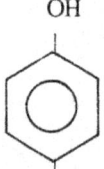

propyl-4-hydroxy-benzoate

It is a white crystalline powder with a fairly aromatic odour. It's uses are similar to those of methyl paraben.

13. Sodium methyl hydroxy benzoate (B.P.) :

The sodium-salt of paraben and sodium propyl paraben. They are highly soluble in water, soluble in alcohol, but insoluble in fixed oils. They are used as an antimicrobial preservatives in syrups and other liquid oral preparations.

14. Phenyl mercuric nitrate (I.P.) :

It is a basic phenyl mercuric nitrate and contains not less than 98 % w/w of $C_{12}H_{11}O_4NHg_2$. It has the appearance of white lustrous plates or white crystalline powder. It is very slightly soluble in water, more in boiling water, it is soluble in alcohol and glycerin and fixed oils. It is stored in well-closed containers, protected form light. It is mainly used as a local antibacterial agent in solutions or creams. It is used as a preservative in solutions used to clean or wet contact lenses, also as a preservative in pharmaceuticals in the concentration 0.0025 %.

15. Sodium benzoate (I.P., B.P., U.S.P.) :

It has the appearance of a white, amorphous, granular or crystalline powder with a faint odour. It is very soluble in water and less in alcohol. It is most extensively used as a food and pharmaceutical preservative, usually in the concentration of 0.50 percent and in most effective in a pH not above 4.0. It has bacteriostatic and fungistatic activity.

II. COLOURING, FLAVOURING AND SWEETENING AGENTS

The addition of colouring and flavouring agents are normally used to enhance the aesthetic appearance of pharmaceutical preparations. The use of these agents has no therapeutic advantage but are important psychologically. A proper use of all the three agents makes the pharmaceutical preparation palatable.

Colouring agents

These may be defined as compounds which are used in pharmaceutical preparations for imparting colour. They are broadly classified as : (i) naturally occuring colouring principles, and (ii) synthetic colouring agents.

Naturally occurring colouring agents are obtained from mineral, plant and animal sources. Mineral colours are called pigments and used mainly in lotions, cosmetics and other external preparations. Examples are yellow ferric oxide, Red ferric oxide and titanium dioxide. The term pigment is also applied to the colouring principle obtained from plants. Examples are chlorophyll giving green colour, anattens obtained from the Annatto seed giving yellow to orange colour, beta carotens imparting yellow colour, indigo obtained from the indigo plant giving a blue odour. Saffron imparts a yellowish orange colour. The coluring principles obtained from animals include cochineal obtained form the insect occus cacti.

The synthetic dyes and coal-tar dyes include a number of well defined groups like nitrosodyes, nitro-dyes, azodyes, anthraquinone, rosanilines, oxazines and many other groups. The synthetic dyes are classified as : (i) acid dyes and basic dyes. Out of thousands of dyes only those which are safe and permitted by the ' Drug and cosmetic Act and Rule ' are actually used. They are often called a certified dyes.

Most of the dyes are relatively unstable due to their unsaturated structure and undergo fading due to light, metals, heat, oxidising and reducing agents and strong acid and bases.

Pharmaceutical formulations which are normally coloured are the liquid preparations, powders, ointment and cosmetics. In liquid preparations, the concentration of dye used is usually 0.0005 to 0.001 % depending upon the depth of the colour needed. The powders usually contain 0.1 % of the dye.

The colouring agents which are official in pharmacopoeias are given below.

1. Amaranth (I.P., U.S.P.) :

It is a dark brown powder, soluble in water, slightly soluble in alcohol. It is one of the permitted red dye and used as a colouring agent for foods, drugs and cosmetic preparations and as an indicator, in hydrazine titration and titratuon of KI in iodine solution (B.P.).

2. Burnt Sugar or Caramel (U.S.P.) :

It is a concentrated solution of a product obtained by heating sugar in the presence of small amount of alkali, alkali carbonate or traces of mineral acids.

It is a thick brown coloured liquid with the odour of burnt sugar and a pleasant bitter taste. It can combine with water in all proportions and imparts a distinct yellowish brown colour. It can be mixed with alcohol, chloroform and ether. It is used as a colouring agent in elixirs, syrup and alcoholic beverages.

3. Cochineal (B.P.) :

It is the dried female insect Dactylopius coccus costa containing the egg and larvae. It has a dark red colour. The colour is due to carminic acid a derivative of anthraquinone.

It is not official in I.P. and U.S.P. and not very much in use.

The other most commonly used colouring agents are tartazine, sunset yellow, erythrosin, indigocarmine and eosin.

FLAVOURING AGENTS

Flavour is a complex mixture of aromatic compounds to form a body which improves the palatability of the dosage forms. Sometimes a single ingredient is used to obtain a desired flavour. A number of essential oils and powders obtained from plants are official in pharmacopoeias and some have other actions besides their use as flavouring agent.

Undesirable changes in taste, odour, colour occur due to the following factors such as enzymatic activity, oxidation, changes in the moisture content, heat and light. The products in general should be stored in tight, light-resistant containers and kept in a cool place. Specific storage conditions are specifed some times in pharmacopoieas to prevent the deterioration of the flavouring agents.

The other most commonly used flavouring agents given below.

Benzaldehyde (B.P., U.S.P.) :

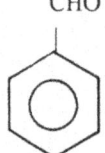

It is a clear colourless liquid with characteristic odour resembling that of bitter almond oil and has a burning aromatic taste. It dissolves slightly in water, but dissolves in alcohol, chloroform, ether and volatile oils. It is steam volatile. In presence of air it gradually oxidises to benzoic acid and is also affected by light. It should be stored in a well-closed containers and is protected from light and ketp below 15°C temperature. It is used as flavouring agent in place of bitter almond oil as it does not contain hydrocyanic acid. It is widely used in the synthesis of many chemicals, drugs and dyes. It also finds use as perfumery chemical.

Methyl salicylate (I.P., U.S.P.) :

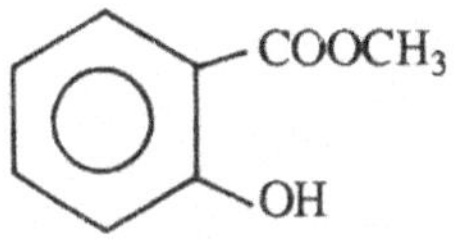

methyl-2-hydroxy benzoate

It is also known as oil of winter green. It is obtained by steam distillation from leavels of *Gaultheria procumbeos* or from the bark of Betula lenta or prepared synthetically. It is difficult to differentiate between the product obtained from plant sources and the synthetic one. The lable should indicate the source.

This occurs as colourless or pale yellowish liquid. The odour is characteristic and has a sweet, warm and aromatic taste. It is slightly soluble in water, but soluble in alcohol and glacial acetic acid. It decomposes in the presence of alkali to methyl alcohol and salicylate. Besides its use as a flavouring agent, it is also used as a counter irritant in creams, solutions and lotions in 5 to 20 % concentration.

Vanillin (B.P., U.S.P.) :

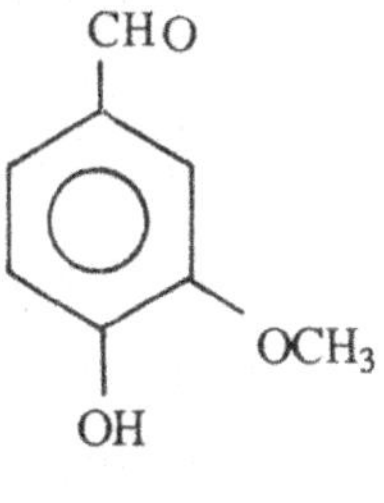

4-hydroxy-3-methoxy benzaldehyde

It is obtained form beans of various vanilla species or prepared synthetically.

It is a white to creamy-white crystalline powder. The odour is characteristic of vanilla. It is soluble in water and glycerine, freely soluble in alcohol and chloroform. Aqueous solutions are acidic in nature. It is slowly oxidised by air and decomposed by alkalies. It is stored in a tight light-resistant container. It is mainly used as a flavouring agent for foods.

SWEETENING AGENTS

Sweetening agents are added to pharmaceutical dosageforms like liquid-orals to improve the taste of preparations and make it more palatable. The following are the commonly used sweetening agents :

1. Sucrose (I.P., B.P., U.S.P.) :

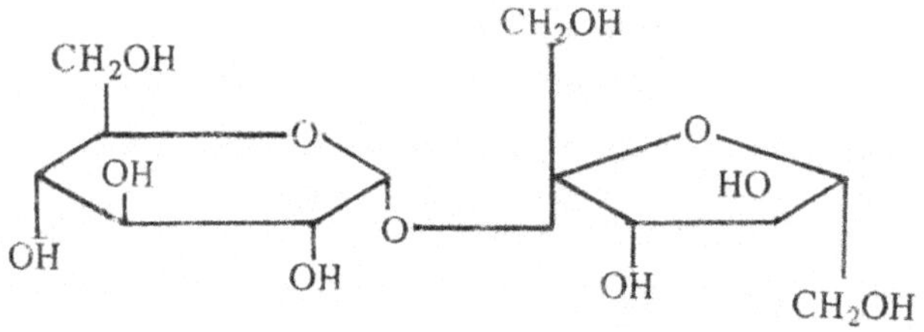

It is obtained from the juice of sugarcane or from beet root. It is made of colourless crystals or crystalline masses or white crystalline powder. It is odourless. It is highly soluble in water, very sparingly soluble in alcohol and insoluble in chloroform and ether. Aqueous solutions are neutral to litmus. As it is affected by moisture, it is stored in a well-closed container. It is a pharmaceutical necessity in the preparation of syrups. It is used as a sweetening agent in various proportions.

Syrup (I.P.) : It is 66.7 % w/w of sucrose in water. It is used as a base in elixirs.

2. Saccharin (B.P., U.S.P.) :

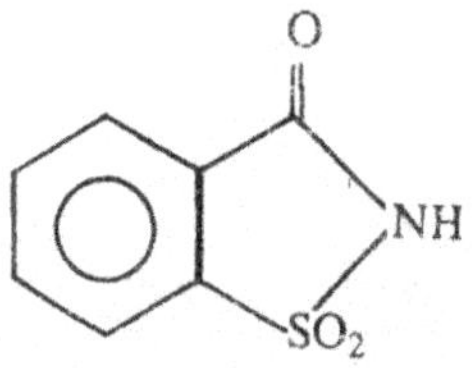

1,2-benzisothiazoline-3-one 1,1-dioxtde

Properties : It is a available as white crystals or a white crystalline powder. It is practically odourless or has very faint odour. It is sparingly soluble in water but more soluble in alcohol and boiling water. It dissolves easily in solutions of ammonia, alkali hydroxides or carbonates forming salts. It is relatively stable in solutions having a pH of 3.3 to 8.0. It is stored in tightly closed containers.

3. Saccharin sodium (I.P., B.P.) :

It is a sodium salt of saccharin and is available as white crystals or white crystalline powder with faint odour. It is highly soluble in water, but less in alcohol. It is efflorscent and thus stored in tightly-closed containers.

Both saccharin and its sodium salt are used as sweetening agents in vehicles and canned foods and beverages. It is particularly useful in diets for diabetic patients to replace sucrose.

4. Sorbitol (B.P., U.S.P.) :

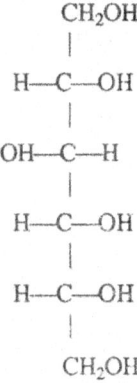

It is a white crystalline powder, odourless, highly soluble in water. Aqueous solutions are neutral to litmus. It should be stored in tightly-closed containers.

Sorbital solution (70 percent) (B.P., U.S.P.) : It is an aqueous solution containing 68-73 % w/w of hexitols as D-sorbitol.

It is a clear, colourless, viscous liquid. It can be mixed with water, glycerin (85 per cent) and propylene glycol, it is soluble but very slightly soluble in the usual organic solvents. It should be stored in tightly-closed containers.

It is used as a vehicle, and sweetener. The other uses are as a laxative, osmotic diuretic and humectant.

III. EMULSIFYING AND SUSPENDING AGENTS

An emulsion can be defined as an intimate mixture of two immiscible phases maintained by means of an intremediate substance which must be present to form a stable emulsion. This intermediate substance is called an emulsifying agent ; or an emulsifying agent is an inert substance used to homogenize two immiscible phases by reducing surface tension.

A suspension is defined as a dispersion containing finely divided insoluble material suspended in liquid media. The presence of another substance is required to overcome agglomeration of dispersed particles and to increase the viscosity of the medium so that the particles settle slowly. The substances which serve the above functions are called suspending agents ; or additives which increase the viscosity of the continuous phase are used extensively in the formulations of elegant pharmaceutical preparations. Some of the compounds may act both as emulsifying and suspending agent.

A number of agents belonging to this class are official in pharmacopoeias. Out of these polysorbates (20, 60, 80), sorbitan esters, (monolaurate, oleate, stearate), glyceryl monosterate and sodium laurylsulphate are described in the category of surface active agents. The remaining agents are discussed below.

1. Acacia (B.P., U.S.P.) :

Indian gum (I.P.). It is a dried exudate obtained from stems and branches of the Acacia species. It consists of irregular and broken tears of varying size, colour is cream brown or brownish red, has brittle fractured surfaces and is odourless. Powder has the light brown or light straw colour. It is nearly soluble in twice its weight of water yielding a viscous solution, which is acidic to litmus. Alcohol and alcoholic solutions cause precipitation of a gummy mass (at about 35 % concentration of alcohol). Heavy metals cause a precipitation from its mucilage. Acacia contains a peroxidase enzyme which forms coloured derivatives with chemicals like aminopyrine, phenol, tannins, thymol, vannilin due to its oxidising property. A number of alkaloids like atropine, cocaine, hyoscyamine, morphine etc. are destroyed to a certain extent. On heating the solution of acacia, the peroxidase is destroyed. It is mainly used as a suspending agent, for preparing emulsions and making pills. It also finds use as a demulcent.

2. Agar (I.P., U.S.P.) :

It is a dried gelatinous substance obtained from *Glelidium amansii (Lamouroux), G. cartilagineum (Linn.), G. pristoides (Turn), Gracilaria contervodes (Linn.).* Greville and other closely allied members of **Rhodophyceae**.

It consists of slender, translucent, nearly colourless strips, or greyish white flakes or coarse powder, odour slight. It is practically insoluble in water but swells to a gelatinous mass and is soluble in boiling water. It is dehydrated and precipitated by alcohol. Electrolytes decrease the viscosity of its solutions. It is mainly used as a stabilizer in mineral oil emulsions. It also finds use in bacteriological medias. In practice it is used as a bulk purgative.

3. Bentonite (I.P., B.P., U.S.P.) :

It is a colloidal hydrated aluminium silicate.

It is a fine pale buff or cream coloured powder free from grit, is odourless and has a slightly earthy taste. It is practically insoluble in water but swells to twelve times its original volume forming viscous suspension or gels. Aqueous suspensions are alkaline to litmus. Acids and acid salts decrease its water absorbing powder. Its suspensions are most stable at a pH of about 7.0. It finds use as a protective colloid for stabilizing suspensions and also as an emulsifier for oil base for plaster and ointments. It is an ingredient of calamine lotion I.P.

4. Carboxymethylcellulose sodium (U.S.P.) :

It is a sodium salt of cellulose carboxymethyl ether and contains 6.5 to 9.5 % sodium. It is made up of white granules or powder, hygroscopic in nature. When added to water it easily forms an aqueous dispersion. A 1.0 % aqueous suspension is slightly acidic or slightly alkaline in nature. It is insoluble in alcohol, ether and other organic solvents. It is stored in a tight container. It finds use as a suspending agent, thickening agent and also as a tablet excipient. its tablets are official in U.S.P. and are used as laxative .

5. Gelatine (I.P., B.P., U.S.P.) :

It is a product obtained by the partial hydrolysis of collegen derived from skin, white connective tissue and animal bones.

It occurs as colourless or pale yellowish, translucent sheets, shreads, flakes or coarse powder with a slight characteristic odour. It is stable in the dry state but undergoes microbial decomposition when it is moist or in solution. It is practically insoluble in water, but when immersed in water it swells, often absorbing 10 times its own weight of water. It is soluble in hot water, which on cooling forms a jelly. It is insoluble in alcohol, ether etc. It is preserved in a well-closed container in a dry place. Gelatin is mainly used to prepare capsules and for coating pills. Sometimes it is used as an emulsifying agent and also in suppositories.

6. Methyl cellulose (U.S.P.) :

It is a methyl ether of cellulose containing 27.5 to 31.0 % methoxy groups. It is a white fibrous powder or granules, soluble in acetic acid and mixture of equal volumes of alcohol and chloroform. It is insoluble in ether, alcohol and chloroform. When added to water. it swells and produces an opalescent viscous solution which is neutral to litmus. It is stable in the presence of alkalies and dilute acids. It is used as an emulsifying, thickening, suspending agent. It is a good stabilizer for o/w emulsions. Clinically it is used as a bulk laxative in treating chronic constipation as a colloidal solution or in the form of tablets (U.S.P.). The usual dose is 1 to 4. Methyl cellulose 20, methyl cellulose 450, methyl cellulose 2500, and methyl cellulose 4500 are official in B.P. They are available as creamy white powder or granules and are hygroscopic in nature. Their properties, and uses are nearly similar to that of methyl cellulose U.S.P. but they differ in their kinematic viscosity. Therapeutically they are used as bulk laxatives except methyl cellulose 20.

7. Povidone (U.S.P.) :

It is also known as polyvinyl pyrrolidone or PVP. It is a polymer of 1-vinyl-2-pyrrolidione.

It is a white odourless powder, very hygroscopic in nature, soluble in water, alcohol and chloroform 1.0 percent aqueous solution has a pH between 3.0 to 7.0. It must be preserved in tight containers, in dry place. It finds use as a suspending and dispersing agent in lotions, creams etc. It is also used as tablet binder and coating agent.

8. Stearyl alcohol (U.S.P.) :

(1-octadecanol) - It consists of not less than 90 % stearyl alcohol and the remainder consists chiefly of cetyl alcohol.

It is found in flakes or granules unctuous to touch with faint and characterisitic odour. It is insoluble in water, soluble in alcohol, chloroform, ether and vegetable oils. It is used to stabilize emulsions and increase their water retaining capacity.

9. Tragacanth (U.S.P.) Indian tragacanth (I.P.) :

It is a dried gummy exudation obtained form the *Astragalus* species.

It is a whitish to off white powder. When added to water it does not dissolve but swells and forms a paste. It is insoluble in alcohol. It is normally used as an emulsifying agent and is used with an emulsifying agent to retard creaming. In mixtures and lotions it is used as a suspending agent.

IV. OINTMENTS AND SUPPOSITORY BASES

Ointments are semisolid preparations for external application of such a consistency that they may be readily applied to skin by inunction. They should be of such a composition that they soften but not necessarily melt, when applied to the skin. The inert bases which are prepared by mixing various materials in judicious combinations for the dispersion of active medicament in semisolid formulation are called ointment bases. The ointment base should be compatible with the skin, stable, permanent, smooth, non-irritating, inert and should be able to absorb water or other liquid preparation and should release the incorporated medicinally active compounds. They can be classified according to their composition into four groups as follows :

1. Oleaginous ointment bases,
2. Absorption ointment bases,
3. Emulsion type ointment bases and
4. Water soluble ointment bases.

Suppositories are solid dosage forms, usually medicated for insertion into the rectum, vaginal cavity or the urethral tract. After insertion they may melt or undergo dissolution in the secretions of the cavity. The substances which are used in the formulation of suppositories are called suppository bases.

(i) Oleaginous ointment bases : They include fixed oils obtained from vegetable origin, fats obtained from animals and semisolid hydrocarbons obtained from the petroleum industry. These are given below.

Arachis oil (I.P., B.P.) :

It is a fixed oil obtained from the seeds of *Arachis hypogaea*.

It is a pale yellow oil with a characteristic odour of nut. It is used as an ingredient of oleoginous ointment base, and also find use as a base (vehicle) for injections of oil soluble substances.

Olive oil (U.S.P.) :

It is obtained from the ripe fruits of *Olea europaea*.

It is a pale yellowish oily liquid with a characterisitic odour. It is used in the preparation of liniments and ointments for its emolient action.

Oleic acid (B.P., U.S.P.) :

It is obtained by the hydrolysis of fixed oils or fats and chiefly consists of octadecanoic acid.

It is a pale brownish to yellowish oily liquid with a characteristic odour. It is insoluble in water, soluble in alcohol, chloroform and petroleum ether. It is incompatible with alkalies as it form soaps and also with heavy metals and calcium to form insoluble salts. It is affected by oxidising agents like nitric acid and potassium permanganate. It should be stored in tightly-closed containers, protected from light. On exposure to air it darkens in colour. It is used in Benzyl benzoate lotion.

Hard paraffin (I.P., B.P.) :

It is a mixture of solid hydrocarbons obtained from petroleum.

It is a colourless or white substance, sometimes showing a crystalline structure, odourless with greasy touch. It is insoluble in water, ethanol and soluble in ether and chloroform. It is an ingredient of ' Paraffin ointment ', ' simple ointment ', and ' wool alcohol ointment ' (I.P.)

White soft paraffin (I.P., B.P.) White petrolactum (U.S.P.)

It is a semisolid mixture of hydrocarbons obtained from petroleum and bleached. It may contain a suitable stabilizer.

It is a white soft translucent in nature, unctuous to the touch, when rubbed on the skin. It is free from fluorescence and is odourless. It is an ingredient of emulsifying ointments, paraffin ointment, simple ointment and wool alcohols ointment.

Yellow soft paraffin (I.P., B.P.) :

It is similar to white soft paraffin except that it has a pale yellowish colour. It is an ingredient of ' Dithranol ointment ', ' Paraffin ointment ', ' simple ointment ' and ' wool alcohols ointment '.

Spermaceti (U.S.P.) :

It is a waxy substance obtained from the head of the sperm whale.

It is a white mass unctuous to touch and has a faint odour and is free from racidity. It is insoluble in water. It is soluble in boiling alcohol, ether, chloroform and fixed oils. It is used to impart a good consistency to creams and ointments.

White bees wax (I.P., B.P.), white wax (U.S.P.) :

It is a product prepared by bleaching and purifying yellow bees wax which is obtained from the honey comb of bees.

It is a yellowish white in colour and has a faint and characteristic odour. It is insoluble in water, partially soluble in alcohol and ether and soluble in fixed oils. It is stored in a well-closed container.

Yellow bees wax (I.P., B.P.) : It is a purified wax obtained from the honey comb of bees having a yellow to greyish brown colour. It is similar in properties to white bees wax and is an ingredient of ' Paraffin ointment ' (I.P.)

(ii) Absorption ointment bases : The substances which are used to prepare these bases have water absorbing properties and are generally anhydrous, which absorb water but still maintain their ointment-like consistency. When water is incorporated as an ingredient they form w/o emulsion.

Wool fat (I.P., B.P.), Anhydrous lanolin (U.S.P.) : It is a purified anhydrous waxy substance obtained form the wool of sheep.

It is a pale yellowish mass, unctuous touch, its odour is faint and characteristic. It is insoluble in water, sparingly soluble in alcohol, freely soluble in ether and chloroform. It must be stored in tightly closed container at

25° C or less. It is used in the preparation of hydrous wool fat and is an ingredient of ' simple ointment ' (I.P.). It is normally used when liquid is to be incorporated in the ointment.

Hydrous wool fat (I.P., B.P.) :

It is prepared by adding 300 ml water to 700 grams of melted wool fat by constant stirring. It has a yellowish white colour and a faint odour. When heated on a water bath the aqueous and oily layer separates. It is practically insoluble in water, soluble in chloroform and solvent ether with separation of water layer. It is preserved in a tightly-closed container in cool place. It is used in emulsion type ointment base.

Wool alcohols (I.P., B.P.) : It is obtained from the waxy substances, from wool of sheep and contains 30 per cent cholesterol and other alcohols.

It is a golden yellow brown solid with a faint odour. When cooled it becomes brittle. It is insoluble in water, soluble in warm alcohol and also in ether and chloroform. It is an ingredient of ' wool alcohol ointment ' (I.P.) which is used to prepare salicylic acid ointment ' (I.P.) .

(iii) **Emulsion type ointment base :** These are actually emulsions and are divided into two types (i) emulsion base o/w type and (ii) emulsion base w/o type. The above type of bases can take up additional amount of water without much affecting the consistency of the base.

Cetosteryl alcohol (B.P.) : It is a mixture of solid aliphatic alcohols consisting mainly of cetyl and stearyl alcohol.

It occurs as a white or cream-coloured mass or as white flakes or granules touch unctuous. It is soluble in ether, less soluble in alcohol and insoluble in water. It is an ingredient of ' cetomaegral emulsifying ointments and cetomaegral emulsifying wax (B.P.), which finds uses as non-ionic emulsifying agents.

Emulsifying wax (I.P., B.P.) : It contains cetosteryl alcohol and sodium lauryl sulphate or sodium salt of sulphated higher primary aliphatic alcohols. It is prepared by adding sodium lauryl sulphate (10 g) to melted cetosteryl alcohol (90 g) at about 95°C and then, 4 ml water is added and heated to 115°C with continuous stirring till frothing ceases and is then cooled. It occurs as white or pale yellow waxy solid or flakes. When warmed, it appears like plastic and has faint characteristic odour. It is insoluble in water, partially soluble in alcohol. It is an ingredient of ' Emulsifying ointment ' and ' Hydrous emulsifying ointment ' (I.P.).

Stearic acid (I.P., U.S.P.) : It is discussed under lubricants.

(iv) **Water soluble ointment bases** : This category includes bases which are prepared from higher ethylene glycols, known as carbowax, which have a wide range of molecular weight, those from 200 to 700 are liquids, and those above 1000 are waxy solid. These are inert, nonvolatile, unctuous and are soluble in water. They have emollient properties and find use in water washable ointment bases. Some examples are polyethylene glycols, polyoxyl stearates and polysorbates, which are discussed under surface active agents.

(V) DILUENTS, BINDERS, DISINTEGRATING AGENTS AND LUBRICANTS

Diluents : *When a single dose is active medicament is to be administered in a small amount, inert substances are* added to it to increase the bulk. Such substances are known as diluents. In tablet manufacture, various diluents are employed. Calcium phosphate dibasic is a commonly used inorganic diluent. Various other substances which are employed as diluents are :

Lactose (I.P., B.P., U.S.P.) : It is a white, amorphous powder, odourless and soluble in water, practically insoluble in alcohol and other organic solvents. It is a general purpose diluent and is used in tablets, lozenges, pills and related preparations.

Starch (I.P., B.P.) : Starch is obtained from various sources, including maize, potatoes, rice and wheat. It occurs as a white amorphous powder, odourless and tasteless. Different starches are identified by using microscopic methods. Starch contains water soluble and water insoluble fractions. Thus in small amounts it is soluble in water on heating and forms a cloudy solution, starch-water mixture when heated, forms a paste. Starch is used in powder from as a diluent, in solution and paste as a binder and also as a disintegrating agent. Starch powder is also used in the preparation of pills, pastilles and lozenges.

Sucrose (I.P., B.P.) : This sweetening agent is used in the powder form as diluent and in syrup from as binding agent.

Binders : Substances which are used to impart cohesive properties to powdered material are called as binding agents or binders. They are mainly used in granulation of materials for tablet making and other purposes. Some pharmaceutically useful binders are :

Acacia powder and mucilage : The powder of acacia and mucilage in 1 to 5 % strength are used as binders in granulation process in tablet making.

Liquid glucose : It is a viscousliquid with a characteristic odour and sweet taste. It is soluble in water and sparingly soluble in ether and alcohol. An aqueous solution is employed in granulation process in 1 – 2 % strength.

Distintegrating agent : This is a substance or mixture of substances which facilitate the break up of tablets. Some commonly used agents are :

Microcrystalline cellulose : It occurs as white crystalline material, odourless and tasteless. It is insoluble in water but swells when added to water. 1 to 2 % in the form of paste is used in tablet-making as a disintegrating agent.

Starch is very commonly used as a disintegrating agent in pharmaceuticals.

Lubricants : Substances which improve the rate of flow of granules, prevent adhesion, cohesion during the tablet-making are known as lubricants. The substances commonly used are :

Stearic acid (I.P., B.P., U.S.P.) : It is fatty acid obtained from natural source as well from synthetic methods. It occurs as whitish lumps or soft powder. It is practically odourless. The acid is soluble in ether, chloroform but is practically insoluble in water. It readily forms salt with sodium or potassium carbonates or hydroxide which are water soluble. Salts with divalent metals are water insoluble. Stearic acid is a common ingredient of certain types of ointments or creams.

Magnesium stearate (I.P.) : It is a salt of stearic acid and occurs as fine white powder. It is insoluble in water. Because of its fine lustering and lubricating property, it is very commonly used in the compression process of tablet-making.

Hydrogenated vegetable oils (U.S.P.) : It occurs as white-waxy like fatty crystalline or grannular material with characteristic odour. It is obtained by hydrogenation of vegetable oils. It is insoluble in water but soluble in oils and organic solvents. It is also used as a lubricant in certain preparations like suppositories.

Talc : The purified magnesium silicate of approximate formula $Mg_6(Si_2O_4)_4(OH)_4$ is widely used as a lubricant in tablet manufacture.

Besides the above mentioned category of substances, cellulose acetate phthalate, Carnauba wax, gelatin, shellac, paraffins etc. are used as coating materials in tablets.

VI. SURFACE ACTIVE AGENTS

Surface-active agents or surfactants include a large and varied group of chemicals having surface active property. They are widely used industrially for various purposes and also for household purposes such as soaps, detergents and shampoos. Some surfactants are used therapeutically and also as antimicrobial agents.

In the structure of surface active agents there is the presence of hydrophilic and lipophilic groups. The presence of groups such as COONa, SO_3Na and OSO_2Na impart strong hydrophilic property, while groups such as OH–CHO, –NO_2, –NH_2, –COOH, Cl, Br, –NR_2 etc. impart weaker hydrophilic property. Alkyl, aryl, alicyclic and hydrocarbons and hydrocarbons having unsaturated linkages as –CH = CH – and – C $\equiv$ C – impart varying degrees of lipophilic property.

In the aqueous dispersions the surfactant concentrates at the interface of the two phases and causes the lowering of the ' interfacial tension between the two phases. The term ' surface tension ' is used for the interfacial tension between air-liquid phases. Another important property associated with surfactants is that in the aqueous dispersion it forms micelles at a critical concentration. All surface-active agents concentrate at interfaces forming micelles which give rise to various applications and they can be classified according to their application as :

1. Emulsifying agents : It forms a interfacial film between two immiscible liquid phase which facilitates the sub-division of liquid particles and stabilizes the system.

2. Wetting agents : It causes a fluid phase to be displaced by another fluid phase (usually air is displaced by an aqueous solution) e.g. this is used to disperse finely divided solids in lotions.

3. Solubilising agents : It increases the solubility of solids or liquids in water, e.g. oils are solubilised as they are incorporated into surfactant miscelles.

4. Detergents : Surfactants acting as detergent involve various processes involving wetting, solubilising, emulsifying dispersing. It also caus foaming.

The surface active agents are classified into four categories such as :

(i) Anionic (ii) Cationic (iii) Non-ionic and (iv) Amphoteric.

If more than one surfactant is to be used, one has to ensure their compatibility. When anionic and cationic agents are mixed the resulting product will have a reduced surfactant property.

ANIONIC SURFACTANTS

Surfactants of this class ionize to given anions which is responsible for its surfactant property. e.g. sodium laurate in aqueous solution ionizes to give $CH_3(CH_2)_{10}COO-$ as a surface active ion. Most of the agents belonging to this class have either a sulphonate, carboxylate or sulphate as its ionising group. In carboxylate derivative sodium, potassium, ammonium or triethanol ammonium salts of naturally occuring fatty acids are very common. These are called soaps and their cations are soluble in water. Soaps with cations like hydrogen, calcium and magnesium have less surfactant property.

Synthetic agents belonging to this class are usually aryl alkyl, sulphonates, alkyl sulphonates, ester amide sulphonates and alkyl sulphates e.g. :

Aryl alkyl sulphonate	Dodecylbenzene sulphonate	
Alkyl sulphonate	sodium acetyl sulphonate	$C_{16}H_{33}SO_3Na$
Ester sulphonate	Sodium lauryl sulphoacetate	$C_{12}H_{25}CO_2CH_2SO_3Na$
Alkyl sulphate	Sodium lauryl sulphate.	$C_{12}H_{25}OSO_3Na$

Sodium lauryl sulphate (I.P., B.P., U.S.P.) :

It is a mixture of sodium alkyl sulphate consisting chiefly of sodium lauryl sulphate $[CH_3(CH_2)_{10}CH_2OSO_2Na]$. It contains up to 8 % of combined sodium sulphate and sodium chloride. It occurs as white or light yellowish flakes or powder with a slight but characteristic odour. It is freely soluble in water forming opalescent solution. It is manly used for its foaming property in shampoos and for cleansing property in dental preparations. Another important use is as emulsifying agent for preparing water miscible ointment bases.

Dioctyl sodium sulphosuccinate (I.P., U.S.P.) :

It is a white wax like solid with a characteristic odour. It is very hygroscopic in nature. It dissolves slowly in water, and is freely soluble in alcohol and glycerine. It is stable in acid and slightly alkaline solutions but decomposes in strongly basic solutions. It is an excellent wetting agent and thus is widely used in many fields. Therapeutically it is used in the form of tablets for treating constipation and is a nonlaxative faecal softener.

Sodium stearate (U.S.P.) :
It is a mixture of sodium sterate $(C_{18}H_{35}NaO_2)$ and sodium palmitate $(C_{16}H_{31}NaO_2)$ which together constitute not less than 90.0 per cent of the total content. The content of sodium stearate is not less than 40.0 per cent. It also contains a small amount of sodium salts of other fatty acids.

It is a white fine powder with a slight tallow like odour and a soapy touch. It dissolves slowly in water and alcohol and readily in hot water and alcohol. The aqueous solutions are alkaline in nature. It is affected by light. It is used as an emulsifying and stiffening agent.

CATIONIC SURFACTANTS

The agents belonging to this class ionise to give cations which have surface active properties. Quarternary ammonium compounds are most important pharmaceutically. Most of the agents belonging to this class have an antimicrobial activity. Cationic surfactants are active against Gram-positive and Gram-negative organisms, fungi and protozoal organisms and also certain pathogenic organisms.

Benzalkonium chloride (U.S.P.) : It is mixture of alkyl dimethyl benzyl ammonium chloride of general formula $[C_6H_5CH_2N(CH_3)_2R]$ Cl where R represents a mixture of alkyl beginning with n-$C_{18}H_{17}$ to n-$C_{12}H_{25}$, n-$C_{14}H_{29}$ and n$C_{16}H_{35}$. It is a white or yellowish white gelatinous with an aromatic odour. It is very soluble in water and alcohol, freely soluble in benzene. Aqueous solutions are alkaline to litmus and foam strongly when shaken. It is incompatible with soaps and other anionic agents. Nitric acid and nitrates cause precipitation. It has a wetting, detergent and emulsifying action. It is used as a surface antiseptic for intact skin and mucous membrane (usual concentration, 1 : 750 to 1 : 20, 000). It is also used for the sterilization of surgical instruments. It has a mild astringent property. It is also effective against many pathogenic non-sporulating bacteria and fungi.

Benzalkonium chloride solution (B.P.) : It contains 49 to 51 % w/v of alkyl benzyl dimethyl ammonium chloride. It is a clear colourless to pale yellow syrupyliquid with an aromatic odour, miscible with water and alcohol. It is mainly used as an ' *Antiseptic detergent.*'

Cetylpyridium chloride (B.P., U.S.P.) :

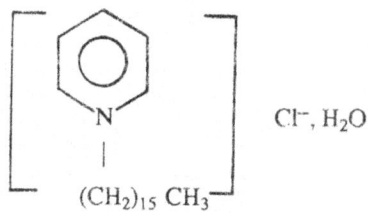

1-hexadecylpyridinium chloride

It is a white powder with a slight characteristic odour. It is very soluble in water, alcohol and chloroform. The aqueous solutions are acidic to litmus paper It is a local anti-infective agent. It has a surface-active as well as an antiseptic action against certain non-sporulating bacteria the solutions of 0.1 to 1 % are applied to intact skin and 0.1 % solutions are used for minor lacerations. It is an Antiseptic detergent. It is available as throat lozenges and in 0.5 % buffered solutions as a mouth wash.

NON-IONIC SURFACTANTS

These agents do not have an ionisable group in their structure. The hydrophilic character is provided by the hydroxyl, ester or a ether groups. As each group has low hydrophilic characters a large number of such groups are present in the structure of the surfactant. In order to get the desired hydrophilicity ether linkages such as the polyoxyethylene group is widely incorporated into the structure of surfactants. Compounds containing polyoxyethylene groups interact with many pharmaceutical agents and change the properties of the agents.

Glycerylmonosterate (B.P.) :

$$C_{17}H_{35}-\underset{\underset{O}{\parallel}}{C}-O-CH_2-\underset{\underset{OH}{|}}{CH}-CH_2OH$$

It is a mixture of mono glycerides of steric and palmatic acids together with variable quantities of di and tri-glycerides. It contains not less than 35.0 % monoglycerides calculated as $C_{20}H_{40}O_4$ and not more than 60 % free glycerine.

It is a white powder or flakes or a hard mass, and it is greasy to the touch It is insoluble in water and soluble in chloroform, benzene and warm alcohol. I is affected by light. So it is stored in light resistant containes. It is dispersable in hot water with the aid of soap or other surface active agents. It has a strong lipophilic property and is used as an emulsifying agent for w/o emulsions. When mixed with suitable surfactant it forms emulsions. Glycerylmonosterate self emulsifying is a combination of glyceryl monosterate with soap or othe surfactants, Glycerylmonosterate also increases the consistency of preparations.

Polyoxyl 40 stearate (U.S.P.) : It is also known as ' Myrj ' 5 polyethylene glycol monosterate PEG-40 etc. It is a mixture of the mono sterat and distearate esters of mixed polyoxyethylene diols and the corresponding fre glycols, the average polymer length being equivalent to about 40 oxyethylen units.

It occurs a white or slightly cream coloured waxy solid, soluble in water alcohol, ether etc. but insoluble in mineral acids and vegetable oils. It is mainly used as an emulsifying agent for preparing o/w emulsions.

Sorbitan fatty acid esters :

Important compounds of this series are given below :
1. Sorbitan monolaurate (Span 20)
2. Sorbitan mono palmitate (Span 40)
3. Sorbitan mono sterate (Span 60)
4. Sorbitan mono oleate (Span 80)

The sorbitans are coloured viscous liquid with characteristic odour. They are insoluble but dispersible in water and are miscible in alcohol. They are useful as emulsifying agents for the preparation of w/o emulsions. If they are blended with more hydrophilic emulsifying surfactants depending upon the proportion they can form either w/o or o/w emulsions.

Polyethylene (20) sorbitan fatty acid esters : The important agents belonging to this class are given below :
1. Polyethylene 20 sorbitan monolaurate (Tween 20)
2. Polyethylene 20 sorbitan monopalmitate (Tween 40)
3. Polyethylene 20 sorbitan monosterate (Tween 60)
4. Polyethylene 20 sorbitan monosterate (Tween 80)

Polysorbate 80 (U.S.P.) Tween 80, polyoxyethylene 20, sorbitan monooleate :

These occurs as yellow to amber coloured oily liquid with a characteristic odour. They are very soluble in water, soluble in alcohol and vegetable oils. These are most stable between 3 to 7.6 pH range. They are used as a solubilising and emulsifying agent. These can be blended with other surfactants to give the desired o/w or w/o type emulsion in cosmetic and other products.

Polysorbate 20, polysorbate 40 and polysorbate 60 are offical in B.P., their properties and uses are similar to polysorbate 80.

Polyethylene glycol 400 monosterate (U.S.P.) : Chemically, it contains ether, alcohol and ester groups in its structure. It occurs as colourless to whitish semitransparent mass. It is insoluble in water, but soluble in ether, chloroform etc. It is used as a surface active agent in the preparation of ointment, creams and other products.

V. SOLVENTS AND VEHICLES

Besides water, a number of organic liquids are used in pharmaceutical preparations as solvents. Some are used for simple dissolution purpose while others are used in extraction and general purpose vehicles. Some commonly used solvents of pharmaceutical importance are :

Acetone (I.P., B.P.) CH_3COCH_3 : It is a colourless sweet smelling liquid. It is inflammable and miscible with water. Fats, fatty substances, resins, rosins etc. are soluble in acetone or can be extracted with acetone. It is employed as a general purpose solvent.

Dimethylsulphoxide (B.P.) CH_3SOCH_3 : It is commonly called as DMSO. It occurs as a colourless, viscous, hygroscopic liquid with characteristic odour. It is a polar solvent and is miscible with water. It should be protected from light. This solvent is used in the preparations intended for topical applications.

Ethanol, ethyl alcohol (I.P., B.P., U.S.P.) : CH_3CH_2OH :

It is colourless, volatile liquid with characteristic odour and taste. It is inflammable and is miscible with water. Absolute alcohol contains over 99 % of ethanol white rectified spirit about 95 % of ethanol. Ethanol diluted with water gives various diluted alcohols (like 10, 20, ... 80 % etc.) and are official. Alcohols, above 70 % strength, act as preservatives while other strengths of alcohol are used for the preparation of tinctures, spirits, extracts and other galenicals and also in external application preparations.

Industrial methylated spirit (B.P.), Specially Denatured spirit (B.P.) : It is ethanol denatured by the addition of wood naphtha, methanol etc. thereby rendered unfit for human consumption. It is mainly used as solvent for external application preparations and for surface coating. A special grade ketone-free industrial methylated spirit is official in B.P.

Glycerol (B.P.), Glycerine (I.P.) $CH_2OH . CHOH . CH_2OH$: It is a clear colourless, odourless, viscous liquid. It is hygroscopic and has sweet taste. Glycerine is soluble in water and alcohol. Since it has moisturising properties it is employed in creams, jellies, pastes etc. It is commonly used as a solvent in ear drop preparations.

Propylene glycol ($CH_3.CH(OH) . CH_2OH$: It is similar in properties and actions to that of glycerine and is used as a substitute for glycerine in various pharmaceutical preparations.

Isopropyl alcohol (B.P.) : It is a clear, colourless liquid, inflammable with a burning bitter taste. It is miscible with water and alcohol. It is used as a solvent in cosmetic preparations, especially in external application preparations of the skin cleansing type. It is also employed in lotions.

Oils : Edible oils like arachies, and sesame are used as solvents in various pharmaceutical preparations.

Solvent ether (I.P., B.P., U.S.P.) $CH_3CH_2 . O . CH_2CH_3$:

It is a clear colourless liquid with a characteristic odour. It is highly inflammable amd volatile in nature. It is used in making solutions of oils, fats, resins and related substances. It is employed as a general purpose solvent in pharmaceutical industry.

Chapter 40

INTRODUCTION TO HETEROCYCLIC COMPOUNDS

In the study of pharmaceutical chemistry, we have come across many drugs and compounds which chemically belong to a class called the heterocyclic. This class comprises of agents from natural sources like alkaloids, proteins, vitamins, several antibiotics, hormones, enzymes and also several synthetic organic compounds which have a heterocyclic ring as a component.

Since there are several heterocyclic rings encountered, both free and fused to other carbocyclic rings, a brief introduction is presented to explain the naming and numbering of compound possessing the heterocyclic ring system.

Classification of organic compounds

Organic compounds are classified as follows :

1. Aliphatic compounds : These are made up of carbon atoms, with or without functional groups, but comprising open chains only.

2. Carbocyclic compounds : The molecules of these compounds contain chains of rings or carbon atoms only. These are subdivided into (a) *Alicyclic compounds:* These include all carbocyclic compounds which have a ring, a fused ring or a closed structure but no aromaticity ; for e.g. cycloalkenes, cycloparaffins, cyclic terpenes, steroids, etc. (b) *Aromatic compounds* : These comprise all carbocyclic compounds which have a ring or a fused ring and an aromatic character ; e.g., naphthalene, anthracene, phenanthrene, etc.

3. Heterocyclic compounds : These are compounds that contain a ring made up of more than one kind of atom. These are sub-divided into heteroparaffin and hetero-aromatic compounds, depending upon the degree of hydrogenation or aromatic character.

The common hetero atoms present in the ring are nitrogen, oxygen and sulphur, with exception of phosphorus, in addition to carbon atoms. There may be present on or more hetero atoms in the ring. The systm may be fused or bridged with homocyclic systems. The heterocyclic rings may have different degrees of unsaturation or may be fully saturated. The ring size may be from 3 to 10 membered. The heterocycles comprising of five to six members are in general stable in nature. Ring compounds containing conjugated double bonds and exhibiting an aromatic character are the most widely encountered. The heterocyclic rings which are easily opened and do not possess any aromatic properties, e.g. ethylene oxide, lactones, etc., are not considered as heterocyclic compounds.

Nomenclature of heterocyclic compounds

General rules in naming the compounds are :

1. When a heterocyclic compound contains only one hetero atom, this hetero atom is always given the number, one.

2. In case more than one heteroatom is present, the numbering runs in such a direction, that the hetero atoms are given the lowest possible numbers.

3. If there are different hetero atoms present in the ring, the order of numbering will be O, S, N, P, etc.

4. The name of monocyclic compounds are derived by a prefix (or prefixes) indicating the nature of the hetero atom present and ending with ' a ', Thus,

Oxygen	Oxa
Sulphur	Thia
Nitrogen	aza
Silicon	Sila
Phosphorus	Phospha ... etc.

5. When two or more of the same hetero atoms are present, the prefixes like di, tri, tetra, penta, etc., are used ; e.g. dioxa. triaza etc.

6. With reference to the order of O, S, N atoms in the rings, the compounds are named as Oxathia for (O and ' S '), thiaza (for ' S ' and ' N '), etc.

7. Endings of the names of simple heterocyclic rings from 3 to 10 atoms is indicated for nitrogenous and non-nitrogenous rings as 3-tridine (irane), 4-etdine (etane), 5-ole, 6-ine (in), 7-epin (epin), 8-Ocine (ocin), 9-onine (onin), 10-ecine (ecine).

8. The state of hydrogenation is indicated in the suffix or by prefixes as dihydro, tetrahydro etc.

Three-membered rings with one heteroatom

A saturated three-membered ring, containing a nitrogen is called Aziridine (*or ethylenimine*), Oxirane (or ethylene oxide, Z = O) and Thirane (or ethylene sulphide, Z = S). These ring compounds, because of the ring strain are very reactive. Under basic or neutral conditions, ring fission takes place. The aziridines are encountered in Thiotepa.

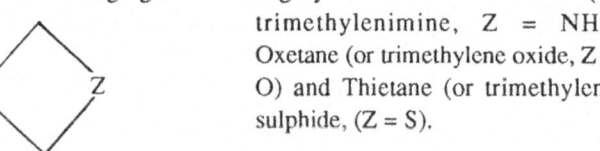

Oxaziridines   **Diaziridines**

Oxazinidines and diaziridines are names for three membered rings with two heteroatoms. These are not, however, encountered in medicinal agents.

Four-membered rings containing one heteroatom

The ring systems belonging to this category are called as Azetidine (or trimethylenimine, Z = NH), Oxetane (or trimethylene oxide, Z = O) and Thietane (or trimethylene sulphide, (Z = S).

The properties of this class are of intermediate between those of aliphatic amines, ethers, etc., and those of the corresponding three-membered ring system. In some reactions the ring is preserved ; while in others, ring fission occurs readily. No medicinal agent is encountered in this category.

Five-membered rings with one heteroatom

The simple five membered heterocyclic compounds are Furan, Thiophene and Pyrrole, each of which contains a single heteroatom.

Furan   **Thiophene**   **Pyrrole**

The position of the side chain substituents is indicated by numbers (or by Greek letters) some examples are :

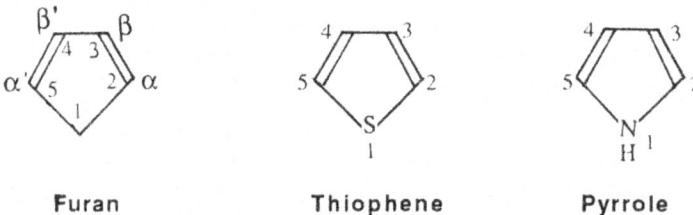

Furfural   **2-Furan**   **2-Acetyl furan**
2-furancarboxyl   **Sulphonic**
aldehyde   **Acid**

      2-benzoylthiophene   **2,5-dimethylthiophene**

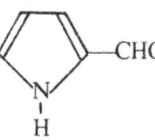  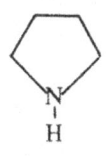

2-pyrrole carboxy-   **3-pyrraline**   **Pyrrolidine**
aldehyde

Thiophenenes occur in coal tar and crude petroleum, furans as a decomposition product of sugar and pyrrole in bone oil. Electrophilic subsstitution of pyrrole, furan and thiophene occurs easily. These can also be reduced. Furan has a lesser aromatic character than thiophene and pyrrole. Medicinally useful drugs like frusemide, nitro-furantoin (furan), cephaloridine, cephalothin (thiophene), viprynium (Pyrrole), pentolnium, triprolidine (pyrrolidine) are some examples of the five-membered heterocyclic class.

Reduced thiophenes and furans are named systematically as 2, 3-dihydro thiophene or 2, 5-dihydrofuran or 2, 3, 4, 5-tetrahydro thiophene.

      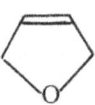   

2, 3-dihydrothiophene   **2, 5-dihydrofuran**   **2, 3, 4, 5-tetrahydro thiophene**

Similarly, reduced pyrroles are called ether Δ^1, Δ^2 and Δ^3- pyrrolines, while tetrahydropyrroles are called pyrrolidines.

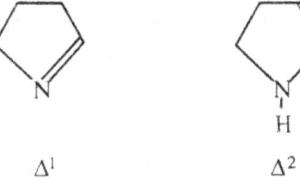 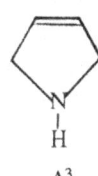

    Δ^1 Δ^2 Δ^3

Pyrrolines

Pyrrolidines

Five-membered rings containing two or more heteroatoms

The compounds containing rings and possessing two or more nitrogen atoms are as follows :

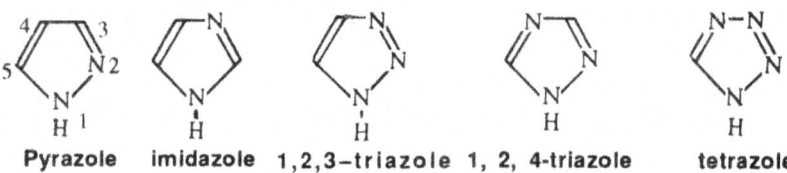

Pyrazole   imidazole   1,2,3-triazole   1, 2, 4-triazole   tetrazole

Some of the reduced forms are :

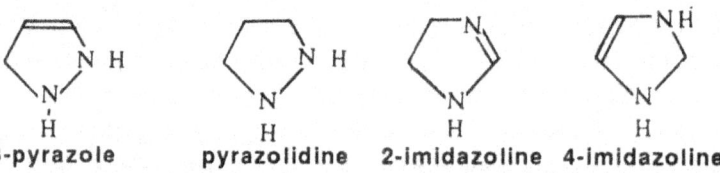

3-pyrazole   pyrazolidine   2-imidazoline   4-imidazoline

Pharmaceutically useful drugs like antipyrine (3-pyrazoline), antazoline, naphazoline (2-imidazoline) are encountered among these compounds.

The ring system containing nitrogen and oxygen atoms are :

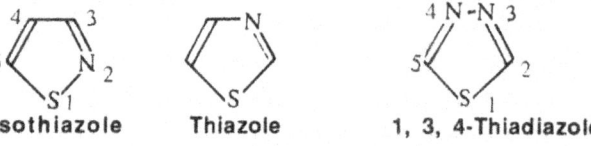

Isoxazole   Isoxazolidine   Oxazole   Oxazolidine

Drugs like sulphafurazole and cycloserine have isoxazole and isoxazolidine rings, while troxidone has oxazolidine skeleton ring. The rings containing nitrogen and sulphur as thiazole and isothiazole are found associated with many drugs.

Isothiazole   Thiazole   1, 3, 4-Thiadiazole

Rings containing more than two heteroatoms, thiadiazole, are found present in drugs like acetazolamide, sulphamethizole, etc.

Five-membered fused ring compounds

The fusion of five-membered heterocyclic rings to a benzonoid nucleus gives various cyclic compounds, like thionaphthene, indole and coumarone, respectively.

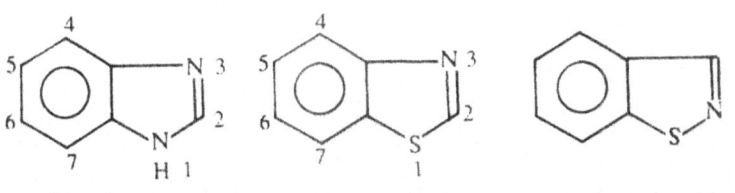

Thionaphthene   **Indole**   **Coumarone**

These rings compounds are aromatic in character. Indomethacin, 5-hydroxytryptamine are the examples of the indole class. Indoline and cumarian are the names given to 2, 3-dihydro derivatives of indole and benzofuran. The indoline ring is encountered in drugs like methisazone and indigo carmine. The isometric form of indoline is called isoindoline (present in chlorthalidone). Fusion of imidazole to the benzene ring gives a nucleus called benzimidazole (found in the drug thiabendazole, in cyanocobalamine nucleus), while the fusion of thiazole to benzene gives benzothiazole. 1, 2-benzisothiazole 2, 3 dihydroform is encountered in saccharin.

Benzimidazole   **Benzothiazole**   **1, 2-benzisothiazole**

The benzoxazole nucleus is found in zoxazolamine.

Benzoxazole

Dibenzo derivatives : When two benzene rings are fused to the two sides of five membered heterocyclic rings, the following ring strutures are obtained, which are named as dibenzothiophene, carbazole and dibenzofuran.

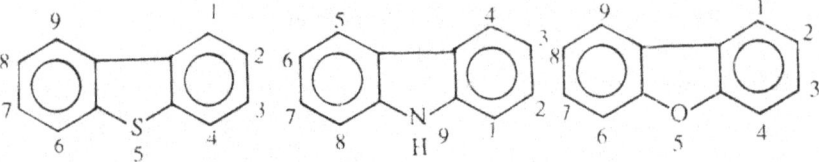

Dibenzothiophene   Carbazole   Dibenzofuran

Six-membered rings with one heteroatom

The nitrogen containing compounds are :

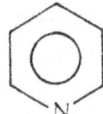

Pyridine

Pyridine nucleus is numbered as,

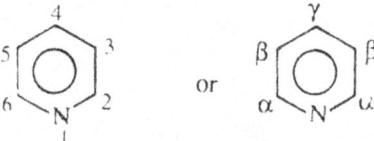

As pyridinium ion is shown as

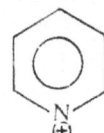

hydrogenated forms are called as dihydro, tetrahydro pyridines and piperidine.

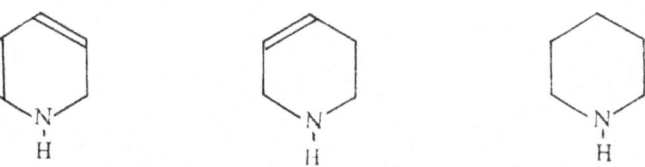

1, 2-dihydro pyridine   1, 2, 3, 6-tetrahydro pyridine   Piperidine

The mono methyl pyridine is called as picolines and depending upon the position it is named as α, β and γ picoline, when the methyl group is at the α, β or γ position respectively. Dimethyl pyridines are called as lutidines (like 2, 6-lutidine) ; while trimethyl pyridines are named as collidines. Sources of these materials are coal tar or bone oil. Some useful pharmaceutical derivatives of pyridine are nicotinamide, isoniazide and of piperidine are benzhezol, halopridol, pethidine, etc.

Some important fused rings and drugs belonging to these are quinine,

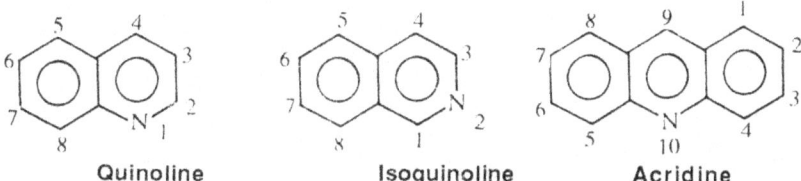

cinchocaine (quinoline), papaverine (isoquinoline), acriflavine, mepacrine (acridine) etc. Fusion of quinoline to the benzene ring gives the nucleus called as benzoquinoline. This has different structures, depending upon the fusion occuring at the sides of quinoline ring. The naming of the nucleus is shown as :

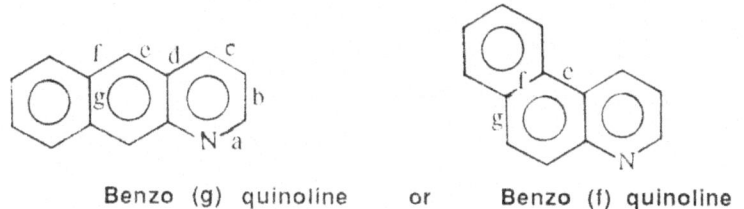

The oxygen and sulphur containing rings and compounds are as follows :

Aromatic oxygen containing ring is pyran and is often called as pyrylium ion. It's reduced forms are 2 dihydropyran, Δ^3 dihydropyran, etc.

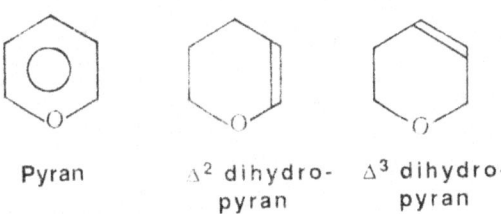

Some benzopyrones of interest are :

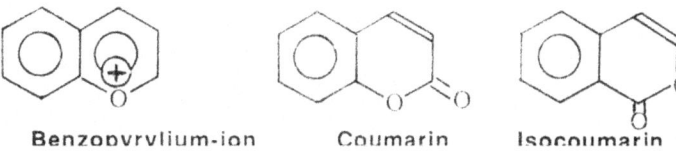

Chromone   Chroman   Flavone

2-H-1-benzopyran

From the pharmaceutical point of view, coumarin and benzopyran are found to be anticoagulants, while vitamin E contains the chroman ring. The sulphur containing a six-membered nucleus is called a thiopyrylium ion. These and its fused ring compounds are not encountered often in pharmaceuticals.

Six membered rings with two or more heteroatoms

There are a number of ring systems in this category, e.g. :

1. Diazines : These are six-membered, with two nitrogen atoms containing rings such as :

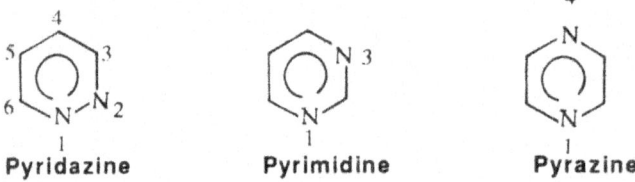

Pyridazine   Pyrimidine   Pyrazine

Drugs containing these rings structures are sulphamethoxy pyridazine (Pyridazine), pyrimethamine, sulphadiazine (Pyrimidine), miloride, pyrazinamide (pyrazine). The reduced ring systems encountered in the pharmaceutical field are 1, 2, 3, 4-tetrahydropyrimidine, which is present in iodxutridine, propylthiouracil, perhydropyrimidines found in primidone, barbituric acid and piperazine encountered in cyclizine, diethylcarbamazine etc.

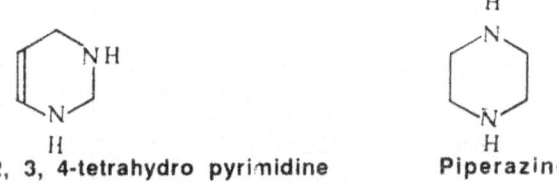

1. 2, 3, 4-tetrahydro pyrimidine   Piperazine

The other rings of interest are:

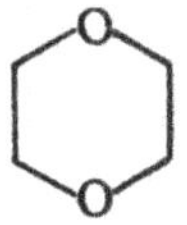

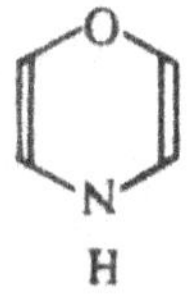

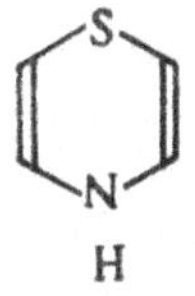

1, 4-dioxon **1, 4-oxozine** **1, 4-thiazine** **S-triazine**

Heterocyclic rings encountered in proteins are:

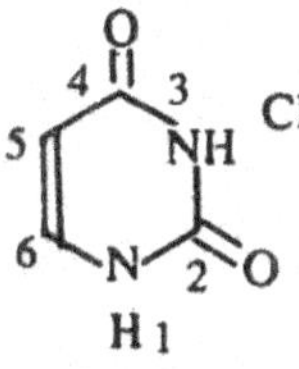

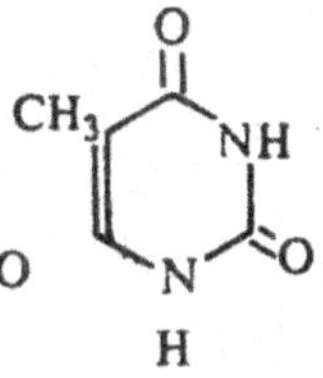

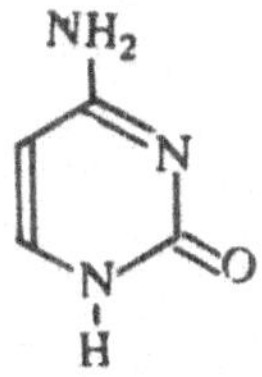

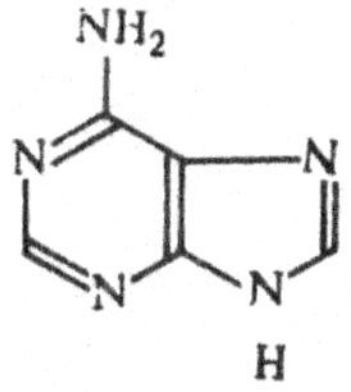

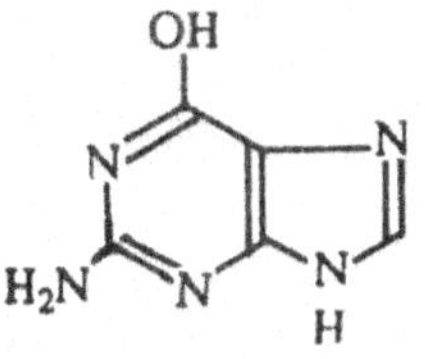

Uracil **Thymine** **Cytosine** **Adenine** **Guanine**

Some fused rings, called as phthalazine (found in hydrazine) quinazoline (present in methaqualone), purine (found in azathiopurine, mercaptopurine), xanthine (present in caffeine), pteridine (encountered in folic acid, triamterance) are of interest in the study of medicinal agents.

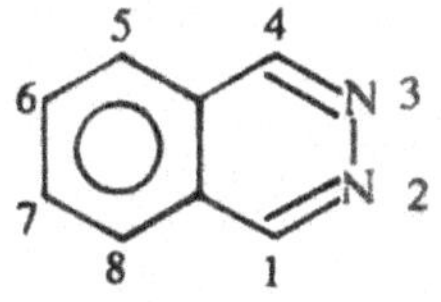

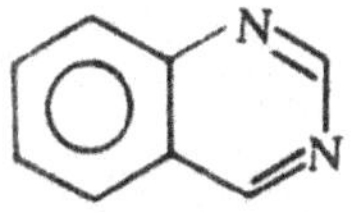

Phthalazine **Quinazoline**

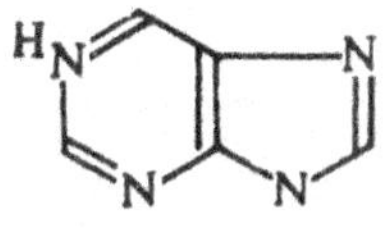

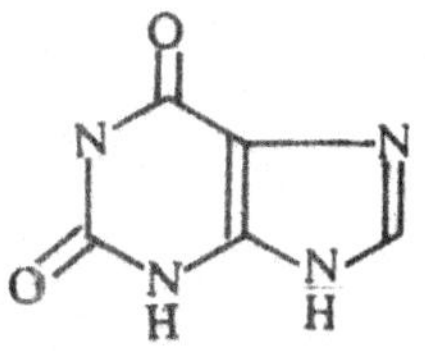

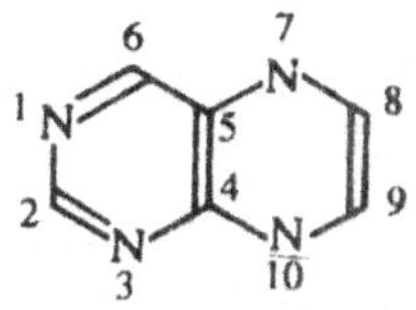

Purine **Xanthine** **Pteridine**

Azepines are the unsaturated, seven membered rings containing one nitrogen atom. Azepine is usually denoted as 1-H-azepine, which undergoes rearrangement into 3-H-azepine.

1-H-azepine   **3-H-azepine**

Fusion of azepine to two benznene rings gives a nucleus called dibenzazepine. The heterocylic ring nucleus is encountered in a number of anti-depressant drugs.

dibenzapine

Octazepine, the 8-membered nitrogen containing rings, is found in guanethidine. Other miscillaneous ring structures encountered in drugs are alloxazine (in riboflavin), phenoxazine, (in chloropromazine, methylene blue, etc.), benzothiadiazine (chlorthiazide) quinuclidine (present in quinine), etc.

alloxozine   **Phenoxozine**

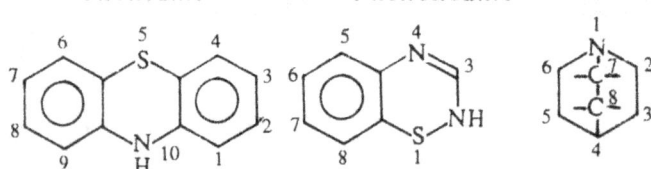

Phenothiazine   **2H, 1, 2, 4-benzothiadiazine**   **Quinuclidine**

Some other tricyclic rings and fused seven-membered ring systems are found in a large number of drugs, from the tranquilising, antidepressant, anti-anxiety categories. The structure of these ring systems are shown as :

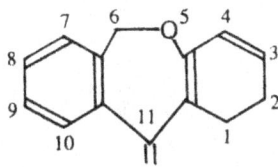   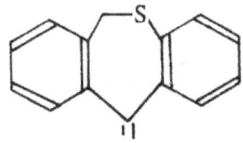

dihydrodibenzoxepin   **Dihydrodibenzothiepin**
e.g. (doxepin)   e.g. (dothiepin)

1, 4-diazapene eg in (chlordiazepoxide)

APPENDIX - I
LIST OF DRUGS WITH OFFICIAL NAME, TRADE NAME, FORM AND USES REFERRED IN THE BOOK

Official Name	Trade Name	Manufacturer	Form	Content in mg	Uses
Theophylline	T. R. PHYLLIN	Natco,Burr-well	T, S	10, 25, 75 125, 250	Bronchial asthma
	THEO - PA		T	100, 300	Chronic bronchitis
Leptazol	CORAMINE	Hind-Ciba	I		Cardiotonic
Amphetamine sulphate	BENZEDRINE	Eskayes	Inhaler		Nasal decongescent
Amitriptyline Hydrochloride	AMITONE	Intas	T	10, 25, 75	Depression
	ELIWEL	Sunpharma	T	25, 75	Anxiety
	TRIDEP	Torrent	T	25, 75	Tension
Nortriptyline hydrochloride	PRIMOX	Sunpharma	T	25	Depression with insomnia,
	SENSIVAL	Wallace	C	25	Neurotic depression
Imipramine hydrochloride	ANTIDEP	Torrent	C	25, 75	Depression,
	DEPSOL	Intas	T	25, 75	Stress with
	IMPRAMINE	Sunpharma	C	25, 75	Insomnia
Mianserin hydrochloride	SERIDAC	Alidac	T	10	Indegenous depression
	TETRADEP	Torrent	T	10, 20	
Meprobamate	EQUANIL	Wyeth	T	200	Insomnia, anxiety, anticonvulsant
Chlordiazepoxide	LIBRIUM	Roche	T	10	Fear anxiety
	CABRIOM	Cadila	T	10	Psychomotor
	EQUILIBRIUM	Jagson	T	10	disorder

			T/S/I	
Diazepam	CALMPOSE	Ranbaxy	T	2, 5, 10
	VALIUM	Roche	T	2, 5
	PLACIDOX	Lupin	T	2, 5, 10	Anxiety insomnia muscle spasm
	ANAXOL	Sigma	T	2, 5, 10
Lorazepam	ATIVAN	Wyeth	T	1, 2	Anxiety
	LARPOSE	Cipla	T	1,	Psychoneurotic disorder,
	TRAPEX	Sunpharma	T	1, 2	Preanesthetic medication
Oxazepam	SEREPAX	Wyeth	T	15	Anxiety, neurotic disorder
Alprazolam	ALPRAX	Torrent	T	0.25, 0.5, 1	Anxiety with depression
	ALZOLAM	Sunpharma	T	0.25, 0.5
	TRIKA	Uniscarch	T	0.25, 0.5, 1
Chlorpromazine	EMETIL	La Pharma	T	25, 50, 100	Sedative in schizophrenia
hydrochloride	SUNPRAZIN	Sun Pharma	T	25, 50, 100
	LARGACTIL	Rhone-Poulence	T	25, 50
Prochlorperazine	STEMETIL	Rhone-Poulence	T	5, 25	in vomiting of pregnancy
maleate	EMIDOXYN	Rallis	I	25
			T	5
Thioridazine	MELLERIL	Sandoz	T	10, 25, 100	Anxiety depression and
hydrochloride	MELOZINE	Intas	T	10, 25, 50	sleep disturbance
	RIDAZIN	Sunpharma	T	25, 50, 100
Trifluroperazine	TRAZINE	Sunpharma	T	5, 10	in halucination
hydrochloride	ESKAZINE	Eskayf	T	1, 5	schizophrenia
	SIQUIL	Sarabhai	T	10

Drug	Brand Name	Manufacturer	Form/Strength	Use
Haloperidal	HALOPIDOL	Ethnor	T 5, 10, 20	Acute and chronic schizophrenia in anxiety
	COMBIDOL	Intas	T 1.5, 5, 10	
	DEPIDOL	Torrent	T 0.25, 1.5, 5	
Metoclopramide	MAXERON	Wallace	T 10	In Gastric irritation
Anesthetic ether	REGLAL	C.F.L	T 10	
	ANESTHETIC ETHER	E. Merck, Alembic Chemical, S. D. fine.	Bottle 250/500 ml	Anaesthetic
Halothane	FLUOTHANE	I. C. I.	Bottle 250	Inhalation anesthesia.
Cyclopropane	CYCLOPROPANE	S. D. fine	Bottle 250	Anaesthetic
Thiopentone sodium	INTERVAL SODIUM	Rhone-Poulence	Vial 0.5 - 1 g	Praenesthetic medication
	PENOTHAL SODIUM	Abbot	Vial 0.5 - 1 g	
Phenobarbitone	GARDENAL	Rhone-Poulence	T 30, 60	epilepsy, hypnotic
	LUMINAL	Bayer	T 30, 60	
Pentobarbitone Sodium	NEMBUTAL	Bayer	T 30 I	hypnotic
Nitrazepam	NITROSUN	Sunpharma	T 5, 10	insomnia
	NITRAZEPAM	FDC	T 5, 10	
Triclofos sodium	TRICLORYL	Glaxo	I 500 mg/5 ml	insomnia and sedation
Paraldehyde	PARALDEHYDE	Glaxo	Bottle 500	insomnia and sedation

Hydrazine hydrochloride	ATARAX	Uni-UCB	T	10, 25	Pruritus, uriticaria
Phenytoin and sodium	DILANTIN	Parke - Davis	Kapscals 100	epilepsy
	DILANTIN - SOD	Parke - Davis	I 100	
	EPTOIN	Boots	T 100	
Primidone	MYSOLINE	ICI	T 250	Grandmal epilepsy
Carbamazepine	TEGRETOL	Hind-Ciba-Gei	T 100, 200	epilepsy and Trigeminal Neuralgia
	ZEPTOL	sunpharma	T 100, 200	
	MAZETOL	S. G. Pharma.	T 200	
Sodium Valporate	VALPROL	Intas	T 200	Grandmal and mixed type
	EPILEX	Reickett and Colman	T 200	
Morphine	MORPHINE	Alembic	I 15 mg/ml	Analgesic
	MORPHINE-SULPH	Biomedica	I 10 mg/ml, 20 mg/ml	
Codeine phosphate	CODEINE PHOSP.	Unicare	Syr. 15 mg	Analgesic and cough supressant
	CODEINE PHOSP.	B. P. Labs	T 10	
Pethidine	PETHIDINE	Alembic	I 50 mg/2 ml	Analgesic
	PETHIDINE	Days	I 50 mg/1 ml 100 mg/2 ml	
Dextropropoxyphene with acetaminophen	PROXY TAB	Wockhardt	T 32.5 + 500	in fever with pain
	PROXYLON	Wockhardt	65 + 500	

Drug	Brand	Manufacturer	Form	Strength	Indication
Pentazocine	PENTAWIN	Biochem	I	30 mg/ml	Post operative pain pain due to trauma, burn
	SOSEGON	Win-medicane	I	30 mg/ml	
	SUSEVIN	Indoco	I	30 mg/ml	
Paracetamol	CALPOL	Burr-well	T	500	
	CROCIN	Duphar-Interferon	T	500	in fevar and pain
	METACIN	Themis Pharma	S	125 mg/ 5ml	
	CORBUTYL	Roussel	T	500	
Aspirin	DISPRIN	Recitt and Colman	Soluble T	300	Pain, Rheumatic fever antiinflammatory
	ASPIRIN	Haffkine	T	300	
	ASPRO	Nicholas	T	300	
Analgin	NOVALGIN	Hoechst	T	500	Headache, muscular pain
	ANALGIN	FDC	T	500	
	ANALGIN	IDPL	T	500	
Phenylbutazone	PHENYLBUTAZONE	Albert-David	T	100	Rhuematic fever
	PHENYLBUTAZONE	Bombay Drug House	T	100	Rhuematic fever
Oxyphenbutazone	OXALGIN	Cadila	T	100 + 500 analgin	Musculo-skeletal injury and pain
	REDUCIN - A	Unique	T	100 + 500 acetaminophen	
	FLAMAP - P	Indoco	T	100 + 325 paracetamol	
Mefenamic acid	MEFTAL	Blue cross	T	250, 500	Chromic muscular pain

Ibuprofen	BRUFEN	Boots	T	200, 400, 600	Rheumatoid Arthritis, Neuralgia, Migraine,
	BREN	Kopran	T	200, 400	
	IBUFLAMAR	Indoco	T	200, 400	
	TABALON	Hoechst	T	400	
Indomethacin	CIPLACID	Cipla	C	25	Rheumatoid arthritis, ankylosing spondylitis
	INDICIN	IDPL	C	25	
	INDOCID	Merind	C	25	
Neproxen	NAPROSYN	Searle	T	250	Chronic muscular pain and inflammation
Piroxicam	BREXIC	Wockhardt	C	20	Rheumatic arthristis, Spondylitis
	DOLONEX	Pfizer	C	10, 20	
	PIROX	Cipla	C	10, 20	
Ibuprophen + Paracetamol	BRUSTIN	Stancare	T	Ibu 400 Para 325	Pain, Spondylitis arthritis
	COMBIFLAM	Roussel	T	Ibu 400 Para 325	
	EMFLAM PLUS	Merck	T	Ibu 400 Para 325	
Adrenaline	ADRENALINE	Belco-pharma	I	1 : 1000	Aresting in fall of B. P.
	ADRENALINE	G. L.	I	1.8 mg/ml	
	ADRENALINE TART	Pharmaceuticals Haffkine	I	1.9 mg/ml	

Naradrenaline acid tart	LEVOPHED	Day's	I	Aresting in fall of B. P.
Isoprenaline	NEO-EPININE	Burr-well	T 20	Bronchial asthama.
	AUTOHALER	Cipla	Inhaler 400 mcg.	
Phenylephrine hydrochloride	SUNPHERINE - Eye	Sunway	Eyedrop 2.5 %, 5 %	in Glucoma, Nasal congestion
	DROSYN	FDC	Eyedrop 5 %	Nasal
Ephedrine hydrochloride	ENDRINE	Wyeth	Nasaldrops 0.75 %	Congestion and bronchodilator
	EPHEDRINE HCl	B. P. L.	Tab 15, 30	
Pseudophedrine	SUDAFED	Burr-well	T/S. 60	Bronchodilator infection
	PSEUDOPHEDRINE	Unicare	S 30 mg/ 5 ml	
			T 60	
Salbutamol	ASTHALINE	Cipla	T 2, 4	Broncheal asthma
	SALBETOL	FDC	T 2, 4	
	BRICANYL	Astra-IDL	T 2.5, 5	
Terbutaline sulphae	TERBUTALINE	Searle-India	T 2.5, 5	Asthma.
Tolazoline hydrochloride	PRISCOL	Ciba-Geigy	T 25	Periferal Vascular disorder
Propanolol hydrochloride	CORBETA	Sarabhai	T 10, 40	Angina Pectoric and hypertension
	BETASPAN	Eskayef	C 40, 80	
	CIPLAR	Cipla	T 10, 40, 80	

Atenolol	ATEN	Kopran	T	25, 50, 100	Cardic arrthemia, hypertension angina pectoris
	ATELOL	Themis Pharma	T	50, 100	
	BETACARD	Torrent	T	25, 50	
	ATENOVA	Lupin	T	56, 100	
Neostigmine	PROSTIGMINE	Roche	T	15	in myasthenia grans, Paralytic ileus
Pilocarpine nitrate	PILOCAR	EDC	Eyedrops 1 %		Congestiva
	BI-MIOTIC	Bell Pharma	Eyedrops 2 %, 4 %		
Antropine methonitrate	BELL PINO-ATRIN-EYE	Bell Pharma	Eyeoint 1 %		Mydriatic
Atropine sulphate	ATROPINE SULPH. Inj	Gluconate India	I	0.6 mg/ml	Mydriatic
Hyoscine butylbromide	HYOSCINE BUTYL BRO	Belco Pharma	I	20 mg/ml	Mydriatic
Homatropine methobromide	BELL HOMATROPINE EYE	Bell Pharma	Oint 1 %, 2 %		Mydriatic
Propantheline bromide	PRO-BANTHINE	Searle	T	15	Peptic ulcer ulcerative
	SPASTHELINE	Sunpharma	T	15	Colitis Gastric ulcer.
Tropicamide	TROPICO EYE	Bell Pharma	Drops 1 %		Eye inflammation
Levodopa	LEVOPA	Wallace	T	500	Perkinsonism
	ELDOPA	Biddle Sawyer	T	500	

Quinidine sulphate	QUINIDINE SULPH	Burr-well	T	200	Cardiac arrhthmia.
	QUINIDINE SULPH	Sandoz	T	200	
Methyldopa	DOPAMET	Stangen	T	250	Hypertension
	ALDOPAN	Cadila	T	250	
	ALPHADOPA	Merrind	T	250	
Clofibrate	CLOFIBRATE	Unicare	C	500	Hypertension
Nifedipine	MYOGARD	Searle	C	5, 10	unstable
	NICARDIA	Unique	C	5, 10	angina
	DEPIN	Cadila	C	5, 10	pectoris
Glyceryltrinitrate	ANGISED	Burr-well	T	0.5	Acute attack of angina
	ANGISPAN TR	Lyka	T	0.5	
Isosorbide dinitrate	ISORDIL	Wyeth	T	10	Angina pectrois and
	MONOTRATE	Sunpharma	T	10, 20, 40	Coronary insufficiency
Histamine phosphate					
Diphehydramine hydrochloride	BENADRYL	Parke Davis	C	25, 50	Allergic conditions
Mepyramine maleate	MEPYRAMINE MALEATE	Paras Pharma	T	50	Allergic conditions
Pheniramine maleate	AVIL PHENIRAMINE	Hoechst	T	22.5, 45	Allergic dermatitis
	MALEATE	B. P. L.	T	25, 50	Antitristaminic

Generic Name	Brand Name	Manufacturer	Dosage	Use
Chloropheniramine maleate	CHLORPHENIRAMINE	Poddar-Pharma	T 4	Antiallergic, antihistaminic
	CHLORPHENIRAMINE	B. P. L	T 4	
Promethazine hydrochloride	PHENERGAN	Rhone-Poulence	T 10, 25	Allergic conditions
	PROMASUN	Sunpharma	T 25	
Cyclizine hydrochloride	MARZINE	Burr-well	Elixir 5 mg/5 ml T 50	in urticaria, rashes
Cyproheptadine hydrochloride	CYDINE	CFL	Liq. 2 mg/5 ml	Allergic disorder
	CYPROWAL	Wallance	Syr. 2 mg/5 ml	
cimetidine	ULCIBAN	Torrent	T 200, 400	duodenal ulcer and hyperacidity
Ranitidine hydrochloride	RANTAC	Unique	T 150, 300	duodenal ulcer and hyperacidity
	RANX	Unisearach	T 150	
	ULTAC	Cipla	T 150, 300.	
	HISTAC	Ranbaxy	I 25 mg/ml.	
Heparin	BEPARIN	B. E.	I 1000 I. U./ ml	Anticoagulant in Blood transfusion
Heparin Sod.	HEPARIN SOD	Biogenic	I 5000 I. U/ml	
Fluoresein sodium	FLOURESTAIN	Bell Pharma.	Opth strips 4 %	to detect damaged area of cornea.
Urea				

Mannitol	MANNITOL	Albert David	I	20 %	Diuretic infusion. to reduce intracrenial pressure.
Frusemide	LASIX	Hoechst	T	40	Congestine heart failure, mild hypertension
	SALINEX	IDPL	T	40	
Hydrochlorthiazide	ESIDREX	Ciba	T	50	Hypertension
Triampterene	DYTIDE	Eskayef	T	50 with 20 benzthiazide	Hypertension
Insulin	INSULIN I. P.	Glaxo	I	40, 80 units/ml	In diabetic conditions, to control sugar.
	INSULIN	Boots	I	40, 80 units/ml	
	INSULIN ISOPHAGE	Boots	I	40 units/ml	
	INSULIN LANTE				
Chlorpropamide	DIABINESE	Boots	I	40 units/ml	As antidiabetics
	CHLOROFORMIN	Pfizer	T	100	
	DIAPONIDE	Cadia	T	250	
		I. D. P. L	T	250	
Tolbutamide	RASTINON	Hoechst	T	500	As antidiabetic
	ARTOSIN	Boehringer	T	500	
Phenfarmin hydrochloride	DBI	USV AND P	T	25	Insulin insufficiency
	DBI - TD	USV AND P	C	50	
Metafarmin hydrochloride	DIAPHAGE	Wallace	T	500, 850	Antidiabetic
Glabenclamide	DAONIN	Hoechst	T	5	Antidiabetic
	IDIMIDE	IDPL	T	5	Antidiabetic

Generic	Brand	Manufacturer	Dosage form & Strength	Use
Benzocaine	HEALEX Spray	Rallis India	Spary 0.36 %	Local anesthetic
Procaine hydrochloride	PROCAINE HCl	Biomedia	I 2 %	Local anesthetic
Lignocaine	XYLOCAINE	Astra. IDL	I 1 % , 2 %	infiltration block anesthesia
			Oint 5 %	
Thyroxin sod.	ROXIN	Cadila	T 100 mcg	Hypothyroidism
	ELTROXIN	Glaxo Allenbury	T 100 mcg	
Thyroid	THYROID	Burr-well	T dry powder 30	Hypothyroidism
Benzalkonium chloride	DECONNASIL	Calila	Drops 0.02 %	Antiinfective
Tolnaftate	TOLNAFTATE	BPL	Solution 10 mg/ml.	Antifungal
		Unicare		
PAS	ISOZONE	Pfizer	Granules 80 %	Antitubercular
	SODIUM PAS	IDPL		
Ethambutal hydrochloride	MYAMBUTOL	Lederle	T 200, 400, 800	Antitubercular
	MYCOBUTOL	Cadila	C 200, 400, 800	
Isoniagid	ISONEX	Pfizer	T 100, 300	Antitubercular
	ISONIAZIDE	Unicare	T 100	Antitubercular
Pyrazinamide	PYZINA	Lupin	T 500, 750	Antitubercular
	PZA - CIBA	Hind-Ciba	T 750	
	P - ZIDE	Cadila	T 500, 750, 1000	
Thiacetazone	THIACETOZONE	Cyperpharma	T 20, 50	Antitubercular
Cycloserine	CYCOSIN	Sunway	C 250	Antitubercular
	THEMISERINE	Themis	C 250	

Clofazimine	HANSEPRAN	S. G. Pharma	C	100	In Leprosy, dapsone resistant
	CLOFOZINE	Astra - IDL	T	50, 100	
Dapsone	DAPSONE	Burr-well	T	25, 50, 100	Antileprotic
	DAPSONE	Day's	T	100	Antileprotic
	PROMINE	Parke-Davis	T	50	
THIAMBUTOSINE					
Clioquinol	AMOCECHIN	Universal Drug House	T	250	in amoebiasis
Diiodohydroxyquinoline	DIODOQUIN	Searle	T	650	Intestinal amoebiasis
			Sus	210 mg/ 5 ml	
Diloxamide furoate	FURAMIDE	Boots	T	500	Intestinal amoebiasis
Metranidazole	FLAGYL	Rhone-Poulence	T	400	in Trichonas vaginitis, urinary tract infection,
	UNIMEZOL	Unichem.	T	200, 400	intestinal infection
Emetine Hydrochloride	EMETINE	Burr-Well	T	200	Amoebetic dysentery.
	EMETINE Hcl in	G. L. Pharma	I	30 mg/ml	
Busulfan	MYLERAN	Burr-well	T	2	Leukemic
Chlorambucil	UKERAN	Burr-well	T	2, 5	Leukemic
Cyclophosphamide	COCYLME	Cadila	T	50	antitumer,
	CYCLOXAN	Biochem.	Vial	100, 200	Hodgkins disease
Azathipurine	IMURAN	Burr-well	T	25, 50	Antitumer, Hodgkins diseas

rouracil	FIVEFLURO	Biddle - Swayer	I	50 mg/ml	Carcinoma of G. I. Tract
	FLURACIL	Biochem.	I	250 mg/ml	
rcaptopurine	PURINAPTHOL	Burr-well	T	50	Anticancer
thotrexate	METHOTREXATE	Cynamide	I	2.5 and 5 mg/5ml	Lymphobastic leukemia
	NEOTREX	Priddle-Swayer	I	50 mg/2ml	
ethylcarbamazine	BENOCIDE	Burr-well	T	50, 100	Anthelmentic in thread and
ate	HETRAZAN	Cynamide	T	50, 100	tape worm infections
bendazole	WORMIN	Cadila	Sus. 100 mg/5 ml		Anthelmentic
	MEBEX	Cipla	T	100	
			granules 200		
erazine adipate	ANTEPAR with lexative	Burr - well	granules 4.5 g/ - 10 g with sennoside		Anthelmentic
	HELMACID	Glaxo			
erazine Phosphate	PIPERAZINE	Burr-well	T 500		
lphacetamide	ALBUCID	Nlolas - Pirmal	Eyedrops 10 %, 20 % 30 %		in infection of eye
lphacetamide	OSUL	BDL	Drops 10 %		
lium	SULPHACETAMIDE	Eye Tablet India	Eyedrops 10 %, 20 %, 30 %		in infection of eye
lphaguanidine	SULPHAGU ANIDINE	Tablet India	T 500		antibacterial sulpha.
ythalyl phathiazole	THALAZOLE	Rhoneal poulene	T 500		for intestinal infection
ccinyl phathiazole			T 500		for intestinal infection
lphadiazine	SULPHADIAZINE	Rhone-Poulence	T 500		Antibacterial sulpha

Silver Sulphadiazine	DUPHAR - SILVER - SULPHA SILVEREX	Duphar Cross lands	Cream 1 % Dusting powder 1 %	Antibacterial for burn injury Antibacterial for burn injury
Sulphadimethoxine (methoxine)	MADRIBON	Rochie	T 500	Antibacterial
Sulphamethoxazole and Trimethoprim	BACTRIM SEPTRAN ORIPRIM	Roche Burr-well Cadila	400 + 80 also 800 + 160 400 + 80 800 + 160 400 + 80	
Quinine sulph.	QUININE QUININE	Nymph Labs. B. P. Labs.	T 100, 300 sugar coated T 100, 300	Antimalerial
Amodiaquine hydrochloride	AMODIAQUINE	Unicare	T 200	Antimalerial
Chloroquine phosphate	NOVAQUIN MELUBRIN RESOCHIN	Rhone-Poulence Ranbaxy Bayer	T 200 I 40 mg/ml T 250 T 250	Antimalerial
Primaquine phosphate	PRIMAQUINE PHOS.	Unicare	T 25	Antimalerial
Pyrimethamine	DARAPRIN PYRAFIN ONLI - 2	Burr-well Lupin Kopran	T 25 T 25 + 400 sulphadoxine T 25 + 400 sulphadoxine	Antimalerial

Drug	Brand	Company	Form	Strength	Use
Cephalexin	CEFF	Lupin	T	250, 500	Antibiotic, used in urinary tract and respiratory tract infections.
	ALCEPHIN	Alembic	T	250, 500	
Cephaloridine	CEPORAN	Glaxo-Pharma	I	0.5 g and 1g/vial	Antibiotic, used in urinary tract and respiratory tract infections.
Benzylpenicillin Benzylpenicillin sod.	CRYSTAPEN	Glaxo		Vial 2, 4 lacks I. U. /vial	Antibiotic, against Gram +ve organisms
Benzylpenicillin Pot.	PENTID	Sarabhai	T	2, 4, 8 lacks I.U./Tab	Antibiotic, against Gram +ve organisms
Benzathine Penicillin	PENCOM	Alembic		Vial 6 lack I. U./vial	
	PENIDURE AD	Wyeth		Vial 6 lack I. U./vial	
Phenoxy-methyl Pencillin (V)	CRYSTAPHEN - V	Glaxo - Pharma	T	250	Antibiotic, against Gram +ve organisms
	PENIVORAL	Franchu-Ind	T	65, Vial, 1 lack I.U./Vial	
Cloxacillin Sod	KLOX	Lyka	C	250, 500	Antibiotic against Streptococus and Stephylococus
Ampicillin	AMPISYN	Cipla	I	500 mg/vial	Stephylococus
	CAMPICILLIN	Cadia	C	200, 500	Stephylococus
	AMPILIN	Lyka	C	250, 500	Stephylococus
Carbenicillin Sod.	BIOPENCE	Biochem.	I	1 g and 5 g/vial	Broad spectrum antibiotic
Gentamycin	GENTICYN	Nicholas	I	40 mg/ml	Broad spectrum antibiotic
Neomycin	NYFUCIN - N	Nymph Lab		Cream 0.5 %	Broad spectrum in skin and eye infection

Erythromycin	ERO - B	Lupin	T	250, 500	Broadspectrum antibioic in upper respiratory tract infections.
	ALTHROCIN	Alembic	T	250, 500	
	EMTHROCIN	Rhone-Poulence	T	250, 500	
	E - MYCIN	Themis-Pharma	T	100, 250	
Tetracyclin	HOESTACYCLINE	Hoechst	C	250, 500	Broad specturm antibiotic
	RESTECLINE	Sarabhai	T	250, 500	
Doxycycline	DOXY - I	U. S. vitamin	C	100	Broad Spectrum antibiotic
Oxytetracyclin	TERAMYCIN	Pfizer	C	250, 500	Broad Spectrum antibiotic
	TERMACYN 1 M		I	50 mg/ml.	
Cycloserine	CYCOSIN	Sunways	C	250	In tuberculosis along with other antitubercular drugs.
Chloramphenical	CHLOROMYCETIN	Parke-Davis	C	250, 500	In typhoid and Eye infection
	CHLORAMPHENICOL	Cadila	C	250, 500	
Griseofulvin	GRIVIN	Associated Pharma	T	125	Antifungal
Rifampicin	RIFAMPILA	Albert-David	C	150, 300, 450	Bacterial infection
streptomycin	AMBISTRIN - S	Sarabhai	I	0.75 g and 1 g/vial	In tuberculoses, along with other antitubercular drugs.
	STREPTOMYCIN	Hindustan Antibiotic	I	0.75 g and 1 g/vial	
Testosterone	TESTOSTERONE Inj.	B. P. L.	I	25 mg/ml	Anabolic hormone
	PERANDREN	Hind-Ciba	I	50 mg/ml	
Nandralone decanoate	DECANEURABOL	Cadila	I	25 /ml	anabolic
	DECABOLINE	Infar	I	25/ml	anabolic

Drug	Brand	Company	Form	Strength	Use
Ethinylestradiol	PROGYNON - C	Schering - AG	T	0.02	Oestrogenic
Estradiol.					Oestrogenic
Progesterone	PROGESTERONE Inj.	BPL	I	25 mg/ml	Progextogenic
	LUTOCYCLIN	Hind-Ciba	I	25 mg/ml	
Hydrocortisone acetate	WYCORT	Wyeth	I	25 mg/ml	In inflammatory conditions
Prednisolone	DELTACORTIL	Pfizer	Y	5	Allergic and in inflammatory disorder.
Betamethasone	BETACORTIL	Pfizer	T	0.5	Allergic and in inflammatory disorder
Betamethasone Sod. Phosph.	SOLUBET	Lupin	T	0.5	Allergic and in inflammatory disorder
Decamethasone	DECADRON	Merind	I	4 mg/ml	Rheumatic and allergic disorders.
Decamethasone sod. Phosph.	DEXONA	Cadila	I	8 ml/2ml	

I - Injection, T - Tablet, C - Capsule. S = Syrup. B. E. = Biologiacal Evans,
B.P.L. - British Pharmaceutical Laboratories, Burr-Well = Burrough - Welcome I.C.I. - Indian Chemical Industries,
I.D.P.L. - Indian Drugs and Pharmaceuticals Limited.

✹ PUBLISHING HOUSE ✹

Pune Office :

Abhyudaya Pragati, 1312 Shivaji Nagar, Off J.M. Road, Pune – 411005,

☎ 25512336/37/39 Fax : (020) 25511379 Email : niralipune@pragationline.com

Mumbai Office :

385, S.V.P. Road, Rasdhara Co-op. Hsg. Society, Girgaum, **Mumbai -** 400004, Maharashtra

✆ (022) 2385 6339 / 2386 9976, Fax : (022) 2386 9976

Email : niralimumbai@pragationline.com

✹ DISTRIBUTION CENTERS ✹

Pune :

* 119, Budhwar Peth, Jogeshwari Mandir Lane, **Pune -** 411002, Maharashtra.
  ☎ (020) 24452044, 66022708; Fax : (020) 2445 1538 Email : niralilocal@pragationline.com
* S. No. 28/27, Dhayari, Near Pari Company, Dhayari, Pune - 411 041, ☎ (020) 24690204
  Fax : 020 - 24690316 Email : bookorder@pragationline.com

✹ DISTRIBUTION BRANCHES ✹

NAGPUR : *Pratibha Book Distributors*

Above Maratha Mandir, Shop No. 3 First Floor, Rani Jhanshi Square, Sitabuldi, Nagpur 440012, Maharashtra, ✆ (0712) 254 7129

JALGAON : *Nirali Prakashan*

34, V. V. Golani Market, Navi Peth, Jalgaon 425001, Maharashtra, ✆ (0257) 222 0395
Mob : 94234 91860

KOLHAPUR : *Nirali Prakashan*

New Mahadvar Road, Kedar Plaza, 1st Floor Opp. IDBI Bank Kolhapur 416 012, Maharashtra.
Mob : 9850046155

BENGALURU : *Pragati Book House*

House No. 1, Sanjeevappa Lane, Avenue Road Cross, Opp. Rice Church, Bengaluru – 560002.
☎ (080) 64513344, 64513355, Mob : 9880582331, 9845021552
Email:bharatsavla@yahoo.com

✹ RETAIL OUTLETS ✹

Mumbai : *Pragati Book Corner*

    Indira Niwas, 111 - A, Bhavani Shankar Road, Dadar (W), Mumbai 400028, Maharashtra
    Tel : (022) 2422 3526 / 6662 5254

Pune : *Pragati Books Center*

* 157, Budhwar Peth, Opp. Ratan Talkies, Pune 411002, Maharashtra
  ☎ (020) 2445 8887 / 6602 2707, Fax : (020) 2445 8887
* 676/B, Budhwar Peth, Opp. Jogeshwari Mandir, Pune 411002, Maharashtra
  ☎ (020) 6601 7784 / 6602 0855
* Amber Chamber, 28/A, Budhwar Peth, Appa Balwant Chowk, Pune : 411002, Maharashtra,
  ☎ (020) 20240335 / 66281669 Email : pbcpune@pragationline.com
* **PBC Book Sellers & Stationers**
  152, Budhwar Peth, Pune 411002, Maharashtra ☎ (020) 2445 2254 / 6609 2463

www.pragationline.com   info@pragationline.com

www.ingramcontent.com/pod-product-compliance
Lightning Source LLC
Chambersburg PA
CBHW060309240426
43661CB00059B/2703